Using *Texas Write Sou*

Your ***Write Source*** book is loaded with information to help you learn about writing. One section that will be especially helpful is the "Proofreader's Guide" at the back of the book. This section covers the rules for language and grammar.

The book also includes four main units covering the types of writing that you may have to complete on district or state writing tests. In addition, a special section provides samples and tips for writing in science, social studies, math, the applied sciences, the arts, and in the workplace.

Write Source will help you with other learning skills, too—such as improving your understanding and use of language and making effective presentations. This makes *Write Source* a valuable writing and learning guide in all of your classes. (The **Quick Tour** on the next two pages highlights many of the key features in the book.)

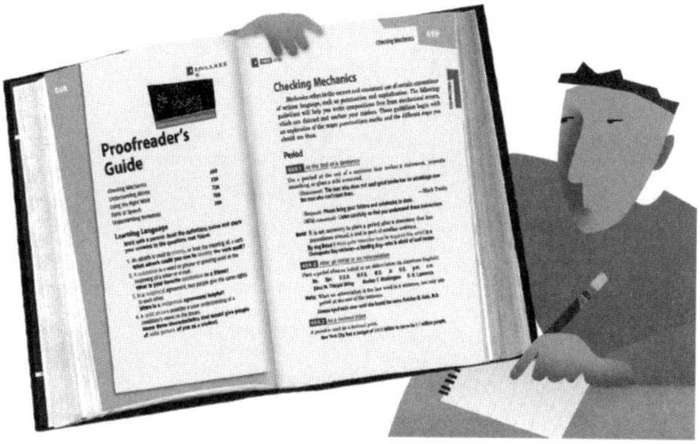

Your *Write Source* guides . . .

With practice, you will be able to find information in this book quickly using the guides explained below.

- The **Table of Contents** (starting on page **vi**) lists the six major sections in the book and the chapters found in each section.
- The **Index** (starting on page **799**) lists the topics covered in the book in alphabetical order. Use the index when you are interested in a specific topic.
- The **Color Coding** used for "A Writer's Resource" (green), and the "Proofreader's Guide" (yellow) make these important sections easy to find. Colorful side tabs also provide a handy reference.
- **Page References** in the book tell you where to turn for additional information about a specific topic. *Example:* (See page **74**.)

If, at first, you're not sure how to find something in *Write Source,* ask your teacher for help. With a little practice, you will find everything quickly and easily.

TEXAS WRITE SOURCE

Authors
Dave Kemper, Patrick Sebranek, and Verne Meyer

Consulting Author
Gretchen Bernabei

Illustrator
Chris Krenzke

GREAT SOURCE®
HOUGHTON MIFFLIN HARCOURT

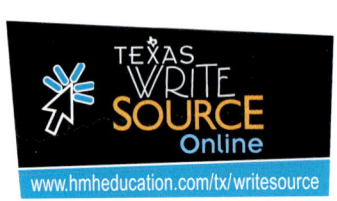

Texas Write Source Online
www.hmheducation.com/tx/writesource

Printed in the U.S.A.

ISBN-13 978-0-547-39497-8

1 2 3 4 5 6 7 8 9 10 0914 19 18 17 16 15 14 13 12 11 10

Quick Guide

A Quick Tour of *Texas Write Source*

Texas Write Source contains many key features that will help you improve your writing and language skills. Once you become familiar with this book, you will begin to understand how helpful these features can be.

Checklists serve as effective revising and editing guides within the writing units.

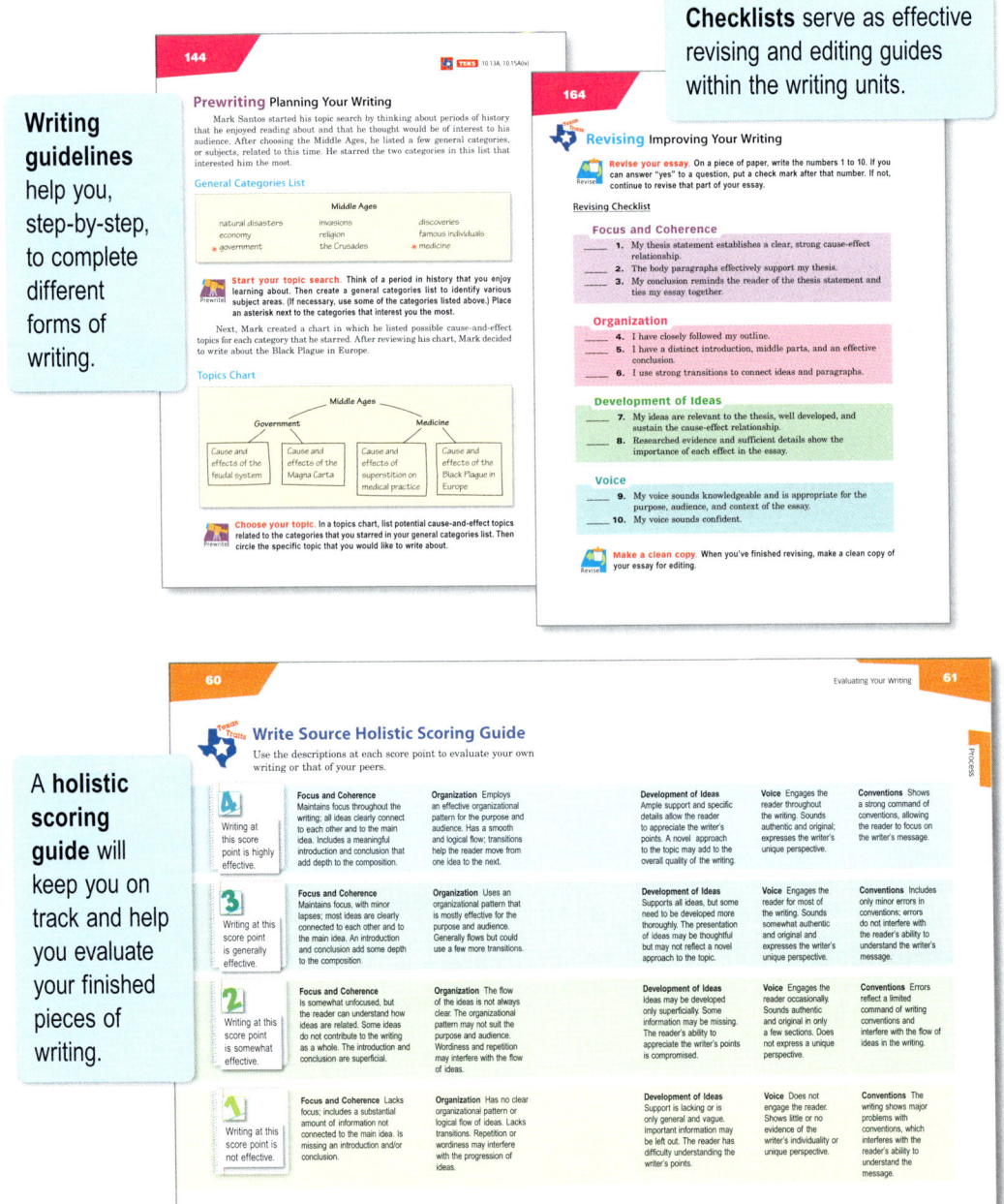

Writing guidelines help you, step-by-step, to complete different forms of writing.

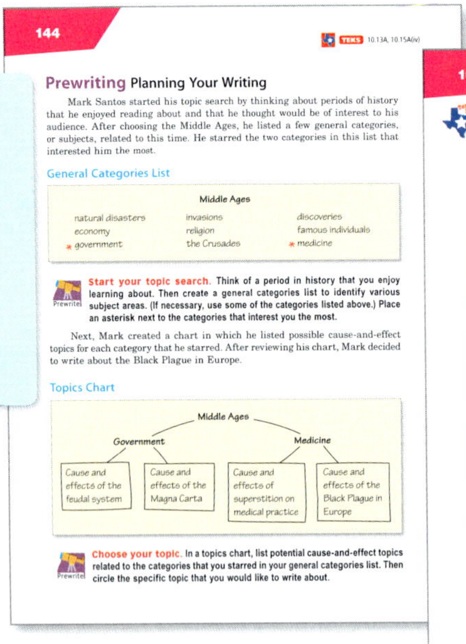
144 TEKS 10.13A, 10.15A(iv)

Prewriting Planning Your Writing

Mark Santos started his topic search by thinking about periods of history that he enjoyed reading about and that he thought would be of interest to his audience. After choosing the Middle Ages, he listed a few general categories, or subjects, related to this time. He starred the two categories in this list that interested him the most.

General Categories List

Start your topic search. Think of a period in history that you enjoy learning about. Then create a general categories list to identify various subject areas. (If necessary, use some of the categories listed above.) Place an asterisk next to the categories that interest you the most.

Next, Mark created a chart in which he listed possible cause-and-effect topics for each category that he starred. After reviewing his chart, Mark decided to write about the Black Plague in Europe.

Topics Chart

Choose your topic. In a topics chart, list potential cause-and-effect topics related to the categories that you starred in your general categories list. Then circle the specific topic that you would like to write about.

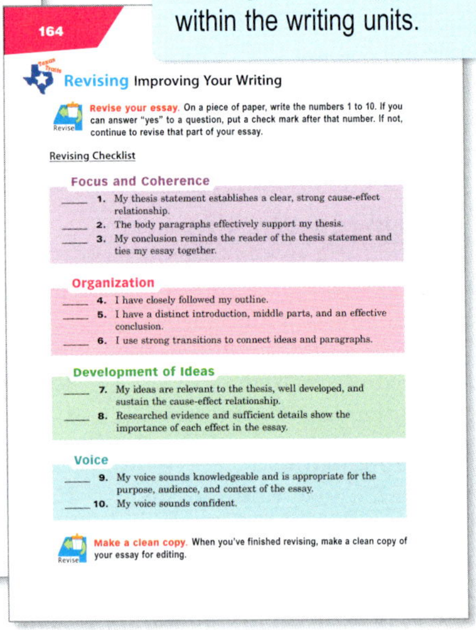
164

Revising Improving Your Writing

Revise your essay. On a piece of paper, write the numbers 1 to 10. If you can answer "yes" to a question, put a check mark after that number. If not, continue to revise that part of your essay.

Revising Checklist

Focus and Coherence

____ 1. My thesis statement establishes a clear, strong cause-effect relationship.
____ 2. The body paragraphs effectively support my thesis.
____ 3. My conclusion reminds the reader of the thesis statement and ties my essay together.

Organization

____ 4. I have closely followed my outline.
____ 5. I have a distinct introduction, middle parts, and an effective conclusion.
____ 6. I use strong transitions to connect ideas and paragraphs.

Development of Ideas

____ 7. My ideas are relevant to the thesis, well developed, and sustain the cause-effect relationship.
____ 8. Researched evidence and sufficient details show the importance of each effect in the essay.

Voice

____ 9. My voice sounds knowledgeable and is appropriate for the purpose, audience, and context of the essay.
____ 10. My voice sounds confident.

Make a clean copy. When you've finished revising, make a clean copy of your essay for editing.

A **holistic scoring guide** will keep you on track and help you evaluate your finished pieces of writing.

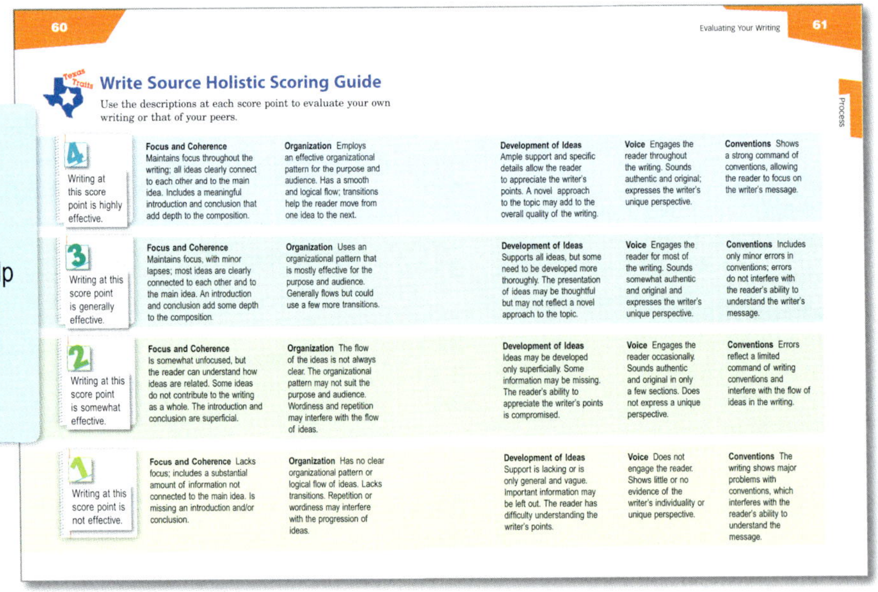
60 Evaluating Your Writing 61

Write Source Holistic Scoring Guide

Use the descriptions at each score point to evaluate your own writing or that of your peers.

4 Writing at this score point is highly effective.	**Focus and Coherence** Maintains focus throughout the writing; all ideas clearly connect to each other and to the main idea. Includes a meaningful introduction and conclusion that add depth to the composition.	**Organization** Employs an effective organizational pattern for the purpose and audience. Has a smooth and logical flow; transitions help the reader move from one idea to the next.	**Development of Ideas** Ample support and specific details allow the reader to appreciate the writer's points. A novel approach to the topic may add to the overall quality of the writing.	**Voice** Engages the reader throughout the writing. Sounds authentic and original; expresses the writer's unique perspective.	**Conventions** Shows a strong command of conventions, allowing the reader to focus on the writer's message.
3 Writing at this score point is generally effective.	**Focus and Coherence** Maintains focus, with minor lapses; most ideas are clearly connected to each other and to the main idea. An introduction and conclusion add some depth to the composition.	**Organization** Uses an organizational pattern that is mostly effective for the purpose and audience. Generally flows but could use a few more transitions.	**Development of Ideas** Supports all ideas, but some need to be developed more thoroughly. The presentation of ideas may be thoughtful but may not reflect a novel approach to the topic.	**Voice** Engages the reader for most of the writing. Sounds somewhat authentic and original and expresses the writer's unique perspective.	**Conventions** Includes only minor errors in conventions; errors do not interfere with the reader's ability to understand the writer's message.
2 Writing at this score point is somewhat effective.	**Focus and Coherence** Is somewhat unfocused, but the reader can understand how ideas are related. Some ideas do not contribute to the writing as a whole. The introduction and conclusion are superficial.	**Organization** The flow of the ideas is not always clear. The organizational pattern may not suit the purpose and audience. Wordiness and repetition may interfere with the flow of ideas.	**Development of Ideas** Ideas may be developed only superficially. Some information may be missing. The reader's ability to appreciate the writer's points is compromised.	**Voice** Engages the reader occasionally. Sounds authentic and original in only a few sections. Does not express a unique perspective.	**Conventions** Errors reflect a limited command of writing conventions and interfere with the flow of ideas in the writing.
1 Writing at this score point is not effective.	**Focus and Coherence** Lacks focus; includes a substantial amount of information not connected to the main idea. Is missing an introduction and/or conclusion.	**Organization** Has no clear organizational pattern or logical flow of ideas. Lacks transitions. Repetition or wordiness may interfere with the progression of ideas.	**Development of Ideas** Support is lacking or is only general and vague. Important information may be left out. The reader has difficulty understanding the writer's points.	**Voice** Does not engage the reader. Shows little or no evidence of the writer's individuality or unique perspective.	**Conventions** The writing shows major problems with conventions, which interferes with the reader's ability to understand the message.

Process

The **writing samples** will stimulate you to write your own effective essays.

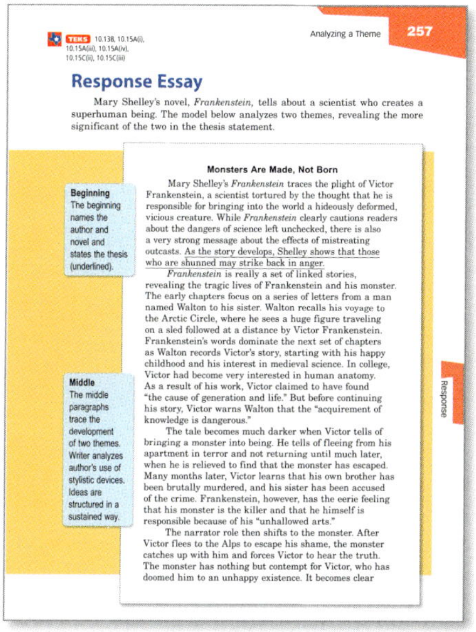
TEKS 10.13B, 10.15A(i), 10.15A(iii), 10.15A(iv), 10.15C(ii), 10.15C(iii)

Analyzing a Theme 257

Response Essay

Mary Shelley's novel, *Frankenstein*, tells about a scientist who creates a superhuman being. The model below analyzes two themes, revealing the more significant of the two in the thesis statement.

Monsters Are Made, Not Born

Beginning The beginning names the author and novel and states the thesis (underlined).

Mary Shelley's *Frankenstein* traces the plight of Victor Frankenstein, a scientist tortured by the thought that he is responsible for bringing into the world a hideously deformed, vicious creature. While *Frankenstein* clearly cautions readers about the dangers of science left unchecked, there is also a very strong message about the effects of mistreating outcasts. As the story develops, Shelley shows that those who are shunned may strike back in anger.

Middle The middle paragraphs trace the development of two themes. Writer analyzes author's use of stylistic devices. Ideas are structured in a sustained way.

Frankenstein is really a set of linked stories, revealing the tragic lives of Frankenstein and his monster. The early chapters focus on a series of letters from a man named Walton to his sister. Walton recalls his voyage to the Arctic Circle, where he sees a huge figure traveling on a sled followed at a distance by Victor Frankenstein. Frankenstein's words dominate the next set of chapters as Walton records Victor's story, starting with his happy childhood and his interest in medieval science. In college, Victor had become very interested in human anatomy. As a result of his work, Victor claimed to have found "the cause of generation and life." But before continuing his story, Victor warns Walton that the "acquirement of knowledge is dangerous."

The tale becomes much darker when Victor tells of bringing a monster into being. He tells of fleeing from his apartment in terror and not returning until much later, when he is relieved to find that the monster has escaped. Many months later, Victor learns that his own brother has been brutally murdered, and his sister has been accused of the crime. Frankenstein, however, has the eerie feeling that his monster is the killer and that he himself is responsible because of his "unhallowed arts."

The narrator role then shifts to the monster. After Victor flees to the Alps to escape his shame, the monster catches up with him and forces Victor to hear the truth. The monster has nothing but contempt for Victor, who has doomed him to an unhappy existence. It becomes clear

Response

258

TEKS 10.13B, 10.15A(i), 10.15A(iv), 10.15C(ii), 10.15C(iii) ELPS 4K

The detailed analysis is more than a summary, and the writer's insights about the novel extend beyond a literal analysis. Writer analyzes the author's use of rhetorical devices.

that the monster begins his existence as a gentle creature trapped in a frightening body. After escaping from Victor's apartment, he is ill treated by everyone he meets. He cannot understand why until one day he sees his reflection in a pool of water and realizes why people loathe him. Longing for companionship, he eavesdrops on happy lives and secretly helps others whenever he can. However, in an awful series of events, the monster is attacked by a mob he has tried to befriend and is shot by the companion of a girl he has saved from drowning. At that point, he declares war on all men, killing Victor's brother and framing his sister.

The monster's story makes it obvious that Victor's creation is vicious not because he is created that way, but because Victor abandons him and because others mistreat him. There is one last chance for Victor to ease the monster's loneliness—by creating another monster to keep him company. But Victor fails to take action. Walton encounters Frankenstein in the Arctic because Victor is chasing down his creation, intent on killing him. Finally, Walton's last report tells how Victor gets sick and dies before he can catch his monster, and the giant, satisfied that Frankenstein is dead, wanders off to perish on the ice.

Ending The ending analyzes the two themes and expresses the importance of the second in quotations from the text.

Through *Frankenstein*, Mary Shelley expresses her fears that science left unchecked could be dangerous. However, in the end, that theme is not nearly as moving as the monster's message—mistreating others is risky. This theme becomes clear when he states, "There was none among the myriads of men that existed who would pity or assist me; and should I feel kindness toward my enemies?" It is the monster's plight that haunts the reader as the monster recalls that he sought shelter from the weather, but "still more from the barbarity of man," and no shelter was given.

Texas Traits

Respond to the reading. Answer the following questions.

Focus and Coherence (1) How is the thesis introduced? (2) How does the conclusion tie the essay together? **Organization** (3) How is the middle part of the analysis organized? **Development of Ideas** (4) What theme becomes the focus of this analysis? (5) Which key quotation from the novel supports this theme? **Voice** (6) Does the writer sound knowledgeable about the topic? Explain.

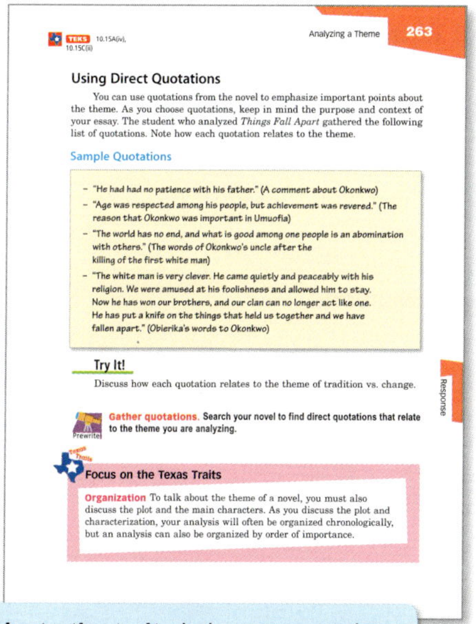
TEKS 10.15A(iv), 10.15C(ii)

Analyzing a Theme 263

Using Direct Quotations

You can use quotations from the novel to emphasize important points about the theme. As you choose quotations, keep in mind the purpose and context of your essay. The student who analyzed *Things Fall Apart* gathered the following list of quotations. Note how each quotation relates to the theme.

Sample Quotations

- "He had had no patience with his father." (A comment about Okonkwo)
- "Age was respected among his people, but achievement was revered." (The reason that Okonkwo was important in Umuofia)
- "The world has no end, and what is good among one people is an abomination with others." (The words of Okonkwo's uncle after the killing of the first white man)
- "The white man is very clever. He came quietly and peaceably with his religion. We were amused at his foolishness and allowed him to stay. Now he has won our brothers, and our clan can no longer act like one. He has put a knife on the things that held us together and we have fallen apart." (Obierika's words to Okonkwo)

Try It!

Discuss how each quotation relates to the theme of tradition vs. change.

Prewrite

Gather quotations. Search your novel to find direct quotations that relate to the theme you are analyzing.

Texas Traits

Focus on the Texas Traits

Organization To talk about the theme of a novel, you must also discuss the plot and the main characters. As you discuss the plot and characterization, your analysis will often be organized chronologically, but an analysis can also be organized by order of importance.

Response

Links to the traits help you appreciate the importance of different traits at different points in the writing process.

Graphic organizers show you how to organize your ideas for writing.

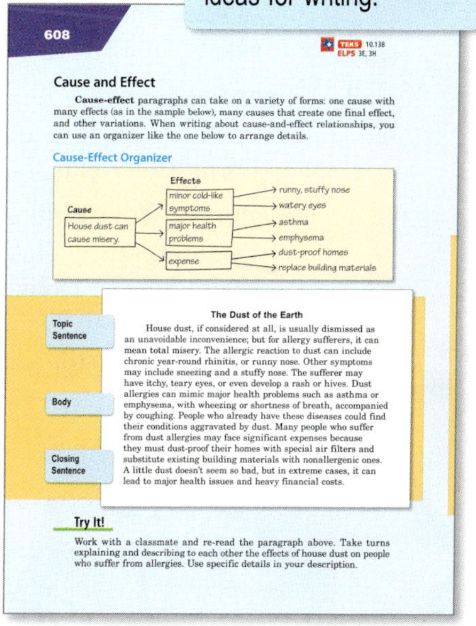
608

TEKS 10.13B ELPS 3E, 3H

Cause and Effect

Cause-effect paragraphs can take on a variety of forms: one cause with many effects (as in the sample below), many causes that create one final effect, and other variations. When writing about cause-and-effect relationships, you can use an organizer like the one below to arrange details.

Cause-Effect Organizer

The Dust of the Earth

Topic Sentence House dust, if considered at all, is usually dismissed as an unavoidable inconvenience; but for allergy sufferers, it can mean total misery.

Body The allergic reaction to dust can include chronic year-round rhinitis, or runny nose. Other symptoms may include sneezing and a stuffy nose. The sufferer may have itchy, teary eyes, or even develop a rash or hives. Dust allergies can mimic major health problems such as asthma or emphysema, with wheezing or shortness of breath, accompanied by coughing. People who already have these diseases could find their conditions aggravated by dust. Many people who suffer from dust allergies may face significant expenses because they must dust-proof their homes with special air filters and substitute existing building materials with nonallergenic ones.

Closing Sentence A little dust doesn't seem so bad, but in extreme cases, it can lead to major health issues and heavy financial costs.

Try It!

Work with a classmate and re-read the paragraph above. Take turns explaining and describing to each other the effects of house dust on people who suffer from allergies. Use specific details in your description.

contents

The Writing Process

The Forms of Writing

NARRATIVE WRITING

contents

EXPOSITORY WRITING

PERSUASIVE WRITING

contents

INTERPRETIVE RESPONSE

CREATIVE WRITING

contents

RESEARCH WRITING

WRITING ACROSS THE CURRICULUM

contents

The Tools of Language

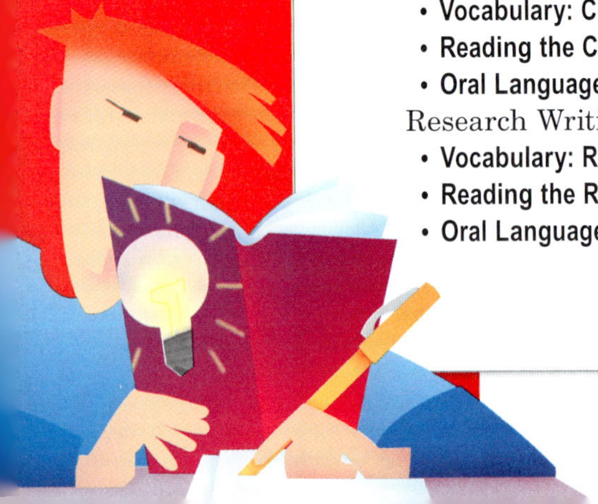

Basic Grammar and Writing

contents

A Writer's Resource

Proofreader's Guide

contents

Why Write?

Wouldn't it be nice if each of your writing assignments meant something to you personally . . . if each one helped you make sense of your life? Unfortunately, that is not the case. You are often asked to summarize facts, recall and interpret information, and explore topics in research papers. These assignments are important for academic reasons. However, they seldom get at your heartbeat—what makes you who you really are.

There is a type of writing that you can control, though, a type of personal writing that will help you explore your cares and concerns. This chapter will help you learn more about this valuable form of writing.

- **Purposes for Writing**
- **Getting Started**
- **Using a Writer's Notebook**

"All glory comes from daring to begin."

—Eugene F. Ware

Purposes for Writing

Experienced writers have their own reasons for writing. Some write in order to sort out their thoughts, while others write simply because it makes them happy. Whatever the reason, writing has a special meaning to them. The following thoughts may help you more fully appreciate the value of personal writing.

Writing helps you . . .

Learn more about yourself.

Writing lets you look deep within yourself, sometimes with surprising results. When you keep a writer's notebook of your thoughts and feelings, you may, as you read your entries later, see yourself in a whole new light.

Learn more about your world.

By recording observations of the world around you (what you hear and see and sense), you can learn from the events that shape you. Your observations also serve as a fascinating record of your time in history. Finally, writing about your classes helps you remember and make sense of what you are learning.

Share your ideas and insights.

Sometimes writing is the best way to share your thoughts with others. Your writing could have many different readers, or audiences. Writing gives you time to decide exactly what you want to say before your audience "hears" it.

Express what you know.

Writing actually helps you become a better thinker. It lets you review what you already know, reflect on it, use new vocabulary words, and add new thoughts. Think of writing as exercise for your mind.

Tip

Remember, writing is a skill. As with all other skills, the more you practice, the better you will become.

Learn to observe. Take a minute to look around you. Write freely for 5 minutes about your surroundings, recording details about the sights and sounds in this setting. Try this activity in a variety of places. Did you make any surprising observations? Discuss your observations with a classmate.

TEKS 10.14A, 10.14B, 10.14C, 10.15B
ELPS 3E, 2I

Getting Started

Think of writing as a skill. Just as you set aside time to improve your musical or athletic skills, do the same with writing. Exercise your mind as well as your body. Your writing will improve if you make an honest effort.

Where should I write?

Write in school. Here are ways you can write throughout your day:

- Listen carefully during your classes and take notes.
- Keep a learning log in each of your classes.
- Complete writing assignments and papers.

Write at home. Writing in your spare time can help you gain fluency—the ability to write quickly and easily. Here are some types of writing or genres you might want to try for fun or in your spare time:

- Write e-mail messages and letters.
- Keep a writer's notebook. (See pages **4–5**.)
- Create short stories and poems. (See pages **314–351**.)

Write wherever you are. Write in a car, on the bus, in a park, or in a coffee shop. In her book *Writing Down the Bones,* Natalie Goldberg suggests that you write wherever you feel comfortable.

What should I write about?

You can write about anything and everything. The more you write, the more you learn. Here are just a few things you can write about:

- **Observations:** What is happening around you right now? What do you think about what is happening?
- **Memories:** What was the best moment of your day? Your week? Your year? What was the worst moment?
- **Hopes and dreams:** What do you want in life? What do you wish for your future?
- **People:** What person means the most to you? What person do you admire? What sort of person do you not understand?
- **Places:** Where are you right now? Where do you wish you were? Where do you never want to be again?
- **Things:** What is your favorite possession? Your least favorite? What one invention would you like to outlaw, and why?

Find inspiration. Write for 5 to 10 minutes about your favorite place. What did you discover through your writing? Discuss your ideas with a partner.

TEKS 10.13A
ELPS 5G

Using a Writer's Notebook

Your most powerful writing tool can be a notebook reserved exclusively for daily writing. A **writer's notebook** (also called a *journal*) is a place to record your thoughts on any topic. As you write regularly in your notebook, you will make countless discoveries about your world.

In his book *Breathing In, Breathing Out: Keeping a Writer's Notebook,* Ralph Fletcher compares a writer's notebook to a compost heap. Over time, all the cuttings and leftovers that a gardener composts turn into rich fertilizer. In the same way, you can use your notes to determine and select topics that you want to write about. Your notes will guide you as your write your thesis statement or controlling idea about your chosen topic. Your notes should also help you pick the best genre for the topic and plan your first draft.

Ensuring Success

To make sure that your writer's notebook is a success, consider the quantity, quality, and variety of your entries. Also follow the rules on this page.

- **Quantity:** Teachers often require a certain number of pages or entries per grading period. Know your teacher's requirements for your notebook.
- **Quality:** Approach each entry with a high level of enthusiasm and interest. Develop your ideas fully with strong supporting details. Try to create vivid images that have sensory appeal.
- **Variety:** Write some of your entries from different points of view. For example, after an argument with a friend, write about it from your friend's point of view, or from the perspective of someone who overheard the argument.

Rules for a Writer's Notebook

- **Date each entry.** The date helps you find an entry and puts those thoughts into perspective with other entries.
- **Write freely.** Don't worry about producing perfect copy. Just get your ideas on paper.
- **Write regularly.** Develop the habit of writing daily.
- **Reflect on your work.** Reread your entries. Consider what you have written and look for ideas for future writing topics.

Taking it Personally

Here is a page from a student writer's notebook. This entry focuses on an old lunch box.

Sample Notebook Entry

April 9, 2011

Last week, Dad announced that it was time for spring-cleaning. As I dug through the garage, I found my old lunch box. Most kids had lunch boxes featuring the latest toys, cartoon characters, or comic-book heroes. My lunch box was different.

My lunch box looked like a pirate's chest. Bright splatters covered the surface because my grandpa used the lunch box when he was a painter. I would look at the paint, trying to imagine each color on an entire house. Mint green was the worst, I thought.

Even though I secretly loved that lunch box, it was so embarrassing to see kids pointing at me and laughing. I remember being relieved when everyone started using brown bags for lunch. Grandpa's lunch box was put on a shelf where it gathered dust.

After wiping the dirt and cobwebs off the lunch box, I realized that it would make a perfect container for my art supplies at school. The funny thing is, now my friends think Grandpa's lunch box is cool.

This notebook entry captures a time in the writer's life. It . . .

- starts with a "seed idea" (an old lunch box),
- describes the object's appearance and uses, and
- reflects on its importance.

Remember: Keeping a writer's notebook lets you look at ordinary things in new ways, describe your feelings, choose good descriptive words, and practice writing until you feel confident.

Write a quick reflection. Think about an object that was once very important to you. Write freely for 5 to 10 minutes about that object. Discuss with a friend what it meant and still means to you.

ELPS 1E, 2C, 3B, 3D, 3E, 4G

Texas Write Source Online
www.hmheducation.com/tx/writesource

Using the Writing Process

Writing Focus

Grammar Focus

Learning Language

Working with a classmate, read the definitions below and discuss your answers to each question.

1. Something is **persuasive** when it convinces you to take a certain course of action.
   What on TV could be described as persuasive?
2. A writer's **voice** is the way a piece of writing sounds.
   What does an author's voice reveal about her attitudes on a topic?
3. A **logical opinion** is one that is sound and it makes sense.
   How can you tell if an argument is logical?
4. A **counter-argument** presents an opposing idea.
   What is one counter-argument to the idea of year-round school?

Understanding the Writing Process

The writing process begins before you put pen to paper. In fact, the writing process begins the day you think your first thoughts, and it never really stops. You are subconsciously involved in the writing process every day of your life. Each of your experiences becomes part of what you know, what you think, and what you have to say. Writing is the process of capturing those thoughts and experiences on paper.

The steps in the writing process discussed in this book include *prewriting, drafting, revising, editing,* and *publishing*. All of these steps are equally important. If you follow the process for each writing project, you (and your audience, your readers) will be pleased with the results.

- **Building Good Writing Habits**
- **Understanding the Writing Process**
- **The Process in Action**
- **Focusing on the Texas Traits**

"Don't think and then write it down. Think on paper."

—Harry Kemelman

ELPS 3E

Building Good Writing Habits

Writing success begins with good writing habits. Follow the tips below and you will see real improvement in your writing.

When to Write

Set aside time each day to write. Regular writing will help you develop fluency—the ability to write quickly and easily.

"Write about it by day, and dream about it by night."
—E. B. White

Where to Write

Write in school and at home. Write on the bus or in a coffee shop. Just keep writing wherever you can.

"I write anywhere, but I still like cafes."
—J. K. Rowling

"Write in a place that you feel safe."
—George Heard

What to Write

Write about anything and everything that interests you—personal experiences, current events, music, books, or sports. Write in a variety of genres: stories, poems, plays, television or movie scripts, and nonfiction.

"If a story is in you, it has got to come out."
—William Faulkner

How to Write

Relax and let the words flow. Share your true feelings and, before long, your distinctive writing voice will develop.

"The beautiful part of writing is that you don't have to get it right the first time, unlike, say, a brain surgeon."
—Robert Cormier

"There are a thousand ways to write, and each is as good as the other if it fits you."
—Lillian Hellman

Read the quotations above and pick one that stands out. Write for 5 to 10 minutes about what this quotation means to you. Discuss with a classmate.

Understanding the Writing Process

Before a piece of writing is ready to share, it should have gone through a series of steps called the *writing process.* Each step is briefly described below.

The Steps in the Writing Process

Prewriting

Prewrite

The first step in the writing process is planning. It involves selecting a specific topic, developing a thesis, and gathering and organizing details to support the writer's position. The writer must also determine who the audience will be and what genre will work best for the topic.

Drafting

Draft

The writer completes the first draft using the prewriting plan as a guide. This is a writer's ***first*** chance to get everything on paper. When drafting, the writer should attempt to include transitions and rhetorical devices such as analogies or repetition to convey meaning.

Revising

Revise

During revising, the writer reviews the draft for key traits: ***focus and coherence, organization, development of ideas, and voice.*** The writer checks that the genre is appropriate for the topic and audience and that the purpose of the writing is clear. Improvements should also be made in style, word choice, use of figurative language, and subtlety of meaning.

Editing

Edit

Check the revised draft for *conventions*—grammar, mechanics, and spelling. Proofread the final copy.

Publishing

Publish

The final step in the writing process is publishing. It is an opportunity for the writer to share work and to respond to additional feedback.

TEKS 10.13A, 10.13B
ELPS 5B

The Process in Action

The next two pages give a detailed description of each step in the writing process. The graphic below reminds you that, at any time, you can move back and forth between the steps in the writing process. Be aware that if you put more effort and care into the early stages of the process, you'll move through the later stages more easily.

Prewriting Planning Your Writing

- Search for topics that meet the requirements of the assignment.
- Plan your writing by selecting a specific topic and genre.

Gathering and Organizing Details

- Gather as many ideas and details as you can about the topic.
- With the purpose of the assignment in mind, find one point to emphasize about the topic—either an interesting part or your personal feeling about it. This will be the thesis, or controlling idea, of your writing.
- Decide which details to include in your writing.
- Organize your details into a writing plan, perhaps using an outline or a graphic organizer.

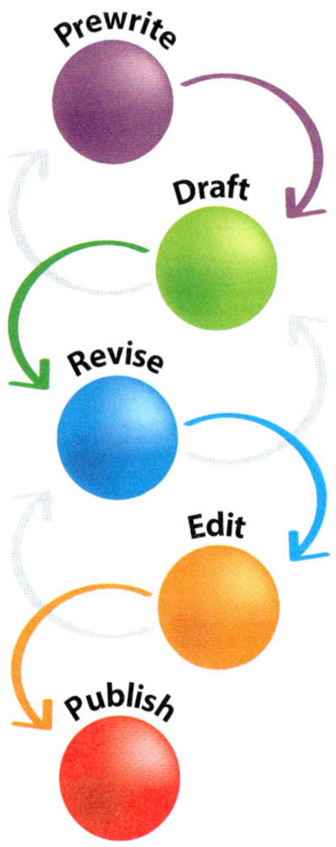

Drafting Developing Your Ideas

- When writing the first draft, concentrate on getting your ideas on paper. Structure your ideas in a persuasive, sustained, and convincing way.
- Use the details you collected to develop your draft. Be sure to include rhetorical devices to help convey and strengthen your ideas.
- Use transitions, and make sure your writing has a beginning, a middle, and an ending.

Tip

Write on every *other* line and on *one* side of the paper when using pen or pencil and paper. Double-space on a computer. This will give you room for revising.

Revising Improving Your Writing

- Set aside your first draft for a while so you can return to it with a fresh perspective.
- Read your first draft slowly and critically.
- Use these questions as a revising guide:
    - Is my topic interesting, and did I use the correct genre?
    - Are my style and word choice appropriate?
    - Are the ideas in order and easy to understand?
    - Have I included enough details to support my controlling idea?
    - Does the ending leave the reader with something to think about?
    - Have I varied my sentence structure?
    - Are the nouns specific and the verbs active?
    - Have I used figurative language and is it clear?
    - Does the piece read smoothly and convey subtlety of meaning?
- Ask another person to review your writing and give suggestions.
- Review for word choice and sentence variety. Make as many changes as necessary to improve your writing.

Editing Checking Grammar, Mechanics, and Spelling

- Check for errors in grammar, punctuation, capitalization, and spelling.
- Have at least one other person check your writing for errors.
- Prepare a neat final copy.
- Proofread the final copy before publishing it.

Publishing Sharing Your Writing

- Ask a classmate to review the final copy, and respond to the feedback.
- Consider submitting your writing to a newspaper or other publication. You may wish to include it in a portfolio of your writing.

Learning Language Reread the last two pages. Discuss the writing process with a classmate, and work together to summarize the steps. Remember, *summarize* means "to say again briefly."

Focusing on the Texas Traits

Writing is complicated, so don't try to focus on everything at once. For example, don't check your punctuation while considering the effectiveness of your beginning and ending paragraphs. Using the writing process will help you focus on each trait of good writing at the appropriate time. (See pages 33–48.)

Connecting the Traits to the Writing Process

Prewrite	
Focus and Coherence	Is my writing focused on the prompt? Have I clearly stated my thesis, or controlling idea? Do all parts of my writing support my thesis statement?
Organization	How should I organize my writing? Which graphic organizer should I use for my planning?
Voice	What is my attitude about the topic?
Draft	
Organization	How do I want to arrange my ideas?
Ideas	What do I want to say? How can I best convey my purpose for writing?
Voice	How do I want to sound?
Revise	
Organization	Do my beginning, middle, and ending work well?
Ideas	Are my ideas clear and complete?
Voice	Have I created an appropriate tone? Have I chosen specific nouns and active verbs? Are my sentences varied? Do they read smoothly?
Edit	
Conventions	Have I used correct grammar, punctuation, capitalization, and spelling?
Publish	
All Traits	What do you think of my work?

Try It!

Reflect on the traits. When you develop a piece of writing, do you consider all of the traits listed above? Are some traits more important than other ones? Explain.

One Writer's Process

Although every individual snowflake is different, all snowflakes are formed by the same natural process. In the same way, although every writer has a unique style, the best writers approach writing with the same writing process. Moving through the process, step-by-step and often back and forth, allows writers to express their ideas clearly, meaningfully, and accurately.

This chapter shows how student writer Nakeisha Williams used the writing process to develop a persuasive essay about saving murals in her community. As you follow her work, you'll see how she shaped her initial ideas into a convincing essay.

- **Previewing the Texas Traits**
- **Prewriting**
- **Drafting**
- **Revising**
- **Editing**
- **Publishing**
- **Assessing the Final Draft**
- **Reflecting on Your Writing**

"Write, write, and write some more. Think of writing as a muscle that needs lots of exercise."

—Jane Yolen

Previewing the Texas Traits

The goal of persuasive writing is to defend a position in a well-organized way. Before Nakeisha began writing, she looked over the writing traits shown below. Nakeisha also looked over the holistic scoring guide on pages 60–61. Considering these points and reminders helped her get started.

Texas Writing Traits

- **Focus and Coherence**
  Select a topic that you care about. Create a thesis statement, or controlling idea. Connect ideas to the thesis statement and to each other. The introduction and conclusion add depth to the writing.

- **Organization**
  Use an organizational pattern that is appropriate for the topic and audience. Create a beginning that states your opinion, a middle that uses facts and examples to support your opinion, and an ending that makes a call for action. Use meaningful transitions.

- **Development of Ideas**
  Develop your ideas thoroughly. Connect all your ideas to the thesis statement and to each other. Use specific details to support your position.

- **Voice**
  Use a confident voice that balances facts and feelings and a tone that is appropriate and engaging for your topic and audience.

- **Conventions**
  Use grammar, capitalization, punctuation, sentence structure, and spelling properly.

Try It!

Answer the following questions about the goals of Nakeisha's assignment, then discuss your answers with a classmate.

1. What must Nakeisha remember when selecting a topic?
2. What should Nakeisha remember about organization?
3. How should she sound (voice) in her essay?

Prewriting Selecting a Topic

Nakeisha's teacher wrote this persuasive writing prompt on the board.

> Write a persuasive essay about a controversy at school or in our community. Choose a current, important issue that you feel strongly about. Your topic should be specific enough to cover in a few paragraphs.

Nakeisha used sentence starters to help her think of controversies. Sentence starters are one of a range of strategies a writer can use to choose a topic and explore ideas. Nakeisha put an asterisk next to her chosen issue.

Sentence Starters

People at my school disagree about . . .

- banning food and drinks in study hall.
- renovating the school theater.

People in my community disagree about . . .

- more lighting in the skate park.
- eliminating the downtown murals.*

Reflecting on the Topic

Nakeisha did some freewriting to explore her ideas on her chosen topic.

Freewriting

> Mom said that the city council is discussing removing the murals because they are chipped and faded. I think the murals should be repaired, maintained, and saved. Hawkins students are proud of the work they did to create those murals. The unity, diversity, and creativity themes are still important today. Too much time and effort were put into this project . . .

Try It!

Complete the two sentence starters above. Write at least two endings for each. Choose one issue that you feel strongly about from your list. Discuss your choice with a classmate and describe your feelings on the issue.

Prewriting Gathering Details

It's important to gather details that support your position. Nakeisha went to the library to find information about the downtown murals. She looked through newspapers, magazines, and Internet sources.

Sources of Information

To keep track of her research, Nakeisha recorded complete source information on note cards.

Sample Source Notes

Olivia Stellpflug. "Mural Masterpiece." Hawkins City Herald. May 3, 2006.

"The Edmund Burke School/HS Community Service," The Edmund Burke School. Visited online April 10, 2009. http://www.eburke.org/pages/sitepage.cfm?page=784

"Corporation for National & Community Service." Corporation for National & Community Service. Visited online April 9, 2009. http://www.nationalservice.org/for_individuals/benefits/index.asp

Quotations

During her research, Nakeisha recorded quotations from interviews. Nakeisha's teacher asked students to use quotations from at least two sources.

Sample Quotations

Interview with a Hawkins student:
"Even though I was only a freshman, I made many friends as we all worked together."
"I thought, wow, these themes are real!"
"It was fun, not work."
Source: Keri Ellings

Interview with a Hawkins teacher:
"The after-school art club could take on the responsibility of restoring and preserving the downtown murals. The city would not have to pay anything."
Source: Ms. Larson, art teacher

Try It!

Look for information about the issue you chose. Find one informative newspaper article and list two people that you could interview.

Developing a Thesis

Once Nakeisha had enough information, she was ready to write a thesis statement for her essay. In persuasive writing, the thesis statement expresses an opinion. It consists of two parts: a specific topic and a particular feeling or an opinion about it.

A specific topic + a particular feeling = an effective opinion statement.

Nakeisha's Opinion Statement

The Hawkins High murals (specific topic) should be saved because they showcase important themes and quality work by students in their own community (particular feeling).

Organizing the Essay

Next, Nakeisha organized her information (main points and supporting details) in a modified outline.

Nakeisha's Modified Outline

Thesis statement: The Hawkins High murals should be saved because they showcase important themes and quality work by students in their own community.

Pride students have about murals
- Quotation from Corporation for National & Community Service
- Entire student body involvement (planning, designing, painting)
- Student interview, Keri Ellings

Sense of importance in community that murals give students
- Teenagers feeling unheard and unseen
- Murals as a positive form of expression
- Destroying murals upsetting to students

Important themes of the murals
- Unity
- Diversity
- Creativity

City's concern about expense of maintaining murals
- Teacher interview, Ms. Larson
- Art Club plan

Drafting Developing Your Ideas

Nakeisha referred to her outline as she wrote her first draft. She wanted to get all her ideas on paper. She also wanted to structure her ideas in a persuasive and convincing way so she could sustain her argument throughout the essay.

Nakeisha's First Draft

The first paragraph states the issue and ends with the opinion statement.

Each middle paragraph covers one part of the issue.

Nakeisha uses a transitional sentence to link the information in this paragraph to her opening paragraph.

Save Our Murals from Sandblasting

Its been nearly three years since students painted the downtown murals. In a suprising move, the city council recently proposed removing the art. The murals have begun to fade and peel The Hawkins High murals should be saved because they showcase important themes and quality work by students in their own community.

The students are proud of the murals. "Pride, satisfaction, and a sense of accomplishment" are valuable benefits of volunteerism, according to the Corporation for National & Community Service. Everybody in the school had a chance to submit possible themes for the murals. Then the art teachers chose twenty of the best ideas for a schoolwide vote. The entire student body voted to choose the themes of unity, diversity and creativity. Three art classes made designs that the school then approved. For an entire month, students volunteered after school to complete the murals. Teachers and parents were impresed by how well students pull together. A student who work on the murals said that she really enjoyed painting.

Allowing the murals to remain would give students a sense of importance in their community. All too often, adults don't realize that teenagers can feel unheard and unseen. If noticed by an adult, some teenagers feel that anything they do or say is negatively viewed. Their music is too loud or their hair is a weird color. The mural project allowed students to express themselves in a positive way. Many schools across the country agree that getting involved gives "student volunteers a sense of community" along with "increased self-esteem and a clearer sense of identity"

Persuasive essays require evidence. Nakeisha sustains her argument with quotations that support her position. She provides her source in parentheses.

("High School Community Service"). If the city sandblasts the murals, students at Hawkins could think that their voice doesn't matter.

A reason to save the murals is the message each one conveys. Every day thousands of people drive through downtown. Before the murals, commuters and shoppers had nothing to look at but brick walls and billboards. Now people can find inspiration in the themes expressed in the murals. Unified Universe shows teenagers. Divine Diversity presents costumed children. Creative Culture features young people. If the city removes the murals, it's saying that these issues aren't important.

By providing a counter-argument, a type of rhetorical device, and addressing that viewpoint, Nakeisha sustains her own position and continues to persuade her audience.

The city says the reason for removing the murals is the estimated expense of maintenance. Art club students have already planned a yearly schedule for fund-raising and maintenance. Since painting will be done after school, any interested students will be encouraged to join in. In response, one of the Hawkins High art teachers, Ms. Larson, said, "The after-school art club will take on the responsibility of restoring and preserving the downtown murals. The city won't have to pay anything." With that kind of support from the school, the city shouldn't remove the one piece of public art created by the students of Hawkins High.

The ending paragraph sums up the issue and closes on a strong note.

The murals give teenagers a sense of pride and belonging, while also sharing a good message with all who pass. In addition, maintaining the murals wouldn't cost the city a single penny, since students would do all of the work. Last weekend, students took petitions to downtown businesses and residential neighborhoods. The 500 signatures prove that the community has united with students at Hawkins.

Try It!

Look through Nakeisha's first draft. Then answer these questions: Does Nakeisha's first draft contain all the information that she outlined (page 17)? Does she add any new details? If so, what are they? What else might she have included? Try to name at least one idea.

ELPS 3E

Texas Traits

Revising Focusing on Ideas

After Nakeisha completed her first draft, she set aside her essay for a day. Then she rechecked the traits on page 14 and reviewed her first draft. Nakeisha's thoughts below reveal the changes she planned to make.

Organization

Use an appropriate organizational pattern. Create a beginning that states your opinion, a middle that uses facts and examples to support your opinion, and an ending that calls for action.

"I need smoother transitions between sentences and paragraphs."

Development of Ideas

Create a thesis statement and connect all your ideas to it and to each other. Develop your ideas thoroughly, and use specific details.

"Some of my details don't fit my opinion statement. I need to add more information from the student interview.

Voice

Use a confident voice that balances facts and feelings and a tone that is appropriate and engaging for your topic and audience.

"I need an opening that sets the right tone (the need for action) for my essay."

Try It!

With a classmate, review and discuss the changes in Nakeisha's first revision on page 21. What other changes in ideas, organization, or voice would you make to Nakeisha's essay? Name two.

Nakeisha's First Revision

Here are the revisions that Nakeisha made in the first part of her essay. As you read, think about how well Nakeisha's draft addresses her purpose, her audience, and the genre in which she is writing.

Using a quotation strengthens the voice in the opening.

A transition helps link two paragraphs.

The specific words from a student worker are added.

"Powerful murals painted by students of Hawkins High School have brought new life to downtown," stated the Hawkins City Herald in a front-page article.

Its been nearly three years since ~~students painted the downtown~~ that article praised the murals. In a suprising move, the city council recently proposed removing the art. The murals have begun to fade and peel The Hawkins High murals should be saved because they showcase important themes and quality work by students in their own community.

~~The~~ First of all, students are proud of the murals. "Pride, satisfaction, and a sense of accomplishment" are valuable benefits of volunteerism, according to the Corporation for National and Community Service. Everybody in the school had a chance to submit possible themes for the murals. Then the art teachers chose twenty of the best ideas for a school-wide vote. The entire student body voted to choose the themes of unity, diversity and creativity. Three art classes made designs that the school then approved. For an entire month, students volunteered after school to complete the murals. Teachers and parents were impressed by how well students pull together. ~~A student~~ Keri Ellings, who worked on the murals said ~~that she really enjoyed painting.~~, "Even though I was only a freshman, I made many friends as we all worked together. I thought, wow, these themes are real!"

TEKS 10.13C
ELPS 3E

Revising Using a Peer Response Sheet

Mario evaluated Nakeisha's essay using the holistic scoring guide on pages 60–61. His suggestions on the response sheet below showed Nakeisha where she could make additional improvements.

Peer Response Sheet

Writer: Nakeisha Williams Responder: Mario Rodriguez

Title: Save Our Murals from Sandblasting

What I liked about your writing:

- Your development of each idea helped me understand the issue and your position on it.
- Your writing is authentic. I can tell you care about this issue.
- You used specific details and gave background information.

Changes I would suggest:

- Wouldn't a transition make the beginning of the fourth paragraph stronger?
- Could you provide more details about the murals?
- Could you use Ms. Larson's quotation earlier in the essay?
- Could you sound more direct at the end of the fifth paragraph?

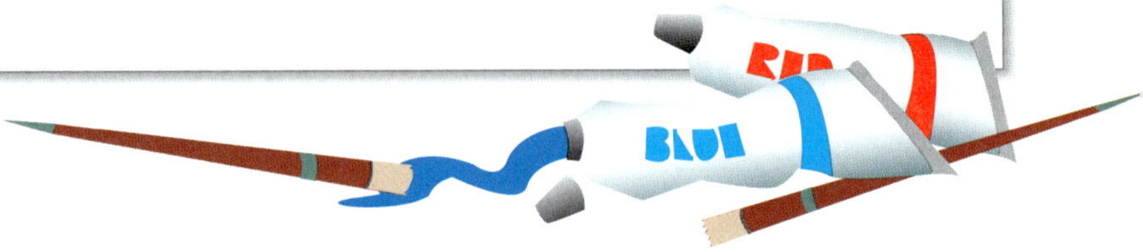

Try It!

Review Mario's suggestions for improvement. Which suggestion seems to be most important? Explain why. With a classmate, discuss at least one new suggestion to improve Nakeisha's writing. Look at the explanation of organization, ideas, and voice on page 20 to help you make a suggestion.

Nakeisha's Revision Using a Peer Response

Using Mario's comments, Nakeisha revised her essay again. The changes she made in two middle paragraphs are shown here.

A topic sentence is strengthened. This change improves the style, and the author clearly states her opinion.

Perhaps the most important ~~A~~ reason to save the murals is the message each one conveys. Every day thousands of people drive through downtown. Before the murals, commuters and shoppers had nothing to look at but brick walls and billboards. Now people can find inspiration in the themes expressed in the murals. Unified Universe shows teenagers supporting the earth. Divine Diversity presents costumed children from around the world. Creative Culture features young ~~people~~ artists, musicians, and dancers. If the city removes the murals, it's saying that these issues aren't important.

Specific details are added.

The city says the reason for removing the murals is the estimated expense of maintenance. Art club students have already planned a yearly schedule for fund-raising and maintenance. Since painting will be done after school, any interested students will be encouraged to join in. In response, one of the Hawkins High art teachers, Ms. Larson, said, "The after-school art club will take on the responsibility of restoring and preserving the downtown murals. The city won't have to pay anything." With that kind of support from the school, the city ~~shouldn't remove the one piece~~ has no excuse to remove the one work of public art created by the students of Hawkins High.

A quotation is moved for greater impact. This change also enhances the author's subtlety of meaning.

Voice is made clearer and stronger. The reader becomes even more engaged in the argument.

TEKS 10.13C
ELPS 3E

Texas Traits

Revising Focusing on Style

Nakeisha also reviewed her writing for its voice and sentence structure. Her thoughts below tell you what changes she planned to make.

Voice

Use a confident voice that balances facts and opinion. Your voice should be appropriate for the topic. Explain important terms that may be unfamiliar to your audience.

"I should find appropriate replacements for overused words (mural). I also want to add more exciting verbs and modifiers."

Conventions

Write clear, complete sentences with varied beginnings. Use grammar, capitalization, punctuation, and spelling properly.

"I should combine some of my short sentences to create a better flow in the text."

Try It!

With a classmate, review Nakeisha's improved essay on page **25**. What other improvements in voice could she make? Name one or two. What other changes in sentence structure could she make? Name one.

Nakeisha's Improvements in Voice

Here are the changes in word choice and sentence structure Nakeisha made in the first part of her essay.

> Sentences are combined to improve sentence structure.

> Changes in word choice improve voice.

"Powerful murals painted by the students of Hawkins High School have brought new life to downtown," ~~stated~~ proclaimed the Hawkins City Herald in a front-page article. Its been nearly three years since that article praised the murals. In a suprising move, the city council recently proposed removing the art~~. The murals have~~, which has begun to fade and peel The Hawkins High murals should be saved because they showcase important themes and quality work by students in their own community.

First of all, students are proud of ~~the murals~~ their efforts. "Pride, satisfaction, and a sense of accomplishment" are valuable benefits of volunteerism, according to the Corporation for National and Community Service. Everybody in the school had ~~a chance~~ an opportunity to submit possible themes for the murals~~.~~ ~~Then~~ before the art teachers ~~chose~~ selected twenty of the best ideas for a schoolwide vote. The entire student body voted to choose the themes of unity, diversity and creativity.

Three art classes ~~made~~ created lively designs that the school then approved. For an entire month, students volunteered after school to complete the ~~murals~~ work. Teachers and parents were impresed by how well students of all ages and abilities pull together. Keri Ellings, who ~~worked~~ assisted on the murals said, "Even though I was only a freshman, I made many friends as we all worked together. . . .

TEKS 10.13D
ELPS 3E

Texas Traits

Editing Checking for Conventions

Finally, Nakeisha was ready to edit her essay. She checked her work for grammar, punctuation, capitalization, and spelling errors.

Conventions

Follow rules of grammar, punctuation, capitalization, and spelling.

"I'll check my essay and correct any errors in grammar, punctuation, capitalization, and spelling."

For help with conventions, Nakeisha used the "Proofreader's Guide" in the back of her *Write Source* textbook and the checklist below.

GRAMMAR

_____ **1.** Do I use proper tense and voice for my verbs?
_____ **2.** Do my subjects and verbs agree in number?
_____ **3.** Do my pronouns clearly agree with their antecedents?

PUNCTUATION

_____ **4.** Do I use punctuation correctly?
_____ **5.** Do I use commas correctly?
_____ **6.** Do I correctly italicize or use quotation marks for titles?
_____ **7.** Do I use apostrophes correctly?
_____

CAPITALIZATION

_____ **8.** Have I capitalized all the proper nouns and adjectives?

SPELLING

_____ **9.** Have I spelled words correctly?
_____ **10.** Have I used the spell-checker on my computer?
_____ **11.** Have I double-checked words my spell-checker may have missed?

Try It!

With a classmate, find four or five errors in Nakeisha's revised draft on page 25. Did you find the same errors as Nakeisha found on page 27?

Nakeisha's Editing for Conventions

Here are Nakeisha's edits in the first part of her essay. See page 641 or the inside back cover of this book for common editing and proofreading marks.

The title of the newspaper is marked for italics.

Punctuation, spelling, and number errors are corrected.

A verb-tense error is corrected.

"Powerful murals painted by the students of Hawkins High School have brought new life to downtown," proclaimed the Hawkins City Herald in a front-page article. It's been nearly three years since that article praised the murals. In a suprising [surprising] move, the city council recently proposed removing the art, which has begun to fade and peel . The Hawkins High murals should be saved because they showcase important themes and quality work by students in their own community.

First of all, the students are proud of their efforts. "Pride, satisfaction, and a sense of accomplishment" are valuable benefits of volunteerism, according to the Corporation for National and Community Service. Everybody in the school had an opportunity to submit possible themes for the murals before the art teachers selected ~~twenty~~ 20 of the best ideas for a schoolwide vote. The entire student body voted to choose the themes of unity, diversity, and creativity. Three art classes created lively designs that the school then approved. For an entire month, students volunteered after school to complete the project. Teachers and parents were impresed [impressed] by how well students of all ages and abilities pull[ed] together. Keri Ellings, who assisted . . .

Publishing Sharing Your Writing

Nakeisha used the information below to produce a clean final draft of her essay.

Tips for Handwritten Copies

- Use blue or black ink and write clearly.
- Write your name according to your teacher's instructions.
- Skip a line and center your title on the first page; skip another line and begin your essay.
- Indent each paragraph and leave a one-inch margin on all four sides.
- Place your last name and the page number on each page after the first.

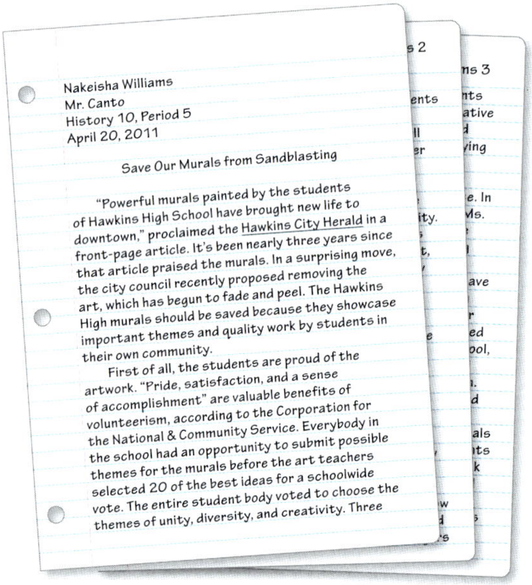

Nakeisha Williams
Mr. Canto
History 10, Period 5
April 20, 2011

Save Our Murals from Sandblasting

"Powerful murals painted by the students of Hawkins High School have brought new life to downtown," proclaimed the Hawkins City Herald in a front-page article. It's been nearly three years since that article praised the murals. In a surprising move, the city council recently proposed removing the art, which has begun to fade and peel. The Hawkins High murals should be saved because they showcase important themes and quality work by students in their own community.

First of all, the students are proud of the artwork. "Pride, satisfaction, and a sense of accomplishment" are valuable benefits of volunteerism, according to the Corporation for the National & Community Service. Everybody in the school had an opportunity to submit possible themes for the murals before the art teachers selected 20 of the best ideas for a schoolwide vote. The entire student body voted to choose the themes of unity, diversity, and creativity. Three

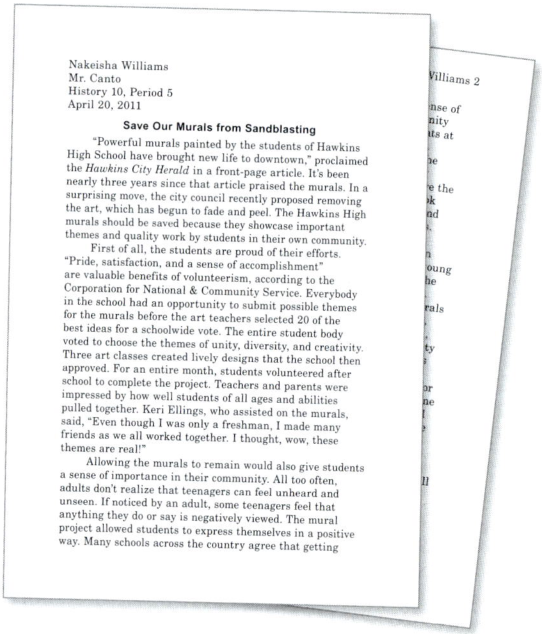

Nakeisha Williams
Mr. Canto
History 10, Period 5
April 20, 2011

Save Our Murals from Sandblasting

"Powerful murals painted by the students of Hawkins High School have brought new life to downtown," proclaimed the *Hawkins City Herald* in a front-page article. It's been nearly three years since that article praised the murals. In a surprising move, the city council recently proposed removing the art, which has begun to fade and peel. The Hawkins High murals should be saved because they showcase important themes and quality work by students in their own community.

First of all, the students are proud of their efforts. "Pride, satisfaction, and a sense of accomplishment" are valuable benefits of volunteerism, according to the Corporation for National & Community Service. Everybody in the school had an opportunity to submit possible themes for the murals before the art teachers selected 20 of the best ideas for a schoolwide vote. The entire student body voted to choose the themes of unity, diversity, and creativity. Three art classes created lively designs that the school then approved. For an entire month, students volunteered after school to complete the project. Teachers and parents were impressed by how well students of all ages and abilities pulled together. Keri Ellings, who assisted on the murals, said, "Even though I was only a freshman, I made many friends as we all worked together. I thought, wow, these themes are real!"

Allowing the murals to remain would also give students a sense of importance in their community. All too often, adults don't realize that teenagers can feel unheard and unseen. If noticed by an adult, some teenagers feel that anything they do or say is negatively viewed. The mural project allowed students to express themselves in a positive way. Many schools across the country agree that getting

Tips for Computer Copies

- Use an easy-to-read font set at 12-point type size.
- Double-space the text and set your margins so that you have a one-inch space around the outside of each page.

Nakeisha's Final Draft

Nakeisha proudly presented a printed draft of her essay to Mr. Canto and volunteered to share her writing about the downtown murals with the class.

Nakeisha Williams
Mr. Canto
History 10, Period 5
April 20, 2011

Save Our Murals from Sandblasting

"Powerful murals painted by the students of Hawkins High School have brought new life to downtown," proclaimed the *Hawkins City Herald* in a front-page article. It's been nearly three years since that article praised the murals. In a surprising move, the city council recently proposed removing the art, which has begun to fade and peel. The Hawkins High murals should be saved because they showcase important themes and quality work by students in their own community.

First of all, the students are proud of their efforts. "Pride, satisfaction, and a sense of accomplishment" are valuable benefits of volunteerism, according to the Corporation for National and Community Service. Everybody in the school had an opportunity to submit possible themes for the murals before the art teachers selected twenty of the best ideas for a schoolwide vote. The entire student body voted to choose the themes of unity, diversity, and creativity. Three art classes created lively designs that the school then approved. For an entire month, students volunteered after school to complete the project. Teachers and parents were impressed by how well students of all ages and abilities pulled together. Keri Ellings, who assisted on the murals, said, "Even though I was only a freshman, I made many friends as we all worked together. I thought, wow, these themes are real!"

Allowing the murals to remain would also give students a sense of importance in their community. All too often, adults don't realize that teenagers can feel unheard and unseen. If noticed by an adult, some teenagers feel that anything they do or say is negatively viewed. The mural project allowed students to express themselves in a positive way. Many schools across the country agree that getting

TEKS 10.13E

Williams 2

involved gives "student volunteers a sense of community" along with "increased self-esteem and a clearer sense of identity" ("High School Community Service"). If the city sandblasts the murals, students at Hawkins could think that their voice doesn't matter.

Perhaps the most important reason to save the murals is the message each one conveys. Every day thousands of people drive through downtown. Before the murals, commuters and shoppers had nothing to look at but brick walls and billboards. Now people can find inspiration in the themes expressed in the paintings. *Unified Universe* shows teenagers supporting the earth. *Divine Diversity* presents costumed children from around the world. *Creative Culture* features young artists, musicians, and dancers. If the city removes the murals, it's saying that these issues aren't important.

The city says the reason for removing the murals is the estimated expense of maintenance. In response, one of the Hawkins High art teachers, Ms. Larson, said, "The after-school art club will take on the responsibility of restoring and preserving the downtown murals. The city won't have to pay anything." Art club students have already planned a yearly schedule for fund-raising and maintenance. Since painting will be done after school, any interested students will be encouraged to join in. With that kind of support from the school, the city has no excuse to remove the one work of public art created by the students of Hawkins High.

The murals give teenagers a sense of pride and belonging, while also sharing a powerful message with all who pass. In addition, maintaining the murals wouldn't cost the city a single penny, since students would do all the work. Last weekend, students took petitions to downtown businesses and residential neighborhoods. The 500 signatures prove that the community has united with students at Hawkins to voice their opinion loud and clear: "Save the murals!" Because the experience of the students working together on the original mural project was so positive, maybe Hawkins High should replace one of the three murals every four years so that more students have a chance to create a mural sometime during their high school years.

Assessing the Final Draft

The teacher used a scoring guide like the one found on pages **60–61** to assess Nakeisha's final draft. Based on this guide a **4** is the very best score that a writer can receive. Nakeisha's teacher included comments under each trait.

Score = 4

Focus and Coherence

The composition is focused on the topic, and you clearly state your opinion in your thesis statement. Your writing contains specific ideas and details that support your thesis .

Organization

Your ideas are organized in a fairly logical pattern and mostly effective. You state your position, offer good support for it, and you make a call for support in the ending.

Development of Ideas

Your ideas are fully developed, and you have included strong supporting details. Your ideas are connected to each other and to the main idea.

Voice

You obviously care about this issue.
Your voice conveys a sense of concern that fits the topic and the audience.

Conventions

Word choice could be stronger. You could use a wider variety of sentences. The writing could flow more smoothly from one idea to another. Your writing follows the rules of grammar, punctuation, capitalization, and spelling.

Review the assessment. Do you agree with the holistic score and the comments made by Nakeisha's teacher? Why or why not? In a brief paragraph, discuss your reaction to Nakeisha's essay and how you would assess it.

Reflecting on Your Writing

After completing her essay, Nakeisha filled out a reflection sheet. This helped her think about the assignment and plan for future writing.

Nakeisha Williams
Mr. Canto
History 10, Period 5
April 20, 2011

Persuasive Essay: Save Our Murals from Sandblasting

1. The best part of my essay is . . .
   my introduction. It uses a powerful quotation to support a solid opinion statement.

2. The part that still needs work is . . .
   my word choice. I should avoid overusing certain words.

3. The most important part of my prewriting and planning was . . .
   exploring the history of the murals and interviewing people who were involved in creating them. That gave me the details I needed to support my position.

4. During revising, I spent a lot of time . . .
   developing better transitions between sentences and between paragraphs.

5. The thing I've learned about this type of essay is . . .
   that it's very important to choose a topic that I care about. If I don't care, it will be difficult to convince others to support my opinion.

6. Here is one question I still have about direct quotations . . .
   How do I handle them if the person I'm quoting wants to remain anonymous?

Understanding the Traits of Writing

An effective piece of writing is like a good stew. Many ingredients combine to create something nourishing and tasty. The ingredients in a piece of writing are known as **traits**, and they include *focus and coherence, organization, development of ideas, voice,* and *conventions*. Only with a proper balance or combination of these traits will you create a piece of writing worth sharing.

The next page in this chapter introduces you to the traits of writing. The pages that follow give writing samples that show the traits in action. Learning about the traits of writing—and putting them into practice—will help you write better in all your classes, whether you are writing a personal narrative, a book review, or a persuasive essay. Think of this chapter as your guide to good writing.

- **Introducing the Traits**
- **The Traits in Action**
- **Understanding the Traits**
- **Guide for Effective Writing**

"When I write . . . it's like driving a team of horses and giving them the lead but not letting them run away in a totally different direction."

—Monica Hughes

Introducing the Texas Traits

The following chart identifies the important traits of effective writing. Write with these traits in mind, and you will be pleased with the results.

Traits of Writing

- **Focus and Coherence**
  Strong writing presents a clear focus. It contains specific, connected ideas that support the thesis and does not include unrelated information. Each paragraph adds depth to the writing.
- **Organization**
  Effective writing creates a meaningful whole—with interesting and distinct beginning, middle, and ending parts. The supporting details are arranged in the best order for the topic and audience. The writing flows smothly from sentence to sentence and paragraph to paragraph.
- **Development of Ideas**
  Good writing contains thoroughly developed ideas that are clearly supported with appropriate details. This type of development helps the reader appreciate and understand the writer's message.
- **Voice**
  Writing that has voice reflects the writer's personality. It is engaging and appropriate for the topic and audience and contains strong words, including specific nouns, verbs, and modifiers.
- **Conventions**
  Strong writing follows the rules for grammar, sentence strucure, capitalization, punctuation, and spelling. It is carefully edited to be free of errors.

FYI

Also consider *presentation*. An effective final copy follows the accepted guidelines for margins, indenting, spacing, and so on. The writing's appearance affects the reader's overall impression. (See pages 72–74.)

The Texas Traits in Action

The following excerpt from an essay by Kendall McGinn displays an effective use of the traits of writing.

The thesis for the essay is clearly stated. The writing focuses on the topic.

The passage is arranged chronologically.

Ideas are well developed, and the included details support the thesis.

The writer sounds interested in the topic.

Varied sentences and word choice add interest. Writing conventions are followed.

Buffalo Nation

Before the Europeans came to North America, the native people of the plains and the buffalo were one *Pte Oyate,* or Buffalo Nation. The big bull *tatanka* was life itself. The Native Americans followed the herds and used the buffalo for food, clothing, shelter, and medicine. A Lakota leader summed up this unity between human and animal: "When the Creator made the buffalo, he put power in them. When you eat the meat, that power goes into you, heals the body and spirit" (qtd. in Hodgson 69).

During the expansion of the United States, however, Europeans nearly eliminated the North American buffalo through a senseless slaughter of the animal. The population of 100 million buffalo in 1700 had, in fact, been reduced to 1,000 by 1889. But surprisingly, the buffalo has made a comeback (Allen 100).

In recent years, the number of buffalo has increased to nearly 400,000. Cable Network News owner Ted Turner raises almost 10,000 buffalo on his Montana and New Mexico ranches. "I guess I've gone buffalo batty," Turner says. He supports the raising of buffalo as an excellent source of low-fat meat (Hodgson 75).

Buffalo ranchers are learning that raising buffalo is more cost-effective and more environmentally safe than raising cattle. Here are four reasons why:

- Buffalo don't overeat.
- Their sharp hooves loosen hard soil.
- Buffalo improve grass crops.
- They adapt to any climate.

Buffalo living in Florida seem just as happy as those living in Alaska. In Hawaii, they even survived a hurricane. Hawaiian rancher Bill Mowry recalls how the buffalo "loved every minute of it" (qtd. in Allen 105).

ELPS 3E

Understanding Focus and Coherence

Strong writing engages the reader and sustains that feeling of engagement by remaining focused on key ideas and making sense throughout. A good thesis hooks the reader. Details (*facts, examples, quotations,* etc.) support the thesis and help create a sense of completeness and coherence.

Establishing Focus and Coherence

Your writing would go on and on if you tried to say everything about a topic. That is why it is important to establish focus and coherence in your writing. Your focus may be based on your main feelings about a topic or on a special part you wish to emphasize. An effective focus gives you a starting point and directs your writing in a coherent manner—that is, in a way that makes sense.

Sample Paragraph

Carefully read the following paragraph, paying close attention to the topic, the focus, and the specific details.

Not to Be Denied

Jackie Robinson's personal attributes allowed him to break major league baseball's color barrier in 1947. When Brooklyn Dodgers president Branch Rickey brought him up to play for the major league club, Robinson courageously faced racism and verbal abuse. Determined and proud, he had the discipline to play through these challenges. Tremendously fast on the base paths, Robinson stole 29 bases his first year. Over his career, he stole home no fewer than 19 times! His excellent defensive skills made him a stellar infielder, playing three different positions during his career. An intelligent and disciplined hitter, he batted .311 for his career. In 1947 he was named Rookie of the Year, and in 1949 won the Most Valuable Player award. His competitive nature helped his team win the pennant in both seasons. His legacy lives on today, as he is the only player to have his number retired by all major league baseball franchises.

Respond to the reading. What is the focus of the paragraph? What details support this focus? Name two. Discuss your choices with a classmate.

Supporting the Focus

Writing has **coherence** when all the supporting details in it are related. Below is a list of types of details you can use to support the focus of your writing.

Types of Details

- **Facts** are details that can be proven.
- **Statistics** present numerical information.
- **Examples** illustrate a main point.
- **Quotations** are direct statements from other people.

Sample Paragraph

Read the paragraph below and note the types of details that it includes.

Hypersonic Travel

The X-15 rocket plane was the most successful and innovative experimental aircraft ever to take to the skies. A total of three X-15's flew 199 missions between 1959 and 1968. The plane looked futuristic with its black color, long, sleek fuselage, and stubby wings and tail. It didn't take off from the ground. Instead, the X-15 was dropped at high altitude from the wing of a B-52 bomber, gliding until the pilot fired a rocket engine that could be throttled up and down like a jet. This was the first rocket with so much pilot control. Unlike any other aircraft, the X-15 was steered by rockets in the plane's nose! According to an expert at the Smithsonian, the X-15 flew "so high that it functioned more as a spacecraft than an airplane." Over its years of service, the X-15 blew away all existing speed and altitude records and pioneered hypersonic technology that aided NASA's Gemini, Apollo, and space shuttle programs. Now retired, the two surviving X-15's are preserved in museums in Washington, D.C., and Dayton, Ohio.

Try It!

Write a paragraph about a topic of your choice. Do some research and use at least three of the four types of details listed above. Be sure your details support the focus of your paragraph.

Understanding Organization

Writer Donald Murray says that strong writing stems from "the solid construction of thoughts." A clear plan of organization gives writing unity, which makes it easy to follow from one point to the next. When you're planning the structure of a piece of writing, think in terms of the three main parts—the beginning, the middle, and the ending. There is a logical flow in the writing, and transitions help the reader move from one idea to the next. Each sentence moves the composition forward and helps the reader understand your ideas.

Connecting the Ending to the Beginning

To close a piece of writing efficiently, remind the reader about the focus, the thesis statement, that was introduced in the beginning. Making this connection brings the writing full circle and helps put everything in perspective.

Sample Paragraph

Pay close attention to the first and last sentences in this paragraph.

Long-Distance Swimmer

A few years ago, a group of scientists hoped to gain insight into the roaming patterns of sharks. To conduct their study, they attached a satellite tracking device to the tail of Nicole, a female great white shark they had located in the Indian Ocean. The tag started recording data in November 2003. It was set to break off, float to the surface, and transmit its recorded information to a satellite in February 2004. Shark experts expected Nicole to migrate a thousand miles or so up the coast of Africa. When the device broke loose and beamed up its report, the marine biologists couldn't believe what they discovered. Nicole had made her way some 7,000 miles (11,265 kilometers) across the Indian Ocean, all the way to Australia! With the device gone, researchers could no longer track Nicole. However, a zoologist in South Africa had collected photo records of the dorsal fin markings of Nicole and many other sharks. Six months later, the zoologist recognized Nicole off the Cape of Good Hope, right back where she had started. This shark had traveled a total of 14,000 miles (22,531 kilometers)! That a marine animal had such an expansive roaming pattern took the scientists completely by surprise.

Respond to the reading. What is the topic of this paragraph? How does the closing sentence connect with the beginning?

"If I can write everything out plainly, perhaps I will myself understand better what has happened."
—Sherwood Anderson

Connecting the Supporting Ideas

Transitions can be used to connect one sentence to another sentence or one paragraph to another paragraph. The type of transitions you use depends on the organization of your writing. Some transitions show time, others compare, still others add information, and so on.

Sample Paragraph

In the following paragraph the transitions (highlighted) help organize the writing chronologically.

Technical Precision

Every time a driver turns the ignition key of a car, he or she puts into action an amazing mechanical sequence. First, the starter motor spins the engine's crankshaft. Immediately, valves open in one cylinder, allowing the perfect mixture of gasoline and air to enter the combustion chamber above the piston. Then that piston rises, compressing the combustible mixture. Next, the car's electrical system discharges power to the spark plug at exactly the right time, and the spark triggers a very powerful explosion in the air-fuel combination. The resulting force drives the piston down. Meanwhile, the process of injection and spark is repeated for the next piston in the firing order, and as that one is propelled downward, the reaction brings the first one up. The rising piston forces the fumes left from the explosion into the exhaust system. Quickly, all of the pistons undergo this four-step action. The process is repeated over and over, many times per second, and when it works well, the engine runs so smoothly that the driver doesn't even have to think about what is occurring under the hood.

Respond to the reading. What is the topic of this paragraph? How do the transitions help organize the details?

Try It!

Write a paragraph that describes a process that you understand well. Use transitions as needed. (See pages 628–629 for a list of transitions.)

Understanding Development of Ideas

The thesis statement, or controlling idea, for your composition should be clearly stated, and you should approach the topic from your own perspective. Each idea should be thoroughly developed, and you should include specific details to help the reader understand and appreciate your ideas. As you have already read, there are different ways to develop your ideas and there are different types of details. These include facts, statistics, examples, and quotations.

Including Facts

Verifiable facts will strengthen your composition. They will show the reader you have done your research and understand the topic.

Sample Paragraph

The writer sounds serious and sincere and wants his audience to act.

Categorical Fury

Tropical cyclones regularly carve destructive paths across our planet. Called hurricanes when they strike the Americas, these massive storms are rated from category one (weakest) to five (strongest) on the Saffir-Simpson Scale. Category-five hurricanes unleash more energy than the combined blast of hundreds of nuclear weapons. The distinctive "eye" of the storm is an area of very low barometric pressure. The winds surrounding this eye can reach speeds greater than 155 mph. Should a category-five hurricane hit land, it can hurl a surge of water 18 to 20 feet high, devastating low-lying areas far inland. Howling winds rip the roofs from buildings, wipe out neighborhoods, and level huge trees. In addition, torrential rains flood vast regions of land. These mighty storms terrify us as few other natural occurrences can.

Try It!

Write freely for 8 to 10 minutes about something powerful and dramatic that you have witnessed. It could be an accident, a storm, a sporting event, or so on. Afterward, underline the facts that you have used in the development of your ideas.

Using Quotations

Using quotations in your writing can help the reader understand the points you are making. They can support your ideas and emphasize your perspective. When you use quotations, you must be careful to cite the source and be accurate with the words.

Sample Paragraph

In the following paragraph, the quotations emphasize the point the writer is making.

Television and Toddlers

One of the most serious problems with television is that it slows social and language development in toddlers. Toddlers need to spend more time playing and less time watching. They need to spend time interacting with their parents. The American Academy of Pediatrics has reinforced this idea. The academy has stated, ". . . research on early brain development shows that babies and toddlers have a critical need for direct interactions with parents and other significant caregivers for healthy brain growth and the development of appropriate social, emotional, and cognitive skills." According to a recent survey, most children under the age of 6 spend about two hours a day watching television or videos, and they watch every day (Kaiser Family Foundation). The Parents as Teachers National Center says that young children need to "explore, move, manipulate, smell, touch, and repeat as they learn." Studies have found that toddlers who are watching TV do none of these things. Parents need to be aware of the dangers of too much TV. They need to take action. They need to turn off the television. They need to take time to play with and talk to their children.

Respond to the reading. **Reread the paragraph. Write the main idea on your own paper, and then copy the quotations. Discuss with a partner the ways in which the quotations help develop the main idea of the paragraph.**

Understanding Voice

Voice is that special quality that makes writing your own. Novelist John Jakes emphasizes the importance of voice when he says, "Be yourself. Above all, let who you are, what you are, what you believe shine through every sentence you write, every piece you finish."

Knowing Your Purpose and Your Audience

Always know why you are writing—your *purpose*. Are you sharing information, arguing for or against something, or explaining a process? Also consider your reader—your *audience*. How much do they know about your subject? How can you gain and hold their attention? When you understand your purpose and audience, it's much easier to know how you should sound.

- For example, if you're writing a personal narrative, you probably want to sound friendly and personable.
- Or, if you're writing a persuasive letter to your school board, you will want to sound respectful, sincere, and concerned.

Sample Paragraph

Save a Life!

Last June, while driving her son home from a baseball game, Pam Withers lost control of her car on wet pavement and skidded into a tree. Her son was unhurt, but Mrs. Withers was rushed to the hospital, bleeding from several deep cuts. Her condition was listed as critical as her family gathered at the hospital. Doctors stitched her wounds, and after a number of transfusions, she finally stabilized. The fully recovered Mrs. Withers is my mother. She is very thankful for the many generous blood donors. Without them, my mother may not have lived. Next week, there will be a blood drive at Northside High School. Please make time to stop in the gymnasium between 8:00 a.m. and 3:00 p.m. and give blood. Your donation could help save a life.

Respond to the reading. Does the voice seem appropriate for the purpose and intended audience of the writing? Discuss your response with a classmate.

"You have to write a million words before you find your voice as a writer."

—Henry Miller

Knowing Your Topic

Your writing voice will hold the reader's attention if you are interested in and knowledgeable about your topic. To sound interested, be sure to choose a topic that you have strong feelings about. To sound knowledgeable, be sure to learn as much as you can about the topic before you start writing.

Sample Paragraph

In this sample, the writer shares knowledge about a topic that clearly interests her.

Fever Pitch

Backpacking into a remote area can be both thrilling and rewarding. However, a trip can be marred for a backpacker who ignores certain important considerations. When pitching a tent, always place it in a spot clear of looming rotten limbs or loose rocks that could be knocked down by wind or rain and crush your shelter. In avalanche country, beware of snowfields or cornices on higher terrain and keep your tent out of any prospective slide paths. The ground under the tent should be dry, of course, but it should also be a little higher than the surrounding area. Otherwise, a sudden rainstorm could leave you sleeping in a puddle. Also, be sure that you securely stake out the corners of your tent and attach a good rain fly. Finally, do not camp on or near an animal trail. Hang food from a tree and always keep food out of your tent. With a little attention to these details, you will minimize any potential risks and maximize your enjoyment of the wilderness experience.

Respond to the reading. What details reveal the writer's knowledge of the topic? Name three. How does she communicate her interest?

Try It!

Write freely for 10 minutes about a topic that truly interests you. When you finish, underline at least four or five ideas that demonstrate your interest in and knowledge about the topic.

"The best metaphors are spontaneous, arising naturally out of the writer's imagination. Some metaphors, though, have become clichés and lost whatever power they once had."
—Scott Rice

Using Metaphors

A metaphor compares an idea or an image in your writing to something new and brings the idea to life for your reader.

- **To Create a Picture** In the example that follows, note how the basic idea becomes a powerful picture when it is stated metaphorically.

  Basic Idea: My presentation was a real disappointment.

  Metaphor: My presentation was a real choke sandwich, all peanut butter and no jelly.

Tip

Avoid overused words or phrases and metaphors such as "The sun was a ball of fire." They have become clichés.

- **To Expand an Idea** An extended metaphor can unify ideas in a series of sentences. Note how the metaphor (comparing family relationships to fabric) is extended in the following passage.

  Metaphor: My family is a rich tapestry of personalities.

  Extended: My family is a rich tapestry of personalities. We were at loose ends last summer, at least until the reunion in August. Whatever feelings had been torn over my brother's divorce and whatever emotions had frayed over my grandmother's illness were mended at the county park.

Respond to the reading. **How is the idea of rich tapestry expanded in the example above? Identify specific metaphoric words and phrases used.**

Try It!

Write a basic metaphor about someone or something that you know well. Then try to extend that metaphor in a short passage. Use the examples above as a guide.

Understanding Conventions

Effective writing is easy to follow because, among other things, it adheres to the conventions for grammar, sentence structure, punctuation, capitalization, and spelling. Writer and editor Patricia O'Conner summarizes the importance of punctuation in this way: "When you write, punctuation marks are the road signs that guide the reader, and you wouldn't be understood without them."

Knowing the Basic Rules

The English language is always growing; it includes more words than any other "living" language. It stands to reason then that there are a lot of rules for using English. The checklist below can guide you as you check your writing for conventions. Also see the "Proofreader's Guide" (pages **642–787**).

Conventions

GRAMMAR

_____ **1.** Do I use correct forms of verbs *(had eaten,* not *had ate)*?

_____ **2.** Do I use the correct word *(their, there, they're)*?

_____ **3.** Do my subjects and verbs agree in number *(the car races* and *the cars race)*?

SENTENCE STRUCTURE

_____ **4.** Do I use a variety of correctly structured sentences?

MECHANICS (PUNCTUATION, CAPITALIZATION, AND SPELLING)

_____ **5.** Do I use end punctuation after all my sentences?

_____ **6.** Do I use commas and semicolons correctly?

_____ **7.** Do I use quotation marks and italics correctly?

_____ **8.** Do I use apostrophes to show possession *(that girl's keys* and *those girls' keys)*?

_____ **9.** Do I start each sentence with a capital letter?

_____ **10.** Do I capitalize the proper names of people and places?

_____ **11.** Do I avoid improper capitalization *(my mom,* not *my Mom)*?

_____ **12.** Have I checked my spelling using a spell-checker?

_____ **13.** Have I also checked my spelling with a dictionary?

TEKS 10.17A, 10.17C, 10.18A, 10.18B, 10.19
ELPS 5C, 5D, 5E

"Don't take commas for granted. They're like yellow lights. If you ignore one, you could be in for a bumpy ride."
—Patricia T. O'Conner

Showing Emphasis

Carefully selected punctuation—especially commas, semicolons, and colons—can be used to emphasize certain words or ideas.

Sample Paragraph

Notice how the commas, semicolons, and a colon are used to add emphasis in the following paragraph.

High Adventure

Who can forget Frodo, the reluctant hero? What about Sam, the best friend ever? Remember Gandalf, and Aragorn, and Legolas, and Gimli! These are just some of the heroes who make up the wonderful fellowship in J. R. R. Tolkien's masterpiece, *The Lord of the Rings*. For some individuals, the epic trilogy provides the best reading they have ever experienced. The three books tell a magnificent story of friendship and courage, betrayal and sacrifice. Tolkien's descriptions of his imaginary world are stunning, and the way he takes the reader to the very edge of doom before pulling him back embodies the essence of high adventure. The tale includes many instances of heart-pounding excitement: terror turns to triumph; opportunities are born from disaster; ultimate evil threatens everything that is good. But the "Rings" trilogy is so much more than an adventure story. Throughout these fantastic books, Professor Tolkien addresses issues of morality, legacy, and history, at a level of depth and breadth that few storytellers have ever attained.

Respond to the reading. How are commas and semicolons used to emphasize certain ideas in the paragraph? Identify specific examples from the writing.

Try It!

Write a brief paragraph about a person you admire. Use punctuation to emphasize the traits and qualities this person exhibits.

Checking for Sentence Variety

Use the following strategy to ensure sentence variety in your writing.

- **Vary sentence beginnings.** In one column on a piece of paper, list the opening words of each sentence in a piece of writing. (Do you need to vary some of your sentence beginnings?)
- **Vary sentence lengths.** In another column, write the number of words in each sentence. (Do you need to change the length of some sentences?)

Sample Paragraph

Read the following sample paragraph, paying attention to the sentence structure. Note the different ways the writer begins various sentences. Also note how the lengths of the sentences are different.

Rite of Passage

The vast marsh seethed with movement, as if a living carpet covered the ground. Wings rustling, heads bobbing, and feathers extended, thousands of Canada geese claimed this wetland for the night. With the new day, they will continue on their journey north, a flight repeated year after year after year. As the sun crests the horizon, several geese will honk. Here and there, a few will take to the air, powerful wing strokes thrashing the waters. More geese will join the chorus in a growing crescendo. Suddenly, hundreds of the big birds will take wing pulling the rest of the flock with them, as all the birds explode into the spring sky.

Respond to the reading. On a piece of paper, analyze the sample paragraph for sentence variety using the strategy above as a guide.

Try It!

Write freely for 10 minutes about animals (wild or domestic) in action. Check your sentence variety using the strategy above.

ELPS 1E, 2C, 2D, 2G, 2H, 2I, 3D, 3E, 3H

Guide for Effective Writing

If a piece of writing meets the following standards, it exhibits the traits of effective writing. Check your work using these standards.

Focus and Coherence

The writing . . .

_____ maintains a clear, specific focus or purpose. The thesis, or controlling idea, is clearly stated.

_____ presents interesting details that support the focus.

Organization

_____ includes a clear beginning, middle, and ending.

_____ arranges the details in the best order for the topic.

_____ flows smoothly from sentence to sentence and paragraph to paragraph, and includes transitions to connect ideas.

Development of Ideas

_____ develops each idea thoroughly, and leaves out no important information.

_____ supports each idea with appropriate details.

Voice

_____ reflects the writer's personality.

_____ engages the audience effectively.

_____ contains strong words, including specific nouns, verbs, and modifiers.

Conventions

_____ adheres to the rules of grammar, punctuation, capitalization, and spelling.

_____ follows established guidelines for presentation.

Learning Language

Take turns with a classmate describing each of the traits of effective writing. When you are listening, ask your partner to clarify any part of the description you don't understand.

Peer Response

Once you've written and revised a paper, you may be quite pleased with the result. You probably made some improvements and even found and corrected a number of mistakes. However, you still may wonder how to make your writing even better. What else can you do?

One of the best things you can do is ask someone else for an opinion. Having one or more classmates read and react to your work is called *peer response*. Often, another person will notice details that you missed. A new point of view can improve your whole approach to a description, an explanation, or an argument.

Peer response works best as a shared project. You read other students' papers, and they read yours. At first, you may find it difficult to offer and receive constructive criticism. Once you try this approach, however, you'll discover the benefit it holds for you as a writer.

"The best advice on writing I've ever received was, 'Rewrite it.' A lot of editors said that. They were all right."

—Robert Lipsyte

TEKS 10.13E
ELPS 3E, 3F, 4G

Peer-Response Guidelines

Use the following guidelines to help you conduct an effective response session. Start by working with one other person or in a small group.

The Author's Role

Bring a meaningful piece of writing to the session and provide one copy for each responder. Keep an open mind and consider all comments. Follow this procedure:

- **Introduce your writing.** Briefly explain the goal of your writing. Tell the group if you have already done some revising and editing.
- **Read your writing aloud.** Alternately, you can ask each group member to read the piece silently.
- **Ask for comments.** Listen to the responses. You don't have to make every suggested change, but keep an open mind.
- **Take notes.** Write comments on your copy where the changes need to be made.
- **Ask for help.** If you are having trouble with a specific part of the writing, ask for suggestions, ideas, and advice from your peers.

Asking for Constructive Criticism

Here are some questions that can produce useful information and create a cooperative relationship between you and the responders. The answers to "Why?" and "How?" give you specific ways to improve your writing.

First ask . . .

What do you like about my writing? Why?

Then ask . . .

What parts do you think could be improved? How?

The Responder's Role

Respond honestly, but be careful of the author's feelings. Be sure that your comments are constructive, not destructive. Follow these tips.

- **Listen (or read) carefully.** Peer response only works if you pay attention to the writing and monitor your own understanding of the writer's words and ideas.
- **Take notes.** Write comments directly on your copy of the writing to show the author exactly where revisions are needed.
- **Start with positive feedback.** Find something good in the writing and make specific comments about what you liked.
- **Ask questions.** Don't hesitate to ask the author about parts that need clarification. Be specific and polite.
- **Avoid "piling on."** Allow one responder to finish before commenting.
- **Make suggestions.** When you point out a problem, try to include a possible solution. (See the chart below.)

Giving Constructive Criticism	
Don't give commands . . . "You should make the beginning grab my attention."	**Do give suggestions . . .** "Wouldn't the beginning be stronger with a different hook?"
Don't focus on the writer . . . "You don't follow any logical order."	**Do focus on the writing . . .** "Is the order of your ideas clear?"
Don't focus on the problem . . . "There aren't enough details to make your main point."	**Do focus on the solution . . .** "More details would help me understand your main point."
Don't give general comments . . . "I thought it was boring."	**Do give specific advice . . .** "Could you use a personal story to support your main point?"

Try It!

Rewrite the unhelpful comments below to make them more constructive.

1. You don't sound like you really believe in your opinion.
2. Your closing sentence doesn't work.
3. I don't understand your solution.

Using the Texas Traits to Respond

When you respond, you are trying to help the author improve his or her writing by rethinking, refocusing, or revising. It can be useful to consider the traits of writing as you respond. Start by thinking about *focus and coherence, organization*, and *development of ideas*.

Addressing Focus and Coherence, Organization, and Development of Ideas

Focus and Coherence: **Help the author maintain focus throughout the writing.**

- How would you state the main idea of your writing?
- I think you're trying to say . . . . Is that right?
- Is . . . the main idea in your writing?
- Do all the ideas support the main idea, the thesis statement?
- Does the writing work together as a whole and have a sense of completeness?
- I got the impression you want the reader to feel . . . . Is that right?

Organization: **Help the author focus on organization.**

- Which sentence is your thesis statement (or controlling idea)?
- I liked the way you got my attention by . . .
- Did you organize your paragraphs by . . . ?
- What main point do these details support?
- Could you make a smoother transition between these two paragraphs?
- What are you trying to say with this ending?

Development of Ideas: **Help the author develop ideas thoroughly.**

- You have developed most of your ideas thoroughly.
- The most important details, to me, are . . .
- Could you give a few more details about . . . ?
- Are you being fair to both sides in this paragraph?

Try It!

Read one of the essays in this book. Write down one or two responses to the essay for each of these traits: *focus and coherence, organization,* and *development of ideas.* Then discuss your response with a classmate.

Addressing Voice and Conventions

Later in the response process, try to address the author's *voice* and *use of writing conventions*. Here are some suggestions for doing this.

Voice: **Help the author focus on voice.**

- I can see your personality in this sentence: . . . .
- You really reveal how you feel about this topic when you . . .
- What audience are you trying to reach with the writing?
- Do you think you might sound too formal (or informal) in this paragraph?
- The writing makes me feel . . . about the topic.

Conventions: **Help the author focus on the conventions of writing.**

- Do you have too many sentences beginning with . . . ?
- In the middle paragraphs, could you combine some short sentences into longer sentences for variety?
- I noticed you used the word . . . three times. Maybe you can find a synonym.
- Did you check for errors in grammar, punctuation, capitalization and spelling?

Try It!

Using the same essay you reviewed on page **52**, write down one response for *voice* and one or two for *conventions*. Discuss your responses with a classmate.

Tip

Listen carefully to your peers' comments, but remember that you don't have to make every change that they suggest. You should weigh the value of each comment and proceed accordingly. The following tips can help you use peer responses effectively.

- Trust your own judgment about your writing.
- Think about which issues are most important to you.
- Pay special attention to comments made by more than one responder.
- Seek another opinion if you are not sure about something.
- Ask questions if you are not sure what a responder means.
- Be patient. Focus on one problem area at a time.

TEKS 10.13E

Sample Peer Response Sheet

Use a response sheet like the one below to make comments about one of your classmate's essays. (The example includes sample responses.)

Peer Response Sheet

Writer: Veronica Gomez Responder: David James

Title: Compromise: Let's Meet in the Middle

What I liked about your writing:

- I liked how you related the topic to history and to everyday life.
- The questions in the first paragraph really got me thinking about your topic.
- The folk saying was kind of funny.
- I'm glad you showed that compromises don't always work.

Changes I would suggest:

- Could you give a specific example about compromising between students and teachers?
- Do you really need to mention that compromise can be a noun and a verb? Does that fact give any insight about your topic?
- "Human social interaction" seems like a complicated phrase. Can you say that another way?

Try It!

Exchange a recent piece of your writing for a classmate's work.

1. Read the paper once to get an overall feel for it.
2. Read it again, paying attention to its strengths and weaknesses.
3. Fill out a response sheet like the one above.
4. Try revising your work using some of your classmate's suggestions.

Evaluating Your Writing

Learning how to evaluate writing is one of the best ways to become a stronger writer. Evaluating writing helps you think like a professional writer and take on the responsibility of making meaningful changes in your work. You learn to evaluate writing by using a scoring guide, which lists the main traits for an effective piece of writing. As you gain more experience with scoring guides, you will come to better understand and appreciate the qualities inherent in effective writing.

Scoring guides aren't just for evaluating completed pieces of writing. They can also direct your early writing and provide specific suggestions for making improvements. By using a scoring guide throughout the writing process, you can expect to produce a quality piece of writing. In this chapter, you will learn about the uses of a scoring guide and you will familiarize yourself with the Write Source Holistic Scoring Guide—the specific evaluation tool that you will be using throughout this book.

- **Understanding Holistic Scoring**
- **Reading a Holistic Scoring Guide**
- **Getting Started with a Holistic Scoring Guide**
- **Understanding the Write Source Holistic Scoring Guide**
- **Evaluating an Essay**

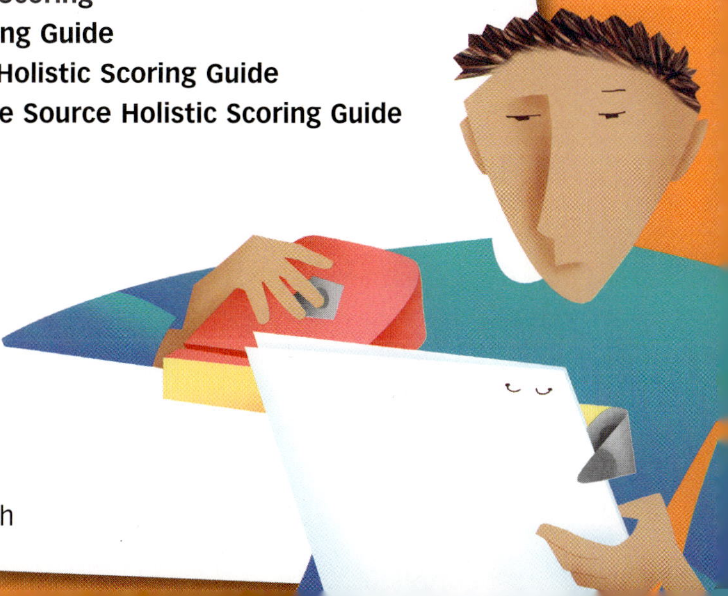

"Rubrics help students and teachers define quality."

—Heidi Goodrich

Understanding Holistic Scoring

Have you ever rated the quality of something on a scale of 1 (not so good) to 10 (fantastic)? Writing can also be rated on a scale. A **scoring guide is a tool used to evaluate and rate a written composition.** With a **holistic scoring guide**, the quality of any piece of writing can be evaluated for its overall impression. The reader does not focus on any individual writing characteristic, but looks at the overall effectiveness of the composition.

The basis of the scoring guide that you will see in this chapter is the five Texas writing traits: *focus and coherence, organization, development of ideas, voice,* and *conventions.* Writing conventions include grammar, usage, capitalization, punctuation, sentence structure, and spelling.

Score Points

The holistic scoring guide in this book uses a 4-point system to evaluate writing. Below, you see a brief description of the score points used. Scores of 4 or 3 indicate strong levels of mastery in most aspects of writing. Scores of 2 or 1 show that the writer has not yet mastered any aspects of writing.

4 A **4** means that the writing is **highly effective.**
It shows an overall mastery of the five writing traits.

3 A **3** means that the writing is **generally effective.**
It shows some mastery of most of the five traits.

2 A **2** means that the writing is **somewhat effective.**
It shows that the writer has little mastery of most traits.

1 A **1** means that the writing is **not effective.**
It shows that the writer needs to work to master most of the traits.

Reading a Holistic Scoring Guide

The scoring guide in this book is based on a four-point scale. At each score point, writing is described in terms of the five traits: *focus and coherence, organization, development of ideas, voice,* and *conventions.* The entire guide is shown on pages **60–61.**

Color-Coded Scoring Guide

4 Writing at this score point is highly effective.	**Focus and Coherence** Maintains focus throughout the writing; all ideas clearly connect to each other and to the main idea. Includes a meaningful introduction and conclusion that add depth to the composition.	**Organization** Employs an effective organizational pattern for the purpose and audience. Has a smooth and logical flow; transitions help the reader move from one idea to the next.
3 Writing at this score point is generally effective.	**Focus and Coherence** Maintains focus, with minor lapses; most ideas are clearly connected to each other and to the main idea. An introduction and conclusion add some depth to the composition.	**Organization** Uses an organizational pattern that is mostly effective for the purpose and audience. Generally flows but could use a few more transitions.

Guiding Your Writing

A scoring guide helps you . . .

- **plan your work**—knowing what is expected;
- **create a strong first draft**—maintaining *focus and coherence, organization,* and *development of ideas;*
- **revise and edit your work**—considering each trait; and
- **assess your final draft**—rating the whole piece of writing in terms of the traits.

Think about the scoring guide. Think about the level-4 descriptions above. According to these descriptions, how does a writer maintain focus? What characterizes the organization of a score-4 paper?

Writing with Scoring in Mind

Each of the writing units in this book includes a page like the one below. This page, which shows the Texas traits of writing, explains the main requirements for developing the composition in the unit. Notice how it also suggests that you refer to the scoring guide as part of your writing process.

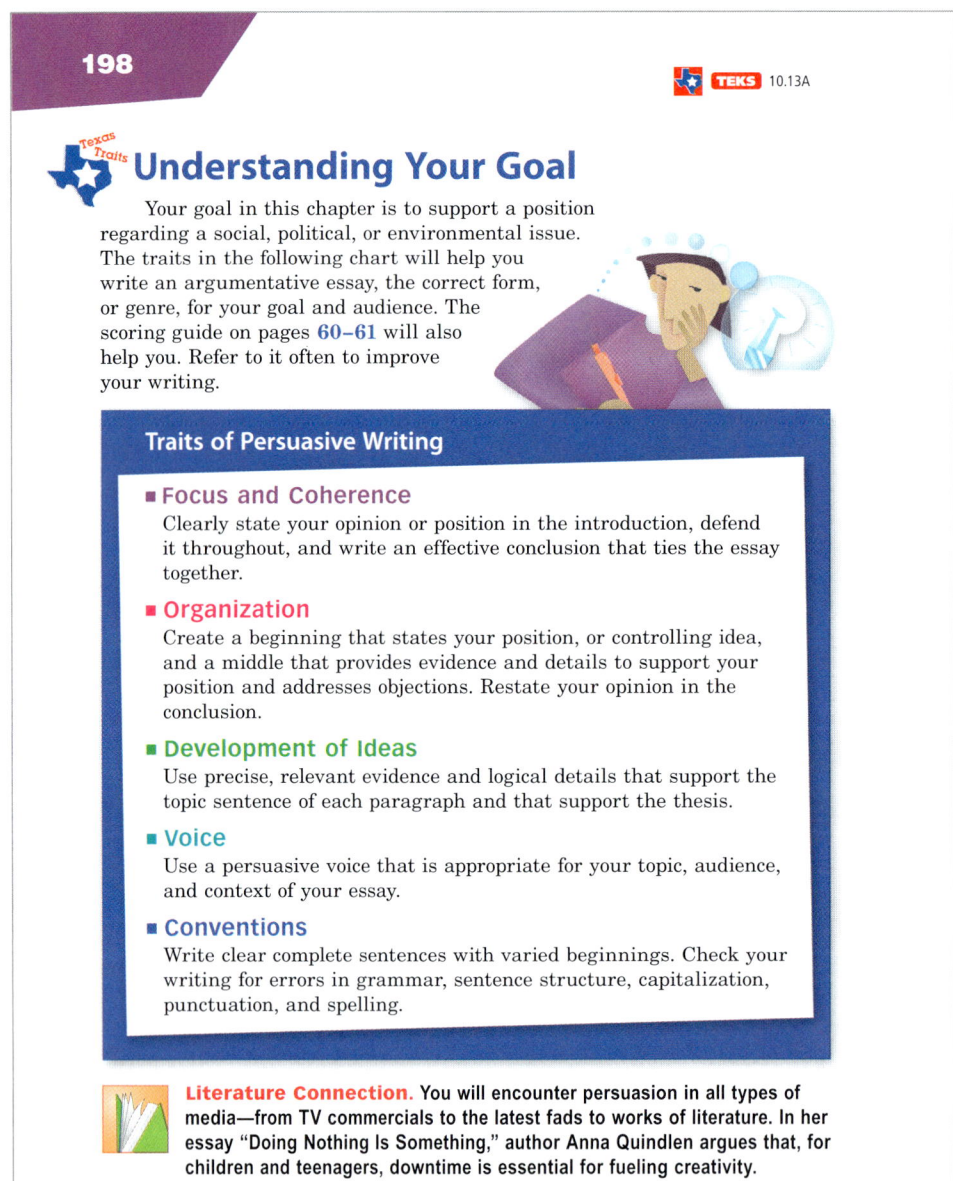

198

TEKS 10.13A

Texas Traits

Understanding Your Goal

Your goal in this chapter is to support a position regarding a social, political, or environmental issue. The traits in the following chart will help you write an argumentative essay, the correct form, or genre, for your goal and audience. The scoring guide on pages **60–61** will also help you. Refer to it often to improve your writing.

Traits of Persuasive Writing

- **Focus and Coherence**
  Clearly state your opinion or position in the introduction, defend it throughout, and write an effective conclusion that ties the essay together.
- **Organization**
  Create a beginning that states your position, or controlling idea, and a middle that provides evidence and details to support your position and addresses objections. Restate your opinion in the conclusion.
- **Development of Ideas**
  Use precise, relevant evidence and logical details that support the topic sentence of each paragraph and that support the thesis.
- **Voice**
  Use a persuasive voice that is appropriate for your topic, audience, and context of your essay.
- **Conventions**
  Write clear complete sentences with varied beginnings. Check your writing for errors in grammar, sentence structure, capitalization, punctuation, and spelling.

Literature Connection. You will encounter persuasion in all types of media—from TV commercials to the latest fads to works of literature. In her essay "Doing Nothing Is Something," author Anna Quindlen argues that, for children and teenagers, downtime is essential for fueling creativity.

A Closer Look at Understanding Your Goal

The following steps will help you get an overview of the assignment in each writing unit.

1. **Read through the Texas traits chart** to familiarize yourself with the unit's goals.
2. Concentrate on ***focus and coherence, organization,*** and ***development of ideas*** at the start of the project, when you are prewriting. As you work on your draft, also think about ***voice*** and ***conventions***. These traits form the foundation of good writing.
3. **Identify specific requirements** for each trait (such as "supporting your opinion with logical reasons" and "sounding persuasive and respectful").
4. **Consult the Write Source Scoring Guide** to see how each trait relates to the four score points.

A Special Note About the Traits

Different traits are important at different stages of the writing process. The following chart shows when the specific traits are important.

During **prewriting**, pay attention to *focus and coherence, organization,* and *development of ideas.* Concentrate on these traits during **drafting** also, but think about *voice* as well.

During **revising**, continue to concentrate on *focus and coherence, organization, development of ideas,* and *voice.* (For some assignments, your teacher may ask you to pay particular attention to one or two of these traits.)

During **editing** and proofreading, concentrate on *conventions*—grammar, sentence structure, capitalization, punctuation, and spelling.

When you, a peer, or your teacher is **assessing** or **reviewing** your final draft, consider all five traits.

Exercise

Review the goals on page **58** and the scoring guide on pages **60–61.** Then write a persuasive paragraph defending your solution for a school-related problem. Keep the traits in mind as you write.

Texas Traits

Write Source Holistic Scoring Guide

Use the descriptions at each score point to evaluate your own writing or that of your peers.

Score	Focus and Coherence	Organization
4 Writing at this score point is highly effective.	**Focus and Coherence** Maintains focus throughout the writing; all ideas clearly connect to each other and to the main idea. Includes a meaningful introduction and conclusion that add depth to the composition.	**Organization** Employs an effective organizational pattern for the purpose and audience. Has a smooth and logical flow; transitions help the reader move from one idea to the next.
3 Writing at this score point is generally effective.	**Focus and Coherence** Maintains focus, with minor lapses; most ideas are clearly connected to each other and to the main idea. An introduction and conclusion add some depth to the composition.	**Organization** Uses an organizational pattern that is mostly effective for the purpose and audience. Generally flows but could use a few more transitions.
2 Writing at this score point is somewhat effective.	**Focus and Coherence** Is somewhat unfocused, but the reader can understand how ideas are related. Some ideas do not contribute to the writing as a whole. The introduction and conclusion are superficial.	**Organization** The flow of the ideas is not always clear. The organizational pattern may not suit the purpose and audience. Wordiness and repetition may interfere with the flow of ideas.
1 Writing at this score point is not effective.	**Focus and Coherence** Lacks focus; includes a substantial amount of information not connected to the main idea. Is missing an introduction and/or conclusion.	**Organization** Has no clear organizational pattern or logical flow of ideas. Lacks transitions. Repetition or wordiness may interfere with the progression of ideas.

Development of Ideas Ample support and specific details allow the reader to appreciate the writer's points. A novel approach to the topic may add to the overall quality of the writing.	**Voice** Engages the reader throughout the writing. Sounds authentic and original; expresses the writer's unique perspective.	**Conventions** Shows a strong command of conventions, allowing the reader to focus on the writer's message.
Development of Ideas Supports all ideas, but some need to be developed more thoroughly. The presentation of ideas may be thoughtful but may not reflect a novel approach to the topic.	**Voice** Engages the reader for most of the writing. Sounds somewhat authentic and original and expresses the writer's unique perspective.	**Conventions** Includes only minor errors in conventions; errors do not interfere with the reader's ability to understand the writer's message.
Development of Ideas Ideas may be developed only superficially. Some information may be missing. The reader's ability to appreciate the writer's points is compromised.	**Voice** Engages the reader occasionally. Sounds authentic and original in only a few sections. Does not express a unique perspective.	**Conventions** Errors reflect a limited command of writing conventions and interfere with the flow of ideas in the writing.
Development of Ideas Support is lacking or is only general and vague. Important information may be left out. The reader has difficulty understanding the writer's points.	**Voice** Does not engage the reader. Shows little or no evidence of the writer's individuality or unique perspective.	**Conventions** The writing shows major problems with conventions, which interferes with the reader's ability to understand the message.

Evaluating an Essay

The essays that follow are examples of writing for each score point on the holistic scoring guide. Study these essays and the notes with them to better understand how to evaluate a written composition. **(Essays will contain errors.)**

Writing that fits a score of 4 is highly effective.

4

The thesis is clearly stated. Writer uses expressive details to create a distinct voice.

Middle paragraphs build upon the thesis. Writer shows knowledge of topic.

Content is arranged from general to specific examples, engaging the reader.

CONSERVING RAIN FORESTS

Every time a tree in the Amazon rain forest is cut down for its wood, or another acre burnt to make way for crops, the earth's climate becomes a little more unbalanced. Rain forests are crucial because they absorb carbon dioxide and release oxygen into the atmosphere. Without rain forests, too much carbon dioxide may lead to climate change, which can affect the whole world.

Rain forests are being destroyed at a rate of 1½ acres per second. At that rate, there may be no more rain forests in another 40 years (Raintree 6)! Besides the effect on climate, many unique plants and animals will become extinct when they are no longer protected by the rain forests' fragile ecosystems. Today, a typical four-square-mile patch of tropical rain forest contains as many as 1,500 flowering plants, 750 species of trees, 400 species of birds and 150 species of butterflies (Nature Conservancy). Tropical rain forests provide us with favorite foods such as coffee, cocoa, and many types of fruits and nuts. Pharmaceutical companies use plants found only in rain forests to create many medicinal and cosmetic products. There are, for example, more than 2000 plants with properties that are used to fight cancer or that might even lead to a cure.

The main causes of rain forest destruction are logging, agriculture, and mining. Of these, illegal logging causes the most problems. Over 105,000 miles of roads have been illegally cut through the Amazon to reach mahogany and other expensive woods that sell for a lot of money on the world market (Wallace). Rain forest wood is also sent to other countries for fuel, charcoal, and paper production. The roads create more illegal activity by opening areas to ranching, farming, and land speculation. People then burn more trees to create more open land.

Ideas are well developed, and details add interest.

Normally, the Amazon produces half of the water it needs, but all the clearing has reduced the amount of moisture released into the atmosphere, causing remaining trees to dry and die out (Wallace 132). This leads to drought and fires. Also, once an area has been cleared, it's very unlikely that it will grow again or recreate the ecosystem that it once supported.

Varied sentences create a smooth flow. Ideas are linked.

Stopping the destruction of the Amazon will be difficult. Many of the problems are due to poverty and greed at all levels. People want free or cheap land to feed their families and to make money growing crops like soybeans or raising cattle. Rich countries like the United States and Japan want to import cheap wood for building and furniture and paper. The governments of countries with rain forests want the money provided by exports and land development and do little to encourage conservation or restrict destructive activities. They also don't have the money to manage and protect their resources.

It's clear that wealthier countries must cooperate with poorer tropical countries to save the rain forests. The United States can do its part by making it more profitable for countries like Brazil to conserve its forests instead of cutting them down. There are a number of ways to do this. One way is to show how more money can be made from the tropical plants that grow naturally in rain forests than from crops and cattle raised on cleared land. According to experts such as Dr. Robert Mendelsohn, an economist at Yale University, and Dr. Michael Balick, Director of the Institute of Economic Botany at the New York Botanical Gardens, there are hundreds of new drugs that could be discovered in rain forests, valued at billions of dollars (Raintree 63).

Conclusion provides sense of completeness.

Much of the destruction of the world's rain forests cannot be reversed, but it's not too late to conserve what we have now. The future of our planet may depend upon it.

Writing that fits a score of 3 is generally effective.

3

The beginning paragraph clearly introduces the thesis.

Details show knowledge of topic and support thesis. Minor grammar and spelling errors do not detract from the message.

Getting Off the Grid

People today are finally becoming more aware of the impact they have on the environment. They are beginning to see that we need to conserve our non-renewable resources in order to save the planet for our children. Electricity is a resource that must be conserved. While electricity itself is not a non-renewable resource, it is often created from non-renewable resources. The use of electricity has gone up a lot because of computers and other new technology, so we have to become more efficient in the ways we create it and use it.

Think of our lives without electricity. We couldn't do much at night because there'd be no electric lights. Food would spoil without refrigeraters to store our food. We couldn't use our computers or watch TV. We'd swelter in the summer without air conditioning. Every time our electricity fails and there's a blackout, we get angry and frustrated. Important information gets lost. Important tasks don't get done. We are completely dependent on it. In 1940, electricity production accounted for 10 % of the energy used in the United States. In 1970, 25% of energy was used to produce electricity. Today it is 40%. Yet, even though our use of electricity is going up, construction of new electric plants have gone down. This situation makes it more likely to have major problems like power outages, poor power quality, and higher bills (Dept. of Energy).

Over 50% of electric power is created by burning coal, which is non-renewable and create a lot of carbon emissions. This is terrible for the environment and adds to global warming. Another 21% is from nuclear power, which is clean energy, but it's also non-renewable and could be dangerous because of the radiation. Only 7% of electric power is from hydroelectric dams and 2% from other renewable sources (Greenpeace). This has to change if we are going to reduce carbon by using cleaner energy.

Some of the renewable energies that we can use are water power, wind power, and solar power. Hydroelectric power is created by damming rivers and using the water to turn turbines.

Idea could have been better developed.

It is a clean and effective way to create electricity, though sometimes damming a river can cause problems. Wind power is becoming more popular. It costs more than fossil fuels, but it is expected to go to 5% by 2020 (Environmental Literacy Council). Solar power is not as efficient as fossil fuels for large electric plants, but people can use it in there own homes to reduce electricity use. Maybe one day they'll be able to use it to generate power plants.

Writer presents solution to problem.

If we cut down our own use of electricity, there wouldn't be as much need to increase production. There are a lot of ways to do this. First, people should start using low energy appliances, especially their refrigerators, which use a lot of electricity. They can use florescent light bulbs. Florescent bulbs cost more than regular bulbs, but they last longer and use less energy. Turning off lights and appliances can also save electricity. Most people don't realize that even unplugging electric cords that their not using can help, for example, you're using electricity when your phone chargers plugged in even when the phone is not charging. In the future, more people might start using solar panels on their own houses to generate a lot of their electricity. That's a lot cheaper than paying the electric company! New kinds of electric meters that monitor usage in real time will help electric companies match supply and demand better, and people can change their usage habits (Dept. of Energy). If people waited to use appliances like their washing machines and dishwashers during non-peak times, there would be less strain on the system and their own costs would go down.

Writer engages the reader with distinct voice.

If there was less need for electricity, there would be less dependence on fossil fuels like coal. There would be less carbon spewing into the atmosphere. By changing our own habits in our homes, we do a lot to conserve electricity and protect the environment.

Writing that fits a score of 2 is somewhat effective.

2

Topic is not clearly stated.

Ideas are not well developed and are not well connected.

There are many errors in writing conventions throughout the essay.

Recycling

Americans are very wasteful. Everyday we throw out tons and tons of paper, glass, and plastic. We use 25 million plastic water bottles alone (http://www.reusablebags.com/facts.php?id=18). This goes into landfills, where it stays forever. Eventually we will run out of places to put all of our garbage! Recycling is the only way to avoid being buried by piles of junk.

Recycling is also important because without it we will use up our natural resourses. Eventually there won't be any trees left for making paper. Today alot of paper products are from recycled paper. Plastic can be reused again and again so there's no need to manufacture it from oil. It can even be turned into clothing! And people are beginning to take cloth bags to the market which can be reused over and over again insted of asking for plastic bags.

Sometimes dangerous items can get put into landfills if their not recycled. For example, computers and cellphones. They have toxic metals in them. Its called e-waste. There are companies that will fix them so they can be donated and reused. Or they take them apart and reuse the good parts and destroy the toxic parts (http://pages.ebay.com/rethink/faq.html#4).

Recycling is getting more common and is becoming a way of live for a lot of lots of people. Its easy to do. Many communities have recycling programs and all you have to do is put your bottles and cans and old newspapers into a special bin then a truck takes it away, just like the regular garbage. Supermarkets often has recycling centers where they even pay you for your bottles.

There is no excuse for people to recycle. They should feel guilty when they throw out a plastic bottle or newspaper. By recycling, they stop creting huge landfills, stop using natural resources, and stop the waste.

Writing that fits a score of 1 is not effective.

1

Thesis is not clearly stated.

Errors in conventions make the essay difficult to understand.

Essay lacks organization. The examples are not clear. Writing does not engage the reader.

Turn Off the Tap!

Its very important to save water these days because we're using up our supply too fast. Water concervation is something we should all think about when we brush our teeth or wash our hands. Its not good to leave the water tap on while you do those things because your just waisting water. You don't have to keep the water running it can save galons of water. And water is expensive.

What are some other ways to concerve water. Don't keep watering your lawn all the time, make sure that water is hitting the grass and plants and not just going on the sidewalk, use a broom to clean your driveway, instead of washing it down with a hose. Just doing little things like that can help alot.

It may seems like we have alot from rain and rivers but its not enough. There are too many people and theres climate change. Those things make it hard to have enough water for everyone even if it rains all the time. Some of the water isn't clean enough to drink, it has to be prosessed first.

Toilets are one of the biggest waisters of water. So use low flush tolets or don't flush all the time. And make sure your toilet isn't leaking because that also waists water.

In conclusion don't assume theirs enough. You can save water by doing a few simple. Like turning off the tap when you brush your teeth. Its easy and its right.

Evaluation Practice

Read the essay below, focusing on its strengths and weaknesses. Then follow the directions at the bottom of the page. **(The essay contains errors.)**

Music and the Arts Make Education Complete

Funding for music and art programs in schools across the country have been cut or greatly reduced (VH1). This is an unfortunate trend. Music and the arts should be supported because they are critical for a well-rounded education.

Persoanlly, I think music and arts are not so important as other subjects, but studies have proven the positive affect of music and the arts in school. Students who participate in music and arts programs are four times more likely to be recognized for academic achievement. (Hills 65). Other studies reveal that music and the arts help develop critical thinking, cognitive development, and a positive self-esteem.

For most students school is the only place they can get instruction in music and the arts because private lessons are very expensive (Americans). Students should not miss out on the benefits of music and the arts just because of their economic status.

Schools support sports programs because sports encourage teamwork. Studies also show that students in sports get better grades. Both of these things are true for music and arts students though, too (Blair and Bruhn 17). Besides, not everyone can shoot hoops well enough to make the basketball team. At the same time, not everyone can play an instrument well enough to be first chair in a jazz band, or sketch a life-like drawing, but anyone with the desire can still participate. I guess we should all have the opportunity.

Music and the arts requires discipline, practice, and studying just like any other subject. They also develop creativity, encourage self-expression, and teach students how to work in a group. A program that can do all of those things should probably be part of every student's education.

Exercise

Assess the persuasive essay you have just read, using the holistic scoring guide on pages 60–61 for reference. To get started, create an assessment sheet like the one on page 31. Remember: After rating each trait, write at least one comment about a strength and one comment about a weakness.

Publishing Your Writing

You've written many essays, articles, and reports since you've started high school. Many of these pieces were probably read by an audience of one, the teacher who made the assignment. But what if the size of your audience was greatly expanded, and included all of your classmates? How would that affect your feelings about writing? More than anything else, it would help you feel part of a writing community, which makes the process of writing a very meaningful and satisfying experience.

Of course, not everything you write is meant to be shared with an audience. You may not want to open up your journal to the world, but you could take a story idea from your journal, develop it, and then post it on your Web page or submit it to a magazine. You might want to finish a poem you started in your personal writing and recite it at an open-mike night at a coffee house.

This chapter will help you with all of your publishing needs—from preparing a piece for publication to launching your own Web site.

"No piece of writing, regardless of how much you polish and fuss with it, comes out exactly as you want it to."

—Tom Liner

Preparing to Publish

Your writing is not ready to share until you have taken it through all the steps in the writing process. The tips below will help you prepare your writing for publication.

Publishing Tips

- **Take advantage of peer response sessions and feedback from your teacher.**
  Make sure that you have addressed the important concerns identified by your teacher and classmates.
- **Check for the traits of writing.**
  Focus and coherence, organization, development of ideas, voice, and conventions are all important in your writing. (See pages 33–48.)
- **Put forth your best effort.**
  Continue working until you feel good about your writing from start to finish.
- **Save all drafts for each writing project.**
  Then you will be able to double-check the changes you have made.
- **Seek editing help.**
  Ask at least one trusted editor to check your work for conventions. Another person may spot errors that you miss.
- **Prepare a neat final copy.**
  Use a pen (blue or black ink) and one side of the paper if you are writing by hand. Select a typestyle that is easy to read if you are using a computer. (Always use a computer when you submit your writing to outside publishers.)
- **Consider different publishing options.**
  There are many ways to publish writing. (See page 71.)
- **Follow all publishing guidelines.**
  Each publisher has certain requirements for publishing. Be sure to follow their guidelines exactly.

Try It!

Prepare to publish. Follow the tips above to get your next piece of writing ready to publish. Before submitting your work, have a friend read your writing out loud. Listen carefully. Does your writing say everything you'd like it to say? Does your personal voice come through in your writing?

Publishing Ideas

The simplest way to publish your writing is to share it with a friend or classmate. Other publishing ideas, such as entering a writing contest, take more time and effort. Try a number of these publishing ideas during the school year. All of them will help you grow as a writer.

Self-Publishing

- Newsletter
- Greeting Cards
- Personal Book
- Web Site
- Blog

Performing

- Sharing with Classmates
- Reading to Other Audiences
- Multimedia Presentation
- Open-Mike Night

Sending It Out

- Local Newspaper
- Magazines
- Web Sites or E-zines
- Writing Contests
- Young Writers' Conferences

Sharing in School

- Literary Magazine
- Writing Portfolio
- Classroom Collection
- School Newspaper/Yearbook

Posting

- Bulletin Boards
- Display Cases
- Business Windows
- Literary/Art Fairs

Think about publishing. How many of these publishing ideas have you tried since you've been in high school? Which other ones would you like to try? Why? Which ones would you not like to try? Why not?

TEKS 10.13E, 10.23C
ELPS 3G

Designing Your Writing

Always focus first on the content of your writing. Then consider its design, or appearance. For most types of publishing, you'll want to use a computer for your final copy. These guidelines will help you to design your writing.

Selecting an Appropriate Font

- **Choose an easy-to-read font.** In most cases, a serif typestyle is best for the text, and a sans serif style works for headings.

  The letters of **serif** fonts have "tails"—as in this sentence.

  The letters of **sans serif** fonts are plain, without tails—as in this sentence.

- **Include a title and headings.** Use the title to introduce your paper and use headings to guide the reader through the text. Headings break a long report into readable parts.

Using Consistent Spacing and Margins

- **Set clear margins.** Use a one-inch margin (top, bottom, left, and right).
- **Indent paragraphs.** Use a half-inch indent.
- **Use one space after every period.** This will improve the readability of your paper.
- **Avoid awkward breaks.** Don't leave a heading or the first line of a paragraph at the bottom of a page or a column. Never split a hyphenated word between pages or columns.

Including Graphic Elements

- **Use lists if appropriate.** Use numbered lists if your points have a clear number order. Otherwise, use bulleted lists (like the ones on this page).
- **Include graphics.** Use tables, charts, or illustrations to help make a point. Keep graphics small within the text. If a graphic needs to be large, display it on its own page.

Try It!

Working with a classmate, compare and discuss the design features of chapters from two different textbooks. How are the design features the same? How are they different? With your partner, decide which design is the most effective, based on the text's audience and purpose.

Effective Design in Action

The following two pages show a well-designed student essay. The side notes explain the design features.

The title is 16-point sans serif type, centered.

Centered subheadings (14-point sans serif type) identify main sections.

The body text is 12-point serif type, double-spaced.

Juan Castillo
Mr. Rodriquez
Computer Technology
Nov. 18, 2011

Warning for Computers: It's Flu Season

How can a computer act "sick"? Maybe its applications aren't working correctly, or it's crashing and restarting every few minutes. If so, a computer might be infected with a virus. Unfortunately, chicken soup and a lot of rest won't do any good. To ensure that a computer remains up and running, users should understand computer viruses so they can protect their computers in the future.

The Culprits

The Internet is an amazing but dangerous tool. With the click of a mouse, a user can communicate with people all over the world. That's also what makes it so dangerous for a computer. On the Internet, everyone is a neighbor, even the computer hacker with criminal intentions. These harmful hackers design destructive software programs called viruses.

The Viruses

Like human viruses, a computer virus can make a copy of itself. Then it spreads from one host to another. Since computer viruses are programs, they have the ability to delete files, format hard drives, or change home pages.

Computer viruses can be spread through floppy discs, CD's, e-mail attachments, and downloads. However, most viruses are spread through e-mail attachments. Once the attachment is opened, the virus activates, and infects a computer. Then the virus can send a copy of itself to everyone in a user's e-mail address book. Since a familiar e-mail address is the sender, friends open the attachment, and the whole process repeats itself. So how can an individual avoid these hidden dangers?

A numbered list helps the reader digest related information.

Protect Your Computer

Just like human viruses, there's no 100-percent-sure way to protect a computer. Following the steps below improve the odds.

1. **Install an anti-virus program from a trusted source.**
   New viruses are discovered every day, so it is important to stay current with all the updates.
2. **Also install firewall software.**
   Without a firewall, hackers can find a way to take control of a computer. Then they rent a "zombie" computer to criminals who want to send spam or attack other computers without having it traced back to them.
3. **Never open spam or unexpected e-mail attachments.**
   Suspicious files should be deleted. Files from a trusted friend can be saved and then opened.
4. **Keep software updated.**
   Over time, "holes" may be discovered in software programs. Download update "patches" from the program's Web site.

Remove a Virus

If a computer does become infected, it should be disconnected from the Internet to keep from infecting others. It's like staying home from school when having the flu. Then run a virus scan and use the removal tool to get rid of the virus. If that doesn't work, get help from a "doctor"—your program's software support.

Don't let the threat of computer viruses keep you from enjoying the World Wide Web. Install anti-virus programs, stay updated, and use caution. A little effort can help keep a computer healthy all year long.

Learning Language

A well-designed essay is often easier to read than a poorly written one. Even so, if the topic is complicated, the essay may still be difficult to understand. Work with a small group of students to reread the essay. Break it into sections and have each student take a section. Then have each student in the group retell or summarize the information in the assigned section. Listen carefully, take notes, and ask questions to clarify the information. If you need help, ask your teacher.

Publishing Online

The Internet offers many publishing opportunities, including online magazines and writing contests. The information below will help you submit your writing for publication on the Net. (At home, always get a parent's approval first. In school, follow all guidelines established by the administration.)

Checking Local Sites

Ask your teacher whether your school has a Web site where students can post work. Also check with local student organizations to see if any of them have Web sites that accept submissions.

Finding Other Sites

Use a search engine to find sites that publish student work. Pay special attention to online magazines for young adults. If you don't have any luck with getting published, consider creating your own Web site. (See pages 76–77.)

Submitting Your Work

Follow these tips for submitting your work.

- **Understand the publishing guidelines for each site.** Be sure to share this information with your teacher and your parents.
- **Become familiar with each site's audience.** Are the site's visitors an appropriate audience for your writing?
- **Send your writing in the correct form.** Some sites have online forms. Others will ask you to send your writing by mail or e-mail. Always explain why you are sending your writing.
- **Provide contact information.** Don't give your home address or any other personal information unless your parents approve.
- **Be patient.** Within a week or so, you should receive a note from the publisher verifying that your work has been received. It may take many weeks for a decision about publishing it.

Try It!

Select a piece of writing that you would like to publish online. Find at least two Web sites that publish this type of student writing. Follow the guidelines, note each site's particular audience, and submit your writing.

Creating Your Own Web Site

To create a Web site on your home computer, check with your Internet service provider to find out how to get started. If you are using a school computer, ask your teacher for help. Then follow these steps.

Planning Your Site

Begin by answering the following questions:

- What will be the purpose of this site, and who will be my audience?
- How are my favorite sites set up?
- How many pages will I include?
- How will my pages be linked together?

Creating the Pages

First plan your pages by sketching them out. Then create each page as a text file. Most word-processing programs let you save a file as a Web page. If yours doesn't, you will have to add hypertext markup language (HTML) codes to format the text and make links to graphics and other pages. You can find instructions about HTML on the Internet.

Testing Your Pages

Use your browser to open your first page. Then follow any links to make sure they work correctly. Finally, check the content and the look of all pages.

Uploading the Site

Ask your Internet provider how to upload your finished pages. (If you're working at home, make sure to get your parents' approval first. If you're using school equipment, work with a teacher.) When you complete this step, visit your site to make sure it still works.

Publicizing the Site

Once your site is up, e-mail your friends and tell them to visit it. Ask visitors to your site to spread the word to other people they know.

Try It!

To create a personal Web site, start planning and sketch out your pages.

Finding Places to Publish

Here are publications that accept student submissions, and the facts about three writing contests. (Refer to *Writer's Market*—found in most libraries—for more places to publish.) Be sure you understand the publishing conditions for a publication or a contest and share this information with your parents.

Publications

Kids Byline: A Magazine for Kids by Kids (Grades 2–12)
FORMS: Fiction, nonfiction, poetry
SEND TO:
P.O. Box 1838
Frederick, MD 21702

Teen Ink (Grades 6–12)
FORMS: Articles, art, photos, reviews, poems, fiction
SEND TO:
P.O. Box 30
Newton, MA 02461

The High School Writer (Grades 9–12)
FORMS: Fiction, poetry, nonfiction
SEND TO:
Senior High Edition
P.O. Box 718
Grand Rapids, MN 55744

Skipping Stones: A Multicultural Children's Magazine (Ages 8–16)
FORMS: Art, stories, photos, and articles in any language
SEND TO:
P.O. Box 3939
Eugene, OR 97403

Writing Contests

Read Writing Contests (Grades 9–12)
FORMS: Short stories, personal essays
SEND TO:
Read Writing and Art Awards
Weekly Reader Corporation
200 First Stamford Place
P.O. Box 120023
Stamford, CT 06912-0023

The American Library of Poetry: Student Poetry Contest (Grades 8–9 and 10–12)
FORMS: One poem (20-line limit) on any subject, and in any form
SEND TO:
Student Poetry Contest
P.O. Box 978
Houlton, ME 04730

Scholastic Writing Awards (Grades 9–12)
FORMS: Short story, essay, poetry, dramatic script, humor, science fiction, fantasy, writing portfolio
SEND TO:
The Scholastic Art and Writing Awards
557 Broadway
New York, NY 10012

Try It!

Which publication sounds the most interesting to you? Why? Which piece of writing could you submit to this publication?

ELPS 2C, 3E, 3G

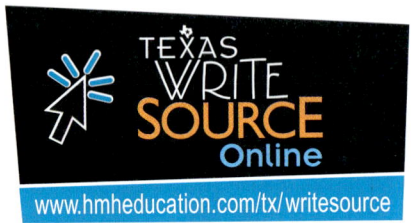

TEXAS WRITE SOURCE Online
www.hmheducation.com/tx/writesource

Narrative Writing

Writing Focus

Grammar Focus

Learning Language

Working with a classmate, read the definitions below and discuss possible answers to each question.

1. A **narrative** tells a story. It can be fiction or nonfiction. **What nonfiction narratives have you read recently?**
2. A **simile** is a comparison of unlike things, using "like" or "as." **Using a simile, what could you compare to a thunderstorm?**
3. **Sensory details** are details that refer to the five senses. **The words "crash" and "bang" appeal to which sense?**
4. To **shed light** on something is to give information about it. **How might you shed light on an accident you observed?**

Narrative Writing

Writing a Phase Autobiography

A phase autobiography re-creates an extended period in your life that changed you. This type of narrative writing invites the reader to experience what you experienced, and it illustrates the lessons you learned from it. If a reader says, "That was an inspiring story. You shed light on the topic, and I know just what you went through," the writer should know that he or she has succeeded.

For this chapter, you will share an extended life-changing experience, such as caring for a sick relative, campaigning for student council president, or surviving summer camp. Your phase autobiography will hold the reader's interest if it includes four key elements: action, sensory details, dialogue, and personal reflection.

Writing Guidelines

Subject: A period that changed you
Purpose: To share a life-changing time in your life
Form: Phase autobiography
Audience: Classmates

"We all have big changes in our lives that are more or less a second chance."

—Harrison Ford

TEKS 10.13A, 10.14A

Narrative Writing Warm-Up: Being Selective

When you write a phase autobiography, it's important to include specific details. However, you don't want to overwhelm the reader with too much information—after all, your life-changing experience could extend over several months. You need to be selective. Choose specific details that build a story to share and shed light on the main focus of your experience.

A writer compiled the list of details below for a narrative paragraph. After reading through his list, he crossed out the ideas that weren't important enough to include.

Sample Details List

Waterskiing

- A friend asked me to go waterskiing with him.
- ~~It was Memorial Day weekend.~~
- I was hoping my parents would say no.
- I didn't want to look silly.
- ~~Even my friend's kid sister can ski.~~
- The boat had 150 hp motor.
- ~~The skis were huge.~~
- ~~My friend's cousins showed up.~~
- My first attempt left me with a mouth full of water.
- I finally got up on the skis and sailed across the lake.
- There was no wind and the water was like glass.
- I even crossed the wake without falling.
- ~~I pulled and leaned so that I was running parallel to the boat.~~
- ~~I waved to people on the shore.~~
- I was so pleased, and my friend celebrated with me.
- After a rest, I was ready to go again.

Note: This final list of details guided the writer as he wrote a paragraph about the experience that changed him. (See the next page.)

Try It!

Think of an experience that changed you. List the details related to the experience. Then review your list and cross out any unimportant ideas. Remember, you don't need to share every detail, just a good story.

Writing a Narrative Paragraph

A narrative paragraph shares an important experience. Remember that a paragraph has three main parts:

- The **topic sentence** introduces the experience.
- The **body sentences** share details that re-create the experience.
- The **closing sentence** reflects on the experience and how it changed the writer.

Sample Narrative Paragraph

In the following narrative paragraph, the writer shares an experience that changed him—water-skiing for the first time.

The **topic sentence** introduces the experience.

The **body sentences** share the important details.

The **closing sentence** reflects on the experience.

Ready to Go Again

I was always a bit nervous about my athletic ability until a friend asked me to go water-skiing with him. At first, I hoped my parents would say no because I was afraid of looking silly, but they thought it was a great idea. I got more worried when I saw the massive 150 hp motor on the back of the boat waiting next to the dock. Bill went first to show me what to do. He sliced through the water, leaped over the wake, and sailed off the ski jump, landing perfectly. All too soon, it was my turn. I jumped in the water, pulled on the skis, and signaled I was ready. The boat surged forward, catching me off guard; I swallowed half the lake. Bill's dad stopped the boat. Patiently, Bill and his dad showed me once more how to use my arms and legs. This time I was ready, and I suddenly found myself standing on skis zipping over the water. The water looked like glass because there were no waves or wind that day. I yelled, "Yahoo!" Carefully, I made my way across the wake, and I didn't fall! When we returned to the dock, I laughed and celebrated. Bill and his relatives shouted, "You were great!" After others had their turns, I was ready to go again. **I suddenly realized that I didn't have to be an expert to enjoy a sport.**

Write your narrative paragraph. Review the three parts of a paragraph (top of page) and what they do. Then use your details list from page 80 to write a narrative paragraph about an experience that changed you.

TEKS 10.14A
ELPS 5G

Texas Traits

Understanding Your Goal

Your goal in this chapter is to write about a period in your life that changed you. The traits in the following chart can help you plan and write your phase autobiography.

Traits of Narrative Writing

- **Focus and Coherence**
  Share an important extended time in your life. Focus on that event. The narrative should tell a story about your life, and the reader should understand how the event you write about changed your life.

- **Organization**
  Develop a clear beginning, middle, and ending that together form a meaningful whole. Use a logical organizational pattern and transitions to move the reader from one idea to the next.

- **Development of Ideas**
  Make sure that each specific event adds to the overall story. Choose sensory details that create a rich description. Consider how storytelling devices such as suspense and conflict can add to your narrative.

- **Voice**
  Use a personal, interested voice appropriate for your topic.

- **Conventions**
  Write sentences of varied length and structure. Check for errors in grammar, punctuation, capitalization, and spelling.

Learning Language As you write, remember that your narrative should show why this was an important event in your life. Using sensory details and dialogue, you can make the event come alive for your reader.

Phase Autobiography

In this phase autobiography, the student writer tells about volunteering at an animal shelter. The side notes explain key parts of the essay.

Beginning The writer starts in the middle of the action and introduces the situation.

Middle Descriptive details pull the reader into the experience.

Middle Details about the dog make him a believeable character.

In the Doghouse

The first time I met Mugsy, I smelled him before I even saw him. He'd just been brought to the animal shelter after getting sprayed by a skunk, and now it was my job to bathe this furry stink bomb. It was only my second day volunteering at the shelter, and I wasn't sure what to do.

The second Mugsy saw me, he wanted to be my best friend. He was an ordinary-looking mutt, about six years old, as big as a shepherd, with long brown matted fur. He bounded toward me, yapping happily, tail wagging like a windshield wiper on hyperspeed. If he hadn't been tethered, I would have had his large skunk-scented muddy feet all over me.

I tried to spray him with the hose, but Mugsy played with the water, running through it, ducking, and generally making me look very incompetent when my supervisor Elena walked by. She quickly grasped the situation. "You're going to have to hold him firmly while you wash him," she said. She looked at me in a way that showed she expected me to do this myself and to do it right.

This was my chance to prove to Elena that she'd made a good choice when she agreed to let me work for her. I was younger than most of the other volunteers, but I'd told her I was ready for the responsibilities of caring for these animals. One day I plan to become a veterinarian, so I thought this would be great preparation. Now I already faced a challenge that I didn't feel ready for. "No problem," I said, hoping that I seemed confident.

I grabbed Mugsy's collar and managed to soap him down. I was surprised to see how skinny he was. One ear was chewed up and he had a sore spot on his hind leg. His life was as a stray must have been really tough. Still soaking wet, Mugsy decided to play again. He jumped up on me, tried to lick my face, and I started laughing. I finally got him clean, but I was a mess. When Elena came back, she looked pleased. "If you want to be successful here, don't try to stay clean," she said with a smile.

Middle
Dialogue moves the story along.

Ending
The writer reflects on how the experience has changed him.

Over the next few months, I hosed down cages and fed and bathed dogs, cats, rabbits, and even snakes that were left at the shelter. My favorite job was helping people find the right pet. I desperately hoped that someone would adopt Mugsy, but during all that time nobody was interested in an ordinary old mutt, no matter how friendly he was. They wanted puppies or purebreds or small dogs or cute dogs. It broke my heart to see families walk right by his cage. Whenever I could, I'd spend time with Mugsy. "Don't worry," I'd say, as I petted him, "Someone will see how special you are." But Mugsy would just lie down. He'd lost his happy goofiness.

One day Elena told me that Mugsy was being sent to a different shelter. They needed his space for more adoptable dogs. I knew I had to do something, so that night, I took Mugsy home with me. My parents took one look at him and I could see the big "no" in their eyes. They didn't want a dog.

I took a deep breath and hoped they could see the new responsible me. "I promise you, I'll take care of him, no matter what. Mugsy needs me." I explained his situation at the shelter. Mugsy seemed to understand that this was his big chance. He walked over to where my dad was sitting, laid his large, soft head on my dad's lap and looked up. Instinctively, my dad petted him, and Mugsy's tail came to life. I knew then that Mugsy had a home. Taking care of Mugsy became the highlight of my day. Having Mugsy and working at the shelter has helped to make my future clearer. I now know without a doubt that I want to become a veterinarian one day.

Respond to the reading. Answer the following questions.

Focus and Coherence (1) Do all the events in the essay work well together? **Organization** (2) What is the organizational pattern? Are any events out of sequence or hard to follow? **Development of Ideas** (3) What kinds of sensory details are used? **Voice** (4) Does this writer sound interested? Explain. **Conventions** (5) Did you find any errors in writing conventions? Were pronouns used correctly?

Prewriting

Go Online!

Your phase autobiography will be about a period of time in your life that changed you. In your prewriting, you will plan your first draft by choosing a specific period, listing the details that capture the phase, and organizing your ideas for writing.

Keys to Effective Prewriting

1. Think about extended periods of time in your life when you went through important changes.
2. Choose one of those periods to write about.
3. List the key events that occurred during this time.
4. Collect sensory details and personal thoughts related to this phase.
5. Consider how you can engage your audience.
6. Organize your ideas in chronological order for writing.

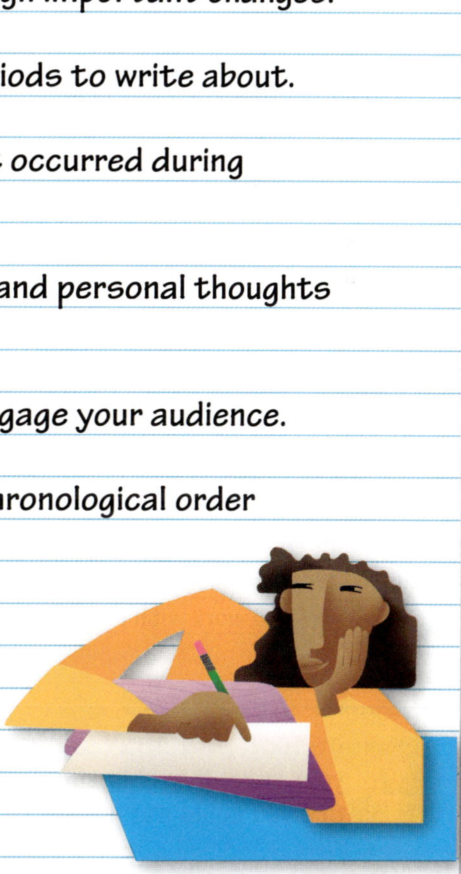

TEKS 10.13A, 10.14A

Prewriting Planning Your Writing

To think of life-changing periods of time, Sarah completed the sentence starter "I experienced an important change when I . . . " in three different ways. She put an asterisk next to the one that she wanted to write about.

Sentence Starter

I experienced an important change when I . . .
overcame homesickness when my family moved.
practiced four hours a day to make the soccer team.
*helped build sets for the school musical.

Prewrite

Complete the sentence starter. Finish the sentence in at least three different ways. Put an asterisk (*) next to the period of time you will choose.

Reflecting on Your Topic

To gather her initial thoughts, Sarah wrote freely about her topic. Then she underlined details that seemed important.

Freewriting

Being on the tech crew for school plays taught me more than construction skills—I also learned patience and how to be part of a team. <u>You had to work your way up to certain jobs. We spent 3 weeks building a fence for "West Side Story."</u> Mr. Morales had built a frame out of pipe, and my job was to cut fencing and attach it to the frame. <u>My arms got scratched up because I wouldn't wear long sleeves—it was too warm in the theater.</u>

When the fence was done, we had to paint a fake brick wall on wooden flats. We drew chalk lines to look like bricks, then painted them red.

<u>But we were running out of time</u>. Opening night was only a week away. Luckily, we made it! I really felt proud when the audience applauded. <u>I had learned how to work with people who had different talents and ideas.</u>

Prewrite

Collect your first thoughts. Write freely for 5 to 10 minutes to gather your initial thoughts about your life-changing period. Underline key details that you could use in your story.

Gathering Details

An effective phase autobiography, one that captures the essence of the time, contains three types of details: actions, sensory details, and personal thoughts.

- **Specific actions or events** move the story forward.
- **Sensory details** show what you saw, felt, heard, smelled, or tasted.
- **Personal thoughts** reveal your feelings and insights at that time.

Sarah completed the following details chart to gather ideas for her story.

Details Chart

Actions or events	Sensory details	Thoughts
Scratched arm on fencing	Sore arm	I'm too hot to cover up with a sweatshirt.
Cutting fencing	Aching arms and hands	Grandpa's voice: "Stick with it!"
Saw other kids goofing off	Annoyed at the goof-offs	I'll just ignore them and keep doing my job.
Had to keep repainting fake brick wall	Frustration about having to repaint	I'm learning patience.
Finished scenery by opening night	Sound of opening night applause	I'm proud of my work and of getting along with everyone.

Prewrite **Create a details chart.** **To gather details for your writing, complete a details chart like the one above.**

Texas Traits

Focus on the Texas Traits

Development of Ideas Actions can keep the reader interested in your story, but be sure to develop your ideas fully. Sensory details and thoughts will make the reader feel part of your experience.

TEKS 10.13A, 10.14A

Prewriting Building Narrative Suspense

A compelling phase autobiography is suspenseful; it makes the reader want to know what happens next. Here's how to build suspense into your story:

Start with a conflict—a task to be accomplished or a problem to be solved. The conflict in Sarah's narrative is the challenge to build sets for a musical.

Respond to the conflict. Sarah does a number of things to address her challenge—working on the fence, ignoring the goof-off kids, repainting the "slipping" brick wall. Each action builds suspense.

Build toward the climax or high point. The climax is the most exciting part of the story. It's the point at which the writer does or does not master the challenge. Sarah's narrative builds to opening night.

Texas Traits

Focus on the Texas Traits

Organization An effective phase autobiography should follow the classic plot line. The beginning gets the reader's attention and introduces the conflict, or challenge. Then a series of actions builds suspense. (Include at least two or three key actions.) At the climax, the writer either does or does not master the challenge. The ending tells how the writer's life is changed.

Plot Line

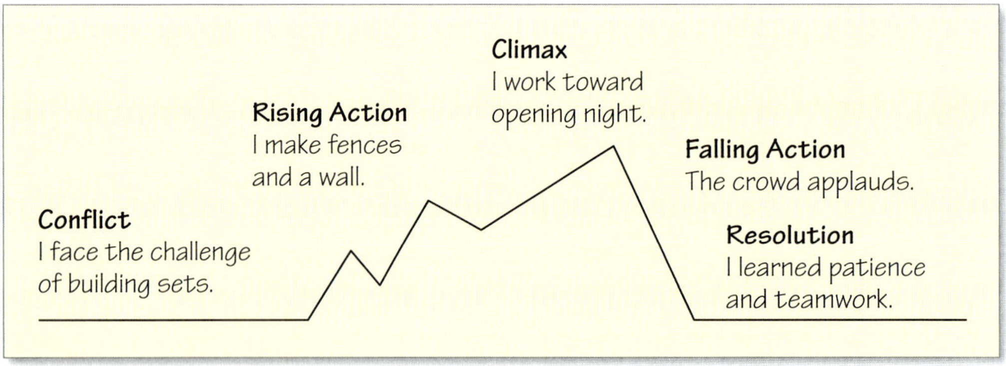
Climax
I work toward
opening night.
Rising Action
I make fences
and a wall.
Falling Action
The crowd applauds.
Conflict
I face the challenge
of building sets.
Resolution
I learned patience
and teamwork.

Prewrite

Create a plot line. Plan the main actions of your phase autobiography in a plot line like the one above. Use your details chart from page 87.

"Of all the subjects available to you as a writer, the one you know best is yourself."

—William Zinsser

Adding Dialogue

Dialogue enriches a phase autobiography by moving the action along, by revealing aspects of the speakers' personalities, and by simply adding information. The chart below shows how Sarah can present the same information without and with dialogue. (The dialogue examples are taken from the model on pages **93–96**.)

	Without Dialogue	With Dialogue
Show a speaker's personality	As the piece of fencing scratched my arm, I began to question why I had joined the tech theater crew.	"Ouch!" I yelped as the piece of fencing scratched my arm, making marks like animal tracks. "Are we having fun yet?"
Keep the action moving	We decided to ask for more help. 	"Please give us more help," we begged Mr. Morales.
Add information	My grandpa told me to always do my best work.	I could hear my grandpa's voice in my head: "You don't want your name on anything you're not proud of."

Prewrite

Consider dialogue for your phase autobiography. For practice, write some realistic dialogue that would be appropriate near the beginning of your story. (See page **654** for information about punctuating dialogue.)

Prewriting Reviewing Features of a Narrative

Read the following excerpt from a phase autobiography, watching for action details, sensory details, personal thoughts, and dialogue.

From "Charting a New Course"

The sixth day dawned with a golden orange sky, flecked with purple clouds. The sea was calm, and a brisk wind filled the sails.

We had been onboard the *John Gray Williamson*, a 64-foot sailing yacht, for nearly a week. Our crew of 12—four adult leaders and eight boys aged 14 to 17—were part of a Boy Scout expedition to the Bahamas. I imagined myself living in a time when sailors relied on wind rather than oil for power. I loved rubbing my fingers along the polished oak decks, which smelled of salt and varnish.

Then I noticed the leaders gazing off the starboard side at a massive cloud formation. Its base melted into the sea in dark columns.

The captain began barking orders: "Break down the sails!" he yelled to three of us standing near him. We had just barely untied the last knot to bring the sail down when the wind began roaring, and we got pelted with rain. I couldn't see my friend. I cried out, "Where are you, Pete?" Then I saw him struggling toward me. The boat rocked back and forth, making it hard to keep firm footing, and the boom swung around wildly. Just before the boom grazed over our heads, I screamed, "Watch out!" and tackled Peter.

Then a tremendous gust of wind struck the starboard side of the ship, tipping it dramatically. "I'm going over!" I shouted. Two scouts called out, "Hold on!" and grabbed my arm to keep me from sliding into the waves. I flopped down on the deck and grabbed a mast, frightened but relieved.

Thirty-five minutes later, we emerged from the storm into bright, blue sky and afternoon sunshine. The captain said that the storm was classified as a "white squall" because of the blinding torrent of rain it produces. It was odd to look back and see the black sky with occasional flickers of lightning. We'd made it!

On your own paper, identify at least one example of each narrative feature—*action details, sensory details, personal thoughts,* or *dialogue*—in the sample above. Be sure to use similar elements in your phase autobiography.

Drafting

With your planning in place, you're ready to write your first draft. This is your first opportunity to put the key elements in place: the beginning, middle, and ending of your story.

Keys to Effective Writing

1. Use the details you gathered and organized as a general guide.
2. Don't tell every detail about this phase in your life. Include just the details that allow the reader to appreciate the essence of this time; otherwise, your writing will go on and on.
3. Avoid getting "stuck" as you write the first draft by not fretting over each word.
4. Build suspense in the middle part of your story to keep the reader interested.
5. Use sensory details and dialogue to help the reader experience the events.

TEKS 10.13B

Drafting Getting the Big Picture

The chart below shows how the parts of a phase autobiography work together. (The examples are from Sarah's essay on pages **93–96**.)

Beginning

The **beginning** gets the reader's attention and identifies the topic of the writing—in this case, a phase.

Opening Paragraphs

"Ouch!" I yelped to my best friend, Angela, as the piece of fencing scratched my arm, making marks like animal tracks. "Are we having fun yet?"

This was my first musical as part of the Riverside High School tech crew. And I was determined, and excited, to help with the backdrops.

Middle

The **middle, or body,** paragraphs use details, description, and dialogue to develop the phase.

At first, I had been disappointed not to be assigned to the carpentry crew.

Mr. Morales, who taught our sixth-hour stagecraft class, had his rules for technical crews.

So for three weeks, day after day, we cut the fencing and attached it, cut and attached. . . .

Ending

The **ending** explains the importance of this time in the writer's life.

Closing Sentences

Working with more than 100 people with different skills and personalities taught me how to get along with others, even some people I didn't especially like. And I had high hopes for being on the carpentry crew for the next show.

Starting Your Phase Autobiography

Beginning
Middle
Ending

Once you've planned the main parts of your phase autobiography, you're ready to write your first draft. An effective opening should do these things:

- Grab the attention of the reader.
- Include relevant background information.
- State the topic, or phase, that you will write about.

Beginning Part

The writer grabs the reader's attention.

"Ouch!" I yelped to my best friend, Angela, as the piece of fencing scratched my arm, making marks like animal tracks. "Are we having fun yet?"

"Well, you could wear long sleeves," she said smugly, looking down at her own protected, sweat-shirted arms.

"Nah," I said. "It's too hot in here." Then I picked up the tools and went back to work.

Background information is given.

Angela and I were working side by side with two other kids, building the fence that would be the backdrop for one of the scenes in our high school musical, West Side Story. Our tech director, Mr. Morales, had welded the frame for the fence out of 1 ½-inch pipe. It was our job to cut the fencing—the kind you see in people's yards—and attach it to the frame with cable ties.

The phase is identified.

This was my first musical as part of the Riverside High School tech crew. And I was determined, and excited, to help with the backdrops.

Draft

Write your beginning. On your own paper, write the beginning part of your phase autobiography. Use transitions to connect your ideas.

Transition Words and Phrases

To shift time: **later, before, then**
To shift location: **between, across, at the edge**
To create a contrast: **however, on the other hand, even so**
To show cause and effect: **because, as a result, due to**
To add information: **in addition, in fact, also**

TEKS 10.13B, 10.14A

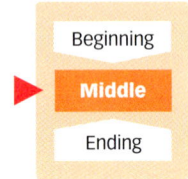

Drafting Developing the Middle Part

Beginning
Middle
Ending

The middle part, or body, of your phase autobiography shares the important information about your experience. *Remember:* Your goal is to tell a good story and hold the reader's interest. Use the tips below as a guide to your writing.

- **Include the key actions,** showing how you tackled your challenge. (See pages 87–88 for help.)
- **Add sensory details** to create vivid images in the reader's mind.
- **Share your personal thoughts** and feelings; use dialogue to show speakers' personalities as appropriate.
- **Maintain suspense!** (See page 88.)

Middle Paragraphs

The writer includes her personal thoughts and feelings.

At first, I had been disappointed not to be assigned to the carpentry crew. I love working with wood, ever since I was ten and my grandpa helped me build a small chair.

But Mr. Morales, who taught our sixth-hour stagecraft class, had his rules for the technical crews. "You have to work your way up to certain jobs," he told us. "But don't worry—by the end of high school, you'll have done a little of everything."

So for three weeks, day after day, we cut the fencing and attached it, cut and attached. Though my hands and arms ached, I could hear my grandpa's voice in my head: "You don't want your name on anything you're not proud of." As a result, I tried to measure and cut the pieces carefully. Angela and I usually worked silently—that's the kind of friends we are —just wanting to get the job done.

The writer's descriptions and dialogue make the scene believable.

At first, it made me mad when other kids goofed off, like when the boys started squirting glue at each other. Turning to them with a scowl, I yelled, "Cut it out, you guys!" They just laughed and kept playing around. Since they ignored me, I just ignored them, too.

Sensory details create effective imagery.

Although it took about three weeks, we could finally step back and look at the finished fence. It was huge—almost 35 feet wide and 15 feet tall!—so it would look real to the audience. Someone else painted signs like graffiti to hang on it. Then the big moment: five or six of us lifted the fence on a pipe, called a fly rail, so it could be moved around. Then Jon, our "fly man," moved it slowly on stage. It really looked like a fence!

Each new action builds suspense.

But there was still more to be done. Our next assignment was to paint a fake brick wall made out of three large wooden flats covered in muslin. If I thought building the fencing had been tedious, that was nothing compared to painting the wall. We spent days drawing chalk lines to look like bricks, then painting them red and adding gray edges for mortar. If we made a mistake, we'd have to whitewash it and start over. "I guess we're learning patience," I sighed.

Other key actions build to the climax.

And as we added more "layers" of brick, the bottom chalk line slipped on the diagonal, making it look like the building was leaning. So we'd erase it and start over, trying to make everything look straight. But time was running out. Opening night was only a week away, and we still had half of the wall to finish. "Please give us more help," we begged. Mr. Morales assigned two of the boys who had played around with the glue—not the most diligent workers. Then we persuaded the janitor to let us stay late, and we asked our teachers for extensions on our homework.

The writer presents a resolution of the conflict as she describes how the situation turned out.

By opening night, the wall was upright and in place, and it looked, well, almost straight. Angela and I were exhausted. At the end of the opening night show, the audience applauded the cast and musicians long and hard. Backstage, the rest of us who made the show happen—the painters, prop people, electricians, sound people, stage managers, costumers, and, of course, we scenery builders—high-fived each other.

Draft

Write your middle paragraphs. Use your prewriting notes to guide your writing. Keep the following drafting tips in mind.

Tip

- Remember that your purpose is to tell about a period that changed you.
- Don't worry about having everything correct in the first draft. Relax and let your ideas flow. If necessary, leave blank spaces and fill them in later.
- Add important ideas that occur to you as you're writing.

Drafting Ending Your Phase Autobiography

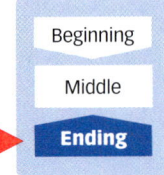

Beginning
Middle
Ending

The ending is your opportunity to reflect on the experience and summarize for the reader what you learned about yourself. Be truthful and sincere. Coming full circle is one idea for an effective ending. You can "come full circle" if you connect the ending with the beginning.

- **Key idea in the beginning**
  "Ouch!" I yelped to my best friend, Angela, as the jagged piece of fencing scratched my arm, making marks like animal tracks. "Are we having fun yet?"
- **Key idea in the ending**
  I'd put blood, sweat, and tears into building those sets, but I got even more out of the experience.

Ending Paragraph

In the conclusion, the writer reflects on how she has grown.

I'd put blood, sweat, and tears into building those sets, but I got even more out of the experience. I learned how to stick with a job until it's finished, and I learned about teamwork. Working with more than 100 people with different skills and personalities taught me how to get along with others, even some people I didn't especially like. And I had high hopes for being on the carpentry crew for the next show.

Draft

Write your ending and form a complete first draft. Complete your phase autobiography by telling what you learned during that period of your life. Put together a complete copy of your story, double-spacing on the computer or writing on every other line so you have room to revise.

Tip

If you have trouble with the ending, put your writing aside for a while. This will give you time to reflect on the importance of the experience. Or ask friends or family members how they saw you change as a result of your experience.

Revising

Go Online!

Your first draft gets the basic story of your phase onto the page. During the revising step, you improve your first draft by reorganizing, rewriting, adding to, or deleting different parts as needed. Concentrate on *focus and coherence, organization, development of ideas,* and *voice.*

Keys to Effective Revising

1. Set your first draft aside for a day or two, if possible, before you begin revising.
2. As you review your draft, think about your purpose, your audience, and the genre, or form, of your writing.
3. Be sure each main part—the beginning, the middle (or body), and the ending—works well.
4. Revise any parts that seem confusing. Add more details to any parts that seem incomplete.
5. Pay special attention to your writing voice. Do you sound interested and sincere?
6. Be sure you have chosen the right words to describe your experience.

TEKS 10.13C, 10.14A

Texas Traits

Revising for Focus and Coherence

When you revise your phase autobiography for *focus and coherence,* be sure that you have introduced the controlling idea in your first paragraph and that your introduction will grab the reader's attention. In addition, you want to cover only the events that relate directly to the controlling idea.

As you begin your revision, look back at the topic and details charts you put together as you planned your phase autobiography. Remember the audience and purpose for your writing. If your essay sticks to your purpose and all the events relate to the controlling idea, your essay will have focus and coherence.

Have I included only necessary events?

You have included only necessary events if each event covers a critical experience during the phase. As you read each event, ask yourself, "What's the point?" If you can't think of the point, cut the event from your narrative.

Exercise

Read through the following time line to get a sense of the total phase. Then reread each event and ask yourself, "What's the point?" Decide which events do not move the narrative along.

Week 1	Aunt Marisa lost her job.
Week 2	My cousin Anna moved in to share my tiny bedroom.
Week 3	Anna and her boyfriend broke up.
Week 4	I caught Anna wearing my favorite sweater.
Week 5	I put a tape line across our bedroom.
Week 6	My favorite sweater was missing, and I accused Anna.
Week 7	Anna and her boyfriend got back together.
Week 8	I found my sweater in the bottom of my locker and apologized.
Week 9	Anna and I made up. We had a good week.
Week 10	Ann's mom got a new job, and Anna moved out.
Week 11	Anna and I get together on weekends.

Revise

Review the events in your phase autobiography. Ask yourself, "What's the point?" for each event. Remove events that do not move the narrative along.

Does my narrative sustain its focus in each paragraph?

Each paragraph in your phase autobiography should communicate, either by restating or suggesting, the focus of your essay. Each paragraph should contain details that support and extend your controlling idea so that the reader will understand and appreciate your viewpoint. The paragraphs should work together to support and sustain your purpose for writing.

Revise

As you revise for focus and coherence, answer each of the following questions. They will help guide your revision and ensure that the focus of the narrative is sustained.

1. What is the controlling idea or conflict that is introduced in the beginning of the essay?
2. How do the main points of each middle paragraph help sustain the narrative's focus?
3. How do these points relate to the controlling idea?
4. How do the details in each paragraph relate to the main idea of the paragraph?
5. How do the details help sustain the narrative's focus?
6. Does the conclusion add meaning and reinforce the writing?

Tip

The conclusion of your phase autobiography should help the reader put the event into perspective. You should leave the reader with something to think about and an understanding of why and how this particular event affected your life.

TEKS 10.13B

Revising for Organization

When you revise for *organization,* check to see that your writing has a clear beginning, middle, and ending. It is also important to use a variety of transitions that lead the reader logically through the narrative.

Is my organization scheme clear to my reader?

A well organized composition is easy for readers to follow. The order in which the ideas are presented is logical and usually sequential. There may be some details from a memory or past event, but they should fit smoothly into the flow of the narrative. The reader should easily be able to understand why these details were included. Transitional words and phrases connecting sentences and paragraphs help the reader understand the action and the flow of ideas.

Exercise

Put the following sentences in a logical, sequential order so that the reader can identify the beginning, the middle, and the ending.

1. Mugsy, who had come into the shelter the day before, had matted fur and needed a bath.
2. I volunteered at the animal shelter because I want to become a veterinarian.
3. My family did not have a dog; in fact, we did not have any pets.
4. I decided that I do want to pursue a career working with animals.
5. It was my job to clean cages and help feed the animals.
6. Lots of dogs arrived at the shelter, and most of them needed loving care and attention.
7. I was surprised that I was the youngest volunteer.
8. It looked like no one would adopt Mugsy, but I hoped that my family would agree to take him in.

Revise

Reread your phase autobiography. Are your ideas logically and sequentially organized? Can your reader easily follow the flow of ideas? If not, rearrange the paragraphs and the details.

Have I used effective transition words and phrases?

Your transitions will be most effective if you use a variety of them in your writing. Using only transitions that indicate time can become tedious. *First* one thing happened, *then* another thing happened, *next* a third thing happened, etc. A variety of transitions will help you indicate not just the order of events but also their *meaning* and importance to the events of the narrative.

Most of the people taking the lifesaving course were members of the swim team. I wasn't on the team, though, and I'd actually taught myself to swim. In the pool, my inexperience showed. As a result, I struggled to swim 12 feet down, put on a mask, and fill it with air. I also gasped as I towed classmates using the cross-chest carry. Because I was the slowest swimmer, I often was still swimming laps after the other students were gone. Usually, my goggles leaked, so my eyes burned with chlorine. Everybody told me I should give up, but I didn't.

Exercise

For each blue transition above, write whether it indicates time, location, contrast, cause and effect, or added information.

Revise

Check your transitions. Review your phase autobiography, underlining transition words or phrases. Decide whether they help to better organize your writing. Revise as necessary.

Organization The writer uses a variety of transitions.

So for three weeks, day after day, ~~W~~we cut the fencing and attached it, cut and attached. Though ~~M~~my hands and arms ached~~.~~, I could hear my grandpa's voice in my head: "You don't want your name on anything you're not proud of." As a result, I tried to measure and cut the pieces carefully. Angela and I usually worked . . .

Narrative

Texas Traits

Revising for Development of Ideas

When you revise for *development of ideas,* you want to be sure that you have covered only the necessary events that relate to the topic. Be sure, however, that you have included enough details to make the narrative clear. Each event should be fleshed out completely and illustrate, or "show," the event.

Does the beginning lead logically to the ending?

The beginning of your phase autobiography connects with the ending if the two parts work together to show how the phase changed you. Here are three strategies for connecting the beginning with the ending.

- Use a question and answer.

  Beginning: When Mom asked me to walk the Appalachian Trail with her, I thought, "Do I really want to do this?"

  Ending: Mom and I looked back over the 400 miles we'd hiked together, and I knew that it was the best thing I'd ever done.

- Use a challenge and an outcome.

  Beginning: I sat shivering, staring at the high school pool, and thought I'd never be strong enough to become a lifeguard.

  Ending: All the chlorine and swallowed water was worth it when I got my lifesaving certificate.

- Use foreshadowing.

  Beginning: When I showed up at my best friend's house on the first day of summer, I should have noticed how pale he looked.

  Ending: We were just kids when that horrible summer began, but as John fought—and beat—cancer, we both grew up.

Revise

Reread your beginning and your ending. If they do not clearly connect, use one of the strategies above to make them work together. If your ending still does not clearly relate to the beginning, reread your narrative and try to see where the connection is lost. Does some event or detail described in the middle part of the narrative interrupt the chain of connections or lead the narrative off course? If so, ask yourself, is this event or detail really important to *this particular* narrative? If I take it out, does my narrative make more sense?

Have I included enough sensory details?

You have included enough sensory details if the reader can truly experience the sights, sounds, and smells associated with the phase. (Depending on your topic, you may or may not cover all of the senses.) Sensory details will also help you define the mood or tone of your narrative.

Exercise

Read the following paragraph from a phase autobiography. Then, on your own paper, list one or two sights, sounds, and smells. Then, briefly describe how those sensory details help define the narrative's mood or tone.

It was so hot that we could feel the scorching sand through our thin sandals. Still, we were very glad to be at the beach. Younger children splashed in the waves, but my brother Pedro and I wandered to a cove about 100 yards from the main beach where we discovered a treasure trove of seashells. Some were creamy colored, but many others were tinted pink, lilac, blue, and pale green. We quickly filled two plastic sacks with a rainbow of shells and made plans to give them to friends as gifts. We hurried back to the main beach, placed the sacks carefully on our towels, and ran off to cool in the water. When it was time to go home, we gathered sandy towels, wet shirts, and our big picnic cooler and dumped everything in the trunk of our car. Every time we went around a corner on the way home, we heard a curious crunching sound. We thought there was something wrong with the car. When we got home, we discovered the source of the sound. Our treasure trove of shells were underneath the cooler, crushed to tiny colorful shell smithereens.

Revise

Check your details. **Review your narrative to be sure that you have included sensory details. If not, add some.**

Development of Ideas
Sensory details make the experience vivid.

But there was still more to be done. Our next assignment was to paint a fake brick wall ^made out of three large flats covered in muslin^. If I thought building the fence had been boring, . . .

Texas Traits

Revising for Voice

When you revise for *voice,* be sure that your voice matches your feeling about the topic and shows your interest. You should state your position clearly so that the reader can recognize your viewpoint. If you do this, you will sound authentic, and the reader will understand your perspective. Your success at conveying your attitude may depend on your choice of words.

Is my voice appropriate for the topic?

Your voice is appropriate for the topic if it matches your attitude or feeling about the phase in your life. Here are adjectives that can describe attitude.

friendly	smart	silly	enthusiastic	bitter	sarcastic
know-it-all	timid	humorous	anxious	sad	flip

Here are some examples of voice:

Sarcastic: Sure, I can wash the dishes. I've got nothing to do tonight except practice the piano, clean my room, and do three hours of homework.

Sad: I wailed, as any seven-year-old would, after finding my goldfish floating upside down.

Enthusiastic: Our student trip to Belize includes a fantastic trek through the rain forest. I can hardly wait!

Exercise

For each sentence, write an adjective that describes the attitude.

1. When we moved to our new neighborhood last summer, I sat on the porch a lot, hoping new friends would simply appear.
2. You are so kind to take time to visit me in the hospital.
3. After rolling down the hill, flattening a marker flag or two, I stood up quickly, like a feline who's fallen from the back of a chair, stretched, and assumed a nonchalant pose.
4. I stepped weakly onto the swaying rope bridge, shaky, eyeing the swollen creek below.

Revise

Check your voice. Read your narrative out loud and think of an adjective to describe your voice. Is that adjective appropriate for the phase?

How can figurative language add to my writing?

Figurative language creates an imaginative comparison between things that are not usually compared to each other. When you use figurative language, you grab the reader's attention and make your writing come alive for the reader. Figurative language helps engage the reader because the reader experiences your unique perspective on events as reflected in your language. There are several different types of figurative language.

A **simile** is a comparison using the words *like* or *as*: *Her hair swished like a velvet curtain.*

A **metaphor** is a comparison of two things in which no word of comparison (*as* or *like*) is used: *He's a bolt of lightning.*

Personification is a literary device in which the author speaks of or describes an animal, object, or idea as if it were a person: *My bicycle was happy to be washed.*

Onomatopoeia is the use of a word whose sound suggests its meaning, as in *clang, buzz,* and *twang*: *The whirring of the buzz saw.*

Caution: Be as original as you can. Avoid cliches like *busy as a bee, on his merry way, the spitting image of his father,* and *right off the bat.*

Exercise

On your own paper, write an example for each figure of speech. Be original!

1. Simile:
2. Metaphor:
3. Personification:
4. Onomatopoeia:

Revise

Use figurative language in your writing. Read through your writing and look for places where you can add an example of figurative language to make your writing come alive.

Texas Traits

Revising Using a Checklist

Revise

Check your revising. On your own paper, write the numbers 1 to 11. Put a check by the number if you can answer "yes" to that question. If not, continue revising that part of your phase autobiography.

Revising Checklist

Focus and Coherence

_____ **1.** Have I focused on an extended period of time that changed me?
_____ **2.** Does each action or event add to the phase autobiography?
_____ **3.** Does my conclusion explain the importance of the event?

Organization

_____ **4.** Do I have a clear beginning, middle, and ending?
_____ **5.** Does the ending connect with the beginning?
_____ **6.** Do I use a variety of transition words and phrases?

Development of Ideas

_____ **7.** Does each action or idea add to the phase autobiography?
_____ **8.** Have I used sensory details and dialogue to help develop my ideas?

Voice

_____ **9.** Is my voice appropriate for the topic?
_____ **10.** Do I sound interested in my topic?
_____ **11.** Have I clearly explained my perspective or viewpoint?

Revise

Make a clean copy. When you've finished revising your story, make a clean draft to edit.

Editing

Go Online!

Once you've made your revisions, you should edit your writing for conventions: grammar, sentence structure, capitalization, punctuation, and spelling.

Keys to Effective Editing

1. To guide your corrections, refer to a dictionary, a thesaurus, and the "Proofreader's Guide" in the back of this book.
2. Watch for any words or phrases that may be confusing to the reader.
3. Check your phase autobiography for the correct use of grammar, sentence structure, capitalization, punctuation, and spelling.
4. Use the editing and proofreading marks inside the back cover of this book.
5. Edit on a computer printout and then enter your changes into the computer.

TEKS 10.13D
ELPS 5D, 5E

Texas Traits Editing for Conventions

When you edit for *conventions*, you should check for grammar, sentence structure, punctuation, capitalization, and spelling.

Grammar

Grammar refers to how language is put together. It also refers to the rules for writing sentences correctly. As you check for grammar errors, be sure to look for correct usage of parts of speech, including nouns, verbs, adjectives, adverbs, and pronouns.

Have I used adjective forms correctly?

You have used adjective forms correctly if you have used the positive form to describe a single noun or pronoun, the comparative form to compare two nouns or pronouns, and the superlative form to rank three or more.

Positive	Comparative	Superlative
hard	harder	hardest
difficult	more difficult	most difficult
good	better	best

Grammar Exercise

For many short adjectives, the comparative form is created by adding *-er,* and the superlative form by adding *-est.* For longer adjectives, the comparative form is created by using the word *more* or *less,* and the superlative form by using *most* or *least.* Some adjectives have irregular forms: *bad, worse, worst.*

Find the adjective-form errors and indicate how each should be corrected.

My desire to get a job was badder than ever. I checked the most late classified ads, I made phone calls, and I set up interviews. But I couldn't land a job, and I was more frustrated than ever. Then I heard about the perfectest job, working as an assistant to the athletic director at the local community center. Believe it or not, the athletic director hired me right after my interview! I couldn't have been happier.

Edit

Edit for adjective forms. Check the adjectives in your narrative and be sure to use the adjective forms correctly.

Do I Use Reflexive and Reciprocal Pronouns Correctly?

A reflexive pronoun refers to the subject of a sentence. First-person reflexive pronouns are *myself,* which refers to the subject pronoun *I,* and *ourselves,* which refers to the subject pronoun *we.* The second-person reflexive pronouns are *yourself* and *yourselves.* Third-person reflexive pronouns are *himself, herself, itself,* and *themselves.*

Examples:

I cut myself with that sharp knife. (The reflexive pronoun *myself* refers to the subject pronoun *I*.)

Cecilia let herself in through the back door. (The reflexive pronoun *herself* refers to the subject, *Cecilia*.)

You need to make that decision by yourself. (The reflexive pronoun *yourself* refers to the subject pronoun *you*.)

They chose costumes for themselves. (The reflexive pronoun *themselves* refers to the subject pronoun *they*.)

A reciprocal pronoun expresses a mutual action or relationship, one that moves or works in each direction. The reciprocal pronouns *each other* and *one another* refer to the individual members of a plural subject.

Examples:

The children exchanged gifts with one another.

Julio and Pedro laughed at each other's jokes.

Grammar Exercise

Rewrite the following sentences, using the correct reflexive or reciprocal pronouns. Your rewrites should eliminate wordiness.

1. Larry gave Natalie a present, and Natalie gave Larry a present. (Rewrite with *each other.*)
2. I bought that bike for me, not for someone else. (Rewrite with *myself.*)

Edit

Check your use of pronouns. Look for places where you could make your sentences flow better by using reflexive or reciprocal pronouns.

Learning Language Work with a partner to create additional example sentences to show correct use of reflexive and reciprocal pronouns.

TEKS 10.13C, 10.17A
ELPS 5F

Sentence Structure

When you edit for *sentence structure,* be sure that you have a variety of sentence beginnings and lengths. As you edit, ask yourself if your sentences will hold the reader's interest. Use different types of phrases and clauses to start your sentences. In addition, use both complex and compound sentences.

Have I varied my sentence beginnings?

You have varied your sentence beginnings if some sentences begin with the subject, some with a phrase, and some with a clause. Also, avoid starting too many sentences with "I." Note how repetitive this paragraph sounds.

I stepped out of my grandfather's car and looked at the farm fields. I saw unending shafts of golden wheat extending to the edge of the world. I could see grain silos standing on the horizon ten miles away. I was used to living in canyons of glass and steel. I wondered if I'd be able to survive out here on the wide-open plains.

Here are the same ideas with varied beginnings.

I stepped out of my grandfather's car and looked at the farm fields. Unending shafts of golden wheat extended to the edge of the world. On the horizon, I could see grain silos. Used to living in canyons of glass and steel, I wondered if I would I be able to survive out here on the wide-open plains.

Exercise

Rewrite the following paragraph to vary the sentence beginnings.

I turned to see the 100-year-old farmhouse with its wooden clapboards and wraparound porch. I could see Grandma sitting on the rocker there, watching the wheat wave. I noticed her cat, weaving through the spindles of the rail. I thought that life here would be tough during the windy hot summers and the stinging cold winters. I would probably go stir-crazy.

Edit

Edit for varied sentence beginnings. Check your phase autobiography for varied sentence beginnings. Begin some sentences with phrases and clauses, and avoid repetitive "I" sentences.

Mechanics: Punctuation

Using correct punctuation is important. If there are errors in punctuation, the reader will have difficulty following your essay and may not be able to understand your message.

How should I punctuate introductory phrases and clauses?

Place a comma after longer introductory phrases and all introductory clauses.

No comma: Soon I decided I couldn't live someone else's life.

Longer introductory phrase: During the summer before my junior year, my weird haircut grew out.

Introductory clause: When stores would take back the clothes or music, I returned them.

Exercise

Indicate where commas should be placed in the following paragraph.

No matter what my friends thought Mr. Foyle was not a control freak. As a matter of fact he gave me a lot of responsibilities right away. I started by setting up the teams for the spring youth basketball league. Then I had to plan a practice schedule for all of the teams. When I finished the scheduling my next task was to help Mr. Foyle set up the league games. Then he had me help him interview people interested in running a concession stand at the games and I learned a lot about the kinds of questions you need to ask in an interview. After my first weekend on the job I knew I was going to like this job.

Edit

Edit for correct punctuation. Reread your phase autobiography. Check for punctuation inside your sentences and at the end the end of each sentence. Make sure you have used commas appropriately after introductory phrases and clauses.

TEKS 10.13D, 10.17C, 10.18A, 10.18Bi, 10.19
ELPS 5C, 5D, 5E

Texas Traits Editing Using a Checklist

Edit

Check your editing. On a piece of paper, write the numbers 1 to 11. Put a check by the number if you can answer "yes" to that question. If not, continue to edit your narrative for that convention.

Editing Checklist

Conventions

GRAMMAR

_____ **1.** Do I use correct forms of verbs *(had gone,* not *had went)*?
_____ **2.** Do my pronouns agree with their antecedents?
_____ **3.** Have I used reflexive and reciprocal pronouns correctly?

SENTENCE STRUCTURE

_____ **4.** Do I use a variety of correctly structured sentences that don't sound repetitive?

MECHANICS (Capitalization and Punctuation)

_____ **5.** Do I start all my sentences with capital letters?
_____ **6.** Do I capitalize all proper nouns?
_____ **7.** Do I use end punctuation after all my sentences?
_____ **8.** Do I use commas after longer introductory word groups?
_____ **9.** Do I punctuate my dialogue correctly?

SPELLING

_____ **10.** Have I spelled all my words correctly?
_____ **11.** Have I consulted a dictionary to check the spellings of words my spell-checker would have missed *(were, we're; to, too, two; its, it's)*?

Creating a Title

- Focus on the tone of your narrative: **Behind the Scenes**
- Give the words rhythm: **Cut and Attach, Draw and Paint**
- Play with words: **Go Along to Get Along**

Publishing

Go Online!

Sharing Your Phase Autobiography

Prewrite · Draft · Revise · Edit · Publish

After you have completed revising and editing, you can make a neat final draft of your story to share. You might ask your teacher or classmates for feedback so that you can make a few final improvements (see pages 72–74). Consider publishing ideas such as recording your narrative, presenting it on a class Web site, or reading it aloud to an audience. (See the suggestions below.)

Publish

Make a final copy. When you write your final draft, follow your teacher's instructions or use the guidelines below. Create a clean copy of your phase autobiography and carefully proofread it.

Focusing on Presentation

- Use blue or black ink and write neatly.
- Write your name in the upper left-hand corner of page 1.
- Skip a line and center your title; skip another line and begin your essay. Double-space your narrative.
- Indent every paragraph and leave a one-inch margin on all four sides.
- Write your last name and the page number in the upper right-hand corner of every page after the first one.

Make a recording

Record your phase autobiography. Be sure to use an expressive voice. Give the recording and a printed copy of it to someone as a gift.

E-mail your story

E-mail your phase autobiography to a small group of friends and relatives not associated with your school. Ask for feedback. Also ask them to share a few details about a period of time that changed them.

Share with a younger audience

Ask if you and several classmates could read your phase autobiographies to younger students. When each author is finished, ask the students what they liked about the story, and why. If you're feeling brave, ask what they didn't like, and why.

Evaluating a Narrative

As you read the narratives that follow, focus on the writers' strengths and weaknesses. Then read the student self-assessment on page 127. **(The essays contain errors.)**

Writing that fits a score of 4 is highly effective.

4

The controlling idea is introduced and clearly states the writer's position.

The conflict is explained logically and descriptively.

Writer shows strong command of writing conventions.

Roll over Beethoven

I would watch the second hand on the clock as I practiced piano. Every minute seemed so slow, and an hour of practice seemed to take forever. "You want to go to a good music school, don't you?" my mom would pointedly remark. "Don't you want to play with a symphony orchestra?" asked my dad—though he wasn't really asking. "Sure," I'd reply. Then I'd start practicing my Bach fugue with a bit more dedication, hiding my deep dark secret from my parents. You see, what I really wanted was to be a rock and roll star.

Both of my parents are classical musicians, as were all four of my grandparents. So, of course, I was expected to carry on the family tradition, especially since I'd won awards for my piano playing since I was five years old. Then I turned thirteen. Suddenly all my friends were listening to music that we never played in my house. I heard keyboards being used in ways that Beethoven never dreamed of. It was loud. It was frenzied. Rock musicians looked like they were having fun when they played. Audiences went wild. It was not like performing to a polite audience in a symphony hall.

When my school announced a music talent night, everyone expected me to perform a complicated classical piece that would make every parent wish his or her child could play the piano. Only my friends knew that I was competing as part of a band called Slam the Doors. We were going to cover songs by the sixties band The Doors. As the day of the talent competition approached, my parents kept asking me what piece I was going to play. I should have just told them the truth, but I didn't have the nerve. I was

Specific examples and details add tension to the story.

sure I would let them down if I told them I was playing "Light My Fire" instead of Mozart's Sonata in C Major. I went ahead and bought them tickets. Even my grandfather was excited about coming to hear me play. I started to feel sick.

On the day of the show, I threw up. My mom was concerned because I'd never had stage fright before. "Is something wrong?" she kept asking. "No . . . yeah . . . no," I'd vaguely reply. As soon as I could, I left the house for our sound check and a final rehearsal. The electric keyboard I was playing was an old rickety one, and I was sure it would collapse on me, if I didn't collapse first.

The reader can understand and appreciate the writer's feelings.

I avoided my parents when they arrived because I knew they'd wonder where my name was on the program. As I listened to the other performers before us, I got more and more nervous. They all sounded so good. I was sure we couldn't compare. Worse, my parents would be out there, judging me, furious with me, disappointed in me.

It was our turn. My bandmates and I went out on stage. I fiddled with the keyboard to avoid looking at the audience. Then Pete, the lead singer, signaled to me and I started the keyboard intro to "Light My Fire." I could feel the audience react to the melody, and I dared to look up and could see the principal nodding along, smiling in recognition. I felt a surge of joy and energy, and suddenly Slam the Doors was really rocking!

Meaningful conclusion adds a sense of completeness.

The applause was thunderous when we finished. At least, it seemed thunderous to me. We came in second place. The winner was a girl who played a Bach Two-Part Invention on the guitar. Triumphant, I finally was ready to face my parents. Before I could apologize, my grandfather ran over. "I saw The Doors play in Dallas," he said gleefully, "and your version of 'Light My Fire' was better." My mom and dad were smiling. I took a deep breath and went to face my newest fans.

Writing that fits a score of 3 is generally effective.

3

The topic is set forth in the introductory paragraph.

Dialogue adds interest and humor.

Essay contains minor errors in writing conventions.

Get Rich Quick?

For my buddy Enrique and me, the beginning of tenth grade was the worst. We were too young to get a work permit or to drive. And we NEVER had enough money to buy the stuff we wanted. Over the summer, we had thought about starting a lawn mowing service, but our parents were too busy to drive us to the jobs, and our neighborhood was spread out, so it wasn't practical to wheel the mowers around. Then, in late September, we hit on the idea of a raking and snow shoveling service. We could easily walk or bicycle around town with the equipment.

"Get rich quick!" said Enrique.

"Video games, here we come!" I said.

So E&M Raking & Snow Shoveling Services was born. We made a professional-looking flyer that listed our rates and even included my next door neighbor as a reference. Then we posted it on some community boards at church and at our local market. We also put flyers in people's mailboxes. By the end of the week, we had six jobs scheduled. The first one, on Monday, was for Mrs. Garcia, a nice, retired school teacher who even brought out cookies while we worked. "I have a bad back, or I'd do this myself," she said. "I'm so happy you boys are here." She had a big lawn, with several trees on the side. It took about three hours, and we split the $20. We congratulated each other over our big success.

Monday night, there was a big storm, and lots of leaves blew to the ground. The phone started ringing, and I say yes to five more jobs. Tuesday, it rains hard all day, so we had to postpone our next job. But Mr. Edgars didn't understand. He called Tuesday night. "I'm disapointed you boys didn't show up," he yelled. "Better be here tomorrow." So we had to do two jobs on Wednesday and didn't get home until after dark. We got only $12 from Mr. Edgars, even though he made us drag brush out to the street in addition to the raking. He also walked around the yard, pointing to the few leaves that were left. "There's a leaf, there's a leaf," he

Examples build on each other.

cried, while Enrique and I took turns picking them up. I hoped he wouldn't call back.

It rained again both Thursday and Friday, so on Saturday we had to rush around doing three jobs. The leaves were soggy and our arms ached. And the five people who called on Monday night all called back, demanding to know when we would be there. I started dreading the sound of the phone. I asked my dad to help us on Saturday. "Sure, just this once," he growls. "But this business was your idea—you've got to figure out how to manage it."

It was only mid November. I wanted to quit but my dad said I couldn't until all the raking jobs were handled. "You can eliminate the snow shoveling," he said, "but you've got to follow through on what you promised people." So even though Enrique and I were exausted, behind in our homework, and tired of being "the boss," we stuck with it. By the time all of the trees were bare, Enrique and I had made $250 each. We were pleased about the money, but glad the work was over.

Writer sounds sincere and has engaged the reader.

Once the pressure was off, I realized that my favorite part of the job was advertising the business and negotiating with customers. It made me realize that I might like a career in business or marketing. Now I'm planning to take some econ courses in high school, maybe major in business at college. My almost disastrous job helped me see a future for myself.

Writing that fits a score of 2 is somewhat effective.

2

The controlling idea is unclear. Writing lacks a clear focus.

Fragments and other errors in conventions interefere with the message.

Detailed descriptions would have added interest.

Ideas are not fully developed, so reader cannot appreciate the writer's position.

A Different Life

Last year my parents decided they want to visit Guatemala where they grew up. I didn't want to go. It was summer and I wanted to spend it with my friends plus I'd have to speak Spanish all the time because no one spoke English there. Also there wouldn't be my favorite TV shows and they didn't have internet service or even a computer! It sounded terrible.

Once we get to Guatemala, it took us three hours to get to my grandparents' house, which was in a small village way out in the country. My heart sunk when we got there. There was nothing to do. No movies, no stores, and not close to any interesting places. It looked like the most intresting thing to do was pick the fruit that was growing everywhere.

Everyone was really happy to see us. They all hugged each other. They all started speaking to me in fast Spanish and when I spoke back they laughed and said I had an American accent! "Great," I thought, "They're going to make jokes about my Spanish the hole time I'm here." But then they started telling me how great it was that I could speak Spanish.

I had to sleep with two of my cousins in a small room. At first it really bugged me, but then we started to talk. I told them about america and they told me they wanted to go to america one day, but they also loved Guatemala. I started meting there friends and we started going out all the time. It was fun and actually a lot less stressful than America. I found out you didn't need to play videogames or talk on cell phones or buy new CDs to have fun with friends.

When I got back I really miss my life in Guatemala. I want to go back son and I've been working hard to improve my Spanish. I found out that life in Guatemala is different from here, but its just as good in its own way.

Writing that fits a score of 1 is not effective.

1

No clear, controlling idea is presented.

The many errors in conventions interfere with understanding.

Passage lacks variety in sentence structure.

Scene lacks description and does not engage the reader.

Team Runt

When I was in middle school I was pretty small for my age. I really like sports though but no one ever picked me for there teams cause I was so small. In PE I was always the last one.

I new that I was a good player even though I was small. But I am always put in the outfild for softball and in soccer no one ever kicked the ball to me. When we played basketball or flag football I would just sit on the bench it was really humilating.

One day we got a new PE teacher who's rule was that everyone plays. That made the kids that got me on there basketball team really mad and they figured if I played they would lose so the teacher made me one of the starters. The other team laughed.

I play basketball all the time with my brothers and dad. I was actually a good shot and could get in close to the basket. I was also good shooting from the fall line. And I'm fast. I guess they didn't know that. I don't think they cared.

When we started playing the big kids thought it was funny to block me and no one would pass me the ball. But once there was a lose ball and I got it. I dribled the ball around the bigger players went up for the shot and scored! Nobody could believe it. They thought it was a one time thing. But after I made a few more baskets they started passing the ball to.

After that basketball game people started picking me for their basketball teams. And me I also grew! Now I play junior varsity basketball and other sports and I'm one of the biggest kids but I'm always nice to the smaller kids!

Evaluating and Reflecting on Your Writing

You've worked hard to write a phase autobiography that your classmates will enjoy. Now take some time to score your own narrative and think about your writing experience. To score your narrative, use the scoring guide on pages 60–61 and refer to the examples on pages 114–119. On another sheet of paper, finish each of the sentence starters below. Reflecting on your writing will help you see how you are growing as a writer.

My Phase Autobiography

1. The focus of my phase autobiography, which I express in my introduction, is . . .

2. My phase autobiography has a logical organizational pattern because . . .

3. One idea I could develop more clearly and completely is . . .

4. In my next personal writing, I would like to . . .

5. One improvement in grammar, usage, or sentence structure that I need to work on is . . .

Narrative Writing

Writing a Historical Narrative

Writer Grace Paley advises that "you write from what you know, but you write *in* what you don't know." This advice is especially helpful when it comes to writing a historical narrative, which re-creates a significant event or experience from the past. While it's important to share accurate details about the event, you were not an eyewitness and so cannot know everything. That's when you need to "expand" the narrative with details that make sense within the context of the story.

This chapter begins with a sample historical narrative based on an event involving Louis Pasteur and one of his patients. The rest of the chapter provides guidelines that will help you write your own historical narrative.

Writing Guidelines

Subject: **An important historical moment**
Purpose: **To share a significant event from the past**
Form: **Historical narrative**
Audience: **Classmates**

"Tell me facts and figures and you touch my mind, but tell me a story and you touch my soul."

—Anne McCaffrey

Sample Historical Narrative

A historical narrative shares a significant experience from the past. In the following sample, DaShawn Mathews shares a lifesaving experience in the life of Joseph Meister, who received the first rabies vaccine from Louis Pasteur. The narrative is told from the point of view of Joseph as a 16-year-old.

Beginning The first paragraph sets the scene.

Middle The second paragraph jumps right into the action.

Descriptive words bring the story to life.

Lurking in the Shadows

In the summer of 1885, I was nine years old, living with my family in the Alsace region of Germany. On the morning of July 4, I was walking alone on the road that led to school. I never even saw the dog lurking in the shadows of the butcher shop.

The snarling beast leapt from nowhere, slamming me to the ground. Pain seared through my body as the huge dog ripped at my arms and legs. "Help! Help!" I shouted. Foam and saliva from the dog's mouth splattered onto me, and blood stained my clothes.

Suddenly, I heard a voice yell, "Someone save little Joseph from that rabid dog!" The vicious attack finally ended when strong hands pulled me to safety. That evening, I screamed in agony as Dr. Weber poured carbolic acid on my wounds to clean them.

Two days later, after traveling nearly 300 miles, my mother and I arrived at the Paris office of Louis Pasteur, who was working on a rabies vaccination. Mother knew that rabies causes seizures, paralysis, and eventually death, so she pleaded with Pasteur to save me. I struggled to stand, because the deep bites on my legs were incredibly painful. Pasteur seemed hesitant, but Mother convinced him to examine me.

Several men in white coats peered down at me as I lay on a cold table. "Due to the severity and number of bites, it's almost inevitable that this boy will come down with rabies and die," whispered a gruff voice.

Pasteur looked uneasy and concerned. He ushered the men over to his desk and explained that he would try a rabies vaccine treatment, even though it hadn't been tried on humans. I heard Pasteur say, "Joseph will be given a series of shots for at least 10 days."

Dialogue adds realism and makes the characters more interesting.

Terrified, I screamed and tried to sit up.

Pasteur quickly came to my side and gently explained that the shots wouldn't hurt much. "Just a tiny sting," he promised. Pasteur's eyes were warm and friendly. His whiskery beard reminded me of my grandfather's beard. I decided that I could trust this man.

For the next 10 days, I received shots of the rabies vaccine. Pasteur grabbed my skin just below my rib cage and pinched it into a fold. I didn't watch as he pushed the needle into my skin. Thankfully, the injections weren't very painful. I didn't understand how the vaccination worked, but I did know that I wasn't getting sick.

My mother was so excited to see me every morning. Pasteur's face drooped with concern because he was so afraid that I would get sick with rabies and die.

Ending The final paragraph explains the significance of the story.

Pasteur shouldn't have worried because I never developed rabies. Less than a month after I was attacked, Pasteur decided that I was healthy enough to go home. Newspapers declared that my amazing recovery was the result of Pasteur's miraculous rabies vaccination. In the months and years ahead, rabies vaccinations were used to treat thousands of people around the world. I was the first of many.

Respond to the reading. Answer the following questions about the historical narrative you have just read.

Focus and Coherence (1) What is the controlling idea of the narrative? (2) How does the conclusion add to the essay? **Organization** (3) What transitions does the writer use to help organize the narrative? **Development of Ideas** (4) What specific facts about this experience does the writer share? Name at least three. **Voice** (5) Does the writer create a believable firsthand experience? **Conventions** (6) How might the writer improve sentence variety? Explain.

TEKS 10.13A, 10.14A

Prewriting Planning Your Writing

After paging through his history book, DaShawn created a chart of possible topics (events) for his historical narrative. He listed only topics that were brief and specific. With each topic, DaShawn chose a specific narrator.

Topics Chart

TOPIC (Specific Events)	NARRATOR
Signing the Declaration of Independence	Thomas Jefferson
Louis Pasteur's first human trial with his rabies vaccine *	Joseph Meister, first person treated with the vaccine
A day in an 1800s tenement sweatshop	Girl working in garment sweatshop

Prewrite

Choose your topic. Create a chart, listing historical events and possible narrators. Put an asterisk next to the event that you would like to write about.

Gathering Details

The next step is to research your topic and take careful notes. Remember that you are writing from the perspective of someone who personally experienced this moment in time. DaShawn used note cards to organize his research. He will use these notes to help him choose a controlling idea for his narrative.

Sample Notes

Pasteur, Louis
- says that germs affect fermentation
- proves his theory
- says that germs cause diseases
- develops anti-rabies vaccine
- treats Joseph Meister with vaccine in 1885
- story of Louis Pasteur pages 8–10

Meister, Joseph
- lives in Meissengott in Alsace
- attacked by a rabid dog while walking to school
- bitten badly, rescued by a local bricklayer
- first person treated for rabies with vaccine
- www.sciencefounder.net/Rabies.htm

Prewrite

Gather details. Research your topic, using a variety of sources to find information for your narrative. Take careful notes.

Organizing Your Details

Historical narratives are usually written in chronological order. DaShawn used a time line to organize the information he had gathered. Above the line, he listed specific dates from the story; below the line, he listed the details.

Sample Time Line

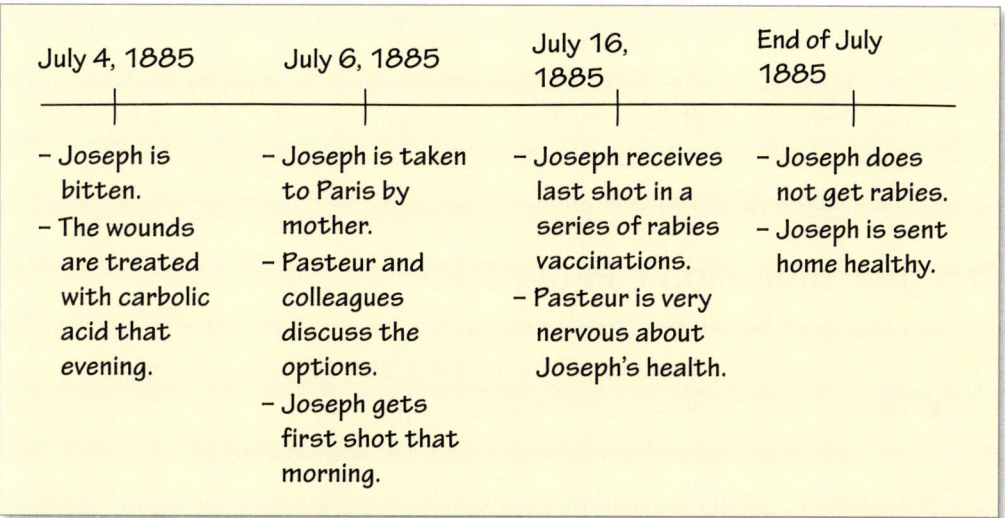

July 4, 1885	July 6, 1885	July 16, 1885	End of July 1885
– Joseph is bitten. – The wounds are treated with carbolic acid that evening.	– Joseph is taken to Paris by mother. – Pasteur and colleagues discuss the options. – Joseph gets first shot that morning.	– Joseph receives last shot in a series of rabies vaccinations. – Pasteur is very nervous about Joseph's health.	– Joseph does not get rabies. – Joseph is sent home healthy.

Prewrite

Organize your details. **Create a time line, listing dates or specific times above the line and details below it. The following types of details will make your story engaging.**

- **Historic details:** facts about *Who? What? When? Where?* and *Why?*
- **Sensory details:** what your character may have seen, heard, smelled, tasted, or touched
- **Reflective details:** what your character may have thought or felt
- **Actions:** what your character may have done or experienced
- **Dialogue:** what your character may have said or heard

Texas Traits

Focus on the Texas Traits

Voice The narrative on pages **122–123** is written from the first-person perspective of a character remembering the experience. This personal voice pulls the reader into the action.

TEKS 10.13B, 10.14A
ELPS 5G

Drafting

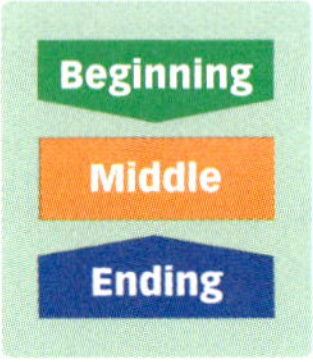

After gathering and organizing your details, read the following tips. They will guide you as you write your first draft.

Writing Your Beginning Paragraph

Introduce the main character and the setting. Provide details to capture the reader's interest and keep him or her reading.

> **In the summer of 1885, I was nine years old, living with my family in the Alsace region of Germany. On the morning of July 4, I was walking alone on the road that led to school. I never even saw the dog lurking in the shadows of the butcher shop.**

Creating Your Middle Paragraphs

- Jump into the action of the moment.

  The snarling beast leapt from nowhere, slamming me to the ground.

- Provide sensory details to create vivid imagery.

  Foam and saliva from the dog's mouth splattered onto me.

- Include realistic, natural-sounding dialogue.

  "Due to the severity and number of bites, it's almost inevitable . . . "

- Add thoughts, feelings, and explanations as needed.

  Pasteur's face drooped with concern because he was so afraid that I would get sick with rabies and die.

Developing a Strong Ending Paragraph

Share the resolution of the conflict and why it was significant.

> **Pasteur shouldn't have worried because I never developed rabies. Less than a month after I was attacked, Pasteur decided that I was healthy enough to go home. Newspapers declared that my amazing recovery was the result of Pasteur's miraculous rabies vaccination. In the months and years ahead, rabies vaccinations were used to treat thousands of people around the world. I was the first of many.**

Write your first draft. Use your time line (page 125) and the tips to guide your writing. Get all of your ideas on paper and don't worry about mistakes.

Texas Traits

Revising Improving Your Writing

Think about your purpose, your audience and the genre, or form, of the writing you have just done. Then use this checklist to improve your writing.

Revising Checklist

Focus and Coherence

_____ **1.** Have I clearly communicated my purpose for writing?
_____ **2.** Do all my ideas relate to the topic?

Organization

_____ **3.** Does my beginning introduce the main character?
_____ **4.** Do the middle paragraphs convincingly re-create the event?
_____ **5.** Does the ending explain the significance of the event?

Development of Ideas

_____ **6.** Have I thoroughly explained the significance of the topic?
_____ **7.** Are my facts, such as names and dates, accurate?
_____ **8.** Are all my ideas connected to each other, and can the reader understand the connection?

Voice

_____ **9.** Does the story sound like a realistic firsthand experience?
_____ **10.** Do I use dialogue effectively?

Creating a Title

- Be clever or humorous: **Vaccine Vanquishes Villain**
- Use an expression or common saying: **A Shot in the Dark**
- Use a line from the narrative: **Lurking in the Shadows**

Revise

Revise your first draft. Use the checklist above to review and make changes to your first draft. Then add a title.

TEKS 10.13D, 10.13E, 10.17C, 10.18A, 10.18B, 10.19
ELPS 5C, 5D, 5E

Texas Traits

Editing Checking for Conventions

After making revisions, you're ready to edit your writing for grammar, sentence structure, punctuation, capitalization, and spelling errors. The following checklist can help you with this step. (See the "Proofreader's Guide" for more about writing rules.)

Editing Checklist

Conventions

GRAMMAR

_____ **1.** Do I use the correct tenses and forms of verbs *(had gone*, not *had went)*?

_____ **2.** Do my subjects and verbs agree in number *(She was running*, not *She were running)*?

_____ **3.** Do I use the right words *(too, to, two)*? Remember, a computer grammar checker does not catch all usage errors.

SENTENCE STRUCTURE

_____ **4.** Do I use a variety of correctly structured sentences that clearly communicate my ideas?

MECHANICS (PUNCTUATION, CAPITALIZATION, AND SPELLING)

_____ **5.** Do I use end punctuation correctly after all sentences?

_____ **6.** Do I use apostrophes to show possession *(Pasteur's beard)*?

_____ **7.** Do I use end commas correctly?

_____ **8.** Do I capitalize all proper nouns?

_____ **9.** Have I used a dictionary to check for spelling errors?

Edit

Correct your narrative. Use the checklist above to find and correct any errors. Also ask a classmate, friend, or teacher to check your work. Then create a neat final draft and proofread it again.

Publishing Sharing Your Writing

Take time to share your work with classmates and family members.

Publish

Share your historical narrative. If you read your narrative to the class, practice first. Then read it clearly and with feeling. Consider using a prop or costume appropriate for the story.

Writing for Assessment

Responding to Narrative Prompts

In one section of his autobiography *Good Old Boy,* Willie Morris states, "Almost every afternoon when the heat was not too bad my father and I would go out to the old baseball field behind the armory to hit flies." Morris's father would hit ball after ball into the outfield, and the author, then a young boy, would try to catch them. Because of all this practice, Morris became a skilled center fielder.

You, too, have learned many skills during your lifetime. You may, for example, have learned how to ride a bike or swim or knit or play the guitar. Narrative writing prompts on assessments often ask you to recall such a learning experience. To respond effectively, you must share the key details related to the experience and tell why it was (or is) important to you. This chapter will guide you through the process of responding to narrative writing prompts.

Writing Guidelines

Subject: **Narrative prompt**
Form: **Response to a prompt**
Purpose: **To demonstrate competence**
Audience: **Instructor or test evaluator**

"Pain is temporary. It may last a minute, or an hour, or a day, or a year, but eventually it will subside and something else will take its place. If I quit, however, it lasts forever."

—Lance Armstrong

Prewriting Analyzing a Narrative Prompt

A prompt is a set of directions that tells you what to write. For example, a narrative prompt is one that tells you to write about a significant personal experience. To effectively respond to the prompt, you must first understand it. The **STRAP questions** below will help you to analyze a narrative prompt.

Using the STRAP Questions

Subject: What specific experience (memorable, life changing, challenging, inspiring) should I write about?

Type: What type of writing (personal narrative, personal essay, autobiographical article) should I create?

Role: What role (student, son or daughter, friend, community member) should I assume as the writer?

Audience: Who (principal, parent, city official, classmates) is the intended reader?

Purpose: What is the goal (share, re-create, entertain, illustrate, inspire) of my writing?

Try It!

Analyze these prompts, answering the STRAP questions for each one.

1. You often hear the phrase "Learn by doing." Recall how you learned a skill, and explain how the skill has benefited you.
2. Think about a time when you wanted something very badly and were not able to obtain or achieve it. What did you learn from the experience? Your response will appear in a booklet for younger students in your school district.
3. "The only way to help yourself is to help others." Share a personal experience that reveals the truth of these words.

Tip

Some prompts do not contain key words for every STRAP question. Use your best judgment to find answers for all the questions.

Planning Your Response

Once you understand a prompt thoroughly, you can plan your response. The following graphic organizers can help you complete your planning.

Narrative Graphic Organizers

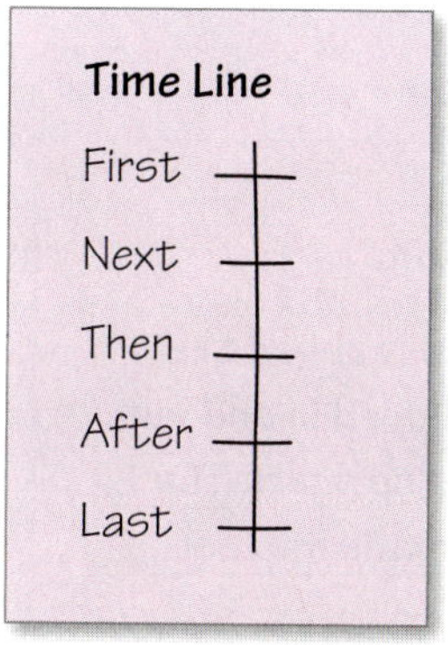

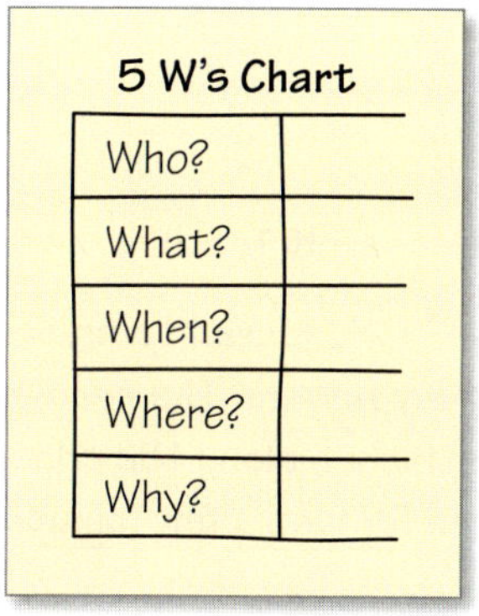

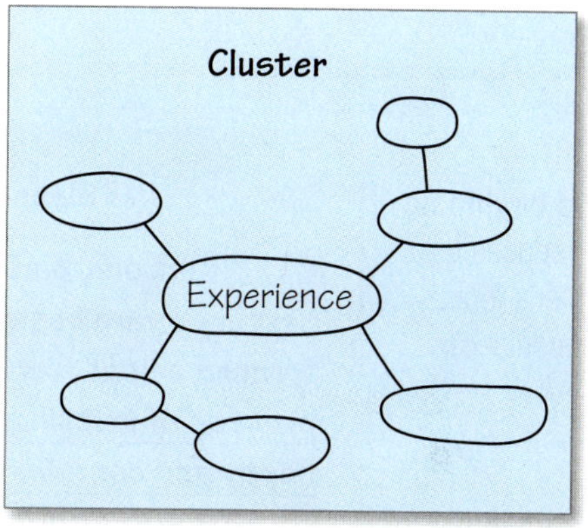

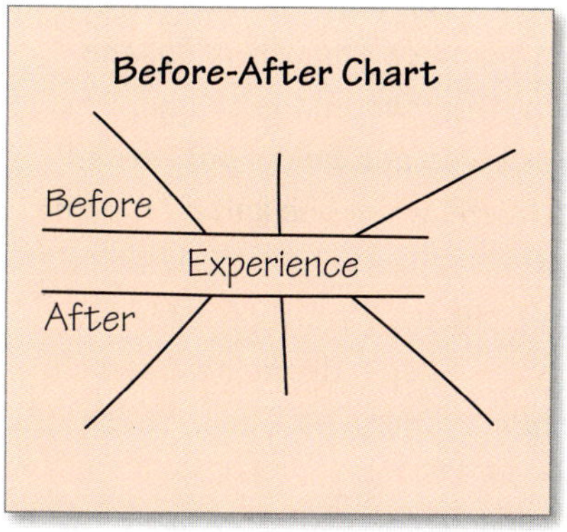

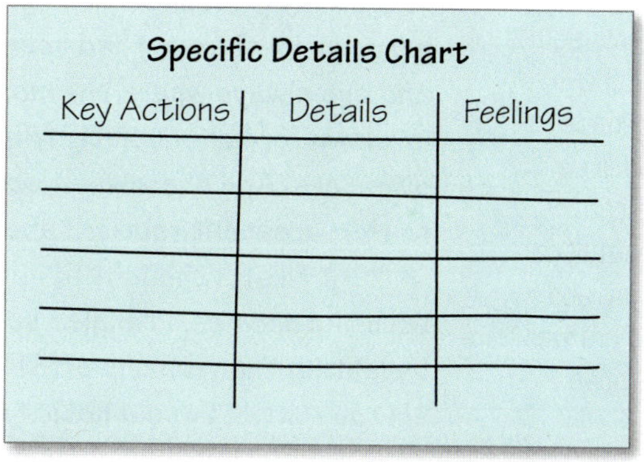

Prewrite

Reread the narrative prompts on page 130. Choose one prompt to respond to, and create a graphic organizer like one of those above to plan your response.

Narrative

Tip

Be sure to use your time wisely. For example, if you have 45 minutes to respond to a prompt, consider using the first 5 to 10 minutes to analyze the prompt and plan your response, and the last 5 minutes to revise and edit it. That leaves 30 to 35 minutes for writing your response.

Drafting Responding to the Prompt

After planning your response, it's time to begin writing. Student writer Ari Marks chose to respond to prompt number 1 on page 130. Ari plans to use dialogue and rich sensory details to make the characters and situations in her narratiive interesting and realistic. Her response to the prompt is below.

Sample Response

The **beginning** introduces the writer's focus (underlined).

Eleanor Roosevelt Teaches Me to Knit

"Knit one, purl two," I whispered to myself as I rubbed the textured yarn between my fingers. The needles dipped in and out, forming a neat row of stitches along the edge of the scarf. <u>The process of knitting, even for just a few minutes, made me feel happy and confident.</u>

Each **middle** paragraph presents details about the experience. There is a logical organizational pattern, and ideas are well developed.

I learned to knit the summer after seventh grade, when I begged my grandmother to teach me. Gran (and she is a very hip gran, by the way) had been knitting since she was in college, and she always wears the most beautiful handmade things. She is known for her elegantly fringed scarves and boldly patterned sweaters. And she always looks content when she knits. "It's the world's greatest relaxer," she says.

At first, I thought I'd never get the hang of it. I fumbled with the needles. I tangled up the yarn. I kept "dropping a stitch" by letting the yarn slip off the needle by mistake. Then, five or six rows later, I would notice a hole, and I'd have to ask Gran to fix it. Every time, she patiently used a crochet hook to work the dropped stitch back up and onto the needle.

Even when I finally mastered the stitches, my first projects weren't always successful. One sweater was too short. The vest I made for my dad was uneven on the bottom. He wore it anyway, mostly when he walked the dog.

The writer has an authentic voice, and details add interest.

The following summer I almost gave up knitting for good. I wanted to knit something spectacular, so I saved my allowance and bought some expensive wool to make a poncho. I used small needles to work the intricate design. When it was time for school to start again, I was really discouraged because I had only finished a piece about 14 inches square!

But Gran's encouragement kept me knitting. She quoted her idol, former First Lady Eleanor Roosevelt. "Eleanor said, 'You must do the thing you think you cannot do,'" Gran said. "I think that applies to knitting as well as to anything else."

I took Gran's advice and continued to knit. But I decided to wait with the poncho. Instead, I perfected my skills on easier patterns that used large needles. Two of my favorite pieces included a silky choker and a backpack made out of a multicolored rayon and cotton. A lot of my friends really liked my backpack. Some people even asked me where I bought it!

The **ending** tells what the writer learned from the experience.

Any frustrations I may have had with learning how to knit were well worth it. Knitting helped me become even closer to Gran. It also helped me learn more about fabrics, colors, and design. Most importantly, it built up my self-confidence and taught me not to be afraid to try new things, even if that meant "dropping a stitch" every now and then.

Draft

Write your own response. Look over the prompt you chose on page 130 and look over the planning you did. Then write a response in the amount of time provided by your teacher.

TEKS 10.13C, 10.13D
ELPS 5C, 5D, 5F

Revising Improving Your Response

Most writing tests allow you to make changes to your response, but be sure you know the number and kinds of changes that are allowed.

Using the STRAP Questions

Return to the STRAP questions to guide your revisions.

Subject: Does my response focus on a specific experience related to the prompt?
Type: Have I written the appropriate type of response (personal narrative, essay, article)?
Role: Have I assumed the role indicated in the prompt (student, friend, son or daughter, community member)?
Audience: Have I kept my intended audience in mind and used language appropriate for that audience?
Purpose: Does my response accomplish the goal called for by the prompt (share, re-create, entertain, illustrate, inspire)?

Revise

Improve your work. Review your response, using the STRAP questions as a guide. Make any changes neatly in the time allowed.

Editing Checking for Conventions

Finally, it is a good idea to read through your draft again to check for punctuation, capitalization, spelling, and grammar errors.

Conventions

_____ **1.** Do my subjects and verbs agree?
_____ **2.** Have I used a variety of correctly structured sentences?
_____ **3.** Have I checked for spelling errors?
_____ **4.** Have I used commas and end punctuation correctly?
_____ **5.** Have I capitalized proper nouns and the first words of sentences?

Edit

Check for conventions. Review your response and correct errors in grammar, sentence structure, punctuation, capitalization, and spelling.

Narrative Writing on Tests

The following tips will guide you whenever you are asked to write a response to a narrative prompt.

Before you write . . .

- **Understand the prompt.**
  Use the STRAP questions and remember that a narrative prompt asks you to share or re-create an experience.
- **Plan your response.**
  Spend several minutes planning your response. Use an appropriate graphic organizer to help you. (See page 131.)

As you write . . .

- **State the focus of your response in the beginning.**
  Keep your purpose *(to share, to illustrate)* in mind as you write.
- **Be selective.**
  Include specific details that effectively re-create your experience. Use dialogue, as well as literary and rhetorical devices (irony, metaphors, and so on) to make your experience interesting.
- **End in a meaningful way.**
  Tell why the experience has been important to you.

After you've written your first draft . . .

- **Check for completeness and correctness.**
  Use the STRAP questions to revise your work. Then check for errors in conventions.

Narrative Prompts

- A Chinese proverb says, "Give a man a fish and you feed him for a day. Teach a man to fish and you feed him for a lifetime." In a personal narrative, share a time in your life when you really learned to do something for yourself. Your audience is your classmates.
- In an article for your school newspaper, describe an accomplishment that made you really proud. Make the experience come alive with vivid details and dialogue.

TEXAS WRITE SOURCE Online
www.hmheducation.com/tx/writesource

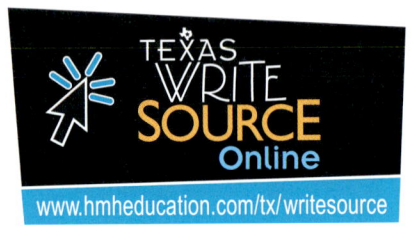

Expository Writing

Writing Focus

Grammar Focus

Learning Language

Learning these words and expressions will help you understand this unit.

1. **Expository** writing explains and informs.
   What are some types of expository writing that you read every day?
2. **Inferences** are logical conclusions drawn from facts that are presented in an essay or an article.
   How does making inferences help you understand a writer's point of view?
3. **Evidence** is the proof that something occurred or is factual.
   What kinds of details would provide strong evidence about a particular event?

A company that is **on the right track** is doing things correctly to be successful.
How can you tell that you are on the right track when you start a new assignment?

Expository Writing

Cause-Effect Essay

You studied thoroughly for your geometry test, so you feel confident that you are on the right track and will do well. You worked hard at swim practice, so you know that you'll be sore tomorrow. Life is a series of actions and reactions, causes and effects. When you reflect upon these actions, you gain a better understanding of your life, and the bigger world around you. That is why keeping a writer's notebook or personal journal can be so enlightening.

In the same way, you can better understand history if you reflect upon the circumstances surrounding important events. What caused the Black Plague to spread across Europe? What effect did Gutenberg's printing press have on literacy and learning? In this chapter you will write a cause-effect essay of sufficient length to discuss an important historical event or time. As you think and write about your topic, you will see how it connects with other times and events.

Writing Guidelines

Subject: A historical event
Purpose: To make connections
Form: Cause-effect essay
Audience: Classmates

"The cause is hidden, but the result is known."

—Ovid

Expository Writing Warm-Up: Focusing on a Specific Topic

Teachers usually base their writing assignments on a general subject that you are studying. For example, your science teacher could ask you to write about the space program in the United States. Before doing any writing, you would have to narrow or limit the subject to a specific topic suitable for the assignment.

Here's how one student narrowed the general subject—the United States space program—to a specific topic suitable for an expository paragraph.

Narrowing a Subject

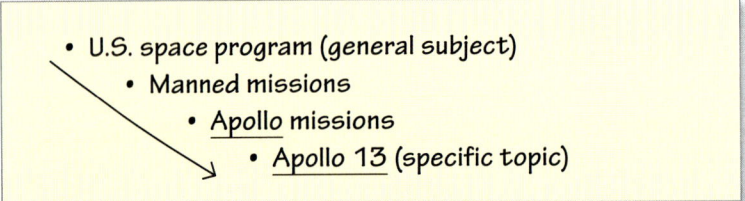

- U.S. space program (general subject)
  - Manned missions
    - Apollo missions
      - Apollo 13 (specific topic)

Try It!

Narrow one of the general subjects listed below until you identify a specific topic suitable for an expository paragraph. (Afterward, research the topic if you don't know a lot about it.)

General subjects: community life, current medicine, high school athletics, weather, movie industry, automobiles, security issues

Writing Your Topic Sentence

Think of the topic sentence as the engine that powers the rest of a paragraph. A topic sentence should identify the specific topic and identify a particular feeling or feature about it that you want to emphasize.

The Apollo 13 spaceflight (specific topic) **nearly ended in disaster** (a particular feature).

Try It!

Write a topic sentence about your specific topic using the sample above as a guide. (Refer to page 599 for more information.)

Writing an Expository Paragraph

An expository paragraph shares information about a specific topic. The paragraph may present facts, give directions, define terms, explain a process, or so on. The following paragraph explains the causes of the *Apollo 13* disaster. Remember that a paragraph has three main parts:

- The **topic sentence** identifies what the paragraph is about.
- The **body sentences** support the idea expressed in the topic sentence.
- The **closing sentence** reminds the reader of the topic or summarizes the paragraph.

"Houston, We Have a Problem"

Topic Sentence

The *Apollo 13* spaceflight on April 17, 1970, nearly ended in disaster.

Body

The problem—an oxygen leak and loss of electricity—was first noted by astronaut Jack Swigert. He calmly informed the mission control center in Houston of the situation. A NASA investigation later determined that the cause of the problem stemmed from inadequate thermostatic switches that somehow were not noticed during the safety inspections. The switches malfunctioned when they overheated, igniting the insulation surrounding the oxygen tank and causing an explosion. The crew had to move from the command module into the smaller lunar module, which was not designed to hold three people. There was limited water and heat in this module, and condensation on the walls created the fear of short circuits. Four tense days passed before the crew landed safely in the Pacific Ocean. As a result of the mission, safety checks of space modules have become more rigorous. In addition, NASA discovered that astronauts were very well prepared to handle such emergencies.

Closing Sentence

More importantly, they learned that respect and teamwork between astronauts and ground control were invaluable.

Draft

Write your own expository paragraph. Use your planning from page 138 and the paragraph above as a guide for your writing.

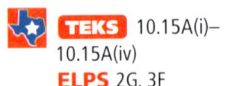

TEKS 10.15A(i)–10.15A(iv)
ELPS 2G, 3F

Understanding Your Goal

Texas Traits

Your goal in this chapter is to write a well-organized expository essay about a historical event that has a clear cause-and-effect relationship. The traits listed in the chart below will help you plan and write your essay. Keep in mind your purpose, audience, and context for writing.

Traits of a Cause–Effect Essay

Focus and Coherence

Select an interesting historical event. Clearly state your controlling idea and the direction your writing will take in your introduction. Plan an essay of sufficient length to cover the topic.

Organization

Include a strong beginning that creates interest and states your thesis. In the middle, support your thesis with reliable, well-researched information. Tie all of your main points together in the conclusion. Be sure to use transitions to connect ideas.

Development of Ideas

Develop your ideas by establishing and sustaining the cause-and-effect relationship related to the event. Support your ideas with researched evidence and carefully thought-out supporting details.

Voice

Sound knowledgeable about and interested in your topic. Use rhetorical devices, and vocabulary appropriate to your audience.

Conventions

Use correct grammar, a variety of sentence structures, correct capitalization, punctuation, and spelling.

Learning Language

Review the scoring guide on pages 60–61. Then using newly acquired vocabulary, discuss possible topics for your essay with your teacher. Ask questions, and listen carefully to the responses.

Cause-Effect Essay

In the following expository essay, the writer identifies the effects of Charlemagne's unification of Europe. The notes in the left margin explain the key parts of the essay. The writer considered audience, purpose, and context.

Beginning
The first paragraph introduces the topic and gives the thesis statement (underlined).

Middle
The middle paragraphs provide background information and discuss three effects. Writer has considered the relative value of data, facts, and ideas that support the thesis. Transitions link paragraphs.

Charlemagne

"By the sword or the cross," proclaimed Charles the Great, one of the most fearless and colorful leaders of the Middle Ages. Better known as Charlemagne, this leader utilized both the sword and the cross to become the first crowned emperor of the Holy Roman Empire, a political area including most of Western and Central Europe. During his 32-year rise to power, he was able to unify the nations of that area into a strong, single entity. Charlemagne's unification of Europe brought peace to all the people, stabilized the European economy, and promoted education.

Charles was the son of Pippin, king of the Franks, whose title he inherited in 768. With this responsibility, Charles developed the leadership and management skills he eventually used to rule much of Europe. He gained control of European lands by political maneuvering and by waging war, also spreading Christianity to unite the people under a common religion. Charles earned the reputation of being a fair-minded, diplomatic leader (Judd 75). In the year 800, Pope Leo III crowned Charles as Emperor *Carolus Magnus*. That Latin name translates to *Charlemagne* in Old French. Charlemagne brought about solidarity among kingdoms and unified continental Europe.

One of Charlemagne's greatest gifts was his skillful peacemaking ability. Prior to his reign, civil uprisings erupted continually as peasants grew weary of funding military campaigns by paying heavy taxes or forfeiting their land. Charlemagne organized the resources of each region to avoid heavy taxing. He started by collecting tolls, custom duties, and tributes from conquered peoples and distributing the funds to the regions where they were most needed (Judd 92). Charlemagne endeared himself to his subjects when he showed mercy to captured invading troops. When peasant and nobleman alike realized that they were being treated fairly, a feeling of trust and peace spread throughout Europe.

TEKS 10.15A(i), 10.15A(ii), 10.15A(vi), 10.15A(v)

The writer uses facts, paraphrases, and rhetorical devices such as quotations to develop and support the thesis.

In order to maintain peace, Charlemagne soon realized that he needed to stabilize the economy in the entire region. He divided larger parcels of land into more manageable estates that were self-contained and administered by a steward or caretaker. Each estate had a bustling center of commerce surrounded by a market, church, guilds, and public buildings. The remaining land was rented to the farmers who produced the crops that fed the people living on the estate. In return, the stewards provided protection and administered justice. The changes instituted by Charlemagne created an intricately balanced system of commerce and trade and stabilized the European economy (Sullivan 115).

With peace and a more stable economy in place, Charlemagne was then able to concentrate his efforts on education. He assembled the greatest minds of the entire region into an "academy" whose members traveled with and advised Charlemagne. Artists, scientists, and teachers, who were educated at the monasteries, were sent to other regions to share their knowledge. Due to Charlemagne's efforts, education was promoted and learning flourished throughout his empire.

Ending
The final paragraph ties all the key points together and connects with the thesis statement.

Charlemagne died in 814 at the age of 72. During his reign as king of the Franks and as emperor, he succeeded in unifying Europe, leaving behind a legacy of peace, economic stability, and an appreciation for the value of education. He cherished the written word and preserved the rich culture of his era. Although historians may judge Charlemagne as a foreign invader rather than a hero, it is difficult to imagine how Europe would have developed without the influence of this dynamic leader who lived "by the sword or the cross."

Texas Traits

Respond to the reading. Answer the following questions.

Focus and Coherence (1) What is the primary focus of this essay? (2) How does the conclusion tie the essay together? **Organization** (3) How does the thesis statement help structure this cause-effect essay? **Development of Ideas** (4) Are the conclusions logical, based on the evidence and research presented? **Voice** (5) How would you rate the writer's level of interest in the topic?

Prewriting

During the initial step in the writing process, you will plan your first draft by selecting a specific topic, gathering details, developing a thesis or controlling idea, and creating a basic structure for your writing.

Keys to Effective Prewriting

1. Choose a specific historical event to write about.
2. Refer to a variety of sources and gather information about your topic. Consider relevant quotations, explanations, and facts.
3. Write a thesis statement that identifies a specific cause-effect relationship related to the topic.
4. Identify the key points that support the thesis statement.
5. Keep in mind your essay's purpose, audience, and context.
6. Organize your details using an outline or another graphic organizer.

Prewriting Planning Your Writing

Mark Santos started his topic search by thinking about periods of history that he enjoyed reading about and that he thought would be of interest to his audience. After choosing the Middle Ages, he listed a few general categories, or subjects, related to this time. He starred the two categories in this list that interested him the most.

General Categories List

Middle Ages

natural disasters	invasions	discoveries
economy	religion	famous individuals
* government	the Crusades	* medicine

Prewrite

Start your topic search. Think of a period in history that you enjoy learning about. Then create a general categories list to identify various subject areas. (If necessary, use some of the categories listed above.) Place an asterisk next to the categories that interest you the most.

Next, Mark created a chart in which he listed possible cause-and-effect topics for each category that he starred. After reviewing his chart, Mark decided to write about the Black Plague in Europe.

Topics Chart

Middle Ages

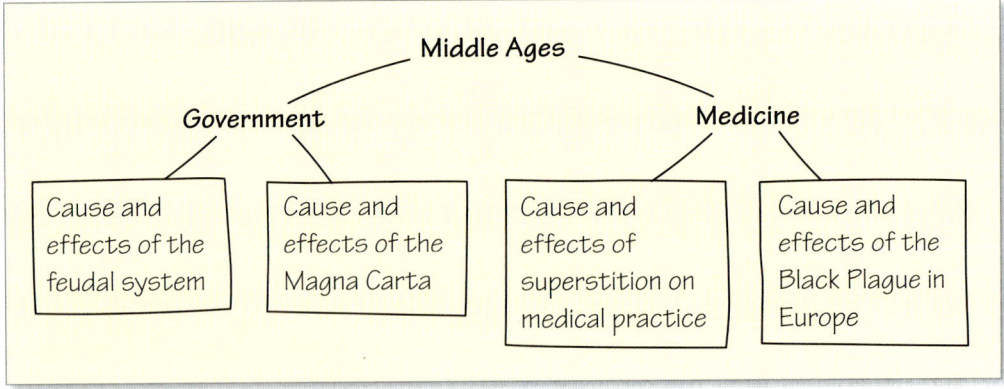

- **Government**
  - Cause and effects of the feudal system
  - Cause and effects of the Magna Carta
- **Medicine**
  - Cause and effects of superstition on medical practice
  - Cause and effects of the Black Plague in Europe

Prewrite

Choose your topic. In a topics chart, list potential cause-and-effect topics related to the categories that you starred in your general categories list. Then circle the specific topic that you would like to write about.

Gathering Your First Thoughts

To gather his initial thoughts about the Black Plague, Mark did the following freewriting. He recorded what he knew about the topic and asked some interesting questions.

Freewriting

The Black Plague pretty much devastated Europe during the 1300s. I read that about a third of the population died. Anyone infected died a horrible, painful death, usually within three days. I know it was spread by fleas on ship rats. That means port cities were probably hardest hit. What about the countryside? Did the farmers get the plague? That must have affected how much food there was. What about the clergy? What happened to religion and education back then? What about the culture of the time? What kinds of treatments were available? Did any of them work, or did the doctors die? Is it still possible to catch the plague today? I think there is an inoculation and a cure.

Prewrite **Freewrite on your topic.** To get started, write down everything you already know about your topic. Write for 5 to 10 minutes.

Listing Your Sources

As you gather your information, keep track of the sources you use so that you can correctly cite them in your essay. You will need the following information.

- **Book:** Author's name. Title. City: Publisher, Copyright date.
- **Magazine:** Author's name. Article title. Magazine title. Date published: Page numbers.
- **Newspaper:** Author's name. Article title. Newspaper title. Date published: Section and page numbers.
- **Internet:** Author's name (if listed). Page title or description of document. Site title. Date posted or copyright date (if listed). Site sponsor. Date of access. Complete URL.
- **DVD or video file:** Title. Format. Distributor or Web site, date.

Prewrite **List your sources.** Keep a list of your sources and include the information shown above. Whenever you find a new source, add it to your list.

TEKS 10.13A, 10.15A(iii)

Prewriting Collecting and Organizing the Details

A gathering grid (see page 383) is an effective way to collect and organize details for an essay. However, sometimes you need more space to record a quotation, to paraphrase important information, or to list important details. In these cases, you should use note cards.

Number each new card and identify the question or main point that the card covers. Then write your notes. If you used a source, identify it at the bottom of the note card.

Sample Note Cards

Details

(1)
How was the disease carried?
- carried by rats and fleas
- infected with lethal bacterium, Pasteurella pestis
- dead rats lined the streets
- fleas on workers' clothing

Quotation

(2)
Did the disease infect just part of the population?
"The disease remained and soon death was everywhere. . . . Friars and nuns were left to care for the sick, and monasteries and convents were soon deserted, as they were stricken, too."
Stevenson, p. 34

Paraphrase

(3)
How did the disease affect the economy?
New construction diminished in the fourteenth century. Most of the great cathedrals begun in the twelfth and thirteenth centuries were left unfinished.
Matthews, p. 129

Prewrite

Collect and organize your information. Use a gathering grid and note cards to collect information for your essay.

Focusing on Causes and Effects

Once you complete your research, find the cause-and-effect relationship in your topic. A cause-effect organizer can help you complete this step. The essays in this chapter put forth one main cause (stated in the thesis) and follow with its effects. However, this is not the only way to develop a cause-effect essay. You can also start with one main effect and follow with its causes.

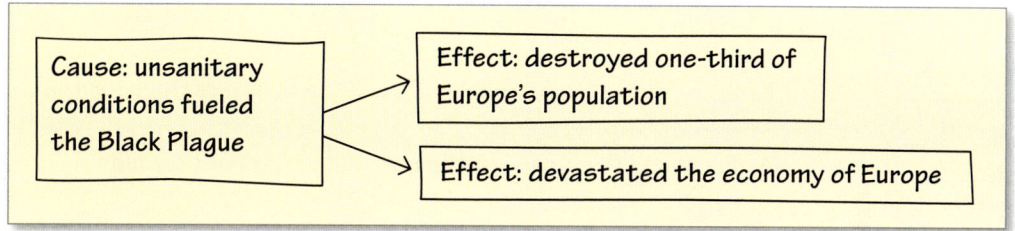

Cause-Effect Organizer

Cause: unsanitary conditions fueled the Black Plague
→ Effect: destroyed one-third of Europe's population
→ Effect: devastated the economy of Europe

Prewrite

Focus your efforts. Use the graphic organizer above (or on page 624) to identify the cause-effect relationship related to your historical event.

Expository

Writing a Thesis Statement

The thesis statement of your essay should establish the focus or direction of your writing. Mark's thesis statement covers the main points included in his cause-effect organizer.

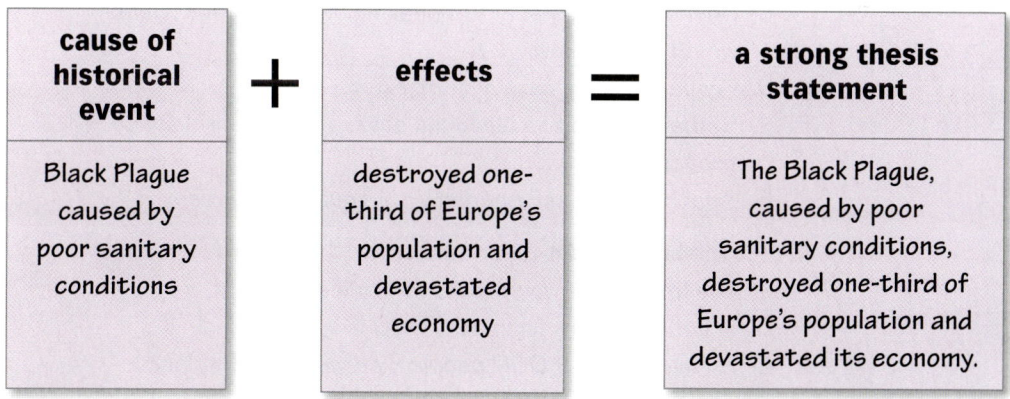

cause of historical event	+	effects	=	a strong thesis statement
Black Plague caused by poor sanitary conditions		destroyed one-third of Europe's population and devastated economy		The Black Plague, caused by poor sanitary conditions, destroyed one-third of Europe's population and devastated its economy.

Prewrite

Write your thesis statement. Use the model above to create a thesis statement for your essay. Try different versions until you are satisfied.

TEKS 10.13A, 10.13B, 10.15A(iii)

Prewriting Outlining Your Essay

Before you write your first draft, you should outline the main information you will use to develop your thesis. (Not all of the specific details need to be included in your outline.) Below is the first page of Mark's sentence outline. (See pages **626–627** for more about outlining.)

Thesis Statement: The Black Plague, caused by poor sanitary conditions, destroyed one-third of Europe's population and devastated its economy.

Background information about cause listed first.

I. Poor sanitation fostered conditions that were perfect for the spread of the disease.
   A. Rats and fleas carried the microbe called *Pasteurella pestis*.
   B. Dead rats lined the streets where children played.
   C. The fleas from rats got on the clothing of workers.
   D. Touching the dead bodies of plague victims was common.
   E. The disease infected multiple family members.

The first effect is explored.

II. Once the outbreak took hold, the disease spread uncontrollably.
   A. The first symptoms of the plague were similar to those of a common cold.
   B. Then more-extreme symptoms would set in.
   C. Once individuals started shaking uncontrollably, death would soon follow.
   D. Proper medical care did not exist.
   E. Some resorted to bleeding; others used astrology to prescribe "cures."
   F. Apothecaries and peddlers sold quack remedies.

III. The disease did not discriminate.
   A. The loss of life was greatest in big cities.
   B. In London, more than 100,000 lives were lost.
   C. An average of 1,000 people died weekly in England.

Prewrite

Prepare a sentence outline. Begin with your thesis statement. Then include the main points (I., II., III.) and supporting details (A., B., C.). You do not need to include every detail in your outline.

Drafting

Go Online!

Now that you have completed your prewriting, you are ready to compose your first draft. As you write, refer to your outline and your research notes.

Keys to Effective Drafting

1. Get all of your ideas down on paper in your first draft.
2. In the first paragraph, state your thesis, identifying a significant cause and its major effects. The middle paragraphs should clarify the cause and discuss the key effects.
3. Include well-reasoned, relevant supporting details in each paragraph.
4. Use smooth transitions to connect your ideas.
5. Write on every other line or double-space to leave room for notes and changes.

TEKS 10.13A, 10.15A(i), 10.15A(iii)–10.15A(v)

Drafting Getting the Big Picture

The graphic that follows shows how the parts of your essay should fit together. (The examples come from the student essay on pages 151–154.)

Beginning

The **introductory paragraph** provides both the topic and the thesis.

Thesis Statement
The Black Plague, caused by poor sanitary conditions, destroyed one-third of Europe's population and devastated its economy.

Middle

The organization and structure of the **middle** paragraphs is appropriate for purpose, audience, and context. Ideas sustain the thesis. Relevant evidence and details provide information and support the thesis.

Topic Sentences
Poor sanitation fostered conditions that were perfect for the spread of the disease. **(Background about cause)**

Once the outbreak took hold, the disease spread uncontrollably, killing millions. **(Effect)**

The disease did not discriminate. **(Effect)**

The plague had a devastating impact on the European economy. **(Effect)**

Ending

The **conclusion** ties all the information together. The essay ends with a memorable final sentence.

Closing Sentences
Today, medicines are available to combat most infectious diseases. Still, the specter of diseases like the Black Plague continues to motivate researchers striving to avert other plagues.

"Write freely and as rapidly as possible and throw the whole thing on paper."

—John Steinbeck

Starting Your Essay

Beginning
Middle
Ending

The introductory paragraph of your essay should effectively capture the reader's interest, introduce your topic, and state your thesis. Here are some ways to start your essay.

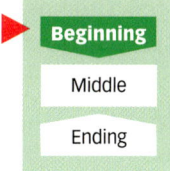

- **Set up a scenario.**
  Imagine a disease that killed millions of people who had no way to defend themselves.
- **Ask a question.**
  What was it really like during the Black Plague?
- **Use rhetorical devices, such as a quotation.**
  "Black Plague brought death and devastation," wrote Boccaccio, "and nary a whimper could be heard."
- **Present unusual or surprising information.**
  During the Middle Ages, the Black Plague descended, and, after only five years, one-third of Europe's people had died.

Beginning Paragraph

Mark starts his beginning paragraph with a *scenario*. He uses a transition phrase and follows the first sentence with information that leads to his thesis statement. It is the final sentence of the paragraph.

The writer captures the reader's interest and leads up to the thesis statement (underlined).

Imagine a disease that killed millions of people who had no way to defend themselves. At its height, from 1348 to 1351, the bubonic plague, better known as the "Black Plague" because of the black spots it caused on the skin, brought Europe to its knees. In The Decameron, Giovanni Boccaccio observed, "Almost everyone expected death. . . . And people said, 'This is the end of the world.'" The Black Plague, caused by poor sanitation, destroyed one-third of Europe's population and devastated its economy.

Draft

Write your introduction. Try one of the suggestions above to capture your reader's attention. Then add information that leads to your thesis statement.

TEKS 10.13B, 10.15A(i), 10.15A(ii)

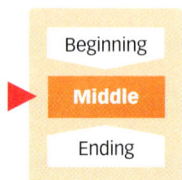

Drafting Developing the Middle Paragraphs

Beginning
Middle
Ending

Refer to your outline and select an organizational pattern that fits the topic and the audience. Expand on key ideas with specific details and evidence. Be sure to include transitions.

Middle Paragraphs

Rhetorical devices engage the reader. Carefully chosen details and relevant evidence make the cause clear and support the thesis.

Transitions link sentences and paragraphs.

The first effect is discussed. Logical inferences are made. A variety of sentence structures sustain interest.

How could one disease travel so quickly? Poor sanitation fostered conditions that were perfect. Rats and fleas carried the microbe called Pasteurella pestis, the lethal bacterium that spread the disease. Dead, infected rats lined the streets like people lining up to watch a parade, and the rats lay within inches of places where little children played. The fleas got on the clothing of workers who then brought the plague into their homes. The fleas spread easily, infecting people through their bites. Since few people understood the nature of diseases, touching the dead bodies of plague victims was a common practice; unfortunately, it was not common practice to wash one's hands afterward. After one family member became infected, it wasn't long before other family members would become sick, too. Cleanup crews often found houses containing several dead—a husband and wife, two or three brothers, a father and a son, and the like (Matthews 87).

Once the outbreak took hold, the disease spread uncontrollably, killing millions. The first symptoms of the plague were similar to those of a common cold, and most people ignored the chills, fever, and coughs. Tragically, this was the period when the disease was most contagious. Then more-extreme symptoms would set in. Victims' bodies would become mottled with blackish spots and swelling boils. Once individuals started shaking uncontrollably, death would soon follow. No one had ever encountered an epidemic as destructive as the Black Plague; as a result, proper medical care did not exist. The most common treatment was bleeding, and many doctors used astrology to prescribe "cures" based on the position of the planets (Matthews 102). Pope Clement VI sat between two fires, which probably saved him, as heat could kill the germs (Cline 67), but this was not understood at the time. Apothecaries and peddlers sold quack remedies, and desperation created a market for anything that offered hope. However, nothing worked, and the death rate soared.

A quotation is included.

As people continued to die, it became clear that the disease did not discriminate. An unknown author stated, "The disease remained and soon death was everywhere. . . . Friars and nuns were left to care for the sick, and monasteries and convents were soon deserted, as they were stricken, too" (Stevenson 34). The loss of life was greatest in the big cities where overcrowding allowed the disease to spread more quickly. John Baker explains that in London alone, more than 100,000 lives were lost. Of 28 monks in Westminster Abbey, 27 died of the plague. An average of 1,000 people died weekly in England, and survivors buried bodies by the hundreds in mass graves (215–216).

The second effect is explored. The writer continues to use transitions and rhetorical devices. Paragraphs are logically organized.

With so many deaths, what was the effect on Europe's economy? By 1363, the plague had affected nearly all business and commerce in Europe. Building came to a halt as workers died or fled. New construction diminished in the fourteenth century, and most of the great cathedrals begun in the twelfth and thirteenth centuries were left unfinished (Matthews 129). Without a source of labor, business people tried to import workers from other countries by offering them financial incentives. The remaining healthy workers, however, were too fearful to accept the offers. With fewer workers available, wages became inflated and most business owners could no longer afford to keep their workers. The cost of goods rose, too. Farmers died because of the plague, decreasing the amount of food available. In turn, food prices skyrocketed. It was not until the late Renaissance, a period of intellectual and artistic revival ending in the 1600s, that most countries began to recover some of the population and economic ground that was lost due to the plague.

Relevant details and solid evidence are offered to explain the effect.

Draft

Write your middle paragraphs. Follow your outline and use transitions to connect your thoughts and paragraphs. Ideas should flow in a logical order and relate to one another. Evidence should support your thesis.

TEKS 10.13B, 10.15A(i)

Drafting Ending Your Essay

Beginning
Middle
Ending

Your conclusion should contain important last thoughts for the reader. Here are some ways to create a strong ending.

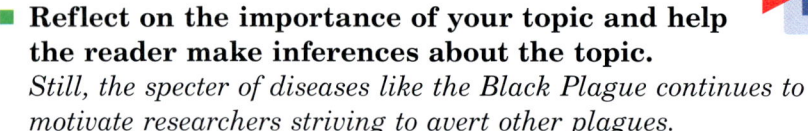

- **Reflect on the importance of your topic and help the reader make inferences about the topic.**
  Still, the specter of diseases like the Black Plague continues to motivate researchers striving to avert other plagues.
- **Include additional information of interest.**
  Tragically, people had little knowledge of how germs, or "wee-beasties," as they were called at the time, were transferred between humans. That critical information would come later.
- **Provide an effective quotation.**
  "How many valiant men, how many fair ladies, breakfasted with their kinfolk and the same night supped with their ancestors."

Ending Paragraph

The writer refers to the thesis and includes additional information of interest. The reader can make valid inferences about the plague.

Unsanitary conditions made the Black Plague one of the worst natural disasters ever to affect Europe. The effects were felt in cities and rural areas alike. Families in both areas were torn apart. The loss of a third of the population had a devastating impact on the European economy, and it took many years to recover. The plague eventually ceased, after having lingered on for almost 300 years. No doubt improved sanitation and an emphasis on personal hygiene helped, but no one knows for sure why the plague ended. Today, medicines are available to combat most infectious diseases. Still, the specter of diseases like the Black Plague continues to motivate researchers striving to avert other plagues.

Draft

Write your conclusion. Write the conclusion, the final paragraph of your essay, using one or more of the strategies above.

"The writing itself has been as important to me as the product. I have always been somewhat indifferent as to whether I have been working on a solemn novel or an impertinent paragraph."
—Sinclair Lewis

Revising

Go Online!

When you revise, you improve your writing. You add relevant details, delete unnecessary ideas, rewrite unclear parts, and reorder passages as needed.

Keys to Effective Revising

1. If possible, set your first draft aside for a day or two before you do any revising.
2. As you look over your draft, always keep your purpose, your audience, and the genre, or form, of your writing in mind.
3. Check your opening paragraph, your introduction. Have you effectively introduced your topic and clearly stated your thesis?
4. Review your middle paragraphs to be sure that they explore the causes and effects related to the topic.
5. Check your ending paragraph, your conclusion. Have you effectively connected with your thesis and provided a memorable final idea?
6. Be sure that you have developed and maintained a knowledgeable, interested voice.

Texas Traits Revising for Focus and Coherence

When you revise for *focus and coherence,* check your thesis statement to see if it shows a clear cause-effect relationship. The controlling idea of your essay must be clearly stated. Also be sure that all your ideas are logically presented. They should clearly connect to each other and support your thesis statement. The effects included in your essay should carry equal weight, meaning that they are of equal importance. In addition, be sure that each paragraph contains relevant evidence and enough supporting detail. Your conclusion should tie the essay together and bring the reader back to the thesis statement.

Does my thesis statement provide the proper focus?

Your thesis statement provides the proper focus if it clearly establishes a cause-effect relationship. In the sample essays in this chapter, the thesis identifies one main cause plus two or three resulting effects. (Each effect carries equal weight.)

Charlemagne's unification of Europe *(cause)* **brought peace to all the people** *(effect)*, **stabilized the European economy** *(effect)*, **and promoted education** *(effect)*.

The Black Plague, caused by poor sanitary conditions *(cause)*, **destroyed one-third of Europe's population** *(effect)* **and devastated its economy** *(effect)*.

Revise

Review your thesis statement. Answer these questions to check the effectiveness of your thesis statement. Revise your thesis as needed.

1. Does the first part of my thesis statement identify the historical event? If so, what is it?
2. Does the second part of my thesis statement identify the main effects? If so, what are they?
3. Do the ideas in the middle paragraphs all relate to and support my thesis statement?
4. Do the details and supporting evidence in the paragraphs relate to and support my thesis statement?
5. Could I state my controlling idea more effectively? Write another version to find out.

Do my body paragraphs maintain the focus set by my thesis statement?

The body of your essay, the middle paragraphs, should show knowledge of and interest in the topic. These paragraphs should work together to show and support the cause-effect relationship you established in your introduction. Your essay should contain sufficient information and be of sufficient length to support your thesis. The effects should be clearly explained and presented logically so that your reader can follow your ideas. The chain of ideas should lead the reader to the conclusion.

Exercise

Read this thesis statement: The community service requirement for graduation benefits both the student and the community.

Then rewrite the following paragraph topic sentences so that each one shows a direct and logical link to the thesis statement.

1. This is a new requirement.
2. Walking dogs at an animal shelter takes a lot of time.
3. People find homeless animals every day.
4. I used a lot more math than I expected at the animal shelter.

Revise **Check your paragraph topic sentences.** Do they clearly convey the point of each paragraph and maintain the focus of the thesis statement?

Focus and Coherence Topic sentences relate directly to the thesis statement.

Once the diesase took hold, the disease sprad uncontrollably, killing millions.
~~It seemed like a lot of people got sick.~~ The first symptoms of the plague were similar to those of a common cold, and most people ignored the chills, fever, and coughs.

The plague had a devastating effect on the European economy.
Many workers died and this affected business. No one expected this to happen. By 1363, the plague had affected nearly all business and commerce in Europe.

Expository

Texas Traits

Revising for Organization

To revise for *organization,* you should first re-read your essay to make sure that the cause-effect pattern that you have chosen is appropriate for the purpose, the audience, and the context of your essay. The reader should be able to see a clear connection from one idea to the next, from the cause to the effects. Check to see that the introduction, middle parts, and conclusion work well together. Also make sure that you have used transition words and phrases to connect the paragraphs in your essay.

Does my ending paragraph, my conclusion, work well?

Your conclusion works well if it helps the reader understand the importance or value of the information presented in the main part of your essay. An effective ending may often do these three things:

- remind the reader of your thesis,
- summarize the important points that you covered, and
- leave the reader with a final thought about the topic.

The thesis is restated.

Main points are highlighted.

The closing adds a final thought.

Unsanitary conditions made the Black Plague one of the worst natural disasters ever to affect Europe. The effects were felt in cities and rural areas alike. Families in both areas were torn apart. The loss of a third of the population had a devastating impact on the European economy, and it took many years to recover. The plague eventually ceased, after having lingered on for almost 300 years. No doubt improved sanitation and an emphasis on personal hygiene helped, but no one knows for sure why the plague ended. Today, medicines are available to combat most infectious diseases. Still, the specter of diseases like the Black Plague continues to motivate researchers striving to avert other plagues.

Revise

Evaluate your ending. As you review your final paragraph, label the different parts, using the information above as a guide. Did you restate your thesis, summarize the main points, and leave the reader with a final thought? Revise as needed.

Are the paragraphs of my essay clearly connected?

When the paragraphs of an essay are organized so that they connect and relate to the thesis statement, the writer has created a strong, logical organizational pattern that has both focus and coherence. When you selected the organizational pattern for your essay, you may have also decided on logical ways to link the paragraphs. The paragraphs of your essay will be clearly connected and lead the reader from one idea to the next if you have effectively used either or both of these linking strategies:

- Choose a key word or phrase from one paragraph and repeat it in the next.
- Start a new paragraph with a transition word or phrase such as *in addition, more importantly,* and so on.

In the sample below, a key word (shown in red) from one paragraph is repeated in the next.

. . . When peasant and nobleman alike realized that they were being treated fairly, a feeling of trust and peace spread throughout Europe.

In order to maintain peace, Charlemagne soon realized that he needed to stabilize the economy in the entire region.

Revise **Check the coherence and organization of your essay.** Review your writing to make sure that you have effectively linked your paragraphs. Make changes as needed. Make sure that your conclusion ties the essay together.

Organization
A key phrase is repeated to connect the paragraphs.

. . . The Black Plague, caused by poor sanitation, destroyed one-third of Europe's population and devastated its economy.

Poor sanitation ~~The way of life~~ fostered conditions that were perfect for the spread of the disease. Rats and fleas carried the microbe called Pasteurella pestis, the lethal bacterium . . .

TEKS 10.13C, 10.15A(iv), 10.15A(v)
ELPS 5G

Texas Traits

Revising for Development of Ideas

When you revise for *development of ideas,* be sure that all your ideas are clearly stated and that enough information is provided to support your thesis. Each paragraph should have a topic sentence that shows an aspect of the cause-effect relationship, and the paragraphs should expand upon your controlling idea. The evidence and supporting details in each paragraph should relate to and support the paragraph's topic sentence. Be sure that inferences you have drawn from your own research are logical. Check to make sure that the reader is also led to make valid inferences from the information in your essay. Check again to make sure that you have chosen the correct genre for the writing.

Does my essay illustrate a clear cause-effect relationship?

Your thesis statement provided the focus for your essay. The body of your essay must make the cause-effect relationship clear. To do this, you will need to provide sufficient evidence and relevant details about each effect.

Exercise

Consider the controlling idea that Charlemagne's unification of Europe brought peace, stabilized the economy, and promoted education. Read the following statements; then label each one relevant or not relevant to the thesis statement. Explain your answers.

1. Charlemagne greatly expanded the territory under his rule by both war and political maneuvering.
2. Charlemagne brought scholars from all over Europe to France.
3. France is now a republic.
4. Charlemagne provided funds to regions that truly needed more resources.
5. Charlemagne was known both as a warrior and as a peacemaker.
6. France is now part of the European Union, which has had a major impact on its economy.

Revise

Revise for Development of Ideas. **Carefully review your essay to make sure that each idea is well developed. Be sure that you have provided sufficient evidence to support the controlling idea. Verify that any inferences you have made from the evidence you gathered for your essay are valid. If not, be sure to correct them, and revise your essay as needed.**

Have I included enough detail?

When you look at the details you have included in your essay, remember the genre you have chosen, a factual cause-effect essay. You have already chosen an organizational pattern that is appropriate for the purpose, audience, and context. Be sure that your essay is long enough to adequately cover the topic. It is important to keep those basics in mind as you begin to examine the details you have chosen to include. You have included enough detail if the body sentences in each paragraph clearly and completely support the topic sentence. A well-written paragraph often contains three levels of detail.

Level 1: Topic sentence: In order to maintain peace, Charlemagne soon realized that he needed to stabilize the economy in the entire region.

Level 2: Clarifying sentence: He divided larger parcels of land into more manageable estates that were self-contained and . . .

Level 3: Completing sentence *(an explanation, a quotation, or a paraphrase)*: Each estate had a bustling center of commerce surrounded by a market, church, guilds, and public buildings.

Note: Most paragraphs include at least two clarifying sentences, each one usually followed by one or two completing sentences.

Revise

Check for levels of detail. As you read through your essay, try putting a *1* next to each topic sentence, a *2* next to each clarifying sentence, and a *3* next to each completing sentence. Then decide if you have included enough detail.

Development of Ideas
A completing detail is added.

. . . The first symptoms of the plague were similar to those of a common cold, and most people ignored the chills, fever, and coughs. Tragically, this was the period when the disease was most contagious. Then more-extreme symptoms would set in. Victims' bodies would become mottled with blackish spots . . .

Texas Traits

Revising for Voice

When you revise for *voice,* be sure that you use the proper informational voice and that you sound knowledgeable and confident. Try to maintain this same knowledgeable, engaging voice throughout your essay. Your writing should engage the reader, and your writing should express your own perspective or viewpoint. Look carefully at the writing style you have used.

Have I used the proper voice in my essay?

If you've "kept your distance," then you've probably used the proper voice. The purpose of a cause-effect essay is to inform the reader, not to get too close and personal with the reader. You'll be right on track if your essay engages the reader with plenty of interesting and relevant facts and draws valid inferences from the evidence you have presented.

Too close and personal: **I've learned about the early battles during the Civil War. Now I know about the Battle of Gettysburg, especially when Pickett's men made their final charge. It was unbelievable.**

Proper distance: **The Union troops on Cemetery Ridge destroyed the ranks of Pickett's men, which meant not only the end of the battle, but also the eventual collapse of the Confederate army.**

Exercise

Read the following statements; then label each one TCP (too close and personal) or PD (proper distance).

1. If you'd been a passenger on that voyage across the Atlantic, you'd have been blown away by the ship's incredible speed.
2. On April 14, 1912, the largest ship ever built, the *Titanic,* collided with an iceberg just before midnight.
3. If I had been scrambling around the deck of the *Titanic,* I would have been scared to death.
4. Tragically, over 1,500 people lost their lives when the ship sank.
5. Can you believe that the *Titanic* only had enough lifeboats for about half the people on board the ship?

Revise

Revise for voice. **Carefully review your essay for voice, making sure that you have engaged the reader and kept the proper distance. Check for word choice and proper use of rhetorical devices. Revise as needed.**

Does my voice sound confident in my essay?

The style of your essay and the voice you choose should be appropriate for the purpose, the audience, and the context. Well-placed and carefully thought-out rhetorical devices, such as quotations, show your research and knowledge; they also help engage the reader. You'll sound confident in your cause-effect essay if you have a clear and thorough understanding of your topic. Simply put, there is a direct link between your knowledge of a topic and the level of confidence in your voice. In the following samples, it's clear which writer is confident and which is not.

Not confident: **When the *Hindenburg* crashed in 1937, many people died. The great airship caught fire, which probably caused the explosion.**

Confident: **When the German zeppelin *Hindenburg* caught fire and crashed on May 6, 1937, 36 people lost their lives. Some people thought the crash occurred on the zeppelin's maiden voyage, but the *Hindenburg* had already made 17 round-trip excursions across the ocean, including 10 trips to the United States and 7 to Brazil.**

Revise

Check for the confidence in your voice. **Carefully review your essay, looking for parts where you don't speak with the proper level of authority. Research and revise as needed.**

Voice
An idea is changed because it is "too close and personal."

Imagine a disease that killed millions of people who had no way to defend themselves.
~~I've had pneumonia and bronchitis, but I've never had to deal with an incurable disease like the bubonic plague.~~ At its height, from 1348 to 1351, the bubonic plague, better known as the "Black Plague" because of the black spots it caused on the skin, brought Europe to its knees. In The Decameron, Giovanni Boccaccio observed, "Almost everyone expected . . ."

Revising Improving Your Writing

Revise your essay. On a piece of paper, write the numbers 1 to 10. If you can answer "yes" to a question, put a check mark after that number. If not, continue to revise that part of your essay.

Revising Checklist

Focus and Coherence

_____ **1.** My thesis statement establishes a clear, strong cause-effect relationship.

_____ **2.** The body paragraphs effectively support my thesis.

_____ **3.** My conclusion reminds the reader of the thesis statement and ties my essay together.

Organization

_____ **4.** I have closely followed my outline.

_____ **5.** I have a distinct introduction, middle parts, and an effective conclusion.

_____ **6.** I use strong transitions to connect ideas and paragraphs.

Development of Ideas

_____ **7.** My ideas are relevant to the thesis, well developed, and sustain the cause-effect relationship.

_____ **8.** Researched evidence and sufficient details show the importance of each effect in the essay.

Voice

_____ **9.** My voice sounds knowledgeable and is appropriate for the purpose, audience, and context of the essay.

_____ **10.** My voice sounds confident.

Make a clean copy. When you've finished revising, make a clean copy of your essay for editing.

Editing

Once you have completed your revisions, you are ready to edit your essay for grammar, sentence structure, capitalization, punctuation, and spelling. These aspects of written English are called *conventions*.

Keys to Effective Editing

1. Edit your essay using a dictionary, a thesaurus, and the "Proofreader's Guide." (See pages 642–787.)
2. Check your writing for grammar, sentence structure, capitalization, punctuation, and spelling errors.
3. Also have a trusted classmate or your teacher check your writing for errors. (Writers usually work with an editor.)
4. If you're using a computer, edit on a printout of your essay. Then enter your changes on the computer.
5. Use the proofreading marks located inside the back cover of this book.

TEKS 10.13D, 10.17A(i)
ELPS 2I, 3C, 3E, 4C, 5D, 5E

Texas Traits

Editing for Conventions

Grammar

When you edit for *grammar,* you make sure that you have used all parts of speech, including verbs and verb tenses, correctly. For example, your cause-effect essay will show relationships related to a particular historical event. Because it is a historical event, most of the verbs you use will be in a past tense. As you write, aim for the active voice, not the passive. Remember that in the active voice, the subject commits the action. The sentence *John hit the ball* is written with an active voice. The sentence *The ball was hit by John* is written in the passive voice. The subject (in this case *the ball*) receives the action.

How do I know when to use more complex verb tenses?

You are already familiar with simple present, past, and future tenses. When you write your cause-effect essay, you will be using more complex verb tenses. To express an action that occurred in the past, there are several complex verb tenses you can use, including past perfect and past progressive.

- To express an action in the past that occurred before another past action, use the past perfect tense.

  After I had completed my homework, I met some of my friends at the mall. My parents had given me a gift certificate.

- To express an action that was happening at a certain time in the past and continued in the past, use the past progressive tense. This is also called the past continuous tense.

  The car engine was making very odd noises. We were traveling on the train.

Grammar Exercise

Rewrite the following sentences, changing the simple past to past progressive tense.

1. Rats and fleas spread the plague.
2. Children played near dead rats.
3. Peddlers sold quack remedies.

Edit

Check verb tenses. Review your essay to be sure you have correctly used past perfect and past progressive verb tenses. Edit for tense and consistency.

When is it appropriate to use the passive voice?

When writing about actual events, try always to use the active voice. In some cases, however, you will need to use the passive voice. For example, in the sentence *Artists, scientists, and teachers were sent from monasteries to other regions to share their knowledge,* we do not know who sent these people. Therefore, the writer correctly used passive voice. We do know that *Charlemagne divided large parcels of lands into more manageable estates,* so that sentence is written in active voice. Just as there are complex active voices, there are also complex passive voices.

- The past perfect in the passive voice is similar to the past perfect in the active voice. It is used to express an action in the past that occurred before another past action.

  Teachers had been sent to outlying regions to teach.

- The past progressive tense in the passive voice is also similar to the past progressive in the active voice. It expresses an action that was happening at a certain time in the past and continued in the past.

  At the same time that teachers were being sent to outlying regions, scientists were being sent away from monasteries to share their knowledge as well.

Grammar Exercise

Rewrite the following sentences, changing the verbs from passive to active voice.

1. Charlemagne was crowned emperor by the Pope.
2. Much of Europe was ruled by Charlemagne.

Edit

Check verb voice. **Review your essay for active and passive voice. When possible, change your verbs to active voice, and make sure you have used active and passive voices and complex tenses correctly.**

Learning Language

Tell a classmate what you did yesterday, what you are doing today, and what you plan to do tomorrow. Use active voice. Have your classmate repeat each sentence, changing the verb from active to passive voice.

Sentence Structure

To edit for *sentence structure*, be sure to avoid series of short, choppy sentences. Your sentences should have a variety of starters, including phrases and clauses.

Do I need to combine or expand any of my sentences?

You may need to combine or expand series of short sentences that sound short and choppy. One way to combine sentences is to use restrictive and nonrestrictive clauses. A restrictive relative clause is essential to the meaning of the sentence. It adds to and limits the meaning of the independent clause. Without the restrictive clause the reader would not understand what the sentence is about. A nonrestrictive clause is not essential to the meaning of the sentence as a whole. In other words, it could be deleted, and the meaning of the sentence would not change.

These clauses are often joined to the independent clause with the relative pronouns *who, whom, whose, that* and *which*. The relative pronoun *which* is used in nonrestrictive clauses.

Restrictive Clauses: The man who is reading the newspaper is my uncle. The book that I read last night was fascinating.

The words ***who is reading the newspaper*** and ***that I read last night*** are essential to the meaning of the sentences because they identify the subject.

Nonrestrictive Clauses: Tennis, which is a popular sport, is not difficult to learn. This novel, which is a best-seller, is about a daughter and her mother.

The words ***which is a popular sport*** and ***which is a best-seller*** are not essential to the meaning of the sentences.

Exercise

Combine the following sentences using a common relative pronoun.

1. I want to attend our local university. It has outstanding teachers.
2. My goal is to become a systems analyst. It is a profitable career.
3. I want to buy a new book. I want a book about Austin, Texas.
4. My uncle is an engineer. You met him last night.

Edit

Check for short, choppy sentences. Review your first draft for series of short, choppy sentences. Rewrite these sentences as needed, adding restrictive and nonrestrictive clauses.

TEKS 10.13D, 10.15A(i), 10.17A(ii), 10.18B(i)
ELPS 5E, 5F

Mechanics: Punctuation

To edit for *mechanics*, you check for correct use of capitalization and punctuation. Be sure to check both end punctuation and punctuation within a sentence. As you know, commas have multiple uses within sentences.

- Commas are used to separate items in a series.
  I bought lettuce, tomatoes, cucumbers, and bell peppers.
- Commas set off participial phrases. For example:
  Panting heavily, the dog flopped onto the cool tile floor.
- Commas are used to separate independent clauses in a sentence.
  I bought a sweater, and my sister bought a jacket. I wanted to go to the movies, but my friends wanted to go bowling.

How do I punctuate restrictive and nonrestrictive phrases and clauses?

- Because nonrestrictive clauses are not essential to the meaning of a sentence, they are set off with commas.
  Pope Clement VI sat between two fires, which probably saved him, as heat could kill the germs. The Black Plague, which was deadly to humans, also killed many farm animals.
- Restrictive clauses are essential to the meaning of a sentence, and they are not separated by commas.
  This method works for people who want to improve their listening skills. Adults who cannot drive often have trouble finding jobs. She accepted all of the suggestions that were practical.

Edit

Check for comma use. **Review your essay to be sure that you have used commas correctly to set off nonrestrictive clauses.**

Grammar Exercise

Decide which of the following sentences have restrictive or nonrestrictive clauses. Add commas as appropriate.

1. The person whom I wanted most to meet could not come to the meeting.
2. My backpack which I left at my friend's house had all my schoolwork inside.
3. The house which was once blue needs painting.
4. The boy who sat next to me did not say a word.

Expository

TEKS 10.13D, 10.15A(i), 10.17A(i), 10.17C, 10.18A, 10.18B(i), 10.19
ELPS 5C–5F

Texas Traits

Editing Checking for Conventions

Edit

Check your editing. On a piece of paper, write the numbers 1 to 9. If you can answer "yes" to a question, put a check mark after that number. Continue editing until you can answer "yes" to all the questions.

Editing Checklist

Conventions

GRAMMAR

_____ **1.** Have I correctly used passive and active voice and more complex verb tenses?

_____ **2.** Have I used the right words *(there, their, they're)*?

SENTENCE STRUCTURE

_____ **3.** Do I correctly use restrictive and nonrestrictive relative clauses to combine sentences?

MECHANICS (Capitalization and Punctuation)

_____ **4.** Do I begin every sentence with a capital letter?

_____ **5.** Have I capitalized proper nouns and adjectives?

_____ **6.** Do I punctuate restrictive and nonrestrictive phrases, clauses, and contrasting expressions correctly?

_____ **7.** Have I correctly cited my sources? (See pages **396** and **407–410**.)

SPELLING

_____ **8.** Have I spelled all my words correctly?

_____ **9.** Have I consulted a dictionary to determine or check the spellings of words my spell-checker may have missed?

Creating a Title

When you write informational essays and reports, it's important to engage your reader with an attention-getting title. Here are some ideas:

- Establish the proper tone: **A Plague for the Ages**
- Catch the reader's attention: **The "Wee-Beasties" of Death**

Publishing

Go Online!

Sharing Your Essay

After editing your essay, make a neat final draft, proofread it, and share it. Ask your teacher or your classmates for feedback so that you can make a few final improvements (see pages 49–54). Then, consider publishing ideas such as posting it on a Web site, submitting your writing for publication, or turning your writing into a multimedia presentation. (See the suggestions below.)

Publish

Make a final copy. **Follow your teacher's instructions or use the guidelines below to format your essay. (If you are using a computer, see pages 72–74.) Create a clean final copy of your essay and carefully proofread it.**

Focusing on Presentation

- Use blue or black ink and write neatly.
- Write your name in the upper left corner of page 1.
- Skip a line and center your title; skip another line and start your writing.
- Indent every paragraph and leave a one-inch margin on all four sides.
- Write your last name and the page number in the upper right corner of every page after page 1.

Ideas for Publishing

Post Your Essay on a Web Site

Upload your paper to a school or personal Web site. Add graphic elements, sounds, and images that will appeal to your audience, show your point of view, and enhance your essay.

Submit Your Essay

Submit your essay to a school publication or create a class anthology.

Create a Multimedia Presentation

Use the information and same point of view in your essay to create a multimedia presentation. Include visual aids, graphics, images, and sounds that will appeal to your audience.

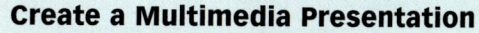

Evaluating a Cause-Effect Essay

To learn how to evaluate a cause-effect essay, you will use the scoring guide on pages 60–61 and the essays that follow. These essays are examples of writing for each score on the scoring guide (1–4).

Notice that the first essay received a score of 4. Read the description for a score of 4 on page 60. Then read the essay. Use the same steps to study the other examples. As you read, concentrate on the overall quality of the writing in each example.

Writing that fits a score of 4 is highly effective.

4

The **beginning** introduces the writer's focus. (underlined)

Thesis is clear and establishes cause-effect relationship.

Each **middle** paragraph presents details about the experience.

Nonrestrictive clauses add sentence variety. Quotations add interest and come from a reliable source.

A Famine That Crushed a Nation

Ever since 1600 when the potato was successfully introduced in Ireland, the Irish had depended upon it for food. In September 1845, an airborn fungus found in the holds of ships traveling from North America to England, created a blight that destroyed crops throughout Ireland. <u>From 1845 to 1850, the Irish potato famine ravaged the country, leading to over a million deaths from starvation and disease and forcing over two million people to emigrate to the United States and Canada.</u>

The five year blight had not only caused crop failure and low food supplies, but it had also driven prices beyond the reach of the poor and destroyed the source of income for small farmers. With the widespread starvation, diseases such as typhus, dysentery, and scurvy began to weaken and kill people of all ages. One man told the British House of Commons in 1847 "a quarter of [Ireland's] population will perish unless you come to her relief" (NBE). Yet many in England, which governed Ireland, did not fully understand the scope of the disaster or even care to help the Irish. Many, like Lord Trevelyan, the British Treasury Secretary, believed that Irish misery was caused by their own "inferior" way of life, and he considered the famine a "sharp but effectual remedy by which the cure is likely to be effected." (Donnelly 6)

Much of the responsibility for the poor was placed on the shoulders of the English landlords, who owned large estates in Ireland and rented small plots of land to tenant farmers. Some

Writer stays on topic as ideas are developed. Specific examples develop ideas and add interest. All ideas are relevant to the topic and evidence is well-documented.

landlords attempted to do their part, but often they did not care about their Irish renters, especially when rents had not been paid because of the blight. Many landlords did not want the expense of caring for tenants. Also, since their potato crops had been destroyed, they could make more money by using the land for sheep or cattle. Landlords had tenants arrested and their families thrown out of their homes. In 1850, over 104,000 people were evicted, and "one landlord, the Earl of Lucan, evicted 187 families (913 people) in 18 months." (NBE) Starving, homeless families roamed the countryside, often having only grass and weeds to eat.

Transitions connect paragraphs and ideas within paragraphs.

The potato blight continued and after a few years, the famine had ruined the economy. Ireland could not handle all of the unemployed poor. Left without choices, thousands began to emigrate to England, but most went to Canada or the United States. Landlords often paid for their tenants to emigrate just to get rid of them. Hundreds of families were crammed onto ships. Conditions on the ships were terrible and many of the people who made the voyage were weak and sick. The ships became known as "coffin ships" because so many passengers died on board. Things weren't much better when they arrived. The sick often died waiting to get into their new coutries, which didn't have the facilities to handle the thousands who arrived.

Each paragraph presents details about the experience.

The potato famine of 1845 to 1850, turned a delicate balance of government policies, economic conditions, and single-crop dependency into a terrible crisis. First, the crop loss and starvation created horrible suffering. Then, England's government failed to grasp the scope of the disaster or come up with policies to help the people. The famine increased Britain's power, which made it possible for self-serving landlords to evict their tenants and forced many people to leave Ireland under terrible conditions. Although the mass migration brought a new mix of people to North America, the huge loss of its population crippled Ireland. Many years passed before the country was able to recover from the damage done to its economy, the food supply, and its people.

Conclusion effectively summarizes the causes and effects of the famine.

Writing that fits a score of 3 is generally effective.

3

The **introduction** presents the controlling idea. Cause-effect relationship is stated.

Each **middle** paragraph continues to develop the thesis statement.

Specific examples add interest and support the thesis. Researched, relevant evidence supports thesis and shows writer's knowledge of topic.

Sugar and the Slave Trade

Today we don't think much about the sugar we put into coffee, but from the 17th to 19th centuries it was a prescious substance, bought with the blood and labor of many African slaves. Sugar and slaves are two sides of whats called the Triangle Trade. "Slaves of the Caribbean sugar plantations produced molasses that was transported to New England for distillation into rum that was shipped to Africa in exchange for the slaves who would endure the final leg of the triangle, the horrific Middle Passage to the sugar islands." (Westfield 69)

Sugar was grown and processed in the Caribbean in the 1500s by the Spanish. English and French colonies also started producing it by the 1600s. By 1700, thousands of slaves were being used to grow the sugar cane. It was very hard and difficult work, and it required a lot of slaves to plant it, harvest it, and grind it. Then the sugar cane had to be boiled to produce sugar. The leftover liquid from this process was molasses.

Molasses was used to produce rum. Merchants in New England bought the molasses cheaply to make rum, which cost very little to produce. "Tiny Rhode Island had more than 30 distilleries, 22 of them in Newport. In Massachusetts, 63 distilleries produced 2.7 million gallons of rum in 1774." (Hooper 72) They would then use the rum to buy slaves. "Slaves costing the equivalent of £4 or £5 in rum or bar iron in West Africa were sold in the West Indies in 1746 for £30 to £80." (Hooper 76) Slave traders from Newport alone had 150 slave ships and traded rum for over 106,000 slaves.

The slave trade was so profitable that it affected the whole economy of New England. "When the British in 1763 proposed a tax on sugar and molasses, Massachusetts merchants pointed out that these were staples of the slave trade, and the loss of that would throw 5,000 seamen out of work in the colony and idle almost 700 ships." (Hooper 94) Many of the important families of New England were involved in the slave trade. For example, the founders of Brown University owned slave ships and used slaves in

Occasional lapses in organization and non-developed ideas detract.

Each **middle** paragraph contains relevant supporting evidence. Errors in conventions may lead to confusion.

Conclusion effectively sums up the thesis and adds an additional effect, the Civil War.

their factories. Boat makers also became wealthy.

The demand for sugar kept the triangle trade going. Slaves were brought in to work on the sugar plantations,. The plantations sent the molasses to New England to make rum, and then the rum was used to trade for more slaves to be sent to the plantations. There were lots of people who thought slavery was immoral and wanted to end it, but the abolition movement really had not become strong enough. In any case, people did not stop buying sugar. Eventually there were so many planatations, though, that there was too much sugar on the market and eventually prices dropped, and plantations went out of business.

Even after slavery had ended in the north (in the late 1700s), the slave trade continued. "Some 156,000 slaves were brought to the United States in the period 1801-08, almost all of them on ships that sailed from New England ports that had recently outlawed slavery." (Hooper 105) Most of the slaves were now sold in the American South.

The sugar industry also led to the first independent nation ruled by former slaves. Haiti was a French colony that was one of the biggest producers of sugar. There were over half a million slaves there by 1789. The American and French revolutions inspired the slaves to revolt in 1791, and they burned down plantations. Even though Napoleon sent troups to the island, the slaves led by Toussaint Louverture, declared independence in 1804.

The production of sugar was one of the major reasons that the slave trade became so important. It created a triangle trade that ended up taking millions of people to work as slaves on sugar plantations in the Caribbean. This, in turn, led to the production of rum in New England, which was traded for more slaves in Africa. The slave trade affected the whole American economy and eventually led to the Civil War.

Writing that fits a score of 2 is somewhat effective.

2

The **introduction** does not present a clear thesis or show a cause-effect relationship.

Middle paragraphs are in chronological order, but organization does not support cause-effect relationship.

Misspellings and errors in verb tenses impede understanding. Sentences do not relate to each other or to the thesis.

Essay lacks conclusion. Paragraphs read more like lists than developed ideas.

The Conquest of Mexico

In 1519, Hernán Cortés sailed from Cuba to Mexico with a fleet of 11 ships and 550 men. In three years he manages to defeat the native tribes who lived in the country, including the powerful Aztecs. He did it by a combination of luck and bravery and skill.

Cortés comes to Mexico because he was looking for gold. His first bit of good luck was finding people who can translate the native languages for him so that helped him make friends with smaller tribes who hated the Aztecs. He also scares the natives by showing them horses and powerful weapons like his cannons. Before going to meet the Aztecs in Tenochtitlán, Cortés burns all his ships so that his men wouldn't dessert him.

Cortés didn't know about his next bit of luck that the Aztec king Moctezuma had omens that something bad was going to happen, and he thought Cortés might be the god Quetzalcoatl who was supposed to return and reclaim his kingdom. So Moctezuma didn't want to fight Cortés at first. He sent gifts instead hoping that would satisfy Cortés. But the gold gifts just made the Spanish want more gold.

When the Spanish gets to Tenochtitlán Cortés took Moctezuma captive, which he thought this would keep the outnumbered Spanish safe. After eight months, though Cortés has to leave the city to fight some Spanish who had come to arrest him for disobeying the governor of Cuba. Cortés defeats the Spanish, but when he got back to Tenochtitlán, things were a mess. Cortés had left someone in charge, but he didn't do a good job and the Aztecs began to rebel.

Many Spanish were killed but they were able to escape from the city. Cortés was lucky once again. While he was gone, the Aztecs came down with smallpox, which was brought by the Spanish. Many of them died. Cortéz returned after about six months. He had more Indian allies. The Aztecs fought for 80 days, but Cortés finally defeated them. (Wood)

Writing that fits a score of 1 is not effective.

1

The **introduction** presents a vague thesis, but ideas are not connected. Incorrect punctuation, grammar errors, and problems in sentence structure detract reader.

Organization is not evident. Paragraphs are out of order. Examples are listed, not developed. No evidence is presented to support ideas.

Conclusion is ineffective and does not tie essay together.

The Silk Road

The Silk Road is one of the worlds oldest trade routes. It goes from China to the Mediteranean. People have traveled on it since around 150 BC, though China stopped using it around 1400 AD and it wasn't just used for silk even though thats what its called. It brought Chinese products and inventions all the way to Europe and visa versa. Religion also spread.

Other things from China besides silk. Spices, paper and gunpowder for example. Eurapean traitors brought Eurapean things back to China too, like glass, ivory and perfume. Many ideas went back and fourth. Religion was very important. Buddism started in India and then it was brought to China.

Around 1 AD silk made it all the way from China to Rome, Italy. No one could figure out how it was made, but everyone in Rome liked to. No one could figure it out until around 400 AD when a princess smuggled silkworms out of China. By the next century they were able to grow silkworms in Europe so it wasn't as important to trade silk anymore.

Most traitors didn't travel over the whole, complete entire road they would just travel over part of the road like the part in there own country and then they would trade off with someone in the next country who would trade with the next county and so on and so on. In 1271 though, Marco Polo travelled from Italy all the way to China. He didn't go home for 24 years! When he got back he wrote a popular book and so he could describe what he had seen on his trip.

Of import for the world's development were the inventions and ideas shared between east and west as the result of the increased trade and communication. Can we underestimate the impact that inventions like the plow, paper or movable type had on the development of the west? Similarly, China was immeasurably enriched by the introduction of Buddism from India.

Evaluating and Reflecting on Your Writing

After you have completed your cause-effect essay, take a few moments to reflect on your writing experience. On your own paper, finish each of the sentence starters below. To score your writing, refer to the scoring guide on pages **60–61** and the examples you just read. Evaluating and reflecting on your writing will help you see how you are growing as a writer.

My Cause-Effect Essay

1. The introduction and conclusion work together because . . .
2. The prewriting activity that worked best for me was . . .
3. The ideas that need better development are . . .
4. I need to use a more confident voice or show more evidence in . . .
5. Reviewing the sentence structure I used and mechanics, in my next cause-effect essay, I would like to . . .
6. One question I still have about writing a cause-effect essay is . . .

Expository Writing
Defining a Concept

What is the real meaning of freedom? How do you explain love, health, or strength? What does it mean to compromise, enjoy, communicate, or celebrate? While you can look up these words in a dictionary, each of them represents a concept that extends far beyond any single definition.

In this chapter, you'll read a sample expository essay that presents a detailed definition of compromise, going well beyond the basic definition of the term. After that, you'll be asked to choose another interesting term and write your own expository essay of definition—one that shows your understanding of the concept and its importance.

Writing Guidelines

Subject: A complex term
Purpose: To define the concept
Form: Essay of definition
Audience: Classmates

"A concept is stronger than a fact."

—Charlotte P. Gillman

TEKS 10.13B, 10.15A(i)–10.15A(v)

Essay of Definition

In the following essay, Veronica Baban explains a concept that is valuable in all aspects of life.

Beginning
The beginning introduces the topic and presents the thesis statement, which is clearly stated (underlined).

Middle
Each middle paragraph presents relevant evidence and well chosen details that support the thesis statement. Rhetorical devices, questions and quotations, help sustain reader interest. The voice and word choice is appropriate for the audience, purpose and context.

Compromise: Let's Meet in the Middle

Do people have to work hard in order to reach an agreement? Do the parties involved often give up something to arrive at common ground? If so, they know what it means to compromise. They understand that they can't always get everything they want in every situation, that life often involves as much "giving" as it does "taking." <u>In fact, the concept of the compromise lies at the very heart of social interaction.</u>

First, to understand the concept of compromise, we need to understand the meaning of the word. The dictionary defines compromise as "a settlement of differences in which each side makes concessions." In terms of usage, compromise is used as a verb or a noun: When someone compromises (*a verb*), he or she reaches an agreement or a compromise (*a noun*). The modern word compromise comes from the Latin word *compromissum*, meaning "mutual promise." Common synonyms for compromise include "settlement," "agreement," "bring to terms," "strike a balance," and "resolve." The opposite of compromising is to act unilaterally, without thinking about the other side.

There is an old saying, "A compromise is an agreement where nobody's happy." As in all sayings, this one has a grain of truth. In a compromise both sides must give up something. Of course, a compromise can be influenced by the relative power of the two sides. For example, an employer or a teacher has more power than an employee or a student, which may affect the eventual agreement. Still, working out compromises is essential in both work- and school-related situations.

Moreover, compromise has played a key role throughout history. The Magna Carta, signed in England in 1215 by King John and his chief nobles, may be the most famous historical compromise. The king had to renounce certain royal powers, respect key legal procedures, and accept that the will of the king could be bound by law. The United States Constitution, framed in the 1700s, is another masterpiece of compromise. This

TEKS 10.13B, 10.15A(i)–10.15A(vi)
ELPS 4K

Middle
Transitions between sentences and paragraphs connect ideas and details. The essay expands the definition from historical to personal, showing the relative value of the ideas, data, and facts presented.

document established the balance of power between the executive, legislative, and judicial branches of government, a critical compromise that is a foundation of American life.

Most agreements between countries or regions represent compromise. Because of deception or different values, these agreements may not always succeed. The Missouri Compromise is a famous agreement in United States history. Northern states allowed the new state of Missouri to be a slave state with the understanding that no other slave states would be admitted to the Union. The compromise lasted for more than 30 years, but slavery was a polarizing issue that eventually led to the Civil War.

Finally, the ability to compromise is critical in all aspects of life—from maintaining friendships to conducting business. It is especially useful within a family. A husband may enjoy professional sports, while his wife may enjoy attending concerts. In a strong marriage there would be a compromise, each partner occasionally sharing in the other partner's interest. Or a teenage son may want more use of the family car. His parents suggest that he work a little harder around the house; in return they will free up the car more often. The son agrees with the compromise, and everyone is satisfied.

Ending
The conclusion puts the concept in perspective and ties the essay to the thesis statement.

In many ways, compromise makes free societies work. Whatever the situation, the two sides must determine what is most important to them and what they will be willing to give up. Then, and only then, the give and take of ideas can take place until a compromise is reached. British statesman Edmund Burke identified the value of compromise best when he stated: "All government—indeed, every human benefit and enjoyment, every virtue and every prudent act—is founded on compromise and barter."

Texas Traits

Respond to the reading. Answer the following questions.

Focus and Coherence (1) How does the conclusion support the thesis statement? **Organization** (2) How is the essay structured? (3) How does the writer show the relative value of ideas, facts, and data that support the thesis? **Development of Ideas** (4) What parts of the definition stand out? Explain you answer to a classmate. **Voice** (5) How would you describe the writer's voice (comical, personal, interested, informative)? Explain your choice to a classmate.

TEKS 10.13A, 10.15A(i), 10.15A(iii)

Prewriting Planning Your Writing

In your expository essay, you will be defining a complex, abstract term. (An *abstract term* is one you can think about but not see or touch.) Your essay needs to be long enough to adequately cover the topic with evidence and details to support your thesis statement. Before writing her essay, Veronica brainstormed possible topics. She started with one word, *freedom*, and added others as quickly as they came to mind. Here is her list.

Concepts List

freedom	compromise	love	humor	enemy
conflict	anger	sadness	friendship	failure
disappointment	happiness	disagreement	weakness	success
liberty	confusion	strength	tragedy	satisfaction

Focusing Your Topic

The topic should be broad enough to discuss in a multiparagraph essay—examining what the term means, how it is important historically, how it relates to real life, and so on. After brainstorming, Veronica looked over her list. She crossed out topics that were either too broad or too narrow. From the remaining words, she chose the one that she wanted to write about and put an asterisk next to it.

~~freedom~~	* compromise	~~love~~	~~humor~~	enemy
conflict	~~anger~~	~~sadness~~	friendship	failure
~~disappointment~~	~~happiness~~	~~disagreement~~	weakness	success
~~liberty~~	~~argument~~	strength	tragedy	~~satisfaction~~

Prewrite

Create your own concepts list. **Brainstorm a list of possible topics to define. Begin with a term that interests you and quickly write down other concepts that come to mind after that. Then look over your list, crossing out concepts that you feel will not give you the right amount of material for an essay. Finally, put an asterisk next to the topic that interests you the most. You may also want to consider the terms in Veronica's list.**

Gathering and Organizing Details

After choosing your topic, consider what the term means, how it is important in history and in everyday life, how it is used in sayings or quotations, and so on. As Veronica researched her term, she took notes.

Notes

Dictionary definition: a settlement of differences; both sides make concessions

Parts of speech: noun and verb

Word history: comes from compromissum, meaning "mutual promise"

Synonyms: settlement, agreement, bring to terms, strike a balance, resolve

Saying: "A compromise is an agreement where nobody's happy."

Historical importance: Magna Carta, Constitution, Missouri Compromise

Quotation: "All government—indeed, every human benefit and enjoyment, every virtue and every prudent act—is founded on compromise and barter."

—Edmund Burke

Note: Even though you may not use the exact dictionary definition in your essay, it is important to your understanding of the concept.

Prewrite

Gather and organize your details. Research your term, taking notes as you go along. Keep in mind your audience, the purpose, and context for your writing. Begin with a dictionary definition; then include your own ideas about the term as well as examples of its historical and everyday importance. Use the information above as a guide. Remember that when you begin your draft, you will need to structure your ideas in a sustained way.

Writing a Thesis Statement

Your thesis statement should introduce the topic and explain its importance. Veronica used this formula to write her thesis statement.

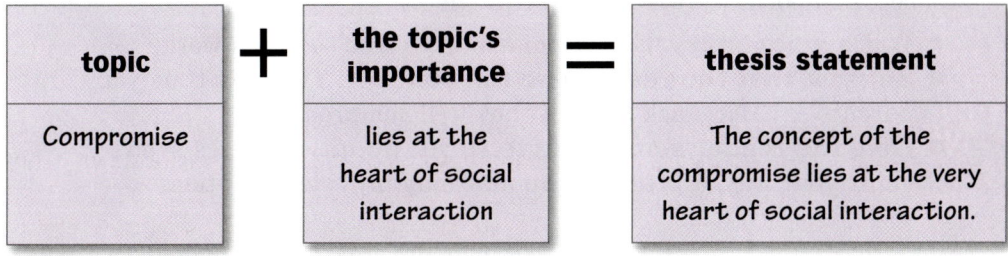

topic	+	the topic's importance	=	thesis statement
Compromise		lies at the heart of social interaction		The concept of the compromise lies at the very heart of social interaction.

Prewrite

Write a thesis statement. Use the formula above to shape your thesis statement for your essay.

TEKS 10.13A, 10.13B, 10.15A(i), 10.15A(ii), 10.15A(iv)–10.15A(vi)
ELPS 5G

Drafting Developing Your Ideas

The tips below can guide your writing of each part of the essay.

Beginning Paragraph

An effective **introduction** should get the reader's attention, give some background, and include the thesis statement, your controlling idea. Your organization should be appropriate for the audience, the purpose, and the context of the essay. Here are some strategies for starting out.

- **Provide a personal story.** My mom and I reached a compromise about the weekend. If I did the laundry, I could go to the movies.
- **Ask a challenging question.** Do people have to work hard in order to reach an agreement? Answer the question in your essay.
- **Refer to a well-known issue.** Many teenagers in El Paso wanted a skate park, but the city officials planned for a picnic area. They compromised by putting some skateboard ramps in one corner.

Middle Paragraphs

The **middle** paragraphs should explain the concept. Be sure to structure your ideas in a sustained way. Consider these directions as you write.

- Develop a paragraph for each part of your definition.
- Write a topic sentence for each paragraph. Consider the relative value of the data, facts, and ideas you plan to include.
- Include plenty of accurate, specific details to explain each part. Be sure to include an appropriate variety of sentence structures.
- Use transitions to link ideas and rhetorical devices for interest.

Ending Paragraph

An effective **conclusion** wraps up the definition and reminds readers of the concept's importance. Use these strategies.

- **Write a summary.** Compromise makes free societies work.
- **Suggest that the reader use the concept.** The next time your parents say "No!" ask them if they will compromise.
- **Give the reader something to think about.** If things aren't going your way, a little compromise may provide a solution.

Draft

Write your first draft. Use your prewriting work (pages 182–183), the sample essay, and these suggestions. Add interesting details and examples.

Texas Traits

Revising Improving Your Writing

Think about your purpose, your audience, and the genre, or form, of the draft you have written. Then use the checklist below to help you improve your essay.

Revising Checklist

Focus and Coherence

_____ **1.** Are my introduction and conclusion effective?
_____ **2.** Have I clearly stated my thesis statement?
_____ **3.** Do all my ideas connect to the thesis statement?

Organization

_____ **4.** Do I include a strong introduction, middle, and conclusion?
_____ **5.** Are my details in a logical order?
_____ **6.** Does each paragraph have a topic sentence?
_____ **7.** Have I used transitions to connect my ideas?

Development of Ideas

_____ **8.** Have I defined the concept clearly?
_____ **9.** Have I included interesting examples, well thought-out details, and relevant evidence that support my thesis?
_____ **10.** Have I used rhetorical devices to sustain reader interest?

Voice

_____ **11.** Does my voice fit the topic, the audience, and the purpose?
_____ **12.** Do I show enthusiasm for the topic?
_____ **13.** Does my word choice adequately convey subtlety of meaning?

Revise

Improve your first draft. Use the checklist above as you review your first draft and make changes. If possible, ask a classmate to review your work.

TEKS 10.13C–10.13E, 10.17C, 10.18A, 10.18B, 10.19
ELPS 5C–5E

Texas Traits

Editing Checking for Conventions

When you have completed your revising, it's time to edit your paper for grammar, sentence structure, capitalization, punctuation, and spelling.

Editing Checklist

Conventions

GRAMMAR

_____ **1.** Do my verbs and subjects agree in number *(they were,* not *they was)*?

SENTENCE STRUCTURE

_____ **2.** Do I use a variety of correctly structured sentences that clearly communicate ideas?

MECHANICS (Capitalization and Punctuation)

_____ **3.** Did I capitalize all proper nouns and proper adjectives?

_____ **4.** Did I capitalize the first word in each sentence?

_____ **5.** Have I used end punctuation correctly?

_____ **6.** Have I used commas correctly, especially in phrases and clauses?

SPELLING

_____ **7.** Did I double-check my spelling and look for errors my spell-checker might miss?

_____ **8.** Did I use a dictionary to double-check the spelling of any special terms?

Edit

Edit your essay of definition. Use the checklist above as you review your work for errors. Ask a partner to check your work, too. Discuss suggested edits, and incorporate feedback from your teacher or peers. Then write a neat final copy and proofread it.

Publishing Sharing Your Writing

After completing your essay and giving it an interesting title, be sure to share it with a number of different audiences. You can also post your work on a personal Web site.

Writing for Assessment
Responding to Expository Prompts

When you explain or inform in a longer piece of writing, you're developing an expository essay. Effective expository writing begins with your complete understanding of a topic, and it ends with a written piece that shows your ability to share this knowledge clearly with your reader. What happens in between is all of the planning, drafting, and revising you do to produce your essay.

On assessment tests, you may be asked to write explanations in response to expository prompts. Of course, your time is limited for this type of expository writing, so you must make the best use of every available minute. This chapter will show you how to complete such a response, adapting the writing process as you work against the clock.

Writing Guidelines

Subject: Expository prompt
Form: Response essay
Purpose: To demonstrate competence
Audience: Instructor

"Good writers are those who keep the language efficient. That is to say, keep it accurate, keep it clear."

—Ezra Pound

Prewriting Analyzing an Expository Prompt

Most writing tests ask you to respond to a prompt. A prompt is a set of directions that tells you what to write. It's crucial for you to analyze the prompt carefully so that you write a response that fits the requirements of the test. When you analyze a prompt, answer the following **STRAP questions:**

Subject: What subject (school, schedule, homework policy, healthy living, friendships) should I write about?

Type: What form (essay, letter, announcement, report, article) of writing should I create?

Role: What position (student, community member, son or daughter, friend) should I assume as the writer?

Audience: Who (classmates, teacher, principal, parents, city council) is the intended reader?

Purpose: What is the goal (inform, explain, evaluate) of my writing?

These key words are often found in **expository** prompts: *explain, analyze, compare and contrast, outline,* and *define.*

Try It!

Analyze these prompts by answering the five STRAP questions above.

1. Aristotle once said, "Happiness depends upon ourselves." Everyone knows the word "happiness," but most of us have a different idea of what it means to be happy. Define the word "happiness" and include two or three clear examples.
2. Many high school students have part-time jobs. Students often choose jobs that are based on economic factors and personal preferences. Identify a part-time job that you would like to have, analyze the duties involved, and explain why you believe the job would suit you.
3. In a letter to a friend, compare and contrast two classes that you are currently taking. In your letter, explain the positive and negative aspects of each class.

Tip

Some prompts do not contain key words for every STRAP question. You will have to use your best judgment to answer these questions.

Planning Your Response

Once you have answered the STRAP questions, you should quickly plan your response. The following graphic organizers can help.

Graphic Organizers

Quick List (Any Essay)

1. First Point
   —Detail 1
   —Detail 2
2. Second Point
   —Detail 1
   —Detail 2
3. Third Point
   —Detail 1
   —Detail 2

Cluster (Definition/Classification)

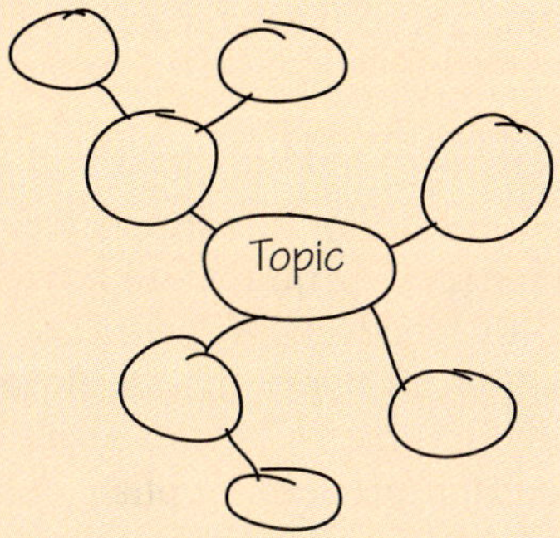

Prewrite

Reread the expository prompts on page 194. Choose one prompt and use one of the graphic organizers above to quickly organize a response to the prompt.

Tip

Manage your time wisely. Allow enough time for prewriting, revising, and editing. For example, if you have 45 minutes to respond, use 5 to 10 minutes to analyze the prompt and plan your response, 30 to 35 minutes for writing, and the last 5 minutes for revising and editing.

TEKS 10.13B, 10.15A(i)–10.15A(iv)

Writing Responding to the Prompt

After using a graphic organizer to plan your response, it's time to begin writing. After analyzing the prompt, Victoria Moreno decided that an expository essay was the best genre to discuss the concept of loyalty. She chose expository because its purpose is to explain and inform, a good match to the prompt.

Sample Response

The **introduction** clearly states the thesis and engages the reader's attention.

Rhetorical devices, like questions, show knowledge and support the thesis. Ideas in the **middle** paragraphs are structured in a sustained way.

The Good and the Bad of Loyalty

Loyalty is a slippery concept. It can be considered an outstanding quality to have in a friend, as in this quote from Woodrow Wilson: "Loyalty means nothing unless it has at its heart the absolute principle of self-sacrifice." Loyalty, however, can also be seen as a quality that can be manipulated, as implied in an old Irish proverb: "The best way to keep loyalty in a man's heart is to keep money in his purse."

The dictionary defines loyalty without any sort of good or bad associations. It is merely "faithfulness to commitments or obligations." (Random House) When is loyalty something to be praised and when should it be condemned?

Few people would question the security of having friends and family who are loyal to them. It is reassuring to know that there are certain people you can always count on no matter what you do or in times of need. Loyalty goes beyond bonds with people though. Sports fans can be loyal to a particular team. Soldiers are loyal to the military and to their country. There are even those who are loyal to particular brands of merchandise, like computers or soda.

Sometimes loyalty is so strong that it can become a problem. People might become so loyal to a product that they refuse to use anything else. Imagine, for example, how difficult that could become when you want to eat out with a friend who will only go to one particular fast-food chain. Further, people sometimes becomes so loyal to a cause, a job, or an organization that it takes over their lives. These people begin to see life in a very limited way

Each **middle** paragraph sustains the thesis. Transitions link ideas from paragraph to paragraph and within paragraphs.

because their faithfulness to these particular commitments become more important than anything else.

This leads to the concept of "blind" loyalty. The Merriam-Webster Dictionary defines this as "unquestioning." Does loyalty have to be unquestioning? The fact that the word "blind" has to be put in front of the word implies that loyalty by itself is not unquestioning. So even though a loyal person is faithful, it does not mean that he or she doesn't question that faithfulness from time to time.

Blind loyalty can happen when someone has gotten so used to supporting a person or an organization or even an idea that he or she just keeps supporting it. The object of loyalty, which might be a person or an object, might change into something that's unpleasant, cruel, or corrupt; still the person continue the support. In such cases, blind loyalty may not be such a good quality.

Loyalty can also be bought, as described in the Irish proverb. Loyalty doesn't necessarily have to be bought with money, though plenty of loyalty is. Many people will overlook bad qualities when they are profiting from a relationship. Loyalty can also be bought by fear. You may stay loyal to an organization because your friends all belong to it, and you don't want to look different. Many employees won't blow the whistle on an employer because they are afraid of being fired.

Effective **conclusion** ties essay together.

Are blind loyalty and bought loyalty the real thing? Most people consider a faithful dog to be the true example of loyalty. Dog love, though, can certainly be blind. If that is the case, then pure, unadulterated loyalty is a special quality that should be reserved for the deserving.

Draft

Now write your own response. **Look over the planning you did for the prompt on page 189, including your use of a graphic organizer. Then write a response to the prompt in the amount of time your teacher gives you.**

TEKS 10.13C, 10.13D, 10.17C, 10.18A, 10.18B(i)
ELPS 5C, 5D, 5F

Texas Traits

Revising Improving Your Response

Most writing tests allow you to make corrections to improve your work, though you should find out ahead of time how many are allowed. Always make changes and corrections as neatly as possible. If the test allows revising and editing, use the STRAP questions to guide your changes.

Subject: Does my response focus on the topic in the prompt? Do my main points support my thesis?
Type: Have I followed the correct form (essay, letter, article)?
Role: Have I assumed the position indicated in the prompt?
Audience: Have I used the right level of language for my audience?
Purpose: Does my writing accomplish the goal set forth in the prompt?

Revise

Improve your work. Reread your response, asking yourself the STRAP questions above. Make neat changes in the time your teacher allows.

Editing Checking Your Response

Check your response for punctuation, capitalization, spelling, and grammar errors. Careless errors can confuse the reader.

Conventions

_____ **1.** Have I used end punctuation for every sentence?
_____ **2.** Have I capitalized all proper nouns and the first word of each sentence?
_____ **3.** Have I checked my spelling?
_____ **4.** Do my subjects and verbs agree *(it does,* not *it do)*?
_____ **5.** Have I used the right word *(there, they're, their)*?

Edit

Check your conventions. Review your response for punctuation, capitalization, spelling, and grammar errors. Make neat corrections in the time your teacher allows.

"If you can read your writing to yourself without wincing, you have probably gotten it right."

—George V. Higgins

Expository Writing on Tests

Use the following tips as a guide whenever you respond to an expository writing prompt.

Before you write . . .

- **Understand the prompt.**
  Review the STRAP questions listed on page **188**.
  Remember that an expository prompt asks you to *explain*.
- **Plan your time wisely.**
  Spend several minutes making notes and planning before starting to write. Use a graphic organizer. (See page **189**.)

As you write . . .

- **Decide on a focus or thesis for your response.**
  Keep your main idea or purpose in mind as you write.
- **Be selective.**
  Use examples and explanations that directly support your focus.
- **End in a meaningful way.**
  Remind the reader about the importance of the topic.

After you've written a first draft . . .

- **Check for completeness.**
  Use the STRAP questions on page **192** to revise your work.
- **Check for correctness.**
  Check your punctuation, capitalization, spelling, and grammar.

Prewrite

Plan and write a response. **Analyze one of the prompts below, using the STRAP questions. Then plan and write a response. Complete your work in the time your teacher gives you.**

Expository Prompts

- Good parents or guardians demonstrate many valuable qualities. Choose three qualities of a good parent or guardian and write an essay that includes examples to support your choices.
- The German poet Johann Wolfgang von Goethe said, "There is nothing insignificant in the world. It all depends on the point of view." Explain why it is important to see a situation from another person's point of view.

ELPS 1E, 2C, 3B, 3D, 3E, 4G

Texas Write Source Online
www.hmheducation.com/tx/writesource

Persuasive Writing

Writing Focus

Grammar Focus

Learning Language

Learning these words and expressions will help you understand this unit.

1. A **mood** is a set of verb forms that tells the writer's attitude about the factuality or possibility that something will occur.
   When do you think you would use the indicative mood?
2. An **argument** is a discussion in which different viewpoints or opinions are expressed.
   Describe a recent argument that you had with a friend.
3. Something that is **precise** is exact and clearly expressed.
   Why do you need to be precise when you give directions to a particular location?
4. **Loaded language** consists of words that have a strong negative or positive connotation and that are intended to influence the reader.
   Describe an advertisement you have seen or heard recently that uses loaded language.

Persuasive Writing
Writing an Argumentative Essay

People have different opinions and take different positions on issues, both big and small. Big issues might include global warming, child labor, or ways to improve education in the United States. Local issues might include whether or not dogs should be allowed in parks. People often disagree over the seriousness of issues, about the consequences, and about the ways to resolve issues that confront them every day.

You are sure to encounter issues that you feel strongly about—topics that are worth debating. Perhaps your school board is deciding whether to eliminate funding for after-school sports or for school bands. Perhaps city leaders are deciding whether or not overnight parking should be allowed in public lots and on public streets. How can you present your ideas and convince others to agree with you?

Persuasive writing helps you address a difference of opinion. By clearly stating a position and defending it with facts and logical reasons, you can convince others to agree with you. In this chapter, you will write an argumentative essay about an issue that affects many people.

Writing Guidelines

Subject: A social, political, or environmental issue
Purpose: To defend a position
Form: Argumentative Essay
Audience: Classmates and community members

"Opinions are made to be be changed or how is truth to be got at?"
—Lord Byron

TEKS 10.13B, 10.16A, 10.16F

Persuasive Writing Warm-Up: Using Support

When you write a persuasive paragraph or essay, it is important to include effective supporting details. You will need to include a range of appropriate appeals: facts, statistics, and case studies that support your position and help persuade your audience. These are considered precise, relevant evidence. Quotations from leading experts on the topic are also considered to be relevant evidence. You may wish to include appropriate anecdotes or analogies as well.

The notebook page below shows evidence and supporting details that one student used to support her position on child labor.

Fact: Worldwide, one in six children aged 5 to 14 is engaged in child labor.
Fact: Girls often work as domestic servants.

Fact: Children who work are not able to attend school.
Fact: Children labor exists in developed countries.
Statistic: According to the UN, in Sub-Saharan Africa, approximately 69 million children work. .

Statistic: Worldwide, approximately 158 million children work.
Statistic: Sixteen percent of children in developing countries work.
Quotation: "Children deserve basic human rights" U.S. Senator Barbara Boxer
Quotation: "Child labor is the bane of modern existence and should be outlawed." Society Against Child Labor

The **solution** is . . .	moderate people should stand up and take charge.
The **problem** with the world today is . . .	limited access to school.
The **solution** is . . .	make it easier for children to attend.
The **problem** with the world today is . . .	third-world countries can't compete.
The **solution** is . . .	third-world debt relief.
The **problem** with the world today is . . .	globalization causes child labor.
The **solution** is . . .	enforce the UN rules on the rights of the child.

Try It!

On your own paper, express an opinion about an important environmental, social, or political problem. Then find precise details and evidence: facts, statistics, and a quotation to support your position. List these appeals.

Writing a Persuasive Paragraph

A persuasive paragraph expresses an opinion about a specific topic and contains logical reasons and precise, relevant evidence to support the position. The ideas are structured to sustain the topic sentence and to persuade the audience. A persuasive paragraph has three parts:

- The **topic sentence** states the position or opinion.
- The **body sentences** support the position.
- The **closing sentence** revisits the position or opinion.

Sample Persuasive Paragraph

Martin wrote the following paragraph about child labor. In his paragraph he considered the relative value of the information he decided to include.

The **topic sentence** names the problem and solution.

The **body sentences** present evidence and details to support the opinion.

The **closing sentence** revisits the opinion.

Certain Inalienable Rights

As globalization sends more children into sweatshops and dangerous factories, it's time for the United States to ratify the United Nations Conventions on the Rights of the Child (CRC). This piece of legislation was created in 1989 to protect those under the age of 18 against bonded labor (slavery) and labor that is dangerous or that interferes with education. Today, one in six children between the ages of 5 and 14 endures forced labor, curtailing any possibility for education and ensuring a life of poverty. Children are forced to work in mines, in fields, and with dangerous machinery. Girls frequently become domestic servants at the age of 5. Such forced labor "crushes the right to normal physical and mental development" (UNICEF Child info), and as U.S. Senator Batbara Boxer has argued, "Children deserve basic human rights." Child labor exists all over the world, in Africa, South Asia, Central Europe, and in the Commonwealth of Independent States (CIS). The United States should ratify the CRC and work with other nations and international groups to stop this practice..

Write a persuasive paragraph. Review the three parts of a paragraph (top of page) and what they do. Then present your opinion and details from page 196 on the topic you selected.

TEKS 10.13A

Understanding Your Goal

Texas Traits

Your goal in this chapter is to support a position regarding a social, political, or environmental issue. The traits in the following chart will help you write an argumentative essay, the correct form, or genre, for your goal and audience. The scoring guide on pages **60–61** will also help you. Refer to it often to improve your writing.

Traits of Persuasive Writing

- **Focus and Coherence**
  Clearly state your opinion or position in the introduction, defend it throughout, and write an effective conclusion that ties the essay together.
- **Organization**
  Create a beginning that states your position, or controlling idea, and a middle that provides evidence and details to support your position and addresses objections. Restate your opinion in the conclusion.
- **Development of Ideas**
  Use precise, relevant evidence and logical details that support the topic sentence of each paragraph and that support the thesis.
- **Voice**
  Use a persuasive voice that is appropriate for your topic, audience, and context of your essay.
- **Conventions**
  Write clear complete sentences with varied beginnings. Check your writing for errors in grammar, sentence structure, capitalization, punctuation, and spelling.

Literature Connection. You will encounter persuasion in all types of media—from TV commercials to the latest fads to works of literature. In her essay "Doing Nothing Is Something," author Anna Quindlen argues that, for children and teenagers, downtime is essential for fueling creativity.

Argumentative Essay

An argumentative essay clearly states where you stand on an issue. By stating and defending your position, you may be able to convince others to agree with you. In this sample essay, the student writer clearly defends his position.

Beginning
The beginning introduces the controlling idea and clearly states the opinion (underlined).

Middle
The first middle paragraph uses precise factual evidence to support the position.

The second, third, and fourth middle paragraphs add more evidence and logical reasons. Ideas are structured according to their relative value.

Conserve Energy and Prevent an Oil Crisis

Gasoline continues to become more and more expensive. The reason is simple—the world's oil supply is slowly being used up. People are using more oil than ever without thinking of the consequences. In fact, many economists believe that an oil crisis is inevitable. When the crisis hits, prices of gasoline, home heating oil, and many other products will rise quickly. People will struggle to heat their homes and buy gas for their cars. Businesses will slow production—or even close down. <u>It is time to address this serious issue and prevent an oil crisis—we must begin conserving oil.</u>

The world's appetite for oil is huge. In 2010, people in the United States used more than 22 million barrels of oil per day to fuel cars, heat homes, and make plastics, clothing, and paint (Cummings 83). The United States government estimates current trends show world wide energy usage will rise to about 98 million barrels a day by 2015. Unless people learn how to conserve, the demand for oil will soon exceed the supply. To avoid a crisis, we must all do our best to conserve oil.

Oil conservation makes sense for many reasons. First of all, oil conservation will help to preserve a valuable resource. In 2008, the average passenger vehicle in the United States got about 22 miles per gallon (Reynolds 3). Today's fuel-efficient vehicles can get more than 30 miles per gallon (Staunton 15). If everyone chose a hybrid, cut out unnecessary car trips, and took public transportation whenever possible, the United States would save millions of barrels of oil every day. That, in turn, would help the nation's oil supply last longer.

TEKS 10.13B, 10.16A–10.16E
ELPS 4K

Middle paragraphs show an analysis of the relative value of data, facts, and ideas.

Conserving oil also helps to protect the environment. Automobiles, home oil burners, and other oil-consuming technologies contribute to air pollution and global warming. When oil and gasoline are burned, polluting gases are released into the atmosphere. One of these gases, carbon dioxide, is a leading cause of global warming. Using less oil for transportation and home heating will reduce air pollution and the effects of global warming.

Finally, conserving oil can save consumers money. Conservation decreases demand for oil, which causes prices of gasoline, heating oil, and other petroleum-based products to drop, or at least to increase at a slower rate. Conservation also saves consumers money directly. At $3 per gallon, using 10 fewer gallons would save $30. Decreased usage increases savings.

The last middle paragraph addresses an objection.

Some people say that the best way to prevent an oil crisis is to drill more oil wells (Miller 86). This is a short-term solution that has its own environmental problems. No one knows how much oil is left, but we do know that the supply is limited. Conservation is smarter. It makes the most of the available oil supply.

Ending The conclusion restates and reinforces the position stated in the introduction.

Gasoline is expensive now, but in the future it could cost $7 per gallon or more. If people don't act now to conserve oil, these prices will soon be here. Conserving oil not only stretches oil supplies and saves consumers money but also cuts pollution. Everyone can help. Drivers can avoid gas-guzzling SUV's and opt for more fuel-efficient hybrid cars. Homeowners can insulate their homes and turn down their thermostats in the winter. Everyone can play a part in preventing an oil crisis.

Texas Traits

Respond to the reading. Answer the following questions. Discuss your ideas with a classmate. **Focus and Coherence** (1) How does the conclusion support the thesis statement? **Organization** (2) Which paragraph explains the problem in detail? (3) Which paragraph answers an objection? **Development of Ideas** 4) What are three logical reasons the writer gives for conserving oil? **Voice** 5) Does the writer sound knowledgeable and persuasive? Explain.

Prewriting

In your prewriting for your argumentative essay, you will select a social, political, or environmental issue, and then gather reasons and details to support your position. It is important to organize your ideas in a sustained, persuasive way. Careful prewriting makes persuasive writing easier and more effective.

Keys to Effective Prewriting

1. Choose a social, political, or environmental topic that interests you. Think about the topic, and decide what your position is.
2. Write a clear position statement to guide your research and your writing.
3. Gather the most logical reasons and the best evidence to support your position. Rank the reasons according to their relative value, 1 for the most important, 2 for the next most important, etc.
4. Address an important objection.
5. Create a list or an outline as a planning guide.

Prewriting Planning Your Writing

Controversies and differing opinions are a part of life. To find a writing topic, student writer Marcela Andrade answered two key questions about important, interesting issues that had been in the news recently. After reviewing her answers, she marked the issue that she would like to write about with an asterisk. Then she stated the position she would take on the issue.

List of Issues

What issues have been covered in the news recently?

- global warming and its damage to the environment
- the increasing cost of health care
- the growth of hunger in the United States *
- a decline in the number of people who vote

What social, environmental, or political issues have we discussed in class?

- increased crime in our state and nation
- the reemergence and spread of tuberculosis
- a lack of good jobs for factory workers

Position statement about hunger in the United States: *I believe that the best way to address the hunger crisis in the United States is to support local food banks.*

Prewrite

Choose an issue. On your own paper, answer each of the questions above in two or three different ways. Then put an asterisk next to the issue that you feel most strongly about. Also write a sentence that states your position or opinion on the issue and the reasons for your choice.

Texas Traits

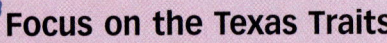

Focus on the Texas Traits

Focus and Coherence Choose an issue that you can discuss clearly with your audience. You may have to do some research before you can write your thesis, or opinion, statement. You can then select relevant evidence and precise details to defend your position.

Gathering Reasons to Support Your Position

After you have you have chosen your topic and stated your opinion, you need to use a range of appeals—facts, data, case studies, anecdotes—to convince your audience. Marcela used a chart to gather and list reasons and evidence.

Reasons Chart

Position: The best way to solve this country's hunger crisis is to support local food banks.

Logical Reasons	Supporting Evidence
Food banks do a great job of getting food to the people who need it.	– 36 million served in 2011 – food banks know local situation – many people work with food banks – food banks deliver food
Food banks help businesses and the environment.	– accept food from restaurants, grocery stores, other businesses – save businesses money every year – keep food out of waste stream
Food banks are economically efficient.	– in Texas alone, people volunteer more than 200,000 hours each year – don't require fancy offices or tons of paperwork

Prewrite

Create a reasons chart. Create your own logical reasons and evidence chart. List a range of appeals, identifying at least three reasons to support your position. Include precise, factual data and logical details that support each reason.

Texas Traits

Focus on the Texas Traits

Organization Persuasive essays are often organized by order of importance and relative value of the information. After you have finished your chart, consider ranking your appeals in order of importance. This will help you plan your essay.

TEKS 10.16B, 10.16C

Prewriting Gathering Objections

As you gather reasons and evidence that support your position, it is wise to gather evidence that will enable you to defend your opinion against at least one strong objection that readers might pose. Addressing objections honestly and accurately can make your position even more persuasive. How can you anticipate and address the objections? Start with a little research.

- Read local newspapers and monitor local television and radio news reports to find arguments that both support and oppose your position.
- Think of class discussions. Recall any opposing arguments and how they were addressed.
- Ask the opinions of your friends and family. Try to debate positions that differ from yours, and listen carefully during the discussion.

Marcela found the following three objections and put an asterisk next to the strongest one.

> – Food banks already have plenty of support.
> – Government programs like food stamps provide all the help people need. *
> – Not many people in the United States use food banks.

Prewrite

Gather objections. Use the strategies above to gather and list three objections to your position. Put an asterisk next to the strongest objection.

Countering an Objection

Countering an objection means arguing against it. Marcela listed three reasons that she could support with evidence to disagree with the objection she chose to address.

> **Objection:** *Government programs like food stamps provide all the help people need.* *
>
> 1. Even with food stamps, the hunger problem has grown.
> 2. Despite government help, millions of people still visit food banks.
> 3. Applying for food stamps takes time. Some people need food right away.

Prewrite

Counter an important objection. Write down the strongest objection to your argument. List several logical reasons why you disagree with it.

Drafting

Go Online!

You have chosen an issue, stated your position, developed support for it, and identified an objection to address. You are ready to begin your draft.

Keys to Effective Drafting

1. Write on every other line or double-space on the computer to make room for changes later on.
2. Introduce the issue and state your position in the first paragraph.
3. Provide background information, specific logical reasons, and supporting evidence in the middle paragraphs.
4. Include precise details to support your reasons.
5. Address an important objection.
6. In the conclusion, reemphasize your position and summarize the support for your position.

TEKS 10.13B, 10.16B–10.16D

Drafting Getting the Big Picture

The graphic below shows how the parts of your argumentative essay should fit together. Be sure that your organizational pattern is appropriate for the purpose, audience, and context of your essay. Use this graphic and your prewriting plan to guide the writing of your first draft. (The examples are from the student essay on pages **207–210**.)

Beginning

The **introduction** states the writer's position about the chosen issue.

Thesis Statement
People can help end hunger in this country by supporting local food banks.

Middle

The **middle** paragraphs explain the issue and supply logical reasons and evidence supporting the writer's position. The objection shows an honest representation of the opposing viewpoint. Ideas are structured in a sustained and persuasive manner.

Topic Sentences
Hunger affects people in the United States, and the problem is worsening.

First and foremost, food banks deserve support because they know how to put food in the hands of the people who need it.

In addition, food banks operate in a very efficient way.

Lastly, food banks serve the environment well.

Some people argue that food banks are not necessary.

Ending

The **conclusion** sums up the writer's position on the issue and offers a final important thought.

Closing Sentence
After all, everyone deserves at least one good meal a day.

Starting Your Essay

Beginning
Middle
Ending

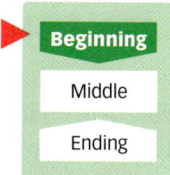

The beginning paragraph of your essay should capture the reader's attention, introduce the topic, and state your position. This three-step process will help you write your introduction.

- **Capture the reader's attention.**
  Consider using a rhetorical device.
  What is it like to be hungry? How does it feel?
- **Provide accurate, relevant background information.**
  Add ideas that help the reader understand the issue.
  Sadly millions men, women, and children in this country face hunger every day.
- **State your position.**
  Your position statement is your thesis statement for the entire essay. Make sure you can support it with logic and evidence.
  People can help end hunger in this country by supporting local food banks.

Beginning Paragraph

The topic is introduced.

Ideas are structured in a persuasive way. Thesis statement is presented (underlined).

Every day, needless hunger devastates families in the United States. What is it like to be hungry? How does it feel? Initially, the stomach starts to rumble, and the mouth waters. Then thoughts of food fill the mind. It becomes hard to concentrate. Most people head for the kitchen or the cafeteria, find some food, and the hunger is history. Now what if there is no food in sight? Sadly, millions of men, women, and children in this country face hunger every day. People can help end hunger in this country by supporting local food banks.

Draft

Write an introduction. Use dramatic, engaging language or rhetorical devices to introduce the topic, state your position, and provide necessary background information.

"Write visually, write clearly, and make every word count."
—Gloria D. Miklowitz

TEKS 10.13B

Drafting Developing the Middle Part

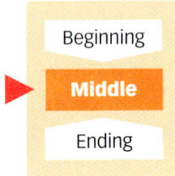

Beginning
Middle
Ending

The middle part of your essay provides the main reasons, relevant evidence, and precise details that support your position. Refer to your reasons and evidence chart. Begin each paragraph with a topic sentence, and then add details that support it. Also address an objection in the last middle paragraph.

Using Transitions

Transitions move your essay smoothly from one paragraph to the next. They can also show the order of importance of your ideas. The following chart includes transitions that could connect your middle paragraphs, depending upon the organizational pattern that you have chosen.

Paragraph 1	Paragraph 2	Paragraph 3
First of all →	Also →	Another reason
One reason →	Another reason →	Most importantly
First and foremost →	In addition →	Lastly

Middle Paragraphs

Facts and precise statistical data support the position.

Hunger affects people in the United States, and the problem is worsening. In 2007, about 33 million Americans did not know how or where they would get the food they needed to stay healthy ("Current News"). By 2011, that number had grown to 36 million. Hunger affects people in many ways. Children who are hungry have a harder time learning, and they may experience delays in physical development. Hunger affects the health of grown-ups, too, and makes it harder for them to work and care for their families (Workman 82).

A topic sentence introduces each middle paragraph (underlined). Transitions link ideas.

First and foremost, food banks deserve support because they know how to put food in the hands of the people who need it. In 2010, one food bank in Texas collected, stored, and distributed enough food to provide over 12 million meals ("East Texas Food Bank"). Feeding the hungry is a massive effort that has been going on for years. Because food banks are local, they often know where to locate and how to reach out to people who need food. People often feel more comfortable visiting a local food bank than they do applying for assistance from a government agency.

In addition, food banks operate in a very efficient way. Because they rely largely on donations and the work of volunteers, food banks keep their costs low. Thousands of people donate hundreds of thousands of hours every year to food banks. That means money donated to a food bank isn't wasted. For example, the Davis City Food Bank uses 90 cents of every dollar donated to buy food for hungry men, women, and children.

Lastly, food banks serve the environment well. Every day, grocery stores, restaurants, and other businesses throw out tons of unneeded food or food beyond its expiration date. The food is safe and edible but often ends up in landfills. Many food banks now collect this food and redistribute it. This process keeps this food from being wasted and filling landfills. Businesses save money, too. Instead of paying a trash hauler, businesses can have the food bank pick up the food for free. There are federal tax incentives for donating, and laws have been passed to protect businesses that donate food.

Some people argue that food banks are unnecessary. They think that government programs such as food stamps are enough to ease hunger. However, not all the people in need qualify for government programs, and applying for help can take time. Hungry people need to be fed, and food banks do just that. Also, even with government help, the hunger problem has escalated. Without food banks, the problem will only keep getting worse.

Each middle paragraph provides logical reasons, relevant evidence, and details to support the position.

The fifth middle paragraph counters an objection.

Draft

Write your middle paragraphs. Create persuasive middle paragraphs that promote your position and give reasons that support it. Start each paragraph with a topic sentence and follow with precise, relevant evidence and details. Your final middle paragraph should respond to a significant objection.

Tip

- Structure your essay so that the most important reasons come first, and use transitions between paragraphs to show order of importance.
- Support reasons with relevant facts, statistics, and quotations from experts. Respond to a significant objection with solid facts and reasons.

TEKS 10.13B, 10.16A, 10.16C

Drafting Ending Your Essay

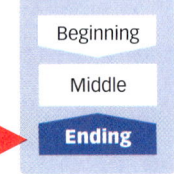

Beginning
Middle
Ending

The main part of your essay should have stated your position and supported it with solid, logical reasons and relevant evidence. With that information in place, you are ready to write your ending. Your conclusion should do all of the following:

- Restate your position and add a final insight.
- Summarize the main reasons that support your position.
- Leave the reader with an important final insight.

Ending Paragraph

The solution is restated.

A final persuasive call is made.

A final insight is provided.

Supporting local food banks is the best way to help ease the hunger problem. Individuals can provide support by volunteering their services or by donating money or food. In either case, hungry people get the food they need, and surplus food gets used. Concerned citizens should contact their local food banks today and offer their help because government programs can't do enough. By backing food banks, people can help to alleviate hunger in this country. After all, everyone deserves at least one good meal a day.

Draft

Write your ending paragraph and prepare a complete first draft. Use the ideas listed above as a guide to develop your final paragraph. Then prepare a copy of your entire essay. Write on every other line or double-space on the computer. This will give you room for revising.

Try It!

If you have followed the traditional persuasive essay structure, your first draft should have turned out well. That structure includes four parts:

1. Introduce the topic and state your opinion.
2. Support your opinion with logical reasons and relevant evidence.
3. Answer an objection.
4. Wrap up your argument.

To make sure that your essay is complete, mark each paragraph with the correct number—a 1 next to your opening paragraph, a 2 next to each supporting paragraph, and so on.

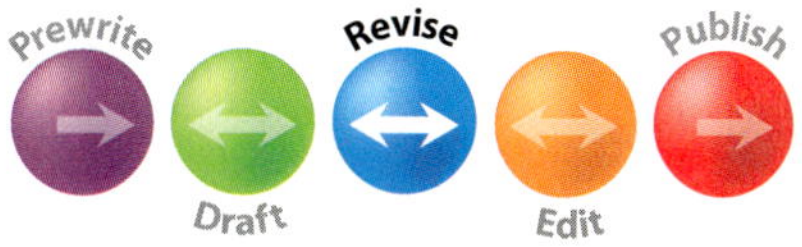

Revising

Go Online!

Revising is the process of improving a first draft. When you revise, you add or delete details, rearrange parts of your writing, and work on developing a more convincing, persuasive voice. You also check your word choice and sentence fluency to make sure you have communicated your ideas effectively.

Keys to Effective Revising

1. As you begin to revise, read your essay to get a feeling for how well it works as a whole. As you begin your revision, keep in mind your purpose, your audience, and the genre, or form, of the writing.
2. Be sure you have clearly stated your position.
3. Check your paragraphs. They should have topic sentences followed by supporting details in logical order, according to their relative value.
4. Be sure you've used an authoritative, respectful voice.
5. Check your writing for precise nouns and direct, active verbs.
6. Be sure you have used different kinds of sentences with varied beginnings.

Revising for Focus and Coherence

When you revise for *focus and coherence,* be sure you have clearly explained the issue and convincingly argued your position. Remember, your job is to convince the audience. Your entire essay should be directed toward this goal. Check your choice of genre. Have you chosen the appropriate form for the writing? If not, you will need to change the genre.

Have I focused on one major issue throughout the essay?

An argumentative essay focuses on one major issue. Your introduction should describe and state your position on that issue. The middle paragraphs should provide more information and give relevant evidence, precise details, and logical reasons to convince your audience. Your conclusion should restate your position and tie the essay together.

- **Review the following thesis statement.**
  Food banks are working together to help solve the problem of hunger in America.
- **The following topic sentences focus on the thesis statement.**
  Hunger affects about 36 million people in the United States, and the problem is worsening. Food banks operate very efficiently.
- **The following topic sentences do not seem to focus on the thesis statement.**
  Our community food bank is running out of food. People in Africa and South America are going hungry, too.

Exercise

Read the paragraph below. How would you revise the paragraph to add focus and coherence?

Food banks also serve the environment well. Every day, grocery stores, and restaurants throw out unwanted food. They want to attract customers, so they run ads with specials in the papers. This unwanted food is safe to eat, but it ends up in landfills. This creates another problem, not enough room to store our trash. Everyone can recycle. Businesses are encouraged to donate to food banks, and many do donate. It saves them money in several ways.

Revise

Check your thesis statement and topic sentences. Re-read your essay to make sure that your topic sentences focus on the thesis statement and that the other sentences support each paragraph topic sentence.

Is my position consistent?

As you re-read your essay and revise it, look carefully to make sure that you have convincingly and consistently argued for your position. As you revise, check to make sure that you accurately explored the issue and considered a wide range of views on the topic. This includes identifying at least one major objection and developing counter-arguments to address it. Be careful not to use loaded language. Check to make sure that your reasons are logical, well documented with factual evidence, and that they support your thesis. The following exercise can help you decide if your position is consistent.

Exercise

Use the following checklist to ensure that you have consistently supported your position.

_____ **1.** After reading the essay, do I still believe in my position? Explain.

_____ **2.** Do I have three compelling reasons that consistently support my position? Underline them in your essay.

_____ **3.** Have I given an honest accounting of views on the issue?

_____ **4.** Do I accurately, logically, and honestly counter a main objection? Circle that part.

_____ **5.** Have I included ideas that do not relate to the main issue? If so, delete them.

Revise

Check your essay. **Revise to make sure that your position is consistent.**

Writer supports the thesis with relevant evidence.

like food stamps are enough to ease the hunger problem.
Some people think that government programs ~~help.~~
applying for government help can take time
However, not all people qualify for government programs.
Hungry people need to be fed when they are hungry, ~~and food banks do just that~~. Also, even with government programs, the hunger problem has escalated.

TEKS 10.13B, 10.13C, 10.16A, 10.16B

Texas Traits

Revising for Organization

When you revise for *organization*, you check the structure of your essay. You make sure that the beginning, middle, and ending parts form a meaningful whole. Your paragraphs should be connected in a logical way, and the reasons you have given to support your position should be arranged by order of importance. Check to make sure that you have used transitions, both words and phrases, to link paragraphs and sentences within each paragraph. Once again, keep in mind the audience, purpose, and context for your writing.

Is my essay unified?

Your essay is unified if all the parts work together. The introduction states your position and describes the issue. The middle paragraphs expand and explore the issue, provide evidence, and address objections. The conclusion and effective transitions tie the essay together. The following checklist will help you evaluate the unity in your essay.

_____ **1.** Does my first paragraph clearly state my position statement?

_____ **2.** Does the topic sentence of each middle paragraph give a key reason to support my position?

_____ **3.** Do the sentences in each paragraph support my position statement?

_____ **4.** Does my conclusion tie the essay together and sum up my position?

Exercise

Rewrite the paragraph below, using transitions to tie the ideas together. Be sure to choose your transition words carefully.

In rush hour, more than 4,000 cars travel down Elm Street. Some people say Elm Street should be closed. Others say it should be widened. The Elm Street Bridge could be widened so that additional lanes can be added. The bridge is only one lane wide with stoplights at either end. Last Thursday, a huge traffic jam on the Elm Street Bridge tied up traffic for four hours. Traffic rolls over the bridge very slowly.

Revise

Check for unity. **Revise your essay using the checklist above. Also check your essay for word choice that leads to unity. Make sure that you have used effective transitions to link ideas.**

TEKS 10.13C, 10.16D, 10.16E

Do I present reasons in the best order?

As you revise for organization, it is important to think about the relative value of the ideas, facts, and data you have included in your essay. As you conducted the research for your essay, you probably noted which were the major arguments in support of your position and which were the major objections against your position. The arguments in your essay should be listed in order of importance. You can check for the order of importance by using the following checklist.

_____ **1.** Does the topic sentence of my first middle paragraph address the least or most important supporting reason? Revise as needed.

_____ **2.** Does the topic sentence of my second middle paragraph address the next most or least or most important reason?

_____ **3.** Have I identified and addressed an objection with a logical counter-argument?

Revise

Check for organization **Make sure you have correctly structured your essay. Rearrange paragraphs that are out of order.**

Organization
A counter-argument is identified and addressed.

Ideas are logically arranged. Writer supports position.

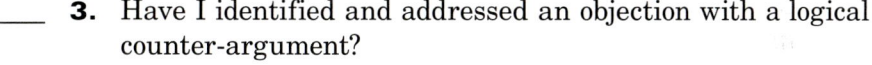

Some people argue that food banks are not necessary. They think that government programs such as food stamps are enough to ease the hunger problem. Not all people qualify. People need to be fed when they are hungry. A lot of money does go to government programs for feeding the hungry, and these programs are worthwhile. They actually work pretty well, but I don't think that they are a very good solution. Even with government programs, the hunger problem has escalated.

Texas Traits

Revising for Development of Ideas

When you revise for *development of ideas*, you make sure that you that you have clearly explained the issue. Further, you check to make sure that the arguments in support of your position are accurate, logical, and well defended. Be sure to check that evidence is relevant and that you have used precise, factual data. Your reasons should be logical, and you should have responded to at least one important objection. Remember your purpose: to convince your audience that your position is the best one. You may even compel your reader to take action and support you. Your word choice will be important as you convince your reader and convey your subtlety of meaning.

Have I effectively explained the issue?

You have effectively explained the issue if the reader understands its importance. Make sure to use revealing facts and precise details in your explanation.

- **Use facts and statistics to make sure the problem is clear and show its significance.**

  In Texas alone, volunteers gave over 200,000 hours of time to food banks.

- **Explain how the problem affects people.**

  Children who are hungry have a harder time learning, and they may experience delays in physical development.

Exercise

Read the paragraph below. How would you revise it so that it more effectively explains the problem of soda consumption?

Increased consumption of soda is causing problems for students at our high school. More and more kids are drinking soda. Not many kids are drinking water, juice, or milk. While milk and juice have important nutrients, soda does not. According to our school nurse, that is bad news for our health.

Revise

Make the issue clear. Read your essay carefully. If necessary add facts and statistics that help explain the issue and persuade the reader.

Have I convincingly argued for my position?

You have convincingly argued for your position if you have included compelling, persuasive reasons and adequate support for your thesis. Check to make sure that you have included logical reasons, relevant evidence, and precise data to support the topic sentence of each paragraph. Precise data is information that is exact, correct, and can be proved using reliable sources.

Use the following checklist to help you decide how well you supported your position.

_____ **1.** Do I still believe in my position? Explain.

_____ **2.** Does the supporting evidence clearly support my position?

_____ **3.** Have I used precise data, as well as compelling and persuasive language, in my essay? Circle examples.

_____ **4.** Do I effectively counter objections with relevant evidence, precise data, and logical reasons? Underline your counter-arguments.

Revise

Check your essay. Answer the questions in the checklist. Continue to revise as needed. Make sure your language is persuasive.

Relevant evidence is supported with precise details.

A final persuasive sentence is added.

over twelve thousand / twelve

In Texas alone, ~~a lot of~~ volunteers serve meals to hungry men, women, and children. Food banks use money donations very efficiently too.

Daly City City food bank uses 90 cents of every dollar to buy food.

While it may be hard to get donations, most of the money goes to purchasing food.

After all, everyone deserves at least one good meal a day.

TEKS 10.13C, 10.16A
ELPS 1G

Texas Traits

Revising for Voice

When you revise for *voice*, remember your purpose for writing this essay. In order to convince people to support your position, you need to use an authoritative, reasonable voice. Because this is an argumentative essay, your voice and word choice should also be more formal. Using a more formal tone will help you sound more authoritative. Think about the way that you speak with a classmate or friend and the way that you speak with a respected adult. With a friend, you are likely to speak informally, using simple vocabulary or slang. If you are discussing a serious issue with an adult, you are more likely to use vocabulary that is formal. It is the same when you write.

Have I used an authoritative voice?

You have used an authoritative voice if you sound knowledgeable and focus on factual information in your essay. Your voice is not authoritative if you use weak, general statements. One way to improve your voice is to include plenty of specific, precise facts and relevant evidence in your essay. When you do this, you will have written with a more formal tone.

Less Authoritative Voice

When a supertanker spills oil, it damages the ocean. It damages beaches, too. The damage caused by an oil spill can last a long time. And it can cost a lot to clean up.

More Authoritative Voice

A supertanker accident can spill as much as 2 million barrels of oil into the ocean. Oil spills cause incredible damage. In 1989, the supertanker *Exxon Valdez* spilled 257,000 barrels of oil. The oil killed thousands of sea birds, hundreds of sea otters, and contaminated 1,300 miles of shoreline. Nine years later, much of that shoreline was still contaminated with oil. Exxon spent $2.1 billion on its cleanup efforts.

Revise

For more authority, add facts. Review your essay. Does your voice sound authoritative? If it doesn't, replace weak, general statements with reliable, specific facts. Use vocabulary that is suited to the topic and audience.

"When your writing is filled with details, it has a lot more impact."
—Ivan Levison

Do I treat my reader with respect?

You have treated your reader with respect if you don't use loaded, emotionally charged, or aggressive language. Using such language may make the reader feel as if he or she were being attacked. Inflammatory language does not serve your purpose for writing, nor does ridiculing people who oppose your position. Inflammatory language and ridicule are ways to lose an argument, not win it. Remember that your goal is to convince your reader. Therefore, treat your audience with respect.

When you revise your essay, look again to make sure that you have supported your position honestly and accurately and that you have considered a wide range of supporting and opposing arguments on the topic.

In the following paragraph, a writer uses an unreasonable, overly aggressive voice to propose a solution.

> **Some people think the Elm Street Bridge doesn't need to be widened to four lanes. They must have rocks in their heads. Get a clue! If the bridge isn't widened, people will continue to sit in traffic forever. Widening the bridge is the only solution, and anyone with any sense knows it.**

Grammar Exercise

Rewrite the paragraph above so that it sounds respectful and reasonable. Trade papers with a classmate. Discuss each other's changes.

Revise

Check your voice for respect. Review your essay, making sure that you don't sound too emotional, aggressive, or inflammatory. Revise as needed.

Voice
An aggressive sentence is deleted and an overemotional one is revised.

Some people argue that food banks are not necessary. They think that government programs such as food stamps are enough to ease the hunger problem. ~~That's completely ridiculous.~~ However, not all the people who need food qualify for government programs, and applying for government help ~~takes forever!~~ can take time.

Texas Traits

Revising Improving Your Writing

Revise

Check your revising. On a piece of paper, write the numbers 1 to 10. If you answer "yes" to a question, put a check mark next to that number. If not, continue to work on that part of your essay.

Revising Checklist

Focus and Coherence

_____ **1.** Do I clearly focus on one significant issue?

_____ **2.** Do I use solid reasons and verifiable evidence to support my position?

_____ **3.** Do my ideas consistently support my position?

Organization

_____ **4.** Have I structured my arguments in order of importance?

_____ **5.** Does my essay have a sense of unity, with an introduction, a middle, and an effective conclusion?

Development of Ideas

_____ **6.** Have I adequately explained the issue?

_____ **7.** Have I presented my argument with convincing details and persuasive language?

Voice

_____ **8.** Do I use an authoritative voice?

_____ **9.** Do I treat the reader with respect?

_____ **10.** Have I avoided overly emotional or inflammatory language?

Revise

Make a clean copy. When you are finished revising, make a clean copy of your essay to edit for conventions.

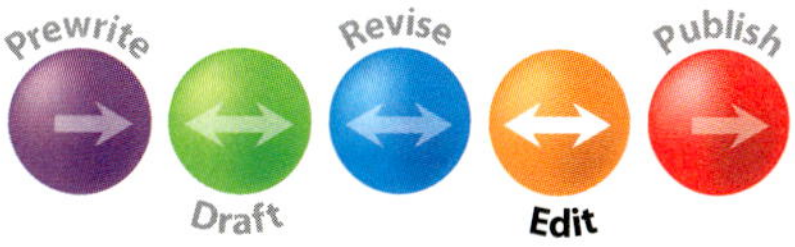

Editing

Go Online!

When you have finished revising your argumentative essay, it is time to edit for conventions: grammar, sentence structure, capitalization, punctuation, and spelling.

Keys to Effective Editing

1. Use a dictionary, a thesaurus, and the "Proofreader's Guide" in the back of this book to check your writing.
2. Check your writing for errors in grammar, sentence structure, capitalization, punctuation, and spelling.
3. Have a classmate edit your writing. You are too close to your writing to catch everything.
4. If you are using a computer, edit your essay on a printed copy and then key in the changes. Otherwise, write a new, final handwritten copy that includes the changes.
5. Use the editing and proofreading marks inside the back cover of this book.

TEKS 10.13D, 10.17B
ELPS 4C, 5E

Texas Traits

Editing for Conventions

Grammar

Editing for *conventions* means checking grammar, sentence structure, capitalization, punctuation, and spelling. Part of the grammar edit means looking carefully at the verb forms you have used.

How and when do I use the subjunctive mood?

The mood of a verb indicates the attitude with which a statement is made. The indicative mood is used to state facts or to ask questions. The subjunctive mood is used to express a condition that is not necessarily a fact. It may be used to express doubts, wishes, or possibilities.

The subjunctive mood is often used in persuasive writing when possibilities and wishes are presented in the form of conditional statements. Conditional statements often begin with *if* clauses. (See pages 752–753 for more information.)

Indicative Mood

I finished my essay. Would you bring in the mail?
(Indicative mood is used for statements of fact and for questions.)

Subjunctive Mood

If I were to volunteer at a food pantry, what would I do?
(The subjunctive mood is used in conditional statements introduced with an *if* clause.)

I wish that I were going to the beach. Everyone would be surprised if our team were to win the game on Friday.
(The subjunctive mood is used to express wishes and possibilities.)

Grammar Exercise

Rewrite the following sentences. Add a conditional *if* clause to express doubts, wishes, or possibilities. Use the subjunctive mood in the clause.

1. I want to go to the movies tonight.
2. We could organize a food drive at school.
3. Volunteers should plan to work 10 hours a week.

Edit

Check for subjunctive mood. Read your essay carefully. Look for proper use of indicative and subjunctive mood. Correct any verb forms that are incorrect.

Have I used verbals correctly?

A verbal is a word that is derived from a verb, but it acts as another part of speech. There are three different types of verbals. Often they make up part of a verbal phrase.

Gerunds

A *gerund* is a verb form that ends in *ing* and is used as a noun.

Walking provides good exercise. Reading is my favorite pastime.

Infinitives

An *infinitive* is a verb form that is usually introduced by the word *to*. Infinitives may be used as nouns, adjectives, or adverbs.

Most people find it fun to cook. To cook a meal for twelve people, however, can be difficult. The desire to cook often comes from enjoying good food.

Participles

A *participle* is a verb form that ends in *ing* or *ed* that acts as an adjective.

The men eating lunch must be very hungry. The tired workers went home.

Grammar Exercise

Rewrite these sentences using gerunds, infinitives, and participles.

1. After they leave the factory, the pollutants flow into the river.
2. The dogs were tired, and they stopped running.
3. The two men were very tired. They had waited at the airport for four hours.
4. The cleanup of the site was costly. It had to be done so that a park could be built.

Edit

Check for verbals. **Make sure that you have included verbals in your essay and used them properly.**

Learning Language

Remember that nouns are names of people, places, or things. Gerunds are also nouns, but they convey actions, like swimming, watching, or playing. Work with a partner to tell about things you like and dislike using gerunds. Then use infinitives to explain how to do chores or everyday activities.

TEKS 10.13B, 10.13C, 10.17C
ELPS 4C, 5E, 5F

Sentence Structure

When you edit for *sentence fluency*, you check to see that you have properly used different kinds of sentences and that they flow smoothly. As you edit, you want to make sure, too, that you have varied your sentence beginnings, and that your sentences spark the reader's interest in your position. (See pages 772–774 for more information about sentence types.)

Have I used a variety of sentence types effectively?

You have used a variety of sentence types effectively if they help you develop your argument. Here are four different types of sentences that you can use. A declarative sentence makes a statement. The situation is worsening. An interrogative sentence asks a question. What does it feel like to be hungry? An imperative sentence makes a command. Imagine that you are hungry. An exclamatory sentence communicates strong emotion or surprise. It is time for us to help out!

Grammar Exercise

Identify each kind of sentence in the following paragraph. Explain how the sentence variety makes the paragraph more effective.

Supporting the clean-water initiative will help solve the spread of cholera. What is cholera? It is an intestinal disease that is caused by bacteria in the water. How dangerous is it? If left untreated, cholera is deadly. But you can help, so take action! Support the clean-water initiative. For people in many parts of the world, clean water makes the difference between life and death.

Edit

Review your sentences. Read your essay carefully. Check to make sure that you have used differerent kinds of sentences correctly and that your sentence starters engage the reader's interest.

Mechanics: Punctuation

When you edit for *mechanics*, you check to make sure that you have followed the correct rules for capitalization and punctuation. You don't want mechanical errors to confuse or distract your readers.

Have I correctly punctuated parenthetical elements?

Parenthetical elements explain or clarify particular words or phrases. Dashes are one way to set off parenthetical material in your writing. Dashes serve other purposes as well. They can indicate a sudden break or change in a sentence. They can indicate interrupted speech. They can be used to emphasize a word, a series, a phrase, or a clause, and they can be used to set off an introductory series or list of items. (See pages **676–677** for more information.)

Grammar Exercise

Read the following sentences. Rewrite them so that the parenthetical material is correctly set off using dashes.

1. The members of the school board all of them agreed to the new schedule.
2. The text plus all of the supplementary material can be purchased at the bookstore.
3. A new bike and a helmet all that I needed to enjoy the day was waiting for me.
4. I was amazed when I saw the guitar the one that I had wanted for so long in my bedroom.
5. After years of hard work, my sister finally reached her goal, to go to college in Europe.

Edit

Check for dashes. Read your essay carefully. Make sure that you have used dashes correctly to set off parenthetical information, emphasize a word, or to set off an introductory series.

TEKS 10.13C, 10.13D, 10.17B, 10.18A, 10.18B(ii), 10.18B(iii), 10.19
ELPS 5C–5F

Texas Traits

Editing Checking for Conventions

Edit

Check your editing. This checklist will help you edit your essay for conventions: grammar, sentence structure, capitalization, punctuation, and spelling. On a piece of paper, write the numbers 1 to 9. If you can answer "yes," put a check after that number. If you can't, continue to edit.

Editing Checklist

Conventions

GRAMMAR

_____ **1.** Do I use the subjunctive mood correctly? *(I wish I were* not *I wish I was)*

_____ **2.** Do I use gerunds, infinitives, and participles correctly?

SENTENCE STRUCTURE

_____ **3.** Do I use a variety of sentence types for their appropriate purposes?

MECHANICS (Capitalization and Punctuation)

_____ **4.** Do I start all my sentences with capital letters?

_____ **5.** Do I capitalize all proper nouns and adjectives?

_____ **6.** Do I use end punctuation after all my sentences?

_____ **7.** Do I use dashes to set off parenthetical material?

SPELLING

_____ **8.** Have I spelled all words correctly?

_____ **9.** Have I consulted a dictionary to determine or check the spellings of words my spell-checker may have missed?

Creating a Title

After your editing is complete, add a title that describes your essay and catches your reader's attention. Here are several ways to approach this task.

- Summarize the issue: **Food Banks Ease Hunger Pangs**
- Call to action: **Back Food Banks and Reduce Hunger**
- Hook the reader: **Help Put an End to Hunger**

Go Online!

Prewrite Draft Revise Edit Publish

Publishing

Sharing Your Essay

After writing, revising, and editing your essay, make a neat final draft. Ask your teacher or your classmates for feedback and make final improvements. When that is done, it's time to share your essay. You can present your essay in a debate, publish it in a newspaper, or send it to an official who can help.

Publish

Format your final copy. To format a handwritten essay, use the guidelines below or follow your teacher's instructions. (If you are using a computer, see pages 72–74.) Make a clean copy and carefully proofread it.

Focusing on Presentation

- Write neatly using blue or black ink.
- Write your name in the upper left corner of page 1.
- Skip a line and center your title; skip another line and start your essay.
- Indent every paragraph and leave a one-inch margin on all four sides.
- Write your last name and the page number in the upper right corner of every page after page 1.

Persuasive

Stage a Debate

Invite a group of friends or family members who have differing viewpoints on the issue. Invite some people who have not yet formed an opinion to come and listen. Present and defend your idea. Then allow others to present and defend their ideas. Finally, ask the audience to form an opinion, based on the debate.

Contact an Official

Identify an official who has authority to take action on your issue. Send your essay to that person along with a cover letter stating your position and asking for help. Remember to use a respectful tone in your letter, and to encourage the official to support your position.

Publish a Letter

Reformat your essay as a letter to the editor of a local newspaper. Make sure your letter conforms to the newspaper's submission guidelines. Then e-mail your letter or send it through the postal service.

Evaluating an Argumentative Essay

To learn how to evaluate an argumentative essay, you will use the holistic scoring guide on pages **60–61** and the essays that follow. These essays are examples of writing for each score on the scoring guide (1–4).

Notice that the first essay received a score of 4. Read the description for a score of 4 on pages **60–61.** Then read the narrative. Use the same steps to study the other examples. As you read, concentrate on the overall quality of the writing in each example.

Writing that fits a score of 4 is highly effective.

4

Put a Stop to Sweatshops

The **beginning** introduces the writer's focus (underlined). Rhetorical question engages reader.

Why do people spend a lot of time choosing the clothes they wear, but little time worrying about where those clothes are manufactured? If people knew, they would be shocked. Many clothes are manufactured in sweatshops, which are factories where the owners treat workers unfairly. Sweatshops pay extremely low wages and demand long hours in conditions that are often unsafe. Workers who complain can be and have been fired (Harris 95). <u>However, it is possible to put a stop to sweatshops by boycotting the clothing made in them</u>.

Each **middle** paragraph presents relevant evidence and precise details about the experience. Writer shows knowledge of topic.

Sweatshops are found around the world. Owners of sweatshops often treat workers badly. At one sweatshop, workers made sneakers for 16 cents an hour, and they were required to work more than 70 hours a week. Workers were fired if they refused to work extra hours even though they were never paid for them. At another factory, workers were paid 1.3 cents for every baseball cap they sewed. By any standard, this is outrageous! American manufacturers, though, buy goods from these factories because the labor is so cheap. They can sell these products at low prices and still make a good profit.

Many people believe that clothes that say "Made in the USA" were not made in a sweatshop. Unfortunately, that is not true. If a garment is made in a U.S. territory like Guam, the label will says "Made in the USA," even though the workers there may work for low wages and are not protected by U.S. labor laws.

The **middle** paragraphs continue to build on and support the thesis.

Boycotting sweatshop clothes—as well as any stores that sell them—will help eliminate sweatshops. Boycotts are effective because they directly affect the profits of clothing manufacturers and retailers. If people refuse to buy clothing made in sweatshops, the manufacturers will in fact lose money. (Anderson 45). It is easy to write to or call the headquarters of your favorite stores, and ask if all the workers who make their garments are treated fairly. If not, tell the stores that you and your friends will no longer buy their products. Do some Web research. A number of organizations are dedicated to opposing sweatshops, and they offer online resources.

Transitions link paragraphs and sentences within paragraphs.

Boycotting sweatshops will also help reward clothing manufacturers and retailers who sell "sweat-free" apparel. Sweat free means that the people who make the garments are paid a fair wage and are treated well. Many universities and colleges now will only sell apparel with their logos if the items come from sweat-free factories. Take a look on the Internet to find retailers and clothing manufacturers who sell sweat-free clothes ("Shop for Sweat Free" 28) Give them your business and your purchases will send a clear message: It pays to treat workers fairly.

Boycotting stores that sell sweatshop goods, and asking others to do the same, focuses media attention on the issue. People need to know that sweatshops abuse their workers. Publicity and coverage in the media that will help spread the word.

An objection is identified and addressed.

Some people insist that sweatshops provide necessary jobs to workers and help them build better lives. They argue that without sweatshops, these workers wouldn't have jobs at all. We all wish that this were true, but it isn't. Instead, companies make huge profits, while workers suffer. Companies could offer higher pay, safer working conditions, and still make a profit.

Effective **conclusion** restates position.

Taking action against sweatshops isn't difficult, and it can make a big difference. Boycott clothing made in sweatshops and, the next time you shop, choose sweat-free clothing and stores that sell it. Help clothing workers everywhere lead better lives.

Writing that fits a score of 3 is generally effective.

3

The **beginning** paragraph clearly states the writer's position. Introducing the controlling idea with a story engages reader's interest.

Each **middle** paragraph supports the position with precise and relevant evidence. Minor errors in conventions do not detract.

Better transitions are needed. Paragraph topic sentences are not always clear.

A Priceless Donation

In 1994, the Green family was traveling in Italy when a terrible tragedy struck. During a robbery, their seven year old son Nicholas was killed. Reg and Maggie Green were grieving, but they decided to donate his organs to Italians, even though they were American. Their act of kindness had unexpected positive effects.

The family and Nicholas were honored all over Italy for their donation. Parks, schools, and streets and even a hospital was named after Nicholas. The president and prime minister thanked the family in person. More important, it helped seven people and their families. Two were saved from blindness and others were on the brink of death. It also made Italians aware of how important it was to donate organs. Since Nicholas's death, organ donations in Italy have quadrupled from 4.2 per million people to 18 per million people. This doesn't seem like a lot, but it has saved the lives of thousands of people. (Greenwood 56)

If more people was to donate organs, I wonder how many sick people would be saved. People use transplanted corneas to see again. People who are on the brink of death can be saved by transplanted organs like hearts and livers and kidneys. Successful transplants have become pretty common, but there are not enough people who will donate organs. So people who are sick have to wait and wait, and sometimes they die while they wait.

In the United States, there are over 100,000 people waiting for organ donations and over a million waiting for donated tissues or corneas. In 2008, 28,000 people—people who might have died without help—had organ transplants. More than a million tissue transplants are performed each year for treating blindness, injuries, and heart surgery. (DLA)

Despite all the success of transplants, though, there are still not enough Americans signing up to donate organs. Many donations come from people who die suddenly and hadn't thought about donating. When that happens, family members may not want to donate. The family may not think of helping other people

Research helps writer provide precise details and creates an authoritative voice.

when they were mourning. They may also have religious reasons for not donating. (Greenwood 61)

That's why health organizations are trying to get people who want to donate to sign up at a state donor registry. Most people signed up when they get a driver's license through their Department of Motor Vehicles. It's easy to do. At the end of 2008, over 38 percent of licensed drivers in the United States were enrolled in state donor registries, which is almost 80 million people. (DLA)

In a survey 51 percent of Americans said they wanted to donate organs or tissues. If a person enrolled in a donor registry program, they could make sure that their wish to donate was honored. I know that I would donate if I was asked. But why then are only 38 percent of people with driver's licenses or state ID enrolled in the program? What keeps people from enrolling?

An objection is identified and addressed. Writer does not use subjunctive mood correctly.

Some of the problem is misinformation. Some people argue that their doctor won't try to save them if they know they want to be a donor. Others think there's a black illegal market in the United States where people can buy and sell organs. And still other people think they're too old or not healthy enough to become donors. None of those rumors are true. Anyone can donate, and donors are safe if that's what they choose.

A single person can donate tissue to help up to fifty people and organs to three people. People might get their sight back or even be able to do simple things without struggling. The lives of children and mothers and fathers could be saved so that families don't have to live in sadness.

Conclusion ties essay together.

Even though the Greens can't get Nicholas back, they have honored his memory by unselfishly donating his organs. They turned a tragedy into something that is beautiful, and it should be a lesson for all of us. Anyone who can should check "Yes" to donate when they get their driver's license.

Writing that fits a score of 2 is somewhat effective.

2

The **beginning** gives an idea of the thesis. Personal story adds interest.

Each **middle** paragraph connects somewhat to the position statement, but organization is lacking. Some evidence and general details are provided, but ideas are not developed.

Errors in conventions lead to confusion.

Conclusion does not sum up the essay or restate the position.

BUY LOCALLY

My parents own a shoe store downtown and it's getting harder and harder for them to get business and stay in business, too. People in town really like the store, but my dad he thinks that even though they like the store they still go to big chain stores to buy their shoes. Other businesses downtown have the same problem. If people want to keep stores like ours open then they need to start buying from us and from other local stores.

There are alot of reason to buy locally. First, "for every $100 spent at a locally owned business, $45 stays in the local economy, creating jobs and expanding the city's tax base. For every $100 spent at a national chain or franchise store, only $14 remains in the community." (Portland) Local businesses put money back in the comunity, like giving to local charities. Our store supports a school baseball team.

My town has a really nice downtown with alot of independant stores. Thats what makes the downtown nice because we give people a lot of choices and people like shopping in that area. "Independent businesses, choosing products based on what their local customers need and desire, not a national sales plan, guarantees a more diverse range of product and service choices." (I Buy Austin)

Alot of people think that it cost way lots more to buy stuff in a small store instead of in a big chain. That just isn't true. To stay in business, small stores have to have competative prices. You also get better service at our small stores. The people who work at the stores give more personal service and know the merchendise plus they know the loyal customers and our customers know us so Its a much more pleasant place to shop.

If shoppers just would start shopping in our small stores instead of just window shopping and then going somewhere else to buy their things it could make a big difference. If everyone shifted only 10% of their shopping from chain stores to local stores, they would make a big difference to their local economy.

Writing that fits a score of 1 is not effective.

1

Thesis is vague, and is not supported or developed.

Essay lacks organization, evidence, and details. Errors in conventions make it difficult to understand. Writer never establishes clear voice.

Essay lacks **conclusion**.

Give Back to the Community

Nobody can graduate from highschool these days unless you have community service credit. I think this is a good thing. Many teenagers don't think of anyone but themselves. Community service makes you think of other peoples.

In my town most kids just want to have fun and don't think if they themselves can do anything for anyone else. Thats why its good that schools are going to make them do community service. At our school we have to do 20 hours in order to gradate. I did my service at a senior citisens center and it was very inspiring work but hard sometimes.

At the center I would help the activities director set up activities and then I would help any of the seniors that had trouble with the activity because a lot of them couldn't here well or they had trubble keeping up or following along. If any of them was having trouble I would help because it was fun sometimes and the people were nice to me and happy to see me so it made me feel good.

My other jobs at the center weren't always so good. Sometimes I had to help clean up or help dress someone and I didn't like that so much. But it was good experience otherwise I might not of learned as much as I did.

The job at the senior center was good experence for other jobs too. It gave me an idea of what I'm good at and what I'm not. I found out I'm good with people and make them happy and also it will also look good when I apply for other jobs or if I apply for college.

Community service is good for highschool students. It makes them think about other people and its good experience for other jobs. They might even like what they do and feel good about helping others.

Evaluating and Reflecting on Your Writing

After you finish your argumentative essay, take some time to reflect on your essay and your writing experience. On your own paper, complete each of the sentences below. To score your writing, refer to the holistic scoring guide on pages 60–61 and the examples you just read. Evaluating and reflecting on your writing will reinforce what you learned from your writing experience and help you apply that knowledge to future assignments.

My Argumentative Essay

1. The paragraphs that best focus on my thesis statement are . . .
2. The paragraphs that need better development are . . .
3. My introduction and conclusion are effective because . . .
4. I should have sounded more knowledgeable and authoritative in paragraphs . . .
5. Word choice, or figurative language, that would have made me sound more confident is needed in . . .
6. One question I still have about writing a persuasive essay is . . .

Persuasive Writing

Writing an Editorial

In six weeks, your city will vote on whether or not to change the zoning regulations for schools. The new zoning would force you to go to a different high school. Do you think you could convince people to vote "no" to the zoning change? You could try—in an editorial for your city's newspaper. An editorial is a persuasive essay that presents your opinion about an important, timely topic and often includes a call for action.

In this chapter, you'll read a sample editorial about the writer's desire to see Valentine's Day celebrated differently at her school. Then you'll write your own editorial to express your opinion about a recent issue or event. Choose a topic that you feel strongly about. Your confidence and conviction will prompt the reader to agree with your point of view.

Writing Guidelines

Subject: Opinion about a school-related issue
Purpose: To present an opinion about a timely and important topic
Form: Editorial
Audience: Classmates

"Sentences are sharp nails, which force truth upon our memories."

—Denis Diderot

TEKS 10.13B, 10.15A(i), 10.15A(iii), 10.15A(iv), 10.16A, 10.16D, 10.16E

Editorial

In the following editorial, Patricia presents her opinion that Valentine's Day should be celebrated differently at her school. Her editorial was printed in the school's February newsletter.

Beginning
The beginning introduces the topic and presents the opinion statement (underlined).

Middle
Each paragraph supports Patricia's opinion.

Let Love Rule

Valentine's Day. Does any other holiday tap into the deepest emotions, bitter or sweet? During the season of chocolates, roses, cards, and stuffed animals, someone always gets left out. Nowhere is the sting more humiliating and unnecessary than at school. <u>At Benchfield High, students should be more sensitive about how they celebrate Valentine's Day.</u>

The first taste of Valentine's Day comes as soon as children can scribble their friends' names. They stuff valentines into decorated shoe boxes. The rules are simple: Students give a valentine to everyone in class. Of course, a student can always add a carefully chosen candy heart, or save the biggest card of the bunch for that special someone. It's impossible to make life completely fair, but at least teachers and parents try to make this situation as fair as possible.

Middle school students have the carnation fund-raiser: white for "friends," pink for "like," and red for "love." The rule, "all or none," no longer applies. Girls with armfuls of floral trophies giggle with valentine glee. Meanwhile, others can only hope that their lack of colorful carnations will just help them fade into the background.

In high school, the carnation parade is bigger than ever, but carnations alone just don't cut it. Now, on Valentine's Day, the pressure is on to do something extraordinary.

During class, the names of the lucky few are called over the intercom. They go to the office to pick up towering arrangements of flowers and balloons. Even if an individual can ignore these huge displays, they probably find themselves wondering, "Will someone special remember me? Will I be the only one without a valentine?" Talk about distracting, and depressing.

TEKS 10.13B, 10.15A(i), 10.15A(iii), 10.15A(iv), 10.16A, 10.16C–10.16E
ELPS 4K

Patricia considers an opposing viewpoint and provides a solution.

A student's love/hate relationship with Valentine's Day can easily change depending on whether or not he or she has a sweetie. Certainly students should show their special someone that they care. But when at school, can't students celebrate Valentine's Day in a way that doesn't flaunt popularity and make others feel excluded?

Introducing a Valentine's Day fund-raiser might be the answer. Instead of carnations, students could buy "Hearts of Hope." Each dollar gets a buyer a paper heart to post on the wall. Each wall represents a different charity. On Valentine's Day, the money would be split between the charities based on the number of hearts on each wall. The money could provide toys for needy children, help for the senior citizen center, and so on. Maybe people can't make life fair, but they can make it a little better?

Ending
The ending leaves the reader with strong, final thoughts.

At its heart, Valentine's Day is about love; it's not a popularity contest. It's time for Benchfield High to put popularity on the bench and let love rule.

Texas Traits

Respond to the reading. Answer the following questions.

Focus and Coherence (1) What is the thesis statement? (2) How does the conclusion tie the essay together? **Organization** (3) How does Patricia organize the middle part of her editorial? **Development of Ideas** (4) What is the main point of Patricia's editorial? (5) How does she inspire the reader to take action? **Voice** (6) What words or phrases convey her feelings about the topic? Name three.

Literature Connection: You might enjoy reading another editorial, "Abolishing the Penny Makes Good Sense," by Alan S. Blinder.

TEKS 10.13A, 10.15A(iii), 10.15A(v), 10.16B

Prewriting Planning Your Writing

The purpose of your editorial is to express your opinion about a timely and important topic. To find a topic for her editorial, Patricia completed a sentence starter about several important issues at her school. After looking over her possible topics, she realized she didn't have enough information about some of the issues, and another matter wasn't up for vote for six months. She chose the Valentine's Day issue, which seemed to be perfect for the school paper.

Sentence Starter

Students at my school are saying that . . .

- the online driver's ed course is a big help.
- Valentine's Day is a popularity contest.*
- we might lose open-campus lunch if students keep skipping class.
- bathroom graffiti is becoming a problem.
- the possible school zoning change for next year is unfair.

Prewrite

Choose your topic. Complete the sentence starter above in three or four different ways. Put an asterisk (*) next to the topic that you would like to write about. Remember that you need a strong opinion in order to present a convincing editorial.

Texas Traits

Focus on the Texas Traits

Development of Ideas An editorial is a form of persuasive writing. An effective persuasive essay includes specific examples that support your opinion. You should consider the whole range of arguments about your position. Your argument will also be more convincing if you do the following:

- **Address an opposing point of view.** Respectfully, honestly, and accurately address and counter objections.
  While it's true that plastic bags are convenient for shoppers, they are more than inconvenient for the environment.
- **Make a final call to action.** Encourage readers to agree with your opinion and take appropriate action.
  Urge friends and family to reuse more durable kinds of shopping bags.

Gathering and Organizing Reasons and Evidence

After choosing your topic, you must gather supporting details to convince your audience. Patricia created a quick list of convincing supporting details. She knew that she would have to build a foundation for her thesis statement in order to convince other students. As you begin to think about your topic, develop a quick list like Patricia's, shown here.

Quick List

- People send flowers and gifts to school.
- In grade school, everyone got a valentine.
- We should do a fund-raiser for a charity.

Next, Patricia arranged her details in order. She knew that in order to convince her audience to support her, she would have to include relevant evidence in her editorial. As you consider ways to support your editorial, create a details chart that you can refer to. Remember your audience, purpose, and context.

Details Chart

early years in school	– stuffed valentines in boxes, all students get cards
middle school	– held carnation fund-raiser
	– popularity contest made some feel left out
high school	– continue carnations
	– give "special someones" bouquets or balloons
other viewpoint	– people with my opinion are just jealous
possible solution	– find another way to celebrate

An editorial needs a strong opinion statement on a timely, important topic.

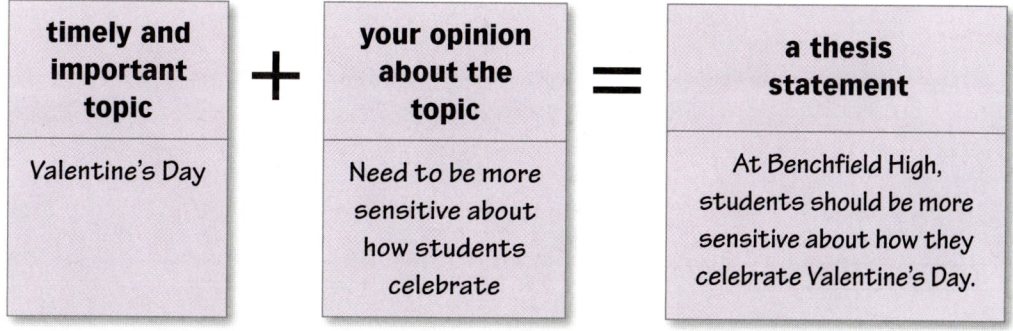

timely and important topic	+	**your opinion about the topic**	=	**a thesis statement**
Valentine's Day		Need to be more sensitive about how students celebrate		At Benchfield High, students should be more sensitive about how they celebrate Valentine's Day.

Prewrite

Gather ideas and build a logical foundation. Using the list and chart above, gather logical and precise, relevant evidence for your position.

TEKS 10.13A, 10.15A(iii), 10.15A(v), 10.16(vi), 10.16A, 10.16B

Prewriting Planning Your Writing

Writing an Opinion Statement

When you write your opinion statement for an editorial, it is critical to keep in mind your audience. For Patricia, the audience was students and administrators at the high school. If you are preparing an editorial for the local newspaper, your audience will be different. Therefore, your voice and the vocabulary that you use should be more formal. The following graphic organizer will help you develop a thesis statement. Also refer to the planning that you did on the previous page.

Review Your Opinion Statement and Your Details Chart

After you have written your opinion statement, think about it carefully. Then look at your details chart to make sure that it includes logical reasons, relevant evidence, and precise details that you can use to support your opinion.

- Does your opinion statement express a single strong opinion?
- Does it accurately express your viewpoint?
- Can you support it sufficiently with relevant evidence and precise details?
- Can you identify a strong objection and counter it with a logical argument?

Prewrite

Write your opinion statement. Use your list and chart to write a strong statement that will engage your reader and that you can support throughout your editorial.

Drafting Creating Your First Draft

The following tips will help you write your editorial. Also refer to the planning that you did on the previous pages.

Writing Your Beginning Paragraph

The beginning paragraph should introduce the topic in an interesting way and present your opinion statement. Here are strategies for capturing your reader's attention.

- Present a question or an interesting detail about the topic. *Does any other holiday tap into the deepest emotions, bitter or sweet?*
- Explain why the topic is important. *During the season of chocolates, roses, cards, and stuffed animals, someone always gets left out.*
- Share a quotation. *"To love and be loved is to feel the sun from both sides."*

Writing Your Middle Paragraphs

The middle paragraphs should build your argument in a logical way, explain the opposing point of view, and offer a possible solution.

- Organize your points in a logical way with relevant examples, precise details, and illustrations. Consider the relative value of the data, facts, and ideas that you include.
- Avoid attacking others or preaching.
- Be brief and direct.
- Offer a reasonable solution.

Writing Your Ending Paragraph

The ending paragraph should sum up the argument in a strong, convincing way. Use the tips below to create a powerful ending.

- Summarize your opinion. *At its heart, Valentine's Day is about love.*
- Put your spin on the opposing viewpoint. *It is not a popularity contest.*
- Create a memorable, positive closing statement. *It's time for Benchfield High to put popularity on the bench and let love rule.*

Draft

Write your first draft. Use your own prewriting work and the tips above to develop your editorial.

Drafting Creating Your First Draft

Convincing Your Audience

There are many ways you can appeal to your audience, make a strong case for your position, and convince your readers to support your position.

- **Emotional appeals try to create strong feeling in the reader.**

When you use an emotional appeal, you use words and phrases that evoke either positive or negative emotions. Consider adding descriptions, analogies, and illustrations that have emotional appeal in your editorial.

- **A testimonial is a kind of appeal in which famous people endorse a product or a cause.**

The positive qualities of the famous person are transferred to the product or the cause. If you add quotations to your editorial, think about them as possible testimonials.

- **The bandwagon technique persuades by convincing the reader that everyone else holds the opinion.**

The bandwagon technique invites readers to "join the winning team." It reinforces people's natural desire to be accepted and admired. Consider using descriptions, case studies, and anecdotes with the bandwagon technique to support your position and help convince your reader.

- **Glittering generalities focus on highly valued concepts and beliefs, such as patriotism, peace, freedom, glory, and honor.**

The "glitter" and positive emotional appeal of these can cause readers to lower their guards and accept information inadequately supported by evidence. Try to avoid generalities that you cannot support with precise detail.

Addressing Objections

In an editorial, it is important to consider a range of views. Identify and address objections to your position. You are trying to convince people to support your position, so you need to identify, describe, and counter objections.

- **Talk to teachers, friends, and family about your position. Listen to what they have to say. Make a list of objections.**
- **Choose at least one objection that you can address. Use counter-arguments in your editorial.**

Choose an appeal to use. Think of appeals you can make to your audience. Jot down descriptions, anecdotes, case studies, analogies, and illustrations you can use to support your position. Include them in your editorial.

Texas Traits

Revising Improving Your Editorial

Once you complete your first draft, set it aside for a while. Then use the guidelines below to revise your editorial.

Revising Checklist

Focus and Coherence

_____ **1.** Have I clearly stated my opinion?
_____ **2.** Have I supported and defended my opinion?

Organization

_____ **3.** Does my editorial have a strong introduction, middle, and conclusion?
_____ **4.** Have I organized my points in a logical way?

Development of Ideas?

_____ **5.** Do I support my position with logical reasons, relevant examples, and precise details?
_____ **6.** Do I address the other side of the argument?
_____ **7.** Have I provided a reasonable call to action?
_____ **8.** Have I included an appropriate range of appeals?

Voice

_____ **9.** Is my voice confident and convincing?
_____ **10.** Does my voice show my interest in the topic?

Revise

Revise your first draft. Use the checklist above as you revise your first draft. Ask a partner to read your editorial and make suggestions as well.

Creating a Title

- Ask a question: **Why Can't We Be Fair?**
- State the topic: **Celebrate Valentine's Day in a New Way**
- Call for action: **Let Love Rule**

TEKS 10.13C–10.13E, 10.17C, 10.18A, 10.18B(ii), 10.19
ELPS 5C–5E

Texas Traits

Editing Checking for Conventions

After you've revised your editorial, it's important to edit it. The following checklist can help you spot any errors in grammar, sentence structure, capitalization, punctuation, and spelling.

Editing Checklist

Conventions

GRAMMAR

_____ **1.** Do I use the correct forms of verbs (*I went* not *I gone*)?
_____ **2.** Do my subjects and verbs agree in number?
_____ **3.** Have I used the right words (*there, their, they're*)?

SENTENCE STRUCTURE

_____ **4.** Have I correctly used a variety of sentence structures?

MECHANICS (Capitalization and Punctuation)

_____ **5.** Do I capitalize the first word in each sentence?
_____ **6.** Do I capitalize all proper nouns and proper adjectives?
_____ **7.** Have I ended my sentences with the correct punctuation?
_____ **8.** Have I used commas correctly?
_____ **9.** Have I punctuated quotations correctly?

SPELLING

_____ **10.** Do I spell all my words correctly?
_____ **11.** Have I double-checked for spelling errors that my spell-checker might miss?

Edit

Edit your editorial. Use the checklist above to edit for conventions. Have a partner check your work, too. Then prepare a final copy and proofread it.

Publishing Sharing Your Editorial

Share your timely editorial with friends and family as soon as possible. If appropriate, consider submitting your editorial to your school or city newspaper, a magazine, or a Web page. Let your voice be heard.

Writing for Assessment

Responding to Persuasive Prompts

Developing a well-organized and convincing persuasive argument can take time. Sometimes, however, you don't have much time to convince people to agree with you. Let's say you're trying to get permission from your parents to spend Saturday night at a classmate's house, or you're trying to convince a friend to go to a concert with you. At times like these, you'll need to organize and present your argument quickly and effectively.

Responding to a persuasive prompt on a test presents a similar problem. Within a set time limit, you'll need to choose a position, structure your argument, and present it in a logical, effective manner. This chapter will show you how to use the writing process to create a clear, effective persuasive response in a timed situation.

Writing Guidelines

Subject: **Persuasive prompt**
Form: **Response essay**
Purpose: **To demonstrate competence**
Audience: **Instructor or test evaluator**

"Good writing is clear thinking made visible."
—Bill Wheeler

Prewriting Analyzing a Persuasive Prompt

In order to respond effectively to a persuasive prompt, you must analyze it carefully, using the following **STRAP questions** as a guide.

Subject: What topic should I write about?
Type: What form (essay, letter, editorial, article, report) of writing should I create?
Role: What position (student, son or daughter, friend, employee, citizen) should I assume as the writer?
Audience: Who (teacher, parents, classmates, employer, official) is the intended reader?
Purpose: What is the goal (persuade, respond, evaluate, tell, describe) of my writing?

Sample Analyzed Prompt

Subject
Type
Role
Audience
Purpose

You are a resident of Bradford. The town's recreation director has announced a plan to close the recreation center during the summer months because not many kids use it. Write a letter to the director arguing for or against this decision.

Try It!

Analyze these prompts by answering the STRAP questions. (Use your best judgment to form an answer for every question.)

1. Your state plans to double license fees for drivers under age 18. The money will be used to fund driver-education programs. Write an editorial for your student newspaper supporting or opposing this decision.
2. The city council is considering a proposal to reduce the number of summer jobs it provides for high school students each year. Write a letter to the editor supporting or opposing this decision.

Planning Your Response

Once you have answered the STRAP questions, you should quickly plan your persuasive response. The following graphic organizers can help you.

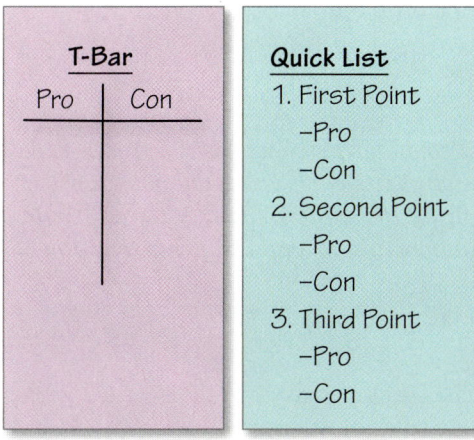

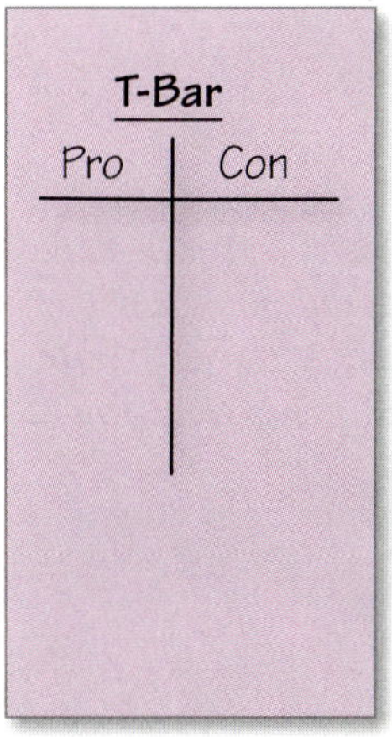

Quick List

1. First Point
   - –Pro
   - –Con
2. Second Point
   - –Pro
   - –Con
3. Third Point
   - –Pro
   - –Con

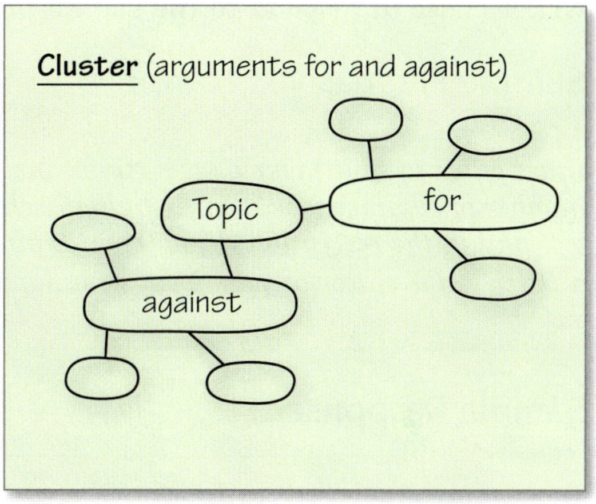

Considering Both Sides

The graphic organizers include space for both pro and con arguments because your response should consider both sides to see where the strongest position lies. In general, facts make the strongest argument, but a reasonable appeal to emotion can also provide strong support.

When planning a persuasive response, you should always present and respond to at least one main objection. By countering the objection, you will strengthen your own position. You will also demonstrate that you have considered both sides of an issue.

Prewrite

Use a graphic organizer to plan a response. Reread the persuasive prompts on page 246. Choose one prompt and use a graphic organizer to plan your response.

Tip

In a timed writing test, plan carefully. Allow yourself time for planning before you write and for revising and editing after you write. For example, if you have 45 minutes to respond to a prompt, use the first 5 minutes to analyze the prompt and plan your response, the last 5 minutes to revise and edit your response, and the time in between to write your response.

Drafting Responding to the Prompt

Once you have answered the STRAP questions and planned your response using a graphic organizer, you can begin writing. In this essay, the student writer chose to respond to the second prompt on page 246.

Sample Persuasive Prompt

In an effort to save money, your city council is considering a proposal to reduce the number of summer jobs it gives to high school students each year. The jobs involve working in the recreation department maintaining the grounds of city parks. Write a letter to the editor of your local newspaper supporting or opposing this decision.

Sample Response

Beginning
The beginning paragraph leads up to the opinion (underlined).

Dear Editor:

When school lets out every summer, the city's high school students go out to look for jobs. For many students, these jobs are important. Summer jobs allow students to make the extra money they need to save for college, maintain a car, or even save for next year's school clothes. But this summer, students in our city might have a harder time finding work. The city council has decided to cut summer jobs in the recreation department. However, for the good of the city and its young people, these jobs should be restored.

Middle
Each middle paragraph presents a logical reason that supports the opinion. Transitions connect ideas.

One reason to restore the jobs is that they may actually end up helping the city and the recreation department save money. Every summer, student workers mow lawns, clean up litter, and help keep parks neat and clean. But they often get paid much less than full-time workers. So hiring a student is like getting a full-time worker for less than full-time pay. And that's a great deal for the city.

Rhetorical devices add interest, and the appeal strengthens the position.

In addition, students who work for the city in the summer are not only earning money, but continuing their education. They learn important job skills such as getting to work on time, following directions, using tools and equipment safely, and working as a team. Learning these skills will help students succeed at college and in their careers. So isn't spending money on summer jobs for students an investment that will pay off for everyone in the future?

Finally, students who work during the summer are less likely to become bored. If kids are busy, they are less likely to get into trouble. Students who work for the city are also more likely to have respect for the city and its property. This respect means that young people will take better care of city facilities.

Objection The final middle paragraph addresses an objection.

Some people might argue that students hired by the city don't work hard enough for their money. Maybe some students don't work as hard as they could, but this is true for adults, too. The fact remains that most students will work hard and gladly contribute to making city parks better for everyone.

Ending The ending summarizes the argument and offers a final plea.

Reducing the number of student summer jobs will not only result in bored students, but it may end up costing the city more in the end. The small amount of money the city pays to hire students for the summer is an investment. And that investment pays off not only in better city parks, but also in students having the skills they need to succeed in the years beyond high school. So please encourage the city council to maintain this program. Everyone in town will benefit.

Sincerely,

Angel Hernandez

Draft

Respond to a persuasive prompt. Review the prompt you chose on page 246, your answers to the STRAP questions, and your graphic organizer. Then write a response to the prompt your teacher gives you. Be sure to plan your time carefully.

TEKS 10.13C, 10.13D, 10.17C, 10.18A, 10.18B(i), 10.19
ELPS 5C, 5D, 5F

Texas Traits

Revising Improving Your Response

Before you begin a writing test, find out whether you will be allowed to make changes in your writing. If this is allowed, always make your revisions and edits neatly. The STRAP questions below can guide your revisions.

Subject: Does my response focus on the topic of the prompt? Do my main points support the opinion stated in my first paragraph?
Type: Have I used the form requested in the prompt (essay, letter, editorial, article, report)?
Role: Have I assumed the position called for in the prompt?
Audience: Have I used appropriate language for my audience?
Purpose: Does my response accomplish the goal of the prompt?

Revise

Improve your work. Reread your response, asking yourself the STRAP questions above. Make necessary changes to your response.

Editing Checking Your Response

Read through your response one final time, checking for errors in grammar, sentence structure, capitalization, punctutation, and spelling.

Editing Checklist

Conventions

_____ **1.** Have I made sure my subjects and verbs agree?
_____ **2.** Have I used the right words *(their, they're, there)*?
_____ **3.** Have I correctly used a variety of sentence structures?
_____ **4.** Have I capitalized all proper nouns and the first word of each sentence?
_____ **5.** Have I used commas and end punctuation correctly?
_____ **6.** Have I spelled all words correctly?

Edit

Check your conventions. Read through your response one final time. In the time allowed, neatly correct any errors in conventions.

Persuasive Writing on Tests

Use this guide when preparing to respond to a persuasive writing prompt.

Before you write . . .

- **Analyze the prompt.**
  Use the STRAP questions. Remember that a persuasive prompt asks you to use facts and logical reasons to persuade or convince.
- **Plan your response.**
  Decide how much time you will spend on planning, writing, revising, and checking conventions. Use a graphic organizer to help you organize your response.

As you write . . .

- **Clearly state your thesis and support your argument.**
  Keep your main idea or opinion in mind as you write. All your reasons should clearly support your opinion.
- **Answer an objection.**
  Make your argument stronger by answering a likely objection.
- **Craft a powerful ending.**
  In the final paragraph, summarize your opinion and supporting reasons and make a final plea to the reader.

After you've written a first draft . . .

- **Revise and edit.**
  Use the STRAP questions to revise your response. Correct any errors in writing conventions.

Try It!

Write a response to the prompt below. Use a graphic organizer to gather details and plan. Then draft, revise, and edit your response.

- Your school lunchroom wants to buy produce from local farmers. It is more expensive but pesticide free. Write a letter to the food service director expressing your support or objection to the plan.

Learning Language

Work with a classmate to review this guide. Take turns reading each tip and then have your classmate retell the tip in his or her own words. If you have questions about any of the words or information, be sure to ask your teacher.

ELPS 1E, 2C, 3B, 3D, 3E, 4G

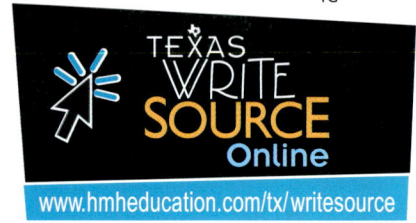

TEXAS WRITE SOURCE Online
www.hmheducation.com/tx/writesource

Interpretive Response

Writing Focus

Grammar Focus

Learning Language

Work with a partner. Read the definitions below and share your answers to the questions that follow.

1. Annotating a text means to add commentary or notes.
   Explain why annotating a text can help focus your reading.
2. Theme is the underlying message about life or human nature that a writer wants the reader to understand.
   What do you think might be a common theme in adventure stories?
3. When you interpret a piece of literature, you explain it.
   Why do you think there could be different interpretations of a literary work?
4. The idiom "hitting the bull's-eye" means getting something exactly right.
   What do you think "missing the bull's-eye" means?

Interpretive Response

Analyzing a Theme

When you tell someone what happens first, second, and third in a novel, you are describing its *plot*. When you talk about the author's message, you are explaining the *theme*. Although reading a compelling story is one of life's great pleasures, the real reward is the new perspective you gain by figuring out its theme. Quality novels are full of insights into life; they can help you think, act, dream, hope, learn, accept, appreciate, and on and on.

In order to understand the theme of a novel, you must examine the interplay between the characters, the plot, the setting, and the symbols. A novel may have one overall theme, or it may have several, each one a significant message and worthy of discussion.

Writing Guidelines

Subject: A novel
Purpose: To analyze a theme
Form: Literary analysis
Audience: Classmates

"Each novel is a kind of voyage of discovery."
—Margaret Lawrence

ELPS 3E

Writing Warm-Up: Subject vs. Theme

First, you need to understand the difference between the *subject* of the novel and its *theme*. The subject describes, in a general way, what the story is about; the theme is the message about life that the story suggests. Study the following chart to discern this difference.

Subject vs. Theme Chart

Novel	Subject	Theme
The Red Badge of Courage	This story is about an inexperienced young man who enlists to fight in the Civil War.	A young soldier learns that courage in war is defined by how a soldier reacts to fear, death, and failure.
A Christmas Carol	An old miserly man is hard-hearted and sees no meaning in Christmas, rejecting any involvement in the holiday.	A bitter old man learns that Christmas is a yearly reminder about the importance of love and the rewards of generosity and kindness toward one's fellow humans.
Fahrenheit 451	This is a story about a society in which free expression is limited by a strong central government.	Government can only control the minds of people who allow themselves to become uninformed and thoughtless.

Try It!

Work with a classmate to create a chart like the one above. Try to list at least three novels that you both have read. For each novel, write a subject statement (what the book is about) and a theme statement (the book's message about life). Remember, a novel may have more than one theme.

"He conceived persons with torn bodies to be peculiarly happy. He wished that he, too, had a wound, a red badge of courage."
—Stephen Crane, *The Red Badge of Courage*

Writing a Paragraph Analysis

You can analyze the theme of a novel in one paragraph by following these guidelines. Include rhetorical devices in your writing to engage your audience.

- In the **opening sentence**, include the title, author, and subject of the novel.
- In the **body sentences**, briefly describe the elements (character, plot, setting, symbols) of the novel and stylistic devices related to those elements that reveal the theme.
- In the **closing sentence**, state the theme of the novel.

Sample Paragraph Analysis

The **opening sentence** introduces the title, author, and subject of the novel.

The **body sentences** describe the elements and devices in the novel that reveal the theme.

The **closing sentence** states the theme (underlined).

Scrooge's Awakening

In Charles Dickens's *A Christmas Carol,* the main character, Ebenezer Scrooge, is a hard-hearted man who sees no meaning in Christmas. Flashbacks reveal that he has become more and more focused on his business, shunning contact with friends and relatives. Scrooge is a character living in a cocoon of selfishness, blinded to the world beyond his counting house. One Christmas Eve Scrooge follows his usual holiday pattern—refusing requests for charity, berating his employee for wanting to take Christmas Day off, and rejecting the holiday dinner invitation of his only nephew. But as darkness falls, the setting shifts to mysterious images of deceased acquaintances, lost youth, and a prophecy of Scrooge's own cold and lonely death. What he sees horrifies him and ironically brings him to his senses. Scrooge learns that Christmas is a yearly reminder about the importance of love and the rewards of generosity and kindness toward one's fellow humans.

Draft

Write a paragraph analysis. Using one of the novels you identified on the previous page, write a paragraph in which you briefly analyze a major theme of the novel. Include the three parts explained above.

TEKS 10.13A

Texas Traits Understanding Your Goal

Your goal in this chapter is to write an essay that analyzes a main theme in a novel. The chart below lists the key traits of a literary analysis essay, with specific suggestions for this assignment.

Traits of a Response to Literature

- **Focus and Coherence**
  Select a novel. Write a thesis statement that explains your interpretation of the novel's theme. Support your interpretation by using relevant, logical evidence. Write an effective conclusion.

- **Organization**
  Include a clear introduction, middle part, and a conclusion. Use transitions to effectively connect sentences and paragraphs.

- **Development of Ideas**
  Use specific details and quotations from the text to support the thesis statement. Make sure each paragraph has a topic sentence and that sentences in the paragraph relate directly to the topic.

- **Voice**
  Show your interest in the novel and a thorough knowledge of its subject and theme. Use literary terms that reveal your understanding of the novel. Choose precise, vivid words to share your ideas.

- **Conventions**
  Correct all grammar, sentence structure, capitalization, punctuation, and spelling errors.

Literature Connection. The essay "Author Brings Back Memories of Not So Long Ago" by Yvette Cabrera provides a literary analysis of the novel *The House on Mango Street* by Sandra Cisneros.

"No matter how disguised, in a certain sense, novel writing is autobiographical."

—Jan Slepian

Response Essay

Mary Shelley's novel, *Frankenstein,* tells about a scientist who creates a superhuman being. The model below analyzes two themes, revealing the more significant of the two in the thesis statement.

Beginning
The beginning names the author and novel and states the thesis (underlined).

Middle
The middle paragraphs trace the development of two themes. Writer analyzes author's use of stylistic devices. Ideas are structured in a sustained way.

Monsters Are Made, Not Born

Mary Shelley's *Frankenstein* traces the plight of Victor Frankenstein, a scientist tortured by the thought that he is responsible for bringing into the world a hideously deformed, vicious creature. While *Frankenstein* clearly cautions readers about the dangers of science left unchecked, there is also a very strong message about the effects of mistreating outcasts. As the story develops, Shelley shows that those who are shunned may strike back in anger.

Frankenstein is really a set of linked stories, revealing the tragic lives of Frankenstein and his monster. The early chapters focus on a series of letters from a man named Walton to his sister. Walton recalls his voyage to the Arctic Circle, where he sees a huge figure traveling on a sled followed at a distance by Victor Frankenstein. Frankenstein's words dominate the next set of chapters as Walton records Victor's story, starting with his happy childhood and his interest in medieval science. In college, Victor had become very interested in human anatomy. As a result of his work, Victor claimed to have found "the cause of generation and life." But before continuing his story, Victor warns Walton that the "acquirement of knowledge is dangerous."

The tale becomes much darker when Victor tells of bringing a monster into being. He tells of fleeing from his apartment in terror and not returning until much later, when he is relieved to find that the monster has escaped. Many months later, Victor learns that his own brother has been brutally murdered, and his sister has been accused of the crime. Frankenstein, however, has the eerie feeling that his monster is the killer and that he himself is responsible because of his "unhallowed arts."

The narrator role then shifts to the monster. After Victor flees to the Alps to escape his shame, the monster catches up with him and forces Victor to hear the truth. The monster has nothing but contempt for Victor, who has doomed him to an unhappy existence. It becomes clear

TEKS 10.13B, 10.15A(i), 10.15A(iv), 10.15C(ii), 10.15C(iii)
ELPS 4K

The detailed analysis is more than a summary, and the writer's insights about the novel extend beyond a literal analysis. Writer analyzes the author's use of rhetorical devices.

that the monster begins his existence as a gentle creature trapped in a frightening body. After escaping from Victor's apartment, he is ill treated by everyone he meets. He cannot understand why until one day he sees his reflection in a pool of water and realizes why people loathe him. Longing for companionship, he eavesdrops on happy lives and secretly helps others whenever he can. However, in an awful series of events, the monster is attacked by a mob he has tried to befriend and is shot by the companion of a girl he has saved from drowning. At that point, he declares war on all men, killing Victor's brother and framing his sister.

The monster's story makes it obvious that Victor's creation is vicious not because he is created that way, but because Victor abandons him and because others mistreat him. There is one last chance for Victor to ease the monster's loneliness—by creating another monster to keep him company. But Victor fails to take action. Walton encounters Frankenstein in the Arctic because Victor is chasing down his creation, intent on killing him. Finally, Walton's last report tells how Victor gets sick and dies before he can catch his monster, and the giant, satisfied that Frankenstein is dead, wanders off to perish on the ice.

Ending
The ending analyzes the two themes and expresses the importance of the second in quotations from the text.

Through *Frankenstein*, Mary Shelley expresses her fears that science left unchecked could be dangerous. However, in the end, that theme is not nearly as moving as the monster's message—mistreating others is risky. This theme becomes clear when he states, "There was none among the myriads of men that existed who would pity or assist me; and should I feel kindness toward my enemies?" It is the monster's plight that haunts the reader as the monster recalls that he sought shelter from the weather, but "still more from the barbarity of man," and no shelter was given.

Texas Traits

Respond to the reading. Answer the following questions.

Focus and Coherence (1) How is the thesis introduced? (2) How does the conclusion tie the essay together? **Organization** (3) How is the middle part of the analysis organized? **Development of Ideas** (4) What theme becomes the focus of this analysis? (5) Which key quotation from the novel supports this theme? **Voice** (6) Does the writer sound knowledgeable about the topic? Explain.

Prewriting

The writing process begins with prewriting—selecting a novel to analyze and planning what you will say about it. Always provide evidence from the novel to support your main ideas.

Keys to Effective Prewriting

1. Select an interesting novel, one that you have recently read and enjoyed.
2. Identify the main theme of the novel.
3. Find the key elements of the novel that reveal the main theme.
4. Look also for the author's use of stylistic or rhetorical devices that make the writing distinctive and help illuminate the theme.
5. Write a clear thesis statement that states the theme.
6. Decide how to organize the information in your middle paragraphs.
7. Write a topic sentence for each middle paragraph.

Prewriting Planning Your Writing

Completing a topics chart like the one below allows you to list novels you have read recently, state what the novels are about, and record possible themes.

Topics Chart

Title and author of the novel	What the novel is about	Possible themes
Brave New World by Aldous Huxley	A future government controls life so that everyone is happy.	– government vs. the individual – the "right" to happiness – life's shortcomings
Things Fall Apart * by Chinua Achebe	A man experiences changes in his Nigerian village during the late 1800s.	– native culture – manhood – evangelism – tradition vs. change

Prewrite

Select a topic. Make a topics chart like the one above. List at least two or three novels. Then put an asterisk next to the novel that you will analyze.

Tip

Choose a novel you have read, understand, and enjoy. You will find it much easier to analyze the theme of such a book.

I picked Things Fall Apart mostly because it's an amazing book. I identify with the main character. I have to struggle for everything I get, and things keep changing around me. I like the book because the main character struggles with the same issues that I struggle with.

Prewrite

Reflect on your choice. As in the example above, write a few sentences that explain the reason for your choice.

Identifying a Main Theme

Your next challenge is to identify the theme you will analyze. Choose one of the possible themes you listed in your topics chart (previous page) or look further by using the three strategies that follow:

- **Look for clues in the title.**
  Paper combusts at 451 degrees Fahrenheit.
  —Ray Bradbury, *Fahrenheit 451*
- **Look in the novel for the author's statement about life.**
  "A man can be destroyed but not defeated."
  —Ernest Hemingway, *Old Man and the Sea*
- **Identify a life lesson that emerges in the novel.**
  Wang Lung sees that genuine happiness is living on the land.
  —Pearl S. Buck, *The Good Earth*

Try It!

Search for a theme. Answer the following questions to find a main theme in your novel.

1. What clues does the title offer about a main theme? Explain.
2. What statements about life does the author make?
3. What lessons about life do the main character's actions reveal?
4. Are there any symbols that play a significant role in the novel? How do they relate to the main character's actions?

Prewrite

Identify a main theme. After answering the "Try It!" questions, complete the sentence below to identify a main theme of your novel.

A main theme of my novel is ______________________.

Texas Traits

Focus on the Texas Traits

Development of Ideas Authors use stylistic or rhetorical devices to make their writing interesting. They also use them to convey ideas to the reader. Among these devices are figures of speech, such as *simile, metaphor, personification,* or *hyperbole.* Look for these figures of speech as you analyze your novel, since they often contain thematic ideas.

TEKS 10.15A(v), 10.15C(ii)

Prewriting Gathering Details

To gather details for your analysis, list the major actions and the significant thoughts and feelings of the main characters in the novel. A character's thoughts and feelings won't always be stated outright, so you may have to infer them. Focus on examples that reflect the theme. The chart below corresponds with the essay on pages 267–270. (The side notes reveal the writer's thoughts about various elements in the plot.)

Plot Chart

Novel Title: Things Fall Apart

Theme: Tradition vs. change

The wrestling match is not important to the theme.

- At 18, Okonkwo becomes famous for winning a wrestling match.
- Okonkwo's father, Unoka, is irresponsible and constantly in debt, and Okonkwo is ashamed of him.
- Okonkwo becomes a powerful, prosperous, respected man.

Tradition is a key idea.

- Tradition rules the village of Umuofia, and Okonkwo follows the rules, except when his temper gets him in trouble.
- Okonkwo becomes a member of *egwugwu,* a powerful, secret cult that dispenses justice in Umuofia.
- At the funeral of the clan's most respected elder, Okonkwo accidentally kills the elder's son and must go into exile for seven years as punishment.

The second part of the story starts when Okonkwo leaves Umuofia.

- Okonkwo goes to a village that his mother came from, and is accepted by her relatives.
- His friend Obierika visits him and tells him about white men who wiped out a neighboring village.
- Later, Obierika returns with stories of white missionaries who have converted many clan members in Umuofia, including Okonkwo's oldest son.

The traditions of the natives and the teachings of the missionaries conflict.

- After seven years, Okonkwo returns to find that life in Umuofia has changed much because of missionaries.
- Europeans have set up a government and courts.
- Mr. Brown, a kind and compassionate missionary, gets sick and is replaced by Rev. Smith, who causes trouble.
- Okonkwo's aggressive ways end in tragedy.

Using Direct Quotations

You can use quotations from the novel to emphasize important points about the theme. As you choose quotations, keep in mind the purpose and context of your essay. The student who analyzed *Things Fall Apart* gathered the following list of quotations. Note how each quotation relates to the theme.

Sample Quotations

- "He had had no patience with his father." (A comment about Okonkwo)
- "Age was respected among his people, but achievement was revered." (The reason that Okonkwo was important in Umuofia)
- "The world has no end, and what is good among one people is an abomination with others." (The words of Okonkwo's uncle after the killing of the first white man)
- "The white man is very clever. He came quietly and peaceably with his religion. We were amused at his foolishness and allowed him to stay. Now he has won our brothers, and our clan can no longer act like one. He has put a knife on the things that held us together and we have fallen apart." (Obierika's words to Okonkwo)

Try It!

Discuss how each quotation relates to the theme of tradition vs. change.

Prewrite

Gather quotations. Search your novel to find direct quotations that relate to the theme you are analyzing.

Texas Traits

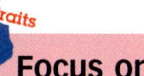

Focus on the Texas Traits

Organization To talk about the theme of a novel, you must also discuss the plot and the main characters. As you discuss the plot and characterization, your analysis will often be organized chronologically, but an analysis can also be organized by order of importance.

TEKS 10.13A, 10.15A(iv), 10.15C(ii)

Prewriting Writing a Thesis Statement

Now that you have gathered details, you are ready to write your **thesis statement**. Your thesis statement should connect an element of the novel—usually character, setting, or action—to the theme.

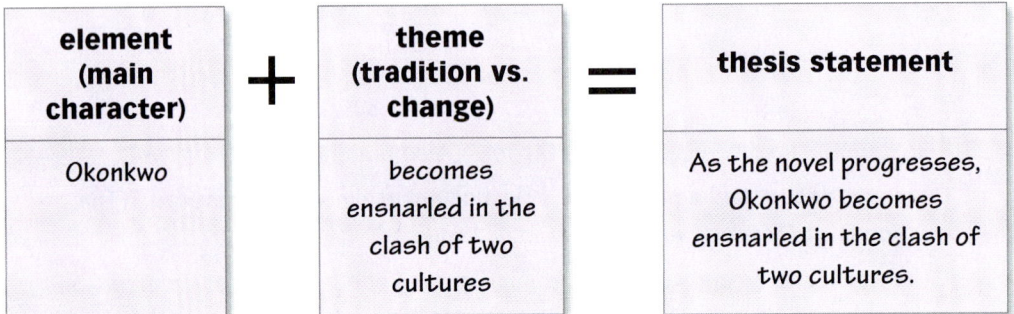

element (main character)	+	theme (tradition vs. change)	=	thesis statement
Okonkwo		becomes ensnarled in the clash of two cultures		As the novel progresses, Okonkwo becomes ensnarled in the clash of two cultures.

Prewrite

Form a focus. Write a thesis statement for your response essay using the formula above.

Organizing the Middle Paragraphs of Your Essay

Each middle paragraph should address a different stage in the explanation of the theme. The writer of the sample essay on pages 267–270 planned her middle paragraphs by writing a topic sentence for each one. Remember that your analysis is much more than a summary of the novel.

Topic Sentence 1 (First middle paragraph)

Okonkwo, the main character, is known far beyond the village of Umuofia for his personal achievements and extraordinary bravery and toughness.

Topic Sentence 2 (Second middle paragraph)

...although Okonkwo feels his exile is the worst thing that could happen to him, the coming of the Europeans proves to be a problem on a much larger scale.

Topic Sentence 3 (Third middle paragraph)

Obierika returns two years later with more stories about missionaries, churches, courts, and converts.

Prewrite

Plan your middle paragraphs. Review your plot chart from page 262. Add any important details you may have left out. Write a topic sentence for each middle paragraph of your essay. Then decide on the best order for your paragraphs.

Drafting

Once you have finished your prewriting, you are ready to write the first draft of your analysis. Your thesis statement, plot chart, quotations, and topic sentences will guide your writing.

Keys to Effective Drafting

1. Write on every other line so that you have room to make changes later.
2. Use your thesis statement and topic sentences as a guide to organize your writing.
3. Support your topic sentences with specific details from the novel.
4. Refer to your plot chart and sample quotations for details, adding more if needed.
5. Get all of your thoughts on paper.
6. Tie your ideas together with transitions.

TEKS 10.13B, 10.15A(i), 10.15A(iv), 10.15C(ii)

Drafting Getting the Big Picture

Remember that an essay includes three main parts—the beginning, the middle, and the ending. You are ready to begin drafting your response if you have . . .

- discovered the theme;
- written a clear thesis statement that ties the theme to the novel;
- planned and organized your paragraphs in a sustained way that is appropriate for your audience, purpose, and context.

The chart below shows how the three parts of a response-to-literature essay fit together. The examples are from the essay on pages 267–270.

Beginning

The **beginning** names the novel and the author, summarizes the plot, and states the thesis.

Thesis Statement
As the novel progresses, Okonkwo becomes ensnarled in the clash of two cultures.

Middle

The **middle** paragraphs show different stages in the development of the theme.

Topic Sentences
Okonkwo, the main character, is known far beyond the village of Umuofia for his personal achievements and extraordinary bravery and toughness.

Although Okonkwo feels his exile is the worst thing that could happen to him, the coming of the Europeans proves to be a problem on a much larger scale.

Obierika returns two years later with more stories about missionaries, churches, courts, and converts.

Ending

The **ending** paragraph analyzes the theme.

Closing Sentences
Okonkwo's plight symbolizes the choice faced by many conquered or controlled peoples—submit to a new way of life or perish. Okonkwo tragically experiences the latter.

Starting Your Analysis

Beginning
Middle
Ending

Your opening paragraph should set the scene for the rest of your analysis. It should include the following information:

- **the title and author of your novel,**
- **background information about the plot and characters, and**
- **your thesis statement.**

Beginning Paragraph

The first paragraph introduces the novel and gives the thesis statement (underlined).

Things Fall Apart by Chinua Achebe focuses on Nigeria in the late 1800s, a time of great change in Africa. Okonkwo, a leader in his village, is a commanding and merciless man deeply involved in the traditional life of his village, Umuofia. The first part of the novel follows Okonkwo's life to the point where an accident threatens to wipe out everything he has worked for. Unknown to Okonkwo, however, something even more disturbing is about to affect his people. White missionaries begin to travel throughout his homeland, bringing their religion. Soon, their laws and their government follow. These missionaries change everything in his village. As the novel progresses, Okonkwo becomes ensnarled in the clash of two cultures.

Draft

Write your beginning. **As you develop your beginning, include the title of the novel and its author, a brief plot summary, and your thesis statement.**

Tip

If you have trouble getting started, try one of these strategies.

- **Talk about your story with a classmate** before you begin to write.
- **Write freely** without trying to produce the perfect analysis right away.
- **Reread the sample on pages 257–258** to see how that writer started his analysis.
- **Think of someone you believe should read this book,** and write with that person in mind.

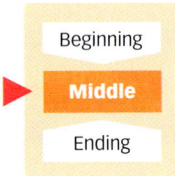

Drafting Developing the Middle Part

Each middle paragraph explores a stage in your explanation of the theme and how it is revealed in the novel. Your writing should focus on the elements of the novel and any stylistic or rhetorical devices that are important to the theme.

Beginning

Middle

Ending

Middle Paragraphs

The first middle paragraph summarizes the first part of the novel dealing with traditional life. Writer uses embedded quotations to support ideas.

Achebe uses vivid imagery and figurative language to draw the reader into the setting, to describe the characters, and to develop the theme. Okonkwo, the main character, is known far beyond the village of Umofia for his personal achievements and extraordinary bravery and toughness. The force that drives him is the fact that he "had no patience with his father," who was irresponsible and constantly in debt, preferring to drink and play the flute. Okonkwo thinks of his father as "effeminate" and is determined that no one will think of him in that way. Because "age was respected among his people, but achievement was revered," Okonkwo works harder than anyone to provide food for his family, reveres the words of the mystic oracles, kills without mercy, and obeys the priestess Chielo. Achebe describes in great detail how hard Okonkwo works and how prudent he is. As a result the reader empathizes with Okonkwo, and is happy when Okonkwo rises to the highest circle of Umuofia's powerful men. Okonkwo is a spiritual man, like his fellow clansmen, and he believes that the living and their ancestors move back and forth between life and death. Unfortunately, he makes a mistake at the funeral of the clan's elder, accidentally killing the elder's son. Knowing that he has done wrong, he immediately takes the step that tradition dictates, exiling himself from Umofia for seven years.

The writer analyzes the development of the theme and the author's stylistic and rhetorical devices.

Achebe develops the theme as he shows how although Okonkwo feels his exile is the worst thing that could happen to him, the coming of the Europeans proves to be a problem on a much larger scale. Again, Achebe uses vivid language to bring readers into the conflict and to make his point. This is particularly important in the scene where a friend Obierika visits Okonkwo in his village of exile two years later and brings news

Each paragraph includes insights into the novel. Using an effective organizational pattern, the writer sustains her thesis and provides details relating to the theme.

that the Abame settlement has been wiped out by white men. This action was done in retaliation for the death of another white man who rode an "iron horse"—a bicycle—through a group of panicked villagers. They apparently attacked him because he did not reply to their questions. Okonkwo's wise uncle Uchendu feels the people of Abame were fools to kill the white man on the bicycle. He says, "Never kill a man who says nothing," for the man's silence holds an ominous secret, whereas "There is nothing to fear from someone who shouts."

Obierika return two years later with more stories about missionaries, churches, courts, and converts. In these scenes, Achebe continues to show the conflicts Okonkwo faces. The reader is drawn into these conflicts and sympathizes with Okonkwo. Achebe uses stylistic and rhetorical devices to emphasize the theme, including the proverb "Blessed is he who forsakes his father and his mother for my sake." Though Kiaga, Okonkwo's son finds it "blessed" to forsake the old ways, Okonkwo feels it is cursed.

Draft

Write your middle paragraphs. **Use your topic sentences, plot chart, and sample quotation list to guide your writing. Try to include an example of a stylistic or rhetorical device to enhance the theme for the reader.**

Tip

Most literary analyses are organized chronologically, providing events in the order they appear in the novel. Use transition words and phrases that show time to connect your ideas.

Transitions That Show Time

After	Before	In the end	That night
As soon as	During	Later	Then
At the start	Finally	Soon	When

Other types of transitions are also useful for connecting ideas. The sample paper uses time transitions (*the first part of the novel, two years later, eventually*) as well as those that show cause and effect (*as a result, because*) and contrast (*however, unfortunately*).

TEKS 10.13B, 10.15A(i), 10.15C(i), 10.15C(ii)

Drafting Ending Your Analysis

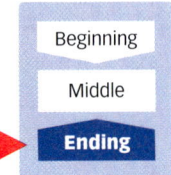

Beginning
Middle
Ending

Your essay starts with a thesis statement that connects the theme to a key element (plot, character, setting) in the novel. In the middle paragraphs, you show how the theme develops during the course of the action. The ending is your final chance to comment on and analyze the theme. Here are some suggestions for this final part of your essay.

- Show how the character has changed because of the theme.
- Use a quotation from the story.
- Predict how the theme might affect the characters in the future.
- State the theme as a basic truth about life.

Theme can be shown through characters or conflict. Theme is a perception about life or human nature that the writer shares with the reader.

Ending Paragraph

A quotation sums up the fatal situation.

The final ideas state the thesis as a basic truth.

Eventually, Okonkwo serves his seven-year exile and returns to Umuofia, inflamed by Obierika's analysis of the situation:

> The white man came quietly and peaceably with his religion. We were amused at his foolishness and allowed him to stay. Now he has put a knife on the things that held us together, and we have fallen apart.

Okonkwo takes up his role as a warrior against the invaders, and in a disastrous series of events, becomes a kind of disgraced martyr. Okonkwo's traditions have been ridiculed and insulted by some of the missionaries, but the damage goes far beyond religious issues. An entire society has been uprooted. The title of a book the English commissioner writes about his African adventures reveals the European attitude toward the natives: The Pacification of the Primitive Tribes of the Lower Niger. Okonkwo's plight symbolizes the choice faced by many conquered or controlled peoples—submit to a new way of life or perish. Okonkwo tragically experiences the latter.

Draft

Write your ending and form a complete first draft. Develop the last paragraph using one or more of the suggestions above. Make a clean copy of your complete essay. Double-space or write on every other line to make room for changes.

Revising

Go Online!

Now that your first draft is complete, you are ready to begin the revision process. Concentrate on focus and coherence, organization, and other key traits to make changes that will improve your writing.

Keys to Effective Revising

1. As you review your draft, consider your purpose, your audience, and the genre, or form, of your writing.
2. Read your essay aloud to see whether it makes sense from start to finish.
3. Check your thesis statement to be sure it includes the theme of the story.
4. Be sure that each middle paragraph supports and explains the thesis statement.
5. Check your ending. Have you given a final analysis of the theme you developed in your essay?
6. Check to see that your voice sounds knowledgeable.

TEKS 10.13C, 10.15A(i), 10.15C(i), 10.15C(ii)

Texas Traits

Revising for Focus and Coherence

When you revise for *focus and coherence,* you make sure that your essay has a sense of unity. The introduction presents a clear and complete thesis statement; the middle paragraphs flow smoothly from one to the next; and the conclusion sums up the points you have made in a final analysis of the theme. All the parts work together to form a whole that supports the thesis, and the reader understand the subtlety of meaning you are conveying.

When you write an interpretive response to a literary text, you are writing more than a summary or a literal analysis of the text. You are providing your reader insights into the author's purpose and theme.

Is my thesis statement clear and complete?

Your thesis statement will be clear and complete if you state the theme and connect it with at least one element *(plot, character, setting)* of the novel. Here are some guidelines to help you evaluate how theme is revealed.

1. Does the **plot** seem to propel the characters? How do the events work together to create the theme? Remember that you are providing an analysis, not a plot summary.
2. Do the **characters** create the conflicts, problems, and solutions? Is there one central character? Be sure to go beyond a simple, literal analysis of the characters.
3. Is the **setting** an important and continuing presence in the novel? How does it impact the characters and their actions? How does the setting help establish the theme of the work?

Try It!

In these thesis statements, identify the theme and the key element.

1. In the end, however, two young sharecroppers demonstrate the hope that happiness can eventually return after terrible loss.
2. The isolated location of the island creates an atmosphere that reveals the fragile nature of society's control over individuals.
3. The moment he discovered the baby on his doorstep, the reclusive Silas Marner began the journey out of isolation and greed, a journey that would reveal the true value of love.

Revise

Check your thesis and your conclusion. Does the thesis statement present a clear, controlling idea? Does the conclusion sum up your analysis of the theme? If not, revise as needed.

Is each paragraph of my analysis coherent?

Remember the meaning of the word *coherent:* orderly and logical. A paragraph will be coherent if the sentences within it flow smoothly, orderly, and logically from one to the next. *Unity* is a key characteristic of coherent paragraphs. It is best to delete any phrase or sentence that does not clearly support the topic of the paragraph.

When you begin revising your paragraphs for focus and coherence, use the following tips.

- **Use rhetorical devices.** Ask yourself how and where you might use rhetorical devices to make the paragraphs and sentences flow more smoothly from one to the next. Rhetorical devices can also help you focus on your thesis statement.
- **Examine your word choice.** Make sure you have used words that appropriately convey subtlety of meaning to the reader. Remember that your choice of words is critical as you support your ideas and share your insights in the essay.

Try It!

Carefully read the following paragraph. Then decide which sentence should be eliminated to make the paragraph more coherent.

The novel is a lesson in how to raise a family. Marmee helps three girls overcome teenage anxiety and tragedy by anchoring them in religion, common sense, and love. Nowadays, people turn to counseling or antidepressants. As adults, the girls carry Marmee's teachings into their own productive lives as a pianist, an artist, and a writer.

Revise

Review your first draft for clear focus and coherence. Be sure that each paragraph is unified, relates to the thesisr, and conveys your meaning. Make sure that your paragraphs flow smoothly from one to the next. Revise any problems.

Focus and Coherence
A sentence is removed to make the paragraph more coherent.

This action was done in retaliation for the death of another white man who rode an "iron horse"—a bicycle—through a group of panicked villagers. ~~Some early bicycles were called velocipedes.~~ They apparently attacked him because he did not reply to their questions. Okonkwo's wise uncle . . .

TEKS 10.13B, 10.13C, 10.15A(iv), 10.15C(ii)

Texas Traits

Revising for Organization

When you revise for *organization,* check the way you have arranged your ideas. Each paragraph should contain a topic sentence. All the sentences in the paragraph should support the topic sentence with insights and relevant evidence from the text. The paragraphs should flow smoothly from one to the next, and the ideas within each paragraph should also flow smoothly from one sentence to the next. As you begin your revision, remember that you are writing an analysis. Keep in mind that your organizational pattern should be appropriate for your purpose in writing the essay and for your audience.

Do my paragraphs flow smoothly from one to the next?

Effective transitions will help your paragraphs flow smoothly from one to the next. Transitions can be used to show location, time, and to compare and contrast things. Transition words and phrases can also be used to emphasize a point, to clarify your meaning, and to add information.

Exercise

Read the following sentences and identify the transitions. Explain how each transition works to move paragraphs smoothly from one to the next.

1. As the novel progresses, Okonkwo becomes ensnarled in the clash of two cultures.
2. Knowing that he has done wrong, he immediately takes the steps that tradition dictates, exiling himself from Umuofia for seven years.
3. ...although Okonkwo feels his exile is the worst thing that could happen to him, the coming of the Europeans proves to be a problem on a much bigger scale.
4. Again, Achebe uses vivid language to bring the readers into the conflict and to make his point.

Revise

Review your first draft. **Check each paragraph and decide if your paragraphs flow smoothly. The opening sentence should connect in some way with the previous paragraph. Then check for the effective use of transitions within paragraphs. Revise accordingly.**

TEKS 10.13C, 10.15A(iv), 10.15C(ii)

Is my organization appropriate for my purpose and audience?

In a literary analysis essay, you are writing about your viewpoint and insights about a particular piece of literature. It is important that you consider who your audience will be and write with appropriate tone and vocabulary. Also consider your purpose: you are not writing a summary or providing a literal analysis of the plot. Therefore, it is important to choose an organizational pattern that matches the purpose for your writing and works best for your readers.

Exercise

Carefully read the following paragraph. Then rearrange the sentences into a logical pattern for the purpose and the audience.

In the poem "Fifteen," William Stafford creates a snapshot of the dreams and realities of a teenager. The speaker describes a motorcycle using human qualities. He then contrasts his dreams with a real accident. The motorcycle is called "a companion, friendly." Its metal parts are called "flanks," and its headlights are described as shy. After the accident, when the adult rider gets back on the cycle, the boy is left with only his dreams.

Revise

Review your first draft for smooth flow and coherence. Be sure that each paragraph is clear and unified. Revise any problems.

Organization
A sentence is moved to make the paragraph more coherent.

Achebe describes in great detail how hard Okonkwo works and how prudent he is. As a result the reader empathizes with Okonkwo and is happy when Okonkwo rises to the highest circle of Umofia's powerful men. Okonkwo works harder than anyone to provide food for his family, reveres the words...

TEKS 10.13B, 10.13C, 10.15A(ii), 10.15C(ii)

Texas Traits

Revising for Development of Ideas

Does my analysis clearly reveal the theme?

Your analysis will clearly reveal the theme if you support your ideas with details from the book. Focus on details that apply directly to the theme. The evidence from the text that you use to support your ideas must be relevant. Use quotations as appropriate to support your insights and to help the reader understand the points you are making. You may wish to use various rhetorical devices, including analogies and figurative language, to convey your insights about the theme.

- **Choose events related to the theme.**
  Knowing that he has done wrong, he immediately takes the step that tradition dictates, exiling himself from Umuofia for seven years.
  not
  Okonkwo had three wives.
- **Mention secondary characters only as they expand the theme.**
  Obierika returns two years later with more stories about missionaries.
  not
  Mr. Brown is a kind and compassionate missionary.

Exercise

Read the paragraph below. Which detail does not apply to the theme?

Word spread that the white men had formed a court in Umuofia to protect followers of their religion. The procedures were different from those used in the natives' system of justice, resulting in anger and misunderstanding when a villager was hanged for killing a missionary. News of the execution was transmitted by *ekwe*, a hollowed-out wooden instrument.

Revise

Review your first draft for development of ideas. Be sure that you have presented sufficent relevant evidence and details from the text to support your thesis.

Have I effectively used literary terms in my analysis?

You have effectively used literary terms if they reveal your understanding of the novel and help you to express yourself. Like science, history, and mathematics, literature has its own set of specialized terms (*conflict, theme, symbol,* and so on). As you discuss conflict, differentiate between internal and external conflicts. Use or identify figurative language, such as similes, metaphors, and hyperbole, that the author uses in the piece of literature, This will help show your understanding of the purpose of literary analysis. Using specific terms, as well as including key quotations from the piece, will help the reader understand your meaning and will also make you sound knowledgeable about the topic.

Try It!

Read the paragraph below and explain how the underlined literary terms add meaning to the analysis.

In *Fahrenheit 451,* Bradbury's references to the natural world serve as symbols of reality. For example, Montag experiences the sensation of smell for the first time when he tries to escape down the river. The nomadic lifestyle also becomes a metaphor for returning to an unstructured, natural existence. Gradually, artificial, urban settings turn out to be less and less real for Montag.

Revise for literary terminology. Review your analysis to be sure that you have used appropriate literary terms as needed.

Revise

Development of Ideas

The writer makes use of literary terms and gives an example of a rhetorical device.

In these scenes, Achebe continues to show the ~~problems~~ conflicts Okonkwo faces. The reader is drawn into the ~~problems~~ conflicts and sympathizes with Okonkwo. Acebe uses ~~good words~~ stylistic and rhetorical devices to emphasize his point; he even uses a proverb: "Blessed is he who forsakes his father and his mother for my sake."

Texas Traits

Revising for Voice

When you revise for *voice,* pay attention to the way your writing sounds. This is an opportunity to improve the style of your writing. You should sound engaging and knowledgeable.

In a literary analysis, it is important to maintain the third-person point of view throughout. Point of view refers to the position or angle from which a story is told. Third-person point of view means that you are outside the story. As an outside observer, your tone should be objective and neutral.

Do I maintain a third-person point of view throughout?

You have maintained a third-person point of view if you have consistently used third-person pronouns *(he, she, it, they).* Avoid using first-person pronouns *(I, we)* or the second-person pronoun *(you).*

Try It!

The paragraph below sometimes drifts away from the third-person point of view. On your own paper, rewrite the paragraph so that the voice is consistently third person. In places, you will need to completely change the sentence structure to correct the point of view.

In *The Old Man and the Sea,* an old fisherman named Santiago is tested beyond normal human endurance. He goes out in his boat one morning, and you catch sight of a huge swordfish. Santiago hooks it, and I thought he was never going to land it, but next thing you know, it's lashed to the boat. Then you see sharks all around, eating pieces of the fish. Santiago must summon every ounce of strength in his struggle against the sharks, and you realize that courage is not limited to young heroes. Santiago says, "Man is not made for defeat. A man can be destroyed but not defeated." You feel he is courageous because of his actions.

Revise

Check for third-person point of view. Read your analysis to see whether you have maintained a third-person point of view throughout. Make any necessary revisions.

Do I sound knowledgeable about the book?

Your voice will sound knowledgeable if you show a clear understanding of the theme and write with confidence about it. Use appropriate vocabulary when you write, and keep these tips in mind.

- **Be direct.** Use the fewest words possible to get your point across. Use figurative language appropriately, but avoid flowery or wordy language.
- **Avoid starting sentences with "It is" or "There is."** These constructions lack energy and direction.
- **Avoid waffle words** such as *kind of, sort of, in a way, maybe, might,* or *seemed like* that overly qualify what you write.
- **Your style should not be too casual.** Remember your audience. Do not include slang or sentence constructions that are not appropriate for an academic essay.

Try It!

Rewrite the following sentence to make it sound more knowledgeable. Use the strategies given above.

It seems like Manolin wants to go along on the fishing trip with Santiago, but there is the problem that his parents think that maybe he shouldn't go because it seems to them that the old man might be bad luck.

Revise

Check your essay for voice. Reread your essay, marking any places that do not sound knowledgeable. Revise as needed.

Voice
Waffle words are deleted.

The force that ~~kind of~~ drives him is ~~probably~~ the fact that he "had no patience with his father," who was ~~sort of~~ irresponsible and constantly in debt, preferring to drink and play the flute. Okonkwo thinks of his father as . . .

Texas Traits

Revising Improving Your Writing

Revise

Check your revising. On a piece of paper, write the numbers 1 to 11. If you can answer "yes" to a question, put a check mark after that number. If not, continue to work with that part of your essay.

Revising Checklist

Focus and Coherence

_____ **1.** Is my thesis statement clear and complete?
_____ **2.** Do my ideas develop the book's theme?
_____ **3.** Does my entire essay present a coherent, unified analysis?

Organization

_____ **4.** Have I written a clear introduction, middle, and conclusion?
_____ **5.** Do my paragraphs flow smoothly from one to the next?
_____ **6.** Is my organizational pattern appropriate for the audience, purpose, and context?

Development of Ideas

_____ **7.** Are all my supporting details related to the theme?
_____ **8.** Have I used key embedded quotations to support my thesis?
_____ **9.** Have I used appropriate literary terms in the analysis?

Voice

_____ **10.** Do I maintain a third-person point of view throughout?
_____ **11.** Do I sound knowledgeable about the novel?

Revise

Make a clean copy. When you finish revising your essay, make a clean copy for editing.

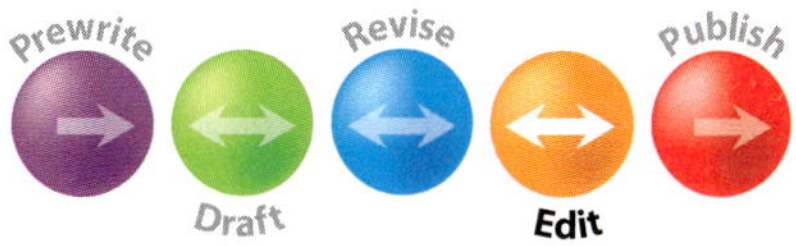

Editing

Go Online!

After you've finished revising your essay, it's time to edit for the following conventions: grammar, sentence structure, capitalization, punctuation, and spelling.

Keys to Effective Editing

1. Use a dictionary, a thesaurus, and the "Proofreader's Guide" in the back of this book (pages 642–787).
2. Use quotation marks correctly for direct quotations.
3. Check all of your writing for correct grammar, sentence structure, capitalization, punctuation, and spelling.
4. If you use a computer, edit on a printout and then enter your changes on the computer.
5. Use the editing and proofreading marks inside the back cover of this book.

Texas Traits

Editing for Conventions

Grammar

When you edit for *grammar,* especially in a literary analysis essay, check to make sure that you have used the correct verb tenses and that you have not shifted from one tense to another in your writing. As you edit, you should also check to make sure that subject and verb in the sentences agree and that your sentences flow smoothly.

When should I shift tenses in my analysis?

A simple rule to follow is that you should not shift tenses in your analysis unless there is good reason to do so. In a response to literature, including a literary analysis, you should usually write in the present tense. The plot unfolds in the same way each you time you read a story, so it makes sense to discuss the story in the present tense. Stories are written, however, in present and past tenses. When you include embedded quotes, you may need to shift to simple or complex past tenses.

- **Present tense (active voice):** Okonkwo works harder…
- **Present tense (passive voice):** Okonkwo is known…
- **Present perfect tense:** Okonkwo's traditions have been ridiculed…
- **Past tense (active voice)** He "had no patience"…

Grammar Exercise

Read the example below. Correct the shift in verb tenses

The narrator in the story started thinking about the situation. He starts to look for the owner of the motorcycle and found him lying in the grass. When the motorcycle rider "thanked the teenager" for his help, we see the contrast between the two characters. The narrator had been dreaming of being an adult. The adult can climb back on the motorcycle and take off for exciting adventures. The narrator, however, is still just a boy.

Edit

Review your first draft. Read your essay and make sure that you have not shifted tenses without good reason.

Should I always avoid split infinitives?

Remember that an infinitive is a verb form that includes the word *to.* The verbals *to write, to walk, to talk, to finish* are infinitives. Infinitives can be used as nouns, adjectives, or adverbs.

- **As a noun:** I want to win the race.
- **As an adjective:** Her desire to win is no stronger than mine.
- **As an adverb modifying an adjective:** People may think it is easy to win a race, but it requires hard work and practice.

The general rule in writing is that infinitives should not be split. In other words, avoid inserting words between the word *to* and the verb itself. The following are examples of split infinitives: *to easily win, to quickly walk, to sharply turn.* The rule about not splitting infinitives comes from Latin, in which infinitives are one word and cannot be split.

There are exceptions, and you will find times when it is almost impossible not to split an infinitive. For example, in the sentence *Economists expect the nation's output to more than double in the coming decade,* not splitting the infinitive would lead to a clumsy sentence.

Exercise

Rewrite the following sentences, so that the infinitives are not split.

1. That loud music is going to certainly harm your hearing.
2. The loss of the game is bound to incredibly damage the team's prospects of winning the championship.
3. The severe drought is going to harmfully affect the crops, and it is going to really hurt the animals.

Learning Language

Work with a partner. Take turns saying the present tense of a verb and have your partner change it into an infinitive. Then ask your partner to say a sentence using the infinitive form. Then say two short sentences and have your partner change them into one sentence using an infinitive. For example, say *He came to the house. He came to have dinner with us. He came to the house to have dinner with us.* Then do the same activity using gerunds. If you have difficulty or questions, ask your teacher for assistance. **Gerund:** a verb form that ends in ing and is used as a noun. **Infinitive:** a verb form that is usually introduced by *to* and that can be used as a noun, an adjective, or an adverb.

Edit

Revise for split infinitives. Check to work to make sure that you have used infinitives and infinitive phrases correctly.

Sentence Structure

When you edit for *sentence structure,* be sure to look at each of your sentences for variety and for correct structure. Using a variety of correct sentence structures will add interest to your writing and engage the reader.

Are my sentences parallel?

You should check each of your sentences to see if its parts are balanced. In other words, check to see if certain elements within each sentence are *parallel,* or stated in the same way. Study the following examples to see the difference that parallel structure can make. Besides adding balance to your sentences, parallel construction can be used as a rhetorical device to emphasize a point in a speech or in your writing.

Unparallel: Granny knew that her love could be seen in the food she cooked, her making all the clothes, and the gardens she liked growing.

Parallel: Granny knew that her love could be seen in the food she had cooked, the clothes she had made, and the garden she had grown.

Unparallel: Granny remembered her life and is preparing for dying.

Parallel: Granny remembered her life and prepared for death.

Grammar Exercise

Revise the following unparallel sentences to make them parallel.

1. Thinking about her life made Granny feel like rolling up her sleeves and she could put the whole place right again.
2. She remembered lighting the lamps, the scrubbing of wooden floors, and how she cared for her little children.
3. Matthew wanted to volunteer at the community center tutoring younger children and he could play outdoor games outdoors with older children.
4. The wind was howling, and the lights began to flicker, and we heard noises as the house creaked in the wind.

Revise

Revise for sentence fluency and parallel construction. Be sure that your sentences are balanced so that they read smoothly.

Mechanics

When you edit for *mechanics,* you check your punctuation and capitalization. Certain phrases and clauses need punctuation after them so that your reader can more easily understand your meaning. Interrupting words and phrases are words that provide detail, emphasis, and transitions. They need to be set off from the main idea of the sentence.

How do I punctuate interrupting words and phrases?

You should place commas before and after any words or phrases that interrupt the flow of your sentences. If the interrupter is in the middle of a sentence, remember to enclose only the interrupting word or phrase in the commas. Common interrupting words and phrases include the following:

however	**in fact**	**by contrast**	**of course**	**for example**
true	**as a rule**	**as a result**	**in response**	**after all**

Try It!

Rewrite the following paragraph, inserting commas as needed for any interrupting words or phrases.

Hobbits are as a rule peaceable people who aren't interested in adventure. When a Black Rider appears in the Shire however Frodo Baggins must journey from his comfortable home. He carries the one ring that can enslave the world. Frodo could use the ring to turn invisible, but doing so would in fact make him easier to detect by the Black Rider. Instead, Frodo and his companions flee across country. At an old watchtower, five Black Riders catch up to them, and Frodo is stabbed by a rider's blade. The tip breaks off in the wound and as a result Frodo becomes ill.

Revise

Edit for punctuation of interrupting words and phrases. Check your essay for words or phrases that interrupt the flow of your sentences. Make sure to set off these words or phrases with commas.

TEKS 10.13C, 10.15D, 10.17B, 10.18A, 10.18B(i), 10.19
ELPS 5C–5F

Texas Traits

Editing Checking for Conventions

Edit

Check your editing. On a piece of paper, write the numbers 1 to 12. Put a check mark by the number if you can answer "yes" to that question. If not, continue to edit your essay for that convention.

Editing Checklist

Conventions

GRAMMAR

_____ **1.** Have I used correct verb tenses throughout?
_____ **2.** Have I used correctly structured verbals, such as infinitives?
_____ **3.** Have I used the right words *(its, it's)*?

SENTENCE STRUCTURE

_____ **4.** Do I use a variety of correctly structured sentences to clearly communicate ideas?

MECHANICS (Capitalization and Punctuation)

_____ **5.** Do I start all my sentences with capital letters?
_____ **6.** Have I capitalized all proper nouns?
_____ **7.** Does each sentence have correct end punctuation?
_____ **8.** Have I used quotation marks correctly with direct quotations?
_____ **9.** Have I used commas to set off interrupting words and phrases?
_____ **10.** Do I use apostrophes to show possession *(in Poe's story)*?

SPELLING

_____ **11.** Have I spelled all my words correctly?
_____ **12.** Have I consulted a dictionary to determine or check the spellings of words my spell-checker may have missed?

Creating a Title

- Focus on the theme: **Good Intentions and Bad Results**
- Refer to a character: **The Pacification of Okonkwo**
- Be creative: **When Cultures Clash, *Things Fall Apart***

Go Online!

Publishing

Sharing Your Essay

Now that you've finished drafting, revising, and editing your essay, it is time to publish it. First, however, share your essay with your classmates. Ask for feedback. Then ask your teacher to review your essay. Make any needed final corrections. See the suggestions in the boxes below for a variety of ways to present your essay.

Publish

Make a final copy. **Follow your teacher's instructions or use the guidelines below to format your paper. (If you are using a computer, see pages 72–74.) Write a final copy of your essay and proofread it for errors.**

Focusing on Presentation

- Use blue or black ink and write neatly.
- Write your name in the upper left corner of page 1.
- Skip a line and center your title; skip another line and start your writing.
- Indent every paragraph and leave a one-inch margin on all four sides.
- Write your last name and the page number in the upper right-hand corner of every page after page 1.

Publish in a Class Literary Magazine

Set up your work in a multicolumn format, add headlines, and include photos or paintings of the author and characters. Consider adding "sidebar" graphics or comments.

Make a Recording

Read your analysis and record it on a CD or DVD. Consider including appropriate music, sound effects, and video clips.

Post Your Essay on the Web

Submit your work to a community, school, or class Web site or post it on a family Web site.

Evaluating an Interpretive Response

To learn how to evaluate a literary analysis, you will use the holistic scoring guide on pages **60–61** and the essays that follow. These essays are examples of writing for each score on the scoring guide (1–4).

Notice that the first essay received a score of 4. Read the description for a score of 4 on pages **60–61.** Then read the literary analysis. Use the same steps to study the other examples. As you read, concentrate on the overall quality of the writing in each example.

Writing that fits a score of 4 is highly effective.

4

The **beginning** gives the novel's title and the author. It also introduces the writer's focus. (underlined)

Each **middle** paragraph supports the thesis with evidence and details from the text. Writer provides insights as the analysis is developed.

Writer consistently uses correct verb tenses.

Land Values

The Good Earth, by Pearl S. Buck, is the story of Wang Lung, a simple farmer who becomes a wealthy man by acquiring more and more land. As he does, he loses his traditional way of life and values. In the end, Wang Lung is haunted by the words he spoke as a young man: "Land is one's flesh and blood." The author sets up the conflict early in the novel, describing Wang Lung's desire for prosperity and the importance of land in his life. As the characters are developed and the plot unfolds, the conflict is fully developed for the reader.

The basic conflict of Wang Lung's life is foreshadowed when his father arranges for him to marry a young woman from the big city. O-lan is a servant girl working for a rich family, the House of Hwang. When Wang Lung goes to get his future bride to take her back to his father's farm, he is shocked by the high prices and the rude ways of the city. The House of Hwang, with its impersonal atmosphere and showy wealth, is a huge contrast to life in the village. When Wang Lung brings O-lan home however, she immediately fits in with the traditional ways of the farm.

Wang Lung's life with O-lan begins happily as they work the land and prosper. They have a son, save their money, and live by the traditional, old-fashioned values that have been in place for centuries. They are so successful, in fact, that Wang Lung buys land from the House of Hwang, although O-lan warns that they already have enough land. Wang Lung does not realize that he has

Middle paragraphs continue to support thesis with evidence from text. Sentences show correct use of infinitives.

begun to turn away from the traditional values toward something new—ambition.

Ambition is so satisfying to Wang Lung that over the years he buys much more land from the failing House of Hwang. One of the ironies in the novel is that, although land is the source of traditional life, obtaining more land leads him from that life. Wang is gradually overcome by lazy relatives, starving villagers, and spoiled children. Although he continues to gain land and wealth, he seems less and less satisfied with his life. Wang Lung goes to the city, seeking escape, and gets involved in fast living, forgetting the morals that he was raised with. At one point, he agrees to cut off his pigtail, a symbol of his traditional, rural background, because an attractive woman in the city laughs at him for wearing one.

Life back on the farm becomes more and more complicated, with huge tracts of land, numerous buildings, and many workers to manage. Because there is so much to keep track of, Wang Lung hires people to take care of business for him, and Wang Lung ends up with nothing to do all day but deal with his family troubles. In the ultimate irony of the novel, Wang Lung decides to move everyone to the old House of Hwang, which has been abandoned by its bankrupt owners. Wang Lung's family has become like the one he despised when he went to bring O-lan home.

Conclusion adds a final analysis. Embedded quotations emphasize writer's point. Correct punctuation is used.

Wang Lung doesn't have much to be happy about, but he does have one remaining comfort—when he picks up a hoe to work in the field, he says, "The land did again its healing work." As an old man, Wang Lung returns to live out his life on the old farm. He still loves the land, thinking, "It is the end of a family—when they begin to sell the land." Wang Lung sees that wealth is not everything; there is more happiness in living on the land—man's true home.

Writing that fits a score of 3 is generally effective.

3

The **introduction** gives the title of the novel and the author. The introductory paragraph provides the thesis statement.

Each **middle** paragraph provides detail and support for the thesis statement. Writer occasionally uses transitions between paragraphs to link ideas. Flow could be smoother.

Writer uses embedded quotes to support ideas and advance the thesis statement. Most ideas are well developed.

Living Off the Land

Pearl Buck has a lot of themes in *The Good Earth*, but she expresses them in a very interesting story that really keeps the reader's attention. As she tells the story of Wang Lung and O-lan, she brings up many of important issues like the way women are treated in China, how traditional ways in China are coming to an end, and how wealth can change a once humble man.

O-lan is not a pretty woman but she is a good wife for Wang Lung. She works side by side with him in the field and she takes care of him and his father at home. Like Wang Lung she is careful with money. Soon the couple's hard work pays off and Wang Lung starts to become wealthy. Money makes Wang Lung more aware of his status. Even though O-lan has done so much for him, Wang Lung starts to slowly feel ashamed of her, particularly her big feet. In China, women bound their feet so they would be tiny. Wang-Lung falls in love with Lotus, a pretty woman who has bound feet. Unlike O-lan, she couldn't work. She could barely walk. "She swayed upon her little feet and to Wang Lung there was nothing so wonderful...as her pointed little feet and her curling helpless hands." Even though he feels bad about what he's done to O-lan, now that Wang Lung doesn't have to work as hard, he is more concerned with Lotus's outer beauty than O-lan's inner beauty.

The richer Wang Lung gets, the less he is interested in traditional ways. Also, his sons are less traditional than he is. In the beginning of the book, Wang Lung lights incense for the gods of the earth. By the end, he stops being thankful to the gods. "Facing him were the small gods and...he noted how...of old he had been afraid of them, but now he was careless, having become prosperous and in no need of gods...." He cuts off his traditional braid to please Lotus. Also the duty and respect that he shows to older family members is corrupted when he gives his uncle opium. He himself is treated with disrespect by his own sons who plan to sell his land and lie to him about it. Selling the land is also the end of traditions. Farming is looked down on by Wang Lung's sons.

Organization is shown by use of transitions.

Errors in conventions do not detract. Reader can understand meaning.

Conclusion does not effectively add to essay.

Finally, the most important theme of the book is how wealth took Wang Lung from being a kind and humble man into the kind of people that he despised. When he first comes for O-lan at the rich home of the Hwangs, he feels humilated and embarrassed by his humble position. Then when he goes back to his farm, he feels comfortable again and he doesn't have to measure his worth by what he sees around him. As Wang Lung gets richer and richer, he moves away from seeing his value from within and begins to judge himself the way he thinks others view him. He begins to dress in fine clothes and spend more money. Finally he buys the Hwang's mansion, which they lost because of there decadent lifestyle. When O-lan, who never changed, dies, Wang Lung really looses his connection to his former self. However, whenever Wang Lung goes back to his farm and works on the land, he feels "healed." But it's too late for his sons to understand this feeling. Wang Lung's family is heading the same downward route as the Hwangs.

The Good Earth was a fascinating story about the people of China, but beneath the story are universal themes about women and beauty, traditional and modern life, and wealth versus happiness. That's why this book won a Pulitzer Prize for the author and will stay a classic for all time.

Writing that fits a score of 2 is somewhat effective.

2

The **beginning** gives an idea of the thesis statement.

Middle paragraphs provide a summary, not an analysis. Writing is difficult to understand. Errors in conventions lead to confusion.

Details are vague and do not support thesis.

Essay lacks **conclusion**.

Real Love Versus Money

The Good Earth, by Pearl Buck, the main charcter Wang Lung has two loves, his land and his wife. By the end of the book he looses both of them. That is what the book is about, a man who gets rich and forgot what he came from and he suffers for it.

Wang Lung married an ugly woman named O-lan and he's upset because she has big feet. They weren't bound to be small, But Wang Lung began to soon appreciate O-lan she is quiet and she works hard in the house and also helps him in the field. He doesn't think he loves her, but he appreciates her and with her help, he begins to make money.

Then Wang Lung falls in love with a beautiful woman named Lotus and he feels embarressed about being a farmer. He begins to ignore O-lan to be with Lotus and finally brings her to the house to live. And he also starts to loose his felings for his land. He uses hired people to do the work for him and his family.

Wang Lung begins to change when he moved away from O-lan and land. Then he cuts off his pigtail and starts worrying about he looks to other people. But when O-lan got sick, he feels terrible because he probably cares for her. And when she died he understands what she really meant to him. Then O-lan dies, Wang Lung moves to a big house in the city. He lived like a rich man. His sons never had to work on the land and want to sell it.

The person who wrote the book showed me how Wang Lung used to appreciate humble pleasures when he was poor. He appreciated his good, but plain wife, and working hard on his land. Having money changed him for the worse Life back on the farm is hard but Wang Lung ends with nothing to do all day but deal with his family troubles. When he decides to move everyone to the old House of Hwang. Wang Lung's family has become like the one he despised when he went to bring O-lan home.

Wang Lung doesn't have much to be happy about, "The land did again its healing work." As an old man, Wang Lung returns to live out his life on the old farm. He still loves the land, "It is the end of a family—when they begin to sell the land."

Writing that fits a score of 1 is not effective.

1

The **beginning** does not provide a thesis. Author's name is misspelled.

Middle paragraphs provide confusing summary; no analysis provided. Errors throughout make essay confusing for reader.

Essay lacks focus, coherence, and organization.

The Good Earth

The Good Earth is a book by Perl Buck. It's about some Chinese farmer who married a woman who's a slave. They had a family he made more and more money from his land. He became rich and lived in the mansion that was owned by the rich people where his wife was a slave but he isn't as happy as he was when he was poor.

The book starts off with Wang Lung' on his wedding day. He's poor so the only woman he can efford to marry is a slave. Her name is O-lan. He's unhappy that she's not pretty but his father wants him to marry a girl who will work in the fields and bare lots of kids. She is strong and helps Wang Lung in the field and she hardly even stops working to have her first baby. That impressed me and Wang Lung was happy.

Soon Wang Lung gets more money. Hes able to buy more land from the rich people. But then there's a drout and Wang Lng loses all his money. The family and him have to go live in a city so they won't starve. But Wang Lung wants go home. He ends up getting some silver and he's able to finally go home.

Wang Lung gets rich again and he bys more land so after a while he doesn't have to work anymore and then he hires people who can work. He gets a pretty young woman instead of O-lan and O-lan then gets unhappy but she still helps Wang Lung and is faithful. Even when she is sick and dying she thinks of him. And when she dies he feels her loss.

By the end of the book Wang Lung is so rich he bys the mansion of the rich people. But he's not the same man he was. He is more concerned about being rich than about his land and then finally he goes back to his first house at the end but its too late so after he dies his sons are going to sell the land

Life back on the farm gets harder, with lots of stuff to do and problems so Wang Lung hires people and he ends up with nothing to except family troubles. and decides to move everyone to an old mansion. Wang Lung is unhappy so he goes back to being a farmer.

Evaluating and Reflecting on Your Writing

Reflect on and score your finished analysis of a theme by completing each starter sentence below. These comments will help you check your progress as a writer.

My Response to Literature

1. The focus of my essay is the theme of the novel, and my thesis statement is . . .
2. The organizational pattern that I chose is appropriate for my purpose, audience, and context because . . .
3. The embedded quotes and relevant details from the text that I used as I developed my ideas emphasize . . .
4. The variety of sentence structures in my essay shows . . .
5. One question I still have about writing an analysis of a theme is . . .
6. Right now I would describe my writing ability as . . . (excellent, good, fair, poor)

Interpretive Response

Interpreting a Nonfiction Text

Nonfiction texts include stories about the lives of real people, the exploration of real places, and descriptions of real events. Nonfiction is written to convey factual information, and you can learn a great deal from reading nonfiction texts. Writers of nonfiction, however, can shape information in accordance with their own views and attitudes. When you read nonfiction, you need to examine it carefully to detect biases, notice gaps in the information, and identify errors in logic. Nonfiction includes a diverse range of writing—newspaper articles, letters, essays, biographies, speeches, true-life adventure stories, and more.

In this chapter, you'll read an essay and a sample interpretation that presents a detailed analysis of the author's ideas. After that, you'll be asked to choose another nonfiction text and write your own interpretation of it.

Writing Guidelines

Subject: Interpretation of nonfiction
Purpose: To analyze a writer's ideas
Form: Literary analysis
Audience: Classmates

"Literature adds to reality, it does not simply describe it."

—C. S. Lewis

Sample Nonfiction Text

From "On Liars" by Michel de Montaigne

I know quite well that grammarians make a distinction between telling an untruth and lying. They say that to tell an untruth is to say something that is false, but that we suppose to be true, and that the meaning of lying is to go against one's conscience, and that consequently it applies to those who say the opposite of what they know; it is of them I am speaking. . . .

Now liars either invent the whole thing, or they disguise and alter an actual fact. If they disguise and alter, it is hard for them not to get mixed up when they refer to the same story again and again because, the real facts having been the first to lodge in the memory and impress themselves upon it by way of consciousness and knowledge, they will hardly fail to spring into the mind and dislodge the false version, which cannot have as firm or assured a foothold. . . .

Lying is indeed an accursed vice. We are men, and we have relations with one another by speech. If we recognized the horror and gravity of an untruth, we should more justifiably punish it with fire than any other crime. I commonly find people taking the most ill-advised pains to correct their children for their harmless faults and worrying them about heedless acts which leave no trace and have no consequences.

Lying—and in a lesser degree stubbornness—are, in my opinion, the only faults whose birth and progress we should consistently oppose. They grow with a child's growth, and once the tongue has got the knack of lying, it is difficult to imagine how impossible it is to correct it. Whence it happens that we find some otherwise excellent men subject to this fault and enslaved by it. I have a decent lad as my tailor, whom I have never heard to utter a single truth, even when it would have been to his advantage.

If, like the truth, falsehood had only one face, we should know better where we are, for we should then take the opposite of what a liar said to be the truth. But the opposite of a truth has a hundred thousand shapes and a limitless field.

There are a thousand ways of missing the bull's-eye, only one of hitting it. . . .

Student Response

In the following essay, student Dominic Montano wrote a careful, detailed interpretation of Montaigne's essay "On Liars." Before he began to write his own essay, Dominic read Montaigne's essay carefully and analyzed each paragraph.

Beginning The first paragraph builds up to the thesis statement (underlined).

Middle The middle paragraphs develop the writer's argument, using a personal anecdote and a reflection.

"An Accursed Vice"

Montaigne's essay "On Liars," brings up some interesting questions. Should we "more justifiably punish [lying] with fire than any other crime"? It seems as though Montaigne might be exaggerating the evils of lying until he defines it: "the meaning of lying is to go against one's conscience." If that is the definition of lying, then perhaps Montaigne is right to believe that there is nothing more important than telling the truth.

One of Montaigne's strongest points is his example of children. According to him, parents need to "consistently oppose" any signs of lying from a child, more than any other act. Whether trying to get out of trouble or to get a special treat, children quickly realize that lying can be in their best interest. That could lead to more serious consequences because lies "grow with a child's growth, and once the tongue has got the knack of lying, it is difficult to imagine how impossible it is to correct it.".

If a lie must go "against one's conscience," it's crucial for parents to explain why lying is wrong. Without understanding what is right and what is wrong, a child might not feel that pang of guilt when he tells a lie. Instead the child might feel gleeful that he got away with something that turned out to be beneficial for him. Montaigne is right when he says that that sort of behavior might be difficult to correct.

The real problem may be that repeated lying changes a person. Like Montaigne's tailor, a liar might get so used to doing it, that he can't tell the truth even when it's to his advantage. That kind of person can never be trusted or taken seriously. Worse, constant liars might not have any conscience left to be concerned about the consequences of their lies. What Montaigne calls the "horror and gravity of an untruth," can lead to terrible behavior, like companies cheating customers, politicians deceiving their citizens, innocent people being killed.

Montaigne clearly demonstrates the power of truthfulness when he states: "If, like the truth, falsehood had only one face, we should know better where we are....But the opposite of a truth has a hundred thousand shapes and a limitless field." His metaphor shows how many ways there are to lie, but how impossible it is to defend any of them. Ultimately the truth must always prevail.

Ending
The ending revisits the thesis and shares a final insight.

Texas Traits

Respond to the reading. Answer the following questions about the student response.

Focus and Coherence (1) What is the thesis statement, and how is it introduced? (2) How does the student writer tie the conclusion back to the main point introduced in the introductory paragraph?

Organization (3) How do the middle paragraphs relate to each other? (4) What transition words and phrases does the writer use to link paragraphs and connect ideas?

Development of Ideas (5) What evidence from the Montaigne essay does the student writer use to support his thesis statement? (6) What quotations does the student writer use from Montaigne's essay? (7) What purpose do the quotations serve?

Voice (8) What rhetorical devices does the student writer use to emphasize his points and engage the reader? (9) What literary terms does the student writer use to make his voice sound knowledgeable?

Prewriting Planning Your Writing

In your interpretation of a nonfiction text, you will be developing a critical analysis of the writer's ideas. Remember the meaning of *analysis*: the separation of a whole into its parts for individual study. The meaning of *interpret* is slightly different: to explain the meaning of something.

Your essay needs to be long enough to analyze and explain the selection. You will need to include sufficient evidence and details from the text to support your controlling idea thoroughly. As you choose your nonfiction text, keep in mind your audience, the purpose, and the genre, or form, your writing will take. It is also important to keep in mind the context of your writing, as well as the context of the nonfiction piece that you have chosen for interpretation. Keep in mind the following:

- **Choose a nonfiction text that interests you.** Your essay needs to show interest in the text, and you should convey both your interest and your understanding to your audience.
- **Decide on the genre of nonfiction that you want to analyze.** Remember that there are a variety of nonfiction genres. Essays, letters, magazine articles, biographies, and adventure stories are just some that you can choose from for your essay.

Choosing a Topic

After thinking about the form of your essay, make a chart of possible topics. This will help you find a suitable text for analysis. Use a two-column chart or a simple outline like the one below to guide you.

- Magazine articles:
- Historical letters:
- Biographies:
- Essays:
- Adventure stories:

Texas Traits

Focus on the Texas Traits

Development of Ideas Remember that your analysis must go beyond a summary or literal analysis. As you plan your essay, make notes about the nonfiction piece you are analyzing. Identify its thesis statement or controlling idea. Note how the author supports his or her position and develops ideas. Look for errors in logic and for any biases that the author may have. Make note of any rhetorical devices the author uses.

TEKS 10.15C(ii), 10.15C(iii)

Prewriting Planning Your Writing

The following tips will help you plan your interpretation. Also refer to the planning that you did on the previous page.

Organizing Your Essay

In your interpretation, be sure to include relevant details and supporting evidence from the text that you have chosen. Citing relevant evidence will be critical as you develop your own analysis. If you find errors in logic or believe that the author shows bias, use quotations from the text to support your explanation. As you plan, be sure to consider the following elements.

- **Start with an effective introductory paragraph that presents your controlling idea. Your conclusion should revisit the thesis statement and tie the essay together.**
- **As you organize the details and relevant evidence from the text, consider the relative value of the specific ideas, facts, and data that you are going to include in your essay to support your thesis.**
- **Plan to include rhetorical devices, and think about transitions you can use to connect ideas and paragraphs.**

Analyzing Nonfiction Text

When you plan your interpretation, you should carefully analyze the nonfiction text that you have chosen. First, look at the author's purpose for writing. For the most part, nonfiction text will not have characters, nor will it have a plot arc. Take notes as you read the text, and use them as you write. Look for the following, and answer these questions.

- How has the author structured his ideas?
- What rhetorical devices has the author used? What purpose do they serve?
- What stylistic devices has the author used? These would include metaphorical or figurative language, anecdotes, allusions, and irony.

Prewrite

Plan your essay. Use the prewriting tips above and from the previous page to plan and organize your essay. Decide which rhetorical and stylistic devices you are going to use and what kinds of transitions will best connect your ideas.

Drafting Creating Your First Draft

The following tips will help you write your interpretation. Also refer to the planning that you did on the previous pages.

Writing Your Beginning Paragraph

The **beginning** paragraph should introduce the nonfiction text that you have chosen. Give both the title and the author of the piece. Present your controlling idea, the thesis statement, completely and clearly.

- **Explain why the topic is important.**
  ...then perhaps Montaigne is right to believe that there is nothing more important than telling the truth.
- **Ask a rhetorical question or share a quotation.**
  Should we "more justifiably punish [lying] with fire than any other crime"?

Writing Your Middle Paragraphs

The **middle** paragraphs should build your interpretation in a logical way. Consider the relative value of the ideas, facts, and data that you are going to include as you create an organizational pattern that is appropriate for your purpose and audience. Use transitions to connect sentences in your paragraphs and to move your essay smoothly from one paragraph to the next.

- **Organize your ideas in a logical, coherent way.**
- **Use relevant evidence and details from the text to support your position.**
- **As appropriate, use embedded quotations to emphasize your points.**
- **Identify faulty logic in the text and discuss why you believe the author introduced these errors.**
- **Identify and discuss any biases that you see in the text.**

Writing Your Ending Paragraph

The **ending** paragraph should tie the essay together into a coherent a whole. Use the tip below to create your conclusion.

- **Summarize your thesis and create a memorable closing.**
  Ultimately, the truth must always prevail.

Draft

Write your first draft. Use your prewriting work and the tips above to develop your essay.

Texas Traits

Revising Improving Your Writing

Always review your writing. Make any changes and corrections neatly. Use the following questions to help you revise your response.

- **Focus and Coherence:** Does my introductory paragraph contain my controlling idea? Do the details and evidence support the thesis? Does the conclusion tie the essay together?
- **Development of Ideas:** Have I adequately analyzed the nonfiction text? Have I supported my ideas with relevant evidence, specific details, and embedded quotations?
- **Organization:** Have I included a beginning, a middle, and an ending? Does each paragraph have a focus? Have I used transitions so that paragraphs flow smoothly from one to the next?
- **Voice:** Do I sound clear in my thinking? Have I used literary terms to express my ideas? Do I sound knowledgeable about the selection that I have analyzed?

Revise

Revise your work. Answer the questions above and revise your work as needed.

Editing Checking Your Writing

Check your final draft for grammar, sentence structure, capitalization, punctuation, and spelling.

Conventions

_____ **1.** Have I used correct and consistent verb tenses?

_____ **2.** Have I correctly used a variety of sentence structures?

_____ **3.** Have I capitalized all proper nouns and first words of sentences?

_____ **4.** Have I put quotation marks around the exact words that I quoted from the selection?

_____ **5.** Have I checked the spelling in my work?

Edit

Check your response. Read over your work, looking for errors in conventions. Make any needed corrections neatly.

Interpretive Response

Analyzing a Poem

A good poem can make us look at the world in a new way. After reading a poem, you may find yourself remembering images that "spoke" to you. When you read a poem closely and analyze it, you will discover how carefully it was crafted.

An analysis goes beyond a mere summary; it explains the way that a poem communicates experiences. You examine a poem's form, the way the words appear on the page. You might consider meter and rhyme. Much of the power of poetry depends upon rhythm—the pattern of syllables in each line. Poets use rhythm to emphasize ideas and to create a mood. Equally important is imagery in a poem—the use of words to create sensory experiences. Figurative language can convey meanings beyond the literal meaning of words. Through these devices and others, poets help us gain a deeper understanding of the beauty of the English language.

In this chapter, you'll read a student analysis of a poem. After that, you'll be asked to write your own poetry

"The poet is a liar who always speaks the truth."

—Jean Cocteau

TEKS 10.13B, 10.15A(i), 10.15A(iii), 10.15(v), 10.15C(i)–10.15C(iii)

Analyzing a Poem

In the following essay, student Gabriel Ferro wrote a detailed analysis of Walt Whitman's poem, "O Captain, My Captain."

Student introduces poem and provides background information. Thesis is introduced.

Embedded quotes support analysis of stylistic devices in the poem. Writer provides detailed analysis of structure and aesthetic effects of poetic, stylistic, and rhetorical devices.

Elegy for a President

Walt Whitman wrote "O Captain! My Captain!" after the assassination of Abraham Lincoln. This short, three-stanza poem expresses the deep grief the poet felt when he heard the news that the president had died. Whitman uses the metaphor of a ship and its captain to represent the country and the president. He then uses these strong visual images to create a moving homage to President Lincoln that is almost like watching a tragic film.

In the first stanza, Whitman sets up the metaphors that carry through until the end. The ship that "has weather'd every rack" is the United States, just recovering from the "fearful trip" of the Civil War. The next line describes the mood of the country after the war and the hope people feel now that the worst is behind them: "the prize we sought is won, The port is near, the bells I hear, the people all exulting." Then, after the first impression of triumph, Whitman expresses the shock of finding the ship's captain, Abraham Lincoln, "Fallen cold and dead."

Once the reader understands that the poem is about President Lincoln and the state of the country after the Civil War, the poem takes on a more tragic tone than it would if it were read without understanding the background. It is easy to picture the president who had been shot and was dying at Ford's Theatre when Whitman exclaims: "But O heart! heart! heart!/ O the bleeding drops of red,/ Where on the deck my Captain lies, Fallen cold and dead." Every time Whitman repeats "O Captain! my Captain!" his anguish gets deeper. The narrator cradles the fallen captain's head with his arm. He calls him "dear father." It's clear that Whitman feels that the country has lost a guiding caring leader.

Throughout the poem, Whitman contrasts the loud colorful celebration of the people on the shore with the still captain on the deck. He moves between the two different feelings by changing the rhythm and the rhyming scheme. The first four lines of each stanza rhyme every two lines. The last four lines have fewer beats and rhyme every other line. The first two stanzas start with the celebration on shore then abruptly change their rhythm and rhyme when Whitman turns to the fallen

Analysis of aesthetic effects of poet's use of stylistic and rhetorical devices continues. Organizational pattern works well for purpose, audience, and context. Embedded quotations support analysis and show rhetorical devices used by poet.

leader. The last stanza is different because it begins with the image of the dead captain. Then when it changes style, it briefly moves back to the celebration, but ends again on the fallen captain.

Whitman structures the poem almost like scenes in a movie. First you watch the victorious ship entering the harbor: "While follow eyes the steady keel, the vessel grim and daring." This is followed by a quick cut to the horror on the ship of seeing their dead captain: "But O heart! heart! heart!" Next you see the people on shore excitedly waiting for their hero to emerge from the ship: "For you bouquets and ribbon'd wreaths—for you the shores a-crowding,/For you they call, the swaying mass, their eager faces turning." But then Whitman cuts back again to the sad scene on the deck: "It is some dream that on the deck,/You've fallen cold and dead." In the final scene, the focus is completely on the people grieving around their leader on the ship. The celebration is now in the background.

Writer **concludes** analysis with a personal opinion.

Whitman has created what looks like a simple poem on the surface. When you look at the symbolism behind it, though, it has a much greater impact. His imagery and techniques draw in the reader so that you feel like you are almost watching the action. I could feel the grief of the nation that was emerging from darkness of war only to be shattered by the tragedy of their leader's death.

Texas Traits

Respond to the reading. Answer the following questions.

Focus and Coherence (1) How is the thesis statement introduced? **Organization** (2) How are the middle paragraphs structured? (3) How is the organization appropriate for the purpose, audience, and context of the essay? **Development of Ideas** (4) What purpose do the embedded quotes serve? (5) Do the examples from the poem support the thesis? **Voice** (6) What devices does the writer use to sound knowledgeable? (7) What imagery does the writer create in the analysis?

Literature Connection. You may wish to read Walt Whitman's letter to his mother, dated January 29, 1865 and his poem "The Artilleryman's Vision."

TEKS 10.13A, 10.13B, 10.15A(ii), 10.15C(i), 10.15C(iii)
ELPS 5E

Prewriting Planning Your Writing

The first step in planning your essay is to choose a poem. Find a poem that you like and that will work for an analysis. Look for a poem that has figurative language, vivid imagery, and language that establishes a mood or theme that you can use in your analysis.

Freewriting

When Gabriel read the poem "O Captain! My Captain!" he began to write some of his ideas about the poem. Turbulent time in the United States; imagery of the Civil War; United States is the ship at sea; President Lincoln is the captain; repetition of line "Fallen cold and dead."

Gabriel also liked the poem "Fifteen" by William Stafford. He wrote the following notes about it.

Teenager dreams of being an adult; sees motorcycle with engine running; wants to ride it; helps owner; teenager knows he is not yet an adult.

Choose Your Topic

After completing the freewriting exercise, Gabriel chose "O Captain! My Captain!" because the figurative language appealed to him, and the poetic devices would lend themselves well to an analysis of meter, figurative language, and other poetic devices.

Gather and Organize Details

Gabriel made the following chart so that he could organize details for his essay. He wanted to include stylistic devices, like rhythm and rhyme, and rhetorical devices, such as repetition of lines and phrases, and diction, which is the word choice and the way that words are arranged in a sentence.

Rhythm "The port is near, the bells I hear, the people all exalting,"

Rhyme "The arm beneath your head!...You've fallen cold and dead."

Repetition "But O heart! heart! heart!

Diction "While follow eyes the steady keel, the vessel grim and daring;"

Prewrite

Plan your analysis. Use the tips above to choose a poem and plan your essay.

Prewriting Writing a Thesis Statement

In your analysis, you will be developing a critical analysis of the ideas and theme in the poem. You will also be developing a detailed analysis of the aesthetics of the rhetorical and stylistic devices the poet has used. When you analyze a poem, be sure to look at all the stylistic and rhetorical devices. These include meter and rhyming patterns, the use of language, and the imagery.

Your essay needs to be long enough to analyze the poem you have chosen. You will need to include details and quotations from the poem to support your controlling idea thoroughly. As you choose a poem, keep in mind your audience, the purpose, and the genre, or form, your writing will take. It is also important to keep in mind the context of your writing.

Developing Your Thesis Statement

Now that you have chosen your poem and gathered and organized the details and quotations that you want to include, you are ready to write your thesis statement.

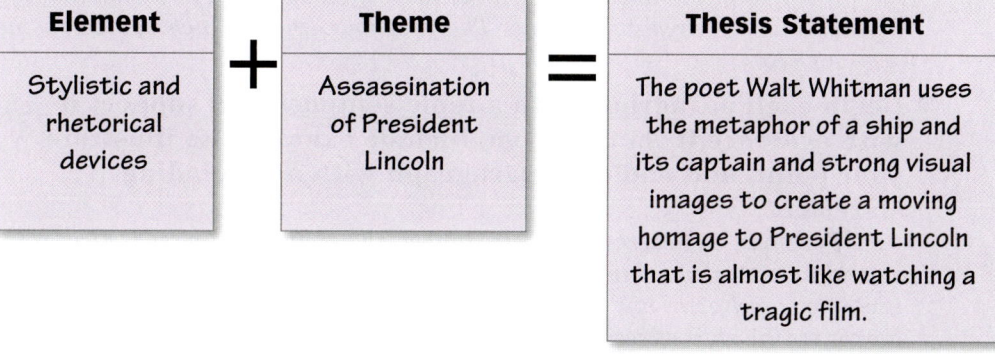

Element	+	Theme	=	Thesis Statement
Stylistic and rhetorical devices	+	Assassination of President Lincoln	=	The poet Walt Whitman uses the metaphor of a ship and its captain and strong visual images to create a moving homage to President Lincoln that is almost like watching a tragic film.

Prewrite

Write your thesis statement. **Using the poem you have chosen, the planning guide from the previous page, and the formula above, write the thesis statement for your analysis. Then write your introductory paragraph.**

Texas Traits

Focus on the Texas Traits

Development of Ideas Remember that your analysis must go beyond a summary, a paraphrase, or a literal analysis. As you plan your essay, make notes about what you want to say in each paragraph. Draft the topic sentence for each paragraph, and then choose quotations from the poem that support the thesis and the paragraph topic sentences.

TEKS 10.15A(iv), 10.15A(v), 10.15C(i)–10.15C(iii)

Drafting Developing Your Ideas

The middle paragraphs should build your analysis in a logical way. Refer to the exercises that you did on the previous pages. Your essay must be long enough to provide a detailed analysis. Remember to use relevant evidence and carefully chosen details to support your ideas.

Writing Your Middle Paragraphs

Develop ideas in each middle paragraph so that you clearly convey your meaning. Be sure to include relevant evidence and well chosen details. The following tips will help you plan your middle paragraphs.

- **First, provide your readers with a brief summary.**

  The ship that "has weather'd every rack" is the United States, just recovering from the "fearful trip" of the Civil War.

- **Other paragraphs should focus on the poem's stylistic and rhetorical devices. Write one paragraph on rhythm, another about diction, another about imagery, and so on.**

  He [Whitman] moves between the two different feelings by changing the rhythm and the rhyming scheme. The first four lines of each stanza rhyme every two lines.

- **Begin each paragraph with a topic sentence and support it with evidence from the poem. Include examples to illustrate your point, and end each paragraph with a concluding statement.**

  Whitman structures the poem almost like scenes in a movie. First you watch the victorious ship entering the harbor: "While follow eyes the steady keel, the vessel grim and daring." This is followed by a quick cut to the horror on the ship of seeing their dead captain: "But O heart! heart! heart!" In the final scene, the focus is completely on the people grieving around their leader on the ship. The celebration is now in the background.

Texas Traits

Focus on the Texas Traits

Organization Choose an organizational pattern in which you can analyze both the theme of the poem and the effects of the rhetorical and stylistic devices. Do not paraphrase the poem in your analysis.

Draft

Write your middle paragraphs. Use the prewriting tips above to draft your middle paragraphs.

Drafting Embedding Quotations in Your Essay

As you draft your analysis, be sure to use quotations from the poem to support your points. Choose quotations and lines that you feel best support the paragraph topic sentence and the controlling idea of your essay. The following tips will help you embed your quotations correctly.

- **If you are including more than one line of poetry, use a slash mark at the end of the line to show the line breaks.**
- **Be sure to use quotation marks correctly around the quotations or lines of poetry. You must also include any punctuation marks that appear in the quotations you are including.**
- **If the poem you are citing has line numbers, embed them in your essay along with the line or quotation.**

Remember, too, to use transitions so that your paragraphs flow smoothly from one to the next and from sentence to sentence within a paragraph.

Writing Your Introductory and Concluding Paragraphs

The following tips will help you write beginning and ending paragraphs.

- **Present your controlling idea in an effective introductory paragraph that gives your reader essential background information about the poem. Be sure to cite the title of the poem and the author's name.**
- **End your essay with an effective conclusion. Revisit the thesis statement and give your own personal opinion about the poem and why and how it "spoke" to you.**
  End with an insight about the poem and why it was important to you.

Draft

Write your opening and closing paragraphs. Use your prewriting work and the tips above to draft effective introductory and concluding paragraphs for your essay.

TEKS 10.13C–10.13E, 10.15A(v), 10.17A(ii), 10.17C, 10.18A, 10.18B(i), 10.19A
ELPS 5C, 5F

Texas Traits Revising Improving Your Response

Always review your writing. Make any changes and corrections neatly. Use the following questions to help you revise your essay.

- **Focus and Coherence:** Does my introductory paragraph contain my controlling idea? Are my ideas well supported? Do they all relate to the thesis? Does the conclusion tie the essay together?
- **Organization:** Have I included a beginning, a middle, and an ending? Does each paragraph have a focus? Have I used transitions so that paragraphs flow smoothly from one to the next?
- **Development of Ideas:** Have I adequately analyzed the poem, including the rhetorical and stylistic devices? Have I used key quotations, relevant evidence, and well chosen details to support the thesis? Have I given the reader background information and explained the theme?
- **Voice:** Have I used literary terms to express my ideas? Do I sound knowledgeable about the poem that I have analyzed?

Revise

Revise your essay. Answer the questions above and revise your work as needed.

Editing Checking Your Conventions

Check your final draft for grammar, sentence structure, capitalization, punctuation, and spelling.

Conventions

_____ **1.** Have I used correct and consistent verb tenses?
_____ **2.** Have I correctly used a variety of sentence structures?
_____ **3.** Have I capitalized all proper nouns and first words of sentences?
_____ **4.** Have I put quotation marks around the exact words that I quoted from the poem?
_____ **5.** Have I checked the spelling in my work?

Edit

Check your response. Read over your work, looking for errors in conventions. Make any needed corrections neatly.

Writing for Assessment

Responding to Prompts About Literature

Some assessments require you to respond to prompts about literature. These prompts may focus on something you have read before the test, something you will read during the test, or a combination of the two. Your response should show how well you understand the literature and how clearly you can form your thoughts within a limited amount of time. To prepare for this type of writing, carefully read your assignments in English class and pay particular attention to terms related to literature, such as *theme, symbol, character, metaphor,* and *irony.*

This chapter will help you to develop responses to literary prompts. You will learn to analyze various types of prompts, to use the writing process in a test situation, and to respond to fiction and nonfiction.

Writing Guidelines

Subject: **Literature prompt**
Purpose: **To demonstrate competence**
Form: **Response to a prompt**
Audience: **Instructor or test evaluator**

"The difficulty of literature is not to write, but to write what you mean."
—Robert Louis Stevenson

"Literature is news that stays news."
—Ezra Pound

Prewriting Analyzing a Literature Prompt

Prompts about literature ask you to respond to specific characteristics of a story, a poem, a novel, or a nonfiction selection. In this chapter, you will be drafting a response to a selection your teacher provides. Look for key words that tell you exactly what the prompt requires. In the sample prompt below, key words and phrases are underlined. The word *analyze* (red) gives the main direction or focus for the response.

Sample Prompt

In Joan Aiken's story "Searching for Summer," the setting and the title are important clues to the theme. When does the story take place? What are the characters really searching for? How does the story suggest a frightening possibility? Analyze how the story serves as a warning about the dangers of present-day technology.

Try It!

Copy the following sample prompts on a sheet of paper. Underline key words and phrases for each prompt and make notes about the kinds of supporting information that you would need for your response.

1. In her essay "Border: A Glare of Truth," Pat Mora discusses her feelings about moving to Ohio from El Paso, the place where she grew up. What is the "truth" that Mora learns about her early life in the border country of the Southwest? Using specific examples from her essay, prove how moving away from the border actually brought her closer to her heritage.

2. The following excerpts from the first chapter of Edith Wharton's novel *Ethan Frome* describe the night Ethan walked to town and caught a glimpse of a church dance. Explain how Edith Wharton uses the setting to help you understand Ethan's emotions. Cite specific examples from the excerpts to support your thesis.

Planning Your Response

Once you analyze and understand the prompt, you are ready to plan your response. If a reading selection is provided, examine it carefully for information related to the prompt. Choose the correct genre, form a topic sentence, and organize the details.

Sample Prompt and Selection

Comparisons are underlined.

In this excerpt from A. Conan Doyle's "A Study in Scarlet," Sherlock Holmes explains the effective use of one's memory. In a paragraph, analyze how he makes his point with comparisons.

"You see," he explained, "I consider that a man's brain originally is like a little empty attic, and you have to stock it with such furniture as you choose. A fool takes in all the lumber of every sort that he comes across, so that the knowledge which might be useful to him gets crowded out, or at best is jumbled up with a lot of other things so that he has a difficulty in laying his hands upon it. Now the skillful workman is very careful indeed as to what he takes into his brain-attic. He will have nothing but the tools which may help him in doing his work, but of these he has a large assortment, and all in the most perfect order.

Writing a Topic Sentence

After reading the prompt and selection, a student wrote this topic sentence.

Sherlock Holmes thinks of the brain (specific topic) **as an empty storage space, where care must be taken to avoid cluttering the memory with useless facts** (particular focus).

Creating a Graphic Organizer

The writer used a T-chart to organize the elements being compared.

Comparisons

Memory	Everyday Objects
– jumbled memory	– "takes in lumber of every sort"
– helpful memory	– "the tools which may help him"

Drafting Responding to a Fiction Prompt

The student writer of the sample essay chose to respond to the second prompt on page 312. The excerpt below shows how the student underlined words and phrases and added some notes on a copy of the selection to address the focus of the prompt (red). You will be responding to a prompt provided by your teacher.

Sample Prompt and Selection

The following excerpts from the first chapter of Edith Wharton's novel *Ethan Frome* describe the night Ethan walked to town and caught a glimpse of a church dance. Explain how Edith Wharton uses the setting to help you understand Ethan's emotions.

From *Ethan Frome* by Edith Wharton

Stillness, cold, shades of black and white except for yellow light from church basement

The village lay under two feet of snow, with drifts at the windy corners. In a sky of iron the points of the Dipper hung like icicles and Orion flashed his cold fires. The moon had set, but the night was so transparent that the white house-fronts between the elms looked gray against the snow, clumps of bushes made black stains on it, and the basement windows of the church sent shafts of yellow light far across the endless undulations.

Young Ethan Frome walked at a quick pace along the deserted street. . . . [T]he church reared its slim white steeple. . . . As the young man walked toward it the upper windows drew a black arcade along the side wall of the building. . . .

At the end of the village he paused before the darkened front on the church. . . . The hush of midnight lay on the village, and all its waking life was gathered behind the church windows, from which strains of dance-music flowed with the broad bands of yellow light. . . .

Heat, movement inside church contrast with cold outside.

Seen thus, from the pure and frosty darkness in which he stood, it seemed to be seething in a mist of heat. The metal reflectors of the gas-jets sent crude waves of light against the whitewashed walls, and the iron flanks of the stove at the end of the hall looked as though they were heaving with volcanic fires. The floor was thronged with girls and young men. . . .

A lively young man and a girl with colorful scarf dance.

The guests were preparing to leave, and the tide had already set toward the passage where coats and wraps were hung, when a young man with a sprightly foot and a shock of black hair shot into the middle of the floor and clapped his hands. The signal took instant effect. The musicians hurried to their instruments . . . and the lively young man, after diving about here and there in the throng, drew forth a girl who had already wound a cherry-coloured "fascinator" about her head, and, leading her up to the end of the floor, whirled her down its length to the bounding tune of a Virginia reel.

Frome's heart was beating fast. . . .

Writing a Thesis Statement

After reading the excerpt and taking notes, the student wrote the following thesis statement for her response essay.

Wharton helps the reader understand the feelings of a man (specific topic) **who sees through a church basement window a scene much different from his colorless world** (particular focus).

Creating a Graphic Organizer

The writer created a T-chart to list important details about the setting.

on the way to the church	in the church basement
"two feet of snow"	"shafts of yellow light"
"hush of midnight"	"strains of dance-music"
"sky of iron," constellations	"broad bands of yellow light"
"hung like icicles"	"seething in a mist of heat"
"flashed his cold fires"	"waves of light," "whitewashed walls"
"black stains"	"stove . . . heaving with volcanic fires"
"white steeple"	"cherry-coloured 'fascinator'"

TEKS 10.13B, 10.15C(i)–10.15C(iii)

Student Response

In this student response to the excerpts from *Ethan Frome*, note how the student writer used details from the novel to support the thesis statement.

Ethan Sees Red

Beginning The first paragraph leads up to the thesis statement (underlined).

In this excerpt from *Ethan Frome*, Ethan walks into a village one cold winter night to get a glimpse of a dance in a church basement. He is definitely portrayed as an outsider in this passage. Wharton helps the reader understand the feelings of this man who sees through a church basement window a scene much different from his colorless world.

Middle One paragraph focuses on the setting outside the church. Writer begins to analyze author's use of stylistic and rhetorical devices.

Ethan was out late at night, as "the hush of midnight lay on the village." Bleak images in shades of black and white mark his journey. He seems to be a part of the quiet landscape as he walks under a "sky of iron" filled with constellations "hung like icicles" or flashing "cold fires." The shadows cast by these night lights are "black stains" on the snow. As he approaches the church, the "white steeple" rises above the black walls of the building. He avoids those walls, attracted by something much different from the night that surrounds him.

The next paragraph focuses on the setting inside the church basement. Writer uses embedded quotes and specific evidence from the text to support thesis.

In contrast with the stark surroundings, the windows of the church basement send out inviting "shafts of yellow light." As Ethan looks in, "strains of dance-music" flow. Inside is a scene "seething in a mist of heat" with "waves of light" washing the walls and a stove, "heaving with volcanic fires." Suddenly, a young man dives into the throng of dancers and pulls out a girl with a "cherry-

Middle
The middle paragraphs include details from the excerpts to support thesis. Transitions move ideas smoothly.

coloured" scarf on her head. The young man and the girl whirl to the "bounding tune of a Virginia reel."

Wharton shows a man as cold and gray as the snowy winter's night in which he finds himself. Then a warm room, snappy music, lively dancing, and a girl in a red scarf give Ethan an emotional wake-up call. As Wharton relates, "Frome's heart was beating fast." The contrast between the winter night and the party has had a dramatic effect on Ethan—an effect that could be important in the rest of the story.

Ending
The closing summarizes the thesis.

Texas Traits

Respond to the reading. Answer the following questions about the student response.

Focus and Coherence (1) How does the thesis statement respond to the focus of the prompt? **Organization** (2) How does the writer organize the middle two paragraphs in the response? (3) What kinds of transitions does the writer use? **Development of Ideas** (4) What types of details does the student use to support her thesis? **Voice** (5) List two words or phrases quoted from the novel that are particularly effective. (6) What kinds of rhetorical devices does the student use?

Draft

Now write your response to the prompt. Use the questions above as a guide.

TEKS 10.13C, 10.13D, 10.17C, 10.18A, 10.18B(i), 10.19
ELPS 5C, 5D, 5F

Texas Traits

Revising Improving Your Response

Always review your response at the end of a writing test. Make any changes and corrections as neatly as possible. Use the following questions to help you revise your response.

- **Focus and Coherence:** Does my thesis statement address the focus of the prompt? Do the details and conclusion support the thesis?
- **Organization:** Have I included an introduction, a middle, and an effective conclusion? Does each paragraph have a focus? Do I use transitions effectively to link ideas between paragraphs? Do my sentences flow smoothly from one to the next?
- **Development of Ideas:** Have I included relevant and precise evidence from the text to support my ideas? Have I included key quotations that support my thesis? Do I conclude with an insight about the literature selection?
- **Voice:** Do I sound clear in my thinking? Have I used correct literary terms? Do I sound confident and knowledgeable?

Revise

Improve your work. **Reread your practice response, asking yourself the questions above. Make any changes neatly.**

Editing Checking Your Response

In your final read-through, check for conventions: grammar, sentence structure, capitalization, punctuation, and spelling.

Conventions

_____ **1.** Have I used proper and consistent verb tenses?

_____ **2.** Have I correctly used a variety of sentence structures?

_____ **3.** Have I capitalized all proper nouns and the first words of sentences?

_____ **4.** Have I put quotation marks around the exact words that I quoted from the selection?

_____ **5.** Have I checked the spelling in my work?

Edit

Check your response. **Read over your work, looking for errors in conventions. Make needed corrections neatly.**

Responding to Literature on Tests

Use the following tips as a guide whenever you respond to a prompt about literature. These tips will help you respond to both fiction and nonfiction selections.

Before you write . . .

- **Be clear about the time limit.**
  Plan enough time for prewriting, writing, and revising.
- **Understand the prompt.**
  Be sure that you know what the prompt requires. Pay special attention to the key word that tells you what you need to do.
- **Read the selection with the focus of the prompt in mind.**
  Take notes that will help you form your thesis. If you're working on a copy of the selection, underline important details.
- **Form your thesis statement.**
  The thesis statement should identify the specific topic plus the particular focus of the prompt.
- **Make a graphic organizer.**
  Jot down main points and possible quotations for your essay.

As you write . . .

- **Maintain the focus of your essay.**
  Keep your thesis in mind as you write.
- **Be selective.**
  Use examples from your graphic organizer and the selection to support your thesis.
- **End in a meaningful way.**
  Start by revisiting the thesis. Then try to share a final insight about the topic with the reader.

After you've written a first draft . . .

- **Check for completeness and correctness.**
  Use the questions on page **318** to revise your essay. Then check for errors in grammar, sentence structure, capitalization, punctuation, and spelling.

Try It!

Plan and write a response. Read a prompt your teacher supplies. Analyze it, read the selection, form a thesis statement, list ideas in a graphic organizer, and write your essay. Then revise and edit your response. Try to complete your work within the time your teacher gives you.

ELPS 1E, 2C, 3B, 3D, 3E, 4G

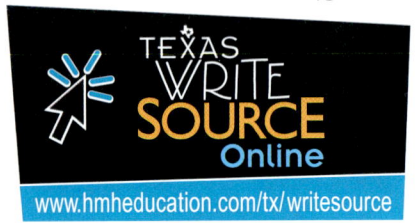

TEXAS WRITE SOURCE Online
www.hmheducation.com/tx/writesource

Creative Writing

Writing Focus

Learning Language

Learning these words and expressions will help you understand this unit.

1. **Mood** is the feeling or atmosphere that a writer creates for the reader.
   What adjectives might a writer use to create a scary mood in a story?
2. **Characters** are the individuals who participate in the action of a literary work.
   Who is your favorite character in short stories or novels that you have read?
3. **Hyperbole** is a figure of speech, an exaggerated statement that is used for humor or to emphasize a point.
   Why is the statement "I am so hungry I could eat a horse," considered to be hyperbole?
4. The expression to **ooh and aah** means to exclaim in wonder or admiration.
   Why do you think people ooh and aah when they see babies?

Writing Stories

You are a born storyteller. You may find that talking about your experiences helps you to make sense out of your life. You may also enjoy making up stories, but that might not be as easy for you as it once was. It's no fault of your own. You're simply more focused on real-life experiences at this point in your life.

Here's the best way to feel inventive again: Sit down and start writing. Write simple stories, crazy stories, stories modeled after the ones you read now and the ones you read when you were younger.

This chapter will help you get started. It discusses the basic plot, offers a sample story and story-writing guidelines, and ends with a discussion of story patterns and important terms related to fiction.

Writing Guidelines

Subject: **A conflict within the main character**
Purpose: **To engage and entertain**
Form: **Short story**
Audience: **Classmates**

"The only way to learn to write short stories is to write them, and then try to discover what you have done."

—Flannery O'Connor

TEKS 10.13A

The Shape of Stories

Think of special experiences in your life: a key game, a family reunion, starting at a new school, getting your driver's license. These experiences build in excitement to a high point that really makes the event memorable. Fiction works in the same way. The story builds until the action reaches the climax, the most intense part of the plot.

Beginning with the Plot

The plot refers to the events or actions that move a story along from start to finish. A plot has five parts: *exposition, rising action, climax, falling action,* and *resolution*. The plot line below shows how these parts work together.

Plot Line

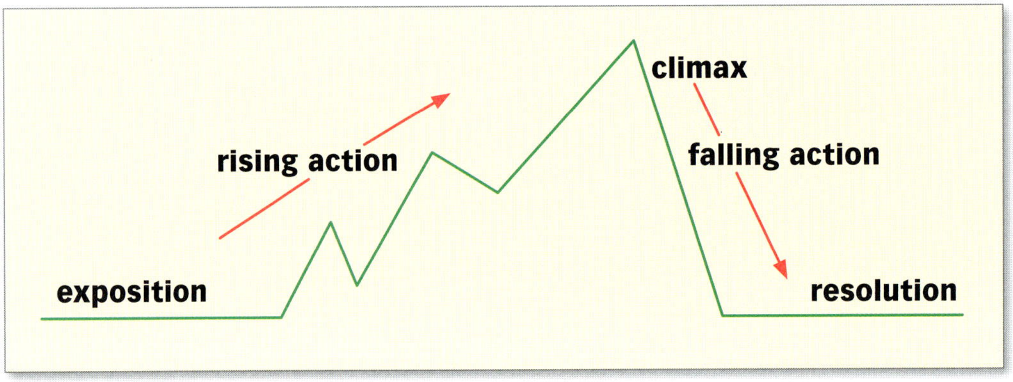

Exposition

The *exposition* is the beginning part of a story. In it, the main character, the conflict, and the setting are introduced. The conflict is the problem that the main character faces. The setting is the place and the time of the action. The following example demonstrates the sort of information that you would share in the exposition.

> Marina is in her room, cuddling her cat, Feather. Feather is very old, has lost his eyesight, and has extreme difficulty moving around. The cat had once belonged to her beloved grandmother, who has since passed away. Marina's parents and the veterinarian have suggested that Feather be put to sleep, but Marina is resisting.

Rising Action

In a short story, the *rising action* usually includes at least two or three important actions involving the main character and his or her problem. This builds suspense into the story.

First Action: Marina talks with her little sister Rosie about their ailing cat, Feather, especially how playful he used to be. Marina tries to play with the cat, but Feather shows no interest.

Second Action: Marina starts to tell Rosie stories about their grandmother. She talks about how much their grandmother had loved Feather.

Third Action: Rosie admits that she doesn't remember much about their grandmother because she was so little when their grandmother died. Marina accuses her sister of forgetting about this special person.

Climax

The *climax* is the moment of truth, or the most exciting part, when the character confronts his or her problem head-on. All the action leads up to the climax. In the best stories, the main character is changed by the climax.

Marina's mother comes in, and Marina confesses that she wants to keep the cat alive because it is her connection with her grandmother. Marina is afraid that if the cat dies, so will her memories. Her mother assures her she won't forget her grandmother, and that it is cruel to make Feather suffer. Marina decides to let the veterinarian put Feather to sleep.

Falling Action

The *falling action* involves the main character as he or she begins to deal with life after the moment of truth.

Marina declares that she will never forget her grandmother. Marina's mother assures her that anyone who is truly loved is never forgotten.

Conflict

A well-developed *conflict* in a story is the struggle between two opposing forces. Almost every story has a major conflict—a conflict that is the story's focus. An *external conflict* involves a character pitted against an outside force, such as nature, a physical obstacle, or another character. An *internal conflict* is one that occurs within a character.

Marina is afraid that she will forget her grandmother. *(internal conflict)* She quarrels with her sister about the cat. *(external conflict)*

Developing Believable Characters

Characters are the people in your story. You can make them come alive through their actions and through the adjectives you use to describe them. Your characters should be believable, and they should be interesting to your readers. Most stories have more than one character. As you will see from the descriptions below, there are different types of characters. As you create your own story, remember that this is fiction, and your characters will become whatever you want them to be.

Types of Characters

Like real people, characters display certain qualities, distinct characteristics that make them come alive. Characters develop and change over time, and they usually have motivations, or reasons for their behaviors.

Main characters

The main character or characters are the most important ones in a story. Generally, especially in a short story, the plot focuses on one main character. A novel, however, may have several main characters.

Minor characters

The less important characters in a literary work are known as minor characters. Their purpose is to support the plot. The story is not centered on them, but they help carry out the action and help the reader learn more about the main character.

Dynamic and static characters

A dynamic character undergoes important changes as the plot unfolds. These changes can be good or bad. They occur because of the character's actions or experiences in the story.

A static character remains the same throughout the story. Static characters may experience events and interact with the other characters, but they do not change.

Alan, the main character in the sample story on pages 326–327, has to work out his feelings toward Tiffany, which is an internal conflict. He is the main character, and he is a dynamic character.

Resolution of the Plot

In a short story or a novel, the *resolution* brings the story to a natural, thought-provoking, or surprising conclusion. In some stories, it's hard to tell the difference between the falling action and the resolution because they are so closely related. As the falling action in a story begins, tensions ease. The final outcome of the story, however, has not yet been fully worked out. It is the events in the falling action that lead to the resolution. In the story about Marina and the cat Feather, the resolution is shown below.

Marina's mother brings out a photo album.

She and Marina sit down with Rosie to tell stories about Grandma.

How the Resolution is Revealed

When you read a short story, you will see that in the resolution the author has revealed the final outcome and tied up any loose ends. In a fairy tale, the outcome is usually a happy one. In many stories, the conflict is resolved, and the characters live happily ever after.

When you write your own short story, ask yourself these questions as you develop the resolution.

1. How have the events and conflicts affected or engaged the characters?
2. How is the conflict resolved?
3. What message are you suggesting for your readers in the resolution?
4. What lesson has the main character learned from the experiences that occurred in the story?

TEKS 10.14A

Sample Story

Read and enjoy the sample story by Thea Karas. The side notes indicate how the story develops from the exposition to the resolution.

Exposition
The writer creates interesting, believable characters. She describes the setting and conflict.

Rising Action
Dialogue and details add to the suspense of the story. They also make characters more believable.

Rising Action
Additional action keeps the reader engaged and enhances plot development. Conflict is well developed.

Building Foundations

Alan sniffed the fragrant blend of open earth, fresh cement, and new wood, almost forgetting how miserable he was feeling. The Construction Class students were actually building a house. As the students grouped around the site for Mr. Hanson's instructions, Alan's friend Sara sidled up and nudged him, her soft lily-of-the-valley cologne mingling pleasantly with the construction smells.

"So, what happened? I thought you were taking Tiffany to the dance," she whispered.

His agony returned. "She got a better offer."

Sara didn't say anything more as Mr. Hanson explained the day's activity: creating foundation walls.

Working in teams, the students began building up the short walls of the crawl space that would serve to support the rest of the house. Alan and Sara worked side by side on the prepared footings, Sara slapping down mortar and Alan setting the cinder blocks.

"I'm sorry about Tiffany," Sara said softly as she tapped her trowel against the mortar bucket. "But why did you ask her to begin with?"

Alan thought about Tiffany, her glossy black hair and amber eyes. Even now, her heady jasmine perfume seemed to fill his senses. "She's just so pretty."

"Pretty boring," Sara snorted. "What do you two have to talk about?"

Alan considered. What *did* they talk about? Tiffany was into international affairs. When they'd eaten lunch together on Friday, all she had talked about was how some country he had never even heard of was being repressed by another country he hadn't heard of! He had sat silent the whole time, just looking at those amber eyes.

"Here." Sara shoved the mortar bucket at him. "Let's switch jobs."

He began slapping the grainy gray mortar on top of the blocks.

Writer continues to develop believable, interesting characters. She uses a variety of literary strategies and devices to enhance the plot.

"I love this class," Sara grunted as she hoisted a cinder block into place. "It's great to build something."

"Yeah, I can't wait to get to the real stuff—putting down the floors, putting up the walls, and fitting windows. This is kinda boring."

"It is pretty tedious," Sara admitted, "but think about it. If we don't do a good job on the foundation, the rest of the house could shift and even fall apart!"

Alan grinned at her enthusiasm. "You're not given to hyperbole, are you?"

Sara blushed, a blond wisp escaping from her hat and curling around her face. "I just think foundations are important." Alan tried to imagine Tiffany working next to him, but the picture wouldn't form. He admired how skillfully Sara skimmed her trowel along, cleaning off the excess mortar.

Climax
Writer creates a believable climax, revealing complex character traits.

"So how's your biology project coming?" he asked.

Alan almost forgot about Tiffany as they discussed genetics. When it was time to get back on the bus, Sara checked her watch. "Wow, time flies . . . "

" . . . when you're having fun!" Alan finished, and they both laughed.

A wayward curl dipped across Sara's eye, and Alan reached over to brush it away. Her eyes were green with little yellow flecks, and looking at them, Alan suddenly felt his knees go weak.

Falling Action and Resolution
With a well-developed resolution, the story comes to a satisfying end.

As they started up the bus steps, he looked back at the wall he and Sara had built together. *It's a good foundation,* he thought to himself. *It will support a good house.* Then he plopped down in the seat next to Sara and caught a delicate whiff of lily-of-the-valley cologne.

"Hey, Sara," he said, "about the dance . . . "

Respond to the reading. Review the story and answer these questions.

Focus and Coherence (1) What is the conflict? How is it introduced and developed? **Organization** (2) What main actions are included in the rising action? Name two. **Development of Ideas** (3) Who are the characters? (4) What details make them interesting and believable? (5) What details make the setting believable? **Voice** (6) How realistic does the dialogue sound? Explain.

TEKS 10.13A, 10.14A

Prewriting Planning Your Writing

Fiction writers plan stories in different ways. For example, C. S. Forester thinks "first of something to be done and then . . . of an interesting character to do it." William Faulkner, on the other hand says he "begins with a character, usually, and once he stands up on his feet and begins to move, all I do is trot along behind." Another writer may start with a particular setting.

No matter how you start, just remember that your short story should include well-developed, interesting, believable characters. As you plan your story, identify at least the main character and his or her problem.

Creating Characters

Who is the central person in your story? You can base the main character on someone you know, but don't embarrass a person by making the main character too much like him or her.

Also decide on one or two supporting, minor characters who will be involved in the action. Including too many characters, however, may make your story unnecessarily complicated. Review the information on types of characters as you plan your story.

Considering a Conflict

For this assignment, your main character should be in conflict with him- or herself. Use a range of strategies to develop your plot. Think about literary strategies and devices you can use to enhance the plot. Consider a number of possible conflicts that your main character could deal with: his or her relationship with someone, peer pressure, stage fright, meeting expectations, and so on.

Establishing a Setting

Your setting can be any place that allows your main character to deal with the conflict. Limit yourself, though, to one main location and a brief span of time. The sample story takes place at a construction site during one class.

Thinking about the Action

The conflict requires the main character to act, so list two or three actions that could move your story along. Also consider the climax, or turning point.

Prewrite

Plan your story. **Using the guidelines above, choose a main character, a conflict, and a setting. Then list actions that result from the conflict.**

Drafting Making Your Story Work

Stories are built with a few interesting characters, realistic dialogue, and believable action. Use a range of literary strategies and devices to develop your plot. Also consider the following points about story writing.

Starting Your Story

To get the reader's attention, start your story in one of these ways.

- **Start in the middle of the action.**
  Without slowing down, Zack artfully dodged the rock flung at his head.
- **Begin with dialogue.**
  "Never flown before, huh?" the flight attendant asked as I clutched the arms of my seat, preparing for takeoff and the end of my young life.
- **Make an attention-grabbing statement.**
  Everyone always oohs and aahs over my cute little brother, but I know the truth: He was sent from an alien planet to destroy the earth.

In the exposition, establish a setting, introduce the characters, and identify the conflict. Once this background is set, write the middle part of your story.

Developing the Action

Place your character in the first challenging action. Build suspense with each new action leading up to the climax.

- Create real, believable, and natural dialogue. Let the words reflect what the characters think and feel.
- Include sensory details and other stylistic and literary devices to enhance the plot.
- Show instead of tell. For example, instead of saying "Alan was sad," say "Alan slumped into his seat." Instead of "Sara felt embarrassed," write "Sara blushed."
- Build to a climax, when the main character confronts the problem.

Bringing the Story to a Close

After the climax, end the story. Show how your character has been changed.

Draft

Write your first draft. Use your planning from page 328 plus the information above as a general guide.

Revising Improving Your Story

Ask yourself the following when you revise your story. (See page 322).

Focus and Coherence

_____ **1.** Do I introduce conflict, setting, and characters and describe them consistently throughout?

Organization

_____ **2.** Have I included a well-developed plot?

Development of Ideas

_____ **3.** Are the characters interesting and believable?

_____ **4.** Is my main character tested? Does my main character change during the story?

_____ **5.** Do all actions build toward the climax?

Voice

_____ **6.** Do I show rather than tell? Do I use descriptive words, images, and figurative language to improve my writing?

Revise

Revise your story. Use the information above to help you revise the first draft of your story.

Editing Checking for Conventions

When you edit your revised story, check grammar, sentence structure, capitalization, punctuation, and spelling.

Conventions

_____ **1.** Are my verb tenses consistent and correct?

_____ **2.** Have I correctly used a variety of sentence structures?

_____ **3.** Have I used correct capitalization, punctuation, and spelling?

_____ **4.** Have I punctuated dialogue correctly?

Edit

Edit your story. Check your story for use of correct conventions.

Story Patterns

Many short stories follow a basic pattern. Here are brief descriptions of some popular short-story patterns.

The Quest

The main character goes on a journey into the unknown, overcomes a number of obstacles, and returns either victorious or wiser. Heroic myths follow this pattern, but so do many modern stories.

A young woman fights for the right to join an all-male sports team.

The Discovery

The main character follows a trail of clues to discover an amazing secret. Mystery and suspense novels use this pattern.

A curious young man discovers that the bully at school is . . .

The Rite of Passage

A difficult experience changes the main character in a significant and lasting way. These stories are also called *coming of age* stories.

A young soldier learns about responsibility while on the battlefield.

The Choice

The focus in this type of story is a decision the main character must make. Tension builds as the decision approaches.

A young adult must decide to follow the crowd or follow her own conscience.

The Union

Two people fall in love, but they are held apart by a number of obstacles. Their struggle to come together only causes their love to grow stronger. Sometimes they succeed, and sometimes they fail.

A young deaf man falls in love with a gifted violinist and then struggles to understand the music he can't hear.

The Reversal

In this pattern, the main character follows one course of action until something causes him or her to think or act in a different way.

A young woman quits school, but then discovers her true love is painting and enrolls in an art school.

Elements of Fiction

The following terms describe elements of literature. This information will help you discuss and write about novels, poetry, essays, and other literary works.

Antagonist The person or force that works against the hero of the story (See *protagonist.*)

Character A person or an animal in a story

Conflict A problem or clash between two forces in a story
- **Person vs. person** A problem between characters
- **Person vs. himself or herself** A problem within a character's own mind
- **Person vs. society** A problem between a character and society, the law, or some tradition
- **Person vs. nature** A problem with an element of nature, such as a blizzard or a hurricane
- **Person vs. destiny** A problem or struggle that appears to be beyond a character's control

Mood The feeling a piece of literature creates in a reader

Narrator The person or character who tells the story, gives background information, and fills in details between dialogue

Plot, Plot Line See pages 322–323.

Point of View The angle from which a story is told
- In **first-person point of view,** one character is telling the story.
- In **third-person point of view,** someone outside the story is telling it.
- In **omniscient point of view,** the narrator tells the thoughts and feelings of all the characters.
- In **limited omniscient point of view,** the narrator tells the thoughts of one character at a time.
- In **camera view** (objective), the narrator records the action from his or her own point of view without any other characters' thoughts.

Protagonist The main character or hero in a story (See *antagonist.*)

Setting The place and time period in which a story takes place

Theme The author's message about life or human nature

Tone The writer's attitude toward his or her subject (*angry, humorous,* and so on)

Writing Scripts

At one time or another, we have all felt that we were sure about something, only to learn that maybe we didn't know as much as we thought. A play is an excellent literary form for exploring such a theme, or underlying message, and for considering what a character might do when things don't work out in the expected way.

In a script for a play, you develop your story almost exclusively through dialogue. Each new exchange between characters moves the story toward the climax or high point of interest. The only other device that you have to work with is stage direction, which provides explanations about the characters' actions onstage.

In this chapter, you will read a brief play script about a student who "thinks" he knows all about the world of work. Then guidelines will help you develop your own script about an individual who learns a lesson about life.

Writing Guidelines

Subject: **Learning a lesson about life**
Purpose: **To entertain and enlighten**
Form: **Brief script**
Audience: **Classmates**

"Drama is life with the dull bits cut out."

—Alfred Hitchcock

TEKS 10.14C

Sample Script

In the following script by student writer Matt Holmes, the main character thinks he knows what it takes to get a job. The side notes identify key points in the development of the play. (See page 339 for an explanation of the abbreviations used in the stage directions.)

Stage Directions
The stage setup and characters are described.

Beginning
The play starts right in the middle of the action. The theme is introduced.

Suiting Up

Characters: **Wesley**, a high school student seeking a job
Luke, his friend
Tori, another friend
Mr. Hayes, a potential employer
Kyle, a student

Scene 1

(The only furniture on the stage is in the UC area—a desk with two chairs, one behind the desk, one in front. At the beginning, Mr. Hayes and Kyle are seated, frozen, in the dark UC area. Tori stands, frozen, in the dark DR area. As the curtain rises, the DL pool of light comes up, where Luke is bouncing a basketball. Wesley enters from DR and comes into the light. He is dressed casually, even a little sloppily, with shirttail untucked and shoelaces untied.)

LUKE: Hey, Wesley, you wanna shoot some hoops?
WESLEY: Can't. I'm heading over to the Food Mart to interview for a job.
LUKE: You joining the ranks of the employed? Cool.
WESLEY: Yeah, I gotta start earning some bucks if I want to get a car.
LUKE: A car? You can't get your license for another six months.
WESLEY: I know, but it'll take me at least that long to get a down payment.
LUKE: What kind of job?
WESLEY: Stocking shelves. I figure a big, strong guy like me . . .
LUKE: You think you look okay for a job interview?
WESLEY: Sure. It's not an executive position, right?
LUKE: Well, good luck, buddy.
WESLEY: Thanks. Catch you later.

Middle
Each new interchange advances the theme and adds tension. The mood is enhanced by figurative language.

Writer continues to develop the mood. The tone, the attitude the writer has toward the main character, is clearly revealed.

(The DL light goes down and Luke freezes as Wesley moves toward the DR section. The light comes up on Tori as Wesley crosses into her area.)

TORI: Hey, Wesley. You seen Luke?
WESLEY: Hi, Tori. Yeah, he's at the park shooting hoops. See ya.
TORI: Where are you headed in such a hurry?
WESLEY: Job interview at Food Mart.
TORI: Er—shouldn't you go home and change first? You look like you just overhauled an engine or something.
WESLEY: Heck, it's only a stocking job. They won't care what I look like.
TORI: Don't you want to make a good impression?
WESLEY: My shining personality will win them over.
TORI: Right. Well, good luck!

(The light goes down and Tori freezes as Wesley moves toward UC. The light comes up on Mr. Hayes and Kyle. Kyle rises, they shake hands, and Kyle turns and leaves.)

MR. HAYES: Next! *(Wesley peeks in.)* Ah, Wesley Jones, isn't it? Come in, son.
WESLEY: Thank you, sir. *(Enters and extends his hand for a handshake, politely sits down.)*
MR. HAYES: *(Eyes Wesley's grungy clothes.)* Well. Let's see here. *(Looks over Wesley's application.)* Hmmm. Ah, you're on the basketball team. Well, we have other students involved in after-school activities. We can always work schedules around.
WESLEY: *(Politely)* Yes, sir.
MR. HAYES: Your grades are good, too.
WESLEY: Yes, sir, I can do that and hold a job.
MR. HAYES: Yes. Well, Wesley, I'll tell you. You seem like a pleasant young man. But I'm not going to give you the job.
WESLEY: *(Surprised)* Sir? But why?
MR. HAYES: There's a lot of competition in this world, Wesley. Did you see that young man who just went out?
WESLEY: Kyle? My grades are better than his!

TEKS 10.14C

MR. HAYES: Maybe, but did you see the way he was dressed?
WESLEY: Heck, I have a suit, too!
MR. HAYES: But you didn't wear it, did you? He took the trouble to be well groomed. That shows me that he wants this job. Your clothes tell me you don't really care.
WESLEY: But I do care! I'd work really hard for you!
MR. HAYES: Maybe you would, Wesley, but I have to *see* that before I can hire you. I'm sorry, son. First impressions do count.
WESLEY: Yes, sir. *(He rises to leave, then turns.)* Thank you, Mr. Hayes.
MR. HAYES: Try again another time, Wesley. *(Wesley nods and goes right as the light goes down and Mr. Hayes exits left.)*

(The light goes up DC. Wesley appears from the right wearing a suit and tie. Luke and Tori move to the area and Luke whistles.)

LUKE: Whoa, who died?
WESLEY: There's another opening at the Food Mart. This time I'm going to get it.
TORI: Ah—
WESLEY: Don't say it, Tori. Okay, so you were right.
TORI: *(Smiling)* I wasn't going to say a thing.
WESLEY: Maybe this time Mr. Hayes'll get the chance to see my shining personality.
TORI: I'm sure of it. After all, you're *suited up* for success! Good luck, Wesley.

Middle
The main character realizes his mistake. The theme is explicit for the reader.

Ending
The main character sets a new course of action. The writer continues to show mood and tone throughout the script.

Texas Traits

Respond to the Reading Answer these questions about the script.

Focus and Coherence (1) When and how is the theme introduced? (2) How is it developed? **Organization** (3) In what part of the play does the climax occur? (4) What happens after this point? **Development of Ideas** (5) How do the action and dialogue advance the theme and tone? **Voice** (6) How does the writer make the dialogue sound natural? (7) How does the writer create the mood?

Prewriting Choosing Your Main Character

In a play script, the main character usually wants something, but faces a problem that keeps him or her from achieving it. As you start your planning, choose a main character and decide on something he or she wants.

The main character of the play is the **protagonist**. This person is changed in some way by the action. Matt decided to write about a teenage boy like himself. He named the character Wesley. Then Matt made a list of things Wesley might want, and starred the one he would write about.

List of Wants

Wesley wants . . .

- to have a girlfriend
- to earn high grades
- to find a job *
- to buy a car

Prewrite

Choose your main character. **Decide on a main character for your play and make a list of things this person may want to achieve or obtain. Choose one that would make an interesting script. Think of how this character will help convey your tone and set a definite mood for your audience.**

Selecting a Conflict

The conflict occurs when something stands in the way of the main character. Matt compiled the following list before selecting a conflict. He starred the problem he thought was most interesting.

Potential Conflicts

Things that could keep Wesley from finding a job

- His parents
- His attitude *
- His grades
- His after-school activities

Prewrite

List possible conflicts. **Be sure these conflicts are believable. Then place an asterisk beside the one that you will use in your play. Consider how your choice of conflict will help to illuminate the theme of your play.**

TEKS 10.13A, 10.14C

Identifying Other Characters

Other characters serve specific purposes. They explain information or complicate the plot. They may help convey theme, either explicitly or implicitly. They can also help set the tone for the play. In the sample, Wesley wants to get a job. Each of the other characters contributes in some way to the action.

Character List

Wesley's friend Luke brings up the idea that Wesley may not be suitably dressed for a job interview.
Wesley's friend Tori reinforces the idea that he is not dressed properly.
Mr. Hayes also points out Wesley's mistake about his attire.
Kyle presents a contrast, showing someone properly dressed for an interview.

Prewrite **List additional characters for your play. Explain what the function of each will be. (Limit yourself to a few additional characters.)**

Planning the Starting Point

Start your play right in the middle of the action. Work in any necessary background information in interchanges between the characters. Matt decided that the action would begin with a conversation between Luke and Wesley about the interview Wesley was going to. Matt also listed background information that he may need to work in early in the play. (Later, Matt crossed out ideas that were unnecessary.)

Background Information

What the audience needs to know:

- Wesley is going on a job interview.
- ~~He has just come from basketball practice.~~
- He wants to work as a stocker at the Food Mart.
- He needs to earn money to buy a car.
- ~~His parents said they would cover his car insurance if he bought a car.~~

Prewrite **Plan how to start your play. Decide which action will begin your play. Also decide what your audience needs to know so they will be able to follow the story line. (Later, you may find that some of these ideas are unnecessary.)**

Considering the Stage Directions

Because a play is a visual as well as an oral medium, the writer must plan the characters' movements onstage. **Stage directions** are the nondialogue parts of a play that identify where the characters are and what they are doing in each scene.

In Matt's play, the action moves smoothly from one location to the next. The opening stage descriptions describe the setup for each acting area that will be used. Remember that the setting and stage directions play a major role in establishing mood.

Stage Directions

(The only furniture on the stage is in the UC area—a desk with two chairs, one behind the desk, one in front. At the beginning, Mr. Hayes and Kyle are seated, frozen, in the dark UC area. Tori stands, frozen, in the dark DR area. . . .)

Prewrite

Plan your opening stage directions. **Describe where and how the opening action of your play takes place. Try to keep things simple.**

Using Proper Stage Terminology

Below is a diagram of the basic acting areas on a stage and the shorthand used to refer to each area. Use this shorthand in your stage directions.

Stage Diagram

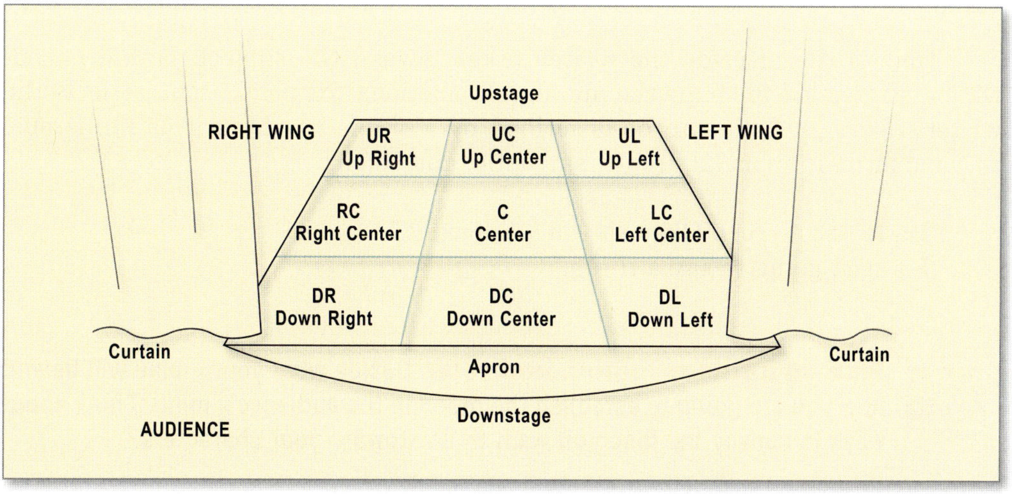

TEKS 10.14C

Developing Theme, Mood, and Tone

As you plan your script, keep in mind three key components: theme, mood, and tone. These components will influence the conflict, the staging and dialogue, and how you portray the characters in your play.

Theme

Theme is the underlying message about life or human nature that a writer wants the reader to understand. In most cases, themes are not explicitly stated but are implied, so they must be inferred by the audience. A theme may imply how a person should live, but theme should not be confused with a moral. Universal themes are those that are found in the literature of all time periods.

Introduce your theme:

"You think you look okay for a job interview?"

Mood

Mood is the feeling or atmosphere that the writer creates for the reader or audience. Descriptive words, imagery, and figurative language contribute to the mood of a play. If the stage is dark, with only a tree or two, and you hear a hooting owl, you can imagine that the mood of the play will be one of dread or fright. Dialogue, too, can convey the mood.

"Well, Wesley, I'll tell you. You seem like a pleasant young man. But I'm not going to give you the job."

Tone

Tone is the attitude the writer takes toward the subject. Unlike mood, which is intended to shape the audience's emotional response, tone reflects the writer's feelings. Tone can be described by a single word, such as humorous, serious, formal, informal, ironic, sarcastic, and so on.

"Don't say it, Tori. Okay so you were right."
"I wasn't going to say a thing."

Prewrite

Plan on a theme, mood, and tone. Decide what your theme will be and how you are going to establish the mood in the audience's mind. Think about ways to convey the tone you want to use toward your characters.

Drafting Creating Your Script

Remember that the characters tell the story. Imagine what they will say and do in response to the play's conflict. Keep in mind that ideas in a script should be structured in a sustained, persuasive way.

Beginning

- **Start right in the middle of the action** and work in the necessary background information. Introduce the theme, either explicitly or implicitly, and use details that will establish a definite mood. As you introduce the characters, include details that will contribute to a definite tone. (See page **340.**)

Middle

- **Use dialogue and action to present the play's ideas.** Make sure the dialogue sounds natural.
- **Add complications (problems) to build suspense.** Don't let the character solve the problem too quickly.
- **Build to the climax.** This is the point where the character comes face-to-face with his or her problem and responds to it in some way.

Ending

- **Bring your play to a close.** Show how your character has changed because of what he or she has learned.

Developing Your Characters

1. **What does the character say and do?** From Wesley's words and actions, we learn that he doesn't think he needs to dress up for the interview. The stage directions tell us what he is doing.

   WESLEY: My shining personality will win them over.
   WESLEY: Thank you, sir. *(Enters and extends his hand for a handshake, politely sits down.)*

2. **What do others say to, or about, the main character?** Their thoughts can reveal personality traits of the character.

   TORI: You look like you just overhauled an engine or something. . . .
   MR. HAYES: Your clothes tell me that you don't really care.

Draft

Write your first draft. Use the tips above to write your first draft.

TEKS 10.14C

Texas Traits

Revising Improving Your Writing

Read your script again. Use these questions to help guide your revision.

Theme

- **How and when did you introduce the theme?**
- **Is the theme stated implicitly or explicitly?**
- **Can your audience infer the theme from the conflict and the actions or dialogue of the characters?**
- **Has your development of the theme been consistent throughout the script?**

Mood

- **What feeling or atmosphere have you created?**
- **Have you used imagery and figurative language to convey the mood to the audience?**
- **Are the descriptions you have created believable and engaging?**
- **Does the mood change during the script? If so, how have you conveyed the change to your audience?**

Tone

- **What is your tone toward the main character? What is your tone toward the other characters?**
- **What words and details have you used to reflect your feelings about the characters?**
- **What one adjective would you use to describe the tone? Have you adequately conveyed it to your audience?**

Revise

Revise for theme, mood, and tone. Use the questions above to guide you as you revise your script for consistent theme. If necessary, add details that contribute to a definite mood and to a definite tone.

TEKS 10.13C, 10.13D, 10.14C

Texas Traits

Revising Improving Your Writing

Read your script out loud or have someone else read it to you. Use this checklist to help with your revision.

Focus and Coherence

_____ **1.** Have I adequately conveyed the theme, mood, and tone?
_____ **2.** Does the plot flow smoothly from beginning to end?

Organization

_____ **3.** Does each complication build on the previous one?
_____ **4.** Is the climax easily recognized?
_____ **5.** Do stage directions help move the action along?

Development of Ideas

_____ **6.** Is the main character's conflict believable?
_____ **7.** Does the action include complications (problems)?
_____ **8.** Does each character serve an important role within the play?

Voice

_____ **9.** Does the dialogue sound natural and believable?
_____ **10.** Does the dialogue flow smoothly from character to character?

Editing Checking for Conventions

Use the following checklist as a guide when you check your script for proper formatting and for conventions.

Conventions

_____ **1.** Have I used correct and consistent verb tenses?
_____ **2.** Are the sentences in my dialogue structured correctly?
_____ **3.** Have I checked for correct capitalization and punctuation?
_____ **4.** Have I checked for spelling errors?

Revise

Revise and edit your writing. Use the checklists above as a guide when you revise and edit the first draft of your script.

TEKS 10.14C

Sample Radio Script

In radio drama, your audience can only imagine the action. Radio scripts have theme, mood, and tone, just like plays.

LIFE IN THE EXPRESS LANE

(SCENE: A GROCERY STORE CHECKOUT LINE. WE CAN HEAR VOICES, THE DING OF THE SCANNER.)

LOUDSPEAKER:	Manager to checkout three, please. Manager to three.
CHECKER:	Er—ma'am, this is the express checkout. Eight items or less. You really should go to the regular line.
GLADYS:	This one's quicker.
CHECKER:	Yes, that's because people only have eight items or less. Usually.
GLADYS:	So how many do I have? It's not that much more.
CHECKER:	Ma'am, your cart is completely full.
GLADYS:	They're big items.
MALE VOICE:	Guess she didn't see the sign.
CHECKER:	Really, ma'am, it's not fair to the others in line.
GLADYS:	Some of my stuff is two-for-one. They should count as one.
FEMALE VOICE:	Hey, is this really the express lane?
GLADYS:	Next, I suppose you'll want to count each of the bananas in a bunch!
CHECKER:	Okay, okay, ma'am. Let's just get going here. (SOUND OF SCANNER BEGINS.)
GLADYS:	I'm a long-time customer. I don't need to be treated so poorly.
CHECKER:	I'm very sorry, ma'am. That'll be $63.47, please.
GLADYS:	Honestly, I don't need to be lectured about—er—oh, my.
CHECKER:	Ma'am? Is there a problem?
GLADYS:	Well, I seem to have forgotten my wallet.
MALE VOICE:	Oh, man! You've got to be kidding!
CHECKER:	(*Sighs.*) I'm sorry, I'll have to close for a few minutes.
VOICES:	(*Background grumbling grows loud; then fades out.*)

Try It!

Write a radio script about an interesting scene from your life.

Prewriting Choosing Your Main Character

In a radio script you may have fewer characters, but there will still be a main character who faces conflict. As you start your planning for a radio script, choose a main character and decide how you want to portray him or her. Think about details you can use to convey tone.

Selecting a Conflict

The conflict is the problem that the main character faces. In the sample script, the problem is that the checker sees Gladys in the express line with too many items. As you plan your own radio script, think about conflicts that your main character might realistically face. Choose a theme you want to address and details you will need to include to create a definite mood for your script.

Considering Sound Effects

Instead of stage directions, in a radio script you will need to consider how to convey action. Think about possible sound effects that will convey the action so that your audience can "see" what is happening.

Prewrite

Plan how to start your radio script. **Decide on your characters and the conflict. Think about ways to effectively convey the action.**

Drafting Creating Your Script

Remember, in a radio script, the characters tell the story.

Beginning

- Start your script in the middle of the action. Background should be provided in the dialogue between characters.

Middle

- Use dialogue and sound effects to convey action.
- Add complications among characters to add tension.
- Build to the climax.

Ending

- Bring your radio script to its conclusion.

Draft

Draft your radio script. **Use the tips above to help guide you as you draft your script.**

TEKS 10.14C

Revising Improving Your Radio Script

Ask yourself the following questions when you revise and edit your script.

Focus and Coherence

_____ **1.** How have I conveyed the theme?
_____ **2.** What details have I included to create the mood of my radio script?
_____ **3.** What is the tone? What details have I used to set my script's tone?

Organization

_____ **4.** Do the actions build toward the climax?
_____ **5.** Does the main character change after the climax?
_____ **6.** Do the sound effects help the audience "see" the action?

Development of Ideas

_____ **7.** Do my characters talk and act like real people?
_____ **8.** Is my conflict believable?

Voice

_____ **9.** Can I improve my style or word choice to make the characters seem more real?

Editing Checking for Conventions

When you edit your revised script, check for correct grammar, sentence structure, capitalization, punctuation, and spelling.

Conventions

_____ **1.** Have I checked for correct verb tenses and grammar?
_____ **2.** Have I structured my sentences and dialogue correctly?
_____ **3.** Have I capitalized proper nouns and first words in sentences?
_____ **4.** Have I correctly punctuated my script, including the dialogue?
_____ **5.** Have I used a print or online dictionary to check my spelling?

Revise

Revise and edit your story. Use the information above to help you revise and edit the first draft of your radio script.

Writing Poetry

Have you ever read a poem and thought, "I know that feeling"? Part of the pleasure of reading poetry is that sense of connection between poet and reader. As Italian poet Salvatore Quasimodo put it, "Poetry is the revelation of a feeling that the poet believes to be interior and personal, which the reader recognizes as his own."

A poem reveals much about a poet's inner feelings, especially when it is an autobiographical poem. In this chapter, you will learn to write an autobiographical free-verse poem. You will also learn about two special forms of poetry: the ballad and the lune poem. No matter what form you work with, you will learn something new about yourself as you develop your thoughts and feelings.

Writing Guidelines

Subject: Self-portrait
Purpose: To entertain
Form: Free-verse poem
Audience: Friends, family, and classmates

"I should not talk so
much about myself if
there were anybody else
whom I knew as well."
—Henry David Thoreau

TEKS 10.14B
ELPS 3G

Sample Free-Verse Poem

Most traditional poetry follows a specific pattern of rhythm and rhyme, two major poetic devices. Free-verse poems, on the other hand, develop a structure of their own. This makes free verse ideal for an autobiographical poem. Eli Pulkkinen wrote the following free-verse poem to tell about a moment of self-discovery.

Perfection

His teeth were not perfect,
so only his lips smiled,
until one day,
laughing at a joke, he
glanced up to find a stranger
laughing with him–
a grin so inviting
that for a moment
he did not recognize
the mirror,
his own reflection.

—Eli Pulkkinen

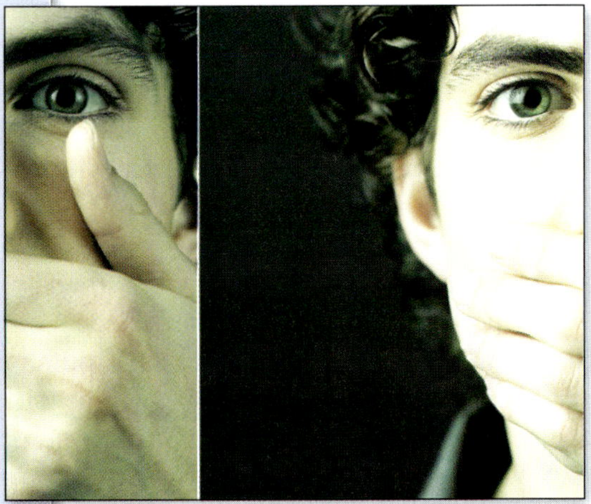

Texas Traits

Respond to the reading. On your own paper, reflect on the focus and coherence, organization, ideas, and voice of the free-verse poem above. Discuss your reflections with a classmate. Listen carefully to what your partner has to say, and ask questions using appropriate vocabulary.

Focus and Coherence (1) The central idea is about a moment of self-discovery. How does the title relate to the poem's message? **Organization** (2) If you were to divide this poem into three parts—beginning, middle, and ending—where would you divide it? Explain why. **Development of Ideas** (3) What does this poem reveal about the writer? **Voice** (4) Why do you think the poet used third-person pronouns (*his, he*) in this poem?

Tip

Some poems rely on many sensory details to build a mental picture. Others are more sparse, like the one above. In either case, the poet must carefully choose the best words to convey the poem's idea.

Prewriting Choosing a Focus

When writing an autobiographical poem, you should focus on one particular idea, event, or feeling that reveals your personality. To choose that focus, you can use one of the following strategies.

Looking in a Mirror

When artists draw a self-portrait, they use a mirror. Poets can do the same. Take time to examine your own face in a mirror and jot down notes about what you see. How would you describe each of your features? What personality do you see looking back at you? How do your features reveal that personality?

Think about poetic techniques you can use to convey these features. Sound devices include alliteration and assonance. Other common poetic devices include metaphors and similes, figurative language, and imagery. Be sure to include a variety of poetic techniques as you plan and write your poem.

Making a Personality Cluster

Write your name in a circle; then list your personality traits around it. Expand your cluster to include ideas about how you reveal each trait.

Reviewing Your Journal or a Photo Album

Browse through your journal to find interesting ideas or events. Or look through a family album for ideas. Eli chose an entry from his journal.

> Sept. 14, 2008
>
> Today at my part-time job, I was sweeping the break room when Rhoda said something that made me bust out laughing. When I looked up, I saw this other guy behind her with a big, amazing grin. For a minute, I didn't realize it was my own reflection in the break-room mirror. Seeing that grin, I don't think I'm going to be so self-conscious about my smile anymore.

Eli boiled down this memory to a purpose statement:

> I want to share the surprise of the moment when I realized the laughing stranger with the great smile was me.

Prewrite

Select a focus. **Use one of the techniques above to choose a specific feature, idea, or memory that reveals something about your personality. Then write a purpose statement to identify the focus of your poem.**

Prewriting Gathering Details

One of the best ways to gather details for a self-portrait poem is to make a list. Eli made the following list of essential details for his poem:

1. Feeling shy about my teeth
2. Laughing at Rhoda's joke
3. Noticing a stranger laughing
4. Being shocked that he was my own reflection

Prewrite

Make a list of details to include in your poem. Put them in the order you want to use in your poem.

Drafting Developing Your Poem

Many poets begin with sentences, focusing on ideas, sounds of words, and imagery. Then they break the sentences into shorter lines to set the rhythm, create rhymes, and make a poem. Eli started with this:

I was shy about my teeth. Then one day, while laughing at a joke, I saw this stranger laughing, too. His smile was so surprising that for a moment I didn't realize it was my own reflection.

Using Poetic Techniques

Rhythm is a special sound technique that separates prose from poetry. One way poets create rhythm is by breaking their writing into unique phrasing for a desired effect and meaning.

Line Breaks

Line breaks help to set the pace and rhythm of a poem. They help control the poem and add emphasis to certain words.

I was shy about my teeth.
Then one day,
while laughing at a joke,
I saw this stranger
laughing, too.
His smile was so surprising
that for a moment
I didn't realize
it was my own reflection.

Draft

Write your first draft. Start with phrases or sentences that get across the idea. Then add line breaks to control the rhythm and add emphasis.

Revising Focusing on the Traits

The first draft of a poem often comes in a rush of creativity. Revision is your chance to polish your work. In particular, look at the following traits.

- **Focus and Coherence**

1. Is my poem focused on my chosen subject?

- **Organization**

2. Do I use line breaks effectively to control the rhythm of my poem?
3. Have I used the correct poetic structure?

- **Development of ideas**

4. Have I used precise details, figurative language, and imagery to convey my meaning?
5. Do I show my feelings without telling the reader what to think?

- **Voice**

6. Does my poem show inventiveness and personality?

Compare the first draft of Eli's poem on page 350 to his final draft on page 348. What changes did he make? Which version seems most effective to you?

Revise your poem. Using the questions above as a guide, keep revising until your poem is the best that it can be.

Editing Checking for Conventions

Because poems are shorter than most other types of writing, every word and punctuation mark is important. Careful editing is necessary.

- **Conventions** Is my poem free from errors in grammar, capitalization, punctuation, or spelling that could distract a reader?

Edit your poem. Poems sometimes break the rules, but never by accident. Edit your poem for careless errors and make a neat final copy.

Publishing Sharing Your Poem

When your poem is finished, share it with others.

- **Post it.** Put it on a bulletin board or a Web site.
- **Submit it.** Send your poem to a contest or magazine.
- **Perform it.** Read your poem to friends and family.

Present your poem. Let other people read or hear what you have created.

TEKS 10.14B

Using Special Poetry Techniques

Poets use a variety of special techniques in their work. This page and the next define some of the most important ones.

Figures of Speech

- A **simile** *(sĭm´ə-lē)* compares two unlike things with the word *like* or *as*.

  She twirled
  across the stage
  like a tornado.

- A **metaphor** *(mĕt´ə-fôr)* compares two unlike things without using *like* or *as*.

  An avalanche of books
  covered the stairs.

- **Personification** *(pər-sŏn´ə-fĭ-kā´shən)* is a technique that gives human traits to something that is nonhuman.

  Brown trees frowned all down the lane.

- **Hyperbole** *(hī-pûr´bə-lē)* is an exaggerated statement, often humorous.

  The test sheet landed
  on my desk
  with a thud.

Sounds of Poetry

- **Alliteration** *(ə-lĭt´ə-rā´shən)* is the repetition of consonant sounds at the beginning of words.

  A bright green blouse

- **Assonance** *(ăs´ə-nəns)* is the repetition of vowel sounds anywhere in words.

  It pleases me to see
  a tree lean in a breeze.

- **Consonance** *(kŏn´sə-nəns)* is the repetition of consonant sounds anywhere in words.

  about what not to wear

- **Line breaks** help control the rhythm of a poem. The reader naturally pauses at the end of a line. There's also added emphasis on the last word in a line.

  laughing at a joke, he
  glanced up to find a stranger
  laughing with him

- **Onomatopoeia** *(ŏn´ə-mät´ə-pē´ə)* is the use of words that sound like what they name.

  Wind hissing on snow

- **Repetition** *(rĕp´ĭ-tĭsh´ən)* uses the same word or phrase more than once, for emphasis or for rhythm.

  You are not my mother.
  You are not my father.
  You are not my teacher.
  You are my friend.

- **Rhyme** *(rīm)* means using words whose endings sound alike.
  End rhyme happens at the end of lines.

  My style's not moderate.
  I've got a doctorate
  in "Color it!"

  Internal rhyme happens within lines.

  Brown trees frowned all down the lane.

- **Rhythm** *(rith´əm)* is the pattern of accented and unaccented syllables in a poem. The rhythm of free-verse poetry tends to flow naturally, like speaking. Traditional poetry follows a more regular pattern, as in the following example.

  I don't fear
  what I hear

Try It!

Write your own example of two or more of the special poetry techniques explained on these two pages. Then expand each of your examples into a complete poem.

Ballad

For centuries, people have composed ballads, stories told in song using the voice and language of everyday people. Ballads were composed orally, and singers often added or changed details to make the songs meaningful for their audience. The earliest ballads are known as folk ballads.

Ballads have characters, setting, and dialogue. Like songs, ballads use repetition and have regular rhyme and meter. A traditional ballad, like "Barbara Allen," consists of four-line stanzas with a simple rhyme scheme, and it narrates a single tragic event.

The ballad "Barbara Allen" has many variations. Several stanzas of the ballad are shown here. Song lyrics today continue to employ the medieval ballad form of poetry.

"Barbara Allen"

All in the merry month of May,
When green buds they were swellin'
Young William Grove on his death-bed lay,
For love of Barbara Allen.

He sent his servant to her door
To the town where he was dwellin'
Haste ye come, to my master's call
If your name be Barbara Allen,

So slowly, slowly got she up,
And slowly she drew nigh him,
And all she said when there she came:
"Young man, I think you're dying!"

He turned his face unto the wall
And death was drawing nigh him.
Good bye, Good bye to dear friends all,
Be kind to Barbara Allen.

Prewriting Planning Your Ballad

- **Select** a single, tragic event for your ballad. Create the characters.
- **Gather and organize details.** Make a list of the events that will be in your ballad. Then organize them in a logical flow. Most ballads are arranged in chronologically.
- Think about the structure and poetic techniques you will use. Most ballads are written in everyday language. Decide on a rhyme scheme and the figurative language you want to use. (Check a rhyming dictionary for help.) Work with the rhythm until the poem reads well aloud.

Prewrite

Plan your ballad. Use the tips and the information about the structure and poetic techniques of a ballad as a guide for your prewriting.

Drafting Writing Your Ballad

Use the information about the structure of ballads, the information about poetic techniques, and the planning you did on the previous page to write your ballad. Structure your ideas in a sustained way, and develop a conflict or tragic event that will engage the reader.

Revising Focusing on the Traits

Ask yourself the following questions when you review and revise the first draft of your ballad.

Focus and Coherence

_____ **1.** Do I narrate a single tragic event in my ballad?
_____ **2.** Can the reader follow the flow of ideas from start to finish?

Organization

_____ **3.** Is there an introduction, middle part, and a conclusion?
_____ **4.** Do I use line breaks to control the rhythm of the poem?
_____ **5.** Have I chosen an effective organizational pattern?

Development of Ideas

_____ **6.** Do I use well-chosen, precise details?
_____ **7.** Do my characters seem real and the event believable?
_____ **8.** Can the reader follow the flow of ideas?

Voice

_____ **9.** Have I used poetic techniques to convey my meaning?

Editing Checking for Conventions

Edit your ballad for grammar, capitalization, punctuation, and spelling.

_____ **1.** Have I used correct verb tenses and capitalized, punctuated, and spelled words correctly in my ballad?

Revise

Revise and edit your ballad. Use the information above to help you revise and edit the first draft of your ballad.

TEKS 10.14B

Lunes

In the 1960s, Robert Kelly decided that the English haiku form (5–7–5 syllables) did not effectively represent the original Japanese form. The problem is that English words have fewer syllables than Japanese words, so an English haiku holds more words. He believed that a new form was needed.

Kelly invented a form with 13 syllables in three lines, in a pattern of 5, 3, and 5 syllables. Because its right edge reminded him of a crescent moon, he called his new form a "lune."

When you're having fun
clocks run fast
not when you're waiting

Trotting by the fence
my new dog
keeps pace with our bus

In a doubtful world
I believe
in you and in me

Prewriting Planning Your Lune

- Select a single image or thought.
- Jot down vivid, descriptive adjectives, and figurative language.
- Think about structure and poetic devices you want to include.

Drafting Writing Your Lune

Use the information about structure, poetic devices, and planning tips to write your lune. Structure your idea to fit the lpattern of 5, 3, and 5 syllables.

Draft

Write a lune. Choose a topic from the list on page 619 and compose a lune about it.

Revising Focusing on the Traits

Ask yourself the following questions when you review and revise the first draft of your lune. (Also see page 332).

Focus and Coherence

_____ **1.** Do I describe a single image, idea, or thought?
_____ **2.** Do all the adjectives relate directly to that image or thought?

Organization

_____ **3.** Have I followed the structure for a lune?
_____ **4.** Have I carefully counted and arranged the words so that the 5, 3, 5 pattern of syllables is correctly followed?

Development of Ideas

_____ **5.** Have I used vivid adjectives to describe the image or thought?

Voice

_____ **6.** Can I improve my word choice or style of writing to better convey my meaning?
_____ **7.** Have I used figurative language to create a powerful image?

Editing Checking for Conventions

When you edit your revised lune, check for correct conventions: grammar, capitalization, punctuation, and spelling.

_____ **1.** Is my lune grammatically correct?
_____ **2.** Have I capitalized proper nouns and the first word of each sentence?
_____ **3.** Have I used correct punctuation, including end punctuation?
_____ **4.** Have I checked my spelling?

Revise

Revise and edit your story. Use the information above to help you revise and edit the first draft of your lune. Pay careful attention to the structure and poetic techniques you have used.

ELPS 1E, 2C, 3B, 3D, 3E, 4F, 4G

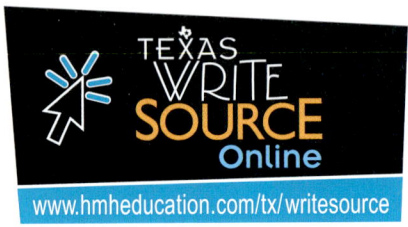

TEXAS WRITE SOURCE Online
www.hmheducation.com/tx/writesource

Research Writing

Writing Focus

Grammar Focus

Learning Language

Learning these words and expressions will help you understand this unit.

1. **Plagiarism** means passing off someone else's ideas as your own.
   Explain why plagiarism is unacceptable.
2. Something that is **valid** is accurate and has been correctly inferred or deduced from a premise.
   Why is it important to check whether or not a source is valid?
3. **To cite** a source means to give credit and to mention the source formally.
   Why must you cite the sources you use in a research report?
4. To be **"plugged in"** means to have access to electricity.
   What do you think it would be like to live in a village that was not "plugged in"?

Research Writing

Research Skills

You can learn a lot simply by observing, but to gain an in-depth understanding of a subject, you must do research. Effective researching in any field of inquiry means knowing where to look for appropriate, reliable information from authoritative sources. The library is an excellent place to start, as is the Internet. While the Internet can make researching easy, however, not every Web site offers solid, verifiable information. You must be careful to use only trustworthy Web sites that post information from authoritative sources.

In this chapter, you will learn how to use the Internet and the library as well as how to discern between reliable and unreliable sources. Knowing how to research efficiently will help you now in school and in the future.

- **Primary vs. Secondary Sources**
- **Evaluating Sources of Information**
- **Using the Internet**
- **Using the Library**
- **Using Reference Books**

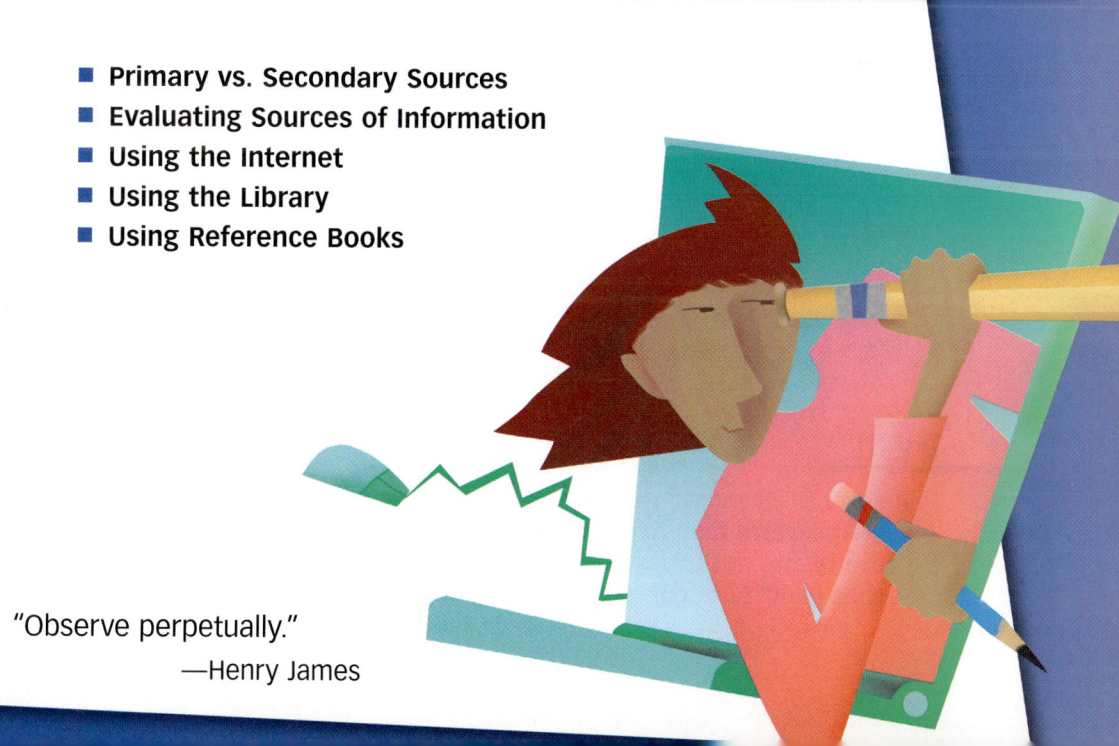

"Observe perpetually."

—Henry James

Primary vs. Secondary Sources

Primary sources are original sources that inform you directly, not through another person's explanation or interpretation. When doing research, use as much primary information as possible.

Primary sources include . . .

- **Diaries, Journals, and Letters** You can often find these in museums, in libraries, or at historic sites.
- **Presentations** An expert at a museum or a historic site can give you firsthand information, but be aware of the presenter's own interpretation of events.
- **Interviews** Talk to an expert about your research topic.
- **Surveys and Questionnaires** These tools help you gather a great deal of data from many people.
- **Observation and Participation** Your own observations of a person, a place, or an event provide excellent firsthand information. Participating in an event can give you insights that cannot be discovered through the reports of others.

Secondary sources are third-person accounts found in research done by other people. Much of the news (*television, radio, Internet, books, magazines*) is secondary information. Keep in mind that secondary sources represent filtered information that may contain biases or misunderstandings.

Primary Sources

1. Reading the journal of the designer of the Aswan High Dam
2. Interviewing someone from Egypt who lived near the dam
3. Watching a documentary with original film footage of the dam's construction

Secondary Sources

1. Reading a magazine article about the dam
2. Watching a TV drama based on the building of the dam
3. Exploring a Web site about dams of the world

Try It!

List several secondary sources you might use to learn about the Civil War. Then list several primary sources you might use to learn about the Alamo. Be sure to cite authoritative sources that would include relevant evidence and that identify major issues within these two fields of inquiry.

Evaluating Sources of Information

You may find a lot of information about your research topic. But before you use any of it, decide whether or not the information is dependable and comes from authoritative sources. Use the following questions as a guide.

Is the source a primary source or a secondary source?

You can usually trust the information you've collected yourself, but be careful with secondary sources. Although many of them are reliable, they can contain outdated or incorrect information.

Is the source an expert?

An expert knows more about a subject than other people. Using an expert's thoughts and opinions can make your paper more believable. If you aren't sure about a source's authority, ask a teacher or librarian what he or she thinks.

Is the information accurate?

Sources that people respect are usually very accurate. Reputable newspapers (*New York Times* or *Chicago Tribune*) and credible Web sites (CNN or ESPN) are reliable sources of information. Sources that do not support their facts or that contain errors may not be reliable.

Tip

Be especially cautious about the accuracy of information on the Internet. While there is an incredible amount of information available on the Net, there is also a lot of misinformation.

Is the information fair and complete?

A reliable, authoritative source should provide information fairly, covering all the major issues within the field of inquiry and all sides of the subject. If a source presents only one side of a subject or has an identifiable bias, its information may not be accurate. To make themselves sound convincing, politicians and advertisers often present just their side of a subject. Avoid sources that are one-sided, and look for those that are balanced.

Is the information current?

Usually, you want to have the most up-to-date information about a subject. Sometimes information changes, and sources can become outdated quickly. Check the copyright page in a book, the issue date of a magazine, and the posting date of online information.

TEKS 10.15A(v), 10.20B, 10.21A, 10.21B

Authoritative Sources

Select reliable and authoritative sources. Respected newspapers and magazines with articles written by experts are considered to be authoritative. Nonfiction books and documentaries are also generally good. The following guidelines will help you determine if a source is authoritative.

- **Is the author an expert on the subject?** Look at the author's credentials. Is the author an expert in the field?
- **What is the level of writing?** Look for scholarly material. A children's book would most likely not be authoritative.
- **Has the author presented complete information?** Look for discussion of all sides of the issue, including controversies or dissenting views. Not all primary and secondary sources present a full view of the issues or the major debates that surround a complex, multi-faceted topic.
- **Is the author unbiased?** Letters or diaries may not be fair. Secondary sources may only discuss one side of an issue.

Compiling Data

After identifying your sources, compile your data. For her report on the Aswan Dam, Isabel consulted several sources and began a list of useful ones that she could consult and include.

	Source	Description
CULTURAL & POLITICAL ISSUES	http://www.washingtonpost.com/wp-dyn/content/article/2006/11/02/AR2006110201657.html	analysis of cultural effects of Aswan High Dam; dam history; includes political issues
TECHNICAL ISSUES	http://www.jstor.org/pss/2010254	"Technological Dimension of Decision Making: The Case of the Aswan High Dam." Johns Hopkins study on technical decisions by Egypt, World Bank, and U.S. about dam.
ECONOMIC ISSUES	http://www.us.sis.gov.eg/En/Pub/magazin/fall2001/ 110 22000000000010.htm	Egyptian Information Service. Book Review of From High Dam to Toshka: The Nile and Man in Egypt between Legend and Reality. Financing; archaeological impact; environmental concerns.

Major Debates

As you begin your research and formulate a plan, think about the issues that surround your topic. When Isabel began her research on the Aswan High Dam, she identified three major issues that surrounded the building of the dam: cultural issues or problems, technical issues, and economic issues.

There will also be major debates surrounding any complex, muti-faceted topic. Debates involve the two sides of the issue. For example, while building the Aswan Dam would protect Egypt from drought and flood, it would, and did, change the salinity of the soil, destroying the fertility of the fields surrounding the Nile forever. As a result, Egypt has had to greatly increase the use of chemical fertilizers, adding to environmental concerns.

As you compile data from authoritative sources, look for those that identify the major debates that exist within your chosen topic.

Pros and Cons

As Isabel began to compile data, she made the following list of pros and cons, listing the major debates surrounding the Aswan High Dam.

PROS	CONS
controls annual flooding and protects against drought	Egypt was forced to agree to using only Soviet engineers and equipment.
made more land available for agriculture	New lake covers irreplaceable archaeological treasures.
enabled urban development along the Nile	Thousands of people had to be relocated.
provides irrigation throughout year	Farmers have to use tons of chemical fertilizer.
provides 50% of Egypt's electricity	decrease in fish and shrimp populations

Try It!

Conduct preliminary research, compile data, and identify major debates that surround your chosen topic. Look for sources that provide information on both sides of the issue. List your sources in a table such as the one on the previous page. Then arrange specific information in a chart of Pros and Cons like the one above, or in another graphic organizer form.

Using the Internet

You can access many resources by surfing the Web. Therefore, the Internet is a valuable research tool, especially as you formulate your plan and conduct research on a complex, multi-faceted topic. You can find government publications, encyclopedia entries, business reports, and firsthand observations on the Internet. Using reliable, authoritative sources, you can quickly identify the major debates and issues within your field of inquiry. When researching on the Internet, keep in mind the following points:

- **Use the Web wisely.** Sites that include *.edu, .org,* and *.gov* in the Web address are often reliable. These sites are usually from educational, nonprofit, or government agencies. If you have questions about a site, talk to your teacher. (Also see page 361.)

- **Try several search engines.** Because there is an enormous amount of information on the Web, no one search engine can handle it all. So employ at least two search engines when you surf the Web. Enter keywords to start your research or enter specific questions to zero in on your topic, especially a complex, multi-faceted research topic.

  When you type a term into a search engine's input box, the search engine scans its database for matching sites. Then the engine returns recommendations for you to explore.
- **Take advantage of links.** When you read a page, watch for links to other sites. These may offer different perspectives on your topic.
- **Experiment with keywords.** Ask different questions or use different keywords to find the information you need. Check the date of the site to make sure the information is current.
- **Ignore Web sites that advertise research papers for sale.** Using these sites is dishonest. Teachers and librarians can recognize and verify when a paper is someone else's work.
- **Learn your school's Internet policy.** Using the computer at school is a privilege. To maintain that privilege, follow your school's Internet policy and any guidelines your parents may have set.

Try It!

Open your favorite search engine and type in the word "Dams." How many sites are listed related to your search? Now type in the phrase "Aswan High Dam." How many sites are listed now? Finally, type in "Aswan High Dam History." How have the numbers changed by focusing your search?

Using the Library

The Internet may be a good place to initiate your research, but a library is often a more valuable place to continue it. Most libraries contain a wide range of authoritative resources on a wide range of multi-faceted topics. Talk to the librarian as you plan your research and begin to compile data.

Books

- **Reference** books include encyclopedias, almanacs, dictionaries, atlases, and directories, plus resources such as consumer information guides and car-repair manuals. Reference books provide a quick overview of research topics.
- **Nonfiction** texts are a good source of facts that can serve as a foundation for your research. Check the copyright dates to be sure you are reading reasonably up-to-date information. (Some libraries organize nonfiction using the Library of Congress system, but most libraries use the Dewey decimal system as shown on page **367**.)
- **Fiction** can sometimes aid or enhance your research. For example, a historical novel can reveal people's feelings about a particular time in history. (Fiction books are grouped together in alphabetical order by the authors' last names.)

Periodicals

Periodicals (*newspapers* and *magazines*) are grouped together in a library. Use the *Readers' Guide to Periodical Literature* to find articles in periodicals. (See page **370**.) You will have to ask the librarian for older issues.

The Media Section

The media section of your library includes DVD's, CD-ROM's, CD's, cassettes, and videotapes. These resources are valuable, but remember that directors and screenwriters may present events from their personal viewpoints.

Computers

Computers are available in most libraries, and many are connected to the Internet, although there may be restrictions on their use.

Try It!

Visit your school or public library. Which sections would you use if you were researching the origin of the moon's craters? Which sections would help you find material on the history of filmmaking? Are there any sections you would use for both topics? List them.

Using the Computer Catalog

Some libraries still use a card catalog located in a cabinet with drawers. Most libraries, however, have put their entire catalog on computer. Each system varies a bit, so ask for help if you're not sure how the system in your library works. A **computer catalog** lists the books held in your library and affiliated systems. It lets you know if a book is available or if you must wait for it.

Using a Variety of Search Methods

When you are using a computer catalog, you can find information about a book with any of the following methods:

1. If you know it, enter the **title** of the book.
2. If you know the **author** of the book, enter the first and last names.
3. A general search of your **subject** will also help you find books on your topic. Enter either the subject or a related keyword.

Sample Computer Catalog Screen

The key to the right identifies the types of information provided for a particular resource, in this case, a book. Once you locate the book you need, make note of the call number. You will use this to find the book on the shelf.

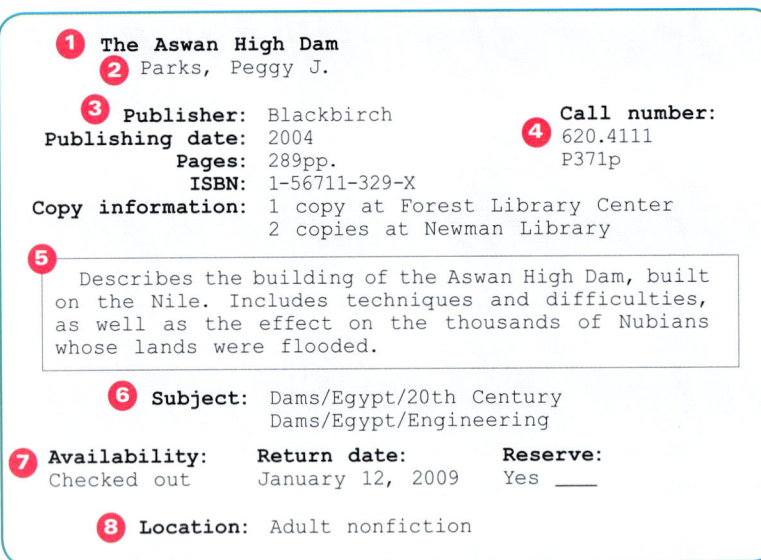

1 **The Aswan High Dam**
2 Parks, Peggy J.

3 **Publisher:** Blackbirch
Publishing date: 2004
Pages: 289pp.
ISBN: 1-56711-329-X
Copy information: 1 copy at Forest Library Center
2 copies at Newman Library

4 **Call number:** 620.4111
P371p

5 Describes the building of the Aswan High Dam, built on the Nile. Includes techniques and difficulties, as well as the effect on the thousands of Nubians whose lands were flooded.

6 **Subject:** Dams/Egypt/20th Century
Dams/Egypt/Engineering

7 **Availability:** Checked out **Return date:** January 12, 2009 **Reserve:** Yes ___

8 **Location:** Adult nonfiction

1. Title heading
2. Author's name
3. Publisher, copyright date, and other book information
4. Call number
5. Descriptive info
6. Subject heading(s)
7. Availability status
8. Location information

Try It!

Look up a topic that interests you on a computer catalog. Identify two authoritative works on the topic and locate them in the library.

Understanding Call Numbers

All nonfiction books are arranged in the library according to their **call numbers**. Call numbers are usually based on the **Dewey decimal classification** system, which divides nonfiction books into 10 subject categories:

000–099	**General Works**	500–599	**Sciences**
100–199	**Philosophy**	600–699	**Technology**
200–299	**Religion**	700–799	**Arts and Recreation**
300–399	**Social Sciences**	800–899	**Literature**
400–499	**Languages**	900–999	**History and Geography**

A call number often has a decimal in it, followed by the first letter of an author's name. Note how the following call numbers are ordered.

Identifying the Parts of a Book

Each part of a book provides valuable information. The **title page** includes the title of the book, the author's name, and the publisher's name and city. The **copyright page** follows with the year the book was published. The **preface**, **foreword**, or **introduction** comes before the table of contents and tells why the book was written. The **table of contents** lists the names and page numbers of sections and chapters in the book. At the end of the book, you may find at least one **appendix**, containing various maps, tables, or lists. Finally, the **index** is an alphabetical list of important topics and their page numbers in the book.

Try It!

Select an authoritative nonfiction book on a topic that interests you. On a note card, write the book's title and call number, the publisher's name and city, and the year it was published. Then select a term related to your topic and find it in the index. Write down the page numbers given there.

TEKS 10.20B, 10.21A

Using Reference Books

A reference book is a special kind of nonfiction book that contains specific facts or background information. The reference section includes encyclopedias, dictionaries, almanacs, and so on. Usually, reference books cannot be checked out, so you must use them in the library.

Referring to Encyclopedias

An encyclopedia is a set of books (or a CD-ROM) that contains basic information on topics from A to Z. Topics are arranged alphabetically. Here are some tips for using encyclopedias.

Tips for Using Encyclopedias

- **At the end of an article, there is often a list of related articles.** You can read these other articles to learn more about your topic.
- **The index can help you find out more about your topic.** The index is usually in a separate volume or at the end of the last volume. It lists every article that contains information about a topic. For example, if you look up "dams" in the index, you would find a list of articles—"Aswan Dam," "Hoover Dam," and so on—that include information on that topic. (See below.)
- **Libraries usually have several sets of encyclopedias.** Review each set and decide which one best serves your needs. (Always check with your teacher first to see if you can use an encyclopedia as a source for your research.)

Sample Encyclopedia Index

Encyclopedia volume — Page numbers — Related topics

Aswan Dam A: 852 with pictures
Egypt **E: 118-132**
Dams **D: 15-20**
Lake Nasser **L: 42**
See also the list of related articles in the Egypt article.
Abu Simbel, Temple of **A: 19**
Ramsas II **R: 135**
Amon-Re **A: 438**
Nubia **N-O: 382**
Delta **D: 147**

Consulting Other Reference Books

Most libraries contain a number of different kinds of reference books in addition to encyclopedias. You may find these very helpful as you plan your research and gather data.

Almanacs

Almanacs are books filled with facts and statistics about many different subjects. *The World Almanac and Book of Facts* contains celebrity profiles; statistics about politics, business, and sports; plus consumer information.

Atlases

Atlases contain detailed maps of the world, continents, countries, and so on. They also contain statistics and related information. Specialized atlases cover topics like outer space and the oceans.

Dictionaries

Dictionaries contain definitions of words and their origins. Biographical dictionaries focus on famous people. Specialized dictionaries deal with science, history, medicine, and other subjects.

Directories

Directories list information about groups of people, businesses, and organizations. The most widely used directories are telephone books.

Periodical Indexes

Periodical indexes list articles in magazines and newspapers. These indexes are arranged alphabetically by subject.

- The *Readers' Guide to Periodical Literature* lists articles from many publications. (See page **370**.)
- The *New York Times Index* lists articles from the *New York Times* newspaper.

Other Reference Books

Some reference books do not fit into any one category:

- *Facts on File* includes thousands of short but informative facts about events, discoveries, people, and places.
- *Facts About the Presidents* presents information about all of the presidents of the United States.
- *Bartlett's Familiar Quotations* lists thousands of quotations from famous people.

TEKS 10.20B, 10.21A

Using Periodical Guides

Periodical guides are located in the reference or periodical section of the library. These guides alphabetically list topics and articles found in magazines, newspapers, and journals. Some guides are printed volumes, some are CD-ROM's, and some are on library Web sites. Ask your librarian for help.

Readers' Guide to Periodical Literature

The *Readers' Guide to Periodical Literature* is a well-known periodical reference source and is found in most libraries. The following tips will help you look up your topic in this resource:

- Articles are always listed alphabetically by author and topic.
- Some topics are subdivided, with each article listed under the appropriate subtopic.
- Cross-references refer to related topic entries where you may find more articles pertinent to your topic.

Sample *Readers' Guide* Format

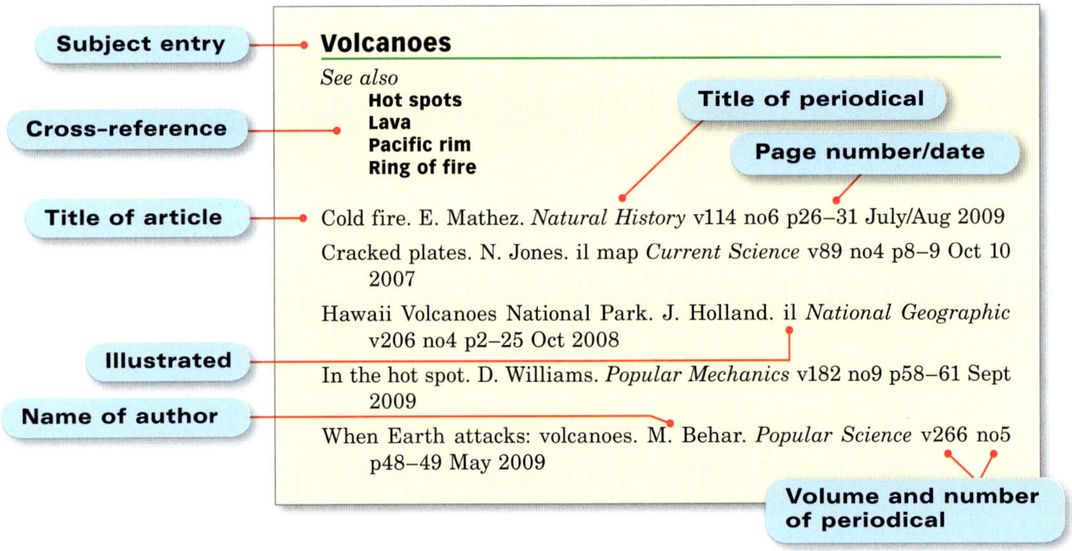
Volcanoes

See also

Hot spots
Lava
Pacific rim
Ring of fire

Cold fire. E. Mathez. *Natural History* v114 no6 p26–31 July/Aug 2009

Cracked plates. N. Jones. il map *Current Science* v89 no4 p8–9 Oct 10 2007

Hawaii Volcanoes National Park. J. Holland. il *National Geographic* v206 no4 p2–25 Oct 2008

In the hot spot. D. Williams. *Popular Mechanics* v182 no9 p58–61 Sept 2009

When Earth attacks: volcanoes. M. Behar. *Popular Science* v266 no5 p48–49 May 2009

Tip

The librarian will have a list of magazines in the library's collection. Check it for the magazine you seek. If you need an older issue, it might be in the archives. If so, ask the librarian to get it for you.

Research Writing
MLA Research Report

Thomas Carlyle, the Scottish essayist and historian, once wrote, "Man is a tool-using animal." He went on to explain, "Nowhere do you find him without tools; without tools he is nothing, with tools he is all." In nature, most creatures adapt to their environment. People, on the other hand, tend to use their tools to adapt the environment to meet their needs. Consider, for example, great works of engineering such as the Empire State Building, the Great Wall of China, or the Hoover Dam. Not only were these monuments built with tools, they are—in effect—tools themselves, helping humans change their environment.

This chapter will help you to write an MLA research report about a great work of engineering that interests you. (MLA is the most common documentation style for research writing.) In the process, you will learn why and how the work came to be, and what effect it has had on the world.

Writing Guidelines

Subject: **A great work of engineering**
Purpose: **To research and present accurate information**
Form: **MLA research report**
Audience: **Classmates**

"It is good to rub and polish our brain against that of others."

—Michel de Montaigne

TEKS 10.13A, 10.20B

Title Page and Outline

After watching a PBS special about dams, Isabel Cotero became interested in Egypt's Aswan High Dam. She decided to write a research paper about that topic. Her paper starts on the next page. Below are the title page and outline of her paper. Some teachers require these additional pages. If your teacher requires them, follow any special instructions he or she may give you.

The Aswan High Dam

Isabel Cotero
Ms. Kai
Language Arts
18 May 2009

Title Page
Center the title one-third of the way down the page. Center and double-space the writer information two-thirds of the way down the page.

i

The Aswan High Dam

THESIS STATEMENT: The Aswan High Dam has solved many important problems for Egypt, but it has also created new ones.

I. Before the dam was built, Egyptians had to live with annual floods along the Nile.
   A. Flooding came after the rainy season in the highlands.
   B. This annual flooding helped to fertilize the land, but sometimes this was too much water.
   C. A dam was needed.

II. In years with little rain, Egypt had less flooding, but that also meant less water for irrigation.
   A. Egypt is mainly desert, so crops are watered by irrigation.
   B. Before the dam, Egyptians stored floodwater for irrigation after the flood season.
   C. In dry years, they could not capture enough water and suffered drought and famine.

Outline
Center the title one inch from the top of the page. Double-space throughout.

Sample MLA Research Report

The entire report is double-spaced.

1" 1/2" Cotero 1 1"

Isabel Cotero
Ms. Kai
Language Arts
18 May 2010

The Aswan High Dam

Humans have been building dams for thousands of years. One of the oldest examples is the Saad El Kafara, built in Egypt around 2700 B.C.E. Its main purpose was to stop catastrophic flooding during wet years, but its water storage also allowed for increased irrigation of croplands. While most dams have been built for these two purposes, huge new dams in the past century have provided the added benefit of hydroelectric power for the world's growing population. However, people are discovering that these large dams also have many detrimental effects on the environment. Egypt's High Dam at Aswan illustrates this critical trade-off. The Aswan High Dam has solved many important problems for Egypt, but it has also created new ones.

1"

Beginning The writer introduces her topic and states her thesis (underlined).

Reasons for the Dam

Before the dam was built, Egyptians had to live with annual floods along the Nile. Each year, after the rainy season, the river would spill over its banks onto the Egyptian countryside. While this annual flooding helped to fertilize the land, sometimes there was just too much water. For example, "between 1860 and 1880, there were four major floods that forced people to flee to higher ground" (Parks 12). They desperately needed a dam to help prevent this recurring damage.

Middle The first middle section explains the historical background. Writer uses embedded quotes to support topic sentence, and she correctly cites researched information.

1"

The writer paraphrases and correctly sites a source of information (Parks, page 11). She addresses major issues in the middle paragraphs.

Headings help guide the reader from section to section.

The second middle section details how the dam came into existence, a major issue.

In years with little rain, Egypt had less flooding, but that also meant less water for irrigation. Egypt is mainly desert, so crops grown there must be watered by irrigation. Before the dam was built, the Egyptians captured floodwater and stored it in pools for irrigation use during the rest of the year. In dry years, however, they could not capture enough water to last. The result was drought and famine (11).

By building a dam, the people of Egypt hoped to accomplish several things. A dam would help to stop catastrophic floods during wet years. It would also prevent Egypt from running out of water during dry years. In fact, it would store enough water to allow even more land to be irrigated. This was important because Egypt's population started to outgrow its crop production during the twentieth century (*Building Big: Dams*).

Building the Dam

The first Aswan Dam was built between 1898 and 1902, while Egypt was a colony of Great Britain. It was designed by William Willcocks, a British engineer who was very familiar with traditional Egyptian irrigation. Willcocks built a dam that would let the silt-laden water of each year's early rains pass through to fertilize the croplands below. The dam then stored later rainwater to be used for irrigation during the rest of the year (Pearce 50). Unfortunately, Willcock's dam didn't hold enough water to last through dry years, even after being raised twice, once in 1912 and again in 1933. Also, the dam almost overflowed in 1946, which happened to be a very wet year (Parks 14).

Page numbers alone (17–20) refer to the last source cited (Parks). Writer continues to cite and summarize information from authoritative sources concerning major debates about her topic.

Each paragraph begins with a topic sentence, followed by relevant evidence and carefully chosen supporting details.

Cotero 3

In 1952, Egypt became independent from Britain, and its new government decided to build a dam that could hold enough water for three years of irrigation. The project quickly became a touchy subject, because Egypt didn't want to hire British engineers to design the dam. As a gesture of friendship, Germany donated plans to the new government. In 1956, the World Bank, Great Britain, and the United States offered to fund the project, but they cancelled those plans when Egypt bought Soviet weapons to fight Israel (17–20). The Soviet Union agreed to fund the dam if Egypt agreed to use only Soviet engineers and equipment. By 1959, plans were complete and the project began ("Aswan Dam" 40).

First, the valley that the dam would flood had to be cleared. This meant moving more than 100,000 Nubian people to new lands. Also, the new lake would cover many ancient temples and other monuments. In 1960, the United Nations Educational, Scientific, and Cultural Organization (UNESCO) asked governments around the world to help move these monuments. In all, 23 were rescued before the reservoir was filled, though many more were lost (*Building Big: Dams*).

Next, preparations had to be made for the dam's actual construction. New roads and railroads had to be built to carry men and equipment to the construction site. In addition, an electrical station had to be built at the old Aswan Dam to supply power for the project. Also, the town of Aswan had to be prepared to host the thousands of workers that would be needed (Parks 27).

Once building began, the construction team faced very harsh conditions. The terrain was extremely

Cotero 4

Dates help the reader follow the development of the dam. By citing and comparing several sources, writer shows that she has considered the reliability, validity, and accuracy of sources she has used.

rugged, rapidly wearing out tires on construction equipment. Daytime temperatures reached 135 degrees Fahrenheit in the shade, so most work had to be done at night. Under these conditions, the Soviet equipment broke down five times faster than expected. This caused expensive delays while replacement parts were shipped from the Soviet Union or equipment was sent back there for repair. In 1961, with little progress made, the Egyptian government brought in Egyptian construction experts to replace the Soviet engineers, and it began using equipment from Sweden and Great Britain (28–29).

The dam was finally completed in July 1970, ten years after the project began. It was by far the largest engineering work of its time, costing over $1 billion (*Building Big: Dams*). More than 50,000 people worked on the dam, using 17 times more material than was used to build the Great Pyramid. The finished dam stretches two miles wide and 364 feet high. The reservoir (holding the water) covers an area larger than the state of Delaware (Parks 35).

The third middle section explains the effects of the dam. Writer again considers major issues and debates about the dam.

Effects of the Dam

The Aswan High Dam immediately helped control flooding. Before the Nile was dammed, floods sometimes forced evacuation of the Nile Valley and its delta, with a great loss of life and property. With the dam in place, however, flooding became a thing of the past. As a result, cities like Cairo, which used to be limited to high ground near the river, have expanded all the way to the Nile's banks. As Michael Sorkin puts it, "By stabilizing the river's banks, the dam not only rescued Egyptian

Writer includes the source of a quotation (Michael Sorkin) in the text, and the page number (82) appears in parentheses.

Writer has abundance of material to choose from, but includes only relevant evidence to support the topic sentence.

Negative effects of the dam are also discussed. Writer shows that she has considered both sides of the issue and is knowledgeable about major debates surrounding the topic.

A technical term (schistosomiasis) is explained for the reader.

agriculture from historic cycles of flood and drought, but enabled extensive urban development along the shore" (82).

The vast reservoir behind the dam makes more irrigation possible in Egypt. In the past, the people could grow crops only as long as their stored water lasted each year. Now the dam provides irrigation throughout the entire year. In fact, Egyptians are able to irrigate two million more acres of land than they could before the dam was built (Parks 41).

Also, the Aswan High Dam provides 50 percent of Egypt's electricity. Once the dam was built, thousands of villages that had never had electricity before were "plugged in." The power station has been important for the swelling populations in Egypt's larger cities (*Building Big: Dams*).

However, there are some significant environmental problems related to the dam. For one thing, without the annual deposit of silt to enrich their fields, Egyptian farmers now have to use tons of chemical fertilizers each year. This has changed the chemistry of the waterways, leading to an excess of waterweeds and a decrease in fish and shrimp. Even the nearby sardine population in the Mediterranean Sea has suffered. The loss of silt has also caused the Nile delta to erode severely (Parks 39–40). Furthermore, industrial building closer to the Nile itself has caused more water pollution. As a result, the soil of the Nile delta, whose crops feed 40 million people, is becoming dangerously contaminated with toxins such as heavy metals (Penvenne 17).

Because the irrigation canals no longer dry up each year, Egyptians suffer from more waterborne diseases than before. One example is schistosomiasis,

TEKS 10.15A(i), 10.15A(ii)

Cotero 6

an intestinal and urinary disease transmitted by microscopic worms that live on snails in the waterways. Before the dam was built, these snails died every year during the dry season. Now they flourish year-round, making the disease seven times more common (Larrson 2). Besides the snails, there are more mosquitoes carrying malaria and other diseases in Egypt since the dam was built (Louria 3).

Transitions such as "in addition" help link paragraphs. Writer effectively uses a variety of sentence structures to engage reader throughout the essay.

In addition, the dam continues to threaten some of Egypt's most important monuments. Year-round irrigation has led to rising groundwater, and this moisture is causing ancient structures like the temples of Luxor to crumble from the bottom up (Brown 22). If this problem isn't corrected, these historical treasures will be destroyed as surely as those that lie beneath the waters of the reservoir.

Ending The closing summarizes the main points of the paper and leaves the reader with a final thought.

Conclusion

No one can deny that the Aswan High Dam has benefited Egypt. Its flood control has prevented loss of life and property in wet years. Year-round irrigation and the expansion of croplands have helped supply food and other goods for Egypt's booming population. The electrical power it provides has helped the country to build and modernize. However, the dam also demonstrates that whenever humans change their environment, they introduce new problems that must be dealt with. The building of the Aswan High Dam teaches people that they have to learn to modernize with caution, and to predict and prepare for the consequences of their actions.

A separate page alphabetically lists the sources cited in the paper.

Second, third, and additional lines are indented five spaces.

Cotero 7

Works Cited

"Aswan Dam." *STC-Link*. University of Colorado at Denver. 15 April 2004. Web. 7 Oct. 2010.

Brown, Jeff. L. "Researchers Unravel Mystery of Eroding Egyptian Monuments." *Civil Engineering* 71.9 (2007): 22. Print.

Building Big: Dams. WGBH Boston Video, 2006. VHS.

Larrson, Birgitta. "Aquaculture and schistosomiasis." *Three Overviews on Environment and Aquaculture in the Tropics and Sub-Tropics*. Food and Agriculture Organization of the United Nations. Dec. 1994. Web. 15 Oct. 2010.

Louria, Donald B. "The Specter of Emerging and Re-Emerging Infection Epidemics." *Healthful Life Project*. The Healthcare Foundation of New Jersey. 15 December 2007. Web. 23 Oct. 2009.

Parks, Peggy J. *The Aswan High Dam*. San Diego: Blackbirch, 2008.

Pearce, Fred. "Dammed Lies." *New Scientist* 175.2361 (2006): 50–51. Web.

Penvenne, Laura Jean. "The Disappearing Delta." *Earth* Aug. 2004: 16–17. Print.

Sorkin, Michael. "Deciphering Greater Cairo." *Architectural Record* 189.4 (2007): 82–87. Print.

Note: This Works Cited page follows MLA documentation style. (See pages 407–410 for more information.)

TEKS 10.20A, 10.20B, 10.21A

Prewrite Draft Revise Edit Publish

Go Online!

Prewriting

Just as every work of engineering begins with a blueprint, every research report must start with some prewriting. Prewriting involves choosing a topic and researching it to gather and organize information for your report.

Keys to Effective Prewriting

1. For your topic, brainstorm, consult with others, and decide on a topic. Choose a complex, multi-faceted, interesting example of a work of engineering.
2. Formulate major research questions you want to have answered about that topic.
3. Formulate a plan for your research. Use a gathering grid to organize your research questions and answers. Use note cards to keep track of longer answers. (See pages 383–386.)
4. Keep track of the sources of information you summarize or quote. You must correctly cite them in your report.
5. Gather plenty of details about your topic, including why and how the work of engineering was built and what the effects of the work have been. You should learn about and address major issues and debates about the topic.

Selecting a Topic

To narrow a general subject to a specific topic, there are a range of strategies that you can use. One strategy is to brainstorm and then cluster. Isabel brainstormed and then made the following graphic organizer.

Cluster Diagram

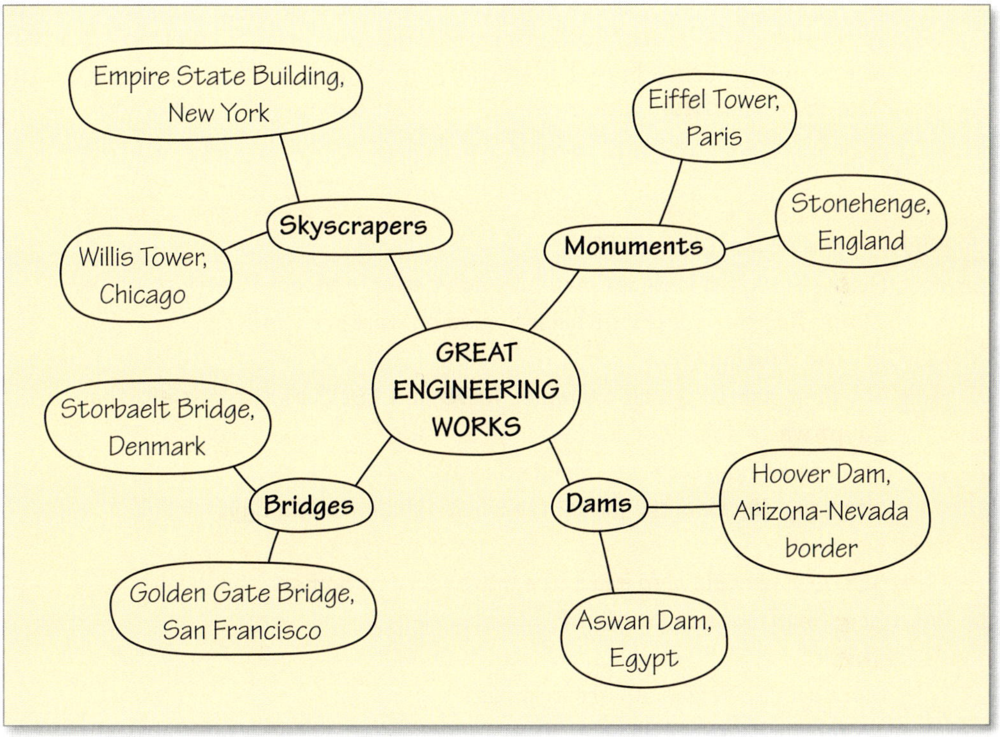

Tip

Great works of engineering aren't limited to skyscrapers, monuments, bridges, and dams. Others include tunnels, cathedrals, pyramids, railways, and so on.

Prewrite

Select a topic. Create a cluster diagram like the one above to identify possible topics (great engineering works) for your research. If necessary, browse through your social studies or history text for ideas. Finally, select a topic from your cluster. (You may also choose one of the works of engineering in the cluster above.)

TEKS 10.13A, 10.20A

Prewriting Selecting a Topic

An effective research report about an important work of engineering should explain the following three things.

- Why was the work built?
- How was it built?
- What are the effects of the work?

To select her topic, Isabel brainstormed and consulted with others. As part of the prewriting process, Isabel also did some quick initial research on the Aswan Dam. She identified the major issues and debates and took notes.

Research Notes

Why was the Aswan Dam built?

- During droughts in Egypt, the Nile didn't supply enough water for crops.
- During floods, people lost their homes or, worse, their lives.

How was the dam built?

- The first dam was built between 1898 and 1902 by the British, when Egypt was a colony.
- The Aswan High Dam was finished in 1970.
- Germany donated the plans; the Soviet Union helped Egypt build the dam.
- 100,000 people also had to be moved to new homes.

What are the effects of the dam?

BENEFITS

- More acres of cropland are irrigated.
- Crops can be grown all year.
- Cities can build closer to the Nile.

PROBLEMS

- Crops need more chemical fertilizers.
- The Nile delta is eroding.
- Fish populations are decreasing.

From this initial research, Isabel could tell that there would be plenty to write about. What interested her most were the good and bad effects of the dam. She was confident that she could write about these issues.

Prewrite

Decide on your topic. Brainstorm, consult with others, and do some initial research about your topic. List major issues and debates about the topic.

Formulating a Research Question

Isabel made a gathering grid during her research about the Aswan Dam. Down the left side, she listed major research questions about the topic. Across the top, she listed sources she found to answer those questions. For answers too long to fit on the grid, Isabel used note cards. (See page 386.)

Gathering Grid

ASWAN DAM	*Building Big: Dams* (video)	*The Aswan High Dam* (book)	"Aswan Dam" (Web site)	"Deciphering Greater Cairo" (magazine article)
1. Why was the Aswan Dam built?	To provide year-round irrigation			British cotton mill owners wanted more cotton.
2. How was the dam built?		See note card #1.	All local material Rock: 28.6 million cubic yards Sand: 20 million cubic yards Clay: 4 million cubic yards	
3. What are the effects of the dam?	Doubled agricultural production Damage to environment		Lake Nasser holds 1.99 trillion cubic yards of water. The lake is 6 miles wide and 310 miles long.	See note card #2.

Prewrite

Create a gathering grid. List your research questions in the left-hand column of a grid or graphic that fits your topic. Across the top of a grid, list sources you will use. Fill in the rest of the grid or graphic with answers you find. Use note cards for longer, more detailed answers.

TEKS 10.13A, 10.20B, 10.21B

Formulating a Plan

As Isabel continued the research for her paper, she realized that the Aswan Dam was a multi-faceted, complex topic. There were economic, political, social, and technical issues involved. The Aswan Dam was years in the making, and all kinds of controversies emerged, including debates over the planning, the financing, and the construction of the dam.

Using her research notes and questions, Isabel created the following graphic organizer so that she could focus her research and formulate a plan that would help her write an analysis that would cover the major issues and debates surrounding the dam.

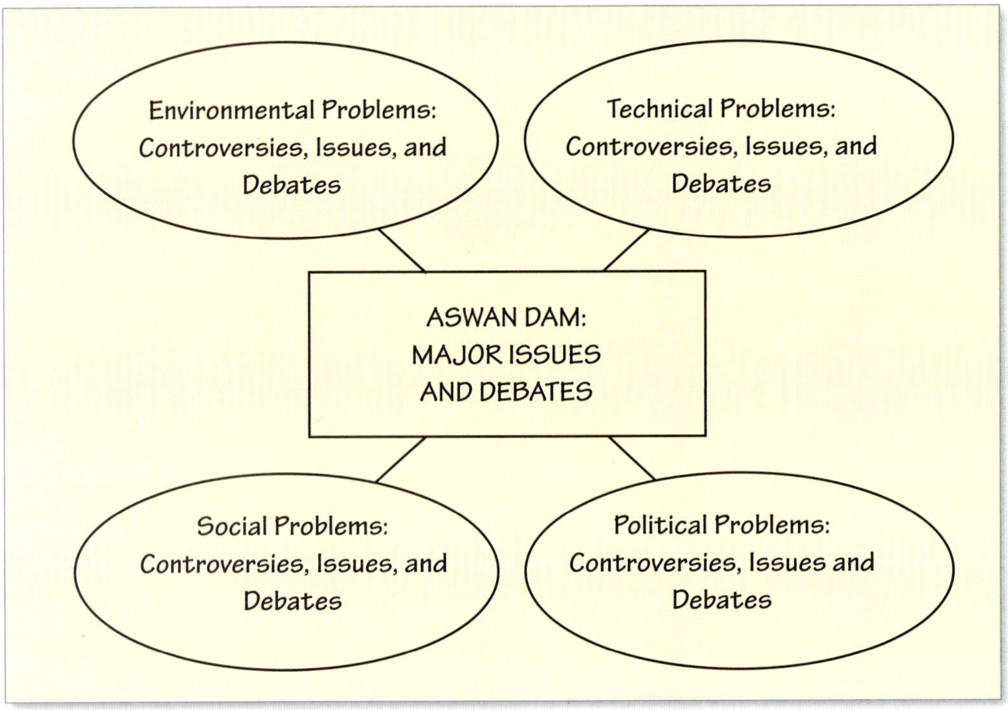

Prewrite

Formulate a plan. Formulate a plan for your research that will enable you to address the major issues and debates surrounding your topic. Then choose a graphic organizer that will help you organize the information about the various facets of the complex topic that you have chosen.

Gathering Sources

From her initial research, Isabel realized that there were a variety of sources to choose from as she conducted her research. She wanted to be sure to use only highly reliable, authoritative sources. She wanted to use different types of printed materials, including books, magazines, journals, and newspapers that were available in her school and local public library. She also wanted to use online sources in her research. Isabel had learned that there was a video about the dam. Isabel's teacher also suggested that she contact Polly Lewis and try to conduct an interview. Isabel decided to pursue a personal interview, e-mailed Ms. Lewis and verified that she was an authority about the dam. Isabel was then able to incorporate the results of that interview in her research paper.

Isabel understood that to gather data about both sides of the issues and debates surrounding the dam, she would need a variety of authoritative sources. She wanted to be able to compare viewpoints and identify writers' biases. She also wanted to show that she had conducted sufficient research to support her viewpoint. Finally, Isabel knew it was critical to use a variety of print and online sources to show mastery of her topic.

Compiling Data

PRINT	Brown, Jeff. "Researchers Unravel Mystery of Eroding Egyptian Monuments." Civil Engineering 2007. Essay on erosion problems resulting from dam. Parks, Peggy. The Aswan High Dam. Book about issues and controversies surrounding planning and building of dam. Penvenne, Laura Jean. "The Disappearing Delta" Earth August 2004: pages 16–17. Discussion of environmental problems caused by dam.
ONLINE	Larsson, Birgitta. "Aquaculture and schistosomiasis." From "Three Overviews on Environment and Aquaculture in the Tropics and Subtropics." Food and Agriculture Organization of the United Nations. Dam's health issues. "Aswan Dam." STC-Link. University of Colorado at Denver. information about history, planning, and construction of dam.
VIDEO	Building Big: Dams. Detailed history of construction and financing controversies

Prewrite

Gather your sources and compile your data. **Create a graphic organizer to show the types and variety of sources that you are using and the kinds of data you will find in each source.**

TEKS 10.21B

Prewriting Creating Note Cards

A gathering grid or similar organizer allows you to see all your research at a glance, but sometimes you need more space for an answer. In that case, use note cards. Number each new card and write a question at the top. Then answer the question with a list, a quotation, or a paraphrase (see pages 387–389). At the bottom identify the source of the information (including a page number if appropriate).

Note cards

Question — Answer (list)

(1)
How was the dam built?
To prepare:
- Thousands of workers had to be summoned and housed at Aswan.
- Roads and railroad lines had to be built to bring heavy equipment.
- For power, an electric station had to be added to the low dam.

…e *Aswan High Dam.*
pages 26-27

Source

(2)
What are the effects of the dam?
"By stabilizing the river's banks, the dam not only rescued Egyptian agriculture from historic cycles of flood and drought, but enabled extensive urban development along the shore."
Sorkin, Michael. "Deciphering Greater Cairo"
Architectural Record April 2007:
page 82

Answer (quotation)

Card number

(3)
Why was the dam built?
The dam would make irrigation around the Nile more modern and much easier. It would allow Egypt to turn large areas of desert into new cropland.
Scientific American
January 2006: page 18

Answer (paraphrase)

Prewrite

Create note cards. Make note cards like the examples above whenever your answers are too long to fit on your gathering grid or graphic.

Paraphrasing

When you *paraphrase*, you restate ideas from a text in your own words. Paraphrasing is a useful tool when you are analyzing poetry. It is also very helpful when you are conducting research and analyzing the finer points of a major debate or issue. Paraphrasing will help you better understand difficult vocabulary and complex texts.

- A paraphrase should be about the same length as the original source
- should contain simpler language
- should contain all of the source's significant information.

Isabel found paraphrasing a useful tool as she conducted her research and compiled her data. For example, Isabel read this information written by Michael Sorkin.

"By stabilizing the river's banks, the dam not only rescued Egyptian agriculture from historic cycles of flood and drought, but enabled extensive urban development along the shore."

She then wrote this paraphrase.

> The dam stabilized the river's banks. It protected Egypt's farming from times of flood and times of drought. The dam also made it possible to build housing and create city life along the shore.

Try It!

Read this excerpt from "To Preserve Egypt's Past." Then write a paraphrase of the selection.

One reason Egypt's history is so well known is that it is so well preserved. Many of Egypt's most ancient monuments were protected for millennia by the dry desert sands that covered them. Unfortunately, in many places those sands are no longer so dry. The year-round irrigation made possible by the Aswan High Dam elevates the local groundwater, which in turn is eroding many standing monuments from the bottom up. No one knows what damage it may be causing to archaeological treasures as yet undiscovered.

Summarizing

When you *summarize*, you restate the main or key ideas. A summary should only include information that appears in the original text. Like a paraphrase, a summary is written in your own words. Unlike a paraphrase, however, a summary is shorter than the original text.

Summarizing is an effective way to take a large amount of material, or a complex issue, and retell the key points in just a few sentences.

Isabel read the quote she had noted from Michael Sorkin and decided to summarize it.

> "By stabilizing the river's banks, the dam not only rescued Egyptian agriculture from historic cycles of flood and drought, but enabled extensive urban development along the shore."

Isabel's summary was shorter: *The dam protected Egypt's agriculture and made urban development possible.*

Try It!

Refer to the excerpt from "To Preserve Egypt's Past" on the previous page. Read the excerpt again and write a summary of the information in the text. When you have finished, compare your summary to your paraphrase. Did your summary capture only the key points? Was it shorter than the paraphrase? If not, you may need to revise both your paraphrase and your summary.

Avoiding Plagiarism

It's always important to give other people credit for their words and ideas. Not doing so is called *plagiarism,* and it is intellectual stealing. Here are two ways to avoid plagiarism.

- **Paraphrase:** Write in your own voice. Use your own words and simpler vocabulary. Always give credit to the source of the ideas.
- **Quote:** Use the exact words of a source to add authority to your paper. Enclose those words in quotation marks and give credit to the source.

Paraphrase

(4)
What are the effects of the dam?
Heavy metals and other dangerous substances are polluting delta croplands and lagoons where Egypt grows a lot of its food.
Earth August 2004
...sappearing Delta."
page 17

Quote

(4)
What are the effects of the dam?
"Thus, the biggest problem . . . is the increasing accumulation of salts, heavy metals, and other pollutants on the delta and in the lagoons where much of Egypt's food is grown."
Earth August 2004
Penvenne, Laura. "The Disappearing Delta."
page 17

Learning Language

Take turns reading the excerpt from "To Preserve Egypt's Past" aloud to a classmate. Pause at the end of each sentence and have your classmate retell the sentence in his or her own words. When you have finished, read the entire excerpt aloud again and have your classmate summarize it in his or her own words. Be sure to listen carefully and ask clarifying questions if you do not understand the summary or any of the vocabulary used by your classmate. Ask your teacher for help if you do not understand the words in the excerpt or the vocabulary used by your classmate.

Prewriting Keeping Track of Your Sources

As you conduct your research, keep track of the sources you use so that you can correctly cite them in your final report. You'll need the following information:

- **Book:** Author's last name, Author's first name. *Book title.* City of publication: Publisher's name, year of publication. Medium of publication.
- **Magazine:** Author's last name, Author's first name. "Article Title." *Magazine Name* day Month year: page number or numbers. Medium of publication.
- **Newspaper:** Author's last name, Author's first name. "Article Title." *Newspaper Name* day Month year: page number or numbers. Medium of publication.
- **Internet:** Author's last name, Author's first name (if known). "Document Title." *Title of Web site* Name of Sponsoring Institution. Date of publication (or last update). Medium of publication (Web). Day month year of access.
- **Videocassette or DVD:** *Film Title.* Dir. first and last name. Distributor, year released. Medium.

Source Notes

Source Notes

Book
Parks, Peggy J. The Aswan High Dam. San Diego: Blackbirch Press, 2008. Print.

Magazine
Sorkin, Michael. "Deciphering Greater Cairo." Architectural Digest April 2007: Pages 82–87. Print.

Internet
"Aswan Dam." STC-Link. University of Colorado at Denver. 15 April 2004. Web. 7 October 2010.

Newspaper
Shenon, Philip. "Digging Up the Ancient Past: Before the Deluge." New York Times 10 September 2004, morning ed: Section A, page 2. Print.

Interview
Lewis, Polly. Personal interview, E-mail. 28 October 2010.

Video
Building Big: Dams. WGBH Boston Video, 2006. VHS.

Prewrite

List sources. Keep a list of each of your sources with the information shown above. Whenever you find a new source, add it to the list.

Writing Your Thesis Statement

With your research completed, you'll be able to write a thesis statement. This statement identifies the controlling idea of your paper and serves as its focus. The rest of your report should explain and support the controlling idea. Use this formula to help you write your thesis statement.

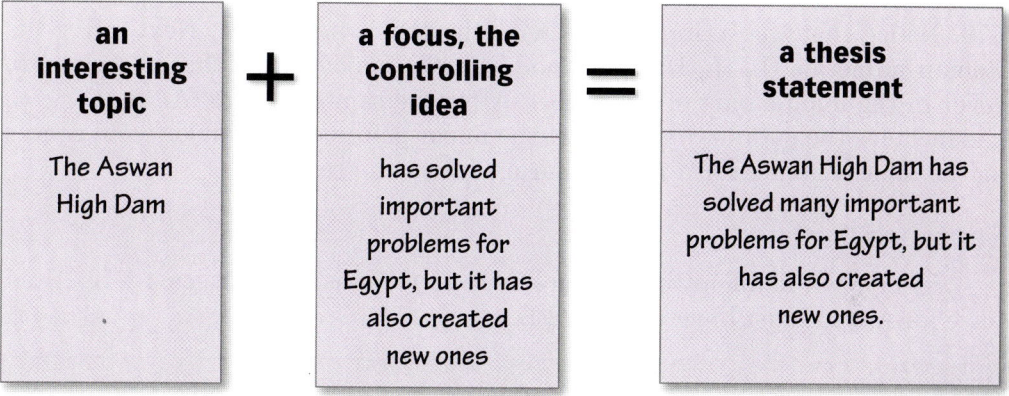

an interesting topic	+	a focus, the controlling idea	=	a thesis statement
The Aswan High Dam		has solved important problems for Egypt, but it has also created new ones		The Aswan High Dam has solved many important problems for Egypt, but it has also created new ones.

Other Possible Thesis Statements

The Aswan High Dam (an interesting, complex topic) **is an important accomplishment in Egypt's use of the Nile** (a focus).

Constructing the Aswan High Dam (an interesting, complex topic) **was a politically charged issue involving many nations** (a focus).

The builder of the first Aswan Dam (an interesting, complex topic) **was an engineer who believed the dam was unnecessary** (a focus).

Prewrite

Form your thesis statement. Review your research notes and choose a main point about your topic to emphasize in your paper. Using the formula above, write a thesis statement for the controlling idea. Revise your thesis statement until it says exactly what you want it to say.

TEKS 10.13B, 10.21B

Prewriting Outlining Your Ideas

One way to organize your research report is to make an outline. An outline maps the ideas you plan to include in your paper and helps organize ideas in a structured, persuasive manner. A topic outline lists ideas as words or phrases; a sentence outline lists them as full sentences.

Below is the first part of a sentence outline for the report on pages 373–379. Notice that the writer begins with the thesis statement. Next, after the Roman numerals (I., II., III., . . .), she lists the major points that she plans to cover in the middle part of her report. After the capital letters (A., B., C., . . .), she includes the details that support the major points. (Each major point serves as the topic sentence for a middle paragraph in the report.)

Sentence Outline

Remember, in an outline, if you have a I, you must have at least a II. If you have an A, you must have at least a B.

Thesis Statement

Major Points (I., II.)

Supporting Ideas (A., B., C.)

THESIS STATEMENT: The Aswan High Dam has solved many important problems for Egypt, but it has also created new ones.

I. Before the dam was built, Egyptians had to live with annual floods along the Nile.
   A. Flooding came after the rainy season in the highlands.
   B. This annual flooding helped to fertilize the land, but sometimes there was too much water.
   C. A dam was needed.

II. In years with little rain, Egypt had less flooding, but that also meant less water for irrigation.
   A. Egypt is mainly desert, so crops are watered by irrigation.
   B. Before the dam, Egyptians stored floodwater for irrigation after the flood season.

Prewrite

Create your outline. Write a sentence outline for your report, using the details you have gathered. Be sure that each topic sentence (I., II., III., . . .) supports the thesis statement and that each detail (A., B., C., . . .) supports the topic sentence. Use your outline as a guide for writing your first draft.

Developing Your Ideas

With your research completed, you will need to organize your note cards and the data you have collected. This will help you see if you have chosen a variety of authoritative sources and consulted enough sources so that you have a thorough understanding of both sides of controversial issues and a variety of viewpoints on the major debates involving your topic.

Isabel chose to create a chart based on her outline so that she could easily see which sources she had consulted for each topic.

Idea	Sources to Support Idea
Annual flooding of the Nile	Parks: The Aswan High Dam, 12
Years with little or no rain; lack of irrigation	Parks: The Aswan High Dam, 11
Erosion	Parks: The Aswan High Dam, 12

Isabel saw that too much information on this particular topic was coming from a single print source. She was then able to include other sources on the same topic. A greater variety of information meant that she could knowledgeably discuss major debates about this topic.

Keeping a Computer Log

You may find it useful to create a computer log to organize information from the sources that you have used. This will enable you to enter data and notes about each source that you consulted. If you choose to develop a computer log, be sure to include a complete citation of the source and detailed summaries or paraphrases of the information and date you gathered. It is easy to include quotes in a computer log. Be sure to enter quotations carefully and correctly. Put them in quotation marks, and provide detailed citations for them. In essence, the computer log becomes a form of electronic note card.

Remember that with any kind of graphic or form that you use to organize information, any and all text that directly uses another writer's ideas must be credited, even if it is not a direct quote. This applies to both print and electronic sources, note cards, and logs.

Prewrite

Organize your information. **Create a chart, graphic, or computer log to organize information from all of the sources you have used. Be sure to include complete citations for each of the sources you consulted in your research.**

Modifying Your Thesis

After you have conducted your research and gathered data, it is important to step back and re-evaluate both your thesis statement and your outline. You may have uncovered important data that will lead you to modify your major research question. As a result, you may need to refocus your research plan, and then rewrite your thesis statement. When this occurs, all or parts of your outline will need to be revised as well.

After you have finished your research, ask yourself the following questions:

- Does my research support the controlling idea and thesis statement?
- If not, what steps should I take to refocus my research plan?
- Do I need to conduct further research?
- How should I revise my thesis statement?

Evaluating Your Research

When you conduct research on a complex, multi-faceted topic, you will learn a great deal about many aspects of the topic. As you gather data, all these aspects and details may seem relevant and important to the topic. After you have re-evaluated the data and modified your thesis, you will be able to distinguish between those details that are relevant to your topic and those that are not.

In conducting her research on the Aswan High Dam, Isabel learned about the archaeological riches of the Nile region in which the dam was to be built. She gathered data about the pharaohs and ancient history of Egypt. As she developed her thesis statement and her outline, she realized that much of the information about the history of Egypt was not relevant to the controlling idea of her research.

Prewrite

Re-evaluate your data. **Take time to review the data you have gathered. Ask yourself whether or not it supports your major research questions. If not, modify your thesis and your outline. Then evaluate your research so that you include only the information that is relevant to your topic.**

Drafting

Go Online!

With your research and planning completed, you are ready to write your first draft. Don't worry about getting everything perfect in this draft. For now, just get your ideas on paper in a way that makes sense to you.

Keys to Effective Drafting

1. Use your first paragraph, your introduction, to get your reader's attention. Introduce your controlling idea and present your thesis statement.
2. In the next section, explain why the work of engineering was built.
3. After that, describe the story of the building process.
4. In the final section, your conclusion, spend a paragraph or more revealing the effects the work has had.
5. Remember to cite, within your report, the sources of any ideas you paraphrase or quote; also list those sources alphabetically on a works-cited page.

TEKS 10.21C, 10.23E

Citing Sources in Your Report

Credit the sources of ideas and facts you use in your report.

When You Have All the Information

- The most common type of citation lists the author's last name and page number.

  Rising groundwater is causing the temples of Luxor to crumble from the bottom up (Brown 22).

- If you name the author in your report, just include the page number in parentheses.

  The town of Aswan, according to Peggy J. Parks, had to be prepared to host the thousands of workers needed for the project (27).

When Some Information Is Missing

- If a source does not list an author, use the title and page number.

  These far-reaching changes indicate the great impact the dam has had on Cairo since 1970 (*Giant and Wonderful Dams* 18).

- If neither the author nor a page number is available, use the title alone.

  In all, 23 were rescued before the reservoir was filled, though many more were lost (*Building Big: Dams*).

- Some sources (especially Internet sites) do not use page numbers. In those cases, include just the author (or, if the author is not listed, the title).

  Now they flourish year-round, making the disease seven times more common (Larrson).

Try It!

Rewrite the following sentence, citing Michael Sorkin's article "Deciphering Greater Cairo" from *Architectural Record,* page 82.

In some ways, modern Cairo's riverfront is similar to Chicago's, with numerous high-rise buildings crowding expensive tracts of land.

Evaluating the Relevance of Sources

As Isabel did her research, she found articles, books, and online sources related to the Aswan High Dam. She knew that she wanted to focus on her major research question, or controlling idea: problems the dam solved and created for Egypt. Besides *Building Big: Dams,* Isabel found another video, *Egypt: Land of Archaeological Riches.* Based on the title, Isabel thought the video might deal with the potential destruction of archaeological sites. She read a review of the video, which said it was a travel documentary produced by Egypt's tourism council. She realized the video would not be a relevant source.

The following tips will help you decide whether or not a resource is relevant.

Read reviews about the source. Look for an overview or summary. Does the content pertain to your topic?

Examine the Table of Contents. How many chapters or pages pertain to your topic?

Examine the Index. Can you find the specific topics that you are looking for? How many pages are devoted to those topics?

Choosing Reliable Sources

After determining the relevance of your sources, you should check their reliability. Reliability means the information is verifiable and accurate. A general rule is that if data can be verified in two sources, the information is reliable and authoritative. When using Web sites, it is critical to check for reliability and accuracy.

As Isabel gathered data, she looked for sources from experts. She also chose data from well-respected sources. Isabel found a travel diary from a tourist who had visited the construction site, but she realized that a tourist would be not be a reliable source about the dam's construction.

To choose reliable sources, look for authors that are well respected. Articles from journals such as *Scientific American* and *National Geographic* are reliable and authoritative. National newspapers such as *The Wall Street Journal, The New York Times,* and *The Washington Post* are considered authoritative and objective. If you have questions about a source, read reviews about the source and its author. You can also check with your teacher or librarian.

Prewrite

Review your sources for relevance and reliability. Use the guidelines and tips on this page to evaluate your sources. Make sure that you have chosen relevant sources of information and that each source is reliable and authoritative.

Evaluating the Validity of Sources

Sources can be relevant and the data within them may be reliable, but they may still contain bias. Valid sources will contain information on both sides of the issue. For Isabel, this meant that sources should discuss both the problems and the advantages of building the dam.

Source/Detail	Data/Details in article
Malin, Matthew. "Consequences of the Aswan High Dam" *Egypt Today* March 2010: page 25. Online.	"Dam will ruin fertility of fields forever." No data provided to support or validate claim. Online magazine provides little information about ownership or authorship of articles.
Parks, Peggy J. *The Aswan High Dam*. pages 39–41.	Agriculture benefits, but there are problems. Farmers use chemical fertilizers, but Egypt can irrigate two million more acres of land than they could before dam was built. Author is well respected in field and provides scholarly footnote for facts,
Baker, Jonathan. "Losing Egypt's Treasures." *Modern Archaeological Disasters*. 18 February 2009. Web. October 15 2010.	Egypt has lost "innumerable monuments and others are at high risk." Terms not defined. Argument not defended with any authoritative sources. No name listed for sponsoring institution of the Web site.
Brown, Jeff. "Researchers Unravel Mystery of Eroding Egyptian Monuments." *Civil Engineering*. page 22. Print.	Rising groundwater and added moisture causing structures to crumble from bottom up. Details added to explain and defend claim. Supported with authoritative, scholarly footnotes. *Civil Engineering* is a well respected journal in the field.

Prewrite

Review your sources for validity. Look again at the data you have collected. Does each source present an honest, unbiased view of the topic? If not, conduct further research to find valid, relevant, and reliable sources.

Evaluating the Accuracy of Sources

Accurate sources contain information that can be verified by more than one source. For example, as Isabel began her research she read two encyclopedias to gain an overview of the history of the dam. She saw that each encyclopedia gave the same dates for beginning and ending the construction. This was the same date that she found in several other scholarly sources. When she saw different dates in an online article, she knew that those dates were inaccurate. In another instance, Isabel noted a 1995 copyright date on one book about the environmental impact of the dam. This meant that the source was dated and would not contain the recent information she needed to complete her research.

The following guidelines will help you as you evaluate the accuracy of your sources.

Nonfiction Books

Examine the copyright date. Check the copyright notice. Look for terms such as revised edition and updated edition on the copyright page or cover. If the book has gone through updates, it is likely to be highly accurate. Checking the copyright date will also tell you if the material is out-of-date.

Look for a bibliography. Examine the sources the author used to write. Some books and articles will also include an appendix—a collection of additional material about the subject. Look for footnotes, endnotes, and cross-references. These will help you determine the accuracy of the information.

Magazines and Periodicals

Is the publication well known and respected? Most large-circulation newspapers and national magazines are reliable and verify the accuracy of the information. Articles in scholarly journals go through a review process to ensure the accuracy of the information.

Was the article originally published in another source? If so, make sure the original source is reliable. For example, articles from news services such as Associated Press might be published in a small newspaper. The source is AP, a reliable news source.

Finally, determine if the facts in the article can be verified. Consult other sources, print or online, to check factual data.

Prewrite

Check for accuracy. Examine your sources. Are the authors experts in their fields? Are the publications authoritative and current? Make notes about the objectivity and authority of each of the sources you have used. Replace sources that are not authoritative or that lack objectivity.

Implementing Changes

As you check your research sources for reliability, validity, and accuracy, you may find that you need to do more research. It is critical to pause before you begin writing to evaluate the information in your sources. Replace any sources that have bias or that do not meet the criteria for reliability, validity, and accuracy.

As you continue your research, ask yourself if your initial inferences and conclusions about the topic are still valid. Often times, as you probe deeper into a topic, you will discover new information that will require a revision of your major research question. When this occurs, you need to refocus your research plan and revise your thesis statement.

As part of the evaluation process, ask yourself the following questions.

- Do I need to implement changes in my research process?
- Do I need to discard any potential source from my research?
- Do I need to find additional reliable, accurate, and valid sources?
- Do I need to change my thesis?
- Do I need to expand a section in my outline, based on my research?

When Isabel began critiquing her research, she was able to apply the lessons that she learned as she conducted new research and evaluated sources. As Isabel went through the process, she realized some of her sources had biases and had not dealt with the health consequence of the dam. After reading several print and online articles about schistosomiasis, Isabel found the following scholarly article and added the information to her research report and listed the information about her new source in her source notes.

Source Notes

Journal Article:
Larsson, Birgitta. "Aquaculture and schistosomiasis."
Three Overviews on Environment and Aquaculture in the Tropics and Sub-Tropics.
Food and Agriculture Organization of the United Nations. December 1994. Web.
15 October 2010.

Disease and the health problems in Egypt resulting from construction of dam.

Prewrite

Critique your research process. Critique each step of your research process and implement needed changes. Modify your research question as needed and refocus your research plan.

"Never underestimate your reader's intelligence or overestimate his or her information."
—Anonymous

Drafting Starting Your Research Report

The opening paragraph of your research report should grab the reader's attention, introduce your topic, and present your thesis statement. Here are three ways to begin . . .

- **Start with an interesting fact.**

  Humans have been building dams for thousands of years. One of the oldest is the Saad El Kafara, built in Egypt around 2700 B.C.E.

- **Ask a thought-provoking question.**

  What's the first thing that comes to mind when you think of Egypt?

- **Start with a quotation.**

  "The Aswan High Dam is known as one of the greatest engineering marvels of the twentieth century," says Peggy J. Parks.

Beginning Paragraph

This beginning paragraph starts with an interesting fact and ends with the thesis statement (underlined). Writer synthesizes information from a variety of sources to create an effective introduction.

Humans have been building dams for thousands of years. One of the oldest examples is the Saad El Kafara, built in Egypt around 2700 B.C.E. Its main purpose was to stop catastrophic flooding during wet years, but its water storage also allowed for increased irrigation of croplands. While most dams over the ages have been built for these two purposes, huge new dams in the past century have provided the added benefit of hydroelectric power for the world's growing population. However, people are discovering that these large dams also have many detrimental effects on the environment. Egypt's High Dam at Aswan illustrates this critical trade-off. The Aswan High Dam has solved many important problems for Egypt, but it has also created new ones.

Draft

Write your opening paragraph. Be sure to grab the reader's interest. Introduce your topic and controlling idea, and present your thesis statement.

Drafting Developing the Middle Part

The middle part of your report should show evidence that supports or explains your thesis statement. Start by explaining why this work of engineering was necessary. Then discuss its development in detail.

Each middle paragraph should cover one major point. Use your sentence outline to guide your writing.

Middle Paragraphs

The first middle paragraphs explain why the dam was built. Writer cites evidence.

Before the dam was built, Egyptians had to live with annual floods along the Nile. Each year, after the rainy season in the highlands, the river would spill over its banks onto the Egyptian countryside. While this annual flooding helped to fertilize the land, sometimes there was just too much water. For example, "between 1860 and 1880, there were four major floods that forced people to flee to higher ground" (Parks 12). They desperately needed a dam to help prevent this recurring damage.

All the details in each paragraph support the topic sentence (underlined). Writer continues to cite evidence.

In years with little rain, Egypt had less flooding, but that also meant less water for irrigation. Egypt is mainly desert, so crops grown there must be watered by irrigation. Before the dam was built, the Egyptians captured floodwater and stored it in pools for irrigation use during the rest of the year. In dry years, however, they could not capture enough water to last. The result was drought and famine (11).

By building a dam, the people of Egypt hoped to accomplish several things. A dam would help to stop catastrophic floods during wet years. It would also prevent Egypt from running out of water during dry years. In fact, it would store enough water to allow even more land to be irrigated. This was important because Egypt's population started to outgrow its crop production during the twentieth century (Building Big: Dams).

Ideas progress logically. The next middle paragraphs tell about how the dam was built.

The first Aswan Dam was built between 1898 and 1902, while Egypt was a colony of Great Britain. It was designed by William Willcocks, a British engineer who was very familiar with traditional Egyptian irrigation. Willcocks built a dam that would let the silt-laden water of each year's early rains pass through to fertilize the croplands below. The dam then stored

Writer includes sources in parentheses and formats them following an accepted style manual. Citations show evaluation of the quality of research.

later rainwater to be used for irrigation during the rest of the year (Pearce 50). Unfortunately, Willcock's dam didn't hold enough water to last through dry years, even after being raised twice, once in 1912 and again in 1933. Also, the dam almost overflowed in 1946, which happened to be a very wet year (Parks 14).

In 1952, Egypt became independent from Britain, and its new government decided to build a dam that could hold enough water for three years of irrigation. The project quickly became a touchy subject, because Egypt didn't want to hire British engineers to design the dam. As a gesture of friendship, Germany donated plans to the new government. In 1956, the World Bank, Great Britain, and the United States offered to fund the project, but they cancelled those plans when Egypt bought Soviet weapons to fight Israel (17–20). The Soviet Union agreed to fund the dam if Egypt agreed to use only Soviet engineers and equipment. By 1959, plans were complete and the project began ("Aswan Dam").

Arrangement of information ensures that the reader can easily follow all ideas and understand the author's point of view.

First, the valley that the dam would flood had to be cleared. This meant moving more than 100,000 Nubian people to new lands. Also, the new lake would cover many ancient temples and other monuments. In 1960, the United Nations Educational, Scientific, and Cultural Organization (UNESCO) asked governments around the world to help move these monuments. In all, 23 were rescued before the reservoir was filled, though many more were lost (Building Big: Dams).

Next, preparations had to be made for the dam's actual construction. New roads and railroads had to be built to carry men and equipment to the construction site. In addition, an electrical station had to be built at the old Aswan Dam to supply power for the project. Also, the town of Aswan had to be prepared to host the thousands of workers that would be needed (Parks 27).

Once building began, the construction team faced very harsh conditions. The terrain was extremely rugged, rapidly wearing out tires on construction equipment. Daytime temperatures reached 135 degrees Fahrenheit in the shade, so most work had to be done at night. Under these conditions, the

TEKS 10.21A, 10.21C, 10.23A, 10.23B, 10.23E

Statistics provide important information for the reader.

The remaining middle paragraphs explain both good and bad effects of the dam. Ideas progress logically, and evidence supports each point.

Writer quotes, summarizes, and paraphrases source material.i Writer clearly communicates her own point of view.

Soviet equipment broke down five times faster than expected. This caused expensive delays while replacement parts were shipped from the Soviet Union or equipment was sent back there for repair. In 1961, with little progress made, the Egyptian government brought in Egyptian construction experts to replace the Soviet engineers, and it began using equipment from Sweden and Great Britain (28–29).

The dam was finally completed in July 1970, ten years after the project began. It was by far the largest engineering work of its time, costing over $1 billion (Building Big: Dams). More than 50,000 people worked on the dam, using 17 times more material than was used to build the Great Pyramid. The finished dam stretches two miles wide and 364 feet high. The reservoir (holding the water) covers an area larger than the state of Delaware (Parks 35).

The Aswan High Dam immediately helped control flooding. Before the Nile was dammed, floods sometimes forced evacuation of the Nile Valley and its delta, with a great loss of life and property. With the dam in place, however, flooding became a thing of the past. As a result, cities like Cairo, which used to be limited to high ground near the river, have expanded all the way to the Nile's banks. As Michael Sorkin puts it, "By stabilizing the river's banks, the dam not only rescued Egyptian agriculture from historic cycles of flood and drought, but enabled extensive urban development along the shore" (82).

The vast reservoir behind the dam makes more irrigation possible in Egypt. In the past, the people could grow crops only as long as their stored water lasted each year. Now the dam provides irrigation throughout the entire year. In fact, Egyptians are able to irrigate two million more acres of land than they could before the dam was built (Parks 41).

Also, the Aswan High Dam provides 50 percent of Egypt's electricity. Once the dam was built, thousands of villages that had never had electricity before were "plugged in." The power station has been important for the swelling populations in Egypt's larger cities (Building).

However, there are some significant environmental problems related to the dam. For one thing, without the annual

The writer shows interest in the subject and point of view through the voice and word choice.

deposit of silt to enrich their fields, Egyptian farmers now have to use tons of chemical fertilizers each year. This has changed the chemistry of the waterways, leading to an excess of waterweeds and a decrease in fish and shrimp. Even the nearby sardine population in the Mediterranean Sea has suffered. The loss of silt has also caused the Nile delta to erode severely (Parks 39–40). Furthermore, industrial building closer to the Nile itself has caused more water pollution. As a result, the soil of the Nile delta, whose crops feed 40 million people, is becoming dangerously contaminated with toxins such as heavy metals (Penvenne 17).

The writer continues to structure ideas in a sustained, persuasive way. Writer provides evidence for thesis statement and for related claims.

Because the irrigation canals no longer dry up each year, Egyptians suffer from more waterborne diseases than before. One example is schistosomiasis, an intestinal and urinary disease transmitted by microscopic worms that live on snails in the waterways. Before the dam was built, these snails died every year during the dry season. Now they flourish year-round, making the disease seven times more common (Larrson). Besides the snails, there are more mosquitoes carrying malaria and other diseases in Egypt since the dam was built (Louria).

In addition, the dam continues to threaten some of Egypt's most important monuments. Year-round irrigation has led to rising groundwater, and this moisture is causing ancient structures like the temples of Luxor to crumble from the bottom up (Brown 22). If this problem isn't corrected, these historical treasures will be destroyed as surely as those that lie beneath the waters of the reservoir.

Draft

Write your middle paragraphs. Keep these tips in mind as you write.

- Use a topic sentence for each paragraph. Support it with evidence.
- Refer to your outline for direction. (See page 392.)
- Give credit to all your sources. (See page 396.)

TEKS 10.15A(i), 10.23A, 10.23B

Drafting Ending Your Research Report

Your ending paragraph, your conclusion, should sum up your research report by doing these three things.

- Remind the reader of the thesis of the report.
- Summarize the main points.
- Leave the reader with a final thought about the topic.

Ending Paragraph

The report's conclusion summarizes the main points and refers back to the thesis statement.

The report ends with a final thought for the reader. Writer shares her viewpoint.

No one can deny that the Aswan High Dam has benefited Egypt. Its flood control has prevented loss of life and property in wet years. Year-round irrigation and the expansion of croplands have helped supply food and other goods for Egypt's booming population. The electrical power it provides has helped the country to build and modernize. However, the dam also demonstrates that whenever people change their environment, they introduce new problems that must be dealt with. The building of the Aswan High Dam teaches humans that they have to learn to modernize with caution, and to predict and prepare for the consequences of their actions.

Draft

Write your ending paragraph and review your first draft. Draft your ending paragraph using the guidelines above. Then read your draft to make sure it is complete. Check your research notes and outline to be sure you haven't forgotten any important details. In the margins and between the lines, make notes about anything you should change.

Tip

Present your ideas honestly and clearly. Allow your writing voice to engage the reader by showing how you feel about the topic and the ideas you've synthesized.

Creating Your MLA Works-Cited Page

The purpose of a works-cited page is to allow the reader to locate the sources you used. The next four pages give standard MLA formats for common types of sources following MLA documentation style. (Your own sources may not always match these formats exactly. In that case, give as much information as possible, in the correct order.)

Books

Author or editor (last name, first name)**. Title** (in italics)**. City of publication: Publisher's name, year of publication. Medium of publication.**

One Author

Parks, Peggy J. *The Aswan High Dam.* San Diego: Blackbirch, 2008. Print.

If a book has two or three authors, list them in the order they appear on the title page. Reverse only the name of the first author. (Example: Brentano, Margaret, and Nicholson Baker.) For a book with four or more authors, list only the first author, followed by "et al."

A Single Work from an Anthology

To list an essay or a short story from an anthology, include the title of that work in quotation marks, followed by the title of the anthology and the editor.

Eisenman, Peter. "Post-Functionalism." *Theorizing a New Agenda for Architecture: An Anthology of Architectural Theory.* Ed. Kate Nesbitt. New York: Princeton Architectural, 2006. 60–68. Print.

An Article in a Familiar Reference Work

It is not necessary to list the editor of familiar reference books, such as dictionaries and encyclopedias. If the article is signed, give the author's name first. If not, give the title first.

Author (if available)**. Article title** (in quotation marks)**. Reference book title** (in italics)**. Edition number** (if available), **year published. Medium of publication.**

"Aswan High Dam." *Columbia Encyclopedia.* 2008. Web.

Periodicals

Periodicals are publications issued on a regular, scheduled basis. This includes magazines, scholarly journals, and newspapers. Again, follow the style guide to document sources and format your works cited list.

A Magazine

If a magazine is published weekly or biweekly, include the full date (day, month, year). If it is published monthly, bimonthly, or less often, include only the month and year. If the article isn't printed on consecutive pages, list the first page followed by a "+" sign.

Author (last name, first name)**. Article title** (in quotation marks)**. Title of the magazine** (in italics) day, Month, year)**: page numbers. Medium of publication.**

Penvenne, Laura Jean. "The Disappearing Delta." *Earth* Aug. 2004: 16-17. Print.

A Scholarly Journal

Scholarly journals are identified by volume number rather than by full date of publication.

Author (last name, first name)**. Article title** (in quotation marks)**. Journal Title** (in italics) **volume number. issue number** (year of publication)**: inclusive page numbers. Medium of publication.**

Sorkin, Michael. "Deciphering Greater Cairo." *Architectural Record* 189.4 (2007): 82-87. Print.

A Newspaper

Author (if available, last name, first name)**. Article title** (in quotation marks)**. Title of the newspaper** (in italics) **Date** (day, Month, year)**, edition** (if listed)**: section and page number or numbers. Medium of publication.**

Rider, Mary. "'Singing' Bridge to Lose Its Song." *Erie Times-News* 22 Nov. 2009: B11. Web.

Online Sources

Online sources include Web pages, documents in Internet databases, and e-mail messages. Follow the style guide to format your Works Cited list.

A Web Page

Author (if known, last name, first name). **Document Title** (in quotation marks). **Title of Web site** (in italics). **Name of Sponsoring Institution. Date of publication (or last update). Medium of publication (Web). day Month year of access.**

> "Aswan Dam." *STC-Link* 15 Dec. 2000. University of Colorado at Denver. 15 Dec. 2000. Web. 17 May 2009

An Article in an Online Service

Libraries often subscribe to online services where articles are kept. To cite such an article, first give any details about the original print version. (See "Periodicals" on page **408**.) Then list the database if known, the service, and the library. Next, give your date of access followed by the URL for the home page of the service (if known). If no URL is given for the article itself, give a keyword or path statement instead, if appropriate.

> Walton, Susan. "Egypt After the Aswan Dam." *Environment* May 1981: 30+. *MasterFILE Premier.* EBSCOHost. Burlington Public Library. 24 Apr. 2009 <http://search.epnet.com>. Keyword: dams environmental aspects schistosomiasis.

Use semicolons to separate the links in a path statement. (Example: Path: Publishing; Journalism; History.)

E-Mail to the Author (Yourself)

Writer (last name, first name). **Type of message** ("E-mail to the author"). **Date received.**

> Mythe, Lewis. E-mail to the author. 31 Jan. 2009.

Other Sources

Your research may include other sources, such as television programs, video documentaries, and personal interviews.

A Television or Radio Program

Episode title, if given (in quotation marks)**. Program title** (in italics)**. Title of the Series** (if any)**. Network Name. Call letters, City of the local station. Broadcast day Month year. Medium of reception.**

"The High Renaissance." *Art of the Western World*. PBS. WMVS, Milwaukee. 29 Nov. 2007. Television.

Video, DVD, Slide Program

Title (in italics)**. Dir. first and last name. Distributor, year released. Medium of reception.** (DVD, Video, slide program)

Building Big: Dams. WGBH Boston Video, 2006. Videocassette.

An Interview by the Author (Yourself)

Person interviewed (last name, first name)**. Description** (Personal interview, Telephone, E-mail, etc.)**. day Month year of interview.**

Mythe, Lewis. Personal interview. 31 Jan. 2009.

Draft

Format your sources. Check your report and your list of sources (page 390) to see which sources you actually used. Then follow these directions.

1. Write out the information for your sources using the guidelines on pages 407–410.
2. Put your sources in alphabetical order.
3. Create your works-cited page. Check the format of each citation on the list to make sure you have followed MLA guidelines. (See the example on page 379.)

Revising

Go Online!

The first draft of a research report is all about getting your thoughts on paper in a logical order. During the revising step, you make changes to ensure that your ideas are clear and interesting, your organization smooth, your voice confident and knowledgeable, your words specific, and the sentences varied.

Keys to Effective Revising

1. Read your entire draft to get an overall sense of your research report. Think about your audience, the purpose, and the genre of your writing.
2. Review your thesis statement to be sure that it clearly states your main point about the topic.
3. Be certain that your beginning engages the reader and that your ending offers an insightful final thought.
4. Check that the middle part clearly and completely supports the thesis statement. Check to see that you have used a variety of sentence types.
5. Review and adjust your voice to sound knowledgeable and interested in the topic. Make sure you have conveyed subtlety of meaning.
6. Check for effective word choice and sentence fluency.

Texas Traits

Revising for Focus and Coherence

When you revise for *focus and coherence,* be sure that your thesis statement is clear and complete. Your research and evidence should support the thesis throughout the essay.

Do I clearly state my thesis?

Your thesis statement should provide your audience with the controlling idea of your research and clearly explain the focus of your research. Here are some guidelines to help you determine if your thesis is clearly stated.

1. Does my thesis explain the direction, or focus, the paper will take?
2. Have I given an overview of the topic and narrowed the controlling idea for my audience?
3. Have I clearly conveyed the purpose for my research?
4. Have I chosen the correct genre for my purpose and audience?

Do my middle paragraphs support my thesis?

Re-read your middle paragraphs. Does each relate to and provide supporting evidence for the thesis statement? If not, review your research notes and revise your middle paragraphs as needed.

Exercise

Read the following paragraph and underline the topic sentence. Cross out the sentences that do not relate to or provide supporting evidence for the topic sentence.

In years with little rain, Egypt had less flooding. That also meant less water for irrigation. In times of old, Egyptians expected that pharaohs and the gods would send rain to help crops grow. This did not always happen, and people suffered. Egypt is mainly desert, so crops grown there must be watered by irrigation. Before the dam was built, Egyptians captured floodwater and stored it in pools for irrigation.

Revise

Revise your essay for focus and coherence. Re-read your thesis statement and your middle paragraphs to make sure that the evidence in each paragraph supports the thesis.

Are my paragraphs coherent?

Each paragraph in your research paper should be coherent, ideas fitting together to form a whole. Each paragraph should have a topic sentence and the rest of the sentences in the paragraph should relate directly to the topic sentence and provide evidence to support it.

- **Check that the evidence is relevant.**
  The details that you use should relate directly to the topic sentence. All the details and supporting evidence should support the controlling idea of your research.
- **Check for unity.**
  Re-read your paper to check for unity. Remember your purpose for writing and look for ways to improve your subtlety of meaning.

Try It!

Read the paragraph below. Revise it so that the paragraph will be coherent and form a unified whole.

Egypt was once a colony of Great Britain. It was still a colony when the first Aswan Dam was built. That happened between 1898 and 1902. Annual flooding during the rainy season meant that the Nile spread over its banks onto the Egyptian countryside. Sometimes there was just too much water. The first dam was designed by William Willcocks, a British engineer who was very familiar with traditional Egyptian irrigation.

Revise

Review your first draft for coherence. Review each paragraph to make sure that it has coherence and unity. Paragraphs should convey your subtlety of meaning, Revise your draft as needed.

Focus and Coherence
Writer deletes a sentence that does not support topic.

There are some significant environmental problems related to the dam. Without the annual deposit of silt to enrich their fields, Egyptian farmers now have to use tons of chemical fertilizers each year. ~~Chemical fertilizers are imported, and this has cost Egypt a good deal of money that the country did not expect to spend.~~ This has changed the chemistry of the waterways, leading to an excess of waterweeds and a decrease in fish and shrimp.

TEKS 10.13B, 10.15A(iv), 10.15C(ii)

Texas Traits

Revising for Organization

When you revise for *organization* in a research paper, it is critical that the ideas be presented in a logical order. Your paragraphs should flow smoothly from one to the next, and the ideas within each paragraph should be presented logically. Use transitions to ensure that the reader can easily follow the progression of ideas.

Do my paragraphs flow smoothly from one to the next?

Your paragraphs will flow smoothly if opening sentences include a transitional phrase or a link to the preceding paragraph.

Exercise

Copy the paragraphs below. Add transitions to make the paragraphs flow smoothly and to help the reader follow the progression of ideas. If needed, reorder the ideas so that they flow in a logical pattern.

In 1952, the government decided to build a dam. By 1959, plans were complete and the project began.

The valley that the dam would flood had to be cleared. This meant moving more than 100,000 Nubian people to new lands. The new lake would cover many ancient temples and other monuments. In all, 23 were rescued, but many more were lost. UNESCO asked governments around the world to help move the 23 monuments that were saved.

Preparations had to be made for the dam's actual construction. New roads had to be built to carry men and equipment to the construction site. An electrical station had to be built at the old Aswan Dam. The town of Aswan had to be prepared to host the thousands of workers that would be needed.

Revise

Review your first draft. Check each paragraph to make sure ideas flow logically. Check for transitions within paragraphs. Make sure that transitions between paragraphs help the reader follow the flow of information. Revise accordingly.

Revising for Organization within Paragraphs

In a research paper, embedded quotations are often used as supporting evidence. Introducing the quotation and then returning to the paragraph or summary will also require transitions. A good organizational pattern will make this process seem seamless to the reader and fit well into the context and purpose for your writing.

Revise

Review your first draft for organization. **Be sure that each paragraph is logically structured. Check that quotations are introduced and integrated into the flow of the paragraph.**

Organization Writer moves a sentence to make the paragraph more coherent. An added transitional sentence introduces the quote and integrates it into the paragraph.

With the dam in place, flooding became a thing of the past. The Aswan High Dam immediately helped control the flooding. Before the Nile was dammed, floods sometimes forced evacuation of the Nile Valley. . . . Cities like Cairo have expanded to the Nile's banks. As Michael Sorkin put it, "By stabililzing the river's banks, the dam not only rescued Egyptian agriculture from historic cycles of flood and drought, but enabled extensive urban development along the shore" (82).

TEKS 10.13C, 10.15C(ii), 10.22C

Texas Traits

Revising for Development of Ideas

When you revise for *development of ideas,* check to make sure that the evidence you have provided to support your ideas is relevant, accurate, and reliable. In a research paper, it is critical to defend or support each point you make with authoritative data and factual, verifiable evidence. Embedded quotations and cited evidence are ways to show that you have used authoritative evidence.

As you re-read and revise your research paper, look at your word choice. Make sure that your words accurately and clearly convey your viewpoint and your subtlety of meaning. At this point, too, it is important to critique your research process to make sure that your research supports your thesis statement.

Try It!

The paragraph below sometimes fails to show clear development of ideas. On your own paper, rewrite the paragraph so that each idea is clearly developed. As you rewrite, keep in mind the purpose, audience, and genre for the writing.

According to one source, the Aswan High Dam was completed in July 1970. It seems to have been the largest engineering project of its time, and it may have cost around $1 billion. A lot of people worked on the dam, and it must have taken a lot of material. We know that it took a lot of material to build the Great Pyramid in Egypt, and that must have taken a lot of workers, too. The finished dam is a couple of miles wide. One of the health problems from the dam is schistosomiasis and it has affected a lot of people. There were other consequences, too, including the need for chemical fertilizers. But, overall I think the dam is a good thing for Egypt.

Revise

Check for well-developed ideas. Read your draft. Make sure that you have supported each idea with evidence. Make sure that your work incorporates factual data and that the data is accurate and reliable. Cite your sources, and embed appropriate quotations to support your thesis and paragraph topic sentences. As you revise, consult your outline or other graphics you created to help you better develop your ideas.

Revising for Drawing Ideas to a Conclusion

The conclusion is a critical component of a research paper. You will provide a final summation of your research and give final support to your thesis statement. The conclusion is the last impression you will leave with your reader. Therefore, all the ideas in your paper need to be pulled together. The conclusion is also your last opportunity to present your own viewpoint on the topic. In a lengthy research paper, the conclusion may be more than one paragraph long.

- **Be direct.** Summarize the ideas and support the thesis statement clearly.
- **Use active verbs.** Leave your reader with strong support for the thesis statement.

Try It!

Rewrite this conclusion so that the reader is left with a strong final impression and a clear idea of the thesis statement.

There were a lot of reasons to build the Aswan High Dam. Egypt needed a dam to help control flooding and help its agriculture. The country also wanted to preserve monuments along the Nile River. Egypt also needed more land for cities to grow.

Revise

Check your conclusion. **Re-read your essay. Is the conclusion effective? Does it summarize your research and clearly support the thesis statement? Revise as needed.**

Development of Ideas
Writer needs more information to support thesis statement and summarize information in middle paragraphs. Final thought also needs to be fleshed out.

No one can deny that the Aswan High Dam has benefited Egypt. Flood control has prevented loss of life and property. Irrigation and the expansion of croplands have helped supply food and other goods. The electrical power it provides has helped Egypt build and modernize. However, the dam also demonstrates There have been problems, that whenever humans change their environment, they ~~too. I think that overall, the dam has been a good thing for~~ introduce new problems that must be dealt with. The building ~~Egypt.~~ of the Aswan High Dam teaches people that they have to lern to modernize with caution, and to predict and prepare for the consequences of their actions.

Texas Traits

Revising for Voice

When you revise for *voice* in a research report, you want to make sure that you sound knowledgable about the topic. You want to show that you have conducted careful research and that you understand the topic thoroughly. Through your voice, you will show that you have synthesized the information and can present it so that your reader can understand it, as well.

Do I maintain an objective, third-person point of view throughout my research essay?

You have maintained an objective point of view if you accurately and honestly discuss both sides of the topic you have chosen. While you will provide your reader with your own viewpoint, that viewpoint should be formed by the evidence from your research.

In a research paper, it is also important to maintain a third-person point of view throughout. Avoid personal pronouns, *I*, and *my*, and use third-person pronouns, *he*, *she*, *they*, and *his*, *her*, *their*.

Try It!

The paragraph below sometimes drifts away from an objective, third-person point of view. On your own paper, rewrite the paragraph so that the voice is consistently third person and objective. In places, you will need to completely change the sentence structure.

The valley that the dam would flood had to be cleared. I was surprised and horrified to learn that this meant moving more than 100,000 Nubian people to new lands. That is a lot of people whose lives were completely disrupted by the building of the dam. Then I learned that many monuments were going to be lost when the valley was flooded. To me, this seemed like a terrible archaeological disaster. In all, however, 23 monuments were rescued before the reservoir was filled.

Revise

Check for objectivity and third-person point of view. Re-read your research paper to see if you have maintained an objective viewpoint and a third-person point of view throughout. Make any necessary revisions.

Do I sound knowledgeable about the topic?

Your voice will sound knowledgeable if you show a clear understanding of the topic and write with confidence about it. Keep these tips in mind.

- **Avoid casual, inappropriate words.** Expressions such as "The Aswan High Dam was the bomb!" would not be appropriate for the purpose, audience, or context for the writing.
- **Define technical terms.** Your audience may not be familiar with the terms you are using. Show your knowledge by defining or explaining special terminology.
- **Support details with specific data.** Words such as *kind of, sort of, in a way* should be replaced with precise, factual data.

Try It!

Rewrite the following sentences to make them sound more knowledgeable. Use the strategies given above.

It seems like there were problems with flooding and with drought. In about 20 years there were several floods that forced people to flee to higher ground. Then when there was a drought, it led to famine and some people died.

Revise

Check your essay for voice. Re-read your essay, marking any places that do not sound knowledgeable. Consult your research notes and revise as needed.

Voice
Writer defines technical terms and uses precise data to support claim.

Because the irigation canals no longer dry up every year, Egyptians suffer from more waterborne diseases than before. One example is schistosomiasis, an intestinal and urinary disease transmitted by microscopic worms that live on snails in the waterways. These snails flourish year-round making the disease seven times more common. There are also more mosquitos carrying diseases in Egypt since the dam was built. (Louria 3) i

Texas Traits

Revising Improving Your Writing

On a piece of paper, write the numbers 1 to 13. If you can answer "yes" to a question, put a check mark after that number. If not, continue to revise your report for that trait.

Revising Checklist

Focus and Coherence

_____ **1.** Is my thesis statement clearly presented?
_____ **2.** Does my research support the thesis statement?
_____ **3.** Is each paragraph coherent and related to the controlling idea?

Organization

_____ **4.** Does my beginning paragraph capture the reader's interest and introduce my topic?
_____ **5.** Do my transitions lead to a smooth flow of ideas?
_____ **6.** Have I introduced and integrated quotations smoothly?
_____ **7.** Do I draw my ideas into an effective conclusion?

Development of Ideas

_____ **8.** Have I chosen an interesting work of engineering to write about?
_____ **9.** Do I include enough relevant, accurate details to support my thesis?
_____ **10.** Do I give credit for ideas that I have paraphrased or quoted?
_____ **11.** Do I clearly support each idea with reliable, authoritative evidence?

Voice

_____ **12.** Does my voice sound knowledgeable and engaging?
_____ **13.** Do I consistently maintain an objective, third-person point of view?

Editing

Go Online!

When you have finished revising your research paper, all that remains is checking for conventions in grammar, sentence structure, capitalization, punctuation, and spelling.

Keys to Effective Editing

1. Read your essay out loud and listen for words or phrases that may be incorrect.
2. Use a dictionary, a thesaurus, your computer's spell-checker, and the "Proofreader's Guide" in the back of this book.
3. Look for errors in grammar, sentence structure, capitalization, punctuation, and spelling.
4. Check your report for proper formatting. (See pages 372–379.)
5. If you use a computer, edit on a printed copy. Then enter your changes on the computer.
6. Use the editing and proofreading marks inside the back cover of this book. Check all citations for accuracy.

Texas Traits

Editing for Conventions

Grammar

In a research paper, you will undoubtedly use complex sentences that contain restrictive and nonrestrictive phrases and clauses.

Have I correctly used restrictive and nonrestrictive clauses and phrases?

As you paraphrase information from your research or embed quotations into your work, it is important to understand the difference between restrictive and nonrestrictive clauses. Here are some tips to guide you.

- A restrictive clause is essential to the meaning of the sentence.
- A nonrestrictive clause or phrase adds information that is not necessary to the basic meaning of the sentence. In other words, the clause could be deleted from the sentence and the meaning would not be changed.
- Use the word *that* to introduce restrictive clauses. Use the word *which* to introduce nonrestrictive clauses.

Exercise

Copy the following sentences onto your own paper. Identify whether the clauses are restrictive or nonrestrictive and explain your answer.

1. The information that is in this particular journal gives details about the dam's construction.
2. This information, which I think you will find useful, is about the UNESCO efforts to save the monuments.
3. The town of Aswan, which had been home to just a few thousand people, experienced incredible growth.
4. Cities like Cairo, which used to be limited to high ground near the river, have expanded.
5. I would like to use a quotation from Michael Sorkin that supports my point about urban development.

Edit

Check for restrictive and nonrestrictive clauses. As you edit your paraphrases and quotations, check for correct use of restrictive and nonrestrictive clauses.

Should I Avoid the Passive Voice?

In a research paper, you should try to use verbs in the active voice. Particularly as you write summaries and paraphrases of the research you have done, think about your word choice and how to convey your ideas so that you can use the active voice. The active voice is stronger and will capture your reader's interest. In a paraphrase you should also try to capture the writer's original voice and communicate to your reader the original writer's opinions.

Try It!

Compare the following sentences from the research paper on the Aswan Dam. The sentences written in active voice are stronger and more engaging to the reader.

In the heat, the Soviet equipment broke down five times faster than expected.

The Soviet equipment was often broken by the heat.

As was reported by Michael Sorkin, "By stabilizing the river's banks, extensive urban development could take place along the river's banks."

As Michael Sorkin puts it, "By stabilizing the river's banks, extensive urban development could take place along the river's banks."

Edit

Edit for active and passive voice. **Review your essay for active and passive voice. When possible, rewrite sentences so that the verbs are in the active voice.**

LEARNING LANGUAGE

Compare the following examples of active and passive voice. Remember that active and passive voice occur in present, past, and future tenses. Explain to a partner how the passive voice is formed. Take turns with your partner saying three verbs in the passive voice and changing them into the active voice. Then say three different verbs in the passive voice and have your partner change them into the active voice.

Active Voice	Passive voice
Engineers observed that	It was observed that
Nubians moved	Nubians were moved
The construction team faced	The construction team was faced with

TEKS 10.13C, 10.17C

Sentence Structure

There are four main types of sentences: simple, compound, complex, and complex-compound. It is important to use a variety of these sentence types in your research paper. It is also important to avoid lengthy compound or complex-compound sentences. Keep your reader in mind as you edit your sentences, and be sure to use correct punctuation.

- A **simple sentence** can have a single subject or a compound subject. It can have a single predicate or a compound predicate. It has no dependent clauses.
  The Aswan High Dam stretches for two miles.
- A **compound sentence** consists of two independent clauses.
  The dam cost over $1 billion, and more than 50,000 people worked on it.
- A **complex sentence** contains one independent clause and one or more dependent clauses.
  Cities like Cairo, which used to be limited to higher ground near the river, have expanded all the way to the Nile's banks.
- A **complex-compound sentence** contains one or more independent clauses and one or more dependent clauses.
  Once the dam was built, thousands of villages gained electricity, and the power station, which has been enlarged several times, has been important to the growing population.

Try It!

Rewrite the following paragraph so that it contains a variety of sentence structures.

The dam was begun in 1960. It was completed in 1970. It took ten years to complete. It was the largest engineering work of its time. It cost over $1 billion. More than 50,000 people worked on the dam. The dam is two miles wide. It is 364 feet high. The reservoir covers an area larger than the state of Delaware.

Edit

Check for sentence variety. Use the information above as a guide to ensure that you have used a variety of sentence structures in your research paper.

Mechanics

How do I punctuate nonrestrictive clauses?

When you edit for *mechanics,* you check for punctuation and capitalization. The punctuation of restrictive and nonrestrictive clauses is different. Knowing how to punctuate clauses and phrases in your research paper will help the reader follow your ideas without distractions.

Always use a comma to set off nonrestrictive clauses. Remember that these are clauses that contain information that is not essential to the meaning of the sentence. In addition, nonrestrictive clauses are introduced by the word *which.*

Austin, which is the capital of Texas, is a vibrant, growing city.

What punctuation do I use with quotations?

To introduce a quotation into your work, use a comma before the quotation marks. Always place commas and periods inside the quotation marks. If you are citing material, however, the period goes after the citation.

As Michael Sorkin puts it, "The dam enabled extensive urban development along the shore" (82).

Edit

Check for mechanics. **As you edit for mechanics, check the punctuation you have used with embedded quotations and with restrictive and nonrestrictive clauses.**

Try It!

Rewrite the following paragraph, inserting punctuation as needed for quotations and clauses.

According to Peggy Parks "between 1860 and 1880, there were four major floods that forced people to flee to higher ground" Egypt desperately needed a dam that would replace the old dam and prevent recurring damage. In dry years, the problems suffered by Egypt were quite different. Without irrigation "the result was drought and famine" problems that could be solved by building a new dam. The Aswan High Dam which was in the planning process for decades seemed to be the perfect solution.

Editing Checking for Conventions

Using a Checklist

On a piece of paper, write the numbers 1 to 12. If you can answer "yes" to a question, put a check mark after that number. Continue editing until you can answer "yes" to all of the questions.

Editing Checklist

Conventions

GRAMMAR

_____ **1.** Do I use the correct forms of verbs *(he saw,* not *he seen)*?

_____ **2.** Do I use active voice whenever possible?

SENTENCE STRUCTURE

_____ **3.** Have I used a variety of sentence structures, including complex and compound sentences?

_____ **4.** Have I avoided run-ons and sentences that are too lengthy?

MECHANICS (Capitalization and Punctuation)

_____ **5.** Have I capitalized proper nouns and adjectives?

_____ **6.** Do I correctly punctuate compound and complex sentences?

_____ **7.** Have I correctly cited sources in my research paper?

_____ **8.** Do I use quotation marks around all quoted words?

_____ **9.** Do I correctly punctuate nonrestrictive clauses?

_____ **10.** Have I correctly formatted a works-cited page?

SPELLING

_____ **11.** Have I spelled all my words correctly?

_____ **12.** Have I double-checked the words my spell-checker may have missed?

MLA Research Papers

In high school English and language arts classes, research papers are usually written in MLA (Modern Language Association) format. However, always follow your teacher's instructions with regard to formatting.

Research Report

Titles and title pages are important parts of your research report. Ask your teacher what he or she wants included in the title page. After you have that information, consider including a title before you share your research report.

Writer Randall VanderMey says that a title, like good fish bait, should entice the reader. Each of the following approaches will help you write an effective title:

- Provide a creative hook:
  Egypt's Modern Marvel
- Focus on a theme that runs through your paper:
  A Trade-Off of Monumental Size
- Highlight a key point of your report:
  Modernize with Caution
- Use alliteration or some other literary device:
  Providing Power to the People

If you are having trouble choosing a title for your research paper, use the following tips to help.

- Brainstorm and consult with others to get ideas.
- When you have decided on possible titles, discuss them with a classmate or friends. Ask for feedback.
- Review possible titles with your teacher and ask for feedback.
- Review your research, your thesis statement, and your outline. Your title should capture the essence of your research and your writing.
- Write down several ideas, think about them overnight or for a few days, and then select the one that best fits your research paper.

Publishing Sharing Your Report

When you finish revising, editing, and proofreading the final copy of your research report, make a neat final copy to share. Be sure to ask your teacher to review your final draft. She or he will be able to provide you with helpful feedback and provide useful ideas for making improvements. Share your report with friends and family. Ask them for ways to improve your report, and incorporate their feedback as well. After you have listened carefully to all the feedback you have been given, make any needed final changes to your report. You are now ready to share your report with others.

A research report can serve as an effective starting point for a speech or a multimedia presentation. (See pages **429–441**.)

Publish

Make your final copy. **Use the following guidelines to format your report. (Also see pages 72–74 for instructions about designing on a computer.) Create a clean final copy and share it with your classmates and family.**

Focusing on Presentation

- Use blue or black ink and double-space the entire paper.
- Write your name, your teacher's name, the class, and the date in the upper left corner of page 1.
- Skip a line and center your title; skip another line and start your writing.
- Indent every paragraph and leave a one-inch margin on all four sides.
- For a research paper, you should write your last name and the page number in the upper right corner of every page of your report.
- If a title page and outline are required, follow your teacher's instructions. (See page **372**.)

Making Presentations

If the very idea of making a presentation in front of a group makes you feel woozy, you're not alone. The fear of speaking in public is probably the most common anxiety around. But you can conquer that fear if you follow the tips and guidance provided in this chapter. Then with preparation and practice, you can make strong, effective presentations that inform and engage your listeners.

In this chapter you will learn to prepare and give a presentation based on a research report you have written. You will then learn how to turn your presentation into a multimedia report.

- **Planning Your Presentation**
- **Creating Note Cards**
- **Considering Visual Aids**
- **Practicing Your Speech**
- **Delivering Your Presentation**
- **Evaluating a Presentation**
- **Preparing a Multimedia Report**

"Be sincere; be brief;
be seated."

—Franklin D. Roosevelt

TEKS 10.15D, 10.23A–10.23C

Planning Your Presentation

To transform a research report into a presentation, you need to consider your purpose, your audience, and the content of your report.

Considering Your Purpose and Your Audience

Your purpose is your reason for giving a presentation. Your audience is all those who will listen to your presentation. As you think about your purpose and audience, keep the following points in mind.

- **Informative** speeches educate by providing valuable information.
- **Persuasive** speeches argue for or against something.
- **Demonstration** speeches show how to do or make something.
- **Be clear.** Listeners should understand your main points immediately.
- **Engage the listeners** through thought-provoking questions, revealing anecdotes, interesting details, and effective visuals.

Conveying Your Point of View

- **Anticipate questions** the audience might have and answer them. This helps keep the audience connected.
- **Speak in your own words.** This helps you convey your own point of view about the topic. It will also keep the audience engaged.

Reviewing Your Report

During a report, your audience obviously cannot go back and listen again to anything you have said, so you must be sure to share your ideas clearly from beginning to end. Review your report to see how the different parts will work in a presentation. Use the following questions as a review guide.

- Will my opening grab the listeners' attention?
- What are my thesis and main points? Is my thesis clearly stated?
- How does my evidence support my claims?
- What visual aids, including graphics and illustrations, can I use to create interest in my topic? (See page **434**.)
- Will the ending have the proper impact on the listeners?

Try It!

Choose a research report to present. Rework any parts that need to be adjusted. Pay special attention to the beginning and ending. Make sure your ideas follow logically and your point of view is clear. (See the next page for example adaptations.)

TEKS 10.15D, 10.23A, 10.23B

Making Presentations

You may need to rewrite certain parts of your report. The new beginning below grabs the listeners' attention by using short, punchy phrases. The thesis is clearly stated for the audience. The new ending makes a more immediate connection to the thesis statement and ties back to the beginning.

Written Introduction (page 373)

Humans have been building dams for thousands of years...main purpose was to stop catastrophic flooding...people are discovering that these large dams also have many detrimental effects on the environment. Egypt's High Dam at Aswan illustrates this critical trade-off. The Aswan High Dam has solved many important problems for Egypt, but it has also created new ones.

Oral Introduction

Dams stop flooding; they provide irrigation; they generate hydroelectric power. In general, dams have proven to be a good thing. But the Aswan High Dam in Egypt is a prime example of how dams, while built to serve humanity, can also have a negative impact on our world.

Written Conclusion (page 379)

No one can deny that the Aswan High Dam has benefited Egypt. . . . However, the dam also demonstrates that whenever humans change their environment, they introduce new problems that must be dealt with. The building of the Aswan High Dam teaches people that they have to learn to modernize with caution, and to predict and prepare for the consequences of their actions.

Oral Conclusion

It's tempting and exciting to find new ways to dominate the physical world. Yet, as the Aswan High Dam has shown, people must modernize with caution. The natural world has a balance of its own, and humans run the risk of destroying their own future when they tamper with that balance.

TEKS 10.15D, 10.23A–10.23C, 10.23E

"To be listened to is, generally speaking, a nearly unique experience for most people. It is enormously stimulating."

—Robert C. Murphy

Creating Note Cards

If you are giving a prepared speech rather than an oral reading of your report, you should use note cards or slides with embedded notes to help you remember your ideas. The guidelines below will help you make effective cards.

Following Note-Card Guidelines

Write out your entire introduction and conclusion on separate note cards. For the body of your speech, write one point per card, along with specific details. Clearly number your cards.

- Place each main point at the top of a separate note card.
- Write supporting evidence on the lines below the main idea, using key words and phrases to help you remember specific details.
- Number each card in a logical sequence.
- Highlight any ideas you especially want to emphasize.
- Mark cards that call for visual aids.
- Cite your sources on your note cards.

Considering the Three Main Parts

As you prepare your note cards, keep the following points in mind about the three parts of your oral presentation: introduction, body, and conclusion.

- **The introduction** should grab the listeners' attention, clearly state the thesis, and provide any essential background information about the topic. (See pages **430–431**.)
- **The body** should contain the main points and supporting evidence from your report. Present these points in a way that impacts listeners. Also jot down the visual aids that you plan to use. (See the bold notes on the sample cards on page **433**.)
- **The conclusion** should restate your focus and leave the listener with a final thought about your topic. (See pages **430–431**.)

Try It!

Create your note cards. Review those on the following page. Then prepare cards for your introduction, main points, and conclusion. Make notes on the cards about where to use visual aids.

TEKS 10.15D, 10.23A–10.23C, 10.23E

Making Presentations

Below are the note cards Isabel used for her presentation.

Introduction 1

Dams stop flooding; they provide irrigation; they generate hydroelectric power. In general, dams have proven to be a good thing. But the Aswan High Dam in Egypt is a good example of how dams, while built to serve humanity, can also have a huge, negative impact on our world.

Reasons to Build 2

- flooding
- water for dry spells
- irrigation

*** Photos of Nile Valley before the dam**

History: Source: Parks 3

- 1898-1902, Britain's William Willcocks
- Not big enough, raised in 1912 and 1933
- 1952—Egyptian independence meant new dam
- Germany gave plans

*** Drawing of early workers**

Preparations for Second Dam: Source: Building Big: Dams 4

- support for machines and workers
- difficult weather and terrain temperatures up to 135° in shade
- 1961—Egyptians took over from the Soviets
- equipment came from Sweden and Great Britain

Completed: Source: "Aswan Dam" 5

- July 1970
- over $1 billion
- more than 50,000 people worked on two-mile-wide, 364-foot-high dam
- reservoir larger than Delaware

*** Photos of finished dam**

Effects *** Show Chart** 6

- Positive: Stabilized banks, controlled irrigation, expanded urban development, electricity for all
- Negative: river pollution, industrial waste, erosion, waterborne diseases, ancient statues crumbling

Conclusion 7

It's tempting and exciting to find new ways to control our physical world. Yet, as the Aswan High Dam has shown, people must modernize very carefully. The natural world has a balance of its own, and humans run the risk of destroying their own future if they tamper with that balance.

TEKS 10.15D, 10.23C

Considering Visual and Audio Aids

Consider using visual and audio aids during your presentation. They can make your presentation clearer, more meaningful, and more appealing to your audience. They can also convey a distinct point of view.

Posters	include words, pictures, or both.
Photographs	help people see what you are talking about.
Charts and Graphs	explain points, compare facts, or show statistics.
Maps	identify or locate specific places being discussed.
Objects	show the audience important items related to your topic.
Audio and Visual clips and slides	project your photographs, charts, and maps onto a screen and turn your speech into a multimedia presentation. (See pages 438–439.)

Indicating When to Present Visuals

Write notes in the margins of your note cards to indicate where a visual aid would be helpful. Isabel considered the following visuals for her presentation.

- Photos of Nile Valley before the dam and of the finished dam
- An illustration of workers on the first dam
- An audio clip of an interview
- A chart comparing the pros and cons of the dam

Try It!

List possible visual aids. Identify two or three visual aids you could use in your presentation. Explain how and when you would use each one.

Tip

When creating visual aids, keep these points in mind.

- **Make them big.** Your visuals should be large enough for everyone in the audience to see.
- **Keep them simple.** Use labels and short phrases rather than full sentences.
- **Make them eye-catching.** Use color, bold lines, and simple shapes to attract the audience.

Making Presentations

Practice is the key to giving an effective presentation. Knowing what to say and how to say it will help eliminate those "butterflies" speakers often feel. Here are some hints for an effective practice session.

- **Arrange your note cards and visual aids in the proper order.**
  This will eliminate any confusion as you practice.
- **Practice in front of a mirror.** Check your posture and eye contact and be sure your visual aids are easy to see.
- **Practice in front of others.** Friends and family can help you identify parts that need work.
- **Record or videotape a practice presentation.** Do you sound interested in your topic? Are your voice and message clear?
- **Time yourself.** If your teacher has set a time limit, practice staying within it.
- **Speak clearly.** Do not rush your words, especially later when you are in front of your audience.
- **Work on eye contact.** Look down only to glance at a card.
- **Speak up.** Your voice will sound louder to you than it will to the audience. Rule of thumb: If you sound *too* loud to yourself, you are probably sounding just right to your audience.
- **Look interested and confident.** This will help you engage the listeners.

Practice Checklist

To review each practice session, ask yourself the following questions.

_____ **1.** Did I appear at ease and convey my point of view?

_____ **2.** Could my voice be heard and my words understood?

_____ **3.** Did I sound like I enjoyed and understood my topic?

_____ **4.** Did my visual aids help explain the concepts? Were the visuals interesting and used effectively?

_____ **5.** Did I clearly convey my thesis and supporting evidence? Did my ideas follow a logical progression?

Try It!

Practice your presentation. Practice your speech in front of family or friends. Also consider videotaping your speech.

Delivering Your Presentation

When you deliver a speech, concentrate on your voice and body language. Voice quality and body language communicate as much as your words do.

Controlling Your Voice

Volume, tone, and *pace* are three aspects of your formal speaking voice. If you can control these three aspects of voice, your listeners will be able to follow your ideas.

- **Volume** is the loudness of your voice. Imagine that you are speaking to someone in the back of the room and adjust your volume accordingly.
- **Tone** expresses your feelings. Be enthusiastic about your topic and let your voice show that.
- **Pace** is the speed at which you speak. For the most part, speak at a relaxed pace. Slow down or pause to make important points.

Considering Your Body Language

Your body language (*posture, gestures,* and *facial expressions*) plays an important role during a speech. Follow the suggestions given below to communicate effectively.

- **Assume a straight but relaxed posture.** This tells the audience that you are confident and prepared. If you are using a podium, let your hands rest lightly on the surface.
- **Pause before you begin.** Take a deep breath and relax.
- **Look at your audience.** Try to look toward every section of the room at least once during your speech.
- **Think about what you are saying** and let your facial expressions reflect your true feelings.
- **Point to your visual aids** or use natural gestures to make a point. Graphics and illustrations play an important role in explaining ideas. Prepare visual aids carefully and practice using them. Make sure any technology is working before you give your presentation so that you will be relaxed as you present the visual aids.

Try It!

Deliver your presentation. As you deliver your speech, make sure to control your voice and exhibit the proper body language. Use technology efficiently. Give the audience time to examine your visual aids and listen to audio clips.

TEKS 10.15D, 10.23A, 10.23B

Making Presentations

Evaluate a presentation using the following evaluation sheet. Circle the descriptions that best fit each assessed area. Then offer two comments: one positive comment and one helpful suggestion.

Peer Evaluation Sheet

Speaker ____________________ Evaluator ____________________

1. Vocal Presentation

Volume:
Clear and loud, loud enough, a little soft, mumbled

Pace:
Relaxed, a little rushed/slow, rushed/slow, hard to follow

Comments:

a. ____

b. ____

2. Physical Presentation

Posture:
Relaxed, straight, a bit stiff, fidgeted a lot, slumped

Eye contact:
Excellent contact, made some contact, quick glances, none

Comments:

a. ____

b. ____

3. Information

Thought provoking, interesting, logical, a few good points, no ideas

Comments:

a. ____

b. ____

4. Visual Aids

Interesting, supporting ideas well, not clear, none used

Comments:

a. ____

b. ____

TEKS 10.15D

Preparing a Multimedia Report

You can enhance an oral report by turning it into a multimedia report. In a multimedia report, graphics, images, video, and sound are used to help convey your ideas. They also appeal to the audience and help convey a distinctive point of view or voice.

Some of the common purposes for multimedia reports include the following: to entertain or to express a theme, observation, or point of view. Audiences could include classmates and teacher, audio/visual program members, Internet video viewers, or community or business leaders. Typical genres or formats include screening for classmates or younger students, online video or podcasts, oral presentations for a class, club, or business or community organizations.

Planning and Preproduction

As you begin to plan your multimedia presentation, it is important to consider the following.

Brainstorming

Consider the potential story resources that you have on hand, such as photographs or illustrations.

Gather technological tools.

A multimedia presentation depends upon technological resources. Look for these resources at home or at school.

Choose your visual format.

Think about which visual format lends itself best to your presentation.

Developing an Outline

Write a brief synopsis or summary of your report. Refer to the outline you prepared for your first draft. Then create a story outline.

Creating a Storyboard

Use your outline to create a storyboard—a visual script that includes descriptions of images, sounds, video, and audio clips. Think about what the audience will see as they hear the words.

Writing a Script

Use your storyboard to create a script. The script will contain the narration that the audience will hear. Be sure to include notes about the graphics, images, and sound clips that you plan to include.

Try It!

Use your research report to develop an outline and a storyboard. Then write a script for your multimedia presentation.

Making Presentations

The following information explains the technological steps involved in producing a multimedia presentation.

Shoot, Scan and Import Images

If you plan to create new photographs or video, shoot in a well-lit location. Scan or import all images—old and new—into your editing software.

Record Sound Effects and Audio

Choose a quiet place in which to record. Adjust the computer's input and output sound settings. Follow software instructions for recording sound. Perform a sound check and adjust the volume as necessary. Record your narration in parts. Stop, save, and play each part. Re-record if needed.

Edit Video

Use the time line in your editing software to place images and sounds. Put compatible images and sound files together on the time line as you work through your presentation. As you work, edit images and sound for timing and pacing by replaying segments.

Add Music and Graphics

Add music to your presentation to support concepts or to create mood. You can collect music files through Web sites that offer royalty-free music.

Add on-screen graphics such as titles, headings, captions, or credits to provide clarity.

Try It!

Choose one of the media listed above and make a rough cut of your multimedia presentation.

Indicating When to Present Visuals

Write notes in the margins of your note cards to indicate where a visual aid would be helpful. Isabel considered the following visuals for her presentation about the Aswan High Dam.

- Photos of Nile Valley before the dam
- A drawing of workers on the first dam
- A photo of the finished dam
- A chart comparing the pros and cons of the dam

List possible visual aids. Identify two or three visual aids you could use in your presentation. Explain how and when you would use each one.

TEKS 10.15D

Revising

As you revise your rough cut, consider how successfully you have combined words, images, sounds, and graphics to support your thesis statement.

The goal is to determine if you have achieved your purpose and effectively communicated your ideas and distinct point of view to your audience. The following questions will help guide your revision.

- Do the visuals support the thesis without distracting from my main points?
- Is the pacing appropriate?
- Is the presentation logically organized with a smooth flow of visuals?
- Have I used transitional techniques that continue the flow of ideas?
- Does the presentation hold the interest of the audience?
- Is my point of view distinct and clear?

Editing

As you revise your rough cut, check for errors in conventions, especially in grammar. Listen carefully to your presentation to check for errors. Ask yourself the following questions.

- Have I used correct grammar throughout?
- Have I used verb tenses consistently and correctly?
- Do I have any other errors in conventions that detract from my presentation?

Publishing

As you have revised and edited your presentation, it is time to hold a screening. Consider one of these ideas.

- Hold a classroom screening of your presentation.
- Host a home screening of your presentation for family and friends.
- Upload your presentation to the Internet.

Try It!

View your rough cut with a partner. As you discuss the presentation, focus on the images, sounds, and graphics. Ask for concrete suggestions for improvement.

Making Presentations

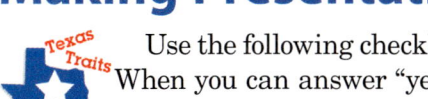

Texas Traits

Use the following checklist to help you improve your multimedia report. When you can answer "yes" to all of the questions, your report is ready.

Revising Checklist

Focus and Coherence

_____ **1.** Is the controlling idea clearly expressed?

_____ **2.** Do all the graphics and other visual elements support the thesis statement?

_____ **3.** Have I chosen the best audio and video for my purpose and audience?

Organization

_____ **4.** Do I state the topic in my introduction?

_____ **5.** Do I include the important main points in the body?

_____ **6.** Have I included transitions to ensure a smooth flow of ideas?

_____ **7.** Do I restate my focus in the conclusion?

Development of Ideas

_____ **8.** Have I included the main ideas of my written report in my multimedia report?

_____ **9.** Have I effectively supported my main ideas with evidence?

_____ **10.** Do my visuals provide relevant details about the topic?

_____ **11.** Does my report flow smoothly from point to point?

Voice

_____ **12.** Do I sound interested and enthusiastic?

_____ **13.** Is my voice clear, relaxed, and expressive?

_____ **14.** Do I convey a clear and distinct point of view?

ELPS 1E, 2C, 3B, 3D, 3E, 4G

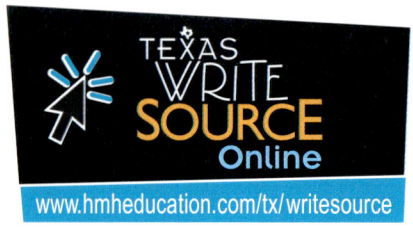

TEXAS WRITE SOURCE Online
www.hmheducation.com/tx/writesource

Writing Across the Curriculum

Writing Focus

Learning Language

Work with a partner. Read the definitions below and share your answers to the questions that follow.

1. **Body language** includes posture and facial expressions.
   If someone is pointing at another person and frowning, what might that body language tell you?
2. A **hypothesis** is an explanation that accounts for a set of facts and that can be tested.
   Why is it important to test a hypothesis?
3. The term **second-class citizen** refers to someone who is economically, socially, or politically deprived.
   When might women in India be considered second-class citizens?

Recording Your Learning

Writing is central to all of your classes, and to your overall success in school and later in life. Writing about what you learn in your classes can deepen your knowledge of the subjects. Writing about each of your classes will give you a strong structure to help you remember what you have learned. Writing will allow you to share your understanding with others.

Learning to take good classroom notes is another skill that will help you in all your classes. Taking notes while you read will help increase your understanding of reading assignments and provide a framework for review. Finally, keeping a learning log will help you connect new material to material you already know.

This chapter explains ways for you to record your learning. The information will help you succeed in all your classes.

- **Taking Classroom Notes**
- **Taking Reading Notes**
- **Keeping a Learning Log**

"He listens well who takes notes." —Dante Alighieri

Taking Classroom Notes

Taking good notes helps you focus on a lecture, remember key points, and understand new material. Here are a few tips on taking good notes in class.

Before you take notes . . .

- **Set up your notes.** Use a three-ring binder so you can add handouts to your notes, or use a notebook with a folder in the back.
- **Date each entry** in your notebook and write down the topic.
- **Organize each page.** Consider using the two-column format, with lecture information on the left and questions on the right.

As you take notes . . .

- **Write information your teacher puts on the board** or on an overhead. This is often the most important material.
- **Use your own words** as much as possible.
- **Write questions** in the second column of your notebook.
- **Draw pictures.** Use quick sketches to capture complex ideas.

After you've taken notes . . .

- **Re-read your notes** after class. Add information to make the notes clear.
- **Research the answers** to any questions you wrote.
- **Review your notes** before the next class to be ready for discussions.
- **Study your notes** to prepare for quizzes and tests.

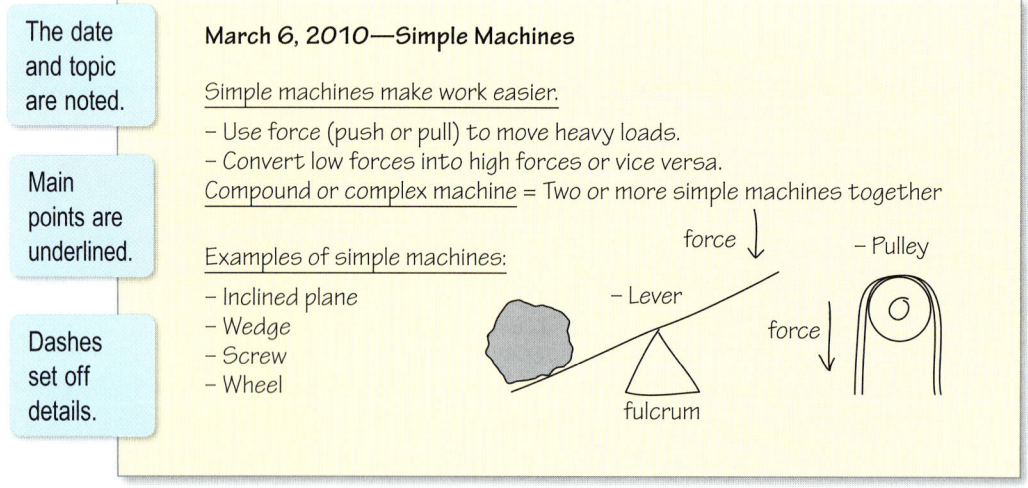

The date and topic are noted.

March 6, 2010—Simple Machines

Simple machines make work easier.

– Use force (push or pull) to move heavy loads.
– Convert low forces into high forces or vice versa.

Main points are underlined.

Compound or complex machine = Two or more simple machines together

Examples of simple machines:

– Inclined plane
– Wedge
– Screw
– Wheel

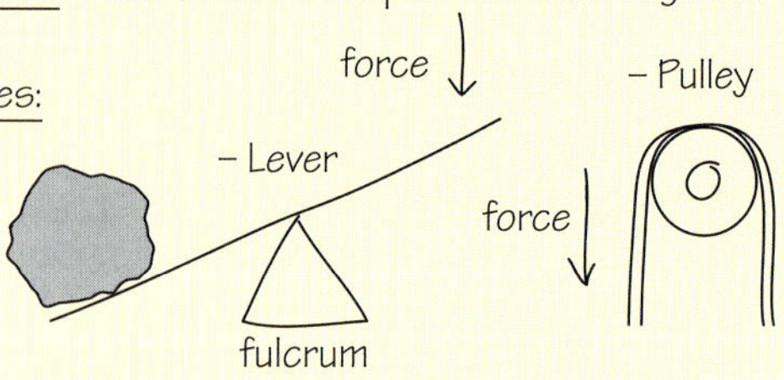

Dashes set off details.

Taking Reading Notes

Note taking can increase your understanding of reading assignments. Here are some tips on taking reading notes.

Before you take notes . . .

- **Write the date, chapter, book, and topic** before each entry.
- **Organize each page.** Try a two-column format with wide margins. Put your notes on the left and your thoughts and questions on the right.
- **Quickly skim the assigned text.** Read the title, introduction, headings, and summaries. Look at the graphics and charts.

As you take notes . . .

- **Write down headings or subtopics.** Note important details under each. Record any questions or thoughts that you have.
- **Use your own words** to help you understand the material.
- **Summarize graphics.** Make a sketch, note the main ideas, or create your own graphic with notes.
- **List vocabulary words.** You can look up definitions later.

After you've taken notes . . .

- **Review your notes.** Then write down any other questions you may have. Find answers and add them to your notes.

Sept. 29, 2010: Exploring Chemistry, chapter 2, section 1
Periodic Table of the Elements*

* The periodic table is a way of classifying elements: a universal language for chemistry. Elements — sorted by rows and columns — organized by similarities in their properties — ordered by increasing atomic numbers — grouped in columns — are liquid, gas, or solid	**Q: How did the periodic table start?** **A: Russian professor Dmitry Mendelyev pioneered a chart to organize elements.**

Questions and thoughts are listed in the second column.

Try It!

Take notes as you complete your next reading assignment.

ELPS 1A, 2H, 2I, 4G, 4I

Keeping a Learning Log

A **learning log** is a specialized journal that lets you reflect on the material you are learning in class. In a learning log, you write about new concepts and connect them to previous knowledge or experiences. Here are some tips for keeping a learning log.

Before you make an entry . . .

- **Set up your learning log** in a binder or notebook. If you use the same binder for different classes, divide it into sections.
- **Write the topic and date of each entry** so you can find it easily.
- **Leave wide margins** for writing thoughts and questions that occur to you later.

As you make an entry . . .

- **Summarize key concepts** and develop meaningful comparisons.
- **Apply new ideas** to what you already know.
- **Write down any questions** you have about the subject.
- **Predict how the new ideas** may prove helpful in the future.
- **Write about** what the ideas mean to you.

After you've made an entry . . .

- **Review your entries** so you can better understand what you are learning.
- **Research any questions** you have and write down the answers.
- **Continue your reflections** by writing new observations or questions in the margins.

Tip

Most topics are like packed suitcases. You can grab the topic by the handle and carry it around without really understanding what's inside it. Writing helps you "unpack" a complicated topic. What are the main ideas? How do these ideas relate to each other? What do these ideas mean to me? When you write answers to questions such as these, you make learning personal—and you begin to understand what is inside the topic you are carrying around.

Try It!

Follow the guidelines above to set up your own learning log. When you have a few minutes during or after class, write about the day's topic in order to "unpack the ideas."

Learning-Log Entries

Here are sample learning-log entries for three classes. The student thinks about the ideas discussed in class, analyzes them, and tries to apply them to current issues and to his own life.

Sample Learning Log: Chemistry

After recording the date and topic, the student reviews ideas from his class.

He writes questions about the topic in the margin.

He reflects on the complex issues.

He finds answers to his questions.

February 18—Chemical Pollution

The class discussion today was about chemicals in the environment. Mrs. Marshall said that fuels, pesticides, paints, cleaners, and other chemicals can cause a lot of harm.

Sometimes natural disasters are to blame. After Hurricane Katrina, many chemicals mixed with floodwaters. When the water drained away, chemicals got into the soil and air. Chlorine, benzene, and gasoline caused huge problems.

Sometimes ignorance is the problem. People pour oil or chemicals into street drains and pollute the water. They dump paint cans in the woods and burn plastics that pollute the air. These actions are as much a problem as natural disasters.

Q: How can polluted soil be cleaned up?

A: The EPA Web site said contaminated soil and sediment would have to be removed, and clean fill would have to be added.

February 22—Exxon Valdez

Mrs. Marshall showed a documentary about the Exxon Valdez oil spill, which occurred when a tanker ran aground in Alaska. Biologists continue to study the long-term effects on area habitats.

Cleaning up after an accident or a disaster is important, but it's more important to prevent these things from happening. One way is to switch to alternative energy sources like wind power.

Another way is to use "green chemistry" to develop environmentally friendly compounds. For example, in Australia, researchers use the genes of pests to make pesticides that target only one creature. Also, natural, nonpolluting cleansers like lemon juice (citric acid) and vinegar (acetic acid) work as well as chemicals do.

Q: What can the government do about spills?

A: Oil doesn't dissolve in water, allowing some spills to be contained. Police and fire departments have "haz-mat" teams for hazardous material spills.

Learning-Log Entries

As with the chemistry sample, the student dated these social studies and math entries, listed the topics, summarized concepts, and made connections.

Sample Learning Log: Social Studies

The date and topic are given.

November 11, 2010 Veterans Day

Today we learned the history of Veterans Day. Uncle James is a veteran, but until today I never gave the holiday any thought.

New information is reviewed.

The holiday was established to honor soldiers who died in World War I, but later it was changed to honor all soldiers. Talking about the holiday made me think more about the men and women who have made sacrifices to defend our country.

A personal connection is made.

It also made me curious about how my town celebrated the first Veterans Day. I think I'll do some research about that topic and write about it for my descriptive report assignment.

Sample Learning Log: Math

November 3, 2010 Pythagorean Theorem

A Greek named Pythagoras developed a formula to calculate the lengths of the sides of a right triangle (a triangle with an angle of 90°).

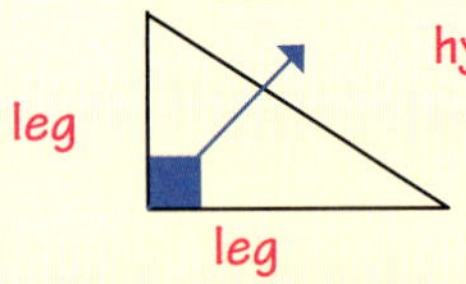

hypotenuse (across from the right angle)

Pythagorean Theorem Formula: $a^2 + b^2 = c^2$
"c" is the side across from right angle (hypotenuse).

Another way to state the formula:
$(\text{length one leg})^2 + (\text{length other leg})^2 = (\text{length of hypotenuse})^2$

Which side is a, and which side is b?

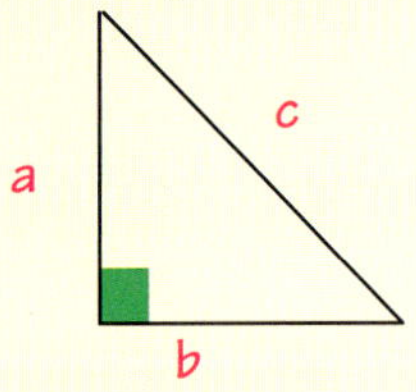

Or is it like this?

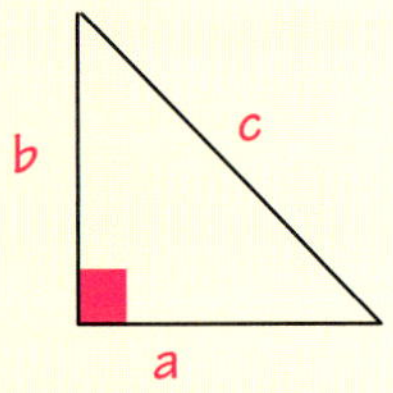

Either one—as long as c is the hypotenuse

Try It!

Try to update your entries and review your class notes every day.

Writing in Science

Writing is central to science. It allows scientists to express their hypotheses, to record their observations, and to communicate their conclusions. In that way, writing gives structure to the scientific method.

Science classes—whether biology, chemistry, physics, geology, astronomy, or life sciences—take you on a journey of discovery into the natural world. Writing lets you chart your course.

This chapter covers the types of writing that will help you in your science classes. Writing about what you learn in lectures and laboratories can deepen your own knowledge of the subject and allow you to share your understanding with others.

"Science is organized knowledge."

—Herbert Spencer

TEKS 10.13A, 10.13B, 10.15A(ii), 10.15A(iii), 10.15A(v)
ELPS 5G

Writing Guidelines Lab Report

A **lab report** outlines the scientific method by stating a hypothesis, setting up a method for testing it, recording observations, and offering conclusions.

Prewriting

- **Select a topic and plan the experiment.** Follow your teacher's assignment. Use a range of strategies (if given a choice) to select a topic. If you have selected the experiment, use a range of strategies to plan it, gather materials, and be sure you understand each step.
- **Follow the proper format.** Use the lab-report format provided by your teacher or follow the lab-report model on page 451.

Drafting

- **Lay the groundwork.** State the purpose (what the experiment is designed to prove), list materials, and note variables. Then write your hypothesis—what you expect the experiment will prove. Organize your ideas in a sustained, logical manner. Use rhetorical devices to engage the reader.
- **Describe procedures.** Use specific language to make each step clear.
- **Record your observations.** Describe what you see, hear, smell, and so forth, in chronological order exactly as it happens. Be sure to use transitions and include only relevant evidence and details.
- **Write a conclusion.** Tell whether your hypothesis was correct or not. Explain why.

Revising

- **Improve your writing.** Review your first draft for *focus and coherence, organization, development of ideas,* and *voice.* Ask these questions: *Have I clearly stated my hypothesis and conclusion? Have I described the experiment in chronological order? Have I included enough details and relevant evidence?*
- **Improve your style.** Check your *word choice* and *sentence fluency.* Ask: *Have I correctly used and explained scientific terms? Have I used transitions to connect my ideas?*

Editing

- **Check for conventions and prepare a final copy.** Proofread and correct errors in grammar, sentence structure, mechanics, and spelling. Make a neat final copy of your lab report.

Lab Report

This lab report describes an experiment on suspensions and emulsions.

Sample Lab Report

The **beginning** states the purpose, the materials, the variables, and the hypothesis.

The well-organized **middle** outlines the procedure and records observations. Details are relevant to the hypothesis.

The **conclusion** tells whether the hypothesis was right or not, and why.

Suspensions and Emulsions

Purpose: To find out which liquids combine and which do not

Materials: 20 ml oil, 20 ml vinegar, egg yolk, two large beakers

Variables: Ingredients

Hypothesis: Oil and vinegar won't mix. When shaken up together, they will form a suspension, but the two parts will separate again. The egg yolk will mix with the vinegar but not with the oil.

Procedure: In the first step, I poured 10 ml of oil into a beaker and added 10 ml of vinegar. Then I shook the liquids and waited for several minutes. I observed the results. In the second step, I combined 10 ml of oil, 10 ml of vinegar, and an egg yolk and shook the liquids. Again, I observed the results.

Observations: When I mixed the oil and vinegar together, the oil and vinegar looked as though they had dissolved. However, minutes later, the oil and vinegar separated. When I combined the oil, vinegar, and egg yolk and shook the beaker, the liquid didn't separate.

Conclusions: My hypothesis that oil and vinegar would not mix was right. They are immiscible. The oil and vinegar made a suspension, but then they separated again.

However, my hypothesis about the egg yolk was wrong. I thought it would mix with the vinegar but not with the oil. The yolk actually mixed with both substances and made them join.

The yolk must be an emulsifier, which allows immiscible substances to blend. The egg yolk, vinegar, and oil form a colloid, which is a stable system of particles dispersed in something else.

Try It!

Perform your science experiment. Describe the experiment and analyze the results completely in a lab report. Make you sure have a clearly stated hypothesis, relevant details and evidence, and a conclusion.

TEKS 10.13A, 10.13B, 10.14C, 10.15D
ELPS 5G

Writing Guidelines Science Script

You may be asked to give a presentation for a science topic, such as a famous discovery, and it might be most effectively presented in the form of a play. You can be creative in your use of setting and dialogue, but remember to keep your script as true as possible to the discovery or moment being dramatized.

Prewriting

- **Select a topic.** As you consider topics, keep your audience in mind. Choose an event or discovery that will engage your audience.
- **Gather details.** Research your topic. Remember that your script must have a theme. In your research, find answers to the *who, what, when, where,* and *how* questions. Look for discussions or conflicts about scientific findings. Note events that will add interest and make your characters come alive.
- **Outline your script.** List characters, conflict, and resolution. Decide on organization. Usually scripts are chronological, but to provide background information, you may decide to include a flashback. Remember to establish theme, mood, and tone.

Drafting

- **Connect your ideas.** Remember your audience and purpose. Your script should be engaging and present factual information. Try to make your dialogue realistic. Characters will convey action, so they need to come alive for your audience. Include details that support your focus and help the audience relate to the characters and topic.

Revising

- **Review your writing.** Check your draft for focus and coherence, organization, development of ideas, and voice. Ask: *Can the audience recognize the topic and follow the dialogue? Do I have a clear beginning and ending? Is the script appropriately organized? Do the characters come alive? Is the dialogue authentic?*
- **Improve your style.** Check your word choice and sentence fluency. Ask these questions: *Have I correctly defined and used scientific terms? Is my language appropriate for the characters?*

Editing

- **Check for conventions.** Proofread for errors in grammar, sentence structure, mechanics, and spelling. Make a neat final copy.

Sample Science Script

In a science script, you have some room to be creative, but you must present factual information about events and the people involved. Remember that the action will be carried through dialogue between characters. The script below dramatizes the discovery of penicillin by Alexander Fleming in 1928.

FLEMING DISCOVERS PENICILLIN

[SCENE: laboratory, London, 1928; lab table, stacks of petri dishes]

[CHARACTERS: Alexander Fleming; colleague Merlin Price]

PRICE: Dr. Fleming, glad to see you back in your lab, but it looks terrible. I don't know how you can find anything in this mess. Trying to straighten it up after your vacation?

FLEMING: Price, old chap, look at this! Who would have thought that a blue mold would have started to grow in this? It is completely different than anything that has grown in my lab before.

PRICE: Fleming, I find molds rather disgusting. Honestly, all molds look the same to me, but you always seem to notice details. In all this mess, things are bound to grow! But you are a careful scientist and an acute observer. I don't think that bit of blue mold would have caught anyone else's eye. You treat research like a game!

FLEMING: Why not play in the lab and have some fun? I am going to keep studying this mold. You never know—it might lead to something big.

PRICE: Like a great discovery and the Nobel Prize?

FLEMING (laughing): That's pretty unlikely, but I am going to try to grow some more and see what happens. I have a spot of meat broth here, some good "mold juice" that will preserve this bit of mold and let it continue to grow. If I can grow enough, I will run it through a few tests and track the results. It almost looks as if this mold might inhibit the growth of bacteria. Lots more work to do, but it might prove to be worth a bit of study.

Try It!

Using the sample above, write a science script about a famous discovery or moment in science. Try to make your characters come alive.

TEKS 10.14C, 10.15D

Delivering Your Presentation

When you deliver an oral presentation in science, even one written as a play, concentrate on your voice and body language. This will convey a mood and set a definite tone. This will also convey your point of view about the topic. Voice quality and body language communicate as much as your words do.

You may also decide to turn your script into a multimedia presentation. As you incorporate graphics, images, and sound into your report, it is still important to consider your audience, mood, and tone.

Controlling Your Voice

Volume, tone, and *pace* are three aspects of your formal speaking voice. If you can control these three aspects of voice, your listeners will be able to follow your ideas.

- **Volume** is the loudness of your voice. Imagine that you are speaking to someone in the back of the room and adjust your volume accordingly.
- **Tone** expresses your feelings. Be enthusiastic about your topic and let your voice show that.
- **Pace** is the speed at which you speak. For the most part, speak at a relaxed pace.

Considering Your Body Language

Your body language (*posture, gestures,* and *facial expressions*) plays an important role during a speech. Follow the suggestions given below to communicate effectively.

- **Assume a straight but relaxed posture.** This tells the audience that you are confident and prepared.
- **Pause before you begin.** Take a deep breath and relax.
- **Look at your audience.** Try to look toward every section of the room at least once during your presentation.
- **Think about what you are saying** and let your facial expressions reflect your true feelings.
- **Point to your visual aids** or use natural gestures to make a point.

Try It!

Deliver your presentation. As you deliver your presentation or script, control your voice and exhibit the appropriate body language and posture.

Preparing a Multimedia Report

You can enhance an oral science report by including electronic aids such as slides, graphics, images, and sound. In order to use these effectively, you must plan exactly where each slide or sound bite will fit into your presentation.

In addition, keep in mind that your graphics, images, and sounds must be appropriate for the topic and audience. Your graphics, images, and sounds must also appeal to your audience and convey a distinct point of view.

Here is a planning script for a multimedia presentation on an experiment about suspensions and emulsions. What will be *seen* appears in the "Video" column, and what will be *heard* appears in the "Audio" column. Note that the directions for the speaker are general, not the actual words to be spoken.

Planning Script

Video	Audio
1. **Title Screen:** "Suspensions and Emulsions"	1. SPEAKER: Introduction and Hypothesis
2. **Slide 2:** Materials on lab bench: oil, vinegar, beakers, egg yolk in dish	2. SPEAKER: Explains materials needed for experiment
3. **Slide 3:** Student mixing oil and vinegar into beaker	3. SPEAKER: Explains procedure for first step SOUND: Liquids being poured into beaker
4. **Slide 4:** Student shaking the liquids	4. SPEAKER: Continues explanation of procedure, revisits hypothesis SOUND: Liquids being shaken and/or upbeat music
5. **Slide 5:** Student mixing and shaking oil, vinegar, and egg yolk.	5. SPEAKER: Explains materials used, revisits hypothesis
6. **Slide 6:** Student examining results	6. SPEAKER: Explains results SOUND: suspenseful music
7. **Slide 7:** Student examining both beakers	7. SPEAKER: Presents conclusions

Try It!

Follow the guidelines above and add graphics, images, and sounds to your science report to create a multimedia presentation.

TEKS 10.13A–10.13D, 10.17C, 10.18A, 10.18B(ii), 10.18B(iii), 10.19, 10.21C
ELPS 4G, 4I, 5C

Writing Guidelines Science-Article Summary

You may be asked to write a summary of a supplied science article in a timed test. Here are some guidelines to help you summarize science articles.

Prewriting

- **Find an article.** Browse through science magazines looking for articles that relate to your class work. Page through your science textbook or visit reliable Internet sites such as *www.nasa.gov.*
- **Read the article.** Quickly read the article you select to get its overall message. Then reread it more carefully for details.
- **Focus on the summary.** Write down the main idea of the article.
- **Gather details.** Select only the most important details that support the main idea of the article. Your summary should be no more than one-third the length of the original article.

Drafting

- **Connect your ideas.** Write your topic sentence, add details to support it. Organize your thoughts logically. Create a closing sentence that wraps up your summary.
- **Paraphrase information.** Use your own words. Avoid plagiarism.

Revising

- **Improve your writing.** Review your first draft for *focus and coherence, organization, development of ideas,* and *voice.* Ask these questions: *Have I identified the main idea of the article? Have I included only important details? Have I used a topic sentence, body sentences, and a closing sentence?*
- **Improve your style.** Check on your *word choice* and *sentence fluency.* Ask these questions: *Have I used transitions so that my summary reads smoothly? Have I used rhetorical devices to convey my meaning? Have I put the ideas in my own words?*

Editing

- **Check for conventions.** Proofread your revised summary for errors in grammar, sentence structure, capitalization, punctuation, and spelling. Be sure that you have used commas correctly in phrases, clauses, and contrasting expressions. Be sure to use quotation marks and dashes correctly.
- **Prepare a final copy.** Make a neat final copy of your summary.

Science-Article Summary

The following professional article from a science news magazine is summarized in the student paragraph below.

Tapping the Earth's Heat

Scientists and environmentalists are increasingly concerned about the limited supply of fossil fuels and the impact of fuel emissions on global warming. As a result, scientists and inventors are looking for alternative sources of energy. One such low-cost, renewable resource—geothermal energy—may be right under our feet.

Geothermal energy has a long history. Early Roman builders and engineers tapped into underground hot springs to help heat homes. Pioneers used underground caves, cooler than the outside air in summer, to store ice and perishable products.

Today, geothermal energy can be used even in areas where there are no hot springs or caves. Modern geothermal systems take advantage of the earth's relatively constant temperature a few feet below ground. Depending on latitude, temperatures underground range from 45 to 75 degrees Fahrenheit.

Geothermal heating and cooling systems exchange heat with the earth rather than with outside air and thus require less energy. These systems often pipe air or water underground (or underwater), where a heat exchanger raises or lowers the temperature. Then a pump transfers the heat from the earth into the building in winter and discharges excess heat from the building into the ground in summer. In summer, the excess heat may also be used to heat the water in the water heater.

Geothermal heating systems may initially cost more to install than fossil fuel systems. However, according to the Environmental Protection Agency (EPA), they save money in operating and maintenance costs. They are also environmentally clean and cost effective.

Sample Summary

Topic Sentence

Body Sentences

Closing Sentence

Geothermal Energy

Geothermal energy can be a low-cost, renewable energy source to heat or cool homes using the earth's own temperature. *Geothermal energy works by drawing heat from the earth or underground water using underground pipes and a heat pump. Because the earth's underground temperature is pretty constant, the underground air or water doesn't have to be heated or cooled as much.* ***That's how geothermal systems can save money and conserve energy.***

Try It!

Write a summary of an assigned article or one of your own choosing in the time allotted. Follow the writing guidelines on the previous page.

Other Forms of Writing in Science

Cause-Effect Essay

Chemistry—Explain the effect of automobile emissions on the atmosphere. Then discuss the effect that hydrogen-powered vehicles would have on the environment.

Classification Essay

Geology, Earth Science, or *Chemistry*—Write a classification essay describing three types of igneous rocks. Describe their appearance, hardness, and composition, and tell how each type of rock is formed.

Definition Essay

Biology or Earth Sciences—Write a definition essay in which you thoroughly explain a concept that you have just learned about. Examine the concept from four or five different points of view.

Process Essay

Chemistry or Geology—Write a process essay describing how scientists create synthetic diamonds. Discuss how synthetic diamonds are used.

Opposing-Views Essay

Physics, Biology, or *Chemistry*—Write an opposing-views essay about a controversial proposal, such as replacing gasoline with ethanol (made from corn). Explain both sides of the argument.

Position Essay

Any Science—Read about controversial new theories in biology, earth-space science, physics, chemistry, or any other area of science that interests you. Choose one theory and write a position essay that provides support for the theory and defends it against opposing viewpoints.

Writing in Social Studies

No two human beings are the same, and no two human societies are either. Social studies focuses on this diversity. As a student of social studies, you may need to survey a variety of documents (speeches, graphs, maps, photos, reports, and so on) and respond to them in writing. You'll need to analyze the documents, summarize and organize the information, and create a response that satisfies the criteria of the assignment.

This chapter models two types of writing you may be asked to do in your social studies classes. It addresses writing a descriptive report and responding to a series of documents.

- **Writing Guidelines: Descriptive Report**
- **Writing Guidelines: Report on Social Studies Research**

"History will be kind to me, for I intend to write it."

—Winston Churchill

TEKS 10.13A–10.13D, 10.17C, 10.18A, 10.18B(ii), 10.19
ELPS 5C, 5G

Writing Guidelines Descriptive Report

Often in social studies, you will need to describe an event or a location. Use the following guidelines to create a descriptive report.

Prewriting

- **Select a topic.** A topic may be assigned by your teacher. If not, use a range of strategies to choose a specific event, time, or place —something you would like to know more about.
- **Gather details.** Learn all you can about your topic. Read books and Web-site articles. Study maps, graphs, and charts. This information will help you write a clear and interesting essay.
- **Outline your essay.** Organize your notes logically to put related details together. If you are describing an event, consider organizing your details in chronological order. If you are describing a place, consider organizing your details by order of location.

Drafting

- **Connect your ideas.** Introduce your topic. Capture your reader's attention with a few interesting details and then write your thesis statement. In the middle paragraphs, describe your topic, one main point at a time. Write an ending that sums up your thesis.

Revising

- **Improve your writing.** Review your first draft for *focus and coherence, organization, development of ideas,* and *voice.* Make sure that you have included relevant details that help the reader clearly understand what you are describing.
- **Improve your style.** Check for *transitions, rhetorical devices, sentence fluency,* and *word choice.* Ask: *Have I correctly used and explained new terms? Do my sentences flow smoothly?*

Editing

- **Check for conventions.** Proofread and correct any errors in grammar, sentence structure, capitalization, punctuation, and spelling. Use quotation marks to indicate irony or sarcasm.
- **Prepare a final copy.** Make a neat final copy of your descriptive report. Proofread this copy and make corrections before sharing it.

Descriptive Report

In this essay, a student writer describes the first Veterans Day celebrated in his hometown.

Sample Report

Morrisville's First Veterans Day

On November 11, 1921, ceremonies in Washington, Paris, and London recognized the sacrifice of soldiers killed in World War I. On that same day, residents of Morrisville also honored their fallen soldiers. That was the first Armistice Day, a holiday that later became Veterans Day.

Armistice Day got its name from the treaty that ended World War I. The day honored the veterans who had lost their lives in the First World War. According to the records of the Carle County Clerk's Office, 83 men from Morrisville served in the United States Expeditionary Force during World War I. Of those 83 men, 14 died serving their country. In a town as small as Morrisville, most people knew at least a few if not all of those men, so it's little wonder that the whole town turned out for the memorial.

Photographs in the archives of the Morrisville Historical Society show the buildings on the town's main street draped with red, white, and blue bunting. Similar decorations covered the horse-drawn wagons and the few automobiles present. The people who gathered in Parish Park, 1,200 according to the *Morrisville Daily Examiner,* dressed in their finest clothing.

The focus of the day's ceremonies was the dedication of the sculpture *Fallen Heroes*. The granite carving, created by Morrisville sculptor Henry O'Brien, depicts a World War I soldier carrying a wounded comrade. The names of Morrisville citizens who died in the war are carved in the statue's base.

Morrisville's mayor, a 50-year-old businessman named Andrew Harrington, dedicated the statue with a stirring speech. In his talk, he called for the citizens to remember "those noble men of our town who set aside the cares of farm, home, and family to serve the greater good of their nation and of the world." He then asked the crowd to observe a minute of silence in honor of the fallen.

In 1954, the holiday was changed to Veterans Day, in memory of U.S. soldiers who died in all wars. Even so, reminders of the first Armistice Day remain in Parish Park. Though worn by time and weather, Henry O'Brien's sculpture still stands, as do a row of memorial oak trees planted by the town's children that day. They still provide shade to park visitors, and a place to pause and remember.

TEKS 10.13A, 10.20A, 10.20B

Writing Guidelines Report on Social Studies Research

In social studies classes, you will often be asked to write a research report on a particular topic or time period. You may be assigned a large, general topic and be asked to narrow it down to a specific focus. Your job is to conduct research and to write an extended essay that thoroughly covers the topic.

The first step in the process is planning and prewriting. In this phase, you will select a topic, form a research question, develop a plan for your research, and conduct research using reliable, authoritative sources.

Selecting a Topic

- **Brainstorm.** Think freely about all the social studies topics that interest you. Make a list of your ideas.
- **Consult with others.** When you have finished your own brainstorming, ask classmates or your teacher what they think about the ideas on your list. They may be able to add ideas and point out ideas that will not work. Listen openly and carefully to what they have to say.
- **Choose your topic.** After you have consulted with others and reviewed or revised your list, choose a topic. Make sure that your topic is broad enough to write a report, but not so broad that you cannot cover it adequately.

Forming a Research Question

- **Narrow your topic.** Remember that your social studies topic must not be so broad that you cannot cover it. One of the strategies that you might use in your planning is to create a general categories list or a cluster diagram about the broad, general topic. Put asterisks next to the particular topics that interest you the most.
- **Conduct initial research.** Use the categories that interest you the most and conduct initial research to learn more about each one.
- **Formulate a major research question.** Using your initial research, formulate a question that will be the focus of your essay.

Forming a Research Plan

- **Gather information.** As you conduct your research, focus on your major research question. Consult a variety of sources that are valid, reliable, and accurate.

Following Your Research Plan

- **Compile your data.** One way to organize the data you have collected is to create a gathering grid like the one shown here. On one side of the grid, list questions you have about the topic. In the other columns, list sources where you found answers to the questions. For answers that are too long to fit on a grid, use note cards.

ASWAN DAM	*Building Big: Dams* (video)	*The Aswan High Dam* (book)	"Aswan Dam" (Web site)	"Deciphering Greater Cairo" (magazine article)
1. Why was the Aswan Dam built?	To provide year-round irrigation			British cotton mill owners wanted more cotton.
2. How was the dam built?		See note card #1.	All local material Rock: 28.6 million cubic yards Sand: 20 million cubic yards Clay: 4 million cubic yards	
3. What are the effects of the dam?	Doubled agricultural production Damage to environment		Lake Nasser holds 1.99 trillion cubic yards of water. The lake is 6 miles wide and 310 miles long.	See note card #2.

- **Identify and research major issues and debates in your field of inquiry.** As you conduct your research, be sure to find valid, reliable, and accurate sources that address both sides of the major issues and debates that involve your topic.
- **Cite your sources.** As you gather information, keep track of the sources you have used so that you can correctly cite them in your essay. Follow the style guide recommended by your teacher to cite and format your sources.

Paraphrasing, Summarizing, and Using Quotations

- **Paraphrasing means to put ideas that you find during your research into your own words.** You must give credit to the source of the ideas.
- **Summarizing means to present the most important ideas from a longer piece of writing.** You must also give credit to the source of the ideas.
- **Using quotations means using the exact words of a source to add authority to your paper.** Enclose those words in quotation marks and give credit to the source.

TEKS 10.13A, 10.13B, 10.22A–10.22C

Prewriting

Developing Your Thesis Statement

- **Write your initial thesis statement.** With your initial research complete, you can write a controlling idea, or focus, for your report. Using your controlling idea, write an initial thesis statement for your report.
- **Evaluate the relevance of your research.** With your thesis statement in mind, look back at your research. Is it all relevant to the thesis statement? Have your sources identified and addressed major issues and debates within your topic?
- **Evaluate your sources for reliability, accuracy, and validity.** Check to make sure that you used unbiased, well-respected works and authors as the sources for your research. Examine each source for authority and objectivity. You may need to do more research to replace sources that do not meet these criteria.
- **Critique your research process.** Evaluate your research process at each step. Make any changes, adjustments, or revisions that are needed.
- **Review and revise your initial thesis statement.** With your research complete and evaluated for relevance, accuracy, and validity, you should review your initial thesis statement. Revise it as needed so that it reflects the major research question, and then, if needed, write a new thesis statement.
- **Create an outline.** Use your thesis statement and your research to create an outline for your report. It will help you organize your details in a logical fashion. Also note if and where you might include graphics or visuals to enhance your report.

Drafting

- **Write your introductory paragraph.** Write an introductory paragraph that contains background information about your topic and clearly presents your thesis statement.
- **Develop your middle paragraphs in a logical order.** Follow or revise your outline so that your essay progresses in a logical way for the reader.
- **Provide relevant, reliable, and accurate details and valid evidence to support the thesis statement.**
- **Clearly state your point of view, based on the research that you have done.**
- **As appropriate, include graphs, charts, illustrations, and other visuals to emphasize or demonstrate your points.** Each visual you include should enhance your meaning and help the reader understand the concepts and points you are making.
- **Connect your ideas with transitions so that your ideas flow smoothly from one to the next.**
- **Follow an approved style guide.** Be sure to cite and format sources correctly within your report and in your works-cited page.

TEKS 10.13C, 10.13D, 10.17C, 10.18A, 10.18B, 10.19, 10.22C, 10.23D
ELPS 5C, 5F

Revising: Improving Your Writing

Review and revise your essay for *focus and coherence, organization, development of ideas,* and *voice.* Use these questions to guide you.

- Is your thesis statement clear to the reader?
- Does your conclusion tie back to the thesis statement and leave the reader with a final thought?
- Do your ideas follow a logical pattern so that the essay forms a cohesive whole?
- Have you used transitions so that ideas flow smoothly from paragraph to paragraph and within paragraphs?
- Does each paragraph have a topic sentence, and are the topic sentences supported with valid, accurate evidence and well-chosen details?
- Have you used a variety of evaluative tools to examine the quality of the research?
- Do you sound knowledgeable and interested in the topic?
- Have you used a more formal tone that is appropriate for the audience and the genre?

Editing: Checking Your Writing

Check for errors in grammar, sentence structure, mechanics, and spelling. Correct as needed.

- Correct any errors in grammar, including verb tenses. Try to use the active voice whenever possible.
- Check your sentence structure and sentence fluency. Try to use a variety of sentence types.
- Check all your mechanics, especially use of commas, quotations marks, and end punctuation. Make sure that proper nouns are correctly capitalized,
- Recheck your spelling to make sure that all words, especially technical terms and specialized vocabulary, are spelled correctly.

Research Report

After thinking carefully about the writing prompt assigned by the teacher, which was to describe one major current global problem and the ways it is being addressed today, one student wrote the following report about the Grameen Bank and microloans.

Sample Report

Thesis statement is clearly stated and background information is provided.

Sources are correctly cited following the style guide.

Transitions are used. Writer uses logical organizational pattern and shows evidence to support thesis.

Ending Poverty One Cent at a Time

In 1976, economics professor Muhammad Yunus was trying to figure out how to reduce poverty in the village near his university in Bangladesh. He spoke to a woman who was so poor that she and her family lived on two cents a day. She made bamboo stools, but had to borrow money from a trader for the material she needed. To pay back the money she owed, she had to sell the stools to the trader, who paid her the two cents for her labor. The trader could then sell the stools for any profit he could make.

Yunus asked the woman how much she needed to buy her own materials. The amount came out to 22 cents. If she could afford her own materials, she could sell the stools herself and make more money. Yunus was shocked that such a small amount might be all a person needed to escape a life of poverty. He realized that because she did not have the cash to buy her raw materials, "Her life was a form of bonded labor, or slavery. The trader made sure certain that he paid Sufiya a price that barely covered the cost of the materials and was just enough to keep her alive. She could not break free of her exploitative relationship with him" (Yunus 48).

The next day, Yunus asked a student to help find other people in the village who had the same sort of arrangement as Sufiya, the woman who made the stools. They found 42 people. The total amount borrowed by all these people came out to less than $27. Yunus donated the amount himself. He hoped that by lending the villagers the money, they could earn more for their labor. They wouldn't have to pay back a trader or moneylender and could sell their products to anyone. It would give the family more money for food and other necessities and maybe help them break out of their cycle of poverty.

TEKS 10.13B, 10.23A, 10.23B

Eventually, Yunus's idea led to his creation of the Grameen Bank in Bangladesh. *Grameen* means "rural" or "village" in the Bengali language. Unlike other banks, the Grameen Bank provided only small loans, or microloans. Borrowers, who were usually illiterate, didn't need to fill out paperwork or prove that they could repay the loan. It was all based on trust. People were expected to pay back the loans in very small amounts every week, and the full amount had to be repaid in a year. This made repayment easier and even allowed people to put some money away to save.

Writer continues to synthesize research and develop controlling idea with specific details.

Yunus added another important element to his banking system that also helped make it successful. In order to get loans from Grameen, borrowers had to form a group with five members. These small groups would then be part of a larger "center" composed of up to eight groups that met weekly in the village with a bank worker. Yunus and his colleagues realized that a group acted as support for its members. It also put peer pressure on each member to follow the rules of the program. "Because the group approves the loan request of each member, the group assumes moral responsibility for the loan. If any member of the group gets into trouble, the group usually comes forward to help" (Yunus 63).

Writer addresses major issues involved in the research topic and continues to cite research.

Despite some trouble recruiting the first borrowers, Grameen's model was soon successful. More and more people began to take out small loans, and almost one hundred percent of the loans were repaid on time. Many borrowers ended up taking out more loans for bigger amounts as their businesses grew. Grameen also found that lending to women was more likely to lead to success. In Bangladesh, women were second-class citizens and the loans were their only chance to make a better life for themselves and their children. Today, over ninety-five percent of Grameen loans are made to women. The group found that "women are more comfortable with the group lending model, are more likely to repay their loans, and are more likely to direct their earnings to providing better clothing, housing, nutrition, health care and education to their families" ("Grameen Lending Model").

Writer uses precise data to support topic sentence.

The Grameen Bank eventually spread to millions of borrowers and thousands of villages in Bangladesh. Its success led to interest from other countries. In the late 1980s and early 1990s, Grameen-style programs began in Malaysia and the Philippines. By the mid 1990s, more programs were developed in India, Nepal, Vietnam, and China. Latin American and Africa started their own programs too. Even the United States became interested.

In 1985, when Bill Clinton was governor of Arkansas, he invited Yunus to discuss ways that he could create new economic opportunities for the low-income people in the state. Yunus helped set up a program called the Good Faith Fund. Very slowly, the new program grew in Arkansas and was adopted in other parts of the United States. At first, it only was aimed at rural people, but some of Grameen's supporters wanted to take the program to urban areas.

Writer continues to synthesize and summarize research to support thesis statement.

Chicago was the first city to start a micro-credit group, called the Full Circle Fund (FCF). Many social activists, community leaders, and economists didn't think that the Grameen model would work in this environment. "They claimed that Chicagoans needed jobs, training, health care, and protection from drugs and violence, not microloans, and that self-employment was a primitive concept lingering only in the Third World. Low-income people in Chicago needed money for rent and food, not for investment. They had no skills anyway" (Yunus 184). They were also skeptical that Americans would take part in the five-person group idea because they were too independent.

Not only was the FCF successful, but many other micro-credit programs sprang up in cities throughout the United States. Not all of these operate using Grameen principles, but in 2008, Yunus founded Grameen America in New York. The United States may be the world's richest country, but nearly 40 million people live in poverty. Around 28 million people do not use banks. They can't borrow money because they don't have the education, collateral, or the credit ratings they need. Often they turn to other sources such as payday lenders or check cashing services, who might charge over 700% interest ("Poverty in the United States."). In a little over a year, Grameen America lent over $2.9 million to over 1,350 borrowers. People used the money to pay for rental space, sewing machines, food carts, beauty parlor supplies, and other

TEKS 10.13B, 10.23E

Conclusion ties back to the thesis statement and leaves reader with a final thought. Writer gives distinct point of view.

business start-up costs. The repayment rate is over 99%. New branches are starting to open across the United States.

In 2006, Muhammad Yunus and the Grameen Bank won the Nobel Peace Prize. The concept of microloans has caught on globally, and many organizations use Yunus's ideas to help poor people in different cultures and situations. Even individuals can now provide their own microloans to small entrepreneurs throughout the world by using online sites like Kiva.org. Although, unfortunately, no program has been able to eliminate poverty, Yunus's organizations have provided a way for millions of people to break the chain of poverty and lead lives of respect and dignity. And it all started with twenty-two cents.

Works Cited list includes all sources actually used and cited in essay.

Works Cited

"The Grameen Lending Model." *Grameen America.* Grameen America. 2008. Web. 16 March 2010.

"Poverty in the United States." *Grameen America.* Grameen America. 2008. Web. 17 March 2010.

Yunus, Muhammad, with Alan Jolis. *Banker to the Poor.* New York: PublicAffairs. 203. Print.

Try It!

The next time you have to write a research report for your social studies class, follow the guidelines on pages **480–484** to conduct and present your research.

Writing in Math

Some people think in numbers. They have no trouble solving quadratic equations or figuring out logarithms. Other people think in words. They have no trouble diagramming complex sentences or writing research reports.

Most of us, though, are somewhere in the middle. We need words to help us with our numbers, and we need numbers to help us with our words. When a kindergartner struggles to solve a story problem, words and numbers have to work together. The same is true when Stephen Hawking writes a mathematical description of the universe.

This chapter will help you understand the different ways writing can help you in math class.

- **Writing Guidelines: Article Summary**
- **Writing Guidelines: Written Estimate**
- **Writing Guidelines: Statistical Argument**
- **Writing Guidelines: Response to a Math Prompt**
- **Other Forms of Writing in Math**

"Nature's great book is
written in mathematics."

—Galileo

TEKS 10.13A–10.13D, 10.17C, 10.18A, 10.18B(i). 10.19, 10.21C
ELPS 4G, 4I, 5C

Writing Guidelines Article Summary

Many magazine articles, books, and news stories include statistics and mathematical concepts. Use the following guidelines to summarize a math-related article.

Prewriting

- **Find an article.** Choose a newspaper or magazine article that uses mathematics to support a story, a position, or an issue.
- **Read the article.** Read the selection first to get its overall message. Then reread it carefully, paying attention to details.
- **Find the focus.** Write down the main idea of the article.
- **Gather details.** Select only the most important details that support the main idea of the article.

Drafting

- **Write your first draft.** Write your topic sentence, putting the main idea of the article in your own words. Supply supporting details. Close with a sentence that summarizes your thoughts.

Revising

- **Improve your writing.** Review your first draft for *focus and coherence, organization, development of ideas,* and *voice.* Ask these questions: *Have I identified the main idea of the article? Have I included only the most important details? Have I explained the math concepts in clear language?*
- **Improve your style.** Check your *word choice* and *sentence fluency.* Ask these questions: *Does my summary read smoothly? Do I sound knowledgeable about the topic?*

Editing

- **Check for conventions.** Proofread your summary for errors in grammar, sentence structure, capitalization, punctuation, and spelling.
- **Prepare a final copy.** Make a neat final copy of your summary.

Try It!

Find an article containing math data. Write a summary and create a graph to illustrate the data. Follow the tips above.

Math Article and Summary

A student read the following article in the newspaper and wrote a brief summary, including a graph to illustrate the statistics in the article.

Where Is All That Money Going?

Every parent of teenagers knows that they are spending quite a bit of money. A recent mall survey shows that suburban teenage boys are spending more than $70 per week on themselves and suburban teenage girls are spending more than $60 per week on themselves. The money is mainly coming from adults in the form of allowance, gifts, or just handouts. However, some teens are earning their own money by working part time.

Since the survey was conducted in a mall, it is not surprising that mall spending figured high for both genders. However, mall spending was nearly matched by online purchases and downloads. The respondents indicated that they engaged in "social" spending at the mall, but often bought "necessities" on the Internet.

So how are teens spending their money? The survey found that the biggest category for teen spending was fashion, which accounted for 41 percent of female spending and 34 percent of male spending. The next biggest category was electronics, including computer programs, video games and players, CD and MP3 players, and other gadgetry. In this category, young men spent 30 percent of their income, and young women spent 26 percent. As for the third biggest category—music—the genders spent nearly evenly, with males spending 21 percent and females spending 20 percent. Both genders tended to save about 10 percent of their income, and they also reported a few "other" purchases (females at 3 percent and males at 5 percent).

Should parents be worried about these spending habits? Some say these spending habits are a concern due to the rising number of bankruptcies filed by those 25 years and younger. Others say it makes sense that teenagers are spending more than saving in the years before they have more financial responsibility. Both groups, however, are asking for better financial lessons in school.

Sample Summary

Tracking Teen Spending

The article "Where Is All That Money Going?" tracks teen spending. Male suburban teens spend about $70 a week while females spend $60.

Although some work part time for the money, most of it comes from adults. Teens spend the most, at malls and online, for fashion, electronics, and music. Males spend slightly more on electronics and females slightly more on fashion. Music spending is nearly identical, and both genders save about 10 percent of their income. Some adults are concerned, and many feel that schools should do more to teach financial responsibility. (Johnson, *Orange County Times*, 7 Jan. 2010)

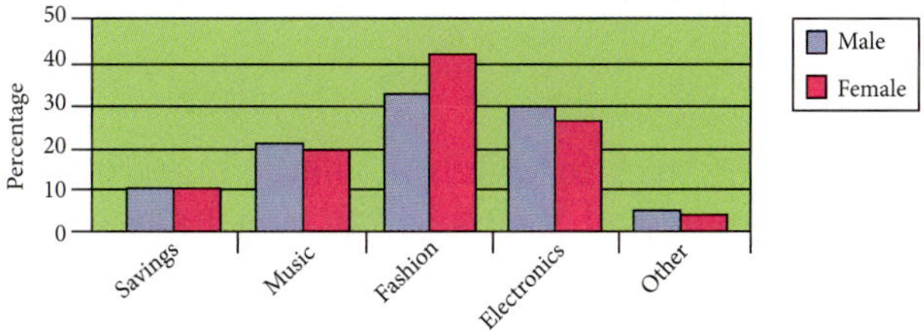

TEKS 10.13A–10.13D, 10.17C, 10.18A, 10.18B(i), 10.19
ELPS 5C, 5F

Writing Guidelines Written Estimate

It is important to learn how to manage money by estimating income and expenses. If you are saving for something you want to buy, making cost estimates and a budget is critical. Making a budget requires several steps.

- **Weekly or Monthly Income:** (actual amount of money earned)
- **Expenditures**: (rent, food, utilities, car payment, gasoline, insurance, replacing a broken cell phone, hosting a party)
- **Evaluations and Explanations:** (step-by-step calculations involved in making a budget and clarification of the information)

Prewriting

- **Select a topic.** Think about a situation in your own life that requires budgeting and estimating expenses.
- **Make assumptions.** Write down the givens as well as the variables of the situation and estimate the costs involved.
- **Plan the steps.** Find a way to arrive at a final cost. Use transitions like *next* and *last* to signal the order of steps.

Drafting

- **Write your first draft.** Introduce the situation and the costs involved. Explain the steps you took to arrive at a final cost and the amount of your budget. Clarify your information.

Revising

- **Improve your writing.** Review your *focus and coherence, organization, development of ideas,* and *voice.* Ask these questions: *Do I identify the situation and explain the budget process clearly? Do I sound knowledgeable?*
- **Improve your style.** Check your *word choice* and *sentence fluency.*

Editing

- **Check for conventions.** Correct errors in grammar, sentence structure, capitalization, punctuation, and spelling.
- **Prepare a final copy.** Make a neat final copy of your work.

Try It!

Ten friends are coming over to watch movies. You will spend $25 on sub sandwiches to feed them and yourself, but you have only budgeted $10. Write an estimate of how much money each person should contribute.

Managing Money

The following estimate was written for a pizza party.

Sample Estimate

You and your friends want to watch the basketball game together next weekend. Your mother has agreed to allow you to invite five friends to your house. You have saved $20 to spend on pizza to eat during the game. That is all the money that you can afford to spend on the party. Write an estimate of the amount of money each person should contribute to provide pizza for everyone.

Given quantities and variables are provided.

Assumptions:

The situation has two given quantities.

Given 1: Five friends and I will eat pizza—six people total.

Given 2: I can afford to spend $20 on pizza.

The situation has three variables that need to be defined.

Variable A: The average number of pieces each person will eat, estimated to be 4

Variable B: The number of pieces in a pizza, estimated to be 8

Variable C: The cost of each large pizza, with tax, delivery, and tip, estimated to be $14

Each step of the calculation is shown.

Evaluations:

The total number of pieces = Variable A × Given 1

4 pieces × 6 people = 24 pieces of pizza needed

The total number of pizzas = 24 ÷ Variable B

24 pieces of pizza ÷ 8 pieces per pizza = 3 pizzas

The total cost of pizzas needed = 3 × Variable C

3 pizzas X $14 = $42

The total amount we need to pay = $42 – Given 2

$42 - $20 = $22

The amount each person needs to pay = $22 ÷ Given 1

$22 ÷ 6 = $3.66 per person

The estimate is explained and clarified.

Explanations:

If my friends and I each eat 4 pieces of pizza, each of us should pay about $3.66. The cost could be higher if the pizzas have multiple toppings. The cost could be lower if we can use a coupon.

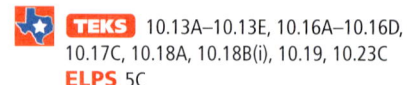

TEKS 10.13A–10.13E, 10.16A–10.16D, 10.17C, 10.18A, 10.18B(i), 10.19, 10.23C
ELPS 5C

Writing Guidelines Statistical Argument

Mathematical statistics are often used—and abused—to argue and prove a point. In an argumentative essay, it is important to include a clear thesis or position that is based on logical reasons and supported by precise, relevant evidence. In statistical arguments, writers must consider the whole range of information on the topic and use statistics to provide an accurate and honest representation of the views on the topic. Often, various kinds of graphics are included to explain concepts and to support points the writer is making.

Prewriting

- **Select a topic.** Use a range of strategies, including brainstorming, as you think about selecting a topic. You might consider statistics related to your school or community: graduation and dropout rates, SAT scores, crime rates, hours spent watching television, attendance rates, and so forth. Choose a topic that interests you.
- **Gather information.** Research the issue, gathering as many facts and figures as you can. Use reliable, valid, and accurate sources of information. Make sure that your sources cover the whole range of information about the topic and that they provide an honest and accurate representation of the viewpoints surrounding the topic.
- **Form an opinion.** After reviewing the research and data, form your opinion about the issue. Write a position statement that is based on logical reasons and that you can support with precise and relevant data from your research.

Drafting

- **Decide on an organizational pattern.** Consider your audience, the purpose of your writing , and the context. Then choose an appropriate organizational pattern for your essay. Structure your ideas in a persuasive, sustained way.
- **Create a first draft.** Write a beginning that introduces the topic and clearly states your position. In your middle paragraphs, support your position with logical reasons and with precise, relevant evidence and data. Show that you have considered the whole range of information and views on the topic and that you have accurately and honestly represented those views. In addition, include counter-arguments that you identified and that are based on your research. Anticipate and address objections raised by the counter-arguments. Include graphics to help explain concepts. Your conclusion should reinforce and tie back to the position statement.

Revising

- **Improve your argument.** Consider *focus and coherence, organization, development of ideas,* and *voice.* Ask these questions: *Is my position statement clear? Do the middle paragraphs connect to and support the position statement? Have I identified and addressed counter-arguments? Is my conclusion effective? Is the organization pattern logical and easy for the reader to follow and understand? Have I developed a convincing argument using statistics? Have I used precise, relevant details and data to support my thesis and cited my sources correctly? Have I varied my sentence structure? Do I sound assured, confident, and knowledgeable?*
- **Improve your style.** Check your *word choice* and *sentence fluency.* Ask these questions: *Have I defined any unfamiliar terms? Is my word choice appropriate for the audience, purpose, and context of the writing? Have I used transitions to connect ideas? Have I used rhetorical devices to convey meaning and engage the reader?*

Editing

- **Check for conventions.** Correct any errors in grammar, sentence structure, capitalization, punctuation, and spelling. Ask yourself these questions: *Have I correctly used verb tenses and active and passive voice? Have I used complex passive voice correctly, but kept as much as possible to active voice? Have I used verbals, including gerunds, infinitives, and participles correctly? Have I correctly punctuated clauses and phrases? Have I checked end punctuation of sentences? Have I correctly used quotation marks and used correct punctuation to introduce quotations? Have I carefully checked my spelling, especially for technical terms and specialized vocabulary? Have I correctly cited, documented, and formatted my sources and sources-cited list following an approved style manual, such as the* MLA Handbook?
- **Prepare a final copy.** After you have checked for all the conventions and answered the questions above, make a neat final copy of your argument and proofread it.

Try It!

Follow the guidelines on these two pages to select a topic and write a statistical argument. Consider the whole range of information and give an honest representation of those views. Include counter-arguments to ancitipate and address objections. Be sure to revise and edit your work.

TEKS 10.13B, 10.16A, 10.16B, 10.16D–10.16F

Statistical Argument

The following persuasive essay uses statistics about young voter turnout to argue a point of view about voter apathy.

Sample Statistical Argument

Background introduces topic and uses statistics to help build an argument. The position statement is given.

Middle paragraphs support thesis with reliable, authoritative evidence. Sources are cited. Writer provides analogies and case studies to support thesis.

Courting the Youth Vote

In the 1960s, the armed services drafted thousands of 18-year-olds to fight in Vietnam, but none of those draftees had the right to vote. Many young people protested this situation. As a result, the minimum voting age was lowered in 1971. That change showed the power of the youth vote in the 1972 elections. Fifty two percent of those 18 to 24 years of age voted, and in order to woo these young voters, candidates had to demonstrate their commitment to ending the war. Although he was unpopular, Nixon still won the election. By 1973 he had withdrawn all American troops from Vietnam and ended the draft. The newest group of voters was obviously an important influence on political policy.

Despite that promising start, over the next 30 years voter turnout among young people slowly declined. By 2000, only 36 percent of young voters went to the polls—a year when their votes could have easily swayed the election. In comparison, 66 to 72 percent of people over the age of 45 voted. ("Voting and Registration"). A survey in colleges conducted that year found that "only a quarter of the students said they discussed political issues as often as three or four times a week. A third said government had no influence on their lives" (Clymer).

Why did young voters become so apathetic? According to the U.S. Census, the people who are most likely to go to the polls are people with the biggest stakes in society: older individuals, homeowners, married couples, and people with more schooling, higher incomes, and good jobs ("Voting and Registration"). Since young people usually don't own property, pay much tax, or have children in public schools, they feel they have less economic stake in the political process.

Often, the issues voters 18 to 24 do care about are not addressed. "The chief reason that young voters give for not voting is that they think nobody is listening to them," writes Jack Doppelt, author of Nonvoters: America's No-Shows. This theory was supported by the brief surge in the youth vote in 1992, which spiked to 48 percent. Young people felt someone

Middle paragraphs continue to build support for the thesis statement. Precise, relevant evidence is presented. Writer considers whole range of views on topic and provides honest representation of views. Writer also provides analysis of relative value of facts, ideas, and data.

was listening. Bill Clinton was a young man who played saxophone on the Tonight Show, appeared on MTV, and answered questions about "guns or butter" and "boxers or briefs."

After Clinton's election, however, the youth vote slid again. Then, in 2004, an even bigger spike occurred. Turnout at the polls for young voters jumped 11 points to 47 percent. This time, the reason was not a charismatic candidate but an issue that young people cared about, specifically the war in Iraq. Political strategists tapped into the growing interest and concern. They began to campaign harder at colleges and targeted potential young voters through organizations like Rock the Vote.

Although the youth vote did not have a significant effect on the 2004 elections, the 2008 elections again saw a rise in voters from 18 to 24. It was the only age group that showed a statistically significant increase in turnout, climbing 2 points from 2004 to reach 49 percent (over 2 million votes). Among young voters, African Americans had the highest turnout rate—55 percent, which was an 8 percent increase from the previous election ("Voter Turnout"). This time, candidates went all out to court the young, spreading their message through new media such as Facebook and YouTube.

It helped that Barack Obama was not only charismatic, but also a potent symbol of change. His ideas reflected a new direction away from the anger that had divided the country after 2004. His ethnicity also represented the often overlooked racial and ethnic populations of the country. Compared to his older rivals, the youthful Obama was more like a peer than a parent—not only someone who listened and was "cool," but also someone who addressed their concerns and understood them.

The conclusion restates the position. Writer's viewpoint is clearly stated.

"Young voters helped form the backbone of the Obama campaign, volunteering in their home towns and on college campuses across the country.... President-elect Obama acknowledged their contribution in his victory speech.... He said his campaign 'grew strength from the young people who rejected the myth of their generation's apathy, who left their homes and their families for jobs that offered little pay and less sleep'" (Falcone). Once again, the youngest group of voters made a difference.

TEKS 10.13B, 10.13D, 10.17C, 10.18A, 10.18B(i), 10.19
ELPS 4G, 5C

Writing Guidelines Response to a Math Prompt

A math prompt is a problem that is solved by writing as well as by mathematics. To answer a prompt, you need to analyze it, decide what you are supposed to do, and then respond to it, working one step at a time. Follow these guidelines.

Prewriting

- **Read the prompt.** Read carefully, paying attention to the directions. Watch for key words such as *find, solve, justify, demonstrate,* or *compare,* and respond only to the questions asked. Also be aware that some prompts have more than one part.
- **Gather details and data.** Write down any values, assumptions, or variables provided in the prompt.

Drafting

- **Build your solution.** Respond to each part of the prompt. Set up formulas or equations, and use diagrams if they will help solve the problem. Perform the necessary calculations to get an answer. Show all of your work.

Revising

- **Improve your response.** Reread the prompt after you do your calculations. If the problem has more than one part, be sure you have answered every part. Work the problem in another way to check that your solution is correct.

Editing

- **Check for conventions.** Check your solution for errors in grammar, sentence structure, capitalization, punctuation, and spelling.
- **Prepare a final copy.** Make a neat final copy of your solution.

Try It!

Find a math prompt and write a response. Choose a practice prompt from your textbook or one recommended by your teacher. Follow the tips above to write your solution.

Response to a Math Prompt

The following math prompt contains three parts. The writer provides a solution using words, mathematics, and a diagram.

Sample Prompt and Response

1. Explain this formula: $(a + b)^2 = a^2 + 2ab + b^2$

a. Using geometry

b. Using algebra

2. Then show how your two explanations are related.

Trevor Hughes
Math 10, period 6

1a. Geometry

The area of the large square below is the length x the width.

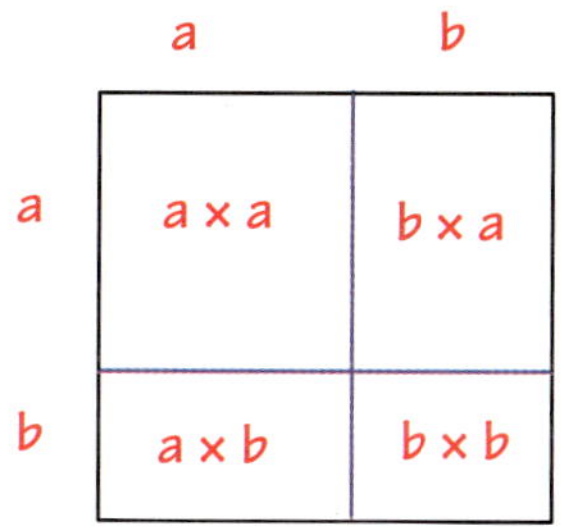

The area = $(a + b)(a + b)$ or $(a + b)^2$

The area is also the sum of smaller boxes:

$(a)(a) + (a)(b) + (b)(a) + (b)(b) =$

$a^2 + ab + ab + b^2 = a^2 + 2ab + b^2$

The area is the same, so

$(a + b)^2 = a^2 + 2ab + b^2$

1b. Algebra

$(a + b)^2 = (a + b)(a + b) =$

$(a)(a) + (a)(b) + (b)(a) + (b)(b) = a^2 + 2ab + b^2$

So $(a + b)^2 = a^2 + 2ab + b^2$

2. Relation

The geometric solution comes from calculating area, while the algebraic solution comes from symbol manipulation. Even so, both solutions have the same middle stage: $(a)(a) + (a)(b) + (b)(a) + (b)(b)$. The underlying math is the same.

Other Forms of Writing in Math

Description

Geometry—Describe a nature scene using geometry.

Definition

Algebra—Write an expository paragraph on the definition of the word *algebra*.

Narrative

Any Math—Write a narrative essay about a time when you used math in daily life.

Classification

Geometry—Write an essay comparing and contrasting the different types of triangles.

Position

Any Math—Read about new theories in math or economics that interest you. Choose one theory and write a position essay that supports the theory and defends it against opposing viewpoints.

Process

Algebra—Write a process paragraph about the details needed to solve a linear equation.

Research

Any Math—Write a report on a famous mathematician. In your report, include at least one interesting fact about the person's life, describe the time period in which she or he lived, and briefly explain the work or discoveries that made the person famous.

Writing in the Applied Sciences

Classes in the applied sciences provide hands-on learning. For example, in a textile arts class, you may learn about fabrics by sewing. In a machine shop, you may learn about internal combustion engines by taking one apart and putting it back together.

Writing is also important in the applied sciences. It can help you plan projects, remember procedures, reflect on successes and failures, and propose new projects for the future.

In this chapter, you will learn about writing essays in the applied sciences. You will discover how writing empowers hands-on learning.

"Jump into the middle of things, get your hands dirty, fall flat on your face, and then reach for the stars."

—Ben Stein

TEKS 10.13A–10.13D, 10.17C, 10.18A, 10.18B(i)–18B(iii), 10.19
ELPS 5C, 5F

Writing Guidelines Descriptive Essay

A descriptive essay describes a person, place, or thing. The goal is to create a clear mental picture for the reader.

Prewriting

- **Select a topic.** If your teacher does not assign a specific topic, review your notes, journal, or textbook to find ideas.
- **Gather details.** Freewrite about the topic using sensory details. Also research the purpose and history of your topic.
- **Plan and organize.** Choose an organizational pattern. If you are describing something physical, consider using spatial organization: front to back, top to bottom, inside to outside, or the whole to the parts. If you are describing something that changes, consider using chronological organization.

Drafting

- **Connect your ideas.** Write a beginning paragraph that introduces your topic and provides your thesis or focus. Then begin your description, following the organizational pattern you selected. Connect your ideas with transitions.

Revising

- **Improve your writing.** Review your first draft for *focus and coherence, organization, development of ideas*, and *voice*. Ask these questions: *Is my thesis or focus clear? Have I chosen the correct organizational pattern for my topic, my audience, and my purpose? Are my ideas fully developed? Have I included details that create a clear mental picture for the reader? Is my level of language appropriate to my audience and topic?* Ask someone else to read your essay and make comments.
- **Improve your style.** Check your *word choice* and *sentence fluency*. Ask these questions: *Have I used vivid descriptive words? Have I used transitions so that my sentences flow from one to the next?*

Editing

- **Check for conventions.** Correct all errors in grammar, sentence structure, capitalization, punctuation, and spelling.
- **Prepare a final copy.** Make a neat final copy of your essay.

Descriptive Essay

In her Home Living class, Andrea described her plan for furnishing a family room.

The **beginning** introduces the topic and leads to a thesis statement (underlined).

The **middle** presents each area and describes its arrangement. Organization is logical.

The **ending** reflects on the arrangement of the room.

Furnishing a Family Room

A family room should be comfortable and inviting—a place that brings the family together. Let's imagine a room 16 feet wide by 20 feet long, with a fireplace on one end and a large bay area on one side. It's a nice space, but it won't be a family room until it is properly furnished.

Creating a gathering spot near the fireplace is the initial focus. On either side of the fireplace should stand two armchairs, with a coffee table between them. Track lighting above the table lights up games and snacks.

Next, it's time to turn the bay area into a quiet place for study. A comfortable chair, a table, and a lamp create a reading nook on one side of the bay. On the other side, a small desk provides a good place for doing homework.

The rest of the room is perfect for larger gatherings. An entertainment center, a couch, and a chair are great for watching TV or listening to music.

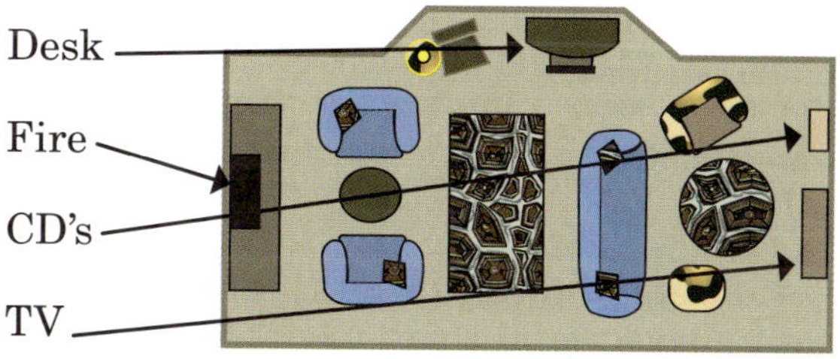

The family room is complete. The furnishings make the space comfortable and inviting for individuals, couples, and the whole family. Whether people want to play cards by the fire, read a book by the window, or watch the Cowboys in the play-offs, this room is waiting for them.

Try It!

Write a descriptive essay about a room or an area you know well. Use spacial organization and follow the guidelines on page 484.

TEKS 10.13A, 10.13B, 10.15A(ii), 10.15A(iii), 10.15A(v)
ELPS 5G

Writing Guidelines Essay of Analysis

An essay of analysis breaks down a topic into its parts and shows how they are related. Complex issues make the best topics for essays of analysis.

Prewriting

- **Select a topic.** If you are not given a topic, think about complex issues related to your class work. Brainstorm, consult with others, and review your class notes or your learning log. For example, in Family and Consumer Science, you could analyze the factors that affect the rising of yeast. In wood shop class, you could analyze the design and function of a piece of furniture.
- **Gather details.** Create a cluster diagram to break down your topic into different components, aspects, and reasons. Think of how each part of the topic connects to other parts.
- **Write your thesis statement.** Using your controlling idea, or focus, and the information you have collected about your topic, create a clear hypothesis for your essay.
- **Plan and organize.** Select an organizational pattern that is appropriate for your purpose, audience, and context for writing. Using the pattern that you have selected, outline your essay. First explain the topic. Use specific, clear language, and then write your hypothesis. Write a topic sentence about one part of the topic for each middle paragraph. Plan ways in which you will present your conclusion.

Drafting

- **Write your introduction.** Write a beginning that introduces your topic and leads to your hypothesis. Develop middle paragraphs by following your outline. Show how the different parts of the topic are related and use transitions to connect your ideas.
- **Write your middle paragraphs.** Follow your outline to develop your middle paragraphs. Show how the different parts of the topic are related. Include relevant, well-chosen details to support your thesis. Be sure to use transitions to connect within paragraphs and to connect one paragraph to the next. Transitional phrases and words might include *next, moreover,* and *finally.* Use rhetorical devices to enhance your writing and engage the reader. Certain rhetorical devices, such as analogies and rhetorical questions, are helpful in explaining scientific concepts and maintaining reader interest.

TEKS 10.13C, 10.13D, 10.15A(i), 10.15A(ii), 10.17A(i), 10.17C, 10.18A, 10.18B(i)–18B(iii), 10.19
ELPS 5C–5F

Revising

- **Improve your writing.** Review your analysis for *focus and coherence, organization, development of ideas*, and *voice*. Ask these questions: *Does my introduction explain the topic? Is my hypothesis clear? After thinking more about my purpose and audience, how I can revise my draft to better fit each one? Does each middle paragraph focus on one part of the topic? Do all the details in each paragraph support the main point of the paragraph? Are the details that I have chosen relevant to the topic, and do they support my hypothesis? Do I show how the parts of the topic are connected?*
- **Improve your style.** Check your *word choice* and *sentence fluency* to make sure that everything is stated clearly and effectively. Look at your sentence starters and sentence types to make sure that you have used a variety of sentence structures. Ask these questions: *Have I used appropriate word choices for my audience, purpose, and context? Have I used transitions so that my sentences flow smoothly and ideas are connected from one paragraph to the next? Have I defined terms associated with my topic? Have I used correct voice in my verbs and shown that I understand the difference between active and passive voice and can use the both correctly?* (See page 750 for information on active and passive voice.) *Have I used the correct tenses and been consistent in my use of verb tenses?*

Editing

- **Check for conventions.** Look for and correct errors in grammar, sentence structure, capitalization, punctuation, and spelling. Check your essay carefully for subject-verb agreement. Make sure that your sentences are correctly structured and all punctuation is correct. Ask these questions: *Have I correctly used commas in phrases and clauses? Have I correctly used quotation marks and used correct punctuation to introduce quotations? Have I correctly used quotation marks to indicate irony and sarcasm? Have I used dashes to emphasize parenthetical information? Have I used various resources, including dictionaries or a computer spell-checker, to check and correct spelling?*
- **Prepare a final copy.** Make a neat final copy of your essay. Proofread it one more time, and make any needed final corrections.

TEKS 10.13B, 10.15A(i), 10.15A(iv)

Essay of Analysis

In Consumer Economics, Nina wrote about the impact of severe weather on consumers. As she planned her essay and wrote her draft, Nina kept in mind her purpose, audience, and context.

The **beginning** presents the topic and provides the thesis statement (underlined).

The **middle** paragraphs analyze the main parts of the topic and show how they are related. Organization is appropriate for audience, purpose, and context.

Precise, relevant evidence supports thesis. Sources are cited.

Weathering High Prices

Most people aren't concerned about bad weather when it happens in another part of the country. A cold snap in Florida, however, or heavy rains in Iowa might end up hurting everyone, no matter where he or she lives. Severe weather can directly affect prices of food, oil, and other consumer goods. When these prices go up, they have ripple effects that can be surprising.

Poor weather can have an effect on food supplies. A sudden freeze in Florida, Texas, or California can ruin the citrus crops in these states. Floods in the midwest can destroy fields of grain or corn. As supplies drop, the prices of these products rise. When there are fewer oranges, grapefruits and lemons in the market, consumers end up paying more for the fruits themselves, for the juice that's made from them, and even for lemon-scented cleaners. If wheat costs more, so does bread, cereal, flour, and even pizza. If farmers pay more for corn to feed their livestock, then the price of meat, leather, and milk can also go up.

In 2005, Hurricane Katrina and a series of hurricanes slammed into the Gulf Coast. This area is one of the major energy producers for the entire country. The hurricanes damaged oil refineries and offshore drilling platforms in the Gulf of Mexico. Some were shut down for weeks and even months. As a result, gasoline prices nationwide skyrocketed (Hermaning 36). Higher gas prices can have a widespread effect. People pay more to drive their cars and heat their houses, which has an impact on family budgets and spending. The cost of airplane flights goes up. Products that are transported by truck or boat cost more to ship. That includes food, mail, and retail products like clothing, toys, and electronic goods. Also, many products are made from oil, including plastic, which is used in everything from zippers to medical equipment. Higher oil prices can cause consumers to pay more for a wide range of products and services (Werner 109).

The **middle** paragraphs continue to sustain thesis with relevant evidence.

Severe weather can spread its economic effects across the nation. According to Nicholas Grierson, "Weather problems and disasters related to weather cost billions each year. Between 1990 and 2008, insurers paid $300 billion for weather-related problems" ("Economic Impact of the Weather"). When disasters hit a community, agencies could spend billions to get things running again. Often the government has to step in to help. Citizens pay for these costs through taxes, insurance hikes, and higher prices. Fortunately, many communities recover quickly after a weather-related disaster.

The **ending** restates the thesis and leaves the reader with a final thought.

Next time you pay more for a pizza, think about the long chain that caused the increase. It could be due to tomato crops damaged by weather. Maybe the delivery driver paid more for gas because oil production slowed. None of us should take for granted the weather report from across the country. When it rains a thousand miles away, we may not have to take an umbrella to work, but when the weather is bad, everyone pays.

Works Cited

Hermaning, Charles. *The Economic Impact of Katrina.* New York: Heath and Sons. 2009. Print.

Werner, Erica. *The High Cost of Oil: Will It Ever Come Down?* Dallas: Midway Press. 2010. Print.

Grierson, Nicholas. "Economic Impact of the Weather: Unplanned Disasters." *Applied Science News* July 2010. Web. 15 March 2010.

Try It!

Write an essay of analysis about a complex issue. Follow the guidelines on pages 486–487.

Other Forms of Practical Writing

Narrative Essay

Child Care—Write an account of your first babysitting experience. Include mistakes you made and techniques that worked best.

Process Essay

Drafting—Explain the steps to create an accurate floor plan of your classroom. Include each step in order, using imperative sentences.

Letter of Application

Career Explorations—Write a cover letter to accompany a résumé. Include an introductory paragraph, a brief background and experience paragraph, and a personal statement about why you want the job.

Classification Essay

Textile Arts—Define and explain the different types of stitches used in needlework. Tell what each is used for and the effect it can create.

Problem-Solution Essay

Machine Shop—Write a problem-solution essay about a motor that isn't working. Explain the cause of the problem and explore possible solutions. Indicate which solution is the best and why.

Proposal

Wood Shop—Design a piece of furniture meant for a specific place or function (for example, a bench along a garden path or a coatrack in a hallway). Write a proposal that explains your design and persuades your teacher to let you build it.

Compare-Contrast Essay

Cooking Class—Write a compare-contrast essay explaining the various leavening agents (yeast, baking powder, baking soda) and their effects on baked goods.

Writing in the Arts

Artists have special powers. A sculptor's chisel can turn rock into skin and cloth, a composer's pen can create landscapes out of sound, and a painter's brush can make a woman immortal. From ancient cave paintings to modern light shows, art empowers human beings to express thoughts and emotions that otherwise would go unspoken.

One way to capture the power of art is to write about it. When you translate paint and stone and notes into words, you understand art more deeply. This chapter will help you write essays and create presentations about the arts.

- **Writing Guidelines: Response to an Art Prompt**
- **Writing Guidelines: Research Report in the Arts**

"I try to apply colors like words that shape poems, like notes that shape music."

—Joan Miro

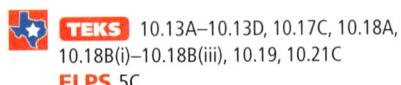

TEKS 10.13A–10.13D, 10.17C, 10.18A, 10.18B(i)–10.18B(iii), 10.19, 10.21C
ELPS 5C

Writing Guidelines Response to an Art Prompt

Responding to a prompt allows you to apply what you know about a specific work. Here are guidelines for planning and writing a response for the arts.

Prewriting

- **Choose the appropriate genre, or form.** Identify your audiences. Read through the prompt and focus on what it is asking you to do. Is the purpose to explain, compare, describe, persuade?
- **Gather your details.** Go through your notes and any research materials you are allowed to use. Highlight or jot down the details you will use in your response. Be sure to record and accurately cite the sources of any quotations or facts you use.
- **Organize your details.** Check the prompt for clues about organizing your response. For example, if the prompt asks you to "describe Cezanne's painting *Girl at the Piano* and tell how the color choices affect the mood," you might begin with a general description of the painting, then zero in on the main figures, and end with a discussion of colors and mood. Make an outline or a graphic organizer to help organize your thoughts.

Drafting

- **Write freely.** Use your notes, outline or graphic organizer as a guide. Some short-response essays are one paragraph long. However, if a prompt calls for several main points, write a separate paragraph for each. Cite and format your sources correctly.

Revising

- **Improve your writing.** Read your draft and cut any details that don't fit the prompt. Also add information that will clarify the ideas in your response. Be as complete as possible.
- **Improve your style.** Check your *word choice* and *sentence fluency* to make sure that your response reads smoothly.

Editing

- **Check for conventions and prepare your final copy.** Look for and correct errors in grammar, sentence structure, capitalization, punctuation, and spelling. Use quotations to set off sarcasm and irony, and use dashes to emphasize parenthetical information. Copy your response paper, and proofread it a final time.

Response to an Art Prompt

Maria wrote this response to a prompt about architecture.

Prompt

Why is Frank Lloyd Wright's house Fallingwater so important to American architecture? Cite the design's special features and techniques and discuss the public's early response to it in a multiparagraph answer.

Sample Response

The writer provides background and her main point. She correctly used quotation marks.

Architect Frank Lloyd Wright designed Fallingwater in 1936 as a country retreat for a Pennsylvania family. In this house, Wright spotlighted his key principle of designing "organic" houses, letting people live in harmony with nature.

Writer supports main point by citing particular details. She summarizes information from her source.

The house stands on top of a waterfall and seems like part of the rock formation. Its central core of stacked sandstone rises out of the rock, and terraces of reinforced concrete mimic the ledges over the waterfall. Glass walls on three sides open the house to the woods around it, and windows framed in a warm red offset the neutral sandstone.

Fallingwater was immediately famous, even appearing on the cover of Time magazine in 1938. The house's design renewed Frank Lloyd Wright's career and shifted the direction of modern architecture back toward natural materials. Critics and fans agree that Fallingwater is a revolutionary design.

The writer uses specific examples and details to demonstrate her understanding.

Many of the features of Fallingwater are still used in home building today. For example, Wright's idea of making walls of glass is popular in modern homes. The natural wood and stone in the home's interior are seen today in stone walls and fireplaces and in wood flooring, paneling, and trim. Wright's idea of making a home part of the natural setting also carries through in much of modern architecture.

Try It!

Respond to a short-essay prompt your teacher will supply about a topic you are studying. Write a multiparagraph answer. Be sure to follow all guidelines for prewriting, drafting, revising, and editing.

TEKS 10.13A, 10.20A, 10.20B

Writing Guidelines Research Report in the Arts

At some point, you may be asked to write a research report in an art or music class. Your topic may be a famous sculptor, painter, composer, or specific style of art or music. The following guidelines will help you with such an assignment.

Selecting a Topic

- **Brainstorm.** Think freely about topics in art or music that interest you. Make a list of your ideas that pertain to the class.
- **Consult with others.** When you have finished your own brainstorming, ask classmates or your teacher what they think about the ideas on your list. They may be able to add ideas and point out ideas that will not work. Listen openly and carefully to what they have to say.
- **Choose your topic.** After you have consulted with others and reviewed or revised your list, choose a topic. Make sure that your art or music topic is broad enough to write a report, but not so broad that you cannot cover it adequately.

Forming a Research Question

- **Narrow your topic.** Remember that your topic must not be so broad that you cannot cover it. One of the strategies that you might use in your planning is to create a general categories list or a cluster diagram about the broad, general topic. Put asterisks next to the particular topics that interest you the most.
- **Conduct initial research.** Use the categories that interest you the most and conduct initial research to learn more about each one.
- **Formulate a major research question.** Using your initial research, formulate a question that will be the focus of your essay.

Forming a Research Plan

- **Gather information.** Use well-known and well-respected authoritative sources in the arts. As you conduct your research, focus on your major research question, which will be a complex, multi-faceted topic. Consult sources that are valid, reliable, and accurate. Plan to use a variety of sources for your research.

Following Your Research Plan

- **Compile your data.** Use a gathering grid like the one shown here. In the left column, list your questions about the topic. In the others, list sources of your answers. For long answers, use note cards.

Gathering Grid

TUVAN THROAT SINGING	Edmonds, Curtis. Rev. of *Genghis Blues.*	Leighton, Ralph. *Tuva or Bust: Richard Feynman's Last Journey.*
1. What is throat singing?	Vocal technique from Central Asia	Single vocalist; two or more distinct pitches simultaneously
2. What does it sound like?	Human bagpipe	

- **Identify and research major issues and debates.** Find valid, reliable, accurate sources that address all sides of the issue.
- **Cite your sources.** Keep track of and correctly cite sources in your essay. Follow the style guide recommended by your teacher.

Paraphrasing, Summarizing and Using Quotations

- **Paraphrasing means to put ideas in your own words.** You must give credit to the source of the ideas.
- **Summarizing means to present the most important ideas.** You must also give credit to the source of the ideas.
- **Using quotations means using the exact words of a source.** Enclose those words in quotation marks and give credit to the source. Expressions of irony and/or sarcasm may also be set off with quotation marks.

TEKS 10.13A, 10.13B, 10.22A–10.22C

Prewriting

- **Write your initial thesis statement.** With your initial research complete, you can write a controlling idea, or focus, for your report. Using your controlling idea, write an initial thesis statement for your report.
- **Evaluate the relevance of your research.** With your thesis statement in mind, look back at your research. Is it all relevant to the thesis statement? Have your sources identified and addressed major issues and debates within your topic?
- **Evaluate your sources for reliability, accuracy, and validity.** Check to make sure that you used unbiased, well-respected works and authors in the arts as the sources for your research. Examine each source for authority and objectivity. You may need to do more research to replace sources that do not meet these criteria.
- **Critique your research process.** Evaluate your research process at each step. Make any changes, adjustments, or revisions that are needed.
- **Review and revise your initial thesis statement.** With your research complete and evaluated for relevance, accuracy, and validity, you should review your initial thesis statement. Revise it as needed so that it reflects the major research question, and then, if needed, write a new thesis statement.
- **Create an outline.** Use your thesis statement and your research to create an outline for your report. It will help you organize your details in a logical fashion. Also note where you might include illustrations, graphics, or other visuals to enhance your report.

Drafting

- **Write your introductory paragraph.** Write an introductory paragraph that contains background information about your topic and clearly presents your thesis statement.
- **Develop your middle paragraphs in a logical order.** Follow or revise your outline so that the ideas in your essay progress in a logical way for the reader.
- Provide relevant, reliable, and accurate details and valid evidence to support the thesis statement. Remember to cite your sources correctly.
- Clearly state your point of view, based on the research that you have done.
- As appropriate, include graphs, illustrations, and other visuals to emphasize or demonstrate your points. Each visual you include should enhance your meaning and help the reader understand the points you are making.
- Connect your ideas with transitions so that your ideas flow smoothly from one to the next.
- Follow an approved style guide, such as the MLA Style Guide. Be sure to cite and format sources correctly within your report and in your works-cited page.

TEKS 10.13C, 10.13D, 10.17C, 10.18A, 10.18B(i)–10.18B(iii), 10.19, 10.22C, 10.23D
ELPS 5C, 5F

Revising

- **Review and revise your essay.** Review and revise your essay for *focus and coherence, organization, development of ideas,* and *voice.* Use the following questions to guide you.
  1. Is your thesis statement clear to the reader?
  2. Does your conclusion tie back to the thesis statement and leave the reader with a final thought?
  3. Do your ideas follow a logical pattern so that the essay forms a cohesive whole?
  4. Have you used transitions so that ideas flow smoothly from paragraph to paragraph and within paragraphs?
  5. Does each paragraph have a topic sentence, and are the topic sentences supported with valid, accurate evidence and well-chosen details?
  6. Have you used a variety of evaluative tools to examine the quality of the research?
  7. Do you sound knowledgeable and interested in the topic?
  8. Have you used a more formal tone that is appropriate for the audience and the genre?

Editing: Checking Your Writing

- **Check for errors in grammar, sentence structure, capitalization, punctuation, and spelling.** Correct all your errors.
  1. Correct any errors in grammar, including verb tenses. Try to use the active voice whenever possible.
  2. Check your sentence structure and sentence fluency. Try to use a variety of sentence types.
  3. Check all your mechanics, especially use of commas, quotations marks, and end punctuation. Make sure that proper nouns are correctly capitalized. Check to make sure that you have introduced and punctuated quotations correctly and set off sarcasm or irony in quotation marks. Dashes should be used to emphasize parenthetical information.
  4. Recheck your spelling to make sure that all words, especially technical terms and specialized vocabulary, are spelled correctly.
- **Prepare a final copy.** Make a neat final copy of your essay.

Research Report

Sean wrote the following report about Tuvan throat singing. After listening to a CD, he had became curious about how this unusual music developed. He decided to research Tuva, its people, and its music.

Sample Report

The introduction presents the thesis statement for the report.

The body of the report explains what throat singing is and how and where it developed. Ideas are fully developed and supported with precise, relevant details. Organization is logical. Sources are cited.

Tuvan Throat Singing: A Unique Vocal Art

The throat singers of Tuva, a remote area of Central Asia, bring a unique musical heritage into the twenty-first century. Throat singing is a vocal technique in which a single vocalist produces two or more distinct pitches simultaneously. One reviewer described the sound as a human bagpipe (Edmonds). This singing technique reflects the lifestyle and the surrounding natural world of the singers.

For many years, throat singing was not well known in the Western world. That's because this technique developed and flourished in places with little contact with the outside world. Tuva is a small Russian republic bordering Mongolia. The remote location and Soviet-era travel restrictions limited visitors but also allowed Tuvans to preserve their musical traditions (Leighton 45).

Throat singing developed among the seminomadic herders who make up much of the area's population. Tuvans herd their horses, sheep, and yaks across dry steppe lands and in the taiga, a cold, mountainous, forested area. Because throat singing produces a musical sound that carries over long distances, the music became a way for shepherds and horsemen to entertain each other and communicate. Variations of throat singing are also found in nearby areas of Mongolia, the Altai region, and other parts of Asia ("Types of Throat Singing").

In Tuva, throat singers use their voices to include the sounds of the natural world—whistling birds, bubbling streams, and blowing wind—in their songs. Because the horse is such an important part of Tuvan culture, many traditional songs have a rhythm that sounds like a cantering horse.

Khoomei, from the Mongolian word for throat singing, is the general name for Tuvan throat singing and also

TEKS 10.13B, 10.23A, 10.23B, 10.23E

Sources are cited in the report. Writer continues to support thesis with well-chosen, relevant evidence. Research sources are accurate, valid, and reliable.

refers to a specific type of simple throat singing. Other styles of throat singing include *sygyt,* which features a whistling tone; *kargyraa,* which uses flaps (the so-called false vocal chords) in the throat to produce notes an octave below the sung note; and *ezengileer,* which incorporates a horseback-riding rhythm ("Types of Throat Singing").

Throat singers perform alone or in groups, often accompanied by traditional Tuvan instruments. Common instruments include the *igil,* a two-stringed fiddle; the *dosh-poluur,* a guitarlike instrument; and the *xomus,* a type of mouth harp ("Types of Throat Singing").

In recent years, scholars, musicians and even tourists have discovered Tuva and its music. An Academy-award-nominated documentary, *Genghis Blues*, brought international attention to Tuva (Edmonds). Tuvan musicians now regularly tour in Europe and the United States as well as in Russia. Tuvan music is even online.

The essay concludes with information on recent developments.

Large music festivals and throat singing competitions each summer bring hundreds of international musicians and fans to Tuva. Tuvan organizations such as the Tuvan Institute for Humanities work with Tuvan musicians and scholars to preserve the country's unique musical form and encourage young singers to learn it (Leighton 55).

Turn to pages **407–410** for more on creating a "Works Cited" page.

Works Cited

Edmonds, Curtis. Rev. of *Ghenghis Blues* by Paul Penn. *TXReviews* 11 July 2006. Web. 16 Jan. 2010.

Leighton, Ralph. *Tuva or Bust: Richard Feynman's Last Journey.* New York: W. W. Norton, 2000. Print.

"Types of Throat Singing." *LandofTuva.com.* Foreign Languages and Education Association. 12 February 2009. Web. 17 Jan. 2010.

Creating a Multimedia Presentation

To transform your written art or music report into a multimedia presentation, you must first consider your purpose, your audience, and the context for your presentation.

Determining Your Purpose

Your purpose is your reason for giving the multimedia presentation.

- **Informative presentations** educate by providing valuable, accurate information about the topic.
- **Demonstration presentations** show your audience how to do or how to make something.

Considering Your Audience and Context

As you think about the audience that will see and hear your presentation, keep the following points in mind.

- **Be clear.** Your audience should understand your main points immediately. They should also be able to see and to hear the presentation easily. Creating good visuals and sound will enable your audience to focus on and understand the key points.
- **Anticipate questions.** As you develop your script and your presentation, think about questions your audience might ask and how you will answer them. This will help keep your audience engaged. It will also show that you are knowledgeable about the topic.

Reviewing Your Report

In a multimedia report, your audience cannot go back to clarify information, re-read paragraphs, or re-examine graphics or illustrations. It is critical to plan visual aids and sounds that will help explain concepts. They should also create interest in the topic.

In a multimedia presentation, you will control the pacing. Your multimedia presentation should move quickly enough to keep the audience engaged, but it should also enable audience members to understand key ideas and concepts.

TEKS 10.14C, 10.15D

Reworking Your Report

When you create a multimedia presentation, you must focus on your message: conveying your thesis statement and supporting ideas. You must also concentrate on the visual and sound elements.

Writing Your Script

- **Transform your written report into a script.** Your written report will serve as the basis for your script. Make sure that you follow a logical pattern for your audience and purpose. Make sure that your ideas in the script are fully developed. Develop graphics, images, and sounds for your presentation. In your script, note where each of these elements will go and give a brief description of each.
- **Develop graphics, images, and sounds.** As you create your script, remember that this is a multimedia presentation. Develop graphics, images, and sounds that are relevant to the topic and that are appropriate for the audience. Make sure that these elements will appeal to your audience.
- **Convey a distinctive point of view.** As you develop your graphics, images, and sounds, make sure that they convey a distinctive point of view. While your report should present an honest and unbiased view of the topic, you should still convey your own point of view. Use your graphics and sound to help accomplish this objective.
- **Convey your theme, or thesis, mood, and tone.** As you write your script and plan your multimedia presentation, clearly establish your thesis, or theme. Set a definite mood. Finally, use details that will contribute to a definite tone. Adding graphics, images, and sounds to your multimedia presentation will enable you to do this. Remember to keep your audience and purpose in mind.

Try It!

Use the guidelines above to develop a script for your multimedia presentation.

Preparing a Multimedia Report

Once your script is completed, you can make an outline for the multimedia presentation. In order to use graphics, images, and sound effectively, you must plan exactly where each slide or sound bite will fit into your speech. Remember that your visuals must appeal to your audience and convey your point of view.

Here is a planning script for a multimedia report on Tuvan throat singing. What will be *seen* appears in the "Video" column, and what will be *heard* appears in the "Audio" column. Note that the directions for the speaker are general, not the actual words to be spoken.

Planning Script

Video	Audio
1. **Title Screen:** "Tuvan Throat Singing: A Unique Vocal Art"	1. SPEAKER: Introduction SOUND: Sample of throat singing begins
2. **Slide 2:** "Where is Tuva" map of Russia, China, Mongolia, Kazakhstan, zoom in on Tuva	2. SPEAKER: Explain location of Tuva SOUND: Babble of language spoken in Tuva
3. **Slide 3:** "History of Tuvan throat singing" images of Tuvans herding horses, sheep, and yak	3. SPEAKER: provide history of Tuvan throat singing, how it developed SOUND: somber, lonely music
4. **Slide 4:** "Throat Singers Perform" image of Tuvan throat singers	4. SPEAKER: Singers use voices to includes sounds of nature SOUND: Tuvan thoat song of birds and bubbling stream
5. **Slide 5:** "Different types of throat singing" Chart explaining types	5. SPEAKER: Explains differences SOUND: sygyt and ezengileer
6. **Slide 6:** "Instruments" chart showing different types of instruments used in throat singing	6. SPEAKER: Explains instruments SOUND: mucic from each instrument
7. **Slide 7:** "Come hear the music!" Pictures/Illustrations of touring Tuvan music groups in U.S.	7. SPEAKER: Discusses how in the U.S. people can hear Tuvan music performed live. SOUND: Tuvan singers; audience clapping
8. **Slide 8:** Tuvan singers performing	8. SPEAKER: Conclusion SOUND: Music up and out

Other Forms of Writing in the Arts

Descriptive Writing

- Describe the use of texture, composition, and color in Vincent van Gogh's *Starry Night*.
- Describe your response to Miles Davis's rendition of "Take Five."
- Describe the varied activity inside a theater from the time you enter until the curtain goes up on a play.

Expository Writing

- Develop a list of tips for making the most of practice time when you're learning a musical instrument.
- Explain how a computer program can turn a digital photo into a new piece of art.
- Explain how origami is created.

Narrative Writing

- Research and write the story of the self-taught quilters of Gee's Bend, Alabama.
- Write about the first time you played a musical instrument.
- Write about a time you viewed a piece of art that really moved you.

Persuasive Writing

- Write an editorial for the school newsletter explaining how dance, art, and music help students learn other subjects.
- Write a letter to the PTA to convince them to sponsor a fund-raiser for new uniforms for the marching band.
- Write a letter to the editor to convince readers that electronic music should be included in the music program.

Creative Writing

- Write a poem inspired by Beethoven's *Moonlight Sonata*.
- Create a short story based on one of the characters in the diner in Edward Hopper's painting *Nighthawks*.
- Write an imaginary letter from Antonin Dvorak to a friend in which he discusses what inspired him to write the *New World Symphony*.
- Pretend you are the girl in Andrew Wyeth's painting *Christina's World*. Write about what you are thinking as you sit in the field.

Writing in the Workplace

Every bit of correspondence in the workplace reflects the business and the professionalism of the people who work there. Memos, e-mail messages, business letters, and procedural documents are common forms of workplace writing. Memos and e-mail messages are brief and quickly composed forms of business writing. Business letters are formal in tone and more carefully worded. Procedural documents usually explain processes or how to accomplish a task.

Effective business communications, no matter what kind, have the same purpose: to get the reader's attention and prompt some action—a meeting, an agreement, a contract, or a solution to a problem. You, too, can use these types of business communications to get things done—both in and out of school. For example, you can write an e-mail requesting information for a school project, write a letter of application for a job, explain procedures, or describe a step-by-step process,

This chapter will give you the basic information about communication in the workplace.

"The word that is heard perishes, but the letter that is written remains."

—Proverb

TEKS 10.13B–10.13D, 10.15B(i), 10.15B(ii), 10.17C, 10.18A, 10.18B(i)–10.18B(iii), 10.19
ELPS 5C

Writing Guidelines Business Letter

A business letter is an effective way to ask for information, resources, or a recommendation. The following tips will help you write a successful letter.

Prewriting

- **Determine your purpose.** Know exactly what you want, need, or intend to ask.
- **Consider your audience.** Word choice, style, and tone should be appropriate for your reader.
- **Gather and organize your information.** Carefully gather details and information. You must also organize the information so that your reader can easily follow and understand your letter.

Drafting

- **State your purpose clearly.** Keep in mind your purpose, and structure your ideas persuasively. Draft a short, concise letter.
- **Format your letter correctly.** Follow the appropriate conventions and correct format for a reader-friendly business letter.
- **Convey information accurately.** Explain clearly what results you expect from the letter. Make sure that you have the exact name of the company and its correct address. Anticipate questions your reader might have and answer them in your letter.

Revising

- **Improve your writing.** Review your essay for *focus and coherence, organization, development of ideas,* and *voice.* Ask these questions: *Have I clearly and accurately stated my purpose? Have I organized and formatted my letter so that it is reader-friendly? Have I used a formal tone and appropriate word choice? Have I varied my sentence structure? Do my ideas flow smoothly?*

Editing

- **Check for conventions.** Correct any errors in grammar, sentence structure, capitalization, punctuation, and spelling, Remember that in business letters, using correct grammar and punctuation, including commas, dashes, and end punctuation is essential.
- **Prepare a final copy.** Make a neat final copy of your letter.

Parts of a Business Letter

Every business letter is made up of the following six parts. Each part follows a specific form and has a specific function within the letter. Follow this format to help ensure that your reader can follow and understand your letter.

1. The **heading** includes the writer's complete address and the date. Write the heading at least one inch from the top of the page, at the left margin.
2. The **inside address** includes the recipient's name, company name, street address or post office box number, city, state, and ZIP code.
   - If the recipient has a short title, include it on the same line as the name, preceded by a comma. If the title is long, write it on the next line.
3. The **salutation** is the greeting. For business letters, use a colon after the salutation, not a comma.
   - If you know the recipient's name, use it in your greeting.
     Dear Dr. Bauer:
   - If you don't know the name of the person who will read your letter, use a salutation such as one of these:
     Dear Veterinarian:
     Dear Sir or Madam:
4. The **body** is the main part of the letter. It is organized into three parts. The beginning states why you are writing, the middle provides the needed details, and the ending focuses on what should happen next. Organize the information in a sustained manner so that your reader can easily follow your letter. Double-space between the paragraphs; do not indent.
5. The **complimentary closing** follows the body of the letter. Use *Sincerely* or *Yours truly* to close a business letter. Capitalize only the first word of the closing and place a comma at the end.
6. Your **signature** ends the letter. If you are typing, leave four blank lines under the closing; then type your name. Write your signature in the space between the closing and your typed name.

Tip

The word-processing program on your computer may have templates that will help you set up your business letters. Be sure the template you choose closely follows the format of the letter on the next page.

TEKS 10.13B, 10.15B(i), 10.15B(ii)

Business Letter

The following is an example of a properly formatted business letter. The write, Katie Mathews, clearly states her purpose, and her reader. She presents accurate information and has carefully organized her information.

The letter is organized and correctly formatted according to the guidelines on page **507**. (The numbers at the right correspond to the guidelines.)

1 617 Crabtree Lane
Plano, Texas 75023
April 15, 2010

2 Mr. Alan DeRosa
Waterloo High School
1123 South Spring Street
Austin, Texas 78702

3 Dear Mr. DeRosa:

The **beginning** introduces the writer.

I am a sophomore at Rio Mesa High School in Plano. I play first trombone in the band and have been involved in the school music programs since I was 10. My goal is to become a band director someday, and I would like to teach and direct at the middle school level.

The **middle** is well organized and conveys important information.

4 Ms. Simenek, our band director, mentioned that you are starting a junior marching band this summer. Would you be interested in hiring an intern? I would appreciate the opportunity to work with younger students.

The new band sounds very exciting, and I would like to know more about your plans. You can reach me at (214) 555-1234 or at my family's e-mail address <tmathews@ourhomeemail.com>.

The **ending** expresses thanks.

Thank you for considering my request. If you could create an internship for me, I would be very grateful.

5 Sincerely,

6 Katie Mathews

TEKS 10.13B–10.13D, 10.15B(i), 10.15B(ii), 10.17C, 10.18A, 10.18B(i)–10.18B(iii), 10.19
ELPS 5C

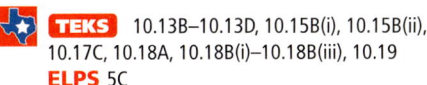

Sending a Letter

Letters will arrive faster if they are properly addressed and stamped. A typed envelope or one with printed address labels is preferred for a business letter. Always include a ZIP Code. If you do not know the ZIP Code, check with the Post Office.

Addressing the Envelope

Place the writer's name and address in the upper left-hand corner of the envelope and the recipient's name and address in the center. Use correct postage.

KATIE MATHEWS
617 CRABTREE LANE
PLANO, TEXAS 75023

MR. ALAN DEROSA
Central High School
1123 South Pine Street
Austin, TEXAS 78702

There are two acceptable forms for addressing an envelope: the older form, often hand-written, and the new form preferred by the postal service.

Traditional Form	Postal Service Form
Mr. Alan DeRosa	MR. ALAN DEROSA
Waterloo High School	WATERLOO HIGH SCHOOL
1123 South Spring Street	1123 S SPRING ST
Austin, Texas 78702	AUSTIN TX 78702

Use the list of common address abbreviations on page 694. Use numerals rather than words for numbered streets and avenues (9TH AVE NE. 3RD ST SW). If you know the ZIP + 4 code, use it.

Try It!

Write a business letter asking for information about summer educational programs or internships. Follow all the guidelines on these pages. Be sure to organize your information and format your letter correctly.

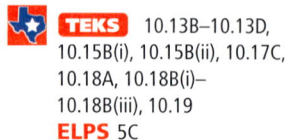

TEKS 10.13B–10.13D, 10.15B(i), 10.15B(ii), 10.17C, 10.18A, 10.18B(i)–10.18B(iii), 10.19
ELPS 5C

Writing Guidelines E-Mail Message

E-mail is a very common form of business communication. It is used to send information inside and outside a company. While e-mail is less formal than business letters, e-mail still requires formal language and a respectful tone. E-mails must follow all the conventions of writing.

Prewriting

- **Jot down your purpose and your main points.** E-mails are short and concise. It is important to state your purpose succinctly and present your ideas clearly and concisely.
- **Organize your ideas.** Organize your ideas, information, or requests so that your reader can quickly grasp your message.
- **Complete the e-mail heading.** Fill in the address line by typing in each character of the address or use your address book's automatic fill-in feature. Check to make sure you have the correct person and the correct address. Then write a subject line that clearly indicates the purpose of the message.

Drafting

- **Format your e-mail.** Format your e-mails so that your reader can quickly and easily grasp your message. Greet your reader and state your reason for writing. Be clear, complete, and accurate. Include only the most important information. Anticipate questions and address them in your e-mail. Close with your name and contact information.
- **Use a proper tone.** Be respectful. Use a formal tone and appropriate word choice.

Revising

- **Improve your writing.** Review and revise your e-mail for *focus and coherence, organization, development of ideas,* and *voice.* Then check for *accuracy, word choice, tone,* and *sentence fluency.*

Editing

- **Check for conventions.** Correct any errors in grammar, sentence structure, capitalization, punctuation, and spelling,
- Proofread one more time and send your e-mail.

E-Mail Message

E-mail has become an important, quick communication tool in the business world. Workers e-mail colleagues within their company. They also send e-mail to people outside their company. It takes time to draft a good, clear message. In the following e-mail message, an employee asks for information and help.

The **heading** includes the recipient's correct address and concise subject line.

New Message

To: mchavez@PAJscompany.com

Cc:

Subject: Information concerning next TXS proejct

The **beginning** greets the reader. Information is well organized, tells the reason for the e-mail message. Writer anticipates question about the project meeting.

Dear Miguel,

As you know I have just been assigned to the upcoming TXS project. I learned from Mark Curtis that a full project description had been prepared. Mark also told me that project precedures and schedules have also been completed.

Could you tell me where these documents have been posted or could you send me a copy of all the available information about the project? I would like to read and digest the information before our project meeting, which has been scheduled for next Tuesday.

The **ending** has a request and thanks the reader.

In addition, I was hoping to schedule a meeting with you to review my responsibilities on this project. Would you be available to meet with me tomorrow or Thursday at 10 a.m.? I look forward to your response. Thank you very much.

Sincerely,
Hillary Markham
Building 203

Try It!

Follow the guidelines and write a business-related e-mail asking for information.

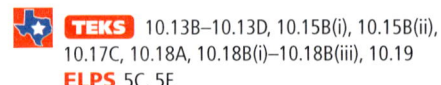

TEKS 10.13B–10.13D, 10.15B(i), 10.15B(ii), 10.17C, 10.18A, 10.18B(i)–10.18B(iii), 10.19
ELPS 5C, 5F

Writing Guidelines Description of Work

Procedural or process documents, either for a volunteer organization or a job, might include a written description of rules and regulations for an organization or company or instructions for coworkers or customers. The following tips will help you write procedural documents.

Prewriting

- **Think about your purpose and audience.** Ask yourself why you are writing this document and who your intended readers are. This will help determine your word choice and tone.
- **Gather all the information you will need.** Process documents are complex. Verify that the information you have gathered is accurate. Choose an organizational pattern that works best for conveying the information.
- **Decide on a format.** Choose a format that will show your organization and be reader-friendly.

Drafting

- **State your purpose clearly.** Keep in mind your purpose for writing, and structure your ideas persuasively.
- **Include needed, relevant, and accurate information.** Explain each detail clearly. Make sure that the information is accurate. Be concise and specific so that readers have no difficulty understanding the information. Show your knowledge of the topic.

Revising

- **Improve your writing.** Review your document for *focus and coherence, organization, development of ideas,* and *voice.* Ask these questions: *Have I explained the purpose or process? Have I organized and formatted my information to make it reader-friendly? Have I used the appropriate tone and word choice? Have I varied my sentence structure?*

Editing

- **Check for conventions.** Correct errors in grammar, sentence structure, capitalization, punctuation, and spelling. Remember that in process documents, correct grammar and punctuation are essential.
- **Prepare a final copy.** Make a neat final copy of your document.

Description of Work

Pablo and Thomas decided to organize a community astronomy club. There was sufficient interest, and the two were asked to write bylaws that would include a description of the organization and detailed information about how the club would operate. They began each section with a heading so that readers could easily find information. They were also very specific so that readers would not misunderstand the rules.

Northwood Community Astronomy Club Bylaws

PURPOSE

1. To understand astronomy
2. To make science enjoyable
3. To inform the community about astronomy

MEMBERSHIP REQUIREMENTS

1. Be a resident of Northwood or a student in a Northwood school
2. Participate in 80 percent of club meetings and club activities

MEETINGS AND RULES OF ORDER

1. Meetings will be held on the third Tuesday of every month.
2. Meetings will be held in the Northwood Library Community Room.
3. All meetings will be conducted according to Robert's Rules of Order.
4. A quorum of ten members must be present for discussion of business items and voting.
5. All officers are voting members of the astronomy club; however, the president votes only when there is a tie.

OFFICERS

1. Officers will be elected at the first meeting of each year.
2. Elected officers will consist of president, vice president, secretary, and treasurer.
3. Officers will meet twice a month.

Try It!

Think of a work-related or volunteer situation that requires a procedural document. Develop the document following the guidelines on page 512. Make sure to choose an appropriate organizational pattern and format. Check your document for all writing conventions, and correct any errors.

ELPS 1E, 2C, 3B, 3D, 3E, 4G

TEXAS WRITE SOURCE Online
www.hmheducation.com/tx/writesource

The Tools of Language

Writing Focus

Learning Language

Learning these words and expressions will help you understand this unit.

1. Academic language is the vocabulary used in learning and education.
   Name two examples of academic language used in math.
2. Prewriting is the planning you do as you think about your purpose for writing, your audience, and the genre that best suits your topic.
   What prewriting strategies work best for you when planning a research report?
3. **Sensory details help your reader visualize sights, hear sounds, and understand smells.**
   What sensory details would you use to describe a garden on a spring day?
4. A call to action is what you make when you ask people to take action to support your position.
   Why do editorials often end with a call to action?

Listening and Speaking

In his book *The Poet at the Breakfast Table*, Oliver Wendell Holmes stated, "It is the province of knowledge to speak, and it is the privilege of wisdom to listen." This famous nineteenth-century poet understood the importance of strong speaking and listening skills. Effective speaking does, in fact, require that you plan what you say, and meaningful listening clearly requires concentration.

This chapter provides tips and strategies that will help you improve your speaking and listening skills. Mastering these skills will make you a better student, leader, coworker, and companion. But remember that true mastery will come only with effort and practice.

- **Listening in Class**
- **Speaking in Class**
- **A Closer Look at Listening and Speaking**

"There is only one rule for being a good talker: learn how to listen."

—Christopher Morley

Listening in Class

When you really listen, you concentrate. You do more than simply hear what is being said. The following tips will help you become a better listener.

- **Know why you're listening.** What is the speaker trying to tell you? Will there be a test? Are you being given an assignment?
- **Listen for the facts.** Listening for the 5 W and H questions—*Who? What? When? Where? Why?* and *How?*—will help you identify the most important information.
- **Take notes.** When you hear important information, write it down in your notebook. In the margins, write down any new vocabulary, expressions, or questions you may have. Review and complete your notes as soon as after class as possible.
- **Put the speaker's ideas into your own words.** Summarize the speaker's key points as you take notes. Add your own comments.

Try It!

The next time you take notes in class, use your own words to record your teacher's ideas. Add comments in the margins.

The Marshall Plan (1947)

known as the European Recovery Program (ERP)	
in effect from 1948-1951	What does *in effect* mean?
designed by George C. Marshall	
– army chief of staff during WWII	
– secretary of state under President Truman	
gave economic aid to parts of Europe	
devastated by WWII	devastated:
– provided about $13 billion	destroyed
– Europe mostly used the money to buy goods from America.	Benefited the U.S. and Europe.
– During Korean War, some of the money helped rebuild the militaries of Western Europe.	

Speaking in Class

Speaking in class is a skill everyone should master. A good classroom discussion depends on cooperation. These basic strategies will help you and your classmates become better speakers.

Before you speak . . .

- **Listen** carefully and take notes.
- **Think** about what others are asking or saying.
- **Wait** until it's your turn to speak.
- **Plan** how you can add something positive to the discussion.

As you speak . . .

- **Use a loud, clear voice.**
- **Stick to the topic.**
- **Express your opinions, ideas, and feelings** with examples, facts, and anecdotes.
- **Narrate, describe, and explain your ideas** with details.
- **Maintain eye contact** with others in the group or class.

Tip

- Summarize what's been agreed upon in the discussion.
- Mention another person's comments and expand on them constructively.

Try It!

Play "Where will you be?" Warm up your impromptu speaking skills by interacting in the following activity.

1. Pair up with a classmate. Take turns interviewing each other about this topic: What do you plan to do after high school?
   - As the interviewer, ask specific questions and get as much information as you can. Take notes as you go along.
   - As the interviewee, answer the questions clearly and completely. Include important facts and interesting details.
2. Exchange roles after the first interview is complete.
3. In a mini-speech, present your partner's future plans to the class. Quickly organize your notes into a beginning, a middle, and an ending. Then follow the "As You Speak" strategies above.

ELPS 1D, 2C, 2D, 2I, 3E, 3G, 3H

A Closer Look at Listening and Speaking

Improving your listening and speaking skills will increase your confidence in and out of the classroom. Follow these basic guidelines to carry on productive conversations and discussions.

Good Listeners . . .	Good Speakers . . .
■ think about what the speaker is saying. ■ take notes of important words, ideas, and expressions. ■ pay attention to the speaker's tone of voice, gestures, and facial expressions. ■ ask for clarification. ■ prepare to respond thoughtfully.	■ speak loudly and clearly. ■ maintain eye contact with their listeners. ■ express their opinions, ideas, and feelings by changing the tone and volume of their voice. ■ use details to describe, explain, narrate, and clarify information. ■ use gestures and body language effectively.

Try It!

Focus on speaking and listening skills with this activity.

1. Pick two classmates and number yourselves 1, 2, and 3.
2. Ask person 1 to take person 2 aside and read the paragraph below.
3. Then ask person 2 to take person 3 aside and try to retell or summarize the paragraph.
4. Finally, ask person 3 to retell or summarize the paragraph to the first two classmates.
5. Compare the original paragraph to what person 3 reports.

In the early 1920s, Roy Chapman Andrews, an explorer from Wisconsin, proposed studying geologic formations in Mongolia. Many fellow scientists felt that this trip would be a waste of time because the shifting sands of the desert would make such research difficult, if not impossible. Even Andrews began to wonder about the wisdom of his proposal, given the distance and the political uncertainties in Asia. Fortunately, he decided to go through with his plan. The scientific community was rewarded with the discovery of many unique fossils in the Gobi Desert of Mongolia. The most important find was a clutch of dinosaur eggs, the first ever discovered.

Using Reference Materials

Since the late 1980s, the use of computers and the Internet has led people to say that we live in the "Information Age." This term refers to the idea that all sorts of information is easily available to anyone who wants to find it. The key is knowing where to look!

When you need to gather information, knowing which print and electronic reference materials are likely to be helpful can save you time and aggravation. You are probably familiar with many common references, such as encyclopedias, newspapers, and atlases. Do you need facts about a specific topic? Do you need to look at maps or read about current events? One of those common references will probably suit your needs.

This chapter will focus on language references that may be useful to you—resources that will help you understand words, expressions, and language structures. The first section provides details about the information found in a dictionary, and the second describes other types of helpful language resources. When you are able to use these kinds of reference materials well, your ability to write clear, engaging, and informative pieces will grow and grow.

- **Checking a Dictionary**
- **Using Other Language Resources**

"Proper words in proper places make the true definition of a style."

—Jonathan Swift

Checking a Dictionary

A dictionary gives many types of information:

- **Guide words:** These are the first and last words on the page. Guide words show whether the word you are looking for will be found alphabetically on that page.
- **Entry words:** Each word defined in a dictionary is called an entry word. Entry words are listed alphabetically.
- **Etymology:** Many dictionaries give etymologies (word histories) for certain words. An etymology tells what language an English word came from, how the word entered our language, and when it was first used.
- **Syllable divisions:** A dictionary tells where to divide a word.
- **Pronunciation and accent marks:** A dictionary tells you how to pronounce a word and also provides a key to pronunciation symbols, usually at the bottom of each page.
- **Illustrations:** Some entries provide an illustration or a photograph.
- **Parts of speech:** A dictionary tells you what part(s) of speech a word is, using these abbreviations:

n.	**noun**	*intr. v.*	**intransitive verb**	*adj.*	**adjective**
pron.	**pronoun**	*tr. v.*	**transitive verb**	*adv.*	**adverb**
conj.	**conjunction**	*interj.*	**interjection**	*prep.*	**preposition**

- **Spelling and capitalization:** The dictionary shows the acceptable spelling, as well as capitalization, for words. (For some words, more than one spelling is given.)
- **Definitions:** Some dictionaries are large enough to list all of the meanings for a word. Most standard-size dictionaries, however, will list only three or four of the most commonly accepted meanings. Take time to read all of the meanings to be sure that you are using the word correctly.

Try It!

Find an article on a topic that interests you and select three words that are unfamiliar to you. Look them up in the dictionary.

1. Identify the part(s) of speech for each word.
2. Give the first two meanings for the word.
3. Explain the etymology (if given) for each word.

Sample Dictionary Page

Guide words — Circle | Circularize

Entry word

Etymology

Syllable divisions

Pronunciation and accent marks

Illustration

Part of speech

Spelling

Definitions

Circle | Circularize 261

cir•cle (sûr′kəl) *n.* **1.** A plane curve everywhere equidistant from a given fixed point, the center. **2.** A planar region bounded by a circle. **3.** Something, such as a ring, shaped like such a plane curve. **4.** A circular course, circuit, or orbit. **5.** A traffic circle. **6.** A curved section or tier of seats in a theater. **7.** A series or process that finishes at its starting point or repeats itself; a cycle. **8.** A group of people sharing an interest, activity, or achievement. **9.** A territorial or administrative division, esp. of a province, in some European countries. **10.** A sphere of influence or interest; domain. **11.** *Logic* A vicious circle. ❖ *v.* **-cled, -cling, -cles** —*tr.* **1.** To make or form a circle around; enclose. **2.** To move in a circle around. —*intr.* To move in a circle. ***—idiom:* circle the wagons** To take a defensive position. [ME *cercle* < OFr. < Lat. *circulus,* dim. of *circus,* circle < Gk. *kirkos, krikos.*] —**cir′cler** (-klər) *n.*

circle graph *n.* See **pie chart.**

cir•clet (sûr′klĭt) *n.* A small circle, esp. a circular ornament. [ME *cerclet* < OFr., dim. of *cercle,* circle. See CIRCLE.]

cir•cuit (sûr′kĭt) *n.* **1a.** A closed, usu. circular line that goes around an object or area. **b.** The region enclosed by such a line. **2a.** A path or route that returns to its starting point. **b.** The act of following such a path or route. **c.** A journey made on such a path or route. **3.** *Electronics* **a.** A closed path followed by an electric current. **b.** A configuration of electrically or electromagnetically connected components or devices. **4a.** A regular or accustomed course from place to place; a round: *the lecture circuit.* **b.** The area or district thus covered, esp. a territory under the jurisdiction of a judge in which periodic court sessions are held. **5a.** An association of theaters among which plays, acts, or films move for presentation. **b.** A group of nightclubs, show halls, or resorts at which entertainers appear in turn. **c.** An association of teams or clubs. **d.** A series of competitions held in different places. ❖ *intr. & tr.v.* **-cuit•ed, -cuit•ing, -cuits** To make a circuit or circuit of. [ME, circumference < OFr. < Lat. *circuitus,* a going around < p. part. of *circumīre,* to go around : *circum-,* circum- + *īre,* to go; see **ei-** in App.]

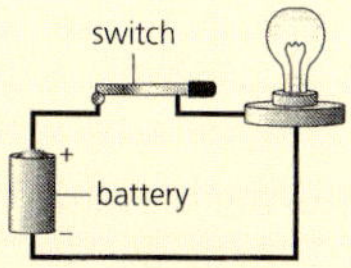

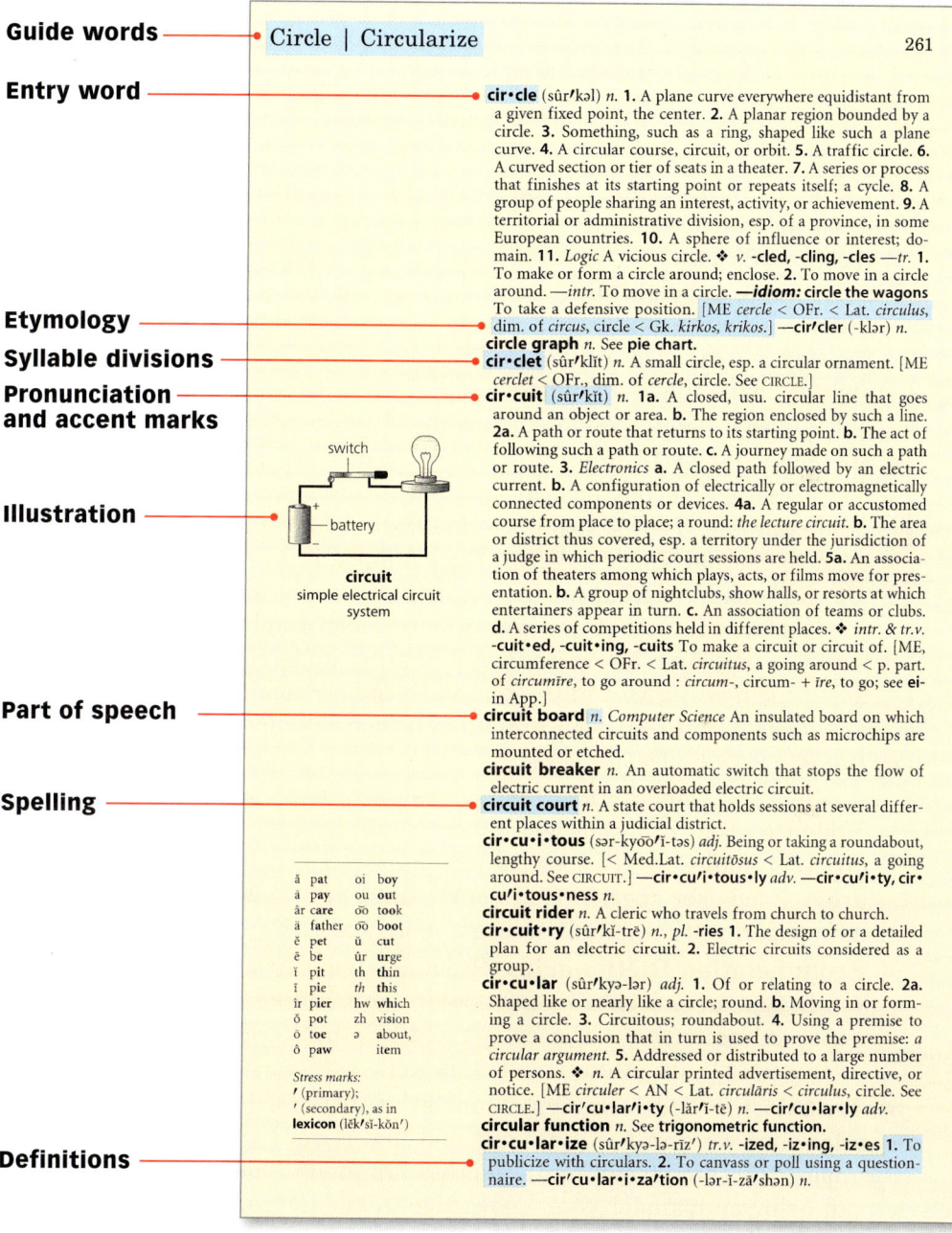

circuit
simple electrical circuit system

circuit board *n. Computer Science* An insulated board on which interconnected circuits and components such as microchips are mounted or etched.

circuit breaker *n.* An automatic switch that stops the flow of electric current in an overloaded electric circuit.

circuit court *n.* A state court that holds sessions at several different places within a judicial district.

cir•cu•i•tous (sər-kyo͞o′ĭ-təs) *adj.* Being or taking a roundabout, lengthy course. [< Med.Lat. *circuitōsus* < Lat. *circuitus,* a going around. See CIRCUIT.] —**cir•cu′i•tous•ly** *adv.* —**cir•cu′i•ty, cir•cu′i•tous•ness** *n.*

circuit rider *n.* A cleric who travels from church to church.

cir•cuit•ry (sûr′kĭ-trē) *n., pl.* **-ries 1.** The design of or a detailed plan for an electric circuit. **2.** Electric circuits considered as a group.

cir•cu•lar (sûr′kyə-lər) *adj.* **1.** Of or relating to a circle. **2a.** Shaped like or nearly like a circle; round. **b.** Moving in or forming a circle. **3.** Circuitous; roundabout. **4.** Using a premise to prove a conclusion that in turn is used to prove the premise: *a circular argument.* **5.** Addressed or distributed to a large number of persons. ❖ *n.* A circular printed advertisement, directive, or notice. [ME *circuler* < AN < Lat. *circulāris* < *circulus,* circle. See CIRCLE.] —**cir′cu•lar′i•ty** (-lăr′ĭ-tē) *n.* —**cir′cu•lar•ly** *adv.*

circular function *n.* See **trigonometric function.**

cir•cu•lar•ize (sûr′kyə-lə-rīz′) *tr.v.* **-ized, -iz•ing, -iz•es 1.** To publicize with circulars. **2.** To canvass or poll using a questionnaire. —**cir′cu•lar•i•za′tion** (-lər-ĭ-zā′shən) *n.*

ă	pat	oi	boy
ā	pay	ou	out
âr	care	o͝o	took
ä	father	o͞o	boot
ĕ	pet	ŭ	cut
ē	be	ûr	urge
ĭ	pit	th	thin
ī	pie	*th*	this
îr	pier	hw	which
ŏ	pot	zh	vision
ō	toe	ə	about, item
ô	paw		

Stress marks:
′ (primary);
′ (secondary), as in
lexicon (lĕk′sĭ-kŏn′)

Using Other Language Resources

As you have seen, dictionaries are an excellent source of information about language. The list below describes other language resources you may find useful.

- **Books of Synonyms, Antonyms, and Homonyms** Thesauruses, or books of synonyms, are probably the most well-known language resource. Synonyms—words that mean the same or almost the same—can be helpful for understanding the meaning of an unfamiliar word, and can add variety to your writing. Many of these resources also include lists of common antonyms (words with opposite meanings) and homonyms (words with the same spelling but different meanings) for thousands of frequently used words.
- **Dictionaries of Idioms** Idioms are used in books, magazines, newspapers, everyday speech—just about anywhere you hear or read language. Phrases that are idioms have a different meaning than the actual words suggest. For example, if you put a project "on the back burner" it means you will work on it later, not that you've placed it on a stove. Learning common English idioms will help you in your reading and your writing; understanding and using them will give you the ability to communicate your thoughts and ideas with expression and imagination.
- **Usage Guides** Usage guides can help you improve your grammar, spelling, and punctuation. Many of these resources also provide guidance about different writing or speaking styles to use for different audiences. Choose a good, multi-purpose guide for general usage issues; for specific types of writing, such as writing for a newspaper, you may want to use a more specific guide as well.
- **Pronunciation Dictionaries** Pronunciation dictionaries allow you to type in or look up a particular word and hear it pronounced, either online or on a CD accompanied by a book. Variations in pronunciation are often included as well.
- **Translation Dictionaries** Translation dictionaries help you take a familiar word in one language and find a word with the same or almost the same meaning in another language. These resources can help you transfer your knowledge in one language into a new language, making your ideas and your writing clearer for your audience.

Learning Language

Has this ever happened to you? You read a page or a chapter in a textbook, put the book down, and say, "I can't remember a thing I just read!" Unfortunately, many students have that experience. The good news, however, is that you can remember the information you read. The way to do it is by reading critically.

Reading for academic success involves a number of steps, including surveying a reading assignment, questioning what the text is about, taking notes as you read, and so on. If you keep these tips in mind and have a tested reading plan, you will be in control of your reading. This chapter gives you an effective critical-reading method to follow.

- **Learning Language: Language Strategies**
- **Language of the Writing Process**
- **Language of the Writing Traits**
- **Language of the Writing Forms**

"Language is the dress of thought."

—Samuel Johnson

ELPS 2C, 2D, 4C

Language Strategies

You hear and read new words every day. Here are some strategies to help you understand, remember, and use the new language correctly.

Use Language Patterns

Listen for patterns others use when speaking English.

You hear: **This morning,** you will practice your presentations. **After school,** the soccer team will hold practice.
You say: **Tomorrow,** I will go on a field trip with my science class.

Try It!

Turn to a partner. Say three sentences that tell what will happen. Start with a word that tells when, as in the examples above.

Look for the Context

You can find the meaning of an unfamiliar word by examining its context, or what surrounds the word.

You read a sign: Pay your co-pay before you see the doctor.
You can conclude that a co-pay is part of the bill you must pay.

Try It!

The next time you read unfamiliar words on a sign, try to identify the meaning of the words by the context in which they appear.

Use Academic Language

Teachers may sometimes use unfamiliar words in class. If your teacher uses a word you don't know, repeat it to yourself and write it down. When you get a chance, look up the word in a dictionary.

You hear: A strong circulatory system is an important part of overall health.
You say and write down: "circulatory."

Try It!

Listen for words you don't understand. Repeat them and write them down. Check with your teacher if you are unsure how to write them.

Say It Again

When your teacher makes an assignment, retell what you have heard so that you can be sure that you fully understand it.

You hear: Your essay must include a works-cited page that follows MLA style.
You can say: I will need to prepare a list of sources that I used in my essay that follows the MLA style guide.

Try It!

Retell the details of a recent assignment to your teacher or another classmate. Listen to any clarifications and retell the clarification.

Look for Word Parts You Know

Many words share prefixes, suffixes, or roots, even across different languages. For example, the prefix *bio-* means "life" in many languages, including French, Spanish, and German.

Try It!

If you hear a word you don't know, try writing it down. See if you recognize any of its parts. If so, use that part to help you determine the meaning of the whole word.

Learn Words in Different Ways

You may hear a word that you know used in a way that is unfamiliar to you. Finding the connection to what you know can help you understand the new use of the word.

You think: Suki has to parallel park on her driving test. In geometry, parallel lines are ones that go in the same direction and never meet. Parallel parking must mean that the car is parallel to the curb, going in the same direction.

Try It!

Listen for familiar words used in unfamiliar ways. Try to find the logical connection between the two uses.

Language of the Writing Process

Read the terms below that identify the steps in the writing process. Then read the description of what you will accomplish at each step.

The first step in the writing process is prewriting, or planning your writing. During prewriting, you will think about your purpose for writing and identify your genre, or form, of writing. You will also plan a topic that will interest your audience. Once you have identified your topic, audience, and genre, you will write your thesis statement, or controlling idea. Finally, you will generate ideas related to your thesis by brainstorming or by using a graphic organizer.

When you write a first draft, you should write freely to get all your ideas on paper. Use your prewriting as a guide and always keep your thesis statement in mind. Organize your basic ideas into paragraphs. Since this is a draft, you don't have to worry that it is exactly right. Include everything you think is important. Always keep your audience and purpose in mind.

Now it is time to read your draft and revise, or make changes, to it. Consider the first four key writing traits: focus and coherence, organization, development of ideas, and voice. When you revise, you make sure that all the parts of your writing support the thesis, that your ideas are fully developed, and that the information is organized to flow well. Finally, check to see that your voice is right for your purpose, genre, and audience.

When you edit, you look for mistakes in your writing. You check for correct use of conventions––grammar, sentence structure, capitalization, punctuation, and spelling. Correct any errors and then proofread your copy. Print or write a neat copy.

Get feedback from your teacher or classmates and make final revisions. Then make a neat final copy that you can share with others.

Vocabulary: Writing Process

draft	edit	feedback
freewrite	organize	prewrite
proofread	publish	revise
traits		

1. **Say the word.** Listen actively and carefully as your teacher reads the words aloud. Pay special attention to your teacher's pronunciation of long and short vowel sounds, silent letters, and consonant clusters. Then repeat the words. Which of these words have you heard before? Which do you already know?

2. **Discover the meaning.** Working with a partner, make a four-column chart. List the vocabulary word, the pronunciation, and the meanings in the first three columns and a sample sentence in the fourth column. Start with the words you already know. Discuss how you can fill in the chart as you find the meanings and pronunciations for any words you do not know.

3. **Learn more.** Listen as your teacher explains each word. Take notes by listening for key words or phrases that help you understand what each word means. Check your understanding by looking each word up in a dictionary or other reference book.

4. **Think about it.** Work with a partner to share ideas and answer the questions below.
   - When might it be good to write more than one draft?
   - When is it important to think about your audience? Why?
   - How could a graphic organizer or outline help organize your thoughts? Explain.
   - What should you think about when you edit your work?

5. **Show your understanding.** Practice explaining how each word in the vocabulary box above fits into the writing process. Then, share your explanation with a partner. Work together to add specific details in order to create an accurate explanation for each word.

The Writing Process in Action

Now that you have learned the language of the writing process, it's time to see and experience the process in action. Your teacher will begin by demonstrating each step of the writing process. Then, you and your classmates will go through the steps of the writing process together. Use the questions below as a guide.

Prewrite

1. What is your topic? Select a topic that interests you or that you know something about.
2. What genre will you use? Sometimes you will be assigned a genre; other times you will be given a prompt, and you must determine the correct genre. Look for clue words in the prompt, such as *describe, explain,* and *give an opinion*, that will help you identify the correct genre, or form.
3. Who is your audience? Will they be interested in your topic? What do they already know about your topic?
4. What is your purpose for writing? Are you writing for a class assignment, for enjoyment, to express an opinion, for a test, and so on.
5. What is your controlling idea or thesis statement? Make sure it is broad enough that you have related ideas to develop and narrow enough to effectively address the thesis statement in the space you have available.
6. How will you generate ideas about your thesis? What graphic organizers can you use to gather and organize your ideas?

Draft

1. Are all your ideas included? Write freely about your topic so that everything you want to write about your topic is included.
2. Are your ideas organized into paragraphs? While your first draft is not polished writing, it is best to keep related ideas in the same paragraph. You may want to start your draft by writing the topic sentences for your paragraphs and then building your paragraphs with the ideas that support those sentences. Remember to use transitions so that your ideas will flow smoothly from one paragraph to the next.
3. Have you considered your audience and purpose as you have written your draft?

Revise

1. Do you maintain focus on your thesis throughout your writing?
2. Do all your paragraphs support your thesis?
3. Is your writing organized with a beginning, a middle, and an ending?
4. Is your organizational pattern effective for your purpose and your audience?
5. Have your developed all your ideas fully?
6. Do your transitions help your readers move from paragraph to paragraph and from idea to idea smoothly?
7. Does your voice seem knowledgeable and engaging? Your word choices should indicate that you understand your topic well. Your voice should reflect your interest in the topic.

Edit

1. Did you check that there is agreement between subjects and verbs?
2. Did you use the correct form of words with more than one spelling, such as *two, to,* and *too*?
3. Did you use a variety of sentence structures?
4. Did you capitalize the correct words, such as the start of sentences and proper nouns?
5. Did you use correct end punctuation for each sentence?
6. Did you use commas correctly?
7. Are all your words spelled correctly?

Publish

1. Did you leave even margins?
2. Did you indent each paragraph?
3. Did you get feedback from your teacher or classmates? Use this feedback to make final improvements before publishing.

Turn and Talk and Listen

Take turns talking with a classmate about what you learned as you used the writing process.

What was easy and what was hard about the writing process?
What do you like about your writing?
What will you do differently the next time you write an essay?
It is important to proofread because ____________________.

Texas Traits Language of the Writing Traits

Read each of these terms. Then read about what they mean.

Focus and Coherence

Focus means that everything in your writing supports the main idea. Your main idea is usually expressed in your thesis statement. **Coherence** means the sentences connect and make sense together. Your writing should always have a clear focus. Include specific ideas and details to support the focus of your topic. Any sentences that don't relate directly to the topic weaken the writing. Remember, everything you write should contribute to the readers' understanding of the topic.

Organization

Your writing should be organized to make it easy to follow from beginning to end. It should have a distinct beginning, middle, and end. Each sentence and paragraph should be logically linked to the ones that come before and after it. Details should support the topic.

Development of Ideas

Include enough details to give your writing depth. **Depth** means you "layer" and "flesh out" ideas so that each sentence adds meaning to the one before it. Good development must also be original. You can't just repeat what someone else has done before you.

Voice

Your writing should express your own voice. It should genuinely express your personality or viewpoint to engage the reader. Voice gives your writing a "face," which establishes a relationship between you and the reader.

Conventions

Think about the basic rules of grammar, sentence structure, punctuation, spelling, and word choice. Edit your work to be sure there are no errors. Writing that has errors is difficult to read and may cause you to lose your reader.

Vocabulary: Writing Traits

coherence	**conventions**	**depth**
development of ideas	**focus**	**organization**
thesis statement	**voice**	

1. **Say the word.** Listen actively and carefully as your teacher reads each word. Pay special attention to your teacher's pronunciation of long and short vowel sounds, silent letters, and consonant clusters. Then repeat the words. Which of these words have you heard before? Which do you already know?

2. **Discover the meaning.** Work with a partner. Write the vocabulary words you already know, and their meanings. Discuss the words with your partner, teaching each other the words you know. Some of these words have more than one meaning. If you are not sure of the correct meaning in this context, list the word with the meaning you know.

3. **Learn more.** Listen as your teacher explains each word. Work with your partner to restate the meaning of each word by putting the meaning in your own words.

4. **Think about it.** Work with a partner to answer the questions below.
   - How do you decide on a thesis statement?
   - How can you be sure that your writing has depth?
   - How can you tell if your writing has coherence?
   - Why is organization important to your purpose?
   - How can you tell if your writing reflects your voice?
   - What conventions are most difficult for you?

5. **Show your understanding.** Use your vocabulary journal to write what you know about each word. Work with a partner to understand each of the words better. When words connect to each other, show the connections with explanations or descriptions. Include sample sentences. You may wish to read your sample sentences to your partner.

Narrative Essays

A narrative essay is writing that tells a true story. A personal narrative essay tells the writer's audience about an important experience in the writer's life. The experience might be one that extended over a period of time and one that changed the writer in some way. Narrative essays have the same basic organization: a beginning that gets the reader's attention and identifies the topic, middle paragraphs that tell about the experience in time order, and an ending paragraph that concludes the story.

Narrative Essay Organization

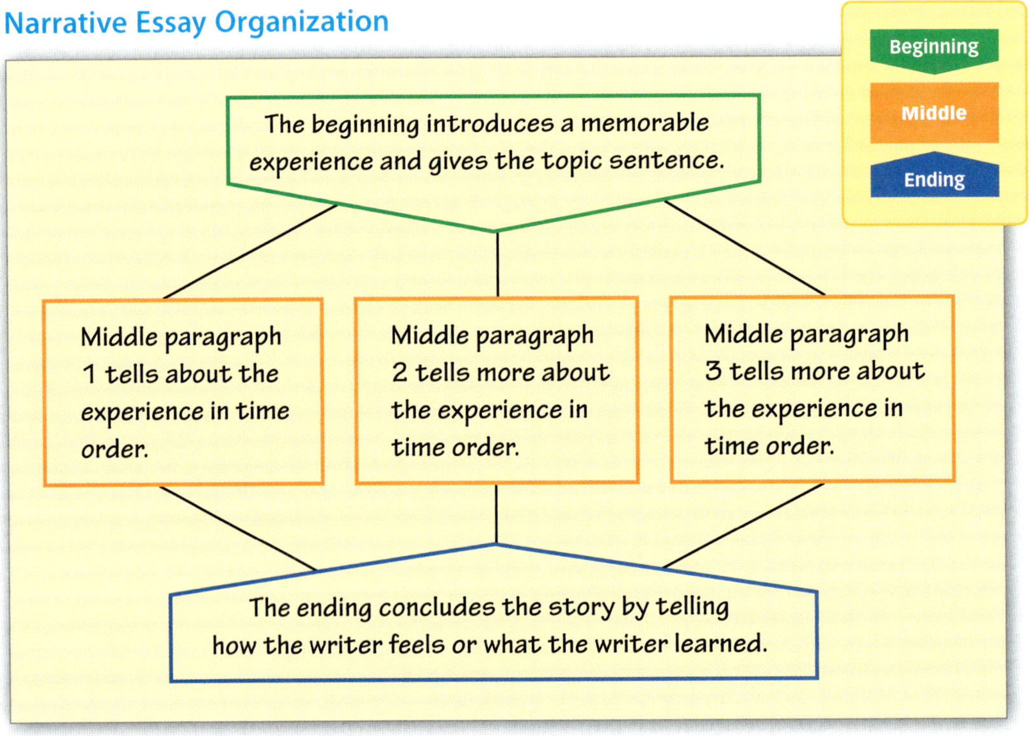

Beginning
Middle
Ending
The beginning introduces a memorable experience and gives the topic sentence.
Middle paragraph 1 tells about the experience in time order.
Middle paragraph 2 tells more about the experience in time order.
Middle paragraph 3 tells more about the experience in time order.
The ending concludes the story by telling how the writer feels or what the writer learned.

Turn and Talk

Talk with a partner about the purpose of each paragraph in a narrative essay as shown in the graphic organizer.

Vocabulary: Narrative Form

action	chronological order	dialogue
experience	narrative	narrator
phase autobiography	sensory details	situation
suspense		

1. **Say the word or phrase.** Listen actively and carefully as your teacher reads the words aloud. Pay special attention to your teacher's pronunciation of long and short vowel sounds, silent letters, and consonant clusters. Then repeat each word.

2. **Discover the meaning.** Work with a partner and make notes about the words you know. Use each of these words in a sentence. Make a list of words that you do not yet know.

3. **Learn more.** Listen as your teacher explains the meaning of each word or phrase. Work with your partner to check and correct your earlier notes. Write the meanings for additional words.

4. **Show your understanding.** Use your notebook to answer the questions below.
   - Where in the narrative does the writer usually reflect upon the situation? Tell why.
   - Why would a narrative be less interesting without suspense?
   - Why is using dialogue important in a narrative essay?
   - Why is chronological order useful in narrative writing?
   - How do sensory details help show the audience what the experience was like?

5. **Write it, explain it.** In your vocabulary journal, list the words that you have learned. Add synonyms, or words that means the same thing, to the right of the word. For example, next to **narrator** you could write "the person who tells a story or a gives a report."

6. **Write about it.** Write a brief paragraph explaining how to write a narrative essay. Use at least three of the vocabulary words above in your paragraph.

The Language of Narrative Essays

What Do You Know?

Next you will read a sample personal narrative essay about an experience volunteering at an animal shelter. Have you ever done any volunteer work? How can you describe it? Why did you do it? How did you feel? What do you know about animal shelters? Are there any in your community? Tell what you know.

Build Background

When people do volunteer work, they offer their time and services for no pay. Volunteering has many benefits to both the community and the volunteers. When you volunteer, you help others in need. Volunteering is also a way to get to know more about people and their life situations. It also allows you to explore what interests you and learn what you can accomplish.

Listening

Listen as your teacher or a classmate reads aloud "In the Doghouse." As you listen, make notes about the order of events. Be prepared to answer the questions below.

1. What are two ways the writer creates effective images for the reader?
2. What challenges does the narrator face and how does he meet them?
3. Why does the writer say, "I thought this would be great preparation"?

Key Words

adoptable	**challenge**	**incompetent**
instinctively	**ordinary**	**preparation**
responsibilities	**shelter**	**volunteers**

Look at the words and phrases in the box. You will see these words and phrases when you read the writing sample. Use the words to tell a partner, in chronological order, about an experience that changed you in some way.

Read Along

Now it's your turn to read. Turn to pages 83–84 in this book. Read the writing model as your teacher or a classmate reads it aloud.

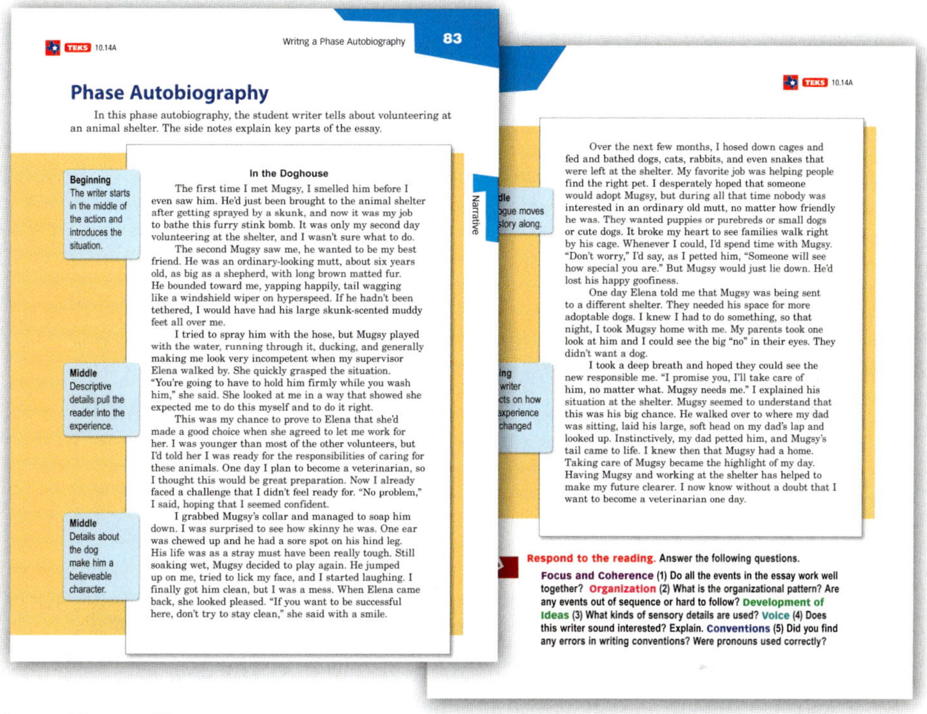
TEKS 10.14A

Writng a Phase Autobiography 83

Phase Autobiography

In this phase autobiography, the student writer tells about volunteering at an animal shelter. The side notes explain key parts of the essay.

Beginning The writer starts in the middle of the action and introduces the situation.

In the Doghouse

The first time I met Mugsy, I smelled him before I even saw him. He'd just been brought to the animal shelter after getting sprayed by a skunk, and now it was my job to bathe this furry stink bomb. It was only my second day volunteering at the shelter, and I wasn't sure what to do.

The second Mugsy saw me, he wanted to be my best friend. He was an ordinary-looking mutt, about six years old, as big as a shepherd, with long brown matted fur. He bounded toward me, yapping happily, tail wagging like a windshield wiper on hyperspeed. If he hadn't been tethered, I would have had his large skunk-scented muddy feet all over me.

Middle Descriptive details pull the reader into the experience.

I tried to spray him with the hose, but Mugsy played with the water, running through it, ducking, and generally making me look very incompetent when my supervisor Elena walked by. She quickly grasped the situation. "You're going to have to hold him firmly while you wash him," she said. She looked at me in a way that showed she expected me to do this myself and to do it right.

This was my chance to prove to Elena that she'd made a good choice when she agreed to let me work for her. I was younger than most of the other volunteers, but I'd told her I was ready for the responsibilities of caring for these animals. One day I plan to become a veterinarian, so I thought this would be great preparation. Now I already faced a challenge that I didn't feel ready for. "No problem," I said, hoping that I seemed confident.

Middle Details about the dog make him a believeable character.

I grabbed Mugsy's collar and managed to soap him down. I was surprised to see how skinny he was. One ear was chewed up and he had a sore spot on his hind leg. His life was as a stray must have been really tough. Still soaking wet, Mugsy decided to play again. He jumped up on me, tried to lick my face, and I started laughing. I finally got him clean, but I was a mess. When Elena came back, she looked pleased. "If you want to be successful here, don't try to stay clean," she said with a smile.

Narrative

TEKS 10.14A

dle ogue moves story along.

Over the next few months, I hosed down cages and fed and bathed dogs, cats, rabbits, and even snakes that were left at the shelter. My favorite job was helping people find the right pet. I desperately hoped that someone would adopt Mugsy, but during all that time nobody was interested in an ordinary old mutt, no matter how friendly he was. They wanted puppies or purebreds or small dogs or cute dogs. It broke my heart to see families walk right by his cage. Whenever I could, I'd spend time with Mugsy. "Don't worry," I'd say, as I petted him, "Someone will see how special you are." But Mugsy would just lie down. He'd lost his happy goofiness.

One day Elena told me that Mugsy was being sent to a different shelter. They needed his space for more adoptable dogs. I knew I had to do something, so that night, I took Mugsy home with me. My parents took one look at him and I could see the big "no" in their eyes. They didn't want a dog.

ing writer cts on how experience changed

I took a deep breath and hoped they could see the new responsible me. "I promise you, I'll take care of him, no matter what. Mugsy needs me." I explained his situation at the shelter. Mugsy seemed to understand that this was his big chance. He walked over to where my dad was sitting, laid his large, soft head on my dad's lap and looked up. Instinctively, my dad petted him, and Mugsy's tail came to life. I knew then that Mugsy had a home. Taking care of Mugsy became the highlight of my day. Having Mugsy and working at the shelter has helped to make my future clearer. I now know without a doubt that I want to become a veterinarian one day.

Respond to the reading. Answer the following questions.

Focus and Coherence (1) Do all the events in the essay work well together? **Organization** (2) What is the organizational pattern? Are any events out of sequence or hard to follow? **Development of Ideas** (3) What kinds of sensory details are used? **Voice** (4) Does this writer sound interested? Explain. **Conventions** (5) Did you find any errors in writing conventions? Were pronouns used correctly?

After Reading

Copy the following chart and fill it in with information about the narrative. Use your chart to summarize the writing model with a partner.

Actions or events	Sensory details	Your thoughts
First:		
Next:		
Next:		
Next:		
Last:		

ELPS 3G, 3I

Oral Language

The person or people who will listen to you or read your writing are called your **audience.** When you speak or write, it is important to choose just the right words that will reach your audience. When you write, the **tone,** or the way you write, will be different for each audience.

Try It!

Read about the situation below. Then choose two audiences from the list below. With a partner, discuss how the words you choose might be different for each audience.

Situation

Your friend has just finished his campaign to run for class president. He told you about the experience, including why he decided to run, the tactics he used to try to win votes, the day of the election, and what he learned from the experience. You will retell his story.

Audiences

- a classmate, an aunt or uncle, an experienced politician

Let's Talk!

When you answer a question, you might use one word, a few words, a sentence, or a few sentences.

Example: What was it like to run for class president?

stressful.

It was stressful.

My experience running for class president was stressful.

Running for class president was a stressful experience. There were many campaign events to prepare for and attend. I was always trying to win the favor of my classmates so that they would vote for me.

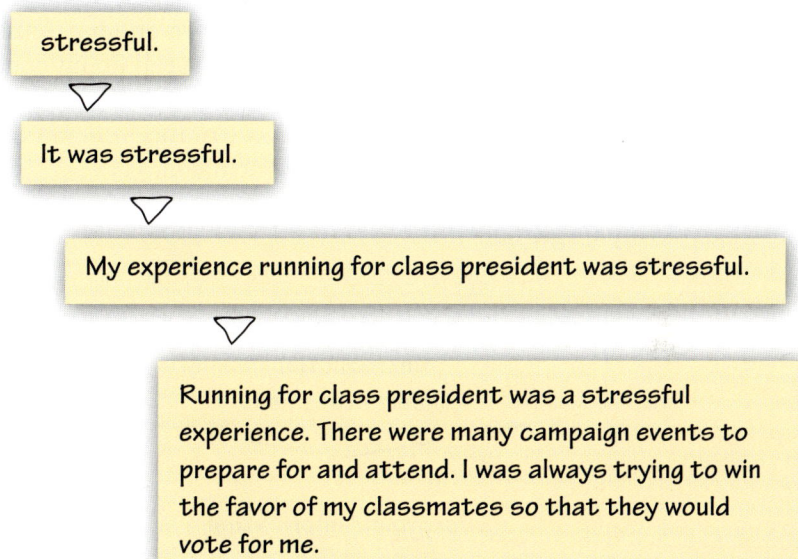

In the first box, there is only a one-word answer. In the other boxes, the writer includes more information. The last box shows the most information. When you use more details to tell about something, the listener will understand it better.

Try It!

Choose a new question that you would like to talk about with a partner. First make notes about details that would make your answer entertaining. Then use your notes to tell your story to your partner.

Here are some ideas to get you started.

1. Have you had an experience, like campaigning for something, from which you learned an important life lesson? Tell what happened and the lesson you learned.
2. Have you ever had to learn something new? Tell why and what happened.

Language of Expository Writing

Expository writing explains something about a specific topic to the writer's audience. This type of writing might explain one particular subject, compare two subjects, explain a process, or it might tell about cause and effect. Expository essays usually have the same basic organization: an introduction that includes a thesis statement and gives background information, body paragraphs with supporting details, and a conclusion.

Expository Essay Organization

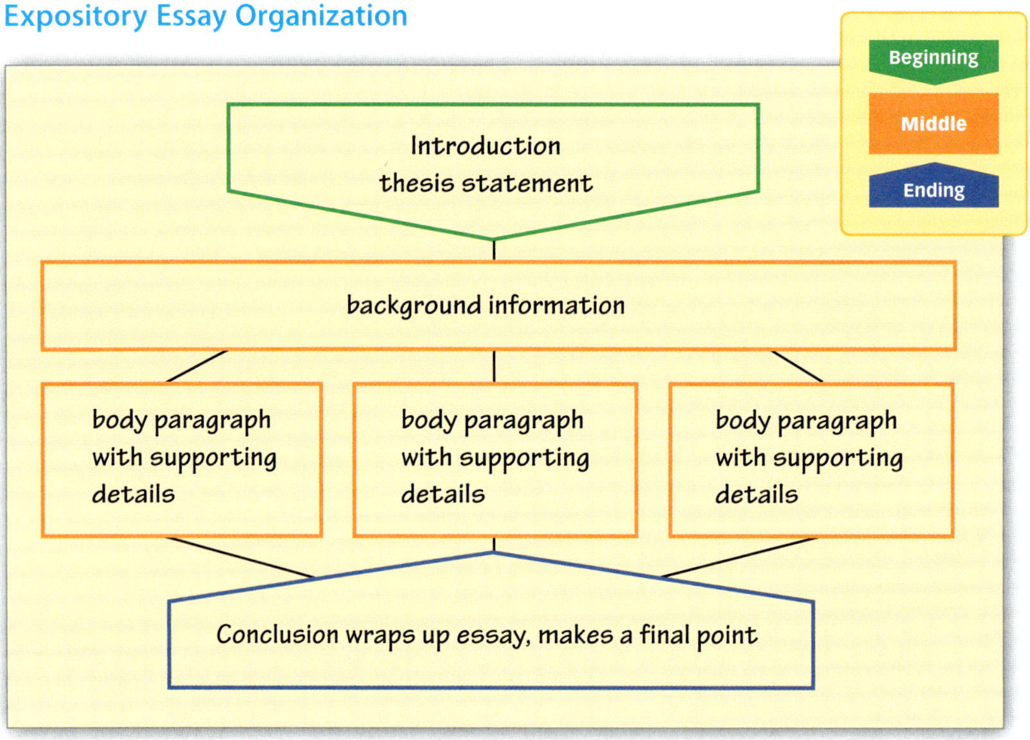

Turn and Talk and Listen

Talk with a partner about why it is important that all parts of the essay work together.

ELPS 2C, 2I, 3A, 3G, 3H, 4C, 4G, 5B, 5G

Vocabulary: Expository Writing

background	**cause**	**effect**
explanation	**expository**	**fact**
paraphrase	**quotation**	**source**
thesis statement		

1. **Say the word or phrase.** Listen actively and carefully as your teacher reads the words aloud. Pay special attention to your teacher's pronunciation of long and short vowel sounds, silent letters, and consonant clusters. Then repeat each word.

2. **Discover the meaning.** Work with a partner. Identify the words you already know. Write notes about their meanings. Review the definitions of terms that you have already heard. Discuss with your partner possible meanings of words you do not yet know.

3. **Learn more.** Listen as your teacher explains the meaning of each word or phrase. Ask for clarification if needed. Work with your partner to review meanings, and correct any misunderstandings.

4. **Think about it.** Use your notebook to answer the questions below.
   - Where should you state your thesis? Why?
   - When and why should you paraphrase and when use quotations?
   - What is the difference between a cause and an effect?
   - Why is the word *opinion* usually not part of expository writing?

5. **Show your understanding.** In your journal, create a graphic organizer that shows the basic structure of an expository essay. Write the vocabulary words in the organizer where they apply. You may wish to add synonyms, or words that mean the same thing. For example, near *paraphrase* you could write *say in your own words.*

6. **Write about it.** Write a brief paragraph explaining how to write an expository essay. Use at least three of the vocabulary words above in your paragraph.

Reading the Expository Model

What Do You Know?

Next you will read a sample expository essay about Charlemagne. Have you ever heard of Charlemagne? What do you already know about him? When and where did he live? What did he do? Talk to a partner about what you know and where you learned it.

Build Background

Charlemagne, or "Charles the Great," was an emperor in Europe during the Middle Ages. He is famous for bringing together many nations into one great empire—the Holy Roman Empire. Charlemagne is known for stabilizing the European economy by balancing trade and commerce. He is also known for his efforts to promote education and learning across the empire.

Listening

Listen as your teacher or a classmate reads aloud "Charlemagne." As you listen, make a note about the thesis statement. Be prepared to answer the questions below.

1. What are two pieces of background information the writer gives?
2. According to the writer, why did Charlemagne stabilize the economy?
3. With what final thought does the writer leave the reader?

Key Words

ability	**by the sword or the cross**	**due to**
in order to	**peace**	**stability**
trust	**when**	

Look at the words and phrases in the box. You will see these when you read the writing model. With a partner, discuss what the words **by the sword or the cross** mean. Use the other words to talk about the effects of another event in history or the effects of an event in your own life, such as an imposed curfew.

Read Along

Now it's your turn to read. Turn to pages 141–142 in this book. Read the writing model as your teacher or a classmate reads it aloud.

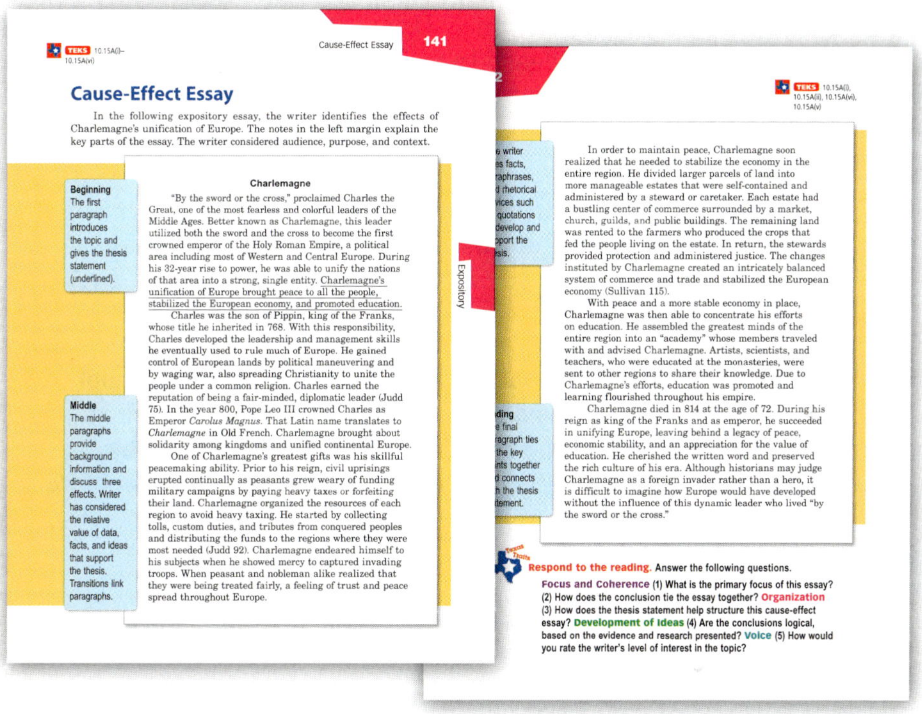

TEKS 10.15A(i)–10.15A(vi)

Cause-Effect Essay 141

Cause-Effect Essay

In the following expository essay, the writer identifies the effects of Charlemagne's unification of Europe. The notes in the left margin explain the key parts of the essay. The writer considered audience, purpose, and context.

Beginning The first paragraph introduces the topic and gives the thesis statement (underlined).

Middle The middle paragraphs provide background information and discuss three effects. Writer has considered the relative value of data, facts, and ideas that support the thesis. Transitions link paragraphs.

Charlemagne

"By the sword or the cross," proclaimed Charles the Great, one of the most fearless and colorful leaders of the Middle Ages. Better known as Charlemagne, this leader utilized both the sword and the cross to become the first crowned emperor of the Holy Roman Empire, a political area including most of Western and Central Europe. During his 32-year rise to power, he was able to unify the nations of that area into a strong, single entity. Charlemagne's unification of Europe brought peace to all the people, stabilized the European economy, and promoted education.

Charles was the son of Pippin, king of the Franks, whose title he inherited in 768. With this responsibility, Charles developed the leadership and management skills he eventually used to rule much of Europe. He gained control of European lands by political maneuvering and by waging war, also spreading Christianity to unite the people under a common religion. Charles earned the reputation of being a fair-minded, diplomatic leader (Judd 75). In the year 800, Pope Leo III crowned Charles as Emperor *Carolus Magnus.* That Latin name translates to *Charlemagne* in Old French. Charlemagne brought about solidarity among kingdoms and unified continental Europe.

One of Charlemagne's greatest gifts was his skillful peacemaking ability. Prior to his reign, civil uprisings erupted continually as peasants grew weary of funding military campaigns by paying heavy taxes or forfeiting their land. Charlemagne organized the resources of each region to avoid heavy taxing. He started by collecting tolls, custom duties, and tributes from conquered peoples and distributing the funds to the regions where they were most needed (Judd 92). Charlemagne endeared himself to his subjects when he showed mercy to captured invading troops. When peasant and nobleman alike realized that they were being treated fairly, a feeling of trust and peace spread throughout Europe.

Expository

TEKS 10.15A(i), 10.15A(ii), 10.15A(vi), 10.15A(v)

In order to maintain peace, Charlemagne soon realized that he needed to stabilize the economy in the entire region. He divided larger parcels of land into more manageable estates that were self-contained and administered by a steward or caretaker. Each estate had a bustling center of commerce surrounded by a market, church, guilds, and public buildings. The remaining land was rented to the farmers who produced the crops that fed the people living on the estate. In return, the stewards provided protection and administered justice. The changes instituted by Charlemagne created an intricately balanced system of commerce and trade and stabilized the European economy (Sullivan 115).

With peace and a more stable economy in place, Charlemagne was then able to concentrate his efforts on education. He assembled the greatest minds of the entire region into an "academy" whose members traveled with and advised Charlemagne. Artists, scientists, and teachers, who were educated at the monasteries, were sent to other regions to share their knowledge. Due to Charlemagne's efforts, education was promoted and learning flourished throughout his empire.

Charlemagne died in 814 at the age of 72. During his reign as king of the Franks and as emperor, he succeeded in unifying Europe, leaving behind a legacy of peace, economic stability, and an appreciation for the value of education. He cherished the written word and preserved the rich culture of his era. Although historians may judge Charlemagne as a foreign invader rather than a hero, it is difficult to imagine how Europe would have developed without the influence of this dynamic leader who lived "by the sword or the cross."

Respond to the reading. Answer the following questions.

Focus and Coherence (1) What is the primary focus of this essay? (2) How does the conclusion tie the essay together? **Organization** (3) How does the thesis statement help structure this cause-effect essay? **Development of Ideas** (4) Are the conclusions logical, based on the evidence and research presented? **Voice** (5) How would you rate the writer's level of interest in the topic?

After Reading

Copy the following chart on a piece of paper. Fill it in with the most important details of each effect of Charlemagne's unification of Europe. Use your chart to summarize the writing model with a partner.

	EFFECTS	DETAILS
peace		
stabilized economy		
education		

ELPS 2I, 3G, 3I

Oral Language: Expository Writing

The person or people who will listen to you or read your writing are called the **audience.** When you speak or write, it is important to choose just the right words that will reach your audience. Use sentence structures that are appropriate for expressing your ideas. In writing and speaking, the **word choice** that you use will be different for each audience.

Try It!

Read about the situation below. Then choose two audiences from the list below. With a partner, discuss how the words you choose might be different for each audience.

Situation

The students at your school would like to have more after-school activities. The student council discussed ways to convince the school board to offer more activities. They decided to focus on benefits by explaining three positive effects of after-school activities on students. You will explain these effects.

Audiences

- a member of the school board, the school principal, a classmate, a younger sibling

Let's Talk!

When you answer a question, you might use one word, a few words, a sentence, or a few sentences.

Example: Why should your school offer more after-school activities?

beneficial

▽

beneficial to students

▽

It would be beneficial to students.

▽

It would benefit the students. They could explore more interests, which would help them make more informed decisions about their futures.

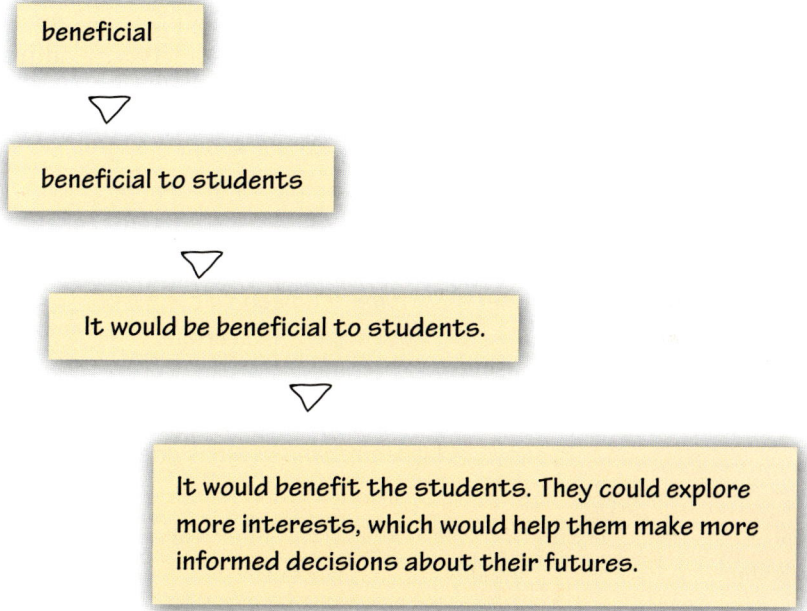

In the first box, there is only a one-word answer. In the other boxes, the writer includes more information. The last box shows the most information. When you use more details to tell about something, the other person will understand it better.

Try It!

Choose a new question that you would like to talk about with a partner. First make notes about details that would give your partner more information about your ideas. Then use your notes to describe your ideas to your partner.

Here are some ideas to get you started.

1. What are the reasons for a school dress code?
2. Why should your school offer more after-school activities?
3. Should your school offer after-school tutoring?

ELPS 3E

The Language of Persuasive Essays

Persuasive essays have a common purpose: to convince the reader to support a position on a topic. The writer uses logical reasons, or arguments, to defend his or her opinion. The writer must also identify and address counter-arguments with logic and reason. The final paragraph usually includes a summary of the reasons to support the writer's position and a call to action.

Persuasive Essay Organization

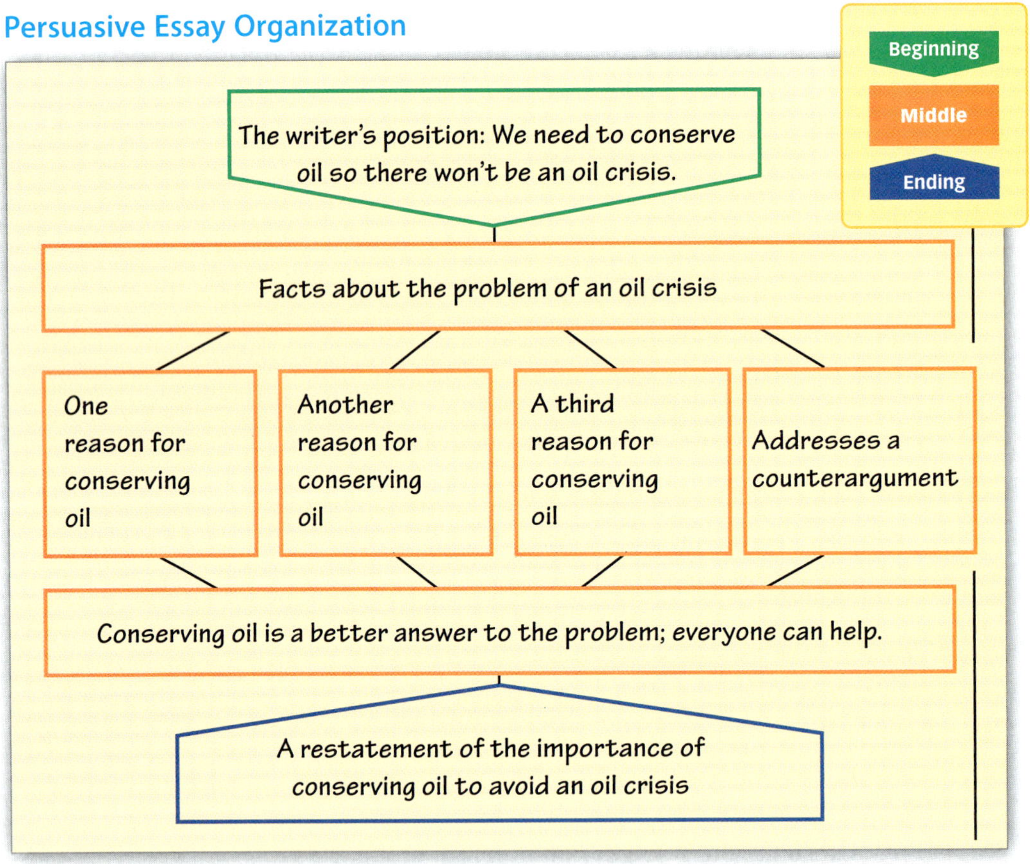
Beginning
Middle
Ending
The writer's position: We need to conserve oil so there won't be an oil crisis.
Facts about the problem of an oil crisis
One reason for conserving oil
Another reason for conserving oil
A third reason for conserving oil
Addresses a counterargument
Conserving oil is a better answer to the problem; everyone can help.
A restatement of the importance of conserving oil to avoid an oil crisis

Turn and Talk and Listen

Talk with a partner about how speeches and debates you might hear during a political campaign are like persuasive essays.

Vocabulary: Persuasive Writing

argument	call to action	counterargument
evidence	objection	opinion
persuade	position	problem
solution	support	

1. **Say the word.** Listen actively and carefully as your teacher reads the words. Pay special attention to your teacher's pronunciation of long and short vowel sounds, silent letters, and consonant clusters. Repeat the words. What part of speech are all of the words? Try to make nouns into verbs and verbs into nouns. Say each word again.

2. **Discover the meaning.** Work with a partner. Define two of the words for your partner. Your partner should then use those words in sentences. Discuss whether or not your partner has used the word correctly.

3. **Clarify.** Listen as your teacher explains the meaning of each word. Work with your partner to find synonyms, words or phrases that mean the same thing, and antonyms, words or phrases that mean the opposite.

4. **Think about it.** Answer the questions below.
   - Which words relate to what the writer thinks?
   - Which word means "to convince"?
   - Which word means "proof or confirmation"?
   - Which word means "the answer to a problem"?
   - Which two words have opposite meanings?

5. **Show your understanding.** Use your vocabulary journal. Write a few sentences about a problem at school and what you think should be done about it and why. Then label parts of your writing with the vocabulary words. Create a graphic organizer that shows the connections among the words. Then write a phrase or give an example of each word from your own writing.

6. **Write about it.** Write a brief paragraph explaining how to write a persuasive essay. Use at least three of the vocabulary words above in your paragraph.

Reading the Persuasive Model

What Do You Know?

What do you and your friends argue about? Are they local or global problems? Think about the issues, and then think of arguments and counterarguments that support and oppose your opinions. What have you learned recently learn about the energy crisis? Do you think it is a serious problem? What are some possible solutions? Talk to your partner, and listen carefully to what your partner has to say, as well.

Build Background

People in America and people around the world use a lot of oil. As well as using oil as fuel, many of the things we use on a daily basis are made from oil. Cleaning supplies, auto parts, eye glasses, and electrical wiring are just a few of the things made from oil. The problem is that there isn't enough oil to supply this huge, growing demand. Running out of oil would cause a world-wide economic crisis. There is a way to avoid this happening—using less oil!

Listening

Listen as your teacher or a classmate reads "Conservation Can Prevent an Oil Crisis" aloud. As you are listening, make notes about the problem and facts that explain the problem. Jot down the solution and three reasons for the solution. Write another solution that the writer doesn't agree with and tell why. What does the writer ask the reader to think about at the end of the essay? Be ready to answer the questions below.

1. What is the writer's position?
2. Name four reasons the writer gives for the proposed solution.
3. What solution to the problem does the writer not agree with? Why?

Key Words

conserve	**economists**	**estimates**
exceed	**gas-guzzling**	**global warming**
short-term	**trends**	**worry**

Look at the words and phrases in the box. You will see them when you read the writing model. With a partner, discuss connections among the words.

Read Along

Now it's your turn to read. Turn to page 199 in this book. Read the writing model as your teacher or classmate reads it aloud.

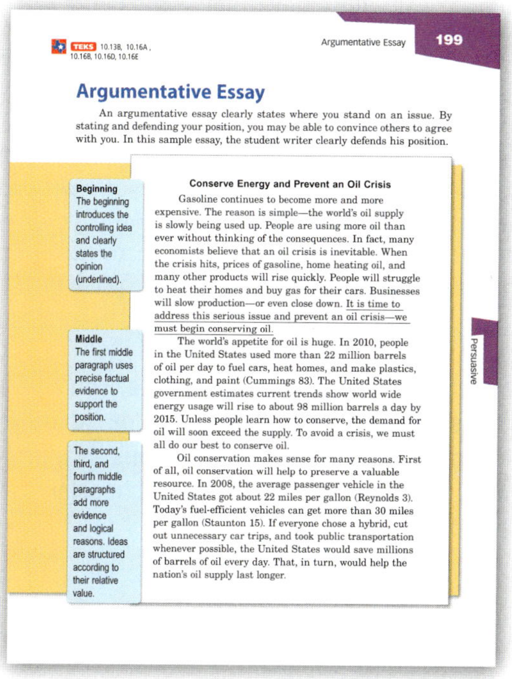

TEKS 10.13B, 10.16A, 10.16B, 10.16D, 10.16E

Argumentative Essay 199

Argumentative Essay

An argumentative essay clearly states where you stand on an issue. By stating and defending your position, you may be able to convince others to agree with you. In this sample essay, the student writer clearly defends his position.

Beginning The beginning introduces the controlling idea and clearly states the opinion (underlined).

Middle The first middle paragraph uses precise factual evidence to support the position.

The second, third, and fourth middle paragraphs add more evidence and logical reasons. Ideas are structured according to their relative value.

Conserve Energy and Prevent an Oil Crisis

Gasoline continues to become more and more expensive. The reason is simple—the world's oil supply is slowly being used up. People are using more oil than ever without thinking of the consequences. In fact, many economists believe that an oil crisis is inevitable. When the crisis hits, prices of gasoline, home heating oil, and many other products will rise quickly. People will struggle to heat their homes and buy gas for their cars. Businesses will slow production—or even close down. It is time to address this serious issue and prevent an oil crisis—we must begin conserving oil.

The world's appetite for oil is huge. In 2010, people in the United States used more than 22 million barrels of oil per day to fuel cars, heat homes, and make plastics, clothing, and paint (Cummings 83). The United States government estimates current trends show world wide energy usage will rise to about 98 million barrels a day by 2015. Unless people learn how to conserve, the demand for oil will soon exceed the supply. To avoid a crisis, we must all do our best to conserve oil.

Oil conservation makes sense for many reasons. First of all, oil conservation will help to preserve a valuable resource. In 2008, the average passenger vehicle in the United States got about 22 miles per gallon (Reynolds 3). Today's fuel-efficient vehicles can get more than 30 miles per gallon (Staunton 15). If everyone chose a hybrid, cut out unnecessary car trips, and took public transportation whenever possible, the United States would save millions of barrels of oil every day. That, in turn, would help the nation's oil supply last longer.

Persuasive

After Reading

Look at the key words in the box. With a partner, choose a social or environmental problem to discuss. Agree about three solutions. Then discuss the problem and solutions. Use the words in the box in your discussion.

On a separate piece of paper, respond to the following questions about the writing model. Share your answers with your partner or in a small group.

1. Why does the writer say that people could struggle in the future to heat their homes and buy gas for their cars?
2. What does the writer say will happen if people don't learn how to conserve?
3. How does the writer say the U.S. could save millions of barrels of oil every day?
4. What is the economic benefit to consumers of conserving oil?
5. Why does the writer of the writing model think it is better to conserve oil than to drill more oil wells?

Oral Language

When you speak or write, the words you choose depend on your audience. Your goal is to create a persuasive message that will influence your audience to support your position. While your persuasive message will stay the same, you should tailor your tone and your language to the audience you are addressing.

Try It!

Read the situation and then select two audiences from the list below. With your partner, discuss how you would vary your persuasive message for two very different audiences. What changes would you make for each audience in tone, voice, and word choice? What arguments and words would you use to convince each audience to support your position?

Role-Play

Imagine that your school doesn't recycle. You and your partner are members of the student council and want to persuade your audience that your school needs to start recycling soda cans, plastic bottles, and paper. Convince your audience that this change is important and that they should support your efforts.

Audiences

- **school principal, community member who wants to help the school, parent, teacher, classmates**

Let's Talk!

When you answer a question, you might use one word, a few words, a sentence, or a few sentences. Below are possible answers to the question **What is one problem in your community?**

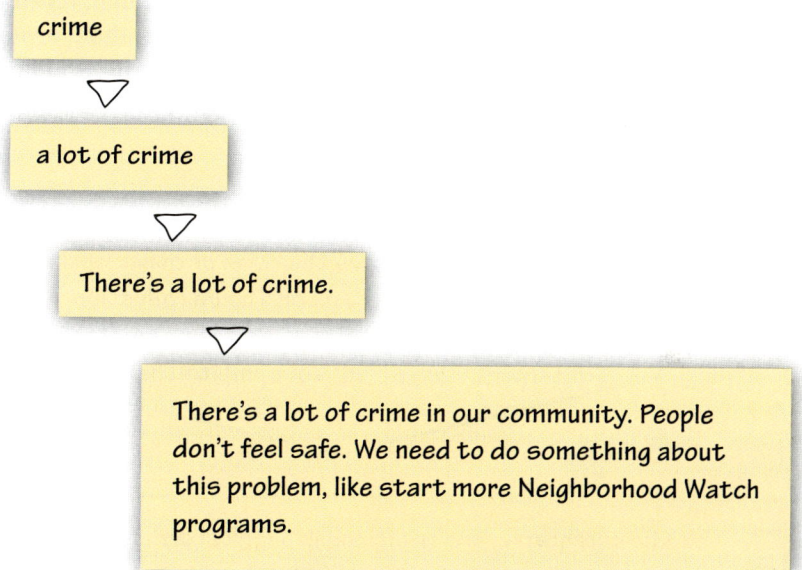

crime

a lot of crime

There's a lot of crime.

There's a lot of crime in our community. People don't feel safe. We need to do something about this problem, like start more Neighborhood Watch programs.

Try It!

Choose an issue that interests you. Answer these questions about the issue: What is my position? What logical solution or call to action can I propose? What arguments can I use to support my position? What are some counterarguments and how can I address them?

Brainstorm words and details that describe your position and your arguments. Use a graphic organizer to rank your arguments from most to least important.

Turn and Talk and Listen

Tell a partner about a problem in your community that concerns you. Remember to use as much detail as you can. You can use the sentence frames below.

________________ is a problem. One way to solve this problem is ________________________.

ELPS 3E

Interpretive Response

An interpretive response is writing that tells about something you have read, usually a novel, short story, poem, or essay. In an interpretive response to a work of literature, you should analyze at least one theme, often two. A theme is the writer's message. A novel or play may have one theme, or it may have several. This type of essay has a beginning, a middle, and an ending. Each part works with the other parts to form a cohesive, coherent whole.

Interpretive Response Essay Organization

Beginning

Middle

Ending

The beginning introduces the novel or other work of literature and the author. The introduction also states the thesis. The thesis is the writer's interpretation of the work and its theme.

Middle paragraphs are organized in a logical order and give specific details from the work to support the thesis statement. Embedded quotations are used to support the writer's interpretation of the theme and to add support for the thesis statement.

The ending analyzes the themes.

Turn and Talk and Listen

Talk with a partner about how to organize an interpretive response essay and how to determine the themes in a literary work.

ELPS 2C, 3A, 3B, 4C, 5B, 5G

Vocabulary: Interpretive Response

analyze	annotate	cohesive
interpretation	plot	quotations
response	summarize	theme

Listen actively and carefully as your teacher reads each word. Pay special attention to your teacher's pronunciation of long and short vowel sounds, silent letters, and consonant clusters. Repeat the words.

1. **Discover the meaning.** Work with a partner. Find some of the vocabulary words on page 550. Write notes about what you think each of the words means. Use the context in which the words appear on page 550 as clues.

2. **Learn more.** Listen as your teacher explains the meaning of each word. Then work with a partner to review the meanings you just heard. Write down any words that you still don't understand. Ask clarifying questions and discuss your questions with your teacher if you do not understand completely.

3. **Think about it.** Use your notebook to answer the questions below.
   - Why is it important for your essay to be cohesive?
   - How does the plot relate to the theme?
   - What is the difference between an analysis and a summary?
   - When does a writer analyze the theme?
   - How can quotations help support the thesis statement and clarify the theme?

4. **Show your understanding.** Use your vocabulary journal. Outline a response to a literature essay using as many vocabulary words as you can. Write a few sentences about any other vocabulary words. Add notes to help you remember and understand the words.

5. **Write about it.** Write a brief paragraph explaining how to write an interpretive response essay. Use at least three of the vocabulary words above in your paragraph.

Reading the Response to Literature Model

What Do You Know?

Next you will read a sample response to a literature essay about a scientist who creates a superhuman being. What stories and movies have you seen that have superhuman beings or monsters? How are they treated by others?

Build Background

For centuries, scientists have been intrigued with the idea of creating life. We know that some of that is possible today. However, when Mary Shelley wrote *Frankenstein,* the idea of actually creating life was true science fiction.

Shelley finished writing *Frankenstein* when she was just 19. Her first edition was published anonymously in 1818 in London. The main character, Victor Frankenstein, is a scientist who learns how to create life. He creates a being in the likeness of man, but larger than average and more powerful.

Listening

Listen as your teacher or a classmate reads aloud "Monsters are Made, Not Born." As you listen, make notes about what decisions Victor Frankenstein made. Think about what the consequences were. Be prepared to answer the questions below.

1. Why does Shelley say the lives of Frankenstein and his monster are "tragic"?
2. Why is Victor relieved that the monster escapes? How does that feeling change later?
3. If Victor Frankenstein were to start over, what do you think he would have done differently?

Key Words

barbarity of man	**deformed**	**eerie**
monster	**outcasts**	**tortured**
unhallowed arts	**vicious**	

Look at the key words in the box. These words appear in the sample. Write a sentence for each word or phrase using the meaning from the essay. Trade sentences with a partner. Discuss how your understandings of each word are the same or different. Consider another meaning for some of the words. Write sentences to reflect those meanings.

Read Along

Now it's your turn to read. Turn to pages 257–258 in this book. Read the writing model as your teacher or classmate reads it aloud.

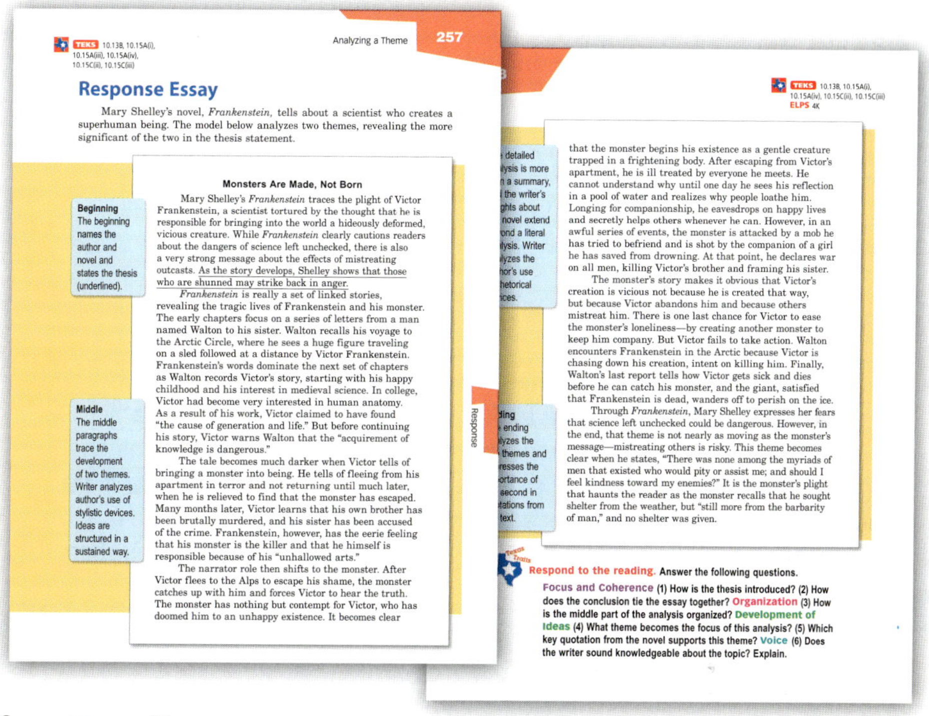
TEKS 10.13B, 10.15A(i), 10.15A(iii), 10.15A(iv), 10.15C(ii), 10.15C(iii)

Analyzing a Theme 257

Response Essay

Mary Shelley's novel, *Frankenstein,* tells about a scientist who creates a superhuman being. The model below analyzes two themes, revealing the more significant of the two in the thesis statement.

Beginning The beginning names the author and novel and states the thesis (underlined).

Monsters Are Made, Not Born

Mary Shelley's *Frankenstein* traces the plight of Victor Frankenstein, a scientist tortured by the thought that he is responsible for bringing into the world a hideously deformed, vicious creature. While *Frankenstein* clearly cautions readers about the dangers of science left unchecked, there is also a very strong message about the effects of mistreating outcasts. As the story develops, Shelley shows that those who are shunned may strike back in anger.

Middle The middle paragraphs trace the development of two themes. Writer analyzes author's use of stylistic devices. Ideas are structured in a sustained way.

Frankenstein is really a set of linked stories, revealing the tragic lives of Frankenstein and his monster. The early chapters focus on a series of letters from a man named Walton to his sister. Walton recalls his voyage to the Arctic Circle, where he sees a huge figure traveling on a sled followed at a distance by Victor Frankenstein. Frankenstein's words dominate the next set of chapters as Walton records Victor's story, starting with his happy childhood and his interest in medieval science. In college, Victor had become very interested in human anatomy. As a result of his work, Victor claimed to have found "the cause of generation and life." But before continuing his story, Victor warns Walton that the "acquirement of knowledge is dangerous."

The tale becomes much darker when Victor tells of bringing a monster into being. He tells of fleeing from his apartment in terror and not returning until much later, when he is relieved to find that the monster has escaped. Many months later, Victor learns that his own brother has been brutally murdered, and his sister has been accused of the crime. Frankenstein, however, has the eerie feeling that his monster is the killer and that he himself is responsible because of his "unhallowed arts."

The narrator role then shifts to the monster. After Victor flees to the Alps to escape his shame, the monster catches up with him and forces Victor to hear the truth. The monster has nothing but contempt for Victor, who has doomed him to an unhappy existence. It becomes clear

Response

TEKS 10.13B, 10.15A(i), 10.15A(iv), 10.15C(ii), 10.15C(iii) ELPS 4K

detailed lysis is more n a summary, the writer's ghts about novel extend ond a literal lysis. Writer lyzes the hor's use hetorical ices.

that the monster begins his existence as a gentle creature trapped in a frightening body. After escaping from Victor's apartment, he is ill treated by everyone he meets. He cannot understand why until one day he sees his reflection in a pool of water and realizes why people loathe him. Longing for companionship, he eavesdrops on happy lives and secretly helps others whenever he can. However, in an awful series of events, the monster is attacked by a mob he has tried to befriend and is shot by the companion of a girl he has saved from drowning. At that point, he declares war on all men, killing Victor's brother and framing his sister.

The monster's story makes it obvious that Victor's creation is vicious not because he is created that way, but because Victor abandons him and because others mistreat him. There is one last chance for Victor to ease the monster's loneliness—by creating another monster to keep him company. But Victor fails to take action. Walton encounters Frankenstein in the Arctic because Victor is chasing down his creation, intent on killing him. Finally, Walton's last report tells how Victor gets sick and dies before he can catch his monster, and the giant, satisfied that Frankenstein is dead, wanders off to perish on the ice.

ding ending lyzes the themes and resses the ortance of second in tations from text.

Through *Frankenstein*, Mary Shelley expresses her fears that science left unchecked could be dangerous. However, in the end, that theme is not nearly as moving as the monster's message—mistreating others is risky. This theme becomes clear when he states, "There was none among the myriads of men that existed who would pity or assist me; and should I feel kindness toward my enemies?" It is the monster's plight that haunts the reader as the monster recalls that he sought shelter from the weather, but "still more from the barbarity of man," and no shelter was given.

Texas Traits

Respond to the reading. Answer the following questions.

Focus and Coherence (1) How is the thesis introduced? (2) How does the conclusion tie the essay together? **Organization** (3) How is the middle part of the analysis organized? **Development of Ideas** (4) What theme becomes the focus of this analysis? (5) Which key quotation from the novel supports this theme? **Voice** (6) Does the writer sound knowledgeable about the topic? Explain.

After Reading

Copy the table below and use some of the key words to describe the actions of Victor Frankenstein. Use other words to describe the monster and how people reacted to him.

Victor Frankenstein	Monster

ELPS 3G, 3I

Oral Language

The person or people who will listen to you or read your writing are called the **audience.** When you speak or write, it is important to choose just the right words that will reach your audience. In writing and speaking, choose words that express your own opinions, ideas, and feelings, and participate in discussions about the literature.

Try It!

Read about the situation below. Then choose two audiences from the list. With a partner, discuss how the words you choose might be different for each audience.

Situation

You read a novel where the main character has an argument with her father. She wants to move to France to be an artist, and her father is against it. She moves to France anyway, but while there, she learns an important lesson, which is one theme of the book. She also learns more about the importance of friends and family, both young and old. Use your imagination to fill in details of the story. Then tell about the book's themes.

Audiences

- teacher or parent, third-grade child, classmate, grandparent

Let's Talk!

When you answer a question, sometimes one word will do. Most often, more details are needed to communicate to your audience.

Example: What is one theme of the novel?

argument

argument about her future

The main character and her dad argue, and she moves to France.

The main character wants to be an artist in France. Her father disagrees, and they argue. She moves to France, but later realizes how much she misses her family and friends.

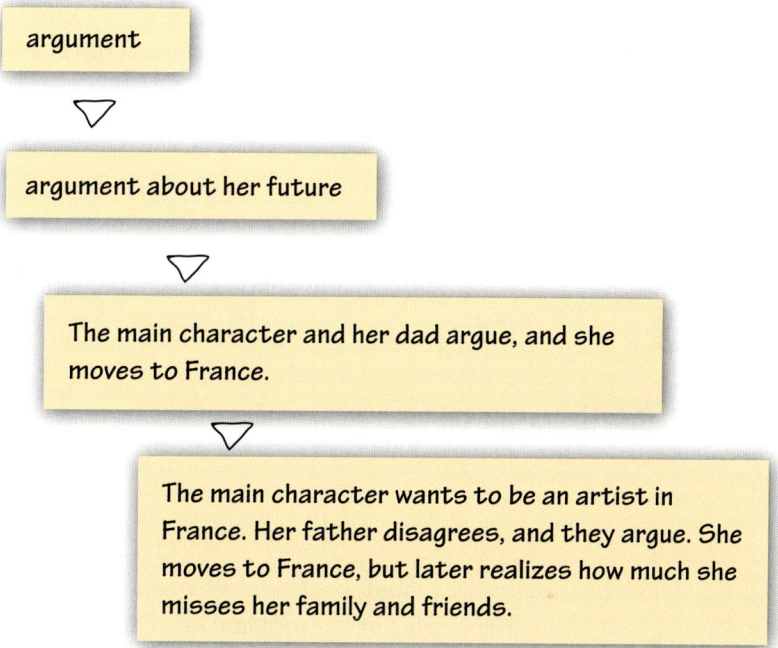

In the first box, there is only a one-word answer. In the other boxes, the writer includes more information. The last box shows the most information. The more details you add to your story, the better the reader or listener will be able to understand and visualize what you mean.

Try It!

Work with a partner. Choose a story that you have both recently read. Choose a new question that you would like to talk about. Make notes about details that would give your partner more information about your ideas. Then use your notes to describe your ideas to your partner.

Here are some ideas to get you started.

1. How can you describe the main character?
2. What is the main theme of the book?
3. What lessons does the main character learn?

ELPS 3E

Creative Writing

Creative writing often tells a fictional story. This type of writing can take the form of a story, a play, or even a poem. Most often, creative writing that tells a story has the same basic organization: an introduction of the characters, conflict, and setting; action that rises, climaxes, and falls; and a resolution. Look at this graphic organizer. It shows what is in each part of a piece of creative writing.

Creative Writing Organization

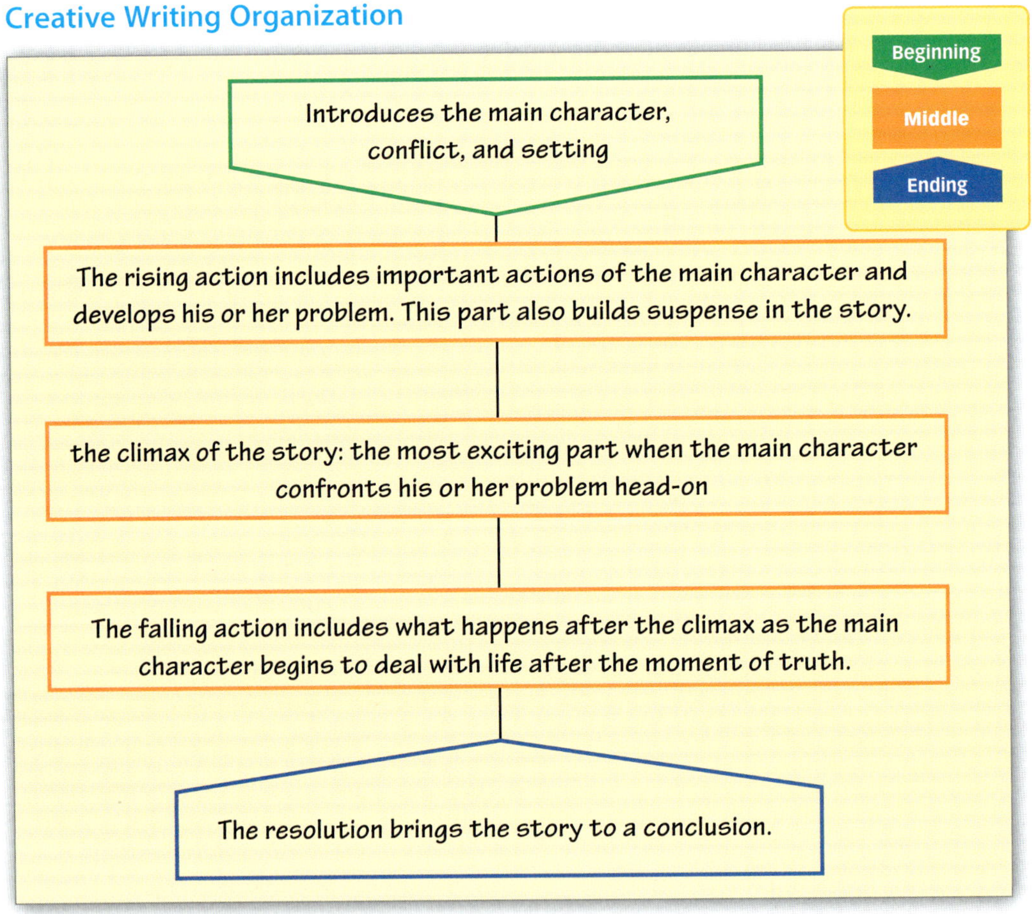

Beginning
Middle
Ending
Introduces the main character, conflict, and setting
The rising action includes important actions of the main character and develops his or her problem. This part also builds suspense in the story.
the climax of the story: the most exciting part when the main character confronts his or her problem head-on
The falling action includes what happens after the climax as the main character begins to deal with life after the moment of truth.
The resolution brings the story to a conclusion.

Turn and Talk and Listen

Talk with a partner about one important part of the graphic organizer. Discuss how the parts of a story build on each other to form a whole.

Vocabulary: Creative Writing

climax	complication	conflict
exposition	falling action	plot
resolution	rising action	tension

1. **Say the word or phrase.** Listen actively and carefully as your teacher reads the words and phrases aloud. Pay special attention to your teacher's pronunciation of long and short vowel sounds, silent letters, and consonant clusters. Then repeat each word or phrase.

2. **Discover the meaning.** Think about what you know about creative writing. Working with a partner, write notes about what you think the words and phrases mean.

3. **Learn more.** Listen carefully as your teacher explains the meaning of each word. Ask questions to ensure that you understand the meaning and use of each word. Work with your partner to make changes and additions to your notes about what the words mean.

4. **Think about it.** Use your notebook to answer the questions below.
   - Which happens first in creative writing—a climax or the falling action? Explain why.
   - How does the conflict or complication add to a story?
   - Why would a writer place the climax near the end of a story?
   - Which term best describes the part of a fairy tale that ends with the words "and they lived happily ever after"?

5. **Show your understanding.** In your vocabulary journal, write short sentences to help you remember the meaning of each of the words and phrases. Where appropriate, list examples or synonyms to show the meaning of the word.

6. **Write about it.** Write a brief paragraph explaining how to write a story, play, or narrative poem (a poem that tells a story). Use at least three of the vocabulary words above in your paragraph.

Reading the Creative Writing Model

What Do You Know?

Next you will read a creative writing script about a boy who is interviewing for a part-time job. Do you think appearances matter when interviewing for a job? Would your opinion change depending on the kind of job it was? Tell what you think.

Build Background

Many students have part-time jobs after school or on the weekends. Not only do these students earn money, but they learn the importance of showing up at work on time and doing a job effectively. If students are interested, they have the opportunity to learn how businesses are run. They may be mopping up in a restaurant, but they can see what the waiters, cooks, and even managers do each day.

Listening

Listen as your teacher or a classmate reads aloud *Suiting Up*. As you listen, make notes about the interchanges between the characters and how the story resolves itself. Be prepared to answer the questions below.

1. How is the format of a script different than a story?
2. Why did Wesley have similar encounters with Luke and Tori?
3. Do you think Wesley got the job in the end?

Key Words

competition	**down payment**	**earn some bucks**
executive position	**frozen**	**impression**
shoot some hoops	**stocking shelves**	**suited up**
well groomed		

Look at the words and phrases in the box. You will see these words when you read the writing sample. With a partner, use the words to talk about jobs and money.

Read Along

Now it's your turn to read. Turn to pages 334–336 in this book. Read the writing model as your teacher or a classmate reads it aloud.

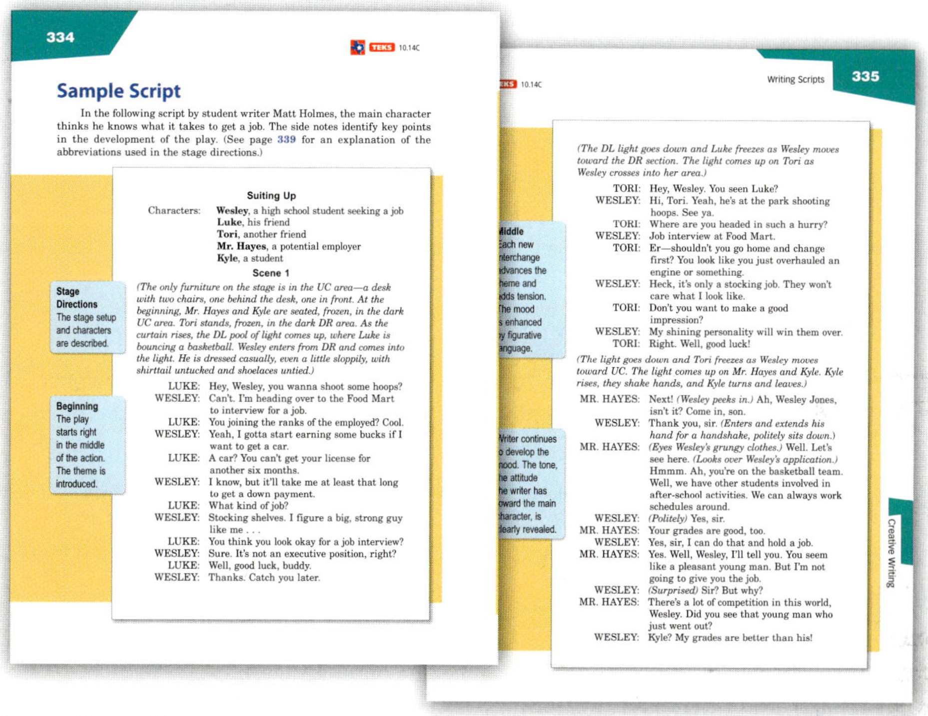
334 TEKS 10.14C

Sample Script

In the following script by student writer Matt Holmes, the main character thinks he knows what it takes to get a job. The side notes identify key points in the development of the play. (See page 339 for an explanation of the abbreviations used in the stage directions.)

Suiting Up

Characters: **Wesley**, a high school student seeking a job
Luke, his friend
Tori, another friend
Mr. Hayes, a potential employer
Kyle, a student

Scene 1

Stage Directions The stage setup and characters are described.

(The only furniture on the stage is in the UC area—a desk with two chairs, one behind the desk, one in front. At the beginning, Mr. Hayes and Kyle are seated, frozen, in the dark UC area. Tori stands, frozen, in the dark DR area. As the curtain rises, the DL pool of light comes up, where Luke is bouncing a basketball. Wesley enters from DR and comes into the light. He is dressed casually, even a little sloppily, with shirttail untucked and shoelaces untied.)

Beginning The play starts right in the middle of the action. The theme is introduced.

LUKE: Hey, Wesley, you wanna shoot some hoops?
WESLEY: Can't. I'm heading over to the Food Mart to interview for a job.
LUKE: You joining the ranks of the employed? Cool.
WESLEY: Yeah, I gotta start earning some bucks if I want to get a car.
LUKE: A car? You can't get your license for another six months.
WESLEY: I know, but it'll take me at least that long to get a down payment.
LUKE: What kind of job?
WESLEY: Stocking shelves. I figure a big, strong guy like me . . .
LUKE: You think you look okay for a job interview?
WESLEY: Sure. It's not an executive position, right?
LUKE: Well, good luck, buddy.
WESLEY: Thanks. Catch you later.

EKS 10.14C Writing Scripts 335

(The DL light goes down and Luke freezes as Wesley moves toward the DR section. The light comes up on Tori as Wesley crosses into her area.)

iddle ach new nterchange dvances the heme and dds tension. he mood s enhanced y figurative anguage.

TORI: Hey, Wesley. You seen Luke?
WESLEY: Hi, Tori. Yeah, he's at the park shooting hoops. See ya.
TORI: Where are you headed in such a hurry?
WESLEY: Job interview at Food Mart.
TORI: Er—shouldn't you go home and change first? You look like you just overhauled an engine or something.
WESLEY: Heck, it's only a stocking job. They won't care what I look like.
TORI: Don't you want to make a good impression?
WESLEY: My shining personality will win them over.
TORI: Right. Well, good luck!

(The light goes down and Tori freezes as Wesley moves toward UC. The light comes up on Mr. Hayes and Kyle. Kyle rises, they shake hands, and Kyle turns and leaves.)

riter continues o develop the ood. The tone, he attitude he writer has ward the main haracter, is early revealed.

MR. HAYES: Next! *(Wesley peeks in.)* Ah, Wesley Jones, isn't it? Come in, son.
WESLEY: Thank you, sir. *(Enters and extends his hand for a handshake, politely sits down.)*
MR. HAYES: *(Eyes Wesley's grungy clothes.)* Well. Let's see here. *(Looks over Wesley's application.)* Hmmm. Ah, you're on the basketball team. Well, we have other students involved in after-school activities. We can always work schedules around.
WESLEY: *(Politely)* Yes, sir.
MR. HAYES: Your grades are good, too.
WESLEY: Yes, sir, I can do that and hold a job.
MR. HAYES: Yes. Well, Wesley, I'll tell you. You seem like a pleasant young man. But I'm not going to give you the job.
WESLEY: *(Surprised)* Sir? But why?
MR. HAYES: There's a lot of competition in this world, Wesley. Did you see that young man who just went out?
WESLEY: Kyle? My grades are better than his!

Creative Writing

After Reading

Copy the table below. In one column, write phrases that describe Mr. Hayes's impression of Wesley. In the second column, write some of the phrases that Tori uses to tell Wesley that he is not dressed appropriately for a job interview.

Use the information in your chart to summarize the script, explaining what lesson Wesley learned.

Mr. Hayes	Tori

Oral Language: Creative Writing

The person or people who will listen to you or read your writing are called the **audience.** When you speak or write, it is important to think about the right words to use so your audience will understand your ideas and opinions. The **tone,** or the way you write, will be different for each audience.

Try It!

Read about the situation below. Then choose two audiences from the list that follows. With a partner, discuss how the words you choose might be different for each audience.

Situation

Everyone knows that Roberta is the best player on the basketball team. She is the one the team turns to when there is a big game. However, Roberta is always late for practice. She misses a lot of games if she knows she isn't going to start as center. The playoffs are beginning, and the team is playing their archrival. The coach asks Stephanie to start as center. Roberta is furious, but the coach tells Roberta that Stephanie is a team player. You will retell the story.

Audiences

- classmate, basketball coach, elementary school student

Let's Talk!

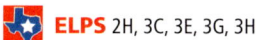

When you answer a question, you might use one word, a few words, a sentence, or a few sentences.

Example: What problem does the coach have with Roberta?

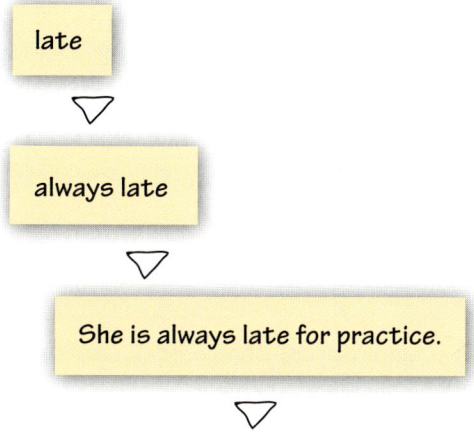

late

▽

always late

▽

She is always late for practice.

▽

Even though Roberta is the best player, she is always late for practice. She misses a lot of games if she knows she isn't going to start as center. The coach doesn't want to reward her bad behavior by letting her start.

In the first box, there is only a one-word answer. In the other boxes, the writer includes more information. The last box shows the most information. It lets you understand what the writer is thinking. When you use more details to tell about something, the person you are addressing will have a much better understanding of what you mean.

Try It!

Choose a new question that you would like to talk about with a partner. Make notes about details that would give your partner more information. Then use your notes to describe your ideas to your partner.

Here are some ideas to get you started.

1. What problem might you have working on a group class project?
2. What problem might you have as a server in a restaurant?

ELPS 3E, 3G, 3H

Research Writing

Research involves exploring a topic of interest in detail using multiple sources and identifying important issues and debates about the topic. Research writing is the presentation of that knowledge to an audience. Research reports need an introduction that includes the thesis statement and sections that develop the topic with supporting evidence and details. Reports end with a conclusion that sums up the paper and leaves the reader with a final thought about the topic. Sections are often separated by headings. A works-cited page is also included.

Research Writing Organization

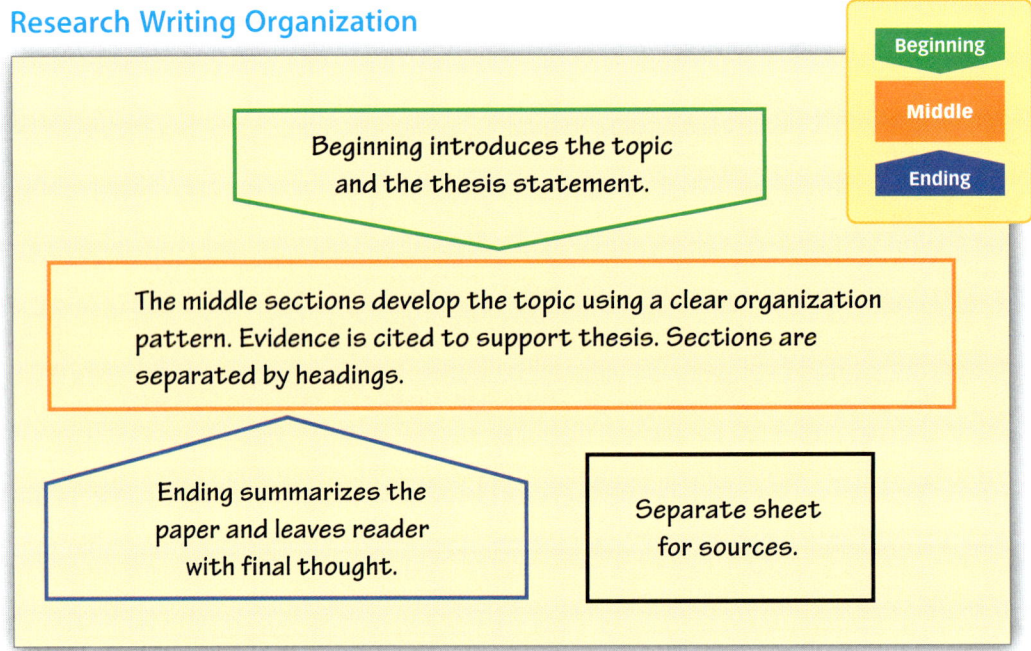

Beginning

Middle

Ending

Beginning introduces the topic and the thesis statement.

The middle sections develop the topic using a clear organization pattern. Evidence is cited to support thesis. Sections are separated by headings.

Ending summarizes the paper and leaves reader with final thought.

Separate sheet for sources.

Turn and Talk and Listen

Talk with a partner about why it is important for a research paper to include plenty of supporting details.

Vocabulary: Research Writing

authoritative	headings	outline
paraphrase	plagiarism	quotation
reliable	source cited	supporting details
transitions	valid	

1. **Say the word or phrase.** Listen actively and carefully as your teacher reads each word or phrase aloud. Pay special attention to your teacher's pronunciation of long and short vowel sounds, silent letters, and consonant clusters. Then repeat each word or phrase.

2. **Discover the meaning.** Work with a partner to discuss meanings of the words that you know. Write notes about what you and your partner think the words mean in the context of research writing.

3. **Learn more.** Listen as your teacher explains each word or phrase. Work with your partner to correct your earlier notes. Ask questions if you still do not understand the words or how they relate to research writing.

4. **Think about it.** Use the information in your notebook to help you answer the questions below.
   - How are headings useful in a research report?
   - What role do transitions play in a research report?
   - When might you paraphrase instead of using an exact quote?
   - Why must you cite sources and create a sources-cited page?
   - What is the difference between paraphrasing and plagiarism?
   - What does it mean when a source is authoritative and valid?

5. **Show your understanding.** In your vocabulary journal, add related words to help you remember what each word means. For example, write **alphabetical order** and **indented** next to **source cited** to remember how sources are listed.

6. **Write about it.** Write a paragraph or two explaining how to write a research essay. Use at least three of the vocabulary words above in your paragraphs.

Reading the Research Writing Model

What Do You Know?

Next you will read a research report about the Aswan High Dam in Egypt. What do you know about dams? Why are they built? How do they help the people who live near them? What problems might they cause?

Build Background

Dams have been around for thousands of years. They are built to prevent flooding and to allow communities to store excess water in rainy years. Some dams provide electric power as well. Modern dams are complicated engineering feats. One of the best-known dams in the United States is the Hoover Dam, completed in 1936. By diverting the water from the Colorado River, the largest reservoir in the United States, Lake Mead, was created.

Listening

Listen as your teacher or a classmate reads aloud "The Aswan High Dam." As you listen, make notes about the dam. Be prepared to answer the questions below.

1. Why was the Aswan High Dam created?
2. Under what conditions did the construction team work? Explain.
3. What is one benefit of the Aswan High Dam to Egypt?

Key Words

catastrophic	contaminated	detrimental effects
fertilize	forced evacuation	hydroelectric power
irrigation	reservoir	toxins
urban development		

Look at the words in the box. You will see these words when you read the writing sample. With a partner, use the words to talk about consequences that may occur when people build dams. Think about whether the benefits always outweigh the problems.

Read Along

Now it's your turn to read. Turn to pages 373–379 in this book. Read the writing model as your teacher or a classmate reads it aloud.

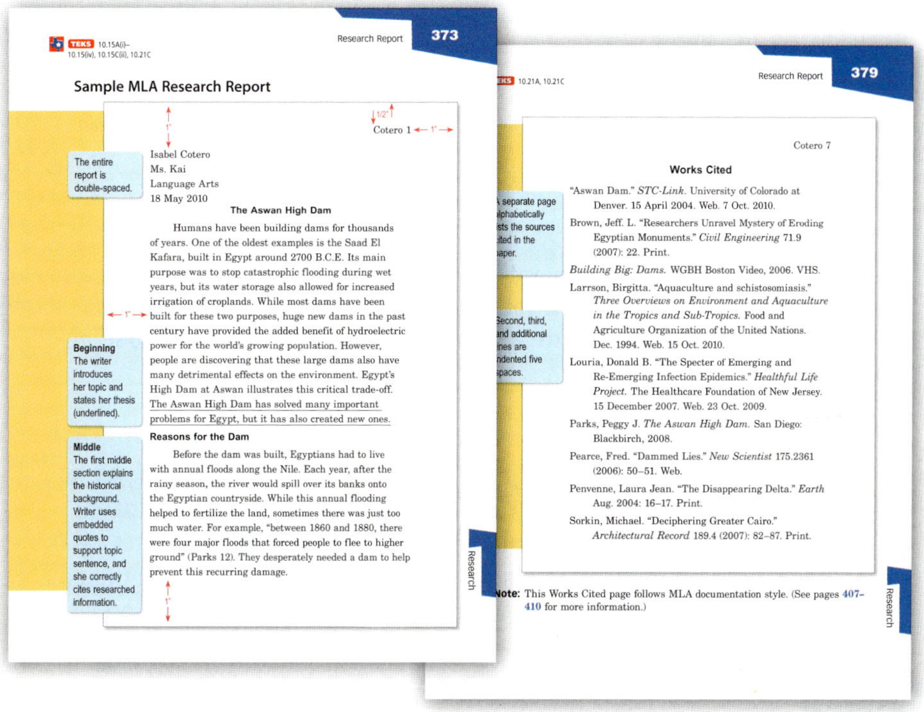

TEKS 10.15A(i)–10.15(iv), 10.15C(iii), 10.21C

Research Report 373

Sample MLA Research Report

Cotero 1

Isabel Cotero
Ms. Kai
Language Arts
18 May 2010

The Aswan High Dam

Humans have been building dams for thousands of years. One of the oldest examples is the Saad El Kafara, built in Egypt around 2700 B.C.E. Its main purpose was to stop catastrophic flooding during wet years, but its water storage also allowed for increased irrigation of croplands. While most dams have been built for these two purposes, huge new dams in the past century have provided the added benefit of hydroelectric power for the world's growing population. However, people are discovering that these large dams also have many detrimental effects on the environment. Egypt's High Dam at Aswan illustrates this critical trade-off. The Aswan High Dam has solved many important problems for Egypt, but it has also created new ones.

Reasons for the Dam

Before the dam was built, Egyptians had to live with annual floods along the Nile. Each year, after the rainy season, the river would spill over its banks onto the Egyptian countryside. While this annual flooding helped to fertilize the land, sometimes there was just too much water. For example, "between 1860 and 1880, there were four major floods that forced people to flee to higher ground" (Parks 12). They desperately needed a dam to help prevent this recurring damage.

The entire report is double-spaced.

Beginning The writer introduces her topic and states her thesis (underlined).

Middle The first middle section explains the historical background. Writer uses embedded quotes to support topic sentence, and she correctly cites researched information.

Research

10.21A, 10.21C

Research Report 379

Cotero 7

Works Cited

"Aswan Dam." *STC-Link.* University of Colorado at Denver. 15 April 2004. Web. 7 Oct. 2010.

Brown, Jeff. L. "Researchers Unravel Mystery of Eroding Egyptian Monuments." *Civil Engineering* 71.9 (2007): 22. Print.

Building Big: Dams. WGBH Boston Video, 2006. VHS.

Larrson, Birgitta. "Aquaculture and schistosomiasis." *Three Overviews on Environment and Aquaculture in the Tropics and Sub-Tropics.* Food and Agriculture Organization of the United Nations. Dec. 1994. Web. 15 Oct. 2010.

Louria, Donald B. "The Specter of Emerging and Re-Emerging Infection Epidemics." *Healthful Life Project.* The Healthcare Foundation of New Jersey. 15 December 2007. Web. 23 Oct. 2009.

Parks, Peggy J. *The Aswan High Dam.* San Diego: Blackbirch, 2008.

Pearce, Fred. "Dammed Lies." *New Scientist* 175.2361 (2006): 50–51. Web.

Penvenne, Laura Jean. "The Disappearing Delta." *Earth* Aug. 2004: 16–17. Print.

Sorkin, Michael. "Deciphering Greater Cairo." *Architectural Record* 189.4 (2007): 82–87. Print.

A separate page alphabetically lists the sources cited in the paper.

Second, third, and additional lines are indented five spaces.

Note: This Works Cited page follows MLA documentation style. (See pages 407–410 for more information.)

Research

After Reading

On a separate piece of paper, write answers to these questions about the writing model.

1. Why is it a problem if water and soil get contaminated?
2. How can dams help urban development?
3. When would it be necessary to have a forced evacuation?
4. How can dams help protect against both flooding and drought?
5. What are some of the health problems associated with the Aswan High Dam? Explain your answer.

Work with a partner to compare the outline on page 392 to the research report. Then discuss with your partner how you think the outline helped the writer create a clear organization pattern for the report.

ELPS 3E, 3G, 3I

Oral Language: Research Report Writing

The person or people who will listen to you or read your writing are called the **audience.** When you speak or write, it is important to think about the right words to use so your audience will relate to and understand your thesis. The **tone,** or the way you write, will be different for each audience and for different types of writing. Research reports should have a more formal tone than many other types of writing.

Try It!

Read about the research topic below. Then choose two audiences from the list that follows the paragraph. Think about what each audience would be interested in knowing about your topic if you had to retell it. With a partner, discuss how the words and examples you choose might be different for each audience.

Topic

Cowboys Stadium in Arlington, Texas, has a retractable roof. As home of the Dallas Cowboys, it has 80,000 permanent seats and can expand seating to 100,000 for all kinds of concerts, including band concerts. It is the largest domed stadium in the world. The architects put in a retractable roof so the stadium could be air conditioned in the hot summer and keep people dry in wet weather.

Audiences

- **middle-school student, architect, teen football fan, college band director, construction foreman**

Let's Talk!

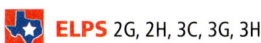

When you answer a question, you might use one word, a few words, a sentence, or a few sentences.

Example: What do you like best about the new Cowboys Stadium?

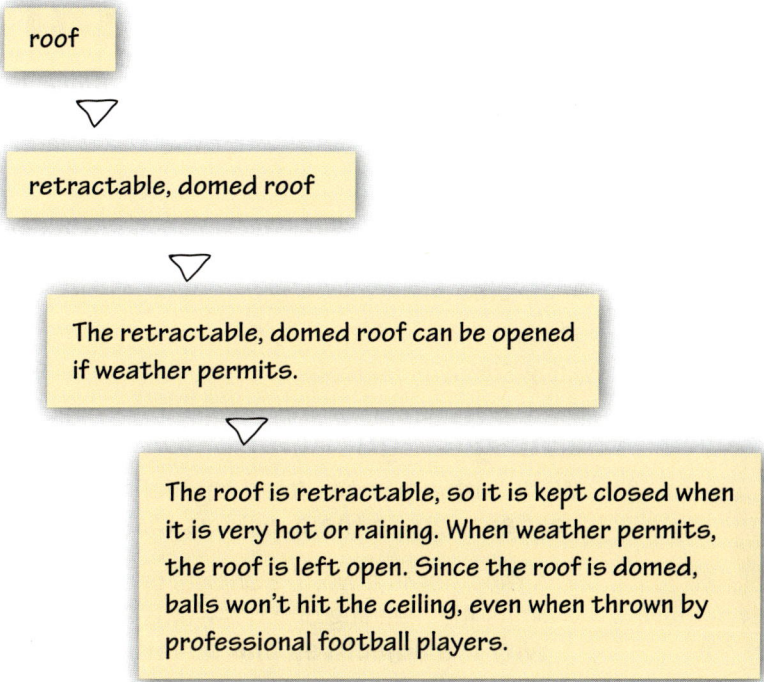

roof

retractable, domed roof

The retractable, domed roof can be opened if weather permits.

The roof is retractable, so it is kept closed when it is very hot or raining. When weather permits, the roof is left open. Since the roof is domed, balls won't hit the ceiling, even when thrown by professional football players.

In the first box, there is only a one-word answer. In the other boxes, the writer tells more. The last box shows the most information. When you use more details to tell about something, the other person will have a better idea of what you are talking about. They are more interested in what you have to say.

Try It!

Choose a famous work of engineering that you would like to research. Make notes about what you want to know about the project and its designers. Then use your notes to describe your ideas to your partner.

Here are some ideas to get you started.

1. How was the Brooklyn Bridge designed and built?
2. How were some of the world's tallest buildings, such as the Willis Tower in Chicago, built?

ELPS 1E, 2C, 3B, 3D, 3E, 4G

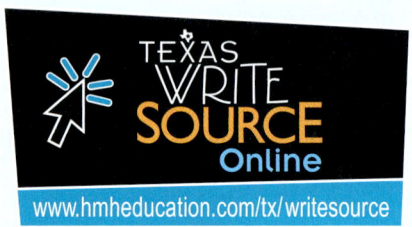

TEXAS WRITE SOURCE Online
www.hmheducation.com/tx/writesource

Basic Grammar and Writing

Writing Focus

Learning Language

Work with a partner. Read the definitions below and share your answers to the questions that follow.

1. A **modifier** is a word, a phrase, or a clause that changes or limits the meaning of other words.
   Why are adjectives and adverbs common modifiers?
2. An **anecdote** is a short account of an interesting or humorous incident.
   How can an anecdote help engage your reader? Explain.
3. **To classify** means to arrange or organize by class or category, based on common characteristics.
   What characteristics would you use to classify bicycles?
4. The idiom **"to hit a home run"** means to succeed or to do well.
   When did you last hit a home run? Describe the incident.

Using Words Effectively

Just as atoms are the fundamental building blocks of matter, words are the building blocks of communication. And like atoms, words have power. Think about the word *yes.* That one little word can change your life forever—for better or for worse. So can the tiny word *no.* And what about the word *ridiculous*? Try shouting that word in just about any situation, and you'll see how powerful a word can be.

English has many types of words: nouns, pronouns, verbs, adjectives, adverbs, prepositions, and conjunctions. This chapter explores these parts of speech, helping you unlock the power each one has to offer.

- **Nouns**
- **Pronouns**
- **Verbs**
- **Adjectives**
- **Adverbs**
- **Prepositions**
- **Conjunctions**
- **Checking Your Word Choice**

"Give me the right word and the right accent, and I will move the world."

—Joseph Conrad

Nouns Using General and Specific Nouns

Since some nouns are general (*man, rock*) and some are specific (*Barnum Brown, sandstone*), they can affect the focus of your writing. As with a camera lens, you can start with general nouns and zoom in to specific nouns, or you can start with specific nouns and zoom out to general ones.

Zooming In (from general nouns to specific nouns)

In the wide *desert*, a *man* crouched under a blazing *sun* and dug. He spent most of his *time* kneeling in the *dirt* holding a small *tool*. Slowly he chipped *sandstone* away from what looked like a *vertebra*. *Stroke* by *stroke*, the *paleontologist Barnum Brown* was uncovering the *skeleton* of a *Tyrannosaurus rex*.

This paragraph starts with general nouns, which paint a broad picture and invite the reader to imagine the scene. Then it zooms in to specific nouns, which provide detailed information.

Zooming Out (from specific nouns to general nouns)

In early *July 1905*, *Barnum Brown* discovered the *skeleton* of a *Tyrannosaurus rex*. An avid *hunter* of dinosaur *bones*, *Barnum* had come to *Hell Creek*, *Montana*, in hopes of finding something special. However, he could not have suspected that his *discovery* would soon visit the *imaginations* of *children* everywhere.

This paragraph starts with specific nouns, providing exact information up front. Then it zooms out to general nouns to reflect on the importance of the discovery.

Try It!

Think of a topic that interests you. Then brainstorm a list of general and specific nouns about the topic. (See the sample chart below.) Afterward, write a paragraph, using the nouns to zoom in or zoom out.

Topic: Dinosaur Hunting

General		Specific	
dinosaur	bones	Tyrannosaurus rex	vertebra
man	desert	paleontologist	Hell Creek, Montana

Creating Metaphors

A **metaphor** is a comparison of two unlike things in which no word of comparison (*as* or *like*) is used. A metaphor represents a high level of thinking and is a powerful writing technique.

Basic Metaphors

A basic metaphor can be a simple noun equation: Noun A = Noun B. In basic metaphors, the nouns are equated using a linking verb such as *is, am, are, was,* or *were*.

Janice is a human calculator.
(Janice = calculator)

Life is a banquet.
(life = banquet)

Advanced Metaphors

Some advanced metaphors *imply* the equation between the nouns. In this example, the highlighted nouns are equated without linking verbs.

The gears in Janice's mind grind through any math test.
(The word *gears* implies that Janice's *mind* is a machine.)

Tip

Create an advanced metaphor by substituting Noun B for Noun A.

Her **lasers** scan problems while her **processor** builds solutions.

Noun A		Noun B
eyes	=	lasers
brain	=	processor

Extended Metaphors

Sometimes an author extends a metaphor, creating a series of pictures for the reader.

Bill's mind is a locker, with his letter jacket hanging from a hook in the center, pictures of his girlfriend covering the inside of the door, and textbooks lying, forgotten, at the bottom.

Try It!

Equate the name of a friend (Noun A) with another noun (Noun B). Then write one basic, one advanced, and one extended metaphor about this person.

Pronouns Engaging Your Reader

Most often, a pronoun should clearly refer to a specific noun (its *antecedent*). However, one special use of pronouns delays mentioning the antecedent, making the reader wonder who or what you are talking about. This technique can work on a sentence level or in a whole paragraph.

Sentence Hook

In the following examples, notice how the pronouns turn the sentences into riddles, causing the reader to wonder, "Who?"

> **When he did a screen test for Paramount, he was told, "[You] can't sing, can't act, but you can dance a little." Still, Fred Astaire was in more than 40 films.**

> **Though she was fired from her first Broadway show after one night, and though Hollywood producers labeled her "box office poison," Katharine Hepburn became a leading lady of twentieth-century film.**

Paragraph Hook

In this paragraph, the reader doesn't discover who *he* is until the end of the paragraph.

> **He was a short, unassuming comedian from New York, but he sat on a train bound for the Soviet Union in 1933. The tools of his trade were simple—a rumpled hat, a curly red wig, a worn-out coat, and a bicycle horn. The young pantomimist was traveling to the Soviet Union to open up a new market to American performers. Arriving in Moscow, he was greeted with suspicion, and when he performed, his audiences were afraid to laugh. In utter frustration, the young American was about to give up, but then the United States and the Soviet Union officially recognized each other. That changed everything. Suddenly, Soviet crowds went wild for Harpo Marx. He later wrote that he had never before played for an audience so desperate to laugh.**

Try It!

Make a list of favorite performers—musicians, actors, comedians, dancers, or friends. Choose one, and think of (or learn) interesting anecdotes about his or her life and career. Write a paragraph about one of these anecdotes, using pronouns to withhold the person's identity until the end.

Persuading Your Reader

In persuasive writing, you can unite people, instruct them, or divide them, depending on the person of the pronouns you use.

Person of Pronouns		
First Person (Unite)	**Second Person** (Instruct)	**Third Person** (Divide)
we us our	you your	they them their

Selecting the Person of a Pronoun

Notice the effect that is created by changing the person of pronouns in the following sentence:

These pronouns **unite** the writer and the reader: "We're all in this together."

When we buy a car, van, truck, or SUV, we must consider how our consumption of gasoline will affect us in the future.

These pronouns **instruct** the reader.

When you buy a car, van, truck, or SUV, you must consider how your consumption of gasoline will affect you in the future.

These pronouns **divide** the reader from those being written about.

When they buy a car, van, truck, or SUV, they must consider how their consumption of gasoline will affect them in the future.

In persuasive writing, use pronouns carefully. Use first-person pronouns to create common ground with your reader. Use second-person pronouns (or the implied "you") to instruct the reader. Use third-person pronouns sparingly, perhaps to point an accusing finger.

Try It!

Check a newspaper opinion/editorial page to find an editorial that uses personal pronouns. Are they first-, second-, or third-person pronouns? Change the pronouns in one of the paragraphs, switching to another person. Then explain how the changes make the paragraph more or less persuasive.

Verbs Affecting the Sense of Time

Verbs and verb tenses can affect the sense of time in a piece of writing. For example, they help express whether an event took place in the past, takes place in the present, or will occur in the future.

Past Tense in Essays

Past-tense verbs work best for most of your writing, showing that events are completed. Past-tense verbs help you to express and analyze solid facts.

> **Throughout history, women have made major contributions to science. For example, in the fourth century C.E., Hypatia of Alexandria created an astrolabe, an instrument for tracking the position of stars and planets. It revolutionized astronomy and navigation.**

Present Tense in Narratives

Present-tense verbs work well for certain narratives. These verbs make action seem immediate, as if it were happening right now.

> **Lise Mitner glances down from the face of Albert Einstein and stares at the paper before her. On it, she has laid out the secrets of the atom. Always shy, Lise covers the equations with her hand. Einstein clucks, shaking his head. "Don't hide your work. You should trumpet it from the rooftops. Don't you know, my dear: You are the German Madame Curie."**

Present Tense in Process Essays

Present-tense verbs also work well for essays that describe action that happens routinely.

> **Every year, more young women decide to study mathematics and science; every year, more female researchers and doctors start their practices; every year, more women make the discoveries that advance human knowledge.**

Try It!

Pull out a recent expository essay or narrative you have written. What verb tense did you use? Choose a paragraph and replace the verbs in it with verbs of a different tense. How does the change affect the sense of time and action?

Creating Verbal Metaphors

Though most metaphors are based on nouns (Noun A = Noun B), some metaphors can be created using verbs.

Verbal Metaphors

My heart galloped in my chest.
(The heart is equated to a running horse.)

The letter ignited my mind.
(The letter is equated to a fire.)

Dad's junker staggered into the driveway, bled transmission fluid, and gasped its last breath.
(The junker car is equated to a dying animal.)

Note: In these examples, verbs that are usually used with one type of noun (the *horse* galloped) are used with nouns of a completely different type (my *heart* galloped).

Try It!

Study the bank of verbs below. Each is strongly associated with a specific noun. Select five verbs and write a sentence for each, creating metaphors by pairing the verb with a completely different type of noun.

Example: The gray sky frowned on our picnic plans.

anchored	eroded	hurdled	rotted
baked	flew	joked	sizzled
bucked	frowned	kindled	sprinted
burned	gargled	laughed	snored
catapulted	groomed	muttered	stomped
danced	hacked	punted	thundered
drummed	hollered	raced	tripped

FYI

When a metaphor implies that a nonhuman thing is performing a human action, the technique is called *personification*.

The day **snored** along, occasionally **muttering** empty promises of adventure before **rolling over** and **drowsing** again.

ELPS 3E

Adjectives Making a Precise Point

Some writers use adjectives like frosting, slathering their nouns as if the adjectives will make them tastier. You will do better to consider how adjectives subtract from a noun, rather than adding to it, by limiting its meaning and making it more precise.

DON'T Write

I had a big, beautiful party.
(The adjectives do not make *party* more precise.)

DO Write

I had a sweet-sixteen birthday party.
(The adjectives tell precisely what *kind* of party.)

Adjective Phrases and Clauses

Phrases and clauses that function as adjectives also need to be precise.

The house rocked like a dryer filled with shoes.
(The phrase *filled with shoes* tells precisely what kind of *dryer*.)

We played a game of truth or dare that resulted in a pillow fight.
(The phrase *of truth or dare* and the clause *that resulted in a pillow fight* tell exactly what kind of *game*.)

Try It!

Think of a special event that you have attended, and make a list of nouns related to it. Add one adjective and one adjective phrase or clause that would make the noun's meaning precise. (See the examples below.) Write a paragraph about the event, using some of the nouns and modifiers from your list. Share and discuss your paragraph with a classmate.

Nouns	Adjectives	Adjective Phrases or Clauses
pool	above-ground	with a ten-foot-deep end
diving board	squeaky	which got a workout
dives	ridiculous	such as the "Spider"
belly flop	blistering	that nearly emptied the pool

Emphasizing the Quality of a Noun

One way to emphasize the quality of a given noun is to use a series of adjectives to describe it.

Series of Adjectives

The sentences below contain adjectives in a series. The first series is separated with commas and the word *and*. The second series is separated without commas, using only the word *and*. This provides special emphasis.

My friend Eva is smart, quirky, funny, and driven.

She says I am kind and patient and totally infuriating.

Series of Phrases or Clauses

Phrases or clauses that function as adjectives can also be used in a series.

Sitting in her living room, propping her feet on the radiator, and balancing a notepad on her lap, Eva writes stories. (Three participial phrases describe *Eva*.)

Eva writes stories about places that she has seen, that she wishes to see, and that she knows don't even exist. (Three relative clauses describe *places*.)

FYI

The quickest way to know whether a phrase or clause is functioning as an adjective is to decide whether it answers one of the adjective questions—*which? what kind of? how many?* or *how much*?

Try It!

Write down the name of a person. Beside the name, write two nouns you associate with that person. Under each noun, list descriptive words, phrases, or clauses. (See the sample chart below.) Then create a sentence that uses an adjective series.

Eva	apartment	places
smart	on the eighth floor	that she has seen
funny	with a view of the alley	that she wishes to see
quirky	in the old downtown	that she knows don't even exist
driven	in Bloomington	

Adverbs Writing Strong Beginnings

Adverbs make great sentence starters because they help create a context. Before the reader knows *what* happens in the sentence, the adverb can tell *how, when,* or *where* it happens. Single-word adverbs (as well as phrases and clauses that act as adverbs) answer these questions: *how? when? where? why? to what degree?* and *how often?*

Adverb Beginnings

Gradually, the glowing twilight surrendered to spangled night. *(How?)*

Afterward, the Perseid meteor shower began. *(When?)*

In the northern sky, meteors were flashing overhead. *(Where?)*

One by one, shooting stars streaked across the sky. *(To what degree?)*

Every few minutes, a new fireball left its fleeting signature. *(How often?)*

Because the earth was passing through the path of a comet, there were hundreds of shooting stars. *(Why?)*

Try It!

Read and then rewrite each sentence below, moving the adverb (or adverbial phrase or clause) to the beginning of the sentence.

1. Dust particles often made slim dashes of light.
2. Marble-sized chunks of matter created bright shooting stars as they crossed the whole sky before burning out.
3. Fist-sized meteorites crossed the sky burning, spinning, and flaming.
4. Earth passes through this cloud of debris every August.

FYI

The regular subject-verb order may be reversed when an adverb starts a sentence.

At the top of the hill lay a clearing. *(A clearing lay at the top of the hill.)*
Overhead were the dancing stars. *(The dancing stars were overhead.)*

Try It!

Think about a natural phenomenon you've witnessed and write a paragraph about what you saw. Try starting a few sentences with adverbs.

Avoiding Adverb Props

Avoid propping up a weak verb with an adverb. Often, the two words can be replaced with a single verb that tells exactly what is happening.

Adverb Props

DON'T Write	DO Write
ran quickly	charged, darted, dashed, scurried, sprinted
walked heavily	marched, plodded, slogged, stomped, trudged
said angrily	growled, hissed, shouted, snarled

Avoiding Redundant Adverbs

A strong verb doesn't need an adverb. When you fix an adverb prop by replacing the weak verb with a stronger one, you can omit the unnecessary adverb.

Redundant Adverbs

DON'T Write	DO Write
dashed quickly (no one dashes slowly)	dashed
plodded heavily (no one plods lightly)	plodded
growled angrily (no one growls happily)	growled

Try It!

Read the passage below and identify the adverb props and redundant adverbs. Suggest how each adverb problem could be corrected.

Afghan refugees staggered unsteadily up the hill. Their world had been changed completely by the war, and now it was rocked deeply by an earthquake. "We are weary," an old man said quietly. Abdullah al Ibin had worked hard to survive the Taliban regime. He thought wishfully that things would become easier. They did not. He put up with robbers until he gave up and escaped away from his hometown. "Now, with this earthquake, even the mountains aren't safe," he murmured sadly.

Prepositions Creating Similes

The preposition *like* allows you to compare two things, creating a simile. For a simile to be effective, it should point out an unexpected similarity.

DON'T Write

Rain is like water that falls from the sky.
(Rain *is* water.)

DO Write

Spring rain is like a mother's voice whispering to the world, "Wake up."

Use similes as good cooks use spices—sparingly to enhance the flavor of the sentence. A simile pushed too far may become tiresome.

DON'T Write

Spring rain is like a mother's voice whispering to the world, "Wake up," and the winds of March are like the rustle of covers drawn back from the slumbering planet.

Try It!

For each of the terms listed below, write a one-sentence simile that shows a surprising similarity. Use the words *is like* or *are like.*

1. lightning
2. warm winds
3. a bird's song
4. new leaves
5. spring flowers
6. umbrellas

FYI

Many similes use the preposition *like* to introduce a prepositional phrase that functions as an adjective.

The winter sky was **like a woolen blanket.**
(The simile modifies the noun *sky.*)

Other similes use the subordinating conjunction *as* to introduce a subordinate clause that functions as an adverb.

Spring draws away the clouds **as a mother draws back a woolen blanket.**
(The simile modifies the verb *draws.*)

Using Prepositional Phrases as Adjectives

Prepositions can turn nouns into modifiers. By placing a preposition before a noun, you can create a phrase that acts as an adjective, answering the questions *which? what kind?* or *how many?*

The proposal with the blue cover is mine.
Which proposal?

Calculations for the construction costs were inaccurate.
What kind of calculations?

Letters from two hundred constituents stopped the bill from passing.
How many?

Prepositional phrases can be used to revise an awkward sentence that strings too many adjectives together.

The city budget debate's end finally came. (awkward)

The end of the debate over the city budget finally came.

Try It!

Rewrite each sentence below, turning at least one of the adjectives into a prepositional phrase. Be sure the new sentence makes sense.

1. The **mayor's hilltop** house needs painting.
2. The **busy street's anxious** residents spoke to the city council.
3. The **school board budget** referendum passed the vote.
4. An **environmental activist student** organization opposes the bypass.
5. The council passed the **2006 property tax reassessment** bill.

FYI

Prepositional phrases also can function as adverbs, answering the questions *how? when? where? why? to what degree?* and *how often?* However, these prepositional phrases can often be replaced by a single adverb—or by a stronger verb.

The mayor replied **with a firm voice** that the budget had been approved.

The mayor replied **firmly** that the budget had been approved.
(adverb)

The mayor **asserted** that the budget had been approved.
(strong verb)

TEKS 10.15A(ii), 10.18B(ii)

Conjunctions Creating Tension

As a writer, you can create tension in a sentence by using certain subordinating conjunctions. The following conjunctions tell the reader that your train of thought will soon shift directions.

although	though	unless	while
even though	whereas	until	

Present a Contrast

In the following examples, ideas pull in opposite directions, building a powerful contrast.

> **Although the French Revolution was meant to provide "liberty, equality, and brotherhood" to all, it actually resulted in repression, inequality, and war.**

> **While royal oppression had been cruel, the mob's remedy for it—gauntlets and guillotines—proved crueler still.**

Create Irony

In this example, the conjunction *even though* sets up a contrast that creates *irony*. Irony is when a writer's actual words say the opposite of what is meant. The writer uses quotation marks to indicate irony.

> **Even though the French thought they had escaped from King Louis XVI's "divine right" to rule France, they found themselves stuck with Emperor Napoleon I's divine right to rule the world.**

Try It!

Select four of the conjunctions listed at the top of the page and use each one at the start of a sentence. Work to create tension and irony in your sentences. Use quotation marks to indicate irony.

FYI

Another way to create tension is to use correlative conjunctions.

not only . . . but also	neither . . . nor
either . . . or	both . . . and
if . . . then	whether . . . or

Creating Pivot Points

The coordinating conjunctions *but* and *yet* can provide pivot points in an essay. They allow the writer to present one line of thought and then create a reversal. In an expository essay, *but* or *yet* can show a shift from background information to the real issue. The technique also works in persuasive writing.

Expository Excerpt

This paragraph gives background and conventional wisdom.

Our climate should be a self-righting system. After all, the main greenhouse gas, carbon dioxide, is also the main food for plants. More carbon dioxide should cause more plant growth. More plants should mean less carbon dioxide and more oxygen. The levels of greenhouse gases should self-regulate.

But signals the shift to new information.

But experiments have shown otherwise. Increased levels of carbon dioxide increase plant growth, but not enough to reduce carbon-dioxide levels. In addition, with global warming, arctic tundras that once were "carbon sinks," absorbing more carbon dioxide than they lost, are becoming "carbon pumps"—accelerating the rise in greenhouse gases.

Persuasive Excerpt

The opposing position is presented.

The politicians are right in this: The world economy is driven by oil, and capitalism is driven by consumption. To keep the economy and capitalism strong, the world needs a great deal of oil now—and an even greater amount in the future.

Yet signals the shift to the writer's opinion.

Yet this argument breaks down. Yes, oil is needed now, but alternative energy sources will reduce the future demands. The standard argument fails to account for one great resource—human ingenuity.

Try It!

Read the paragraphs above, and think of an issue with two sides. Write a paragraph that explains one side. Then write a second paragraph, beginning with *but* or *yet,* to explain the other side of the issue.

TEKS 10.13C

Word Choice Using a Checklist

After you finish a writing assignment, you can check your word choice by using the following checklist.

Word-Choice Checklist

_____ **1.** Have I used nouns to set my focus (zooming in or out)?

_____ **2.** Have I included any metaphors? List examples: The Calcutta massacre was a last gasp of the dying imperial beast.

_____ **3.** Have I used pronouns occasionally to create suspense? List examples: He was a small man of noble birth, but Mohandas Gandhi became a titan who fought for the common people.

_____ **4.** Have I used pronouns persuasively? List examples:
To unite: We wonder if the world holds more Gandhis.
To instruct: "Live as if you were to die tomorrow. Learn as if you were to live forever."
To divide: Though some may say passive resistance cannot stand up to armies and bombs, they have forgotten the lessons of Gandhi.

_____ **5.** Have I used verb tense to establish time?

_____ **6.** Have I used adjectives to make precise points?

_____ **7.** Have I used an adjective series?

_____ **8.** Have I started any sentences with adverbs?

_____ **9.** Have I used any similes? List examples: Gandhi's heart was like a magic box, larger on the inside than on the outside.

_____ **10.** Have I used prepositional phrases as adjectives?

_____ **11.** Have I used subordinating conjunctions to create contrast or irony where needed?

_____ **12.** Have I used *but* or *yet* to create pivot points in my writing?

Understanding Sentence Style

Close your eyes, and imagine a carefully handwoven scarf or shawl. Try to visualize how each stitch works with the next one to create a unique design. Now imagine that the sentences you write are like those stitches. As you weave them together, your design—your message—takes form, leaving a lasting impression on your reader.

Good writing holds sentences that are clear, creative, and effective. To become sentence-smart, look for well-crafted sentences as you read. Then write sentences of your own modeled after some of these published gems. If you read and write often, your writing style will continue to improve—one sentence at a time. The guidelines in this chapter will help.

- **Sentence Patterns**
- **Sentence Length**
- **Sentence Variety**
- **Sentence Combining**
- **Sentence Problems**
- **Sentence Agreement**
- **Sentence Modeling**

"The best advice on writing I've ever received is: 'Knock 'em dead with the lead sentence.'"

—Whitney Balliet

ELPS 4C, 5E

Sentence Patterns Understanding the Basics

In the English language, sentences follow basic patterns. Combining a variety of sentence patterns adds interest to your writing.

1. Subject + Action Verb

S AV
Armin coughed. (Some action verbs, like *coughed*, are intransitive. They *do not need* a direct object to express a complete thought. See **744.1**.)

2. Subject + Action Verb + Direct Object

S AV DO
Omaya directs the play. (Some action verbs, like *directs* in this sentence, are transitive. They *do need* a direct object to express a complete thought. See **744.2**.)

3. Subject + Action Verb + Indirect Object + Direct Object

S AV IO DO
The teacher read the students a description of the test. (The direct object *description* names who or what receives the action; the indirect object *students* names to whom or for whom the action is done. See **744.2**.)

4. Subject + Action Verb + Direct Object + Object Complement

S AV DO OC
The class found the presentation entertaining. (The object complement *entertaining* describes the direct object.)

5. Subject + Linking Verb + Predicate Noun

S LV PN
Serafina is a dancer. (The predicate noun *dancer* renames the subject. See **732.3**.)

6. Subject + Linking Verb + Predicate Adjective

S LV PA
Our parents are interested in contributing to the fund. (The predicate adjective *interested* describes the subject. See **756.1**.)

Note: In the patterns below, the subject comes after the verb.

LV S PN
Is Dominic a sports fan? (A question)

LV S
There were three limousines in the parking lot. (A sentence beginning with *there*)

"Whatever sentence will bear to be read twice, we may be sure was thought twice."
—Henry David Thoreau

Sentence Length Varying Sentence Lengths

Using sentences of different lengths adds interest to your writing. If too many of your sentences have the same number of words, your writing may sound monotonous.

In this paragraph, all of the sentences have the same basic length.

Being a veterinarian is hard work. Sometimes the veterinarian has to handle heavy animals. Some dogs can weigh more than 100 pounds. Rural veterinarians must care for large farm animals on-site. That means they must travel from farm to farm. Of course, there are also late-night emergencies. Still, there are many rewards. Veterinarians know the joy of helping animals. They have the satisfaction of relieving their pain.

The same paragraph has been improved below because the sentences now vary in length. The writer added and deleted words as needed.

Being a veterinarian is hard work. A veterinarian must be able to handle heavy animals, including dogs that can weigh more than 100 pounds. In addition, rural veterinarians must care for large animals on-site, which means they must travel from farm to farm. Of course, there are also late-night emergencies to deal with. Still, there are many rewards, especially knowing the joy and satisfaction of helping animals and relieving their pain.

Try It!

Read and then rewrite the following paragraph using a variety of sentence lengths.

Thad is starting an internship as an audio/video technician. Technicians are part of the production crew for television shows. Thad will work on both live and taped television events. He is very excited about learning some new job skills. He will set up sound and video equipment. Thad's math and science skills will help him set up complicated productions. It is Thad's job to regulate and monitor audio levels. He is also responsible for setting up television video signals. Thad would like to work as an audio engineer.

TEKS 10.17C
ELPS 4C, 5F

Sentence Variety Using Sentences for Effect

Short and long sentences can be used for special effect in your writing. Short sentences build tension and speed while longer ones add meaning in a paced way.

Using Short Sentences

- Short sentences grouped together build tension.
  The TV screen was lying. It couldn't be true. I blinked once, twice. The trail of puffy smoke remained. *The Challenger,* its crew, hope—were all gone.
- Short sentences pick up the pace of the action.
  The finish line lay just ahead. We ran close enough to smell each other's sweat. Four arms pumped hard. Four feet slapped the ground. We breathed only to win.

Using Long Sentences

- A long sentence builds layers of meaning.
  We hauled out the boxes of food and set up the camp stove, all the time battling the hot wind that would not stop, even when we screamed to the sky.
- Long sentences slow down the pace and facilitate reflection.
  Although I have no memory of the ordeals I faced during my first years of life, I shall always bear the orthopedic deformities that I was handed at birth. These deformities have been difficult to accept, but they have provided me with a unique life and greatly influenced the development of my character.
- A long sentence with a central idea forms a complex thought.
  "To those peoples in the huts and villages across the globe struggling to break the bonds of mass misery, we pledge our best efforts to help them help themselves, for whatever period is required—not because the Communists may be doing it, not because we seek their votes, but because it is right."

—President John F. Kennedy

Try It!

Carefully read the examples above. Then write a series of short sentences that build tension. Write a long sentence that builds layers of meaning or slows down the pace.

"How can we combine the old words in new order so that they survive, so that they create beauty, so that they tell the truth?"

—Winston Weathers

Writing Loose Sentences

A loose sentence expresses the main idea near the beginning and adds details as needed. In loose sentences, the thoughts seem to be presented as they occur to the writer. When used effectively, this type of sentence can add a special style and rhythm to your writing. In the examples below, the main ideas are underlined. (See page 776.)

Example Loose Sentences

Sam was studying at the kitchen table, memorizing a list of vocabulary words, completely focused, intent on acing tomorrow's Spanish quiz.

"They are wonderfully built homes, aluminum skin, double-walled, with insulation, and often paneled with walls of hardwood."

—John Steinbeck, *Travels with Charley*

"Jeff couldn't see the musician clearly, just a figure on a chair on the stage, holding what looked like a misshapen guitar."

—Cynthia Voight, *A Solitary Blue*

Tip

Remember these important points when writing loose sentences.

1. Structure the sentence carefully. If a sentence begins to ramble, the reader will lose track of the main idea.
2. Avoid using too many long, loose sentences. Remember that varying your sentence lengths will keep the reader interested.

Try It!

Read the examples and the tip above. Then write four loose sentences using these brief sentences as starting points.

1. Nayara gasped.
2. Storm clouds surged through the sky.
3. Ari wrote a free-verse poem.
4. Mr. Groves sauntered away.

TEKS 10.15A(i), 10.17A(i), 10.17C
ELPS 5F

Sentence Combining
Using Infinitive and Participial Phrases

Ideas from shorter sentences can be combined into one sentence using an infinitive phrase or a participial phrase.

Using an Infinitive Phrase

An infinitive phrase is a group of related words introduced by the word *to* plus a verb form—*to conquer* my fears. (See page 768.)

- **Short Sentences:**
  Annetta searched the Internet. She needed information about the Serengeti Plain.
  I would really like to go to Africa. That's my dream vacation.
- **Combined Sentence:**
  Annetta searched the Internet to find information about the Serengeti Plain.
  To go to Africa is my dream vacation.

Using a Participial Phrase

A participial phrase is a group of related words introduced by a participle (a verb form ending in *–ing* or *–ed*)—*circling* the date. (See page 768.)

- **Short Sentences:**
  Kyle walked barefoot in the garden. He stepped on a hornets' nest.
  Shannon covered her ears. She was annoyed by the sound of the air hammer.
- **Combined Sentence:**
  Kyle, walking barefoot in the garden, stepped on a hornets' nest.
  Annoyed by the sound of the air hammer, Shannon covered her ears.

Try It!

Combine these sentences using an infinitive or a participial phrase.

1. Marcus went to the ballet. He did it to please his mother.
2. The ring was locked in a safety deposit box. It was safe for many years.
3. A cold front swept through Michigan. It sent temperatures plummeting below zero.
4. The tornado swept through a small town. It left a trail of death and destruction.

Creating Complex Sentences

Ideas from shorter sentences can also be combined into a complex sentence. A complex sentence is made up of two clauses that are not equal in importance. The more important idea should be included in the *independent clause,* which can stand alone as a single sentence. The less important idea should be included in the *dependent clause,* which cannot stand alone. (See pages 770 and 774.)

The two clauses in a complex sentence can be connected with a subordinate conjunction (*after, although, because, before, even though, until, when*, and so on) or a relative pronoun (*who, whose, which,* or *that*).

- **Even though LeBron sprained his ankle, he sunk the winning free throw.**
  [dependent clause, independent clause]
- **It isn't funny when a practical joke continues until someone's feelings are hurt.** [independent clause, two dependent clauses]

Using a Complex Sentence

- **Two Short Sentences:**
  Mt. McKinley rises 20,320 feet above sea level.
  It is the highest peak in the United States.
- **Combined Sentence:**
  Mt. McKinley, which rises 20,320 feet above sea level, is the highest peak in the United States.

Try It!

Read the sentences below. Combine each set of short sentences into a complex sentence using the subordinating conjunction or relative pronoun in parentheses.

1. Mrs. Lopez returned to work.
   School lunch tasted good again. (because)
2. We found a village called "Pity Me."
   The village is located in County Durham. (which)
3. I want my sister to proofread my report.
   I will give it to Ms. Belmont. (before)
4. My aunt loves to travel.
   She is planning a trip to France. (who)
5. We had to leave the golf course.
   The storm finally started. (when)

TEKS 10.17C, 10.18B(i)
ELPS 5F

Sentence Problems Avoiding Sentence Errors

Avoid sentence problems as you write—or correct them when you revise.

Correcting Run-On Sentences

Run-on sentences occur when two sentences are joined without punctuation or without a connecting word *(and, but, or, so).*

- **Run-on Sentence:** Lightweight cookware soon came on the market the idea of casserole cooking became popular.
- **Corrected as Two Sentences:** Lightweight cookware soon came on the market. The idea of casserole cooking became popular.
- **Corrected as a Compound Sentence:** Lightweight cookware soon came on the market, so the idea of casserole cooking became popular.

Eliminating Comma Splices

Comma splices occur when two independent clauses are connected with a comma and no conjunction.

- **Comma Splice:** Casseroles took little preparation time, women's magazines began promoting easy-to-prepare meals.
- **Corrected as Two Sentences:** Casseroles took little preparation time. Women's magazines began promoting easy-to-prepare meals.
- **Corrected as a Compound Sentence:** Casseroles took little preparation time, and women's magazines began promoting easy-to-prepare meals.

Try It!

On your own paper, rewrite the following paragraph, correcting the run-ons and comma splices.

(1) The word "soup" comes from the Old English word "sopp" it means a slice of bread over which roast drippings are poured. (2) Soup was eaten even in ancient times the first evidence of it dates back to around 6000 B.C.E. (3) The main ingredient of "ancient" soup may surprise you it was hippopotamus bones. (4) Soup is easily digested, so it is often prescribed as a nutritious meal for sick people. (5) Many families eat a lot of soup, most often it comes in cans and boxes and can be quickly heated.

Fixing Fragments

A fragment is not a sentence because it does not form a complete thought. In a sentence fragment, a subject, a predicate, or both are missing.

Fragment: **Was introduced in 4 B.C.E.** (The subject is missing.)
The mathematical decimal system was introduced in 4 B.C.E.

Fragment: **Roman emperors many lighthouses.** (A predicate is missing.)
Roman emperors built many lighthouses.

Fragment: **Including schools.** (A subject and predicate are missing.)
All public institutions, including schools, were closed.

Try It!

Rewrite each fragment as a complete sentence.

1. Under the Golden Gate Bridge.
2. About 200 feet deep.
3. Served in Iraq.
4. Steven Spielberg.
5. Is celebrated on November 11th.
6. John Philip Sousa his own band.

Rewriting Rambling Sentences

Rambling sentences seem to go on and on. Their parts are connected by coordinating conjunctions. While not grammatically incorrect, these sentences can be hard to read. As a rule, if a sentence links more than two complete ideas with *and, but,* or *so*, try to divide it into shorter sentences.

Rambling: **I saw my band director, Mr. Sandoval, at the jazz concert, and I called to him but he didn't hear me and then he disappeared into the crowd.**

Better: **I saw my band director, Mr. Sandoval, at the jazz concert. I called to him, but he didn't hear me. Then he disappeared into the crowd.**

Try It!

Rewrite this rambling sentence by eliminating one or more of the connecting words. Punctuate the new sentences correctly.

I wanted to be on the prom committee so I went to the first meeting and I knew I was on time and in the right place and I waited around for almost an hour but nobody showed up.

Correcting Double Subjects

Be careful not to use a pronoun immediately after the subject. The result is usually a double subject.

Double Subject: The Presidential election it is this Tuesday.

Corrected: The Presidential election is this Tuesday.

Double Subject: Barry he plays college football.

Corrected: Barry plays college football.

Correcting Double Negatives

Avoid sentences that contain double negatives. Double negatives occur when two negative words are used together in the same sentence (*not never, barely nothing, not no,* and so on). Double negatives also occur if you use contractions ending in *n't* with a negative word (*didn't never, can't not*).

Negative Words

nothing	nowhere	neither	never	not	barely	hardly	nobody	none

Double Negative: I could not go nowhere.

Corrected Sentence: I could not go anywhere.

Negative Contractions

don't	can't	won't	shouldn't	wouldn't	couldn't	didn't	hadn't

Double Negative: He didn't hear nothing unusual.

Corrected Sentence: He didn't hear anything unusual.

Try It!

Rewrite each sentence below, correcting the double-subject or double-negative errors.

1. King Richard he was known as "Richard the Lionhearted."
2. I didn't do nothing about the mistake on my application.
3. Why don't you never listen to hip-hop?
4. I hadn't never heard of The Hanging Gardens of Babylon. The gardens they are one of the Seven Wonders of the Ancient World.
5. We can't go nowhere without Steve's brother coming along.
6. Oscar and I we went to the rock concert on Friday night.

Sentence Agreement

Making Subjects and Verbs Agree

A verb must agree in number (singular or plural) with its subject. The basic rules for subject-verb agreement are listed below.

- A **singular subject** needs a singular verb, and a plural subject needs a plural verb.

  Singular Subject and Verb: Los Angeles is the second-most populated city in the United States.

  Plural Subject and Verb: Most Los Angeles beaches provide plenty of sun.

- A **compound subject connected by the word *and*** usually needs a plural verb.

  Compound Subject and Verb: Ty and Janelle are going to Europe.

- A **compound subject connected by the word *or*** needs a verb that agrees in number with the subject nearest to the verb.

  Compound Subject and Verb: Either the pool managers or a Red Cross volunteer teaches the lifeguard class.

- An **indefinite pronoun** can be singular or plural when used as a subject. (See **780.2**.)

  Singular Subject and Verb: Almost everyone in school likes the new coach.

  Plural Subject and Verb: Many of the parents appreciate his approach.

Try It!

Number your paper from 1 to 5. Write the correct verb choice for each of these sentences.

1. Some sodas or a juice container *(remains, remain)* in the refrigerator.
2. Kindra and Lawson *(is, are)* my friends from Mahone High School.
3. Vegetarians *(has, have)* some great recipe ideas.
4. Two coffee shops on our block *(sells, sell)* fair-trade coffee.
5. Each of the tourists *(has, have)* moved to another hotel.

Draft

Write a sentence using each of the subjects below. Remember to use verbs that agree in number with the subjects.

1. drivers
2. musician
3. Washington and Lincoln
4. the principal or counselors
5. everyone
6. all

Sentence Modeling Writing Stylish Sentences

Many painters learn to paint by copying famous works of art. Student writers, too, can learn to write better by modeling sentence patterns used by professional writers.

Model: **Eventually, all things merge into one, and a river runs through it.**

—Norman Maclean, *A River Runs Through It*

New Sentence: **Slowly, new players develop into a unit, and a team forms among them.**

Try It!

Choose three of the sentences below and write your own sentences, modeling the sentence structure as closely as possible.

1. I neither marched up to the stage like a conquering Amazon, nor did I look in the audience for Bailey's nod of approval.
   —Maya Angelou, *I Know Why the Caged Bird Sings*

2. A leftover smile of moon hides in the bottom branches of the sugar maple, teasing her to smile back.
   —Barbara Kingsolver, *Pigs in Heaven*

3. Then from behind the black and wavy line of the forests a column of golden light shot up into the heavens and spread over the semicircle of the eastern horizon.
   —Joseph Conrad, "The Lagoon"

4. I awoke that morning from a bizarre dream in which I had climbed down the stairs in our house, lifted the piano high above my head, then dropped it onto my right big toe.
   —Joel Ben Izzy, *The Beggar King and the Secret of Happiness*

5. If General Jackson hadn't run the Creeks up the creek, Simon Finch would never have paddled up the Alabama, and where would we be if he hadn't?
   —Harper Lee, *To Kill a Mockingbird*

6. I came, I saw, I conquered, as the first baby in the family always does.
   —Helen Keller, *The Story of My Life*

Writing Strong Paragraphs

In the real world of literature, the paragraph is not considered a form of writing. You wouldn't, for example, head to the local bookstore to buy a book of paragraphs. Nor would you pursue a writing career because you wanted to write award-winning paragraphs.

But paragraphs are very important as building blocks for other kinds of writing. When you write an essay, for instance, you develop paragraphs to organize your thoughts into manageable units. The paragraphs work together to build a clear, convincing argument or explanation. Learning how to write effective paragraphs will give you control of all your academic writing—from essays to articles to research papers.

"Excellence is doing ordinary things extraordinarily well."
—John W. Gardner

ELPS 4G, 4I

The Parts of a Paragraph

A typical paragraph consists of three main parts: a **topic sentence**, the **body sentences**, and a **closing sentence**. A paragraph can develop an explanation, an opinion, a description, or a narrative. Whatever form a paragraph takes, it must contain enough information to give the reader a complete picture of the topic. The following expository paragraph provides information about a remarkable ancient sculpture. As you read, notice how each detail in the body supports the topic sentence.

Topic Sentence

Body

Closing Sentence

Power and Glory

The huge, leonine sculpture known as the Great Sphinx prompts feelings of awe and curiosity from visitors to Giza, Egypt. At 200 feet long and 65 feet high, the statue, depicting a lion's body with the head of a man, is the world's earliest known sculpture. The man was probably the pharaoh Kahfre, who also built the nearby pyramids around 2500 B.C.E. No records or building plans of the Great Sphinx have been found, and scientists are not sure what tools would have been used to create such a huge sculpture. Because the body consists of soft limestone, wind and sand have caused terrible erosion. Several attempts have been made to save it, including restoration work done by ancient Egyptians and, later, by Roman invaders. The 13-foot-wide head was sculpted from a harder rock, so it is in better shape, although it is missing its nose. Scientists also believe the head may have included a plume and a curled beard. Because of the blowing desert sand, the body of the Sphinx has been covered and dug out several times over the centuries, with the latest excavation occurring in 1905. The world seems to agree that this statue is just too magnificent and mysterious to hide beneath shifting sands.

Respond to the reading. What main idea about the topic does this paragraph communicate? What specific details are included to support this idea? Name two or three of them.

A Closer Look at the Parts

Whether a paragraph stands alone or is part of an extended piece of writing, it contains three elements.

The Topic Sentence

A **topic sentence** tells the reader what your paragraph is about. The topic sentence should do two things: (1) name the specific topic of the paragraph and (2) identify a particular feeling or feature about the topic. Here is a simple formula for writing a topic sentence.

a specific topic
\+ a particular feeling or feature about the topic
= an effective topic sentence

The huge, leonine sculpture known as the Great Sphinx
\+ prompts feelings of awe and curiosity from visitors
= The huge, leonine sculpture known as the Great Sphinx prompts feelings of awe and curiosity from visitors to Giza, Egypt.

Tip

The topic sentence is *usually* the first sentence in a paragraph. However, it can also be located elsewhere. For example, you can present details that build up to an important summary topic sentence at the end of a paragraph.

The Body

The sentences in the **body** of the paragraph should all support the topic sentence. Each sentence should add new details about the topic.

- Use specific details to make your paragraph interesting.
  At 200 feet long and 65 feet high, the statue, depicting a lion's body with the head of a man, is the world's earliest known sculpture.
- Organize your sentences in the best possible order: time order, order of importance, classification, and so on. (See pages 607–610.)

The Closing Sentence

The **closing sentence** comes after all the body details have been presented. This sentence can remind the reader of the topic, summarize the paragraph, or link the paragraph to the next one.

The world seems to agree that this sculpture is just too magnificent and mysterious to hide beneath shifting sands.

TEKS 10.13B
ELPS 4G, 4I, 4J, 5G

Types of Paragraphs

There are four basic types of paragraphs: *narrative, descriptive, expository,* and *persuasive.*

Narrative Paragraph

A **narrative paragraph** tells a story. It may draw from the writer's personal experience or from other sources of information. A narrative paragraph is almost always organized chronologically, or according to time.

My First Driving Lesson

Topic Sentence

I began my first driving lesson thinking I would hit a home run my first time in the car.

Body

I got into the car and immediately turned the key. The instructor made a mark on his clipboard because in my excitement, I hadn't buckled my seat belt. After buckling up, I put the car into gear, which led to another mark. I hadn't checked my mirrors or looked to see if someone else was coming. After looking around, I stepped on the gas, and we sort of lunged to the practice area marked by orange highway cones. As I started through the practice course, I jerked the wheel to avoid one cone and knocked down two others. Then, in my panic, I hit the gas pedal instead of the brake! Two more cones went down before my instructor slammed on his master brake pedal. Unfortunately, the rest of my lesson didn't go any smoother. My instructor's pencil scratched noisily as he wrote on the clipboard. I figured I would never get my license. But when we finally stopped, he just handed me a copy of the checklist and said we would work on all my mistakes. I was relieved to know that they didn't expect perfection right away.

Closing Sentence

Suddenly, I couldn't wait for my second lesson.

Respond to the reading. What transitional words or phrases does the writer use to indicate the passage of time? Find three. What tone does the writer use—serious, entertaining, or surprising? Explain.

Write a narrative paragraph. Share your first driving experience or some other "first" experience. (Follow the guidelines on page 604.)

Descriptive Paragraph

A **descriptive paragraph** provides a detailed picture of a person, a place, an object, or an event. This type of paragraph should contain a variety of sensory details—specific sights, sounds, smells, tastes, and textures.

The Northside Youth Center

Topic Sentence

Body

Closing Sentence

The Northside Youth Center is the perfect place to spend time after school and on weekends. When entering the multipurpose room, one's eyes are immediately drawn to the bank of six computers along the left wall. There, students play games or do homework on the softly humming machines, while nearby a teacher/supervisor sits at a desk, ready to help. Beneath the tall, narrow windows on the back wall is the art area, with glow-in-the-dark metal cabinets that contain art supplies. To the right of the cabinets are several vending machines, their flashy windows offering fruit, sandwiches, and juice. A table with a microwave oven sits next to the machines, and the inviting scent of a warming sandwich or popping popcorn often fills the air. A large door on the wall to the right is open, and echoing shouts mixed with a chorus of bouncing basketballs spill in from the gym. Games of a quieter nature are played at tables stacked with colorful board games along this wall. Next to the tables, an area dominated by a bookshelf sprawling behind comfortable chairs spreads out into the middle of the room. This is a favorite spot. Students usually occupy these chairs, reading, studying, or talking with a friend. The Northside Youth Center provides many positive opportunities for students, all in a safe, inviting environment.

Respond to the reading. What senses are covered in this paragraph? Which two or three details seem especially descriptive?

Write a descriptive paragraph. Write a paragraph that describes a place that is important to you. Use sensory details in your description and structure your ideas in a sustained way. (Follow the guidelines on page 604.)

TEKS 10.13B
ELPS 4G, 4I, 5G

Expository Paragraph

An **expository paragraph** shares information about a specific topic. Expository writing presents facts, gives directions, defines terms, explains a process, and so forth. It should clearly inform the reader.

Topic Sentence

Body

Closing Sentence

Step, Toe, Heel

There are many types of dance shoes, but three of the most popular types are specially designed for ballet, jazz, and tap. Ballet shoes are soft, leather-soled slippers that have an adjustable tie to help them fit the foot. They often have ribbons sewn on to wrap around the leg for an elegant look. Some ballet slippers are designed especially for *pointe,* which is dancing on the tips of the toes. These have a more structured toe box that is heavily padded at the base to prevent damage to the toes. Jazz shoes, which lace on and look like street shoes, are generally made of leather with a rubber sole and heel. The sole might be whole or split to offer more flexibility. Jazz shoes may be boot height to give the dancer firmer ankle support. Tap shoes also vary in style and construction, but they usually include a layer of fiberboard glued and stapled to the leather sole. The extra layer provides a hard surface for the screws holding the metal taps. Men's tap shoes can be almost any style, while those for women generally have a stacked heel and a strap. A rubber pad is sometimes attached to the bottom of the sole to prevent slipping. Whether a dancer chooses to leap, glide, or tap, there is a shoe that will help get the "pointe" across.

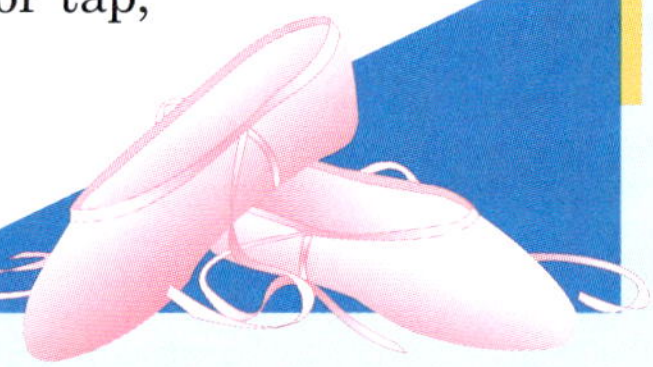

Respond to the reading. What is the specific topic of this paragraph? What supporting facts or examples does the writer include? Name at least three of them.

Write an expository paragraph. Write a paragraph that shares information about a specific topic. Be sure to include plenty of supporting details and structure your ideas in a sustained way. (Follow the guidelines on page 604.)

Persuasive Paragraph

A **persuasive paragraph** expresses an opinion and tries to convince the reader that the opinion is valid. To be persuasive, a writer must include effective supporting reasons and facts.

Topic Sentence

Body

Closing Sentence

Helping One Child Helps the World

The Midtown High School Spanish Club should sponsor a needy child in a Spanish-speaking country, working through the Save the Children Foundation. Such sponsorship would be extremely beneficial to all. Club members would be encouraged to communicate with the child. Sending and receiving letters in Spanish would enhance our Spanish reading and writing skills. In addition, we could ask questions and receive information about the child's city and country, further expanding our understanding of another culture. Finally, we would be doing something important. Offering humanitarian aid is one of the most selfless and beneficial things a person can do, and sponsoring a child could even prove to be life saving. Our sponsorship would help assure the child's nutritional and educational needs are met, giving that child a better life. Some members have said that our club could not afford to sponsor a child, but the cost of $18 a month could easily be covered for an entire year by our club's treasury. We could also do additional fund-raising to send extra materials and supplies to our adopted child. This shared sense of purpose would draw club members closer together, creating a family feeling. The Spanish Club sponsoring a needy child would benefit everyone and should begin as soon as possible.

Respond to the reading. What is the writer's opinion in the paragraph? What reasons does the writer include to support the opinion? Name two.

Write a persuasive paragraph. Write a paragraph expressing your opinion about an event or an activity. Include at least two or three strong reasons that support your opinion. Be sure to structure your ideas in a sustained, persuasive way. (Follow the guidelines on page 604.)

TEKS 10.13A–10.13D, 10.17C, 10.18B(i)–10.18B(iii), 10.19
ELPS 5C

Writing Guidelines Developing a Paragraph

Before you begin your writing, make sure you understand the requirements of the assignment. Then follow the steps listed below.

Prewriting Planning Your Writing

- Select a specific topic that meets the assigned requirements.
- Collect facts, examples, and other details about your topic.
- Write a topic sentence stating what your paragraph will be about. (See page 599.)
- Decide on the best way to organize the supporting details. (See pages 607–610.)

Drafting Developing Your Ideas

- Start your paragraph with the topic sentence.
- Follow with sentences that support your topic. Use your details and organizational plan as a general guide.
- Connect your ideas and sentences with transitions.
- Close with a sentence that restates your topic, gives a final thought, or, in the case of an essay, leads into the next paragraph.

Revising Improving Your Writing

- Add information if you need to say more about your topic or better convey your subtlety of meaning.
- Move sentences that aren't in the best order.
- Delete sentences that don't support the topic.
- Rewrite any sentences that are unclear.

Editing Checking for Conventions

- Check the revised draft for grammar, sentence structure, capitalization, punctuation, and spelling. Correct all errors.
- Write a neat final copy and proofread it one last time.

Tip

When you write a paragraph, remember that the reader wants to . . .

- learn something new and interesting and hear the writer's voice. *(Let your personality come through in the writing.)*

Types of Details

There are many types of details you can include in paragraphs (and in longer forms of writing). The purpose of your writing determines which details you should use. The key types are explained below and on the following page.

Facts are *details* that can be proven.

The Great Chicago Fire began on October 8, 1871.

Eating blueberries helps lower cholesterol and prevent infections.

Statistics present *numerical information* (numbers) about a specific topic.

In 2010, more than 400 people in the United States were hit by lightning, and on average, lightning strikes result in approximately 50 deaths per year in our country. (National Safety Council; CNN.com)

Examples are *statements that illustrate a main point.*

A pancake may not always be called a pancake *(main point)*. **In Wales, pancakes are called Welshcakes and might be served flat or split and spread with jam. France has its crepes, and Italy, its cannelloni. In the Middle East, you'll find sweet wedding pancakes called ataif. In Russia or Poland, you can enjoy delicious blini, but if you're hungry in Hungary, ask for palacsinta.**

Anecdotes are *brief stories* that help to make a point about a topic. They can be much more effective than a matter-of-fact list of details.

Members of the media might try to influence us, but they often find that they should not underestimate the American voter. Perhaps the best example of this occurred during the presidential election of 1948. Harry Truman was running for re-election against Thomas Dewey, the popular governor of New York. All the polls and commentators had predicted a landslide victory for Dewey, and even Truman's wife, Bess, felt her husband could not win.

Truman refused to give up, and set off on a "whistle stop" campaign, traveling the country to talk to the people face-to-face. The night of the election, Truman went to bed early, convinced he would lose. Dewey's victory seemed such a sure thing, the ***Chicago Tribune*** **even printed the next day's headline early: "Dewey Defeats Truman." But in the morning, the results showed that Truman had won. The American people had ignored the polls and had made the decision for themselves.**

Quotations are *people's statements* repeated word for word. Quotations can provide powerful supporting evidence.

Hunger is a great motivator for change, as witnessed by the French Revolution and by the rise of Nazi Germany. Both governmental changes were precipitated by the poverty of the common people, who resorted to violence to improve their lives. As O. Henry wrote, "Love and business and family and religion and art and patriotism are nothing but shadows of words when a man's starving." People who are fed and comfortable will accept the status quo, while those who are in need often demand violent change.

Definitions give the *meaning* of unfamiliar terms. Definitions of technical terms are especially important for the reader. Defining such terms makes your writing clear.

Chiaroscuro—the play of light and shade—to create mood was used effectively in films by Orson Welles and Alfred Hitchcock.

Reasons answer *why* and can explain or justify ideas.

Carpeting the school would be an excellent idea. A good indoor-outdoor carpet would muffle noise in hallways and classes, creating an atmosphere conducive to learning. Carpeting creates a more formal feel, subtly encouraging better behavior and reducing litter. Carpeting is also easier to repair than hard flooring, as a damaged or stained area can simply be cut out and a new patch set in.

Comparisons address the *similarities* or *differences* between two things. It is especially helpful to compare something new or unknown to something your reader understands.

Regular broadcast television and satellite television both depend on radio waves to deliver the signal to your TV. Broadcast television is limited because the waves transmitted follow a straight path, eventually heading into space. Satellite TV, however, uses a fixed-location space satellite to catch the waves and bounce them back, allowing for a greater number of signals and, consequently, a larger choice of TV stations.

Try It!

Find examples in this book's writing samples of any four types of details listed on the previous two pages. On your own paper, write the examples and the pages where you found them.

Patterns of Organization

On the following four pages, sample paragraphs show basic patterns of organization. Reviewing these samples can help you organize your own writing.

Chronological Order

Chronological (time) **order** is effective for explaining a process or sharing a story. The paragraph below, from a procedural document written for customers, explains how to change the oil and the oil filter in a car.

Graphic Organizer: Time Line

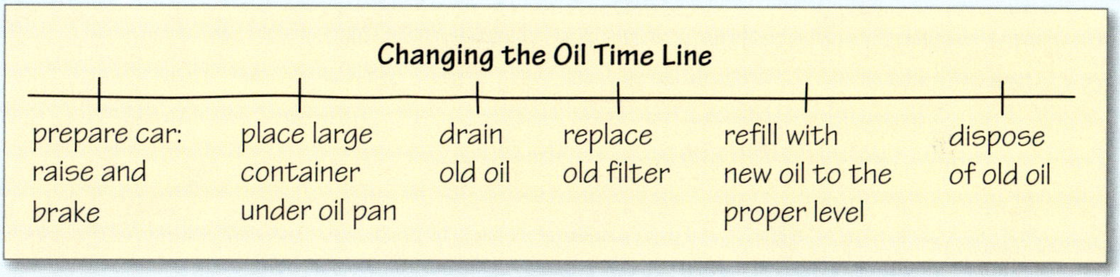
Changing the Oil Time Line
prepare car: raise and brake
place large container under oil pan
drain old oil
replace old filter
refill with new oil to the proper level
dispose of old oil

Topic Sentence

Body

Closing Sentence

Change Is Good

Changing the oil and oil filter in a car is easy. First, put several newspapers under the engine to catch any oil accidentally spilled while the oil is drained. Then place a large container under the oil pan to catch the old oil. Lie on some newspaper and use a wrench to loosen the plug. Wear rubber gloves and use your fingers to gently unscrew the plug and pull it quickly away, allowing the old oil to pour into the container beneath. When all the oil has drained, replace the plug, tightening it with the wrench. Next, loosen the old oil filter with a filter wrench. Finish removing the filter by hand and empty the contents into the used-oil container. Spread a small amount of oil around the new filter's gasket to create a good seal and hand-turn the new filter into place. Finally, remove the engine's oil cap and pour in the new oil to the proper level. Be sure to properly dispose of the old oil at a recycling center. With a little care and regular oil changes, an engine will continue to run smoothly for a long time.

TEKS 10.13B
ELPS 3E, 3H

Cause and Effect

Cause-effect paragraphs can take on a variety of forms: one cause with many effects (as in the sample below), many causes that create one final effect, and other variations. When writing about cause-and-effect relationships, you can use an organizer like the one below to arrange details.

Cause-Effect Organizer

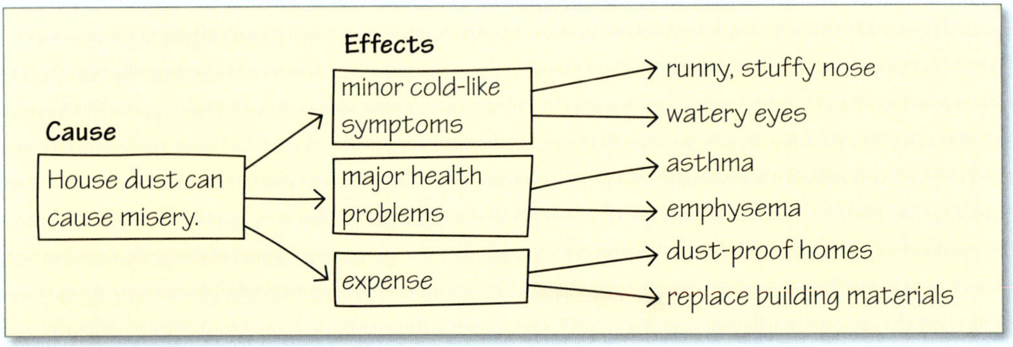

Topic Sentence

Body

Closing Sentence

The Dust of the Earth

House dust, if considered at all, is usually dismissed as an unavoidable inconvenience; but for allergy sufferers, it can mean total misery. The allergic reaction to dust can include chronic year-round rhinitis, or runny nose. Other symptoms may include sneezing and a stuffy nose. The sufferer may have itchy, teary eyes, or even develop a rash or hives. Dust allergies can mimic major health problems such as asthma or emphysema, with wheezing or shortness of breath, accompanied by coughing. People who already have these diseases could find their conditions aggravated by dust. Many people who suffer from dust allergies may face significant expenses because they must dust-proof their homes with special air filters and substitute existing building materials with nonallergenic ones. A little dust doesn't seem so bad, but in extreme cases, it can lead to major health issues and heavy financial costs.

Try It!

Work with a classmate and re-read the paragraph above. Take turns explaining and describing to each other the effects of house dust on people who suffer from allergies. Use specific details in your description.

Classification

Classification is a technique used to break down a topic into categories. The following paragraph classifies the different types of pyramids. The writer used a line diagram to plan her writing.

Line Diagram

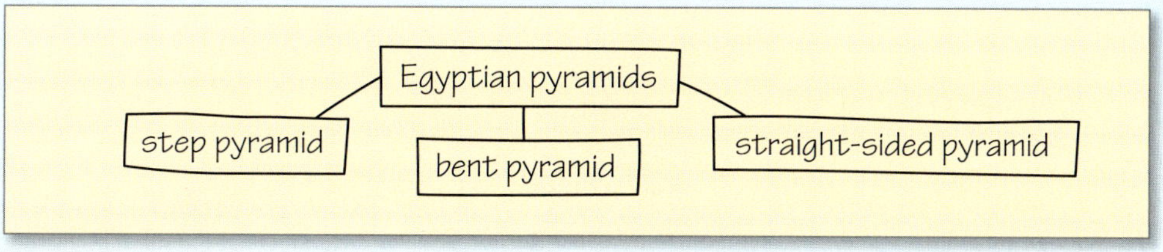

Topic Sentence

Body

Closing Sentence

Types of Pyramids

Three distinct styles of pyramids were created in ancient Egypt: the step pyramid, the bent pyramid, and the more commonly recognized straight-sided pyramid. The step pyramid actually evolved from the earliest burial chambers, the *mastabas,* which were low, flat structures built of mud brick. Around 2780 B.C.E., the architect Imhotep stacked six successively smaller mastabas, creating the first step pyramid as a burial chamber for King Djoser. This pyramid can be seen near Saqqara, south of Cairo. The next attempt at a pyramid came in Dashur, also south of Cairo, during the reign of Pharaoh Snefru. The limestone-faced sides were straight, but they changed angle and cut sharply inward about halfway up, creating a bent, squashed-looking top. Not satisfied with this design, Snefru ordered another pyramid to be built, this time with straight sides that met at a tip. The result was the first straight-sided pyramid, called the red pyramid because the sun gave it a reddish tint. Snefru's son, Khufru, also known as Cheops, perfected the pyramid, creating the magnificent Great Pyramid of Giza, today known as one of the Seven Wonders of the Ancient World. Whether step, bent, or straight-sided, the pyramids of Egypt are magnificent reminders of a great ancient nation.

Respond to the reading. What facts or details did you learn about the straight-sided pyramid? Name three.

TEKS 10.13B

Comparison and Contrast

Organizing by **comparison** shows the similarities or differences between two subjects. To compare trolleys with modern buses, one student used a Venn diagram. After organizing her details, she found the two modes of transportation had key similarities, which became the focus of her paragraph.

Venn Diagram

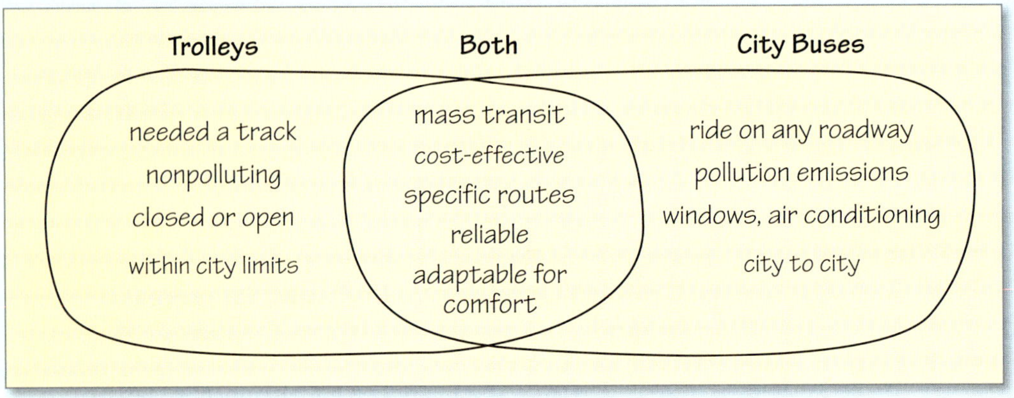

Trolley Cars and Buses

Topic Sentence

Today's buses might seem like a huge improvement over the trolley cars of a century ago, but in some ways the old mode of transportation was very similar to its modern counterpart.

Body

Trolleys were an early form of mass transportation, and, like modern buses, they were able to move large numbers of people across cities in an efficient, cost-effective manner. Like buses, trolleys had established routes with specific schedules, making both modes of transportation convenient and reliable for commuters. Today's buses provide air-conditioned relief from hot weather and comfortable heat when the weather is cold. Similarly, trolleys also adapted for rider comfort, though they had to rely on removable wooden panels to let in cool summer breezes or to shut out cold winter winds.

Closing Sentence

So while modern buses offer comfortable, efficient transportation, trolleys served well as a moving force of yesterday. The two really aren't that different after all, showing, perhaps, that the more things change, the more they stay the same.

TEKS 10.13A–10.13C, 10.13E, 10.14A
ELPS 5G

Modeling Paragraphs

When you come across paragraphs that you really like, practice writing examples of your own that follow the author's pattern of writing. This process is called **modeling**. Follow these guidelines:

Guidelines for Modeling

- **Find a paragraph** you would like to model.
- **Think of a topic** for your practice writing.
- **Follow the pattern** of the paragraph.
- **Build your paragraph** one sentence or idea at a time.
- **Review your work** and change any parts that seem confusing.

Using an Anecdote

An anecdote is a brief story that can be used to illustrate a point. The following paragraph uses an anecdote in this way.

I had always thought I lacked the genes for artistic expression. My artwork was chaotic and my sculptures misshapen. Even coloring inside the lines when I was little was an exercise in futility. Then I had an art class with Ms. Edelman. She laughed at my mistakes and encouraged me to try again. I learned to carefully follow her directions, but also to experiment with new ideas. Sometimes the results were awful, but Ms. Edelman said that failure is only a stepping-stone to success. She taught me to look at art not as a finished product, but as a creative process, and that I should value and have confidence in my efforts. Most important, I learned that everyone has the ability for creative expression, even if that expression is unconventional or unappreciated. Ms. Edelman taught me that a good, caring teacher can make a huge difference in a student's life.

Respond to the reading. What is the topic of the above paragraph? In which sentence is the topic identified? Which main points provide the strongest support of the topic? Name two.

Try It!

Write a paragraph modeled on the sample above. Consider your audience and refer to the modeling guidelines to help you complete your writing.

ELPS 4I, 4K

"Good writing has an aliveness that keeps the reader reading from one paragraph to the next."
—William Zinsser

Creating a List Paragraph

A creative way to develop a paragraph is to provide supporting sentences, one after another, almost in list form. In the following paragraph, the writer "lists" her friends like a lineup of television programs.

I was just . . .
After that . . .
MILK

Lunchtime with my friends is like watching television—with a complete lineup of television programs. Drew supplies the news and commentary, advising us all of the latest school happenings, along with his sometimes sarcastic "editorials." Keisha provides us with our own private sitcom, as she hilariously describes her ups and downs of the morning, along with some dead-on impersonations of teachers and other students. Gabriel is our public service announcer, serenely reminding us of the importance of our music and drama departments, and trying to get us involved. Meanwhile, Yolanda rattles off sports anecdotes and updates for the current teams, including who is starting, injured, or benched because of grades. Squeezed in between all these formidable conversations, Leanne manages to give us a celebrity update, dropping in gossipy little tidbits about the social life of various CHS students. So what is my function while all this chatter is going on? I serve as the audience, appreciating the array of friends who offer me such varied programming.

Respond to the reading. **What is the topic of this paragraph? What do all of the sentences in the body have in common?**

Try It!

Write your own list paragraph modeled after the sample above. Refer to the guidelines for modeling on page **611** to help you complete your writing.

Connecting Paragraphs in Essays

To write strong essays, you must organize the ideas within each paragraph and then organize the paragraphs within the essay. The guidelines that follow will help you connect the paragraphs in your essay.

- **Be sure that your paragraphs are complete.** Each one should contain an effective topic sentence and supporting details.
- **Identify the topic and thesis (focus) of your essay** in the beginning paragraph. Start with some interesting details to get the reader's attention. Then share the focus of your writing.
- **Develop your ideas** in the middle paragraphs. Each middle paragraph should include information that explains and supports your focus. Often, the paragraph that contains the most important information comes right after the beginning paragraph or right before the final paragraph.
- **Review one or more of the main points in your essay** in the closing paragraph. The last sentence usually gives the reader a final interesting thought about the topic.
- **Use transition words or phrases** to connect the paragraphs. Transitions help the reader follow an essay from one paragraph to the next. In the sample below, the transitions are shown in red.

. . . Suddenly, sports enthusiasts discovered they did not need a boat to go sailing.

In addition to skateboard sailing, people started adding sails when they went skiing, snowboarding, or roller-skating. Using the principles of water sailing, they were able to increase their speed and skills, moving rapidly across the landscape. . . .

Because of several factors, wind sports have gained in popularity through the past decade. For one, wind power is free, and all the sailor needs is a sail and something to slide or glide on. Another reason for the popularity of wind sports is the availability of places to practice. Any snowy area, flat or hilly, works for winter sailing, while parking lots and quiet streets offer excellent summer conditions. . . .

Try It!

Turn to pages **628–629** to see examples of transition words and phrases. Find one or two writing samples that use some of these transitions.

TEKS 10.13B, ELPS 4G, 4I, 4J

Sample Essay

Read this sample essay about coffee production. Notice how the three parts—the beginning, the middle, and the ending—work together.

Java Crisis

The production of coffee beans is a huge, profitable business, but, unfortunately, full-sun production is taking over the industry and leaving destruction in its wake. The change in how coffee is grown endangers the very existence of certain animals and birds, and even alters the world's environmental equilibrium.

On a local level, the devastation of the forest required by full-sun fields affects the area's birds and animals. The forest canopy of shade trees provides a home for migratory birds and other species that depend on the trees' flowers and fruits. Full-sun coffee growers destroy this forest home. Many species have already become extinct due to deforestation, and many more are quickly dying out.

On a more global level, the destruction of the rain forest for full-sun coffee fields also threatens human life. Medical research often makes use of the forests' plant and animal life, and the destruction of such species could prevent researchers from finding cures for certain diseases. In addition, new coffee-growing techniques are contributing to toxic runoff that is poisoning the water locally—a poison that could eventually find its way into much of the world's groundwater.

Both locally and globally, the continued spread of full-sun coffee plantations could mean the ultimate destruction of the rain-forest ecology. The loss of shade trees is already causing a slight change in the world's climate, and studies show that the loss of oxygen-giving trees also contributes to air pollution and global warming. In addition, the new growing techniques are contributing to acidic soil conditions and erosion.

It is obvious that the way much coffee is grown affects many aspects of life, from the local environment to the global ecology. But consumers do have a choice. They can purchase shade-grown coffee whenever possible, although at a higher cost. The future health of the planet and its inhabitants is surely worth more than an inexpensive cup of coffee.

Look at the transitions. What specific words does the author use to move from one paragraph to the next? Identify them.

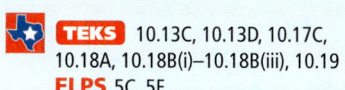

TEKS 10.13C, 10.13D, 10.17C, 10.18A, 10.18B(i)–10.18B(iii), 10.19
ELPS 5C, 5F

Texas Traits

Paragraph Traits Checklist

Use the checklist below as a basic guide when you review your paragraphs. If you answer "no" to any of the questions, continue to work with that part of your paragraph.

Revising and Editing Checklist

Focus and Coherence

_____ **1.** Do I have a clear topic sentence and an effective conclusion?
_____ **2.** Does the body of my paragraph or essay support the thesis?
_____ **3.** After I have thought more about the purpose for my writing, do I need to revise my writing?

Organization

_____ **4.** Is my organizational pattern appropriate for my audience and topic?
_____ **5.** Have I used transitions to connect my ideas?

Development of Ideas

_____ **6.** Have I included specific, relevant details to support both my topic sentences and my thesis statement?
_____ **7.** Have I fully developed each of my ideas?

Voice

_____ **8.** Do I sound interested in and knowledgeable about my topic?
_____ **9.** Does my voice fit the assignment and my audience?
_____ **10.** Is my word choice appropriate for my topic and audience?

Conventions

_____ **11.** Have I checked for and corrected errors in grammar, sentence structure, capitalization, and punctuation?
_____ **12.** Have I checked carefully for spelling errors using a dictionary or my computer spell-checker?

ELPS 1E, 2C, 3B, 3D, 3E, 4G

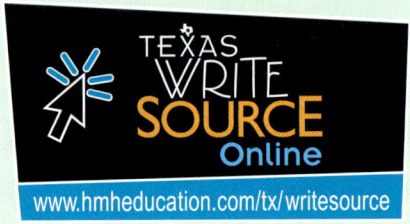

TEXAS WRITE SOURCE Online
www.hmheducation.com/tx/writesource

A Writer's Resource

Writing Focus

Learning Language

Work with a partner. Read the definitions below and share your answers to the questions that follow.

1. A **commitment** is a pledge or an agreement to do something.
   What commitments have you made for the coming week?
2. **To incorporate** means to combine into an organized whole.
   What is one of the ways to incorporate evidence into an essay?
3. **Subsequent** means following in time or order.
   What are your plans subsequent to graduating from high school?
4. A "**red-letter day**" is an important or very good day.
   Why is the first day of high school considered a red-letter day?

A Writer's Resource

Personal narratives, persuasive essays, short stories, poetry, reports—writing assignments come in all shapes and sizes. Some assignments come together quite easily because you know a lot about the topic; others are more challenging because they require thoughtful planning and research. Whatever the situation, you should approach *all* writing assignments in the same way—with a commitment to do your best work.

This chapter contains tips and guidelines to help you complete any writing assignment creatively and effectively. Once you become familiar with this material, you'll find it easier to write essays, articles, research papers, and more.

- **Finding a Topic**
- **Knowing the Different Forms**
- **Collecting and Organizing Details**
- **Creating an Outline**
- **Using Transitions**
- **Writing Thesis Statements**
- **Writing Great Beginnings and Endings**
- **Integrating Quotations**
- **Learning Key Writing Terms**
- **Using Writing Techniques**
- **Adding Graphics to Your Writing**

"When everything seems to be going against you, remember the airplane takes off against the wind, not with it."

—Henry Ford

TEKS 10.13A

Finding a Topic

Searching for a topic can be a challenge even if the teacher provides a general writing subject. For example, you might be asked to write about the westward development of the United States in the 1800s. This subject is too broad to cover well in one paper. It would be necessary to narrow the focus to find a manageable topic. Here are some ideas to help you.

Using a Cluster Diagram

A cluster diagram can help you identify a topic. Place the general subject in the center and then break it down into categories. Break each category into yet smaller topics. Choose one that has enough information and is the most interesting to you.

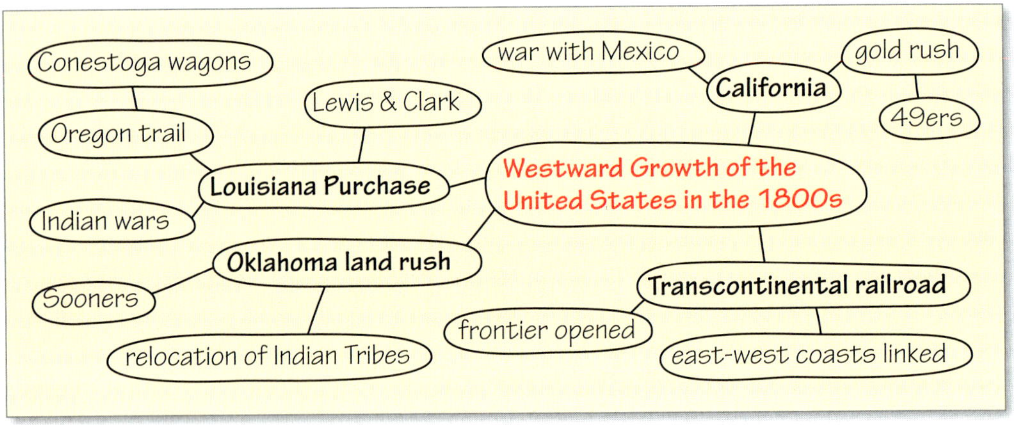

Trying Freewriting

Freewriting can help you identify a topic. Take a few minutes to write what you can remember about a general subject. Incorporate questions and ideas that occur to you as you write. The freewriting below led one student to write about the relocation of Native American tribes.

> The book Bury My Heart at Wounded Knee really made me think. I knew that people came from other countries to start a new life here and that the transcontinental railroad made it much easier to open the West to settlement. But why couldn't Native Americans and settlers share the land? The ownership of land seemed to make cooperation impossible. Were reservations the only answer? How long did it take to settle the West?

Reviewing a "Basics of Life" List

Most people find they need a few basic things in order to live a full life. The list below, a "Basics of Life" list, could help you focus on a topic. For example, choosing "trade/money" might lead you to explore and write about ranching and cattle drives.

family	warmth	food	shelter
friends	work	community	art/music
faith/religion	love	machines	natural resources
tools	education	clothing	health
hobbies	identity	trade/money	literature
water	rules/laws	freedom	government

Studying Visual Images

Paintings and visuals can give you topic ideas as well. The paintings and photographs of the Old West by nineteenth-century artists could prompt you to write about changes brought to the West by the transcontinental railroad.

Using Writing Prompts

Every day is full of experiences that make you think. You do things that you feel good about. You hear things that make you angry. You wonder how different things work. You are reminded of a past experience. These everyday thoughts can make excellent starting points for writing. As you write about one of these prompts, a number of specific topics will come to mind.

Best and Worst

My most memorable day in school
My best hour
My encounter with a bully

It could only happen to me!

A narrow escape from trouble
I was so shocked when . . .
My life began in this way.
My strangest phone conversation
If only I had done that differently
Whatever happened to my . . .

Quotations

"Someone who makes no mistakes does not usually make anything."

"When people are free to do as they please, they usually imitate each other."

"More is not always better."

"It is easier to forgive an enemy than a friend."

"Never give advice unless asked."

"Honesty is the best policy."

"Know thyself."

"Like mother, like daughter."

"Like father, like son."

I was thinking.

Everyone should know . . .
Where do I draw the line?
Is it better to laugh or cry?
Why do people like to go fast?
I don't understand why . . .

First and Last

My first game or performance
My last day of ____________
My last visit with __________

School, Then and Now

The pressure of tryouts
Grades—are they the most important part of school?
Finally, a good assembly
What my school really needs is . . .
A teacher I respect
I'm in favor of more . . .

People and Places

Who knows me best? What does he or she know?
Getting along with my brother, sister, or friend
A person I admire
My grandparents' house
The emergency room
A guided tour of my neighborhood

Using Sample Topics

People, places, experiences, and information you encounter all offer springboards for writing. Here are some topic ideas for descriptive, narrative, expository, and persuasive writing.

Descriptive

People: friend, cousin, favorite uncle, minister, boss, cashier, waiter, parent, bus driver, librarian, professional athlete

Places: store, diner, river, amusement park, religious building, train station, airport, city center, zoo, cemetery

Things: video game, CD, bike, wrench, skateboard, basketball, warehouse, movie, shoes, spoon, book, bench, kiosk, postcard

Animals: elephant, walrus, pigeon, zebra, mouse, spider, moth, poodle, penguin, cat, lobster, rat, raccoon, squirrel

Narrative

Stories: entering an abandoned building, saving an injured bird, helping a lost child, attending the ballet, entering a contest, attending a concert, riding on the train, visiting a museum

Expository

Comparison-Contrast: private school and public school, taxis and buses, apartments and condominiums, butterfly and moth, mopeds and motorcycles, two different city neighborhoods

Cause/Effect: thunder, street potholes, echo, sonic boom, hurricane, sunburn, erosion, capillary action, flooding

Classification: types of volcanoes, kinds of television shows, groups of invertebrates, types of birds, branches of the military, kinds of cameras

Persuasive

School: banning the use of cell phones in school, keeping cars out of the school bus loading area, eliminating all carbonated drinks

Home: getting an electric guitar, negotiating rules about visitors when parents aren't around, sleeping in on Saturdays, taking the bus by yourself, getting a job, going downtown with friends

Community: relocating the stop sign by the library, creating a skateboard park, closing the city center to cars, setting up a teen advisory board for the city

Knowing the Different Forms

Finding the right form, or genre, for your writing is just as important as finding the right topic. When you are selecting a form, be sure to ask yourself who you're writing for (your *audience*) and why you're writing (your *purpose*).

Anecdote	A brief story that helps to make a point
Autobiography	A writer's story of his or her own life
Biography	A writer's story of someone else's life
Book review	An essay offering an opinion about a book, not to be confused with *literary analysis*
Cause and effect	A paper examining an event, the forces leading up to that event, and the effects following the event
Character sketch	A brief description of a specific character showing some aspect of that character's personality
Descriptive writing	Writing that uses sensory details that allow the reader to clearly visualize a person, a place, a thing, or an idea
Editorial	A letter or an article offering an opinion, an idea, or a solution
Essay	A thoughtful piece of writing in which ideas are explained, analyzed, or evaluated
Expository writing	Writing that explains something by presenting its steps, causes, or kinds
Eyewitness account	A report giving specific details of an event or a person
Fable	A short story that teaches a lesson or moral, often using talking animals as the main characters
Fantasy	A story set in an imaginary world in which the characters usually have supernatural powers or abilities
Historical fiction	An invented story based on an actual historical event
Interview	Writing based on facts and details obtained through speaking with another person
Journal writing	Writing regularly to record personal observations, thoughts, and ideas

Literary analysis	A careful examination or interpretation of some aspect of a piece of literature
Myth	A traditional story intended to explain a mystery of nature, religion, or culture
Novel	A book-length story with several characters and a well-developed plot, usually with one or more subplots
Personal narrative	Writing that shares an event or experience from the writer's personal life
Persuasive writing	Writing intended to persuade the reader to follow the writer's way of thinking about something
Play	A form that uses dialogue to tell a story, usually meant to be performed in front of an audience
Poem	A creative expression that may use rhyme, rhythm, and imagery
Problem-solution	Writing that presents a problem followed by a proposed solution
Process paper	Writing that explains how a process works, or how to do or make something
Profile	An essay that reveals an individual or re-creates a time period
Proposal	Writing that includes specific information about an idea or a project that is being considered for approval
Research report	An essay that shares information about a topic that has been thoroughly researched
Response to literature	Writing that is a reaction to something the writer has read
Science fiction	Writing based on real or imaginary science and often set in the future
Short story	A short fictional piece with only a few characters and one conflict or problem
Summary	Writing that presents the most important ideas from a longer piece of writing
Tall tale	A humorous, exaggerated story about a character or an animal that does impossible things
Tragedy	Literature in which the hero fails or is destroyed because of a serious character flaw

Collecting and Organizing Details

Using Graphic Organizers

Graphic organizers can help you gather, organize, and structure your ideas and details for writing. Clustering is one method (see page 618). These two pages show other useful organizers.

Cause-Effect Organizer

Use to collect and organize details for cause-effect essays.

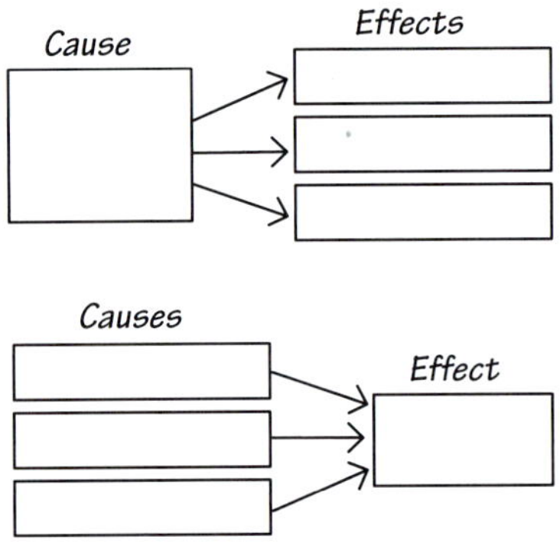

Problem-Solution Web

Use to map out problem-solution essays.

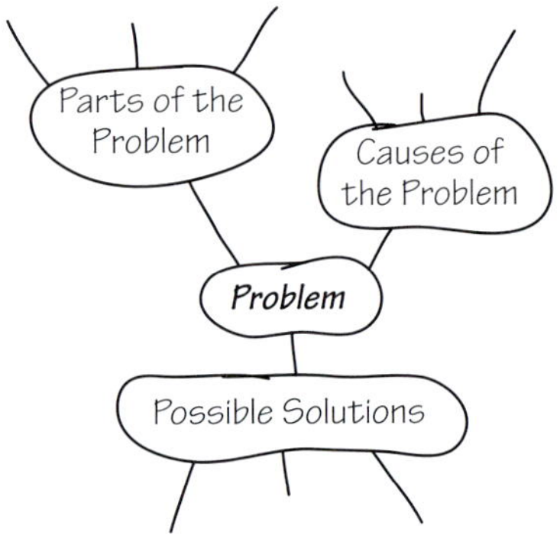

Time Line

Use for personal narratives to list actions or events in the order they occurred.

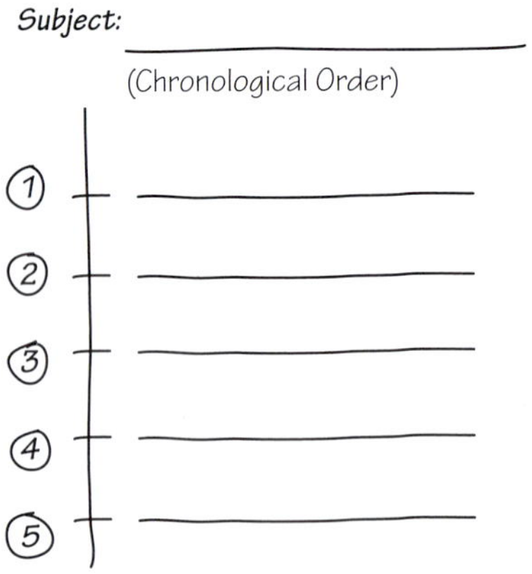

Evaluation Collection Grid

Use to collect supporting details for essays of evaluation.

Subject:

Points to Evaluate	*Supporting Details*
1.	
2.	
3.	
4.	

Venn Diagram

Use to collect details to compare and contrast two topics.

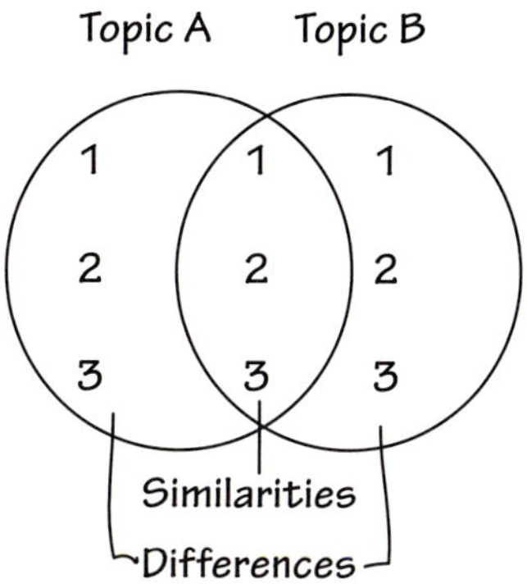

Line Diagram

Use to collect and organize ideas and details for academic essays.

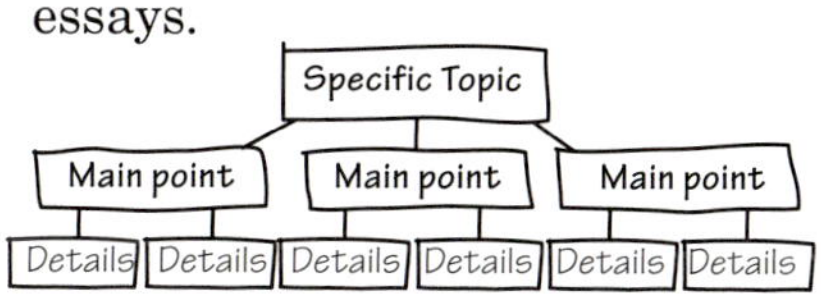

Process (Cycle) Diagram

Use to collect details for science-related writing, such as how a process or cycle works.

Topic: ____________________

(Chronological Order)

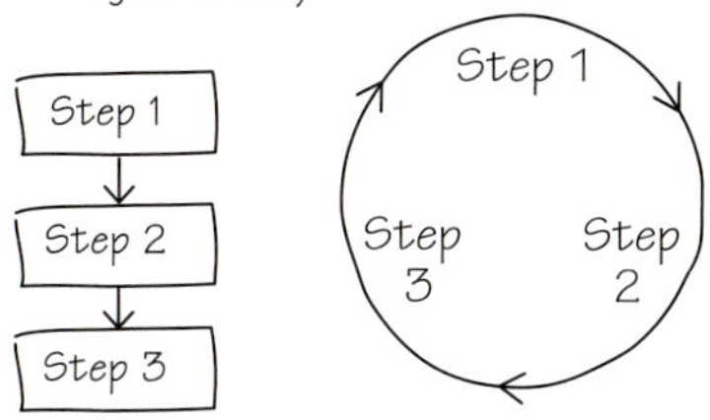

5 W's Chart

Use to collect and structure the *Who? What? When? Where?* and *Why?* details for personal narratives and news stories.

Subject: ____________________

Who?	What?	When?	Where?	Why?

Definition Diagram

Use to gather information for extended definition essays.

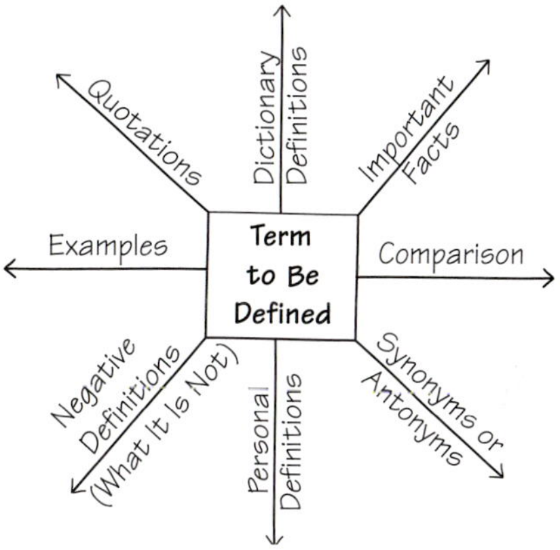

Sensory Chart

Use to collect details for descriptive essays and observation reports.

Subject: ____________________

Sights	Sounds	Smells	Tastes	Textures

Creating an Outline

An **outline** organizes a set of facts or ideas by listing main points and subpoints. An effective outline shows how topics or ideas fit together. A well-designed outline helps you structure your ideas in a sustained way, and it serves as a frame for an effective essay. There are two types of outlines: *topic outlines* and *sentence outlines.* (See the samples below and on the next page.)

A Topic Outline

In a **topic outline**, main points and details appear as phrases rather than as complete sentences. Topic outlines are useful for short essays, including essay-test answers. The information after the Roman numerals (I., II., III., and so on) identifies the main points in the essay. The information after the capital letters (A., B., C., and so on) identifies the details that support the main points.

Sample Topic Outline

I. Effects of malnutrition on the body
- A. Extreme weight loss and stunted growth
- B. Frequent infections
- C. Lower resistance to life-threatening diseases

II. Marasmus—a form of malnutrition
- A. Extremely underweight
- B. Lack of body fat or defined muscles
- C. Puppet-like appearance
- D. Increased internal problems

III. Kwashiorkor—another form of malnutrition
- A. Badly swollen bellies
- B. Pale or red skin
- C. Thinning hair

IV. Effects of malnutrition on development
- A. Limited ability to walk and to talk
- B. Stunted intellectual development
- C. Ongoing effects into adulthood

Note: Information for the opening and closing paragraphs is not included in this outline for an essay on malnutrition.

Tip

In an outline, if you have a "I.," you must have at least a "II." If you have an "A.," you must have at least a "B.," and so on.

A Sentence Outline

A **sentence outline** is a detailed plan for writing. In this type of outline, the ideas are explained in complete sentences. This type of outline is useful for longer writing assignments like research reports and formal essays.

Sample Sentence Outline

I. Malnutrition limits the physical development of children.
  A. Malnutrition causes extreme weight loss and stunted growth.
  B. It can result in children suffering from frequent infections.
  C. It can lower children's resistance to diseases.
II. Marasmus is one form of malnutrition.
  A. Children with this condition lack body fat and muscle.
  B. They appear puppet-like.
  C. This condition causes the skin to sag and wrinkle.
  D. It also decreases the size of internal organs.
III. Kwashiorkor is another form of malnutrition.
  A. Children with this condition have swollen bellies.
  B. Kwashiorkor causes pale or red skin and thinning hair.
  C. This condition causes growth to stop.
IV. Malnutrition limits the mental development of children.
  A. It hinders toddlers' ability to walk and to talk.
  B. Iron and iodine deficiencies stunt intellectual development.
  C. Malnutrition in early childhood affects ongoing learning.

A Quick List

Use a **quick list** when there is no time for an outline. A quick list organizes ideas in the most basic way, but it will still help you organize or structure your writing.

Sample Quick List

Malnutrition
- *effects on body (physical)*
- marasmus
- kwashiorkor
- *effects on development (mental)*

Using Transitions

Transitions can be used to connect one sentence to another sentence within a paragraph, or to connect one paragraph to another within a longer essay or report. The lists below show a number of transitions and how they are used.

Each **colored list** below is a group of transitions that could work well together in a piece of writing.

Words used to show location

above	around	between	inside	outside
across	behind	by	into	over
against	below	down	near	throughout
along	beneath	in back of	next to	to the right
among	beside	in front of	on top of	under

Above	In front of	On top of
Below	Beside	Next to
To the left	In back of	Beneath
To the right		

Words used to show time

about	during	yesterday	until	finally
after	first	meanwhile	next	then
at	second	today	soon	as soon as
before	to begin	tomorrow	later	in the end

First	To begin	Now	First	Before
Second	To continue	Soon	Then	During
Third	To conclude	Eventually	Next	After
Finally			In the end	Subsequent

Words used to compare things

likewise	as	in the same way	one way
like	also	similarly	both

In the same way	One way
Also	Another way
Similarly	Both

Words used to contrast (show differences)

but	still	although	on the other hand
however	yet	otherwise	even though

On the other hand	Although
Even though	Yet
Still	Nevertheless

Words used to emphasize a point

again	truly	especially	for this reason
to repeat	in fact	to emphasize	

For this reason	Truly	In fact
Especially	To emphasize	To repeat

Words used to conclude or summarize

finally	as a result	to sum it up	in conclusion
lastly	therefore	all in all	because

Because	As a result	To sum it up	Therefore
In conclusion	All in all	Because	Finally

Words used to add information

again	another	for instance	for example
also	and	moreover	additionally
as well	besides	along with	other
next	finally	in addition	

For example	For instance	Next	Another
Additionally	Besides	Moreover	Along with
Finally	Next	Also	As well

Words used to clarify

in other words	for instance	that is	for example

For instance	For example
In other words	Equally important

Writing Thesis Statements

An effective thesis statement tells the reader specifically what you plan to write about. In a longer essay or research report, your thesis statement generally comes at the end of the opening paragraph. It serves as a guide to keep you on track as you develop your writing. You will be supporting your thesis statement with logical reasons and relevant evidence as your write your essay.

The Process at Work

A thesis statement usually takes a stand or expresses a specific feeling about, or feature of, your topic. Write as many versions as it takes to hit upon the statement that sets the right tone for your writing. The following formula can be used to form your thesis statements.

A specific topic *(The Lincoln Memorial)*
\+ **a particular stand, feeling, or feature** *(is being damaged by pollution.)*
= **an effective thesis statement.**

Sample Thesis Statements

Writing Assignment: Research report about aviation
Specific Topic: The DC-3 airplane
Thesis Statement: The DC-3 airplane established many structural standards for propeller aircraft.

Writing Assignment: Expository essay on cooking
Specific Topic: Gourmet meal
Thesis Statement: A gourmet meal results from careful preparation.

Writing Assignment: Analysis of a poem
Specific Topic: "Old Ironsides" by Oliver Wendell Holmes
Thesis Statement: Oliver Wendell Holmes wrote "Old Ironsides" to support the restoration of a historic warship.

Thesis Checklist

Be sure that your thesis statement . . .

_____ identifies a limited, specific topic,
_____ focuses on a particular feature or feeling about the topic,
_____ is stated in one or more clear sentences,
_____ can be supported with logical reasons, convincing facts and details, and meets the requirements of the assignment.

Writing Great Beginnings

There are a variety of rhetorical devices you can use as you write your opening paragraph. Try one of these approaches to grab the reader's attention, introduce your topic, and present your thesis.

- **Start with an important or an interesting fact.**
  A catalytic converter is a key component in reducing automobile exhaust emissions.
- **Ask an interesting question.**
  How many people know that the internal temperature of a catalytic converter can reach 1,200 degrees Fahrenheit?
- **Start with a quotation.**
  George Wilson, a technician at Miller Motors, warned us, "A badly timed engine can raise catalytic temperatures to more than 1,200 degrees Fahrenheit!"

Trying a Beginning Strategy

If you have trouble writing your first paragraph, follow the example below.

First sentence—Grab the reader's attention.
Write a sentence that will draw the reader into the topic. (See above.)

Did you know that the internal temperature of a catalytic converter can reach 1,200 degrees Fahrenheit?

Second sentence—Give some background information.
Supporting information will add clarity and interest to your paper.

A catalytic converter is enclosed in stainless steel, so it should last a long time.

Third sentence—Introduce the specific topic of the essay.
Introduce the topic in a way that builds up to the thesis statement.

Car companies have installed this device in automobiles to meet emission standards.

Fourth sentence—Give the thesis statement.
Clearly present the thesis statement. (See page 630).

Fortunately, the installation of catalytic converters has greatly reduced exhaust emissions in cars.

TEKS 10.13B

Developing Great Endings

The closing paragraph of a paper should summarize your thesis and leave the reader with something to think about. When writing your closing paragraph, use two or more of the following ideas.

- Reflect on the topic.
- Restate your thesis.
- Review your main supporting points.
- Emphasize the special importance of one main point.
- Answer any questions the reader may still have.
- Draw a conclusion and put the information in perspective.
- Provide a final significant thought for the reader.

Trying an Ending Strategy

If you have trouble coming up with an effective closing paragraph, follow the step-by-step example below. Remember that in your conclusion, as in the body of your essay, you must structure your ideas in a sustained way.

First sentence—Reflect on the topic.

Start by reflecting on the material presented previously about the topic.

Emission controls have greatly improved air quality in major cities.

Second sentence—Add another point.

Include a significant point of interest that you didn't mention before.

Along with clearer skies, catalytic converters have also offered the bonus of greater fuel economy.

Third sentence—Emphasize the most important point.

Stress the importance of one or more key points that support the thesis.

Continued improvements of the catalytic converter will mean longer equipment life and increased pollution control.

Fourth sentence—Wrap up the topic or draw a conclusion.

Add one final thought about the topic or draw a conclusion from the points you've presented in the writing.

Although the cost of developing the catalytic converter may be substantial, there is no price too high to pay for cleaner, breathable air.

Integrating Quotations

Always choose quotations that are clear and appropriate for your writing. Quotations should *support* your ideas, not replace them.

Trying Strategies for Using Quotations

Use the strategies below to get the most from quoted material in your writing.

- **Use quotations to support your own thoughts and ideas.** Effective quotations can support your main points and arguments.

  Doing what you know to be right will build your self-esteem. As Mark Twain noted, "A man cannot be comfortable without his own approval." That is why it is so important to let your conscience guide your actions.

- **Use quotations to lend authority to your writing.** Quoting an expert shows that you have researched your topic and understand its significance.

  Albert Einstein observed the growth of nuclear power with concern, stating, "I know not with what weapons World War III will be fought, but World War IV will be fought with sticks and stones." His disturbing comment reminds people that a nuclear war would result in unthinkable destruction.

- **Use quotations that are succinct and powerful.** Any quotation that you use must add value to your writing.

  Clearly, the education provided for today's students will determine the success of the future. As Benjamin Franklin put it, "An investment in knowledge always pays the best interest." A well-funded education system greatly benefits and enriches society.

Common Quotation Problems to Avoid

Keep these problems in mind when you consider using quotations.

- **Don't plagiarize.** Accurately cite sources for all quotations (and paraphrases). Follow an approved style guide for your citations.
- **Don't use long quotations.** Keep quotations brief and to the point.
- **Don't overuse quotations.** Use a quotation only if you can't share the idea as powerfully or effectively in another way.

Learning Key Writing Terms

Here's a glossary of terms that describe aspects of the writing process.

Balance	Arranging words or phrases in a way to give them equal importance
Body	The main part of a piece of writing, containing details that support or develop the thesis statement
Brainstorming	Collecting ideas by thinking freely about all the possibilities; used most often with groups
Central idea	The main point of a piece of writing, often stated in a thesis statement or a topic sentence
Closing sentence	The summary or final part in a piece of writing
Coherence	The logical arranging of ideas so they are clear and easy to follow
Dialogue	Written conversation between two or more people
Emphasis	Giving great importance to a specific idea in a piece of writing
Exposition	Writing that explains and informs
Figurative language	Language that goes beyond the normal meaning of the words used, often called "figures of speech"
Focus (thesis)	The specific part of a topic that is written about in an essay
Generalization	A general statement that gives an overall view, rather than focusing on specific details
Grammar	The rules that govern the standard structure and features of a language
Idiom	A phrase or an expression that means something different from what the words actually say That answer was really out in left field. (This means the answer was not even close to being correct.) Next year you'll sing a different tune. (This means you'll think differently.)
Jargon	The special language of a certain group or occupation The weaver pointed out the fabric's unique warp and weft. Computer jargon: byte icon server virus

Limiting the subject	Narrowing a general subject to a more specific one
Literal	The actual dictionary meaning of a word; a language that means exactly what it appears to mean
Loaded words	Words slanted for or against the subject The new tax bill helps the rich and hurts the poor.
Logic	Correctly using facts, examples, and reasons to support a point
Modifiers	Words, phrases, or clauses that limit or describe another word or group of words
Objective	Writing that gives factual information without adding feelings or opinions (See *subjective.*)
Poetic license	A writer's freedom to bend the rules of writing to achieve a certain effect
Point of view	The position or angle from which a story is told (See page 332.)
Prose	Writing in standard sentence form
Purpose	The specific goal of the writing
Style	The author's unique choice of words and sentences
Subjective	Writing that includes the writer's feelings, attitudes, and opinions (See *objective.*)
Supporting details	Facts or ideas used to sustain the main point
Syntax	The order and relationship of words in a sentence
Theme	The main point or unifying idea of a piece of writing
Thesis statement	A statement of the purpose, or main idea, of an essay
Tone	The writer's attitude toward the subject
Topic	The specific subject of a piece of writing
Topic sentence	The sentence that carries the main idea of a paragraph
Transitions	Words or phrases that connect or tie ideas together
Unity	A sense of oneness in writing in which each sentence helps to develop the main idea
Usage	The way in which people use language (*Standard language* follows the rules; *nonstandard language* does not.)
Voice	A writer's unique personal tone or feeling that comes across in a piece of writing

TEKS 10.13B, 10.14A, 10.15A(ii), 10.15C(iii)
ELPS 4C

Using Writing Techniques

Become familiar with these common literary and rhetorical devices. Experiment with some of these techniques in your own essays and stories.

Allusion A reference to a familiar person, place, thing, or event
Mario threw me my mitt. "Hey, Babe Ruth, you forgot this!"

Analogy A comparison of similar ideas or to help aid clarification.
"There is no frigate like a book, to take us lands away."
—Emily Dickinson

Anecdote A brief story used to illustrate or make a point
It is said that the last words John Adams uttered were "Thomas Jefferson survives." Ironically, Jefferson had died just a few hours earlier. Both deaths occurred on July 4, 1826—the 50th anniversary of the Declaration of Independence. (This anecdote intensifies the importance of both men.)

Colloquialism A common word or phrase suitable for everyday conversation but not for formal speech or writing
"Cool" and "rad" are colloquialisms suggesting approval.

Exaggeration An overstatement or a stretching of the truth to emphasize a point (See *hyperbole* and *overstatement*.)
We opened up the boat's engine and sped along at a million miles an hour.

Flashback A technique in which a writer interrupts a story to go back and relive an earlier time or event
I stopped at the gate, panting. Suddenly I was seven years old again, and my brother was there, calling me "chicken" from the edge of the stone well. Then I opened my eyes and heard only the crickets chirping.

Foreshadowing Hints about what will happen next in a story
As Mai explained why she had to break their date, she noticed Luke looking past her. Turning, she saw Meg smiling—at Luke.

Hyperbole (hi-púr-bə-lē) Exaggeration used to emphasize a point
The music was loud enough to make your ears bleed.

Irony An expression in which the author says one thing but means just the opposite
As we all know, students love nothing better than homework.

TEKS 10.13B, 10.14A, 10.15A(ii), 10.15C(iii)
ELPS 4C

Juxtaposition	Putting two words or ideas close together to create a contrasting of ideas or an ironic meaning **Ah, the sweet smell of fuel emissions!**
Local color	The use of details that are common in a certain place
Metaphor	A figure of speech that compares two things without using the words *like* or *as* **The sheep were dense, dancing clouds scuttling across the road.**
Overstatement	An exaggeration or a stretching of the truth (See *exaggeration* and *hyperbole*.) **On this red-letter day, if I eat one more piece of pie, I will burst!**
Oxymoron	Connecting two words with opposite meanings **small fortune, cruel kindness, original copy**
Paradox	A true statement that says two opposite things **As I crossed the finish line dead last, I felt a surge of triumph.**
Parallelism	Repeating similar grammatical structures (words, phrases, or sentences) to give writing rhythm **We cannot undo, we will not forget, and we should not ignore the pain of the past.**
Personification	A figure of speech in which a nonhuman thing is given human characteristics **The computer spit out my disk.**
Pun	A phrase that uses words that sound the same in a way that gives them a funny effect **I call my dog Trousers because he pants so much.**
Simile	A figure of speech that compares two things using *like* or *as* **Her silent anger was like a rock wall, hard and impenetrable.**
Slang	Informal words or phrases used by a particular group of people **cool it hang out shoot the curl**
Symbol	A concrete object used to represent an idea
Understatement	The opposite of exaggeration; using very calm language to call attention to an object or an idea **The car broke down, we were stranded for two days, and missed the wedding. Other than that we had a great trip.**

Adding Graphics to Your Writing

Graphics and illustrations can enhance your writing by explaining your ideas in a visual manner. You can create graphics and illustrations by hand or design them on a computer and paste them into your document. Be sure to refer to the graphic in the text of your paper, either in the body of a paragraph or in a parenthetical reference.

Line Graphs

Line graphs show change or trends across a period of time. A line graph is drawn as an L-shaped grid. The horizontal axis shows time, and the vertical axis denotes quantity. Dots are plotted and connected to show changes. The stages are clearly labeled as well as the quantity figures.

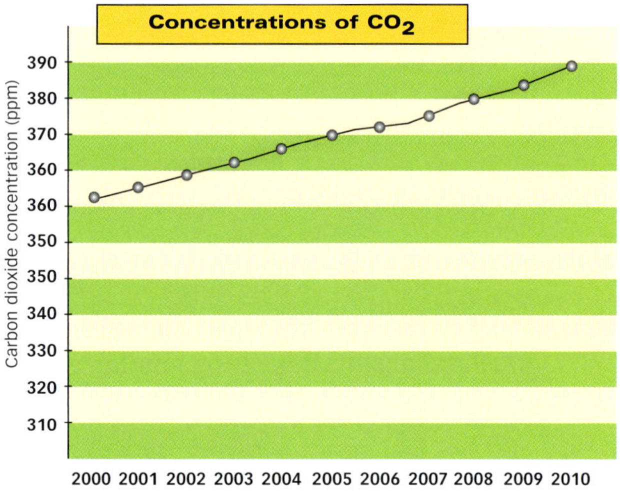

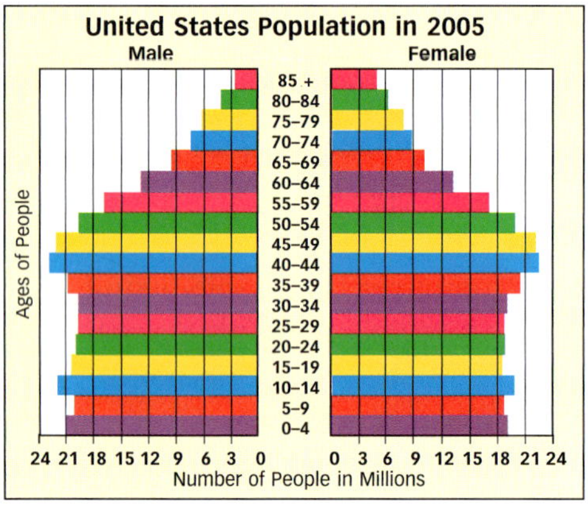

Bar Graphs

Bar graphs use columns representing the subjects of the graph. Unlike the line graph, it does not show how things change over time but is used to show comparisons. The bars may run horizontally or vertically. Label each axis clearly so the reader can easily see and understand the information.

Pie Graphs

Pie graphs show all the proportions and percentages of a whole, along with how those percentages relate to each other. Use a different color for each section. You can either add a key explaining each color or label the graph itself if the graph is large enough.

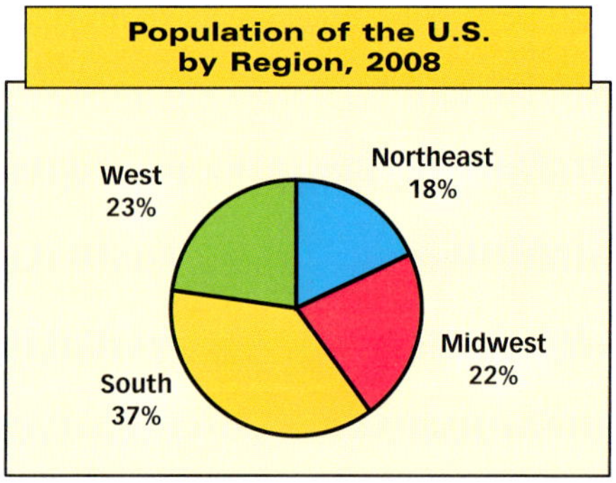

Tables

Tables can organize information in a convenient manner. Most tables have rows (going across) and columns (going down). Rows contain one set of details, while columns contain another. At the right is a sample flight table, showing how far it is from one place to another. Check one place's column against the other's row.

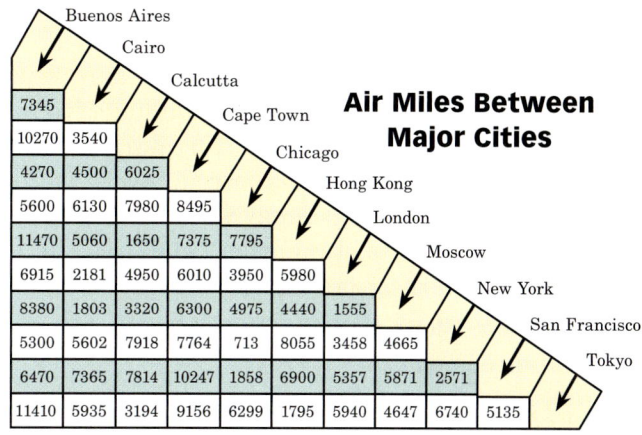

Air Miles Between Major Cities

	Buenos Aires	Cairo	Calcutta	Cape Town	Chicago	Hong Kong	London	Moscow	New York	San Francisco
Cairo	7345									
Calcutta	10270	3540								
Cape Town	4270	4500	6025							
Chicago	5600	6130	7980	8495						
Hong Kong	11470	5060	1650	7375	7795					
London	6915	2181	4950	6010	3950	5980				
Moscow	8380	1803	3320	6300	4975	4440	1555			
New York	5300	5602	7918	7764	713	8055	3458	4665		
San Francisco	6470	7365	7814	10247	1858	6900	5357	5871	2571	
Tokyo	11410	5935	3194	9156	6299	1795	5940	4647	6740	5135

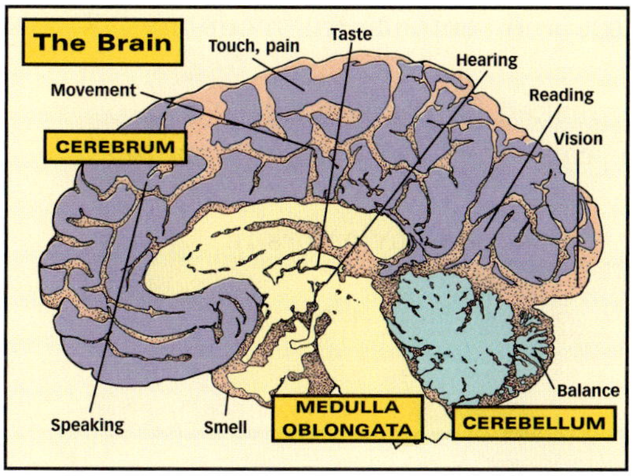

Diagrams

Diagrams are drawings that show how something is constructed, how it works, or how its parts relate to each other. A diagram may leave out parts to show you only what you need to learn.

Maps

Maps can be used to illustrate many different things, from political boundaries to population issues to weather conditions. Use color or patterns to show differences.

U.S. Weather Map

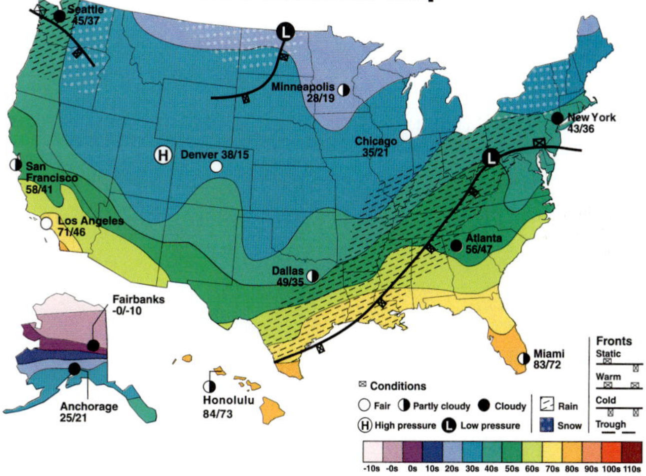

TEKS 10.13D, 10.18A, 10.18B(i)–10.18B(iii), 10.19
ELPS 5C, 5E

Using Editing and Proofreading Marks

You may be asked to review the work of peers or to mark corrections on a draft of your own work. As you edit for grammar, sentence structure, capitalization, punctuation, and spelling, you should mark your suggested changes clearly and consistently using the proofreader's marks on the next page.

Editing requires that you read every word of an essay carefully, looking specifically for errors. You may want to read the draft several times, looking for a different type of mistake each time. Use the following questions to help you identify and mark errors.

- Have I found and marked for correction any errors in subject-verb agreement?
- Have I found and marked for correction any errors in pronoun-antecedent agreement?
- Are the correct verb tenses used? If not, have I marked corrections?
- Have I found any run-on sentences and sentence fragments and marked changes?
- Are any errors in capitalization marked for correction?
- Have I identified and marked for correction any errors in ending punctuation?
- Have I identified and marked for correction any errors in punctuation within sentences?
- Have I used quotation marks and dashes correctly?

Tip

If possible, let your writing sit overnight before proofreading it. When you return to your writing, it will be easier to identify and correct mistakes.

Try It!

Work with a partner. Exchange a piece of writing that you have recently drafted. Edit your partner's work for grammar, sentence structure, mechanics, and spelling. Use the proofreader's marks shown on the next page. Then, correct your writing following the proofreader's marks and changes indicated by your partner.

TEKS 10.13D, 10.18A, 10.18B(i)–10.18B(iii), 10.19
ELPS 5C, 5E

Editing and Proofreading Marks

Use these symbols and letters to show where and how your writing needs to be changed. Your teachers may also use these symbols to point out errors in your writing. (This chart also appears inside the back cover of your book.)

Symbols	Meaning	Example	Corrected Example
≡	**Capitalize a letter.**	Willa Cather wrote *my* *Antonia.*	Willa Cather wrote *My* *Antonia.*
/	**Make a capital letter lowercase.**	Her novel tells the story of a Pioneer woman.	Her novel tells the story of a pioneer woman.
⊙	**Insert (add) a period.**	The story focuses on the right thing to do Antonia is . . .	The story focuses on the right thing to do. Antonia is . . .
⬭ or sp.	**Correct spelling.**	Jim Burden narates the story.	Jim Burden narrates the story.
ℓ	**Delete (take out) or replace.**	Jim he tells about his relationship with Antonia.	Jim tells about his relationship with Antonia.
∧	**Insert here.**	Antonia represents Jim's childhood on the ∧ frontier. (western)	Antonia represents Jim's childhood on the western frontier.
∧ ∧ ∧ (, : ;)	**Insert a comma, a colon, or a semicolon.**	Antonia's family, the Shimerdas came from Bohemia.	Antonia's family, the Shimerdas, came from Bohemia.
∨ ∨ ∨ (' " ")	**Insert an apostrophe or quotation marks.**	They are friends with Jims family on the frontier.	They are friends with Jim's family on the frontier.
?∧ !∧	**Insert a question mark or an exclamation point.**	Why is Antonia condescending toward Jim ∧ (?)	Why is Antonia condescending toward Jim?
¶	**Start a new paragraph.**	¶ Their friendship changes when . . .	Their friendship changes when . . .
∽	**Switch words or letters.**	Jim goes away to college attend.	Jim goes away to attend college.

Resource

ELPS 1E, 2C, 3B, 3D, 3E, 4G

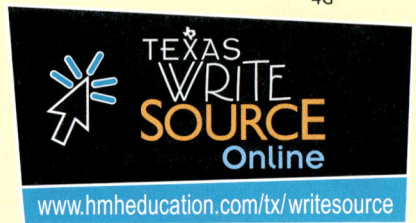

Texas Write Source Online
www.hmheducation.com/tx/writesource

Proofreader's Guide

Writing Focus

Learning Language

Learning these words and expressions will help you understand this unit.

1. An acronym is a word formed by the first letter or the first few letters of words in a phrase.
   Explain what the letters in the acronym "NASA" represent.
2. Function refers to the purpose or role of a person or thing.
   What is the function of a hospital emergency room?
3. The idiom on board means to agree or to be on the job.
   Describe a recent group project in which all the members were on board with the idea for the project.

Checking Mechanics

Period

643.1 At the End of a Sentence

Use a **period** at the end of a sentence that makes a statement, requests something, or gives a mild command.

(Statement) **The man who does not read good books has no advantage over the man who can't read them.**

—Mark Twain

(Request) **Please bring your folders and notebooks to class.**

(Mild command) **Listen carefully so that you understand these instructions.**

NOTE: It is not necessary to place a period after a statement that has parentheses around it and is part of another sentence.

My dog Bobot (I don't quite remember how he acquired this name) is a Chesapeake Bay retriever—a hunting dog—who is afraid of loud noises.

643.2 After an Initial or an Abbreviation

Place a period after an initial or an abbreviation (in American English).

Ms. Sen. D.D.S. M.F.A. M.D. Jr. U.S. p.m. a.m.

Edna St. Vincent Millay Booker T. Washington D. H. Lawrence

NOTE: When an abbreviation is the last word in a sentence, use only one period at the end of the sentence.

Valerie eyed each door until she found the name Fletcher B. Gale, M.D.

643.3 As a Decimal Point

A period is used as a decimal point.

New York City has a budget of $59 billion to serve its 8.4 million people.

Exclamation Point

643.4 To Express Strong Feeling

Use the **exclamation point** (sparingly) to express strong feeling. You may place it after a word, a phrase, or a sentence.

Imagine the sheer joy of shouting "Finished!" when you turn in your last assignment of the school year.

Question Mark

644.1 Direct Question

Place a **question mark** at the end of a direct question.

> **Where do I go now? I wondered. Do I climb the stairs or take the elevator? Why is there no escalator in this building? Why should I be discouraged by the sound of ringing in my ears?**

When a question ends with a quotation that is also a question, use only one question mark, and place it within the quotation marks.

> **On road trips, do you remember driving your parents crazy by asking, "Are we there yet?"**

NOTE: Do *not* use a question mark after an indirect question.

> **While I was crossing through the park, I found a friendly looking woman and asked her where nearest the bus stop was.**

644.2 To Show Uncertainty

Use a question mark within parentheses to show uncertainty.

> **This summer marks the 20th season (?) of the American Players Theatre.**

644.3 Short Question Within a Sentence

Use a question mark for a short question within parentheses.

> **We crept so quietly (had they heard us?) past the kitchen door and back to our room.**

Use a question mark for a short question within dashes.

> **Maybe somewhere in the pasts of these humbled people, there were cases of bad mothering or absent fathering or emotional neglect—what family surviving the '50s was exempt?—but I couldn't believe these human errors brought the physical changes in Frank.**
>
> —Mary Kay Blakely, *Wake Me When It's Over*

Practice

Periods and Question Marks

Write a period where it is needed to end a sentence and after an abbreviation. Write a question mark where it is needed to end a sentence or for a short question within parentheses.

Example: Ms Henson is teaching a course in forensic science this year
Ms. year.

1. With the popularity of television shows featuring forensic science (isn't *CSI* one), many high schools have begun offering classes in the subject
2. What is forensic science
3. It's any area of science that could be used in a court of law
4. For instance, a forensic psychologist (Dr Sam Waters of *Profiler* is a TV example) studies a crime scene to determine clues to the criminal's personality
5. Have you heard of a *criminalist*
6. A criminalist, who uses chemical and microscopic techniques to examine physical evidence, can identify an individual through DNA analysis
7. A forensic pathologist is an MD and examines samples removed from the body to establish the time and cause of death
8. He or she might also be able to determine if a death was a homicide or a suicide
9. Ms Henson asked me if I'd like to be a forensic pathologist someday

Model

Model the following sentences to practice using the correct punctuation for direct and indirect questions.

Have you given any consideration to joining the military?

I asked him why he wants to join the armed forces.

Comma

646.1 Between Two Independent Clauses

Use a **comma** between two independent clauses that are joined by a coordinating conjunction *(and, but, or, nor, for, yet, so)*.

I wanted to work in the garden, but it was raining too hard.

NOTE: Do not confuse a sentence containing a compound verb for a compound sentence.

I decided to plant flower bulbs and then mow the yard.

646.2 To Separate Adjectives

Use commas to separate two or more adjectives that *equally* modify the same noun. (Note: Do not use a comma between the last adjective and the noun.)

Miriam saw the kind, curious look in her grandmother's eyes as they discussed her plans for the future.

—Julio Namente, student writer

A Closer Look

To determine whether adjectives modify equally—and should, therefore, be separated by commas—use these two tests:

1. Shift the order of the adjectives; if the sentence is clear, the adjectives modify equally. (In the example below, *hot* and *smelly* can be shifted and the sentence is still clear; *usual* and *morning* cannot.)
2. Insert *and* between the adjectives; if the sentence reads well, use a comma when the *and* is omitted. (The word *and* can be inserted between *hot* and *smelly*, but *and* does not make sense between *usual* and *morning*.)

Matty was tired of working in the hot, smelly kitchen and decided to take her usual morning walk.

646.3 To Separate Contrasted Elements

Use commas to separate contrasted elements within a sentence. Often the word or phrase that is set off is preceded by *not*.

Since the book was about children and their antics, and not the problems that teenagers face, I was not that interested.

Practice

Commas 1

- To Separate Adjectives
- To Separate Contrasted Elements

Indicate where commas are needed in the following sentences by writing the commas along with the words that surround them.

Example: Marianna was very smart though not a genius.
smart, though

1. One of her favorite things was learning unfamiliar interesting words.
2. Marianna unlike many of her friends could solve tough word puzzles with little effort.
3. Putting together challenging complex word puzzles was her favorite pastime.
4. Marianna created her puzzles for personal satisfaction not for financial gain.
5. The puzzles she made had thought-provoking entertaining themes.
6. They included fascinating little-known facts about countries of the world.
7. Books of her puzzles were published overseas not in the United States.
8. She was pleasantly surprised when her hobby became a serious profitable business.
9. Now Marianna is a busy successful business owner.

Model

Model the following sentences to practice using commas to separate contrasted elements.

Be a first-rate version of yourself, not a second-rate version of someone else.

—Judy Garland

Strive not to be a success, but rather to be of value.

—Albert Einstein

Comma *(continued)*

648.1 To Set Off Appositives

A specific kind of explanatory word or phrase called an **appositive** identifies or renames a preceding noun or pronoun.

> Benson, our uninhibited and enthusiastic Yorkshire terrier, joined our family on my sister's fifteenth birthday.
>
> —Chad Hockerman, student writer

NOTE: Do not use commas with *restrictive appositives.* A restrictive appositive is essential to the basic meaning of the sentence.

> Sixteen-year-old student Ray Perez was awarded an athletic scholarship.

648.2 Between Items in a Series

Use commas to separate individual words, phrases, or clauses in a series. (A series contains at least three items.)

> Dad likes meat, vegetables, and a salad for dinner. (words)
>
> I took her for walks, read her stories, and made up games for her to play. (phrases)
>
> —Anne Moody, *Coming of Age in Mississippi*

NOTE: Do not use commas when all the words in a series are connected with or, nor, or and.

> We washed the car and waxed the car and changed the oil.

648.3 After Introductory Phrases and Clauses

Use a comma after an introductory participial phrase.

> Determined to finish the sweater by Friday, my grandmother knit night and day.

Use a comma after a long introductory prepositional phrase or after two or more short ones.

> In the oddest places and at the strangest times, my grandmother can be found knitting madly away.

NOTE: You may omit the comma if the introductory phrase is short.

> Before breakfast my grandmother knits.

Use a comma after an introductory adverb (subordinate) clause.

> After the practice was over, Tina walked home.

NOTE: A comma is not used if an adverb clause follows the main clause and is needed to complete the meaning of the sentence.

> Tina practiced hard because she feared losing.

However, a comma is used if the adverb clause following the main clause begins with *although, even though, while,* or another conjunction expressing a contrast.

> Tina walked home, even though it was raining very hard.

Practice

Commas 2

- To Set Off Appositives
- Between Items in a Series
- After Introductory Phrases and Clauses

Indicate where commas are needed in the following paragraph by writing the commas along with the words that surround them.

Example: Sharks probably the oldest predators in the sea live in every ocean in the world.

Sharks, probably   sea, live

Sharks belong to a family that includes dogfish skates and rays. They are distinguished from other fish by their cartilaginous skeletons. Besides this unusual feature the skin of a shark feels much like sandpaper. Throughout the world's seas sharks search for something to eat. Sharks bite off chunks of food and then swallow the pieces whole. A tiny seven-inch-long shark the pygmy is dwarfed by the fifty-foot-long variety the whale shark within this intriguing group. Though there are more than 360 species most people have only heard of the great white the tiger the hammerhead and the mako. Although it is foolish to ignore them most sharks are not interested in eating every person who steps into the sea.

Model

Model the following sentences to practice using commas in a series, after an introductory phrase, and to set off an appositive.

Only through experience of trial and suffering can the soul be strengthened, ambition inspired, and success achieved.

—Helen Keller

If you don't know where you are going, any road will take you there.

—Lewis Carroll

What we're all striving for is authenticity, a spirit-to-spirit connection.

—Oprah Winfrey

Comma *(continued)*

650.1 To Enclose Parenthetical Elements

Use commas to separate parenthetical elements, such as an explanatory word or phrase, within a sentence.

> **The two children played together on the sand, away from the high, rough waves that were crashing onto the shore, and they laughed as their sand castles grew higher and higher.**
>
> **Allison meandered into class, late as usual, and sat down.**

650.2 To Set Off Nonrestrictive Phrases and Clauses

Use commas to set off **nonrestrictive** (unnecessary) clauses and participial phrases. A nonrestrictive clause or participial phrase adds information that is not necessary to the basic meaning of the sentence. For example, if the clause or phrase (in red) were left out in the two examples below, the meaning of the sentences would remain clear. Therefore, commas are used to set them off.

> **The Altena Fitness Center and Visker Gymnasium, which were built last year, are busy every day.** (nonrestrictive clause)
>
> **Students and faculty, improving their health through exercise, use both facilities throughout the week.** (nonrestrictive phrase)

Do not use commas to set off a **restrictive** (necessary) clause or participial phrase, which helps to define a noun or pronoun. It adds information that the reader needs to know in order to understand the sentence. For example, if the clause and phrase (in red) were dropped from the examples below, the meaning wouldn't be the same. Therefore, commas are *not* used.

> **The handball court that has a sign-up sheet by the door must be reserved.**
> The clause identifies which handball court must be reserved. (restrictive clause)
>
> **Individuals wanting to use this court must sign up a day in advance.**
> (restrictive phrase)

A Closer Look: *That* and *Which*

Use *that* to introduce restrictive (necessary) clauses; use *which* to introduce nonrestrictive (unnecessary) clauses. When the two words are used in this way, the reader can quickly distinguish necessary and unnecessary information.

> **The treadmill that monitors heart rate is the one you must use.**
> (The reader needs the information to find the right treadmill.)
>
> **This treadmill, which we got last year, is required for your program.**
> (The main clause tells the reader which treadmill to use; the other clause gives additional, unnecessary information.)

Practice

Commas 3

- To Enclose Parenthetical Elements
- To Set Off Nonrestrictive Phrases and Clauses

Indicate where commas are needed in the following sentences by writing the commas along with the words that surround them. If no commas are needed, write "none."

Example: Patrick who loves science tried to get me interested in astronomy.

Patrick, who loves science, tried

1. He has a Dobsonian telescope which he built from a kit.
2. Last July having time on my hands I stayed at his country home.
3. With Patrick's telescope we spotted the International Space Station which I was surprised to be able to see.
4. The "Dob" as my cousin affectionately calls it is popular among amateur astronomers.
5. When I got home, my dad helped me buy a telescope that is similar to the Dobsonian.
6. Patrick attempting to help me put it together accidentally broke one of the legs.
7. Dad's coworker whose experience with telescopes is amazing fixed it easily.
8. Next month armed with my new telescope I'll be searching the heavens for new planets and moons.

Model

Model the following sentences to reinforce the difference between restrictive and nonrestrictive phrases and clauses and their correct punctuation.

Those who don't believe in magic will never find it.

—Roald Dahl

The hardest thing to explain is the glaringly evident, which everybody has decided not to see.

—Ayn Rand

Comma *(continued)*

652.1 To Set Off Dates

Use commas to set off items in a date.

> **On September 30, 2010, my little sister entered our lives.**
>
> **He began working out on December 1, 2010, but quit by May 1, 2011.**

However, when only the month and year are given, no commas are needed.

> **He began working out in December 2010 but quit by May 2011.**

When a full date appears in the middle of a sentence, a comma follows the year.

> **On June 7, 1938, my great-grandfather met his future wife.**

652.2 To Set Off Items in Addresses

Use commas to set off items in an address. (No comma is placed between the state and ZIP code.)

> **Mail the box to Friends of Wildlife, Box 402, Spokane, Washington 20077.**

When a city and state (or country) appear in the middle of a sentence, a comma follows the last item in the address.

> **Several charitable organizations in Fort Worth, Texas, pool their funds.**

652.3 In Numbers

Use commas to separate numerals in large numbers in order to distinguish hundreds, thousands, millions, and so forth.

> **1,101　　25,000　　7,642,020**

652.4 To Enclose Titles or Initials

Use commas to enclose a title or initials and names that follow a surname (a last name).

> **Letitia O'Reilly, M.D., is our family physician.**
>
> **Hickok, J. B., and Cody, William F., are two popular Western heroes.**

Practice

Commas 4

- To Set Off Dates
- To Set Off Items in Addresses
- To Enclose Titles or Initials

Indicate where commas are needed in the following sentences by writing the commas along with the words that surround them.

Example: Thomas Bonnicksen Ph.D. has written extensively about the forests that grew after the last ice age.

Bonnicksen, Ph.D., has

1. Professors in Austin Texas answered some questions about the role of carbon dioxide in warming the atmosphere.
2. Although many think the world is going to warm up considerably, Chronis Tzedakis Ph.D. believes we may be headed into a new ice age.
3. On April 30 2011 a science magazine reported the earth's climate has changed dramatically over the last 9,000 years.
4. You can get information about glaciers and ice ages by writing to World Data Center for Glaciology University of Colorado Campus Box 449 Boulder Colorado 80309.
5. The coldest temperature on record for North America—81 degrees below zero Fahrenheit—occurred near the town of Beaver Creek Yukon Territory on February 3 1947.
6. John Margolies CPA counsels against buying investment property in the Yukon.

Model

Model the following sentences to practice using commas to enclose titles or initials.

Richard Swenson, D.D.S., advises his patients to put their toothbrushes in the dishwasher.

For his daughter's graduation gift, Mr. Blade had her office door painted with her new title: Miranda K. Blade, J.D.

TEKS 10.18B(i)

Comma *(continued)*

654.1 To Set Off Dialogue

Use commas to set off the speaker's exact words from the rest of the sentence. (It may be helpful to remember that the comma is always to the left of the quotation mark.)

> **"It's as if people no longer care about the problems of city life," added Monica Torres, an urban studies student.**

654.2 To Set Off Interjections

Use a comma to separate an interjection or a weak exclamation from the rest of the sentence.

> **Hey, how am I to know that a minute's passed?**
>
> —Nathan Slaughter and Jim Schweitzer, *When Time Dies*

654.3 To Set Off Interruptions

Use commas to set off a word, a phrase, or a clause that interrupts the movement of a sentence. Such expressions usually can be identified through the following tests: (1) They may be omitted without changing the meaning of a sentence. (2) They may be placed nearly anywhere in the sentence without changing its meaning.

> **For most of the students, well, it was just another normal day at school.**
>
> **The safest way to cross this street, as a general rule, is with the light.**

654.4 In Direct Address

Use commas to separate a noun of direct address from the rest of the sentence. A *noun of direct address* is the noun that names the person(s) spoken to.

> **I don't think you understand, my friend, how important it is for me to do well in school and create a successful life for myself.**

654.5 For Clarity or Emphasis

You may use a comma for clarity or for emphasis. There will be times when none of the traditional rules call for a comma, but one will be needed to prevent confusion or to emphasize an important idea.

> **Those who can see tomorrow, can find the energy to continue.** (emphasis)
>
> **What the crew does, does affect our voyage.** (clarity)

Practice

Commas 5

- To Set Off Dialogue
- To Set Off Interjections
- In Direct Address

Indicate where commas are needed in the following sentences by writing the commas along with the words that surround them.

Example: Hey do you have a hero?
Hey, do

1. "My hero" said Jolene "is the science-fiction author Ray Bradbury."
2. In his introduction to *The Circus of Dr. Lao,* Bradbury stated "Science fiction balances you on the cliff. Fantasy shoves you off."
3. Writer Miriam Allen de Ford said "Science fiction deals with improbable possibilities."
4. Mr. Castillo says "Science fiction entertains and provides insights into sciences and society."
5. The main elements in science fiction may be real or imagined Jolene.
6. People often attribute the following words to the television show *Star Trek:* "Beam me up Scotty!"
7. Well did you know it was never said on the show?
8. Hey are you sure about that?

Model

Model the following sentences to practice using commas to set off dialogue and interjections.

"I need to rake the leaves again," I inanely said to my old friend.
—Patricia Cornwell, *Black Notice*

Oh, life is a glorious cycle of song . . .
—Dorothy Parker

TEKS 10.18B

Semicolon

656.1 To Join Two Independent Clauses

Use a **semicolon** to join two or more closely related independent clauses that are not connected with a coordinating conjunction. (Independent clauses can stand alone as separate sentences.)

A heart attack is a medical emergency; immediate attention and care is required.

Silence coated the room like a layer of tar; not even the breathing of the 11 Gehad made any sound.

—Gann Bierner, "The Leap"

NOTE: When independent clauses are especially long or contain commas, a semicolon may punctuate the sentence, even though a coordinating conjunction connects the clauses.

We waited all day in that wide line, tired travelers pressing in from all sides; and when we needed drinks or sandwiches, I would squeeze my way to the cafeteria and back.

656.2 With Conjunctive Adverbs

A semicolon is used *before* a conjunctive adverb (with a comma after it) when the word connects two independent clauses in a compound sentence. (Common conjunctive adverbs are *also, besides, finally, however, indeed, instead, meanwhile, moreover, nevertheless, next, still, then, therefore,* and *thus.*)

I know that I need to finish the research for my essay; however, our Internet service is down and the library is closed on Sunday.

656.3 To Separate Groups That Contain Commas

A semicolon is used to separate groups of words that already contain commas.

Every Saturday night my little brother gathers up his things—goggles, shower cap, and snorkel; bubble bath, soap, and shampoo; tapes, stereo, and rubber duck—and heads for the tub.

Practice

Semicolons

- To Join Two Independent Clauses
- To Separate Groups That Contain Commas

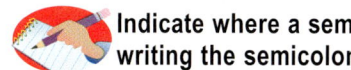

Indicate where a semicolon is needed in the following sentences by writing the semicolon along with the words that surround it.

Example: "It's not what I can do it's what I *will* do." —Kyle Maynard
do; it's

1. Kyle Maynard has a rare disorder called "congenital amputation" he has been limbless since birth.

2. He wrestles, swims, and plays baseball competes in athletic contests and has written a book.

3. Kyle is a normal young man despite having no elbows or hands and no knees or legs below them, he has become an outstanding role model.

4. He stands only three feet tall and weighs 120 pounds those who know him hardly notice his unique proportions.

5. Kyle has traveled cross-country as a motivational speaker won an ESPN ESPY Award, a Courage Award, and wrestling awards and modeled for Vanity Fair and Abercrombie & Fitch.

6. What makes Kyle different isn't his body it's his heart.

7. His story goes way beyond athletics his story serves as an inspiration to anyone who must overcome huge odds.

8. Kyle's book is titled *No Excuses* it is a revealing autobiography.

Model

Model the following sentence to practice using a semicolon to join two independent clauses.

His brows came together; his mouth became a thin line.
—Harper Lee, *To Kill a Mockingbird*

TEKS 10.18B

Colon

658.1 After a Salutation

Use a **colon** after the salutation of a business letter.

Dear Judge Parker: **Dear Governor Whitman:**

658.2 Between Numerals Indicating Time

Use a colon between the hours, minutes, and seconds of a number indicating time.

8:30 p.m. **9:45 a.m.** **10:24:55**

658.3 For Emphasis

Use a colon to emphasize a word, a phrase, a clause, or a sentence that explains or adds impact to the main clause (also see 684.3).

The newest candidates announced their platforms today: Lower taxes and more efficient services are the consistent themes.

658.4 To Introduce a Quotation

Use a colon to formally introduce a quotation, a sentence, or a question.

Directly a voice in the corner rang out wild and clear: "I've got him! I've got him!"

—Mark Twain, *Roughing It*

658.5 To Introduce a List

A colon is used to introduce a list.

I got all the proper equipment: scissors, a bucket of water to keep things clean, some cotton for the stuffing, and needle and thread to sew it up.

—Joan Baez, *Daybreak*

A Closer Look

Do not use a colon between a verb and its object or complement, or between a preposition and its object.

Incorrect: Min has: a snowmobile, an ATV, and a canoe.
Correct: Min has plenty of toys: a snowmobile, an ATV, and a canoe.
Incorrect: I watch a TV show about: cooking wild game.
Correct: I watch a TV show about a new subject: cooking wild game.

658.6 Between a Title and a Subtitle

Use a colon to distinguish between a title and a subtitle, volume and page, and chapter and verse in literature.

***Encyclopedia Americana* IV: 211** **Psalm 23:1–6**

Practice

Colons

- Between Numerals Indicating Time
- For Emphasis
- To Introduce a Quotation

Indicate where a colon is needed in the following sentences by writing the colon along with the words that surround it.

Example: The Orloj is a glorious old clock tower in Prague, unique for this reason It dates back to medieval times.
reason: It

1. The clock was built in 1410 by Mikulas of Kadan, royal clock maker under the reign of a familiar ruler King Wenceslas IV.
2. Whether it's 1200 midnight, 1200 noon, or any hour between, the Orloj will astound you with its moving statues.
3. After "The Walk of the Apostles," a rooster flaps and crows, and the clock chimes 900, 1000, 1100 . . .
4. Other moving figures include a Turk shaking his head, a miser watching his bag, and an individual admiring his reflection in a mirror Vanity himself.
5. The clock also has a calendar dial and an astronomical dial that displays the current state of the heavens sort of an ancient planetarium.
6. Otakar Zamecnik, a keeper of the Orloj, relates "The Orloj will soon be 600 years old, and I'm proud to be continuing the work of some 100 Orloj keepers before me."

Model

Model the following sentence to practice using a colon for emphasis.

Humanity's true moral test, its fundamental test, consists of its attitude toward those who are at its mercy: animals.
—Milan Kundera, *The Unbearable Lightness of Being*

TEKS 10.18B

Hyphen

660.1 In Compound Words

Use the **hyphen** to make some compound words.

great-great-grandfather **maid-in-waiting** **three-year-old**

660.2 To Create New Words

Use a hyphen to form new words beginning with the prefixes *self-*, *ex-*, *all-*, and *half-*. Also use a hyphen to join any prefix to a proper noun, a proper adjective, or the official name of an office. Use a hyphen before the suffix *-elect*.

self-contained **ex-governor** **all-inclusive** **president-elect**
pre-Cambrian **mid-December** **half-painted**

Use a hyphen to join the prefix *great-* only to the names of relatives.

great-aunt, great-grandfather (correct) **great-hall** (incorrect)

660.3 To Form an Adjective

Use a hyphen to join two or more words that serve as a single adjective (a single-thought adjective) before a noun.

When I am on the field, I see myself as a tall, well-built quarterback armed with magic plays and an incredible ability to throw the ball.

Use common sense to determine whether a compound adjective might be misread if it is not hyphenated. Generally, hyphenate a compound adjective that is composed of . . .

- a phrase **heat-and-serve meal** **off-and-on relationship**
- a noun + adjective **oven-safe handles** **book-smart student**
- a noun + participle (*ing* or *ed* form of a verb) **bone-chilling story**

A Closer Look

When words forming the adjective come after the noun, do not hyphenate them.

In real life I am large and big boned.

When the first of these words is an adverb ending in *-ly*, do not use a hyphen.

delicately prepared pastry

Also, do not use a hyphen when a number or a letter is the final element in a single-thought adjective.

class B movie

660.4 To Join Letters and Words

Use a hyphen to join a capital letter or lowercase letter to a noun or participle. (Check your dictionary if you're not sure of the hyphenation.)

T-shirt **Y-turn** **G-rated** **x-axis**

Practice

Hyphens 1

- In Compound Words
- To Create New Words
- To Join Letters and Words

For each sentence below, write the words that should be hyphenated.

Example: Robert Ripley is best known for his vast collection of mind boggling artifacts.
mind-boggling

1. Ripley was a self taught artist who won fame as a cartoonist.
2. As a so called world traveler, Ripley collected innumerable oddities.
3. Each year, thousands take self guided tours through his 27 "odditoriums."
4. Each odditorium, or museum, contains improbable, far flung rarities.
5. The museums are filled with eye popping exhibits.
6. A miniature Rolls Royce made of 1,016,711 matchsticks took 4,609 man hours to complete over a fifteen month period.
7. A close up of *Self Portrait in Front of Easel,* 1888, reveals that this work of art is made up of thousands of postcards.
8. Most of the exhibits are G rated, but some visitors might find a few of them disturbing.

Model

Model the following sentences to practice using a hyphen to create new words.

"Slumgullion" was the name given by the miners to a certain soft, half-liquid mud . . .
—Bret Harte, *The Queen of the Pirate Isle*

"The spring of 1885 a new wave of settlers broke and spread over the hard-land table of the upper Niobrara."
—Mari Sandoz, *Old Jules*

TEKS 10.18B

Hyphen *(continued)*

662.1 Between Numbers and Fractions

Use a hyphen to join the words in compound numbers from *twenty-one* to *ninety-nine* when it is necessary to write them out (see 692.3).

Use a hyphen between the numerator and denominator of a fraction, but not when one or both of those elements are already hyphenated.

forty-five **five-sixteenths** **seven thirty-seconds (7/32)**

662.2 In a Special Series

Use hyphens when two or more words have a common element that is omitted in all but the last term.

The ship has lovely two-, four-, or six-person cabins.

662.3 To Join Numbers

Use a hyphen to join numbers indicating the life span of a person or the score in a contest or a vote.

We can thank Louis Pasteur (1822–1895) for pasteurized milk.

In the 2009 Fiesta Bowl, Texas defeated Ohio State 24–21.

662.4 To Prevent Confusion

Use a hyphen with prefixes or suffixes to avoid confusion or awkward spelling.

re-create (not *recreate*) the image **re-cover (not *recover*) the sofa**

662.5 To Divide a Word

Use a hyphen to divide a word, only between its syllables, at the end of a line of print. Always place the hyphen after the syllable at the end of the line—never before a syllable at the beginning of the following line.

Guidelines for Dividing with Hyphens

1. Always divide a compound word between its basic units: **sister-in-law**, not **sis-ter-in-law.**
2. Avoid dividing a word of five or fewer letters: **paper, study, July.**
3. Avoid dividing the last word in a paragraph.
4. Never divide a one-syllable word: **rained, skills, through.**
5. Never divide a one-letter syllable from the rest of the word: **omit-ted**, not **o-mitted.**
6. When a vowel is a syllable by itself, divide the word after the vowel: **epi-sode**, not **ep-isode.**
7. Never divide abbreviations or contractions: **shouldn't**, not **should-n't.**
8. Never divide the last word in more than two lines in a row.

Practice

Hyphens 2

- In a Special Series
- To Divide a Word

In the sentences below, write the numerals or words that should be hyphenated.

Example: The golfers received first, second, and third place trophies.
first-, second-, and third-place

1. Asra found fabric remnants in two, three, and four yard lengths.
2. The assignment requires 4, 8, and 16 ounce measuring cups.
3. The department store is hiring both full and part time employees for the holidays.
4. We heard pro and anti war speeches at the convention.
5. Both English and Spanish speaking citizens attended the rally.

Use a slash (/) as shown below to indicate where each word should be divided at the end of a line of print. If the word should not be divided, explain.

Example: mass-produced
mass- / produced

6. gasoline
7. duty
8. father-in-law
9. marched
10. haven't

Model

Model the following sentence to practice using hyphens in a special series.

Goran was curious about the Russian Revolution as well as pre- and post-war history.

—Jean Fischer, *Vladimir's Reign*

TEKS 10.18B

Apostrophe

664.1 In Contractions

Use an **apostrophe** to show that one or more letters have been left out of a word group to form a contraction.

hadn't — *o* is left out   they'd — *woul* is left out   it's — *i* is left out

NOTE: Use an apostrophe to show that one or more numerals or letters have been left out of numbers or words in order to show special pronunciation.

class of '99 — *19* is left out   g'day — *ood* is left out

664.2 To Form Singular Possessives

Add an apostrophe and *s* to form the possessive of most singular nouns.

Spock's ears   Captain Kirk's singing   the ship's escape plan

NOTE: When a singular noun ends with an *s* or a *z* sound, you may form the possessive by adding just an apostrophe. When the singular noun is a one-syllable word, however, you usually add both an apostrophe and an *s* to form the possessive.

San Carlos' government (or) San Carlos's government (two-syllable word)

Ross's essay (one-syllable word)   The class's field trip (one-syllable word)

664.3 To Form Plural Possessives

The possessive form of plural nouns ending in *s* is usually made by adding just an apostrophe.

students' homework   bosses' orders

For plural nouns not ending in *s*, an apostrophe and *s* must be added.

children's book   men's department

A Closer Look

It will help you punctuate correctly if you remember that the word immediately before the apostrophe is the owner.

girl's guitar (*girl* is the owner)   boss's order (*boss* is the owner)

girls' guitar (*girls* are the owners)   bosses' order (*bosses* are the owners)

664.4 To Show Shared Possession

When possession is shared by more than one noun, use the possessive form for the last noun in the series.

Hoshi, Linda, and Nakiva's water skis (All three own the same skis.)

Hoshi's, Linda's, and Nakiva's water skis (Each owns her own skis.)

Practice

Apostrophes 1

- To Form Singular Possessives
- To Form Plural Possessives

Correctly write the words from the following sentences that need apostrophes.

Example: An ice climbers helmet is an essential piece of equipment.
climber's

1. For some, a mountains icy walls or frozen waterfalls are a real test.
2. A climbers tools include crampons, hard boots, an ice pick, ice screws, cold-weather clothes, and goggles.
3. Although articles in mens magazines focus on men who lead the sport of ice climbing, many women love the challenge as well.
4. An ice climber must make sure his or her crampons spikes are strong and sharp.
5. Enthusiasts also depend upon each ice screws holding power.
6. These screws give climbers a measure of safety on a walls icy face.
7. The American Alpine Institute is one of North Americas best climbing schools.
8. The Institutes programs teach beginners as well as seasoned climbers.
9. Marchs longer days and slightly higher temperatures make it an ideal month for ice climbing.

Model

Model the following sentences to practice using apostrophes in contractions.

Twenty years from now you will be more disappointed by the things that you didn't do than by the ones you did do.
—Mark Twain

If you wait to do everything until you're sure it's right, you'll probably never do much of anything.
—Win Borden

Apostrophe *(continued)*

666.1 To Show Possession with Indefinite Pronouns

Form the possessive of an indefinite pronoun by placing an apostrophe and an *s* on the last word (see **734.1** and **736.3**).

everyone's **anyone's** **somebody's**

666.2 To Show Possession in Compound Nouns

Form the possessive of a compound noun by placing the possessive ending after the last word.

the secretary of the interior's (singular) **agenda**
her lady-in-waiting's (singular) **day off**

If forming a possessive of a plural compound noun creates an awkward construction, you may replace the possessive with an *of* phrase. (All four forms below are correct.)

their fathers-in-law's (plural) **birthdays**
or **the birthdays of their fathers-in-law** (plural)

the ambassadors-at-large's (plural) **plans**
or **the plans of the ambassadors-at-large** (plural)

666.3 To Express Time or Amount

Use an apostrophe and an *s* with an adjective that is part of an expression indicating time or amount.

a penny's worth **today's business** **this morning's meeting**
yesterday's news **a day's wage** **a month's pay**

666.4 To Form Certain Plurals

Use an apostrophe and *s* to form the plural of a letter, a number, a sign, or a word discussed as a word.

B — B's **C — C's** **8 — 8's** **+ — +'s** ***and* — *and's***

Ms. D'Aquisto says our conversations contain too many *like's* and *no way's*.

NOTE: If two apostrophes are called for in the same word, omit the second one.

Follow closely the *do's* and *don'ts* (not *don't's*) on the checklist.

Practice

Apostrophes 2

- To Show Possession with Indefinite Pronouns
- To Express Time or Amount

Write the possessive form of the underlined words in the following sentences.

Example: Who will succeed Coach Marshall is anyone guess.
anyone's

1. This morning paper included a story about the Animal Rescue League.
2. At times, it is best to keep one opinions confidential.
3. Kendra found somebody gym shoes on the bench near Mr. Mariano's office.
4. Today advanced geometry exam was easier than I'd expected.
5. Rob is everyone first choice as a geometry tutor.
6. When I get this week paycheck, I'll have enough to buy a new CD.
7. Latisha and Petra usually share each other oil paints.
8. It was nobody fault but my own.
9. Yesterday chemistry lab turned out better than I expected it would.
10. Because of the tough competition, no one artwork from our school won an award.

Model

Model the following sentences to practice using apostrophes to express time or amount.

After a day's walk, everything has twice its usual value.

—George Macauley Trevelyan

A single conversation with a wise man is worth a month's study of books.

—Chinese Proverb

Quotation Marks

668.1 To Set Off Direct Quotations

Place **quotation marks** before and after the words in direct quotations.

> **"Come with me to the concert tonight," Michaela suggested. "You'll come away with a totally different opinion about classical music."**

In a quoted passage, put brackets around any word or punctuation mark that is not part of the original quotation. (See **680.1**.)

If you quote only part of the original passage, be sure to construct a sentence that is both accurate and grammatically correct.

> **Much of the restructuring of the Postal Service has involved "turning over large parts of its work to the private sector."**

668.2 Placement of Punctuation

Always place periods and commas inside quotation marks.

> **"Dr. Slaughter wants you to have liquids, Will," Mama said anxiously. "He said not to give you any solid food tonight."**
>
> —Olive Ann Burns, *Cold Sassy Tree*

Place an exclamation point or a question mark *inside* quotation marks when it punctuates the quotation and *outside* when it punctuates the main sentence.

> **"Am I dreaming?" Had she heard him say, "Here's the key to your new car"?**

Always place semicolons or colons outside quotation marks.

> **I wrote about James Joyce's "The Dead"; I found it thought provoking.**

668.3 For Long Quotations

If you quote more than one paragraph, place quotation marks before each paragraph and at the end of the last paragraph (Example A). If a quotation has more than four lines on a page, you may set it off from the text by indenting 10 spaces from the left margin (block form). Do not use quotation marks either before or after the quoted material, unless they appear in the original (Example B).

Example A

"______________________

____

____________.

"______________________

____

____________.

"_________________."

Example B

______________________.

____

____

____

____

____________.

____

Practice

Quotation Marks 1

- To Set Off Direct Quotations
- Placement of Punctuation

Write the following conversation, placing quotation marks correctly.

Example: Calvin, would you please get that? his mom asked.
"Calvin, would you please get that?" his mom asked.

The phone had already rung four times; Calvin picked it up.

Hello? he greeted the caller. He listened for a bit, and then said, Yes, I think so. What's the problem?

Calvin's mom came into the room and asked, Who is it?

Calvin gestured to his mom to wait a second and continued to speak into the phone. No, we'd prefer the black one. . . . Right. OK, hold on, please. He covered the mouthpiece and said to his mom, It's the repair shop. They can't fix our car by this weekend, but they have a rental car for us.

Calvin's mom said, Ask them when our car will be ready.

Calvin talked again to the mechanic. Did Calvin hear him right? Did he say, It won't be ready for at least a week?

We have to special order a part, the mechanic explained. I wish I had better news for you.

Exercise

Continue the phone conversation between Calvin and the mechanic. Use quotation marks correctly.

Quotation Marks *(continued)*

670.1 Quotation Marks Within Quotations

Use single quotation marks to punctuate a quotation within a quotation. Use double quotation marks in order to distinguish a quotation within a quotation within a quotation.

"For tomorrow," said Mr. Botts, "read 'Unlighted Lamps.'"

Sue asked, "Did you hear Mr. Botts say, 'Read "Unlighted Lamps"'?"

670.2 For Special Words

You may use quotation marks (1) to distinguish a word that is being discussed, (2) to indicate that a word is unfamiliar slang, or (3) to point out that a word is being used in a special way, i.e., to indicate irony or sarcasm.

(1) If I had to choose a word to describe his attitude, it would be "stoic."

(2) The next time I hear a New Zealander say "ta," I will know that I am being thanked.

(3) Tom pushed the wheelchair across the street, showed the lady his "honest" smile . . . and stole her purse.

NOTE: You may use italics (underlining) in place of quotation marks in each of these three situations. (See **672.3**.)

670.3 To Punctuate Titles

Use **quotation marks** to punctuate titles of songs, poems, short stories, one-act plays, lectures, episodes of radio or television programs, chapters of books, unpublished works, electronic files, and articles found in magazines, newspapers, encyclopedias, or online sources. (For punctuation of other titles, see **672.2**.)

"Santa Lucia" (song)

"The Chameleon" (short story)

"Twentieth-Century Memories" (lecture)

"Affordable Adventures" (magazine article)

"Dire Prophecy of the Howling Dog" (chapter in a book)

"Dancing with Debra" (television episode)

"Miss Julie" (one-act play)

NOTE: Punctuate one title within another title as follows:

"Clarkson's 'Breakaway' Hits the Waves"
(title of a song in title of an article)

Practice

Quotation Marks 2

- Quotation Marks Within Quotations
- For Special Words
- To Punctuate Titles

Write the word or words that should be enclosed in quotation marks in the following sentences.

Example: The players stood on the sidelines as Olivia sang the Star-Spangled Banner.
"Star-Spangled Banner."

1. Ms. Rupka said, "The exam will include Hills like White Elephants and other short stories by Hemingway."

2. He called himself benevolent, but everyone knew he was exaggerating his measly donations.

3. Hazim was featured in the *Trumpet* magazine article Flags to Riches.

4. No one answered correctly when asked to define the word pidgin.

5. I like Usher's new song Truth Hurts.

6. The coach shouted, "I called Ty, and he said, Madison West won 28–10!"

7. Merina asked, "Who sings Happy Ever After?"

8. My three-year-old nephew calls dogs oggies.

9. According to the newspaper, gasoline prices are expected to increase just twenty-five percent this summer..

Model

Model the following sentence to practice using quotation marks within quotations.

"'The Duke's Daughter' paid the butcher's bill, 'A Phantom Hand' put down a new carpet, and the 'Curse of the Coventrys' proved the blessing of the Marches in the way of groceries and gowns."

—Louisa May Alcott, *Little Women*

Italics (Underlining)

672.1 Handwritten and Printed Material

Italics is a printer's term for a style of type that is slightly slanted. In this sentence, the word *happiness* is printed in italics. In material that is handwritten or typed on a machine that cannot print in italics, underline each word or letter that should be in italics.

> ***My Ántonia*** **is the story of a strong and determined pioneer woman.**
> (printed)
> **Willa Cather's <u>My Ántonia</u> describes pioneer life in America.**
> (typed or handwritten)

672.2 In Titles

Use italics to indicate the titles of magazines, newspapers, pamphlets, books, full-length plays, films, videos, radio and television programs, book-length poems, ballets, operas, paintings, lengthy musical compositions, sculptures, cassettes, CD's, legal cases, and the names of ships and aircraft. (For punctuation of other titles, see 670.3.)

> ***Newsweek*** (magazine)
> ***X-Men Origins: Wolverine*** (film)
> ***Caring for Your Kitten*** (pamphlet)
> ***Chicago Tribune*** (newspaper)
> ***Cold Sassy Tree*** (book)
> ***Law & Order*** (television program)
> ***Hedda Gabler*** (full-length play)
> ***The Thinker*** (sculpture)

672.3 For Special Uses

Use italics for a number, letter, or word that is being discussed or used in a special way. (Sometimes quotation marks are used for this reason. See 670.2.)

> **I hope that this letter *I* on my report card stands for *incredible* and not *incomplete*.**

672.4 For Foreign Words

Use italics for foreign words that have not been adopted into the English language; also use italics for scientific names.

> **The voyageurs—tough men with natural *bonhomie*—discovered the shy *Castor canadensis*, or North American beaver.**

Practice

Italics (Underlining)

- In Titles
- For Special Uses
- For Foreign Words

Write and underline the word or words that should be italicized in the following sentences.

Example: Kelly's embroidered jeans were très chic.
très chic

1. Jennifer Aniston was in last month's issue of People magazine.
2. We are studying Antigone, a Greek tragedy by Sophocles.
3. Sodium aluminum sulfate, also known as soda alum, is used in baking powder.
4. In the 1857 legal case Dred Scott v. Sandford, the Supreme Court claimed that African Americans were not considered United States citizens.
5. The first episode of The Real World aired on MTV in 1992.
6. When did the word props become slang?
7. My brother was stationed on the United States Navy ship the USS Richard Bonhomme.
8. The workshop featured an art technique called trompe l'oeil, which means "trick of the eye."

Model

Model the following sentence to practice using italics (underlining) for special uses.

> **I had no faith in pie charts or diagrams of humanity wherein the wicked were divided from the good and the *forever after* was in direct opposition to the *here and now*.**
>
> —Alice Hoffman, *The Ice Queen*

Parentheses

674.1 To Set Off Explanatory Material

You may use **parentheses** to set off explanatory or added material that interrupts the normal sentence structure.

> **Benson (our dog) sits in on our piano lessons (on the piano bench), much to the teacher's surprise and amusement.**
>
> —Chad Hockerman, student writer

NOTE: Place question marks and exclamation points within the parentheses when they mark the added material.

> **Ivan at once concluded (the rascal!) that I had a passion for dances, and . . . wanted to drag me off to a dancing class.**
>
> —Fyodor Dostoyevsky, "A Novel in Nine Letters"

674.2 With Full Sentences

When using a full sentence within another sentence, do not capitalize it or use a period inside the parentheses.

> **Since the judging has already begun (the judges have narrowed their selection to the top six), you'll have to wait until next year to enter your apple pie in the contest.**

When the parenthetical sentence comes after the period of the main sentence, capitalize and punctuate it the same way you would any other complete sentence.

> **Register for the event by completing this application. (Use blue or black ink.)**

NOTE: For unavoidable parentheses within parentheses (. . . [. . .] . . .), use brackets. Avoid overuse of parentheses by using commas instead.

Diagonal

674.3 To Show a Choice

Use a **diagonal** (also called a *slash* or forward *slash*) between two words, as in *and/or*, to indicate that either is acceptable.

> **Press the load/eject button.**
> **Don't worry; this is indoor/outdoor carpet.**

674.4 When Quoting Poetry

When quoting more than one line of poetry, use a diagonal to show where each line of poetry ends. (Insert a space on each side of the diagonal.)

> **"In Venice behind, / Fall the leaves, / Brown, / And yellow streaked with brown."**
>
> —Amy Lowell, "The City of Falling Leaves"

Practice

Parentheses and Diagonals

Write the word or words that should be enclosed in parentheses or divided by a diagonal. (Use the correct punctuation.)

Example: I tried tekka maki a kind of sushi at the restaurant.
(a kind of sushi)

1. Julia Alvarez she wrote *How the Garcia Girls Lost Their Accents* is my favorite author.
2. Push the up down button on the control panel to change the time.
3. Captain Chuck Yeager made famous as a test pilot was also a World War II flying ace.
4. Pizza and or lasagna will be served at the open house.
5. Raymond our Chihuahua likes to sleep in the bathroom sink.
6. Aunt Jo she's not really my aunt but a family friend is coming for a visit.

Model

Model the following sentence to practice using parentheses with full sentences.

> **"One day he brought the teacher a dead chicken snake in a burlap sack, and a chicken was still in the snake's belly (or whatever snakes call bellies).**
>
> —Willie Morris, *Good Old Boy*

Model

Write the lyrics to a favorite song to practice using diagonals when quoting poetry.

> **Tell them at home I long to be there, / While thro this wide world ever I roam; / Only to meet my darling so fair, / Only to see the dear folks at home.**

TEKS 10.18B, 10.18B(iii)

Dash

676.1 To Indicate a Sudden Break

Use a **dash** to indicate a sudden break or change in the sentence.

> Near the semester's end—and this is not always due to poor planning—some students may find themselves in a real crunch.

NOTE: Dashes are often used in place of commas. Use dashes when you want to give special emphasis; use commas when there is no need for emphasis.

676.2 To Set Off an Introductory Series

Use a dash to set off an introductory series from the clause that explains the series.

> A good book, a cup of tea, a comfortable chair—these things always saved my mother's sanity.

676.3 To Set Off Parenthetical Material

You may use a dash to set off parenthetical material—material that explains or clarifies a word or a phrase.

> A single incident—a tornado that came without warning—changed the face of the small town forever.

676.4 To Indicate Interrupted Speech

Use a dash to show interrupted or faltering speech in dialogue.

> Why—why are you doing this to me?

676.5 For Emphasis

Use a dash to emphasize a word, a series, a phrase, or a clause.

> After years of trial and error, Belther made history with his invention—the unicycle.

> After several hours of hearing the high-pitched yipping, Petra finally realized what it was—coyote pups.

Practice

Dashes

- To Indicate a Sudden Break
- To Set Off Parenthetical Material
- For Emphasis

A word, a phrase, or a clause follows each sentence below. Write the sentences to include those words, set off by one or two dashes.

Example: The ingredients he cooked with were strange and unfamiliar. (mustard oil and fenugreek seeds)

The ingredients he cooked with—mustard oil and fenugreek seeds—were strange and unfamiliar.

1. This machine was destined to change the world. (the computer)
2. Suddenly I realized exactly what he was telling me. (a lie)
3. The tsunami came without any warning. (caused by an underwater earthquake)
4. In the distance, a mournful cry echoed through the woods. (and this is not to say that it was miles away)
5. *The Greensboro Gazette* is doing a feature article on Blaine High School senior Todd Davis. (winner of the Langston Hughes Poetry Award)
6. Tears filled his eyes as he recognized the ring in the pawnshop window. (the emerald ring he had given Tamara)

Model

Model the following sentences to practice using a dash to show emphasis.

The ancient sea-faring cultures—the Phoenician, the Greek, and the Roman, all used ships driven by three sets of oars.

The manager of the hotel—I can't remember his name—switched us to a room with a view of the ocean.

TEKS 10.18B

Ellipsis

678.1 To Show Omitted Words

Use an **ellipsis** (three periods with one space before and after each period) to show that one or more words have been omitted in a quotation.

(Original)

We the people of the United States, in order to form a more perfect Union, establish justice, insure domestic tranquility, provide for the common defense, promote the general welfare, and secure the blessings of liberty to ourselves and our posterity, do ordain and establish this Constitution for the United States of America.

—Preamble, *U.S. Constitution*

(Quotation)

"We the people . . . in order to form a more perfect Union . . . establish this Constitution for the United States of America."

678.2 At the End of a Sentence

If words from a quotation are omitted at the end of a sentence, place the ellipsis after the period that marks the conclusion of the sentence.

"Standing at the entrance were small groups of students. . . . As Will walked by, he could not help but overhear the murmurs of discontent as they continued to wait for the signal to return to classes."

—Pamela Brown, student writer

NOTE: If the quoted material is a complete sentence (even if it was not complete in the original), use a period, then an ellipsis.

(Original)

I am tired; my heart is sick and sad. From where the sun now stands I will fight no more forever.

—Chief Joseph of the Nez Percé

(Quotation)

"I am tired. . . . From where the sun now stands I will fight no more forever."

or

"I am tired. . . . I will fight no more. . . . "

678.3 To Show a Pause

Use an ellipsis to indicate a pause.

I brought my trembling hand to my focusing eyes. It was oozing, it was red, it was . . . it was . . . a tomato!

—Laura Baginski, student writer

Practice

Ellipses

- To Show Omitted Words
- At the End of a Sentence
- To Show a Pause

For each of the following paragraphs, select the least important information to replace with ellipses. Write the shortened paragraphs on your paper.

Example: Joseph Geissman, a local deputy sheriff who has been on the force for five years, was honored for his bravery during the recent flood.

Joseph Geissman, a local deputy sheriff . . . was honored for his bravery during the recent flood.

1. Plan now to land a part-time summer job. First, decide on what kind of job you want in terms of location, hours, and pay. Then think about what you have to offer—in particular, your skills and past experience. Next, write a résumé using one of the many online or printed guides. Then look for suitable jobs: Ask around, read newspaper job ads. Apply for any jobs that interest you. Finally, prepare for your interviews. Decide how you will make a great impression on potential employers.

2. Ancient Olympic events were different from modern games. For example, one of the most popular events was chariot racing. There were two-horse races and four-horse races. There were other types of races as well—with foals and mules, for example. The course was 9 miles long (12 laps around the track). Only rich people could afford the horses, equipment, and jockey. It was the owners, and not the winning jockey, who received the olive wreath of victory.

Model

Model the following sentence to practice using an ellipsis to show a pause.

When the student is ready . . . the lesson appears.

—Gene Oliver

Brackets

680.1 To Set Off Clarifying Information

Use **brackets** before and after words that are added to clarify what another person has said or written.

> **"Those annoying pests [the mosquitoes] ruined our day fishing at the lake."**
>
> —Will Shepherd, student writer

NOTE: The brackets indicate that the words *the mosquitoes* are not part of the quotation but were added for clarification.

680.2 Around an Editorial Correction

Place brackets around an editorial correction inserted within quoted material.

> **"Brooklyn alone has 8 percent of lead poisoning [victims] nationwide," said Marjorie Moore.**
>
> —Donna Actie, student writer

NOTE: The brackets indicate that the word *victims* replaced the author's original word.

Place brackets around the letters *sic* (Latin for "as such"); the letters indicate that an error appearing in the material being quoted was made by the original speaker or writer.

> **"When I'm queen," mused Lucy, "I'll show these blockheads whose [*sic*] got beauty and brains."**

680.3 To Set Off Added Words

Place brackets around comments that have been added to a quotation.

> **"Congratulations to the astronomy club's softball team, which put in, shall we say, a 'stellar' performance." [groans]**

Punctuation Marks

´	Accent, acute	,	Comma	( )	Parentheses
`	Accent, grave	†	Dagger	.	Period
'	Apostrophe	—	Dash	?	Question mark
*	Asterisk	/	Diagonal/Slash	" "	Quotation marks
{ }	Brace	¨ (ü)	Dieresis	§	Section
[ ]	Brackets	. . .	Ellipsis	;	Semicolon
^	Caret	!	Exclamation point	~	Tilde
(ç)	Cedilla	-	Hyphen	___	Underscore
^	Circumflex	...	Leaders		
:	Colon	¶	Paragraph		

Practice

Brackets

- To Set Off Clarifying Information
- Around an Editorial Correction
- To Set Off Added Words

Follow the directions for each activity below.

Example: In the following quotation, the speaker is talking about the English Industrial Revolution. Use words in brackets to clarify the quotation.

"The productive capacity of England was changed dramatically," Dr. Bates said. "Every class of people was touched by it."

. . . was touched by it [the English Industrial Revolution]."

1. In the following quotation, the speaker is talking about satellites. Use words in brackets to clarify the quotation.

   "There has been some damage to them," the astrophysicist explained. "For the most part, it has been minor."

2. In the following quotation, replace the speaker's use of the word *repartee* with *witty reply*.

   Mr. Daly reported, "She responded to my commentary with a repartee."

3. Quote the following statement and show that the error was made by the original writer, Joy Thayer.

   James Monroe's secratary of state was John Quincy Adams.

4. Add the comment *sigh* to the following quotation.

   "I'm so tired that I can't concentrate."

Model

Model the following sentence to practice using brackets to set off clarifying information.

Nobody thought that it [the airline strike] would last as long as it did.

TEKS 10.18A

Capitalization

682.1 Proper Nouns and Adjectives

Capitalize proper nouns and proper adjectives (those derived from proper nouns). The chart below provides a quick overview of capitalization rules. The pages following explain some specific rules of capitalization.

Capitalization at a Glance

Names of people	**Alice Walker, Matilda, Jim, Mr. Roker**
Days of the week, months	**Sunday, Tuesday, June, August**
Holidays, holy days	**Thanksgiving, Easter, Hanukkah**
Periods, events in history	**Middle Ages, the Battle of Bunker Hill**
Official documents	**Declaration of Independence**
Special events	**Elgin Community Spring Gala**
Languages, nationalities, religions	**French, Canadian, Islam**
Political parties	**Republican Party, Socialist Party**
Trade names	**Oscar Mayer hot dogs, Pontiac Vibe**
Official titles used with names	**Mayor John Spitzer, Senator Feinstein**
Formal epithets	**Alexander the Great**
Geographical names	
Planets, heavenly bodies	**Earth, Jupiter, the Milky Way**
Continents	**Australia, South America**
Countries	**Ireland, Grenada, Sri Lanka**
States, provinces	**Ohio, Utah, Nova Scotia**
Cities, towns, villages	**El Paso, Burlington, Wonewoc**
Streets, roads, highways	**Park Avenue, Route 66, Interstate 90**
Landforms	**the Rocky Mountains, the Sahara Desert**
Bodies of water	**Yellowstone Lake, Pumpkin Creek**
Buildings, monuments	**Elkhorn High School, Gateway Arch**
Public areas	**Times Square, Sequoia National Park**

Practice

Capitalization 1

- Proper Nouns and Adjectives

For each sentence below, write the words that should be capitalized.

Example: On tuesday, mayor henke declared that all city offices would be closed on martin luther king day.
Tuesday, Mayor Henke, Martin Luther King Day

1. Edward the confessor ruled england from 1042 to 1066.
2. Admittance to the independence ball required a ticket from the presidential inaugural committee.
3. When sylvie attended carlton college, she learned to speak greek and latin.
4. I wish stores would not decorate for christmas until after thanksgiving.
5. A severe earthquake hit san francisco on april 18, 1906.
6. The missouri river flows from its source in the rocky mountains to the mississippi river near st. louis.
7. Ancient greeks called mercury, venus, mars, jupiter, and saturn "wandering stars."
8. The teachings of the chinese philosopher confucius (551 to 479 B.C.E.) are called confucianism.

Model

Model the following sentences to practice capitalizing proper nouns and adjectives.

Though Africa and Egypt were popular destinations, Carlos decided to travel to Chile, the country where his father was born.

While in Rome, Larissa saw the Colosseum, the Vatican, the Arch of Constantine, and the Roman Forum.

Capitalization *(continued)*

684.1 First Words

Capitalize the first word of every sentence, including the first word of a full-sentence direct quotation.

> **The crowd was quiet. A girl whispered, "I hope it's not Nancy," and the sound of her whisper reached the edges of the crowd.**
>
> —Shirley Jackson, "The Lottery"

684.2 Sentences in Parentheses

Capitalize the first word in a sentence enclosed in parentheses, but do not capitalize the first word if the parenthetical appears within another sentence.

> **In a bygone era, a fortunate New Orleans visitor could be entertained by a young Louis Armstrong playing the cornet. (A cornet is a kind of small trumpet with a mellower sound.)**
>
> **Damien's aunt (she's a wild woman) plays bingo every Saturday night.**

684.3 Sentences Following Colons

Capitalize the first word in a complete sentence that follows a colon when (1) you want to emphasize the sentence or (2) the sentence is a quotation.

> **When we quarreled and made horrible faces at one another, Mother knew what to say: "Your faces will stay that way, and no one will marry you."**

684.4 Sections of the Country

Capitalize words that indicate particular sections of the country; do not capitalize words that simply indicate direction.

> **Mr. Johnson is from the Southwest.** (section of the country)
>
> **After moving north to Montana, he had to buy winter clothes.** (direction)

684.5 Certain Religious Words

Capitalize nouns that refer to the Supreme Being, the word *Bible,* the books of the Bible, and the names for other holy books.

> **God   Jehovah   the Lord   the Savior   Allah   Bible   Genesis**

684.6 Titles

Capitalize the first word of a title, the last word, and every word in between except articles (*a, an, the*), short prepositions, and coordinating conjunctions. Follow this rule for titles of books, newspapers, magazines, poems, plays, songs, articles, films, works of art, photographs, and stories.

> ***Washington Post***   **"The Diary of a Madman"**   ***Nights of Rain and Stars***

Practice

Capitalization 2

- Sentences Following Colons
- Certain Religious Words
- Titles

For the paragraphs below, write the line number along with the words that should be capitalized.

Example: 2. What

When my grandfather was young, everyone asked the same question: what would he be when he grew up? Hans was interested in many things. He studied the bible and the torah. He considered becoming a religious philosopher. When he read *a tale of two cities, for whom the bell tolls,* and other great novels, he decided to be an author. He also wanted to be an architect, an engineer, and even a horse trainer! So what profession did my grandfather finally choose? He became a typesetter!

Hans thought typesetting was a way to be a part of great events in the world. He set type for some amazing headlines: "Pearl Harbor attacked," "Yankees win the Series." He set articles about coronations and the first astronauts' ventures into space. Yes, Hans was there for all the great happenings. Shortly before he died, he summed it up this way: "if it happened in the last 40 years, I was there—a mere shadow, perhaps, but that was me."

Model

Model the following sentences to practice capitalizing certain religious words, titles, and sentences following colons.

Allah, Jehovah, Jah, and the Lord are different names for God.

The class was stunned by the teacher's statement: "We'll be reading *Notes from the House of the Dead, Crime and Punishment,* and *The Idiot* this semester."

TEKS 10.18A

Capitalization *(continued)*

686.1 Words Used as Names

Capitalize words like *father, mother, uncle,* and *senator* when they are used as titles with a personal name or when they are substituted for proper nouns (especially in direct address).

We've missed you, Aunt Lucinda! (*Aunt* is part of the name.)

I hope Mayor Bates arrives soon. (*Mayor* is part of the name.)

A Closer Look

To test whether a word is being substituted for a proper noun, simply read the sentence with a proper noun in place of the word. If the proper noun fits in the sentence, the word being tested should be capitalized; otherwise, the word should not be capitalized.

Did Mom (Sue) say we could go? (*Sue* works in this sentence.)

Did your mom (Sue) say you could go? (*Sue* does not work here.)

NOTE: Usually the word is not capitalized if it follows a possessive —*my, his, your*—as it does in the second sentence above.

686.2 Letters

Capitalize the letters used to indicate form or shape.

U-turn I-beam S-curve T-shirt V-shaped

686.3 Organizations

Capitalize the name of an organization, an association, or a team.

Lake Ontario Sailors American Red Cross Democratic Party

686.4 Abbreviations

Capitalize abbreviations of titles and organizations. (Some other abbreviations are also capitalized. See pages 694–696.)

AAA CEO NAACP M.D. Ph.D.

686.5 Titles of Courses

Capitalize words like *sociology* and *history* when they are used as titles of specific courses; do not capitalize these words when they name a field of study.

Who teaches History 202? (title of a specific course)

It's the same professor who teaches my sociology course. (a field of study)

NOTE: The words *freshman, sophomore, junior,* and *senior* are not capitalized unless they are part of an official title.

Rosa is a senior this year and is in charge of the Senior Class Banquet.

Practice

Capitalization 3

- Words Used as Names
- Organizations
- Letters

For each of the following sentences, correctly write any word or word groups that are incorrectly capitalized or lowercased.

Example: The a-frame house, popularized by Architect Andrew Geller, was a popular style for vacation homes in the 1960s.
A-frame, architect

1. The American institute of architects has more than 74,000 members.
2. Last week, vice president Shannon Kraus from that Organization visited our school.
3. My Dad wanted to meet her; he was once a member of his high school's Future architects club.
4. That, of course, was before his stint on the School's lacrosse team, the Arlington eagles.
5. Back then, dad was so good that he was recruited by the Long island lizards.
6. He had to put his lacrosse career on hold, however, when he burned his hand while changing an o-ring on grandma's motorcycle.
7. Now he and mom own their own Cycle-repair Shop.
8. They also belong to the Canadian motorcycle association.

Model

Model the following sentences to practice capitalizing organizations and words used as names.

We met Senator Blanche Lincoln at an American Heart Association fund-raiser.

After the last election, Uncle Ray said he was going to vote for the Green Party next time.

Plurals

688.1 Most Nouns

Form the **plurals** of most nouns by adding *s* to the singular.

cheerleader — cheerleaders **wheel — wheels** **crate — crates**

688.2 Nouns Ending in *sh, ch, x, s,* and *z*

Form the plurals of nouns ending in *sh, ch, x, s,* and *z* by adding *es* to the singular.

lunch — lunches **dish — dishes** **mess — messes** **fox — foxes**

Exception: When the final *ch* sounds like *k*, add an *s* (*monarchs*).

688.3 Nouns Ending in *y*

The plurals of common nouns that end in *y* (preceded by a consonant) are formed by changing the *y* to *i* and adding *es*.

fly — flies **jalopy — jalopies**

Form the plurals of nouns that end in *y* (preceded by a vowel) by adding only an *s*.

donkey — donkeys **monkey — monkeys**

NOTE: Form the plurals of all proper nouns ending in *y* by adding *s (Kathys).*

688.4 Nouns Ending in *o*

The plurals of nouns ending in *o* (preceded by a vowel) are formed by adding an *s*.

radio — radios **rodeo — rodeos** **studio — studios** **duo — duos**

The plurals of most nouns ending in *o* (preceded by a consonant) are formed by adding *es*.

echo — echoes **hero — heroes** **tomato — tomatoes**

Exception: Musical terms always form plurals by adding *s*.

alto — altos **banjo — banjos** **solo — solos** **piano — pianos**

688.5 Nouns Ending in *ful*

Form the plurals of nouns that end in *ful* by adding an *s* at the end of the word.

two tankfuls **three pailfuls** **four mouthfuls**

NOTE: Do not confuse these examples with *three pails full* (when you are referring to three separate pails full of something) or *two tanks full.*

688.6 Compound Nouns

Form the plurals of most compound nouns by adding *s* or *es* to the important word in the compound.

brothers-in-law **maids of honor** **secretaries of state**

Mechanics

Practice

Plurals 1

- Regular Nouns
- Nouns Ending in *sh, ch, x, s,* and *z*
- Nouns Ending in *y, o,* and *ful*

Write the correct plural of the underlined word in each sentence.

Example: The art portfolioes of seven students were on display.
portfolios

1. The keyes for the table saw are in the industrial arts office.
2. Lila poured five cansful of water into the kettle and carefully stirred the soup.
3. We followed our guide across three mountain pass's to get to Blaine's Ridge.
4. The landscaping staff will plant lilac bushs along the walk to the main entrance.
5. The Wilmores looked at five different patioes before picking out a design they liked.
6. Harbor authoritys reported that ship traffic increased by 50 percent during the last quarter of 2005.
7. The home economics class used six different cake mixs to make one large cake.
8. A cow does not have four stomaches; it has one stomach with four parts.
9. No one can explain all the mysterys of the universe.
10. Use this paint to make 20 dashs across the wall.
11. Jayleen and Francine found five dust-covered piccoloes in the band's storage room.

Exercise

Write a sentence for the plural of each of the following words.

ray, tress, glassful, territory

TEKS 10.19

Plurals *(continued)*

690.1 Nouns Ending in *f* or *fe*

Form the plurals of nouns that end in *f* or *fe* in one of two ways: if the final *f* sound is still heard in the plural form of the word, simply add *s;* but if the final *f* sound becomes a *v* sound, change the *f* to *ve* and add *s*.

Plural ends with *f* sound: roof — roofs; chief — chiefs

Plural ends with *v* sound: wife — wives; loaf — loaves

NOTE: Several words are correct with either ending.

Plural ends with either sound: hoof — hooves/hoofs

690.2 Irregular Spelling

A number of words form a plural by taking on an irregular spelling.

crisis — crises	**child — children**	**radius — radii**
criterion — criteria	**goose — geese**	**die — dice**

NOTE: Some of these words are acceptable with the commonly used *s* or *es* ending.

index — indices/indexes **cactus — cacti/cactuses**

Some nouns remain unchanged when used as plurals.

deer moose sheep salmon aircraft series

690.3 Words Discussed as Words

The plurals of symbols, letters, numbers, and words being discussed as words are formed by adding an apostrophe and an *s*.

Dad yelled a lot of *wow's* and *yippee's* when he saw my A's and B's.

NOTE: You may omit the apostrophe if it does not cause any confusion.

the three R's or Rs YMCA's or YMCAs

690.4 Collective Nouns

A collective noun may be singular or plural depending upon how it's used. A collective noun is singular when it refers to a group considered as one unit; it is plural when it refers to the individuals in the group.

The class was on its best behavior. (group as a unit)

The class are preparing for their final exams. (individuals in the group)

If it seems awkward to use a plural verb with a collective noun, add a clearly plural noun such as *members* to the sentence, or change the collective noun into a possessive followed by a plural noun that describes the individuals in the group.

The class members are preparing for their final exams.

The class's students are preparing for their final exams.

Practice

Plurals 2

- Irregular Spelling
- Words Discussed as Words
- Collective Nouns

For each sentence below, write the plural form of the word in parentheses.

Example: How many (child) attend the Bayshore Science School?
children

1. When Diego opened the musty trunk, he was startled to see four (mouse) staring back at him.
2. It was disturbing to me to hear the president continue his incorrect pronunciation of all the *(nuclear)* in his speeches.
3. Isle Royale, an island in Lake Superior, supports a population of about 550 (moose).
4. Many of the university's (alumnus) donate money to help keep the school competitive both academically and athletically.
5. Mr. Lake pointed out that the writer had used six *(and)* in quite a rambling sentence.
6. Scientists count the number of protons and neutrons to distinguish between the (nucleus) of atoms.
7. Kev plans to ask the five (W) during the interview.
8. Najib and Sylvia were pleased with their catch of 15 (fish).

Model

Model the following sentences to practice using collective nouns correctly.

Make sure you have finished speaking before your audience has finished listening.

—Dorothy Sarnoff

After their honeymoon was interrupted by a hurricane, the couple were happy to be back home.

Numbers

692.1 Numerals or Words

Numbers from one to nine are usually written as words; numbers 10 and over are usually written as numerals. However, numbers being compared or contrasted should be kept in the same style.

8 to 11 years old   eight to eleven years old

You may use a combination of numerals and words for very large numbers.

1.5 million   3 billion to 3.2 billion   6 trillion

If numbers are used infrequently in a piece of writing, you may spell out those that can be written in no more than two words.

ten   twenty-five   two hundred   fifty thousand

692.2 Numerals Only

Use numerals for the following forms: decimals, percentages, chapters, pages, addresses, phone numbers, identification numbers, and statistics.

26.2	8 percent	Highway 36	chapter 7
pages 287–89	July 6, 1945	44 B.C.E.	a vote of 23 to 4

Always use numerals with abbreviations and symbols.

8%   10 mm   3 cc   8 oz   90° C   24 mph   6' 3"

692.3 Words Only

Use words to express numbers that begin a sentence.

Fourteen students "forgot" their assignments.

NOTE: Change the sentence structure if this rule creates a clumsy construction.

Clumsy: *Six hundred thirty-nine* teachers were laid off this year.

Better: This year, 639 teachers were laid off.

Use words for numbers that come before a compound modifier if that modifier includes a numeral.

They made twelve 10-foot sub sandwiches for the picnic.

692.4 Time and Money

If time is expressed with an abbreviation, use numerals; if it is expressed in words, spell out the number.

4:00 A.M., 4:00 a.m., (or) four o'clock

If an amount of money is spelled out, so is the currency; use a numeral if a symbol is used.

twenty dollars (or) $20

Practice

Numbers

- Numerals or Words
- Numerals Only
- Words Only
- Time and Money

For each sentence below, write the underlined numbers the correct way. If a number is already correctly presented, write "correct."

Example: In 1 year, an acre of trees produces enough oxygen for eighteen people.
one, 18

1. In that same year, those trees can absorb as much carbon as is produced by a car driven up to 8,700 miles.
2. A tree does not reach its most productive stage of carbon storage until it is ten years old.
3. Over its life, a seventy-year-old tree absorbs over three tons of carbon.
4. Trees that provide shade and shelter reduce yearly heating and cooling costs by $2.1 billion dollars.
5. A giant redwood in California, the world's tallest tree, measures 378 feet high.
6. The largest tree in the world, a sequoia in California, has a volume of fourteen hundred eighty-seven cubic meters.
7. Found in the White Mountains of California, bristlecone pines are the world's oldest trees at more than four thousand, eight hundred years old!
8. The *Apollo 14* mission of January thirty-first, 1971, had tree seeds among its cargo.

Exercise

Complete these sentences with your own numbers.

Please read chapter ____ in your science book. Remember, the test next week will count for ____ percent of your grade.

Abbreviations

694.1 Formal and Informal Abbreviations

An **abbreviation** is the shortened form of a word or phrase. Some abbreviations are always acceptable in both formal and informal writing:

Mr. Mrs. Jr. Ms. Dr. a.m. (A.M.) p.m. (P.M.)

NOTE: In most of your writing, you do not abbreviate the names of states, countries, months, days, or units of measure. However, you may use the abbreviation *U.S.* after it has been spelled out once. Do not abbreviate the words *street, company,* and similar words, especially when they are part of a proper name. Also, do not use signs or symbols (%, &, #, @) in place of words. The dollar sign, however, is appropriate with numerals ($325).

694.2 Correspondence Abbreviations

United States

	Standard	Postal
Alabama	Ala.	AL
Alaska	Alaska	AK
Arizona	Ariz.	AZ
Arkansas	Ark.	AR
California	Calif.	CA
Colorado	Colo.	CO
Connecticut	Conn.	CT
Delaware	Del.	DE
District of Columbia	D.C.	DC
Florida	Fla.	FL
Georgia	Ga.	GA
Guam	Guam	GU
Hawaii	Hawaii	HI
Idaho	Idaho	ID
Illinois	Ill.	IL
Indiana	Ind.	IN
Iowa	Iowa	IA
Kansas	Kan.	KS
Kentucky	Ky.	KY
Louisiana	La.	LA
Maine	Maine	ME
Maryland	Md.	MD
Massachusetts	Mass.	MA
Michigan	Mich.	MI
Minnesota	Minn.	MN
Mississippi	Miss.	MS
Missouri	Mo.	MO
Montana	Mont.	MT
Nebraska	Neb.	NE
Nevada	Nev.	NV
New Hampshire	N.H.	NH
New Jersey	N.J.	NJ
New Mexico	N.M.	NM
New York	N.Y.	NY
North Carolina	N.C.	NC
North Dakota	N.D.	ND
Ohio	Ohio	OH
Oklahoma	Okla.	OK
Oregon	Ore.	OR
Pennsylvania	Pa.	PA
Puerto Rico	P.R.	PR
Rhode Island	R.I.	RI
South Carolina	S.C.	SC
South Dakota	S.D.	SD
Tennessee	Tenn.	TN
Texas	Texas	TX
Utah	Utah	UT
Vermont	Vt.	VT
Virginia	Va.	VA
Virgin Islands	V.I.	VI
Washington	Wash.	WA
West Virginia	W.Va.	WV
Wisconsin	Wis.	WI
Wyoming	Wyo.	WY

Canadian Provinces

	Standard	Postal
Alberta	Alta.	AB
British Columbia	B.C.	BC
Labrador	Lab.	NL
Manitoba	Man.	MB
New Brunswick	N.B.	NB
Newfoundland	N.F.	NL
Northwest Territories	N.W.T.	NT
Nova Scotia	N.S.	NS
Nunavut		NU
Ontario	Ont.	ON
Prince Edward Island	P.E.I.	PE
Quebec	Que.	QC
Saskatchewan	Sask.	SK
Yukon Territory	Y.T.	YT

Addresses

	Standard	Postal
Apartment	Apt.	APT
Avenue	Ave.	AVE
Boulevard	Blvd.	BLVD
Circle	Cir.	CIR
Court	Ct.	CT
Drive	Dr.	DR
East	E.	E
Expressway	Expy.	EXPY
Freeway	Fwy.	FWY
Heights	Hts.	HTS
Highway	Hwy.	HWY
Hospital	Hosp.	HOSP
Junction	Junc.	JCT
Lake	L.	LK
Lakes	Ls.	LKS
Lane	Ln.	LN
Meadows	Mdws.	MDWS
North	N.	N
Palms	Palms	PLMS
Park	Pk.	PK
Parkway	Pky.	PKY
Place	Pl.	PL
Plaza	Plaza	PLZ
Post Office Box	P.O. Box	PO BOX
Ridge	Rdg.	RDG
River	R.	RV
Road	Rd.	RD
Room	Rm.	RM
Rural	R.	R
Rural Route	R.R.	RR
Shore	Sh.	SH
South	S.	S
Square	Sq.	SQ
Station	Sta.	STA
Street	St.	ST
Suite	Ste.	STE
Terrace	Ter.	TER
Turnpike	Tpke.	TPKE
Union	Un.	UN
View	View	VW
Village	Vil.	VLG
West	W.	W

695.1 Other Common Abbreviations

abr. abridged; abridgment
AC, ac alternating current
ack. acknowledge; acknowledgment
acv actual cash value
A.D. in the year of the Lord (Latin *anno Domini*)
AM amplitude modulation
A.M., a.m. before noon (Latin *ante meridiem*)
ASAP as soon as possible
avg., av. average
BBB Better Business Bureau
B.C. before Christ
B.C.E. before the Common Era
bibliog. bibliographer; bibliography
biog. biographer; biographical; biography
C **1.** Celsius **2.** centigrade **3.** coulomb
c. **1.** circa (about) **2.** cup
cc **1.** cubic centimeter **2.** carbon copy
CDT, C.D.T. central daylight time
C.E. of the Common Era
chap. chapter
cm centimeter
c.o., c/o care of
COD, C.O.D **1.** cash on delivery **2.** collect on delivery
co-op. cooperative
CST, C.S.T. central standard time
cu., c cubic
D.A. district attorney
d.b.a. doing business as
DC, dc direct current
dec. deceased
dept. department
DST, D.S.T. daylight saving time
dup. duplicate
DVD digital video disc
ea. each
ed. edition; editor
EDT, E.D.T. eastern daylight time
e.g. for example (Latin *exempli gratia*)
EST, E.S.T. eastern standard time
etc. and so forth (Latin *et cetera*)
ex. example
F Fahrenheit
FM frequency modulation
F.O.B., f.o.b. free on board
ft foot
g **1.** gram **2.** gravity
gal. gallon
gloss. glossary
GNP gross national product
hdqrs, HQ headquarters
HIV human immunodeficiency virus
Hon. Honorable (title)
hp horsepower
HTML hypertext markup language
Hz hertz
ibid. in the same place (Latin *ibidem*)
id. the same (Latin *idem*)
i.e. that is (Latin *id est*)
illus. illustration
inc. incorporated
IQ, I.Q. intelligence quotient
IRS Internal Revenue Service
ISBN International Standard Book Number
Jr., jr. junior
K **1.** kelvin (temperature unit) **2.** Kelvin (temperature scale)
kc kilocycle
kg kilogram
km kilometer
kn knot
kW kilowatt
l liter
lat. latitude
lb, lb. pound (Latin *libra*)
l.c. lowercase
lit. literary; literature
log logarithm
long. longitude
Ltd., ltd. limited
m meter
M.A. master of arts (Latin *Magister Artium*)
Mc, mc megacycle
M.C., m.c. master of ceremonies
M.D. doctor of medicine (Latin *medicinae doctor*)
mdse. merchandise
mfg. manufacturing
mg milligram
mi. **1.** mile **2.** mill (monetary unit)
misc. miscellaneous
ml milliliter
mm millimeter
mpg, m.p.g. miles per gallon
mph, m.p.h. miles per hour
MS **1.** manuscript **2.** Mississippi **3.** multiple sclerosis
Ms., Ms title of courtesy for a woman
MST, M.S.T. mountain standard time
neg. negative
N.S.F., n.s.f. not sufficient funds
oz, oz. ounce
PA **1.** public-address system **2.** Pennsylvania
pct. percent
pd. paid
PDT, P.D.T. Pacific daylight time
PFC, Pfc. private first class
pg., p. page
P.M., p.m. after noon (Latin *post meridiem*)
P.O. **1.** personnel officer **2.** purchase order **3.** postal order; post office **4.** (also **p.o.**) petty officer
pop. population
POW, P.O.W. prisoner of war
pp. pages
ppd. **1.** postpaid **2.** prepaid
PR, P.R. **1.** public relations **2.** Puerto Rico
P.S. post script
psi, p.s.i. pounds per square inch
PST, P.S.T. Pacific standard time
PTA, P.T.A. Parent-Teacher Association
qt. quart
RF radio frequency
RN registered nurse
R.P.M., rpm revolutions per minute
R.S.V.P., r.s.v.p. please reply (French *répondez s'il vous plaît*)
SASE self-addressed stamped envelope
SCSI small computer system interface
SOS **1.** international distress signal **2.** any call for help
Sr. **1.** senior (after surname) **2.** sister (religious)
ST standard time
St. **1.** saint **2.** strait **3.** street
std. standard
syn. synonymous; synonym
TBA to be announced
tbs, tbsp tablespoon
TM trademark
tsp teaspoon
UHF, uhf ultra high frequency
UPC universal product code
UV ultraviolet
V **1.** *Physics:* velocity **2.** *Electricity:* volt **3.** volume
V.A., VA Veterans Administration
VHF, vhf very high frequency
VIP *Informal:* very important person
vol. **1.** volume **2.** volunteer
vs. versus
W **1.** *Electricity:* watt **2.** *Physics:* (also **w**) work **3.** west
whse., whs. warehouse
wkly. weekly
w/o without
wt. weight
yd yard (measurement)

Acronyms and Initialisms

696.1 Acronyms

An **acronym** is a word formed from the first (or first few) letters of words in a phrase. Even though acronyms are abbreviations, they require no periods.

radar	radio detecting and ranging
CARE	Cooperative for American Relief Everywhere
NASA	National Aeronautics and Space Administration
VISTA	Volunteers in Service to America
LAN	local area network

696.2 Initialisms

An **initialism** is similar to an acronym except that the initials used to form this abbreviation are pronounced individually.

CIA	Central Intelligence Agency
FBI	Federal Bureau of Investigation
FHA	Federal Housing Administration

696.3 Common Acronyms and Initialisms

ADD	attention deficit disorder
AIDS	acquired immunodeficiency syndrome
AKA	also known as
ATM	automatic teller machine
BMI	body mass index
CD	compact disc
DMV	Department of Motor Vehicles
ETA	expected time of arrival
FAA	Federal Aviation Administration
FCC	Federal Communications Commission
FDA	Food and Drug Administration
FDIC	Federal Deposit Insurance Corporation
FEMA	Federal Emergency Management Agency
FTC	Federal Trade Commission
FYI	for your information
GPS	global positioning system
HDTV	high-definition television
IRS	Internal Revenue Service
IT	information technology
JPEG	Joint Photographic Experts Group
LCD	liquid crystal display
LLC	limited liability company
MADD	Mothers Against Drunk Driving
MRI	magnetic resonance imaging
NASA	National Aeronautics and Space Administration
NATO	North Atlantic Treaty Organization
OPEC	Organization of Petroleum-Exporting Countries
OSHA	Occupational Safety and Health Administration
PAC	political action committee
PDF	portable document format
PETA	People for the Ethical Treatment of Animals
PIN	personal identification number
PSA	public service announcement
ROTC	Reserve Officers' Training Corps
SADD	Students Against Destructive Decisions
SUV	sport utility vehicle
SWAT	special weapons and tactics
TDD	telecommunications device for the deaf
VA	Veterans Administration

Practice

Abbreviations, Acronyms, and Initialisms

For each abbreviation, acronym, or initialism below, write out what it stands for. Then write whether it is an abbreviation, acronym, or initialism. (Do as many as you can before referring to the previous pages.)

Example: MI
Michigan, abbreviation

States/Provinces

1. NC

2. AK

3. QC

4. MA

5. MS

6. VI

7. IA

8. ON

9. PR

Addresses

10. PKY

11. CT

12. LK

13. HTS

14. RV

Miscellaneous

15. OPEC

16. B.C.E.

17. d.b.a.

18. PETA

19. DVD

20. i.e.

21. IRS

22. PIN

23. lb.

24. POW

25. pct.

26. UPC

27. avg.

28. SWAT

Model

Model the following acronyms and initialisms to come up with your own abbreviations. (Write at least one acronym and one initialism.)

HTML – hypertext markup language
HRH – Her Royal Highness
PERT – program evaluation review technique
MERCAD – measurement electronically recorded computer-aided design

TEKS 10.19
ELPS 5C

Spelling Rules

698.1 Write *i* before *e*

Write *i* before *e* except after *c*, or when sounded like *a* as in *neighbor* and *weigh*.

relief receive perceive reign freight beige

Exceptions: There are a number of exceptions to this rule, including these: *neither, leisure, seize, weird, species, science.*

698.2 Words with Consonant Endings

When a one-syllable word *(bat)* ends in a consonant *(t)* preceded by one vowel *(a)*, double the final consonant before adding a suffix that begins with a vowel *(batting)*.

sum — summary god — goddess

NOTE: When a word with more than one syllable *(control)* ends in a consonant *(l)* preceded by one vowel *(o)*, the accent is on the last syllable *(con trol′)*, and the suffix begins with a vowel *(ing)*, the same rule holds true: double the final consonant *(controlling)*.

prefer — preferred begin — beginning
forget — forgettable admit — admittance

698.3 Words with a Silent *e*

If a word ends with a silent *e*, drop the *e* before adding a suffix that begins with a vowel. Do not drop the *e* when the suffix begins with a consonant.

state — stating — statement like — liking — likeness
use — using — useful nine — ninety — nineteen

Exceptions: *judgment, truly, argument, ninth*

698.4 Words Ending in *y*

When *y* is the last letter in a word and the *y* is preceded by a consonant, change the *y* to *i* before adding any suffix except those beginning with *i*.

fry — fries — frying hurry — hurried — hurrying lady — ladies
ply — pliable happy — happiness beauty — beautiful

When *y* is the last letter in a word and the *y* is preceded by a vowel, do not change the *y* to *i* before adding a suffix.

play — plays — playful stay — stays — staying employ — employed

Important reminder: Never trust your spelling even to the best spell-checker. Use an online or print dictionary to determine or check the spelling of words your spell-checker does not cover.

TEKS 10.19
ELPS 4G, 5C

Practice

Spelling 1

Find the 10 words that are misspelled in the following paragraph and write them correctly. (Each misspelled word is in the "Commonly Misspelled Words" list on pages 700–701.)

Example: 1. wholly

The Kyoto Protocol is an international agreement to avert climate change caused by greenhouse gases. Enforcement began in February 2005. More than 150 countries are wholey on board with this effort to aleviate global warming. Among those countries not joining are Australia and the United States. These two priviledged countries, with approxamitely 5 percent of the world's population, account for more than 20 percent of the world's fossil fuel emissions. Yet leaders in niether of these two industreal nations agree with the Protocol's approach. They claim that the effort would cost too much money and would hurt the economy. In addision, these leaders believe China and India should not be exempt from emisions' controls because China alone will soon become the largest emitter of greenhouse gases. Many other government leaders beleive the costs of the Kyoto Protocol are affordable, but no one relly knows if the Protocol will make any differince.

Learning Language

Work with a partner and re-read aloud the spelling rules on the previous page. Take turns retelling each rule in your own words. Ask your partner to listen carefully and correct any errors you might have made as you retold the rules. With your partner, identify and discuss patterns in the spelling rules. Ask questions that you have about any of the rules and answer any questions your partner might have. Ask your teacher for clarification, if needed. Finally, work with your partner to summarize each of the spelling rules. Provide your own examples of each rule, and be sure to spell each of your own words correctly.

TEKS 10.19
ELPS 5C

Commonly Misspelled Words

A

abbreviate
abrupt
absence
absolute (ly)
absurd
abundance
academic
accelerate
accept (ance)
accessible
accessory
accidentally
accommodate
accompany
accomplish
accumulate
accurate
accustom (ed)
ache
achieve (ment)
acknowledge
acquaintance
acquired
across
address
adequate
adjustment
admissible
admittance
adolescent
advantageous
advertisement
advisable
aggravate
aggression
alcohol
alleviate
almost
alternative
although
aluminum
amateur
analysis
analyze
anarchy
ancient
anecdote
anesthetic
annihilate
announce
annual
anonymous
answer
anxious
apologize
apparatus
apparent (ly)
appearance
appetite
applies
appreciate
appropriate
approximately
architect
arctic
argument
arithmetic
arrangement
artificial
ascend
assistance
association
athlete
attendance
attire
attitude
audience
authority
available

B

balance
balloon
bargain
basically
beautiful
beginning
believe
benefit (ed)
biscuit
bought
boycott
brevity
brilliant
Britain
bureau
business

C

cafeteria
caffeine
calculator
calendar
campaign
canceled
candidate
catastrophe
category
caught
cavalry
celebration
cemetery
certificate
changeable
chief
chocolate
circuit
circumstance
civilization
colonel
colossal
column
commercial
commitment
committed
committee
comparative
comparison
competitively
conceivable
condemn
condescend
conference
conferred
confidential
congratulate
conscience
conscientious
conscious
consequence
consumer
contaminate
convenience
cooperate
correspondence
cough
coupon
courageous
courteous
creditor
criticism
criticize
curiosity
curious
cylinder

D

dealt
deceitful
deceive
decision
defense
deferred
definite (ly)
definition
delicious
descend
describe
description
despair
desperate
destruction
development
diameter
diaphragm
diarrhea
dictionary
dining
disagreeable
disappear
disappoint
disastrous
discipline
discrimination
discuss
dismissal
dissatisfied
dissect
distinctly
dormitory
doubt
drought
duplicate
dyeing
dying

E

earliest
efficiency
eighth
elaborate
eligible
eliminate
ellipse
embarrass
emphasize
employee
enclosure
encourage
endeavor
English
enormous
enough
enrichment
enthusiastic
entirely
entrance
environment
equipment
equipped
equivalent
especially
essential
eventually
exaggerate
examination
exceed
excellent
excessive
excite
executive
exercise
exhaust (ed)
exhibition
exhilaration
existence
expensive
experience
explanation
exquisite
extinguish
extraordinary
extremely

FG

facilities
familiar
fascinate
fashion
fatigue (d)
feature
February
fiery
financially
flourish
forcible
foreign
forfeit
fortunate
forty
fourth
freight
friend
fulfill
gauge
generally
generous
genuine
glimpse
gnarled
gnaw
government
gradual
grammar
gratitude
grievous
grocery
guard
guidance

H

happiness
harass
harmonize
height
hemorrhage
hereditary
hindrance
hoping
hopping
hospitable
humorous

hygiene
hymn
hypocrisy

IJ

ignorance
illiterate
illustrate
imaginary
immediately
immense
incidentally
inconvenience
incredible
indefinitely
independence
indispensable
industrial
industrious
inevitable
infinite
inflation
innocence
inoculation
inquiry
installation
instrumental
intelligence
interesting
interfere
interrupt
investigate
irregular
irresistible
issuing
itinerary
jealous (y)
jewelry
journal
judgment

KL

knowledge
laboratory
laugh
lawyer
league
legacy
legalize
legitimate
leisure
liaison
license
lightning
likable
liquid
literature
loneliness

MN

maintenance
maneuver
manufacture
marriage
mathematics
medieval
memento
menagerie
merchandise
merely
mileage
miniature
miscellaneous
mischievous
misspell
moat
mobile
mortgage
multiplied
muscle
musician
mustache
mutual
mysterious
naive
nauseous
necessary
neither
neurotic
nevertheless
ninety
nighttime
noticeable
nuclear
nuisance

OP

obstacle
obvious
occasion
occupant
occupation
occurred
occurrence
official
often
omitted
opinion
opponent
opportunity
opposite
optimism
ordinarily
organization
original
outrageous
pamphlet
parallel
paralyze
partial
particularly
pastime
patience
peculiar
pedestal
performance
permanent
permissible
perseverance
personal (ly)
personality
perspiration
persuade
petition
phenomenon
physical
physician
picnicking
planned
playwright
plead
pneumonia
politician
ponder
positively
possession
practically
precede
precious
preference
prejudice
preparation
presence
prevalent
primitive
privilege
probably
proceed
professional
professor
prominent
pronounce
pronunciation
protein
psychology
puny
purchase
pursuing

QR

qualified
quality
quantity
questionnaire
quiet
quite
quizzes
recede
receipt
receive
recipe
recognize
recommend
reference
referred
regard
regimen
religious
repel
repetition
residue
responsibility
restaurant
rheumatism
rhythm
ridiculous
robot
roommate

S

sacrifice
salary
sandwich
satisfactory
scarcely
scenic
schedule
scholar
science
secretary
seize
separate
sergeant
several
severely
sheriff
shrubbery
siege
signature
signify
silhouette
similar
simultaneous
sincerely
skiing
skunk
society
solar
sophomore
souvenir
spaghetti
specific
specimen
statue
stomach
stopped
strength
strictly
submission
substitute
subtle
succeed
success
sufficient
supersede
suppose
surprise
suspicious
symbolism
sympathy
synthetic

TU

tariff
technique
temperature
temporary
tendency
thermostat
thorough (ly)
though
throughout
tongue
tornado
tortoise
tragedy
transferred
tremendous
tried
trite
truly
unanimous
undoubtedly
unfortunately
unique
unnecessary
until
urgent
usable
usher
usually

V

vacuum
vague
valuable
variety
vengeance
versatile
vicinity
villain
visibility
visual

W

waif
Wednesday
weird
wholly
width
women
wrath
wreckage

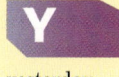

Y

yesterday
yield
yolk

TEKS 10.19
ELPS 4A, 5C

Steps to Becoming a Better Speller

1. **Be patient.**
   Becoming a good speller takes time.

2. **Check the correct pronunciation of each word you are attempting to spell.**
   Knowing the correct pronunciation of a word can help you remember its spelling.

3. **Note the meaning and history of each word as you are checking the dictionary for pronunciation.**
   Knowing the meaning and history of a word provides you with a better notion of how the word is properly used, and this can help you remember its spelling and pronunciation.

4. **Before you close the dictionary, practice spelling the word.**
   Look away from the page and try to "see" the word in your mind. Then write it on a piece of paper. Check your spelling in the dictionary; repeat the process until you are able to spell the word correctly.

5. **Learn some spelling rules.**
   For four of the most useful rules, see page 698.

6. **Make a list of the words that you often misspell.**
   Select the first 10 and practice spelling them.

   STEP A: Read each word carefully; then write it on a piece of paper. Check to see that you've spelled it correctly. Repeat this step for the words that you misspelled.

   STEP B: When you have finished your first 10 words, ask someone to read them to you as you write them again. Then check for misspellings. If you find none, congratulations! (Repeat both steps with your next 10 words, and so on.)

7. **Write often.**

Practice

Spelling 2

Find the 10 words that are misspelled in the following paragraphs and write them correctly. (Each misspelled word is in the "Commonly Misspelled Words" list on pages 700–701.)

Example: 1. *scenic*

In the early part of the twentieth century—before air travel, before the interstate highway system, before cars—people took the train to travel long distances. Rail service provided passengers with a comfortable, seenic trip accross the country. Slowly, however, private railroads were dieing as ridership decreased.

In 1970, the goverment agreed to subsidize the passenger rail service that became Amtrak. A network of 23,000 miles of track connected 314 communities with 184 trains. The number of trains and cities served by them has grown since then, but skedules are always subject to change. Maintainance of the aging equippment has also become a problem. Allthough the railroad has always struggled finantially (it has never made a profit), it remains a prominint part of many Americans' transportation options.

Model

Model the following sentences to practice using the "words with a silent *e*" spelling rule. (Use the underlined words in your sentences, too.)

Behind every <u>argument</u> is someone's ignorance. —Louis D. Brandeis

Journal <u>writing</u> is a voyage to the interior. —Christina Baldwin

Understanding Idioms

Idioms are phrases that are used in a special way. You can't understand an idiom just by knowing the meaning of each word in the phrase. You must learn it as a whole. For example, the idiom *bury the hatchet* means "to settle an argument," even though the individual words in the phrase mean something much different. This section will help you learn some of the common idioms in American English.

apple of his eye	Eagle Lake is the apple of his eye. (something he likes very much)
as plain as day	The mistake in the ad was as plain as day. (very clear)
as the crow flies	New London is 200 miles from here as the crow flies. (in a straight line)
at a snail's pace	My last hour at work passes at a snail's pace. (very, very slowly)
axe to grind	The manager has an axe to grind with that umpire. (disagreement to settle)
bad apple	There are no bad apples in this class. (a bad influence)
beat around the bush	Don't beat around the bush; answer the question. (avoid getting to the point)
benefit of the doubt	Everyone has been given the benefit of the doubt at least once. (another chance)
beyond the shadow of a doubt	Beyond the shadow of a doubt, this is my best science project. (for certain)
blew my top	When I saw the broken statue, I blew my top. (showed great anger)
bone to pick	Alison had a bone to pick with the student who copied her paper. (problem to settle)
brain drain	Brain drain is a serious problem in some states. (the best students moving elsewhere)
break the ice	The nervous ninth graders were afraid to break the ice. (start a conversation)
burn the midnight oil	Ryan had to burn the midnight oil to finish his report. (work late into the night)

bury the hatchet	My sisters were told to bury the hatchet immediately. (settle an argument)
by the skin of her teeth	Diana avoided an accident by the skin of her teeth. (just barely)
champing at the bit	The skiers were champing at the bit to get on the slopes. (eager, excited)
chicken feed	The prize was chicken feed to some people. (not worth much money)
chip off the old block	Frank's just like his father. He's a chip off the old block. (just like someone else)
clean as a whistle	My boss told me to make sure the place was as clean as a whistle before I left. (very clean)
cold shoulder	I wanted to fit in with that group, but they gave me the cold shoulder. (ignored me)
crack of dawn	Tony delivers his papers at the crack of dawn. (first light of day, early morning)
cry wolf	If you cry wolf too often, no one will believe you. (say you are in trouble when you aren't)
dead of night	Hearing a loud noise in the dead of night frightened Bill. (middle of the night)
dirt cheap	A lot of clothes at that store are dirt cheap. (inexpensive, costing very little money)
doesn't hold a candle to	That award doesn't hold a candle to a gold medal. (is not as good as)
drop in the bucket	The contributions were a drop in the bucket. (a small amount compared to what's needed)
everything from A to Z	That catalog lists everything from A to Z. (a lot of different things)
face the music	Mario had to face the music when he broke the window. (deal with the punishment)
fish out of water	He felt like a fish out of water in the new math class. (someone in an unfamiliar place)
fit for a king	The food at the athletic banquet was fit for a king. (very special)

ELPS 1H, 2C

flew off the handle	Bill flew off the handle when he saw a reckless driver near the school. (became very angry)
floating on air	Celine was floating on air at the prom. (feeling very happy)
food for thought	The boys' foolish and dangerous prank gave us food for thought. (something to think about)
get down to business	After sharing several jokes, Mr. Morales said we should get down to business. (start working)
get the upper hand	The wrestler moved quickly on his opponent in order to get the upper hand. (gain the advantage)
give their all	Student volunteers give their all to help others. (work as hard as they can)
go fly a kite	Rosa stared at her nosy brother and said, "Go fly a kite." (go away)
has a green thumb	Talk to Mrs. Lopez about your sick plant. She has a green thumb. (is good at growing plants)
has a heart of gold	Joe has a heart of gold. (is very kind and generous)
hit a home run	Rhonda hit a home run with her speech. (succeeded, or did well)
hit the ceiling	When my parents saw my grades, they hit the ceiling. (were very angry)
hit the hay	Exhausted from the hike, Jamal hit the hay without eating supper. (went to bed)
in a nutshell	Can you, in a nutshell, tell us your goals for this year? (in summary)
in one ear and out the other	Marcella, concerned about her pet, let the lecture go in one ear and out the other. (without really listening)
in the black	My aunt's gift shop is finally in the black. (making money)
in the nick of time	Anna caught the falling vase in the nick of time. (just in time)
in the red	Many businesses start out in the red. (in debt)
in the same boat	The new tax bill meant everyone would be in the same boat. (in a similar situation)

iron out	Martin will meet with the work crew to iron out their complaints. (solve, work out)
it goes without saying	It goes without saying that saving money is a good idea. (it is clear)
it stands to reason	It stands to reason that your stamina will increase if you run every day. (it makes sense)
keep a stiff upper lip	Keep a stiff upper lip when you visit the doctor. (be brave)
keep it under your hat	Keep it under your hat about the pop quiz. (don't tell anyone)
knock on wood	My uncle knocked on wood after he said he had never had the flu. (did something for good luck)
knuckle down	After wasting half the day, we were told to knuckle down. (work hard)
learn the ropes	It takes every new employee a few months to learn the ropes. (get to know how things are done)
leave no stone unturned	The police plan to leave no stone unturned at the crime scene. (check everything)
lend someone a hand	You will feel good if you lend someone a hand. (help someone)
let the cat out of the bag	Gabe let the cat out of the bag during lunch. (told a secret)
let's face it	Let's face it. You don't like rap. (let's admit it)
look high and low	We looked high and low for Jan's dog. (looked everywhere)
lose face	In some cultures, it is very bad to lose face. (be embarrassed)
needle in a haystack	Trying to find a person in New York is like trying to find a needle in a haystack. (something impossible to find)
nose to the grindstone	With all of these assignments, I have to keep my nose to the grindstone. (work hard)
on cloud nine	After talking to my girlfriend, I was on cloud nine. (feeling very happy)
on pins and needles	Elizabeth was on pins and needles during the championship game. (feeling nervous)

out the window	Once the rain started, our plans were out the window. (ruined)
over and above	Over and above the required work, Will cleaned up the lab. (in addition to)
pain in the neck	Mark knew the report would be a pain in the neck. (very annoying)
pull your leg	Cassie was only pulling your leg. (telling you a little lie as a joke)
put his foot in his mouth	Alex put his foot in his mouth when he answered the question. (said something embarrassing)
put the cart before the horse	Tonya put the cart before the horse when she sealed the envelope before inserting the letter. (did something in the wrong order)
put your best foot forward	When applying for a job, you should put your best foot forward. (do the best that you can do)
red-letter day	Taylor had a red-letter day because she did so well on her math test. (very good day)
rock the boat	I was told not to rock the boat. (cause trouble)
rude awakening	Jake will have a rude awakening when he sees the bill for his computer. (sudden, unpleasant surprise)
save face	His gift was clearly an attempt to save face. (fix an embarrassing situation)
see eye to eye	We see eye to eye about the need for a new school. (are in agreement)
shake a leg	I told Enrique to shake a leg so that we wouldn't be late. (hurry)
shift into high gear	Greg had to shift into high gear to finish the test in time. (speed up, hurry)
sight for sore eyes	My grandmother's smiling face was a sight for sore eyes. (good to see)
sight unseen	Liz bought the coat sight unseen. (without seeing it first)
sink or swim	Whether you sink or swim in school depends on your study habits. (fail or succeed)

spilled the beans	Suddenly, Kesia realized that she had spilled the beans. (revealed a secret)
spring chicken	Although Mr. Gordon isn't a spring chicken, he sure knows how to talk to kids. (young person)
stick to your guns	Know what you believe, and stick to your guns. (don't change your mind)
sweet tooth	Chocolate is often the candy of choice for those with a sweet tooth. (a love for sweets, like candy and cake)
take a dim view	My sister will take a dim view of that movie. (disapprove)
take it with a grain of salt	When you read that advertisement, take it with a grain of salt. (don't believe everything)
take the bull by the horns	It's time to take the bull by the horns so the project gets done on time. (take control)
through thick and thin	Those two girls have remained friends through thick and thin. (in good times and in bad times)
time flies	Time flies as you grow older. (time passes quickly)
time to kill	Grace had time to kill, so she read a book. (extra time)
to go overboard	The class was told not to go overboard. A $50.00 donation was fine. (to do too much)
toe the line	The new teacher made everyone toe the line. (follow the rules)
tongue-tied	He can talk easily with friends, but in class he is usually tongue-tied. (not knowing what to say)
turn over a new leaf	He decided to turn over a new leaf in school. (make a new start)
two peas in a pod	Ever since kindergarten, Lil and Eva have been like two peas in a pod. (very much alike)
under the weather	Mike was feeling under the weather this morning. (sick)
wallflower	Maria knew the other girls thought she was a wallflower. (a shy person)
word of mouth	Joseph learns a lot about his favorite team by word of mouth. (talking with other people)

TEKS 10.19A
ELPS 1C, 4C, 5C

Using the Right Word

a lot ■ *A lot* (always two words) is a vague descriptive phrase that should be used sparingly.

> **"You can observe a lot just by watching."**
>
> — Yogi Berra

accept, except ■ The verb *accept* means "to receive" or "to believe"; the preposition *except* means "other than."

> **The principal accepted the boy's story about the broken window, but she asked why no one except him saw the ball accidentally slip from his hand.**

adapt, adopt ■ *Adapt* means "to adjust or change to fit"; *adopt* means "to choose and treat as your own" (a child, an idea).

> **After a lengthy period of study, Malcolm X adopted the Islamic faith and adapted to its lifestyle.**

affect, effect ■ The verb *affect* means "to influence"; the verb *effect* means "to produce, accomplish, complete."

> **Ming's hard work effected an A on the test, which positively affected her semester grade.**

The noun *effect* means the "result."

> **Good grades have a calming effect on parents.**

aisle, isle ■ An *aisle* is a passage between seats; an *isle* is a small island.

> **Many airline passengers on their way to the Isle of Capri prefer an aisle seat.**

all right ■ *All right* is always two words (not *alright*).

allusion, illusion ■ *Allusion* is an indirect reference to someone or something; *illusion* is a false picture or idea.

> **My little sister, under the illusion that she's movie-star material, makes frequent allusions to her future fans.**

already, all ready ■ *Already* is an adverb meaning "before this time" or "by this time." *All ready* is an adjective meaning "fully prepared."

NOTE: Use *all ready* if you can substitute *ready* alone in the sentence.

> **Although I've already had some dessert, I am all ready for some ice cream from the street vendor.**

TEKS 10.19A
ELPS 1C, 4C, 5C

Practice

Using the Right Word 1

accept, except; affect, effect; all right; allusion, illusion; already, all ready

Write the correct word if the underlined word is not used correctly. If it is, then write "OK."

Example: 1. already

The small group of people staggering across the hot sand had **(1)** all ready been without water for a day. One said, "I refuse to **(2)** except this situation! We must find water!"

They forced themselves to continue—**(3)** accept for one man, who was **(4)** all ready to give up. The other members of the group persuaded the despairing man to keep up. If he stayed behind, surely his loss would **(5)** effect the others negatively. A woman said, "This is not Gilligan's Island, you know, where we could survive in huts." He didn't quite get the **(6)** illusion, but he went along anyway.

Soon the lack of water would begin to have an adverse **(7)** affect on them. Many times, of course, they would "see" water—only to realize that it was just an **(8)** illusion. They knew that if they could only find water, they'd be **(9)** all right.

Model

Model the following sentences to practice using *allusion* and *illusion* correctly.

I think we must quote whenever we feel that the allusion is interesting or helpful or amusing.

—Clifton Fadiman

If power was an illusion, wasn't weakness necessarily one also?

—Lois McMaster Bujold, *A Civil Campaign*

TEKS 10.19A
ELPS 1C, 4C, 5C

altogether, all together ■ *Altogether* means "entirely." The phrase *all together* means "in a group" or "all at once."

> **"There is altogether too much gridlock," complained the Democrats. All together, the Republicans yelled, "No way!"**

among, between ■ *Among* is typically used when speaking of more than two persons or things. *Between* is used when speaking of only two.

> **The three of us talked among ourselves to decide between going out or eating in.**

amount, number ■ *Amount* is used for bulk measurement. *Number* is used to count separate units. (See also *fewer, less.*)

> **A substantial amount of honey spilled all over a number of my CD's.**

annual, biannual, semiannual, biennial, perennial ■ An *annual* event happens once every year. A *biannual* or *semiannual* event happens twice a year. A *biennial* event happens every two years. A *perennial* event is one that is persistent or constant.

> **Dad's annual family reunion gets bigger every year.**
> **We're going shopping at the department store's semiannual white sale.**
> **Due to dwindling attendance, the county fair is now a biennial celebration.**
> **A perennial plant persists for several years.**

anyway ■ Do not add an *s* to *anyway.*

ascent, assent ■ *Ascent* is the act of rising or climbing; *assent* is "to agree to something after some consideration" (or such an agreement).

> **We completed our ascent of the butte with the assent of the landowner.**

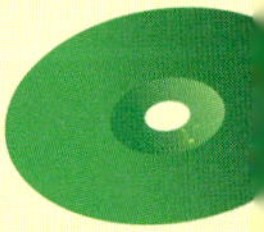

bad, badly ■ *Bad* is an adjective. *Badly* is an adverb.

> **This apple is bad, but one bad apple doesn't always ruin the whole bushel.**
> **In today's game, Ross passed badly.**

base, bass ■ *Base* is the foundation or the lower part of something. *Bass* (pronounced like *base*) is a deep sound. *Bass* (pronounced like *class*) is a fish.

beside, besides ■ *Beside* means "by the side of." *Besides* means "in addition to."

> **Mother always grew roses beside the trash bin. Besides looking nice, they also gave off a sweet smell that masked odors.**

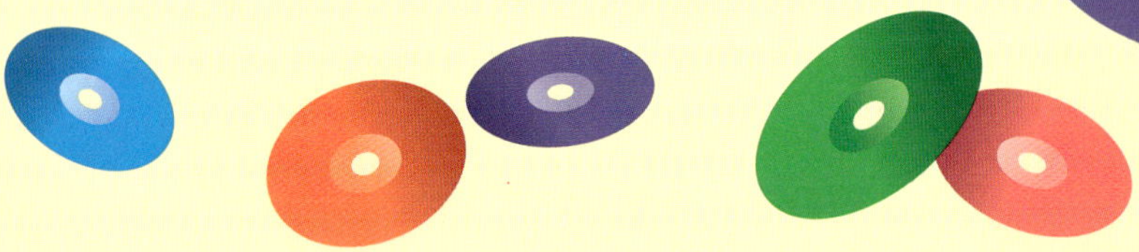

TEKS 10.19A
ELPS 1C, 4C, 5C

Practice

Using the Right Word 2

among, between; amount, number; anyway; bad, badly; base, bass; beside, besides

Write the correct choice from those given in parentheses.

Example: The team talked *(among, between)* themselves as they watched Lamar being carried off the field.
among

1. Lamar was hurt *(bad, badly)* when he was tackled during the game.
2. A cut near the *(base, bass)* of his skull caused concern.
3. *(Beside, Besides)* the cut, Lamar had also fractured his leg.
4. *(Anyway, Anyways),* he had to stay in the hospital for several days.
5. His classmates sent him a huge *(amount, number)* of get-well cards.
6. Lamar spotted a letter *(beside, besides)* his water pitcher.
7. It was from the player who tackled him—he felt *(bad, badly)* about the incident.
8. The player suggested that he and Lamar go *(base, bass)* fishing when Lamar felt better.
9. Now, *(beside, besides)* getting out of the hospital, Lamar had something else to look forward to.
10. *(Among, Between)* the medical treatment and the good *(number, amount)* of support from his friends, he knew he would be well soon.

Model

Model the following sentences to practice using the words *among* and *between.*

And in the midst of it, out sprang from among the trees and bushes the great white body of a man, who dashed into the stream and swam like a dolphin.
—Frances Hodgson Burnett, *His Grace of Osmonde*

The shortest distance between two points is under construction.
—Noelie Altito

board, bored ■ *Board* is a piece of wood. *Board* is also an administrative group or council.

The school board approved the purchase of fifty 1- by 6-inch pine boards.

Bored is the past tense of the verb "bore," which may mean "to make a hole by drilling" or "to become weary out of dullness."

Watching television bored Joe, so he took his drill and bored a hole in the wall where he could hang his new clock.

brake, break ■ *Brake* is a device used to stop a vehicle. *Break* means "to separate or to destroy."

I hope the brakes on my car never break.

bring, take ■ *Bring* suggests the action is directed toward the speaker; *take* suggests the action is directed away from the speaker.

Bring home some garbage bags so I can take the trash outside.

can, may ■ *Can* suggests ability while *may* suggests permission.

"Can I go to the mall?" means "Am I physically able to go to the mall?"

"May I go to the mall?" asks permission to go.

capital, capitol ■ The noun *capital* refers to a city or to money. The adjective *capital* means "major or important." *Capitol* refers to a building.

The state capital is home to the capitol building for a capital reason. The state government contributed capital for its construction.

cent, sent, scent ■ *Cent* is a coin; *sent* is the past tense of the verb "send"; *scent* is an odor or a smell.

For forty-four cents, I sent my girlfriend a mushy love poem in a perfumed envelope. She adored the scent but hated the poem.

cereal, serial ■ *Cereal* is a grain, often made into breakfast food. *Serial* relates to something in a series.

Daniel enjoys reading serial novels while he eats a bowl of cereal.

chord, cord ■ *Chord* may mean "an emotion" or "a combination of musical tones sounded at the same time." A *cord* is a string or a rope.

The guitar player strummed the opening chord to the group's hit song, which struck a responsive chord with the audience.

chose, choose ■ *Chose* (chōz) is the past tense of the verb *choose* (cho͞oz).

Last quarter I chose to read Chitra Divakaruni's *The Unknown Errors of Our Lives*—a fascinating book about Indian immigrants.

TEKS 10.19A
ELPS 1C, 4C, 5C

Practice

Using the Right Word 3

brake, break; bring, take; can, may; chord, cord; chose, choose

Write the correct choice from those given in parentheses.

Example: The *(chord, cord)* on these blinds doesn't work right.
cord

1. *(Can, May)* I get you something to drink?
2. Cheng wants to *(brake, break)* the old school record for consecutive free throws.
3. Make sure we *(bring, take)* some sunscreen with us to the beach.
4. Wilson *(choose, chose)* a bright blue, sparkling sweater for his girlfriend's birthday present.
5. At the first *(chord, cord),* the audience knew the song and went wild.
6. This printer *(can, may)* make two-sided copies.
7. I would not *(choose, chose)* a career as a septic-tank cleaner.
8. Tristan should *(bring, take)* his suit to the cleaners on his way to the concert.
9. Most often, a vehicle does not come to an immediate stop when the *(brake, break)* is applied.
10. You *(can, may)* leave the room when you are done with the test.

Model

Model the following sentences to practice using *brake* and *break* correctly.

Even though you may want to move forward in your life, you may have one foot on the brake. In order to be free, you must learn how to let go.
—Mary Manin Morrissey

A hole is nothing at all, but you can break your neck in it.
—Austin O'Malley

coarse, course ■ *Coarse* means "rough or crude"; *course* means "a path or direction taken." *Course* also means "a class or a series of studies."

> **Fletcher, known for using coarse language, was barred from the golf course until he took an etiquette course.**

complement, compliment ■ *Complement* refers to that which completes or fulfills. *Compliment* is an expression of admiration or praise.

> **Kimberly smiled, thinking she had received a compliment when Carlos said that her new Chihuahua complemented her personality.**

continual, continuous ■ *Continual* refers to something that happens again and again with some breaks or pauses; *continuous* refers to something that keeps happening, uninterrupted.

> **Sunlight hits Texas on a continual basis; sunlight hits Earth continuously.**

counsel, council ■ When used as a noun, *counsel* means "advice"; when used as a verb, it means "to advise." *Council* refers to a group that advises.

> **The student council counseled all freshmen to join a school club. That's good counsel.**

desert, dessert ■ The noun *desert* (dĕz′ərt) refers to barren wilderness. *Dessert* (dĭ zûrt′) is food served at the end of a meal.

> **The scorpion tiptoed through the moonlit desert, searching for dessert.**

The verb *desert* (dĭ zûrt′) means "to abandon"; the noun *desert* (dĭ zûrt′) means "deserved reward or punishment."

> **The burglar's hiding place deserted him when the spotlight swung his way; his subsequent arrest was his just desert.**

die, dye ■ *Die* (dying) means "to stop living." *Dye* (dyeing) is used to change the color of something.

different from, different than ■ Use *different from* in a comparison of two things. *Different than* should be used only when followed by a clause.

> **Barry is quite different from his brother.**
> **Life is different than it used to be.**

farther, further ■ *Farther* refers to a physical distance; *further* refers to additional time, quantity, or degree.

> **Alaska extends farther north than Iceland does. Further information can be obtained in an atlas.**

fewer, less ■ *Fewer* refers to the number of separate units; *less* refers to bulk quantity.

> **Because we have fewer orders for cakes, we'll buy less sugar and flour.**

TEKS 10.19A
ELPS 1C, 4C, 5C

Practice

Using the Right Word 4

complement, compliment; counsel, council; desert, dessert; farther, further

Write the correct choice from those given in parentheses.

Example: Saaid needs *(farther, further)* information for his essay.
further

1. Nadia's energy *(deserted, desserted)* her as she approached the end of the triathlon.
2. The student *(council, counsel)* sponsored this year's food drive.
3. Dylan *(complemented, complimented)* Renee on her new hairstyle.
4. Zach can punt the ball *(farther, further)* than any of his teammates.
5. Mr. Garcia *(counciled, counseled)* our class on the SAT tests.
6. Jorge's sly smile was a *(complement, compliment)* to his secretive disposition.
7. Mrs. Lang's *(deserts, desserts)* were first to go at the bake sale.
8. Soo got her just *(deserts, desserts)* when she missed the last bus.
9. To *(complement, compliment)* her costume, Yvette dyed her hair an outrageous purple.
10. My Panhandle town is a *(desert, dessert)* compared to a rain forest.

Model

Model the following sentences to practice using the words *further* and *farther* correctly.

Gratitude is merely the secret hope of further favors.
—Francois de La Rochefoucauld

Men came from the east and built these American towns because they wished to go no farther, and the towns they built were shaped by the urge to go onward.
—Rose Wilder Lane, *Old Home Town*

TEKS 10.19A
ELPS 1C, 4C, 5C

flair, flare ■ *Flair* refers to style or natural talent; *flare* means "to light up quickly" or "burst out" (or an object that does so).

> **Ronni was thrilled with Jorge's flair for decorating—until one of his strategically placed candles flared, marring the wall.**

good, well ■ *Good* is an adjective; *well* is nearly always an adverb. (When *well* is used to describe a state of health, it is an adjective: He was happy to be *well* again.)

> **The MP3 player works well.**
>
> **Our team looks good this season.**

heal, heel ■ *Heal* means "to mend or restore to health." A *heel* is the back part of a foot.

> **Achilles died because a poison arrow pierced his heel and caused a wound that would not heal.**

healthful, healthy ■ *Healthful* means "causing or improving health"; *healthy* means "possessing health."

> **Healthful foods build healthy bodies.**

hear, here ■ You *hear* with your ears. *Here* means "the area close by."

heard, herd ■ *Heard* is the past tense of the verb "hear"; *herd* is a large group of animals.

hole, whole ■ A *hole* is a cavity or hollow place. *Whole* means "complete."

idle, idol ■ *Idle* means "not working." An *idol* is someone or something that is worshipped.

> **The once-popular actress, who had been idle lately, wistfully recalled her days as an idol.**

immigrate, emigrate ■ *Immigrate* means "to come into a new country or environment." *Emigrate* means "to go out of one country to live in another."

> **Martin Ulferts immigrated to this country in 1882. He was only three years old when he emigrated from Germany.**

imply, infer ■ *Imply* means "to suggest or express indirectly"; *infer* means "to draw a conclusion from facts." (A writer or speaker implies; a reader or listener infers.)

> **Dad implied by his comment that I should drive more carefully, and I inferred that he was concerned for both me and his new car.**

Practice

Using the Right Word 5

good, well; heard, herd; idle, idol; immigrate, emigrate; imply, infer

Choose the correct words from the list above to fill in the blanks.

Example: Let the engine ______ for a few minutes.
idle

1. Have you ______ the latest news?
2. My little sister's ______ is Blue of Blue's Clues.
3. Some people think the government should tighten restrictions on those wishing to ______ to the United States.
4. Everyone agrees that Dena has a ______ head on her shoulders.
5. If Yadira declined Al's invitation, she would ______ that she didn't want to spend time with him.
6. Victims of civil wars have every reason to ______ from their countries.
7. I had never seen a ______ of any kind of animal until we saw the buffalo in South Dakota's Custer State Park.
8. I ______ from your silence that you do not agree.
9. Granddad actually plays the violin quite ______, but he calls it "fiddling."
10. Dallas was suffering from the flu last week, but he is ______ again.

Model

Model the following sentences to practice using *imply* and *infer* correctly.

> **The fact that some geniuses were laughed at does not imply that all who are laughed at are geniuses.**
>
> —Carl Sagan

> **That man is the noblest creature may also be inferred from the fact that no other creature has yet contested this claim.**
>
> —G. C. Lichtenberg

insure, ensure ■ *Insure* means "to secure from financial harm or loss." *Ensure* means "to make certain of something."

To ensure that you can legally drive that new car, you'll have to insure it.

it's, its ■ *It's* is the contraction of "it is." *Its* is the possessive form of "it."

It's hard to believe, but the movie *Shrek* still holds its appeal for many kids.

later, latter ■ *Later* means "after a period of time." *Latter* refers to the second of two things mentioned.

Later that year we had our second baby and adopted a stray kitten. The latter was far more welcomed by our toddler.

lay, lie ■ *Lay* means "to place." *Lay* is a transitive verb. (See **744.1**.)

Lay your books on the big table.

Lie means "to recline," and *lay* is the past tense of *lie*. *Lie* is an intransitive verb. (See **744.1**.)

In this heat, the children must lie down for a nap. Yesterday they lay down without one complaint. Sometimes they have lain in the hammocks to rest.

lead, led ■ *Lead* (lēd) is the present tense of the verb meaning "to guide." The past tense of the verb is *led* (lĕd). The noun *lead* (lĕd) is a metal.

We were led along the path that leads to an abandoned lead mine.

learn, teach ■ *Learn* means "to acquire information." *Teach* means "to give information."

I learn better when people teach with real-world examples.

leave, let ■ *Leave* means "to allow something to remain behind." *Let* means "to permit."

Would you let me leave my bike at your house?

lend, borrow ■ *Lend* means "to give for temporary use." *Borrow* means "to receive for temporary use."

I told Mom I needed to borrow $18 for a CD, but she said she could only lend money for school supplies.

like, as ■ When *like* is used as a preposition meaning "similar to," it can be followed only by a noun, pronoun, or noun phrase; when *as* is used as a subordinating conjunction, it introduces a subordinate clause.

You could become a gymnast like her, as you work and practice hard.

medal, meddle ■ *Medal* is an award. *Meddle* means "to interfere."

Some parents meddle in the awards process to be sure that their kids get medals.

Practice

Using the Right Word 6

it's, its; lay, lie; lead, led; learn, teach; leave, let; like, as

Write the correct choice from those given in parentheses.

Example: Let your mind wander *(like, as)* a bird searching for food.
like

1. In my opinion, an apple is a snack at *(it's, its)* best.
2. After dinner, Grandpa *(leaves, lets)* scraps on the porch for our cat.
3. The mountain guide *(lead, led)* the inexperienced campers down a winding path.
4. Mia wants Ms. Benke to *(learn, teach)* her how to play the flute.
5. Just as I *(lay, lie)* my head on the pillow, the smoke alarm went off.
6. I wish I could fly on my own *(like, as)* the birds do.
7. The dogs enjoy being out this time of year; they *(lay, lie)* in the shade of the maple tree.
8. Children can *(learn, teach)* a foreign language more easily than adults can.

Learning Language

With a partner, re-read the information on the previous page. Note the differences in each word pair. Choose four pairs and tell a story with the words. Have your partner write the story as you narrate it and retell it to you. When you have finished, discuss and correct the retelling. Check the spelling in the written story; discuss and correct any errors. Have your partner choose a different set of words and tell another story with clear, precise details. Follow the same process as your partner tells the new story.

TEKS 10.19A
ELPS 1C, 4C, 5C

metal, mettle ■ *Metal* is a chemical element like iron or gold. *Mettle* is "strength of spirit."

Grandad's mettle during battle left him with some metal in his shoulder.

miner, minor ■ A *miner* digs for valuable ore. A *minor* is a person who is not legally an adult. A *minor* problem is one of no great importance.

moral, morale ■ A *moral* is a lesson drawn from a story; as an adjective, it relates to the principles of right and wrong. *Morale* refers to someone's attitude.

Ms. Ladue considers it her moral obligation to go to church every day.

The students' morale sank after their defeat in the forensics competition.

passed, past ■ *Passed* is a verb. *Past* can be used as a noun, an adjective, or a preposition.

That old pickup truck passed my sports car! (verb)
Many senior citizens hold dearly to the past. (noun)
Tilly's past life as a circus worker must have been . . . interesting. (adjective)
Who can walk past a bakery without looking in the window? (preposition)

peace, piece ■ *Peace* means "tranquility or freedom from war." *Piece* is a part or fragment.

Grandma sits in the peace and quiet of the parlor, enjoying a piece of pie.

peak, peek, pique ■ A *peak* is a high point. *Peek* means "brief look" (or "look briefly"). *Pique*, as a verb, means "to excite by challenging"; as a noun, it is a feeling of resentment.

The peak of Dr. Fedder's professional life was his ability to pique children's interest in his work. "Peek at this slide," he said to the eager students.

pedal, peddle, petal ■ A *pedal* is a foot lever; as a verb, it means "to ride a bike." *Peddle* means "to go from place to place selling something." A *petal* is part of a flower.

Don Miller paints beautiful petals on his homemade birdhouses. Then he pedals through the flea market every weekend to peddle them.

personal, personnel ■ *Personal* means "private." *Personnel* are people working at a particular job.

plain, plane ■ *Plain* means "an area of land that is flat or level"; it also means "clearly seen or clearly understood."

It's plain to see why settlers of the Great Plains had trouble moving west.

Plane means "flat, level"; it is also a tool used to smooth the surface of wood.

I used a plane to make the board plane and smooth.

TEKS 10.19A
ELPS 1C, 4C, 5C

Practice

Using the Right Word 7

moral, morale; passed, past; peak, peek, pique; plain, plane

Write the correct word if the underlined word is not used correctly. If it is, then write "OK."

Example: 1. passed

The jet from Boston **(1)** past the mid-Atlantic states and crossed the Great **(2)** Plains on its way to Denver. After another short ride, we finally reached our **(3)** plane yet beautiful mountain lodge, greatly improving our **(4)** morale. An elderly gentleman spoke to some children gathered about him. "A ghost named Ahote lives on the mountain **(5)** peek," he said. I didn't catch much else of his speech, but it **(6)** peaked my curiosity, so I decided to do some research upon my return home.

I was not able to find much. An Internet search led me to a book about Native Americans of the **(7)** passed century. I found a copy at the city library and took a **(8)** pique. Yes, there was an Ahote—meaning "restless one"—from the area where we vacationed. He guided non-natives across the mountain. When he died, his grave was placed at the highest mountain pass. Pioneers knew they were headed in the right direction when they came upon it. I thought of this **(9)** morale: A guiding spirit can make its presence known in more ways than one.

Model

Model the following sentences to practice using *peak* and *peek* correctly.

Simplicity is the peak of civilization.
—Jessie Sampter

I've stayed in the front yard all my life.
I want a peek at the back
Where it's rough and untended and hungry weed grows.
—Gwendolyn Brooks, "A Street in Bronzeville"

TEKS 10.19A
ELPS 1C, 4C, 5C

poor, pour, pore ■ *Poor* means "needy or pitiable." *Pour* means "to cause to flow in a stream." A *pore* is an opening in the skin.

> **Tough exams on late spring days make my poor pores pour sweat.**

principal, principle ■ As an adjective, *principal* means "primary." As a noun, it can mean "a school administrator" or "a sum of money." *Principle* means "idea or doctrine."

> **His principal concern is fitness. (adjective) The principal retired. (noun)**
> **During the first year of a loan, you pay more interest than principal. (noun)**
> **The principle of *caveat emptor* is "Let the buyer beware."**

quiet, quit, quite ■ *Quiet* is the opposite of "noisy." *Quit* means "to stop." *Quite* means "completely or entirely."

quote, quotation ■ *Quote* is a verb; *quotation* is a noun.

> **The quotation I used was from Woody Allen. You may quote me on that.**

real, really, very ■ Do not use *real* in place of the adverbs *very* or *really.*

> **Mother's cake is usually very (not *real*) tasty, but this one is really stale!**

right, write, wright, rite ■ *Right* means "correct or proper"; it also refers to that which a person has a legal claim to, as in copyright. *Write* means "to inscribe or record." A *wright* is a person who makes or builds something. *Rite* refers to a ritual or ceremonial act.

> **Write this down: It is the right of the shipwright to perform the rite of christening—breaking a bottle of champagne on the stern of the ship.**

ring, wring ■ *Ring* means "encircle" or "to sound by striking." *Wring* means "to squeeze or twist."

> **At the beach, Grandma would ring her head with a large scarf. Once, it blew into the sea, so she had me wring it out.**

scene, seen ■ *Scene* refers to the setting or location where something happens; it also may mean "sight or spectacle." *Seen* is a form of the verb "see."

> **Serena had seen her boyfriend making a scene; she cringed.**

seam, seem ■ *Seam* (noun) is a line formed by connecting two pieces. *Seem* (verb) means "to appear to exist."

> **The ragged seams in his old coat seem to match the creases in his face.**

set, sit ■ *Set* means "to place." *Sit* means "to put the body in a seated position." *Set* is transitive; *sit* is intransitive. (See 744.1.)

> **How can you just sit there and watch as I set all these chairs in place?**

Practice

Using the Right Word 8

principal, principle; real, really, very; ring, wring; set, sit

In each sentence, a word is misused. Write the correct word.

Example: My parents are trying to pay down the principle on their mortgage.
principal

1. I am real excited about my sister's engagement ring.
2. In this game, you must find something to set on when you hear a bell ring.
3. "That is a very interesting painting," remarked the principle to the art student.
4. Reina's hair is really long—she has to ring it out one section at a time when she washes it.
5. My ears are starting to wring; I think I'd better sit down.
6. Rosa Parks was a real hero who adhered to the principal of fairness.
7. Don't sit that candle on the wooden table . . . it could lead to a very bad situation.
8. The principle reason to recycle is really quite simple: it saves natural resources.

Model

Model the following sentences to practice using *real* and *really* correctly.

A man always has two reasons for doing anything—a good reason and the real reason.
—J. P. Morgan

All that is really necessary for survival of the fittest, it seems, is an interest in life—good, bad, or peculiar.
—Grace Paley

TEKS 10.19A
ELPS 1C, 4C, 5C

sight, cite, site ■ *Sight* means "the act of seeing"; a *sight* is what is seen. *Cite* means "to quote" or "to summon," as before a court. *Site* means "location."

In her report, the general contractor cited several problems at the downtown job site. For one, the loading area was a chaotic sight.

sole, soul ■ *Sole* means "single, only one"; *sole* also refers to the bottom surface of the foot. *Soul* refers to the spiritual part of a person.

As the sole inhabitant of the island, he put his heart and soul into his farming.

stationary, stationery ■ *Stationary* means "not movable"; *stationery* refers to the paper and envelopes used to write letters.

steal, steel ■ *Steal* means "to take something without permission"; *steel* is a type of metal.

than, then ■ *Than* is used in a comparison; *then* tells when.

Abigail shouted that her big brother was bigger than my big brother. Then she ran away.

their, there, they're ■ *Their* is a possessive personal pronoun. *There* is an adverb used to point out location. *They're* is the contraction for "they are."

They're a well-dressed couple. Do you see them there, with their matching jackets?

threw, through ■ *Threw* is the past tense of "throw." *Through* means "from beginning to end."

Through seven innings, Janelle threw just seven strikes.

to, too, two ■ *To* is a preposition that can mean "in the direction of." *To* is also used to form an infinitive. (See **754.2**.) *Too* means "also" or "very." *Two* is a number.

vain, vane, vein ■ *Vain* means "valueless or fruitless"; it may also mean "holding a high regard for oneself." *Vane* is a flat piece of material set up to show which way the wind blows. *Vein* refers to a blood vessel or a mineral deposit.

The vain prospector, boasting about the vein of silver he'd uncovered, paused to look up at the turning weather vane.

vary, very ■ *Vary* means "to change." *Very* means "to a high degree."

Though the weather may vary from day to day, generally, it is very pleasant.

TEKS 10.19A
ELPS 1C, 1E, 3B, 3E, 3H, 4C, 5C

Practice

Using the Right Word 9

sole, soul; than, then; vain, vane, vein; vary, very

Read the following paragraphs. If the underlined word is used incorrectly, write the correct word. If it's correct as is, write "OK."

How do credit cards work? Essentially, you (the card user) borrow money to buy something. The card issuer, a bank, agrees to the loan and **(1)** than deposits the money into the merchant's bank account.

If you cannot pay the full amount of the bill, the bank charges interest on the unpaid balance. Interest rates typically **(2)** vary from 11 to 23 percent. The next bill will be for the unpaid amount plus interest. The amount owed, even if you don't borrow a dollar more, keeps going up! It can be **(3)** vary difficult to pay off a balance. You may begin to think that you're making payments in **(4)** vein. You may even feel you owe your heart and **(5)** sole to the credit card company.

Banks also charge credit card users fees for cash advances and late payments. Anyone who uses credit cards should be aware of how easy it is to incur more debt **(6)** then he or she can comfortably repay. List your charges on some paper. **(7)** Than learn to use credit responsibly to build a positive credit record.

Learning Language

Work with a partner and re-read the information on the previous page. Discuss the differences in meaning among the words. Then choose four words from different groups and use them to describe a particular person or thing. Be sure to include specific details in your narration. Have your partner retell the description to you. Have your partner tell which words you used and how those words would be spelled. Then have your partner choose a different set of words, and repeat the activity.

vial, vile ■ *A vial* is a small container for liquid. *Vile* is an adjective meaning "foul, despicable."

It's a vile job, but someone has to clean these lab vials.

waist, waste ■ *Waist* is the part of the body just above the hips. The verb *waste* means "to spend or use carelessly" or "to wear away or decay"; the noun *waste* refers to material that is unused or useless.

Her waist is small because she wastes no opportunity to exercise.

wait, weight ■ *Wait* means "to stay somewhere expecting something." *Weight* refers to a degree or unit of heaviness.

ware, wear, where ■ *Ware* refers to a product that is sold; *wear* means "to have on or to carry on one's body"; *where* asks "in what place?" or "in what situation?"

The designer boasted, "Where can anybody wear my ware? Anywhere."

way, weigh ■ *Way* means "path or route." *Weigh* means "to measure weight" or "to have a certain heaviness."

My dogs weigh too much. The best way to reduce is a daily run in the park.

weather, whether ■ *Weather* refers to the condition of the atmosphere. *Whether* refers to a possibility.

Due to the weather, the coach wondered whether he should cancel the meet.

which, that ■ Use *which* to refer to objects or animals in a nonrestrictive clause (set off with commas). Use *that* to refer to objects or animals in a restrictive clause. (For more information about these types of clauses, see **650.2**.)

The birds, which stay in the area all winter, know where the feeders are located. The food that attracts the most birds is sunflower seed.

who, whom ■ Use *who* to refer to people. *Who* is used as the subject of a verb in an independent clause or in a relative clause. *Whom* is used as the object of a preposition or as a direct object.

To whom do we owe our thanks for these pizzas? And who ordered anchovies?

who's, whose ■ *Who's* is the contraction for "who is." *Whose* is a pronoun that can show possession or ownership.

Cody, whose car is new, will drive. Who's going to read the map?

your, you're ■ *Your* is a possessive pronoun. *You're* is the contraction for "you are."

Take your boots if you're going out in that snow.

TEKS 10.19A
ELPS 1C, 4C, 5C

Practice

Using the Right Word 10

vial, vile; ware, wear, where; weather, whether; which, that; who, whom

In each numbered paragraph below, some words are used incorrectly. Write the correct word for each.

Example: This is my dad, Emerson Whitley, who you probably recognize from his work in commercials.
who—whom

1. Willis had been feeling a bit under the weather lately. He went to the doctor, whom ordered some tests. The doctor told him wear the blood lab was because Willis needed to provide a vile or two of blood to be tested.

2. "I don't know weather you're aware of this or not, but there is a vile odor coming from the science lab," Lupe informed Ms. Yiel.

"I'll have to talk to Dario, who I allowed to perform an experiment," Ms. Yiel said. "He must have used the sodium chloride instead of the potassium chloride, which I *did* warn him about!"

3. Aunt Yolanda's utensils are agate wear, that is not agate at all but enameled steel. Her plates are real china, and she uses the glasses which she got in Ireland. Mom thinks Aunt Yolanda's table settings are very beautiful, so she makes us where nice clothes whenever we eat there.

Model

Model the following sentences to practice using *who* and *whom* correctly.

A jury consists of twelve persons chosen to decide who has the better lawyer.

—Robert Frost

We cannot really love anybody with whom we never laugh.

—Agnes Repplier, *Americans and Others*

Parts of Speech

Words in the English language are used in eight different ways. For this reason, there are eight parts of speech.

730.1 Noun

A word that names a person, a place, a thing, or an idea

Governor Smith-Jones   Oregon   hospital   religion

730.2 Pronoun

A word used in place of a noun

I   you   she   him   who   everyone   these   neither
theirs   themselves   which

730.3 Verb

A word that expresses action or state of being

float   sniff   discover   seem   were   was

730.4 Adjective

A word that describes a noun or a pronoun

young   big   grim   Canadian   longer

730.5 Adverb

A word that describes a verb, an adjective, or another adverb

briefly   forward   regally   slowly   better

730.6 Preposition

The first word or words in a prepositional phrase (which functions as an adjective or an adverb)

away from   under   before   with   for   out of

730.7 Conjunction

A word that connects other words or groups of words

and   but   although   because   either, or   so

730.8 Interjection

A word or phrase that shows strong emotion or surprise

Oh no!   Yipes!   Good grief!   Well, . . .

Parts of Speech

Noun

A **noun** is a word that names something: a person, a place, a thing, or an idea.

governor   Oregon   hospital   Buddhism   love

Classes of Nouns

The five classes of nouns are *proper, common, concrete, abstract,* and *collective.*

731.1 Proper Noun

A **proper noun** names a particular person, place, thing, or idea. Proper nouns are always capitalized.

Jackie Robinson	**Brooklyn**	**World Series**
Christianity	**Ebbets Field**	**Hinduism**

731.2 Common Noun

A **common noun** does not name a particular person, place, thing, or idea. Common nouns are not capitalized.

person   woman   president   park   baseball   government

731.3 Concrete Noun

A **concrete noun** names a thing that is tangible (can be seen, touched, heard, smelled, or tasted). Concrete nouns are either proper or common.

child   Grand Canyon   music   aroma   fireworks   Becky

731.4 Abstract Noun

An **abstract noun** names an idea, a condition, or a feeling—in other words, something that cannot be touched, smelled, tasted, seen, or heard.

New Deal   greed   poverty   progress   freedom   awe

731.5 Collective Noun

A **collective noun** names a group or a unit.

United States   choir   team   crowd   community

Forms of Nouns

Nouns are grouped according to their *number, gender,* and *case.*

732.1 Number of a Noun

Number indicates whether the noun is singular or plural.

A **singular noun** refers to one person, place, thing, or idea.

actor stadium Canadian bully truth child person

A **plural noun** refers to more than one person, place, thing, or idea.

actors stadiums Canadians bullies truths children people

732.2 Gender of a Noun

Gender indicates whether a noun is masculine, feminine, neuter, or indefinite.

Masculine: uncle brother men bull rooster stallion

Feminine: aunt sister women cow hen filly

Neuter (without gender): **tree cobweb garage closet**

Indefinite (masculine or feminine): **president plumber doctor parent**

732.3 Case of a Noun

Case tells how nouns are related to other words used with them. There are three cases: *nominative, possessive,* and *objective.*

- A **nominative case** noun can be the subject of a clause.

  Andrew's jacket was soaking wet. . . . His new umbrella had broken in the wind and was useless in the pouring rain.

  A nominative noun can also be a predicate noun (or predicate nominative), which follows a "be" verb *(am, is, are, was, were, be, being, been)* and renames the subject. In the sentence below, *type* renames *Mr. Cattanzara.*

  Mr. Cattanzara was a different type than those in the neighborhood.

  —Bernard Malamud, "A Summer's Reading"

- A **possessive case** noun shows possession or ownership.

  Unlike John's new baseball mitt, mine is old and dirty, but it still serves me very well each time we take the field.

- An **objective case** noun can be a direct object, an indirect object, or an object of the preposition.

  Keisha always gives Mylo science-fiction books for his birthday.

  (*Mylo* is the indirect object and *books* is the direct object of the verb "gives." *Birthday* is the object of the preposition "for.")

Grammar Practice

Nouns

- Classes of Nouns
- Number of a Noun
- Case of a Noun

For each underlined noun, write its class (there will be at least two classes for each), number, and case.

Example: The Bill of Rights refers to the first ten amendments of the United States Constitution.
Class: proper, concrete; Number: singular; Case: nominative

1. Checks and balances in the United States government allow Congress to override a presidential veto.
2. During the American Revolution, George Washington was commander of the Continental army.
3. The tax laws imposed on the colonists by the British government were viewed as unfair.
4. The Civil War began when the Confederates shelled Fort Sumter.
5. Frederick Douglass made the argument that African Americans should be allowed to serve in the army.
6. The Great Wall of China formed a boundary between China and Mongolia.
7. In feudal Japan, a shogun had more military power than an emperor.
8. A megalopolis is an area made up of adjoining cities and suburbs.

Learning Language

Working with a partner, re-read the information on the two previous pages. Take turns describing a concept or a particular process using at least one proper, one common, one concrete, and one abstract noun. Have your partner listen carefully, name the nouns, and identify the classification of each.

TEKS 10.17A(iii)
ELPS 4C, 5E

Pronoun

A **pronoun** is a word used in place of a noun.

I, you, she, it, which, that, themselves, whoever, me, he, they, mine, ours

The three types of pronouns are *simple, compound,* and *phrasal.*

Simple: I, you, he, she, it, we, they, who, what
Compound: myself, someone, anybody, everything, itself, whoever
Phrasal: one another, each other

All pronouns have **antecedents**. An antecedent is the noun that the pronoun refers to or replaces.

Ambrosch was considered the important person in the family. Mrs. Shimerda and Ántonia always deferred to him, though he was often surly with them and contemptuous toward his father. —Willa Cather, *My Ántonia*

(*Ambrosch* is the antecedent of *him, he,* and *his.*)

NOTE: Each pronoun must agree with its antecedent. (See page 782.)

734.1 Classes of Pronouns

The seven classes of pronouns are *personal, reflexive and intensive, reciprocal, relative, indefinite, interrogative,* and *demonstrative.*

Personal

I, me, my, mine / we, us, our, ours
you, your, yours / they, them, their, theirs
he, him, his, she, her, hers, it, its

Reflexive and Intensive

myself, yourself, himself, herself, itself, ourselves, yourselves, themselves

Reciprocal

each other, one another

Relative

what, who, whose, whom, which, that

Indefinite

all	both	everything	nobody	several
another	each	few	none	some
any	each one	many	no one	somebody
anybody	either	most	nothing	someone
anyone	everybody	much	one	something
anything	everyone	neither	other	such

Interrogative

who, whose, whom, which, what

Demonstrative

this, that, these, those

ELPS 4C, 5E

Grammar Practice

Pronouns 1

- **Antecedents**

For the following paragraphs, write the antecedent of each underlined pronoun.

Example: 1. Marian Anderson

In the early 1900s, nobody imagined that "Baby Contralto" would grow up to be the first African American to sing a leading role with the Metropolitan Opera. "Baby Contralto" is what the Baptist parishioners called Marian Anderson when **(1)** she began singing at **(2)** their church at age six.

Marian's family had a piano, but **(3)** they could not afford lessons, so Marian taught **(4)** herself. Soon she became a popular singer in her community. After graduating from high school, she applied to a local music school. **(5)** It coldly rejected Marian because of her color.

Prejudice did not stop her. She stalwartly pursued a successful singing career, and in 1930, **(6)** she became the first black female to perform at Carnegie Hall. Famed composer Jean Sibelius was so moved by her work that **(7)** he dedicated a song to her. Marian went on to perform all over the world. Audiences loved her, and **(8)** they demanded even more performances. In 1955, at the age of 58, she performed at the New York Metropolitan Opera as Ulrica in Guiseppe Verdi's *The Masked Ball.*

Model

Model the following sentence to practice using a pronoun and an antecedent in the same sentence.

There are many persons ready to do what is right because in their hearts, they know it is right.

—Marian Anderson

TEKS 10.17A(ii), 10.17A(iii)
ELPS 4C, 5E, 5F

736.1 Personal Pronouns

A **personal pronoun** can take the place of any noun.

Our coach made her point loud and clear when she raised her voice.

- A **reflexive pronoun** is formed by adding *-self* or *-selves* to a personal pronoun. A reflexive pronoun can be a direct object, an indirect object, an object of the preposition, or a predicate nominative.

  Miss Sally Sunshine loves herself. (direct object of *loves*)

  Tomisha does not seem herself today. (predicate nominative)

- An **intensive pronoun** is a reflexive pronoun that intensifies, or emphasizes, the noun or pronoun it refers to.

  Leo himself taught his children to invest their lives in others.

736.2 Relative Pronouns

A **relative pronoun** relates or connects a relative clause to the noun or pronoun it modifies.

Students who study regularly get the best grades. Surprise!

The dance, which we had looked forward to for weeks, was canceled.

(The relative pronoun *who* relates the restrictive relative clause to *students; which* relates the nonrestrictive relative clause to *dance*.)

736.3 Reciprocal Pronouns

A **reciprocal pronoun** refers to the individual parts of a plural antecedent and expresses mutual actions or relationships between the parts.

The students decided not to exchange holiday cards with one another this year.

John and Toby often do favors for each other.

736.4 Indefinite Pronouns

An **indefinite pronoun** refers to unnamed or unknown people or things.

I have never known anybody that well. (antecedent of *anybody* is unknown)

736.5 Interrogative Pronouns

An **interrogative pronoun** asks a question.

Who are you? What do you want? What do you expect to find here?

736.6 Demonstrative Pronouns

A **demonstrative pronoun** points out people, places, or things without naming them.

This shouldn't be too hard. That looks about right.
These are the best ones. Those ought to be thrown out.

NOTE: When one of these words precedes a noun, it functions as an adjective, not a pronoun. (See 756.1.)

That movie bothers me. (*That* is an adjective.)

TEKS 10.17A(iii)
ELPS 4C, 5E

Grammar Practice

Pronouns 2

- Indefinite Pronouns
- Interrogative Pronouns
- Demonstrative Pronouns
- Reciprocal Pronouns

Identify each underlined pronoun as *indefinite, interrogative, reciprocal*, or *demonstrative*.

Example: Whom do you think is the funniest woman in America?
interrogative

1. Many of today's actresses have been cast in comedy roles.
2. These are a few well-known women comedians: Ellen DeGeneres, Rosie O'Donnell, Tina Fey, and Lucille Ball.
3. They all seem to know one another quite well.
4. Which of the above-named comedians was the voice of Dory in *Finding Nemo*?
5. Who would have guessed that *I Love Lucy* would still be on the air 50 years after it was made?
6. This is a famous quotation from comedian Gilda Radner: "I base most of my fashion taste on what doesn't itch."
7. Those are my favorite kind of clothes, too.
8. None of the women believed that they would grow up to be famous.
9. All of them became famous for their ability to make people laugh.
10. I wonder if Ellen and Tina correspond with each other about comedy routines.

Model

Model the following sentence to practice using indefinite and interrogative pronouns.

Who is rich? He that is content. Who is that? Nobody.

—Benjamin Franklin

ELPS 4C, 5E

Forms of Personal Pronouns

The form of a personal pronoun indicates its *number* (singular or plural), its *person* (first, second, third), its *case* (nominative, possessive, or objective), and its *gender* (masculine, feminine, or neuter).

738.1 Number of a Pronoun

Personal pronouns are singular or plural. The singular personal pronouns include *my, him, he, she, it*. The plural personal pronouns include *we, you, them, our*. (*You* can be singular or plural.) Notice in the caption below that the first you is singular and the second you is plural.

"Larry, you need to keep all four tires on the road when turning. Are you still with us back there?"

738.2 Person of a Pronoun

The **person** of a pronoun indicates whether the person, place, thing, or idea represented by the pronoun is speaking, is spoken to, or is spoken about.

- **First person** is used in place of the name of the speaker or speakers.

  I went to the movies with some friends, but when we arrived at the theatre, we realized the movie we wanted to see was not playing.

- **Second-person** pronouns name the person or persons spoken to.

  "If you hit your duck, you want me to go in after it?" Eugie said.

  —Gina Berriault, "The Stone Boy"

- **Third-person** pronouns name the person or thing spoken about.

  He did not understand what was happening to him. It wasn't even noon, and here he was in the hospital with a broken leg.

ELPS 4C, 5E

Grammar Practice

Pronouns 3

- Number of a Pronoun
- Person of a Pronoun

Identify the person and number of each underlined pronoun in the paragraphs below.

Example: 1. *second person, plural*

"Mom and Dad!" Greg yelled. "Are **(1)** you ready yet?" Greg, his sister, and **(2)** their folks were going to a football game; they were late. Greg was almost ready to say **(3)** he would leave without **(4)** them. The kickoff was less than an hour away, and Greg would be mad if he missed **(5)** it.

When they were finally on their way, Greg's dad said, "Uh-oh, I forgot **(6)** our tickets. We'll have to go back."

"**(7)** I can't believe it," Greg sighed, shaking his head.

"Why are **(8)** you so worried?" Greg's mom asked **(9)** him.

Before Greg could answer **(10)** her, his sister said, **(11)** "We don't have to turn around. I have the tickets."

Model

Model the following sentences to practice using first-, second-, and third-person pronouns.

Computers are useless; they can only give you answers.

—Pablo Picasso

We are so vain that we even care for the opinion of those we don't care for.

—Marie Ebner von Eschenbach

ELPS 4C, 5E

740.1 Case of a Pronoun

The **case** of each pronoun tells how it is related to the other words used with it. There are three cases: *nominative, possessive,* and *objective*.

- A **nominative case** pronoun can be the subject of a clause. The following are nominative forms: *I, you, he, she, it, we, they.*

  I like life when things go well. You must live life in order to love life.

A nominative pronoun is a *predicate nominative* if it follows a "be" verb (*am, is, are, was, were, be, being, been*) or another linking verb (*appear, become, feel,* etc.) and renames the subject.

"Oh, it's only she who scared me just now," said Mama to Papa, glancing over her shoulder.
"Yes, it is I," said Mai in a superior tone.

- **Possessive case** pronouns show possession or ownership. Apostrophes, however, are not used with personal pronouns. (Pronouns in the possessive case can also be classified as adjectives.)

  But as I placed my hand upon his shoulder, there came a strong shudder over his whole person.
  —Edgar Allan Poe, "The Fall of the House of Usher"

- An **objective case** pronoun can be a direct object, an indirect object, or an object of the preposition.

  The kids loved it! We lit a campfire for them and told them old ghost stories. (*It* is the direct object of the verb *loved*. *Them* is the object of the preposition *for* and the indirect object of the verb *told*.)

Number, Person, and Case of Personal Pronouns

	Nominative	Possessive	Objective
First Person Singular	I	my, mine	me
Second Person Singular	you	your, yours	you
Third Person Singular	he	his	him
	she	her, hers	her
	it	its	it
	Nominative	Possessive	Objective
First Person Plural	we	our, ours	us
Second Person Plural	you	your, yours	you
Third Person Plural	they	their, theirs	them

740.2 Gender of a Pronoun

Gender indicates whether a pronoun is masculine, feminine, or neuter.

Masculine: **he him his** Feminine: **she her hers**
Neuter (without gender): **it its**

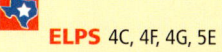

ELPS 4C, 4F, 4G, 5E

Grammar Practice

Pronouns 4

- Case of a Pronoun

Identify each underlined pronoun as *nominative, possessive,* or *objective.*

Example: 1. *possessive*

Mr. Lee, a neighbor, was taking out **(1)** his garbage. **(2)** He saw **(3)** me beginning to rake our yard and asked, "Do you need any help, Maria?"

Not one to turn down such an offer, **(4)** I accepted. The next thing I knew, he came from his garage with a new "toy." **(5)** It was a noisy, smelly leaf blower.

"Have **(6)** you ever seen one of these things?" he asked. He demonstrated **(7)** its powerful wind, aiming **(8)** it at a pile of leaves I had just raked.

"Well, I've seen people use them," I admitted, "but **(9)** we only have rakes at **(10)** our house. I guess we're a little old-fashioned that way."

Learning Language

With a partner, review the information about pronouns on the previous page. As you re-read the information, take notes about each case and the corresponding pronouns. This will help you remember the information. In your notes use your own words to write a brief definition of the word *case* and an explanation of its function. Write new example sentences, and share and explain your sentences. Listen as your partner reads his or her sentences to you. If you have questions about pronoun cases, ask your teacher for clarification.

ELPS 4C, 5E

Verb

A **verb** is a word that expresses action (*run, carried, declared*) or a state of being (*is, are, seemed*).

Classes of Verbs

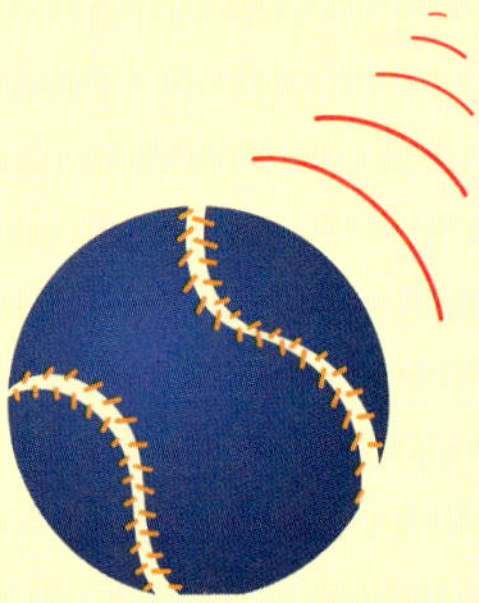

742.1 Linking Verbs

A **linking verb** links the subject to a noun or an adjective in the predicate.

In the outfield, the boy felt confident.
He was the best fielder around.

Common Linking Verbs

is	are	was	were	be	been	am

Additional Linking Verbs

smell	seem	grow	become	appear	sound
taste	feel	get	remain	stay	look	turn

742.2 Auxiliary Verbs

Auxiliary verbs, or helping verbs, are used to form some of the **tenses** (**746.3**), the **mood** (**752.1**), and the **voice** (**750.2**) of the main verb. (In the example below, the auxiliary verbs are in **red**; the main verbs are in **blue**.)

The mud had flowed quickly down the mountain, covering everything in its path. By the time the rain had stopped, the rescue crews were faced with the daunting task of slogging through the mud to help those who had survived.

Common Auxiliary Verbs

is	was	being	did	have	would	shall	might
am	were	been	does	had	could	can	must
are	be	do	has	should	will	may	

Grammar Practice

Verbs 1

Linking and Auxiliary Verbs

Write whether each underlined word is a linking verb or an auxiliary verb.

Example: The earth's solid inner core is surrounded by a fluid outer core about 4,200 miles across.
auxiliary

1. Researchers have recently discovered that the core spins 1/4 to 1/2 of a degree faster than the rest of the planet.
2. Magnetic interaction is the most likely reason for the different spin rates.
3. The researchers had arrived at their discovery by studying the travel times of earthquake waves through the earth.
4. There are differences not only in the times but also in the shapes of the waves.
5. The researchers theorized there must be differences in the core as the waves pass through it.
6. The small difference in the rotation speed means that it would take 700 to 1,400 years for the core to get one full revolution ahead.
7. The rate, however, could vary from one decade to the next.
8. The inner core appears to spin slower than the outer core at other times.

Model

Model the following sentences to practice using linking and auxiliary verbs.

Thought is only a flash between two long nights, but this flash is everything.

—Henri Poincare

A loud voice cannot compete with a clear voice, even if it's a whisper.

—Barry Neil Kaufman

ELPS 4C, 5E

744.1 Action Verbs: Transitive and Intransitive

An **intransitive verb** communicates an action that is complete in itself. It does not need an object to receive the action.

The boy flew on his skateboard. He jumped and flipped and twisted.

A **transitive verb** (**red**) is an action verb that needs an object (**blue**) to complete its meaning.

The city council passed a strict noise ordinance.

While some action verbs are only transitive *or* intransitive, some can be either, depending on how they are used.

He finally stopped to rest. (intransitive)

He finally stopped the show. (transitive)

744.2 Objects with Transitive Verbs

- A **direct object** receives the action of a transitive verb directly from the subject. Without it, the transitive verb's meaning is incomplete.

  The boy kicked his skateboard forward. (*Skateboard* is the direct object.)

  Then he put one foot on it and rode like a pro.

- An **indirect object** also receives the action of a transitive verb, but indirectly. An indirect object names the person *to whom or for whom* something is done. (An indirect object can also name the thing *to what or for what* something is done.)

  Ms. Oakfield showed us pictures of the solar system. (*Us* is the indirect object.)

  She gave Tony an A on his project.

NOTE: When the word naming the indirect receiver of the action is in a prepositional phrase, it is no longer considered an indirect object.

Ms. Oakfield showed pictures of the solar system to us. (*Us* is the object of the preposition *to*.)

Grammar Practice

Verbs 2

■ Transitive and Intransitive Verbs

Write whether each underlined verb is transitive or intransitive. For a transitive verb, also write the direct object and, if present, the indirect object.

Example: The customer provided the cash.
transitive — direct object: cash

1. Nasha jogs around the track every day after school.
2. My dad found the map under the front passenger seat.
3. Look at the sky!
4. Simone guessed correctly.
5. Veronica guessed the answer exactly.
6. We bought my mom a new leather briefcase.
7. Kumar allowed me the use of his cell phone for one afternoon.
8. I'm not feeling well; I should lie down.
9. Juana opened the jar of pickles quite easily after Alex couldn't.
10. Mario sent his brother an autographed program from the game.

Model

Model the following sentences to practice using transitive and intransitive verbs.

I don't like to write, but I love to have written.
—Michael Kanin

Life shrinks or expands in proportion to one's courage.
—Anaïs Nin

ELPS 4C, 5E

Forms of Verbs

A verb has different forms depending on its *number, person, tense, voice,* and *mood.*

746.1 Number of a Verb

Number indicates whether a verb is singular or plural. In a clause, the verb (in **blue** below) and its subject (in **red**) must both be singular or both be plural.

- **Singular**

  One large island floats off Italy's "toe."

  Italy's northern countryside includes the spectacular Alps.

- **Plural**

  Five small islands float inside Michigan's "thumb."

  The Porcupine Mountains rise above the shores of Lake Superior.

746.2 Person of a Verb

Person indicates whether the subject of the verb is first, second, or third person (is speaking, is spoken to, or is spoken about). The form of the verb usually changes only when a present-tense verb is used with a third-person singular pronoun.

	Singular	Plural
First Person	**I sniff**	**we sniff**
Second Person	**you sniff**	**you sniff**
Third Person	**he/she/it sniffs**	**they sniff**

746.3 Tense of a Verb

Tense indicates time. Each verb has three principal parts: the *present, past,* and *past participle.* All six tenses are formed from these principal parts. The past and past participle of regular verbs are formed by adding *ed* to the present form. For irregular verbs, the past and past participle are usually different words; however, a few have the same form in all three principal parts (see page 748.2).

746.4 Simple Tenses

- **Present tense** expresses action that is happening at the present time, or action that happens continually, regularly.

  In September, sophomores smirk and joke about the "little freshies."

- **Past tense** expresses action that was completed at a particular time in the past.

  They forgot that just ninety days separated them from freshman status.

- **Future tense** expresses action that will take place in the future.

  They will recall this in three years when they will be freshmen again.

Grammar Practice

Verbs 3

- Person of a Verb
- Simple Tenses

Write the verb or verbs in the sentences below. Then identify the person and tense of each.

Example: Every year sophomores plan a scuba diving trip.
plan: third person, present tense

1. Jacques-Yves Cousteau invented the Aqua-Lung® in 1942.
2. One day scientists will make artificial gills for divers.
3. Today, no one believes that is possible.
4. Scuba divers enjoy the freedom to dive without restraints.
5. If you dive deep into the ocean, make a series of timed stops on your way back to the surface.
6. Otherwise, nitrogen in your air mixture dissolves under pressure and enters your blood stream.
7. Rising directly to the surface will result in nitrogen narcosis.
8. Without special treatment in a decompression chamber, this dangerous condition will almost always lead to death.
9. A diver who follows proper diving protocol is in no danger.
10. Thousands of people safely dived last year with scuba gear and experienced the marvels of the undersea world.

Model

Model the following sentence to practice using past-tense verbs effectively.

In a sky of iron the points of the Dipper hung like icicles, and Orion flashed his cold fires.

—Edith Wharton, *Ethan Frome*

TEKS 10.17A(i)
ELPS 4C, 5E

Forms of Verbs (continued)

748.1 Perfect Tenses

- **Present perfect tense** expresses action that began in the past but continues in the present or is completed in the present.

  Our boat has weathered worse storms than this one.

- **Past perfect tense** expresses an action in the past that occurred before another past action.

  They reported, wrongly, that the hurricane had missed the island.

- **Future perfect tense** expresses action that will begin in the future and be completed by a specific time in the future.

  By this time tomorrow, the hurricane will have smashed into the coast.

748.2 Irregular Verbs

Common Irregular Verbs and Their Principal Parts

Present Tense	Past Tense	Past Participle	Present Tense	Past Tense	Past Participle	Present Tense	Past Tense	Past Participle
am, be	was, were	been	go	went	gone	shrink	shrank	shrunk
begin	began	begun	grow	grew	grown	sing	sang, sung	sung
bite	bit	bitten	hang (execute)	hanged	hanged	sink	sank, sunk	sunk
blow	blew	blown	hang (suspend)	hung	hung	sit	sat	sat
break	broke	broken	hide	hid	hidden, hid	slay	slew	slain
bring	brought	brought	know	knew	known	speak	spoke	spoken
buy	bought	bought	lay	laid	laid	spring	sprang, sprung	sprung
catch	caught	caught	lead	led	led	steal	stole	stolen
choose	chose	chosen	leave	left	left	strive	strove	striven
come	came	come	lie (recline)	lay	lain	swear	swore	sworn
dive	dove	dived	lie (deceive)	lied	lied	swim	swam	swum
do	did	done	lose	lost	lost	swing	swung	swung
draw	drew	drawn	make	made	made	take	took	taken
drink	drank	drunk	ride	rode	ridden	teach	taught	taught
drive	drove	driven	ring	rang	rung	tear	tore	torn
eat	ate	eaten	rise	rose	risen	throw	threw	thrown
fall	fell	fallen	run	ran	run	wake	waked, woke	waked, woken
fight	fought	fought	see	saw	seen	wear	wore	worn
flee	fled	fled	shake	shook	shaken	weave	weaved, wove	weaved, woven
fly	flew	flown	show	showed	shown	wring	wrung	wrung
forsake	forsook	forsaken				write	wrote	written
freeze	froze	frozen						
get	got	gotten						
give	gave	given						

These verbs are the same in all principal parts: *burst, cost, cut, hurt, let, put, set,* and *spread.*

Grammar Practice

Verbs 4

- Irregular Verbs
- Perfect Tenses

Write the correct form (past tense or past participle) of the verb shown in parentheses to complete each sentence. Decide if any perfect tenses have been created. If not, write *simple*.

Example: Thirty-five students had ______ the bus to the wrestling match. *(ride)*
had ridden = *past perfect*

1. Salina ______ off her cold by getting lots of rest. *(fight)*
2. Nadia discovered that her backpack had been ______. *(steal)*
3. Owen ______ to get a perfect score on his algebra exam. *(strive)*
4. Rajan ______ to taste the egg roll, but it was too hot. *(begin)*
5. The fastest swimmers had ______ in the first heat. *(dive)*
6. Dontriece ______ at the assembly about the upcoming tournament. *(speak)*
7. My mom has a blanket that my great-great-grandmother ______ on a loom. *(weave)*
8. Martin had ______ the book on the shelf and forgotten about it. *(lay)*
9. He knew he had ______ a good story by the look on his teacher's face. *(write)*
10. I liked the suit that my cousin ______ to my brother's wedding. *(wear)*

Model

Model the following sentence and perfect tenses to practice using irregular verbs.

He has chosen to run many marathons, and he has run with the best.

TEKS 10.17A(i)
ELPS 4C, 5E

750.1 Continuous Tenses

- A **present continuous tense** verb expresses action that is not completed at the time of stating it. The present continuous tense is formed by adding *am, is,* or *are* to the *-ing* form of the main verb.

  Scientists are learning a great deal from their study of the sky.

- A **past continuous tense** verb expresses action that was happening at a certain time in the past. This tense is formed by adding *was* or *were* to the *-ing* form of the main verb.

  Astronomers were beginning their quest for knowledge centuries ago.

- A **future continuous tense** verb expresses action that will take place at a certain time in the future. This tense is formed by adding *will be* to the *-ing* form of the main verb.

  Someday astronauts will be going to Mars.

  This tense can also be formed by adding a phrase noting the future *(are going to)* plus *be* to the *-ing* form of the main verb.

  They are going to be performing many experiments.

750.2 Voice of a Verb

Voice indicates whether the subject is acting or being acted upon.

- **Active voice** indicates that the subject of the verb is, has been, or will be doing something.

  For many years Lou Brock held the base-stealing record.

Active voice makes your writing more direct and lively.

- **Passive voice** indicates that the subject of the verb is being, has been, or will be acted upon.

  For many years the base-stealing record was held by Lou Brock.

NOTE: Passive verbs also have tense—the same simple, perfect, and continuous tenses as active verbs. (The chart below shows simple tenses.)

The ordinance had been overturned. (passive past perfect)

	Active Voice		Passive Voice	
Tense	Singular	Plural	Singular	Plural
Present	I see you see he/she/it sees	we see you see they see	I am seen you are seen he/she/it is seen	we are seen you are seen they are seen
Past	I/he saw you saw	we/they saw you saw	I/it was seen you were seen	we/they were seen you were seen
Future	I/you/he will see	we/you/they will see	I/you/it will be seen	we/you/they will be seen

TEKS 10.17A(i)
ELPS 2I, 3E–3H, 4C, 5E

Grammar Practice

Verbs 5

- Active and Passive Voice
- Continuous Tenses

If a sentence below is in the passive voice, rewrite it in the active voice. If it is already in the active voice, write "active."

Example: By then, the pizzas will have been eaten by my brothers.
By then, my brothers will have eaten the pizzas.

1. The announcement was heard by only half of the students.
2. My geometry textbook has been lost.
3. The student council is considering action on the proposal.
4. Most of the class is going to the afternoon assembly.
5. Winners' names will be published in the next issue of *The Bugle*.
6. The new menu was tested last week by the cooks.
7. A fossil of an unknown dinosaur was recently discovered by scientists in a remote area of New Mexico.
8. Stefan will perform his composition at the fall concert.
9. Since we hadn't missed any school all semester, we had been given movie passes by the attendance office.
10. You may use my computer today after school.

Learning Language

Although the active voice is more direct and forceful, the passive voice is appropriate in some situations. Read and think about the following sentence.

It was learned that Patrick was being followed by a detective.

Explain to a partner why you think the passive voice and the present continuous tense are or are not appropriate in this sentence. Then ask your partner to share his or her opinions.

TEKS 10.17B
ELPS 4C, 5E

752.1 Mood of a Verb

The **mood** of a verb indicates the tone or attitude with which a statement is made.

- **Indicative mood** is used to state a fact or to ask a question.

  Sometimes I would ride my old bicycle to school, but my friends would laugh and ask, "What's the matter? Your parents bought you a car for your birthday." The answer was simple: I wanted the exercise I got from riding the bike.

- **Imperative mood** is used to give a command.

"Whatever you do, don't fly your kite during a storm."
—Mrs. Abiah Franklin

- **Subjunctive mood** is used to express a condition that is contrary to fact or highly doubtful, a wish, a possibility, a suggestion, or a necessity.

  Use the subjunctive *were* to express a condition that is contrary to fact or highly doubtful.

  If I were finished with my report, I could go to the movie.

  The young lady looked as if she were at least 14 years old, but her childish behavior suggested otherwise.

  Use the subjunctive *were* to express a wish or a possibility.

  Oh, how I wish I were rich!

  Were your circumstances to change, you could reapply for admission.

  Use the subjunctive *be* in "that" clauses to express a suggestion or a necessity.

  Carlos suggested that we be ready to go when he arrives."

  It is essential that everyone be seated by the time the bell rings.

TEKS 10.17B
ELPS 4C, 5E

Grammar Practice

Verbs 6

- Mood of a Verb

Write whether each statement shows *indicative, imperative,* or *subjunctive* mood.

Example: Mr. Cerminera closes the windows, even on the nicest days.
indicative

1. He moved as if he were a deer running from a hunter.
2. Don't forget to read chapters eight and nine before the test tomorrow.
3. What is wrong with Lamont's car?
4. The city councilwoman amended the proposal to include schools in our district.
5. Whatever happens, don't forget to call me tonight.
6. She acted as though the exam weren't important.
7. Everyone must attend the meeting.
8. Sarena arrived on time.
9. Where in Kansas is Cottonwood Falls?
10. Katrina would have gotten the part if she were a Redford or an Eastwood.
11. Will your family plan a trip to New York City next summer?
12. If it were to rain, we will have to change the plans for the outdoor concert.

Model

Model the following sentence to practice using the subjunctive mood.

When there is no news, [newscasters] give it to you with the same emphasis as if there were.

—David Brinkley

TEKS 10.17A(i)
ELPS 4C, 5E

Verbals

A **verbal** is a word that is derived from a verb but acts as another part of speech. There are three types of verbals: *gerunds, infinitives,* and *participles.* Each is often part of a verbal phrase.

754.1 Gerunds

A **gerund** is a verb form that ends in *ing* and is used as a noun.

> **Swimming is my favorite pastime.** (subject)
>
> **I began swimming at the age of six months.** (direct object)
>
> **Swimming in chlorinated pools makes my eyes red.** (gerund phrase used as a subject)

754.2 Infinitives

An **infinitive** is a verb form that is usually introduced by *to*; the infinitive may be used as a noun, an adjective, or an adverb.

> **Most people find it easy to swim.** (adverb modifying an adjective)
>
> **To swim the English Channel must be a thrill.** (infinitive phrase as noun)
>
> **The urge to swim in tropical waters is more common.** (infinitive phrase as adjective)

754.3 Participles

A **participle** is a verb form ending in *ing* or *ed* that acts as an adjective.

> **The workers raking leaves are tired and hungry.** (participial phrase modifies *workers*)
>
> **The bags full of raked leaves are evidence of their hard work.** (participle modifies *leaves*)

TEKS 10.17A(i)
ELPS 4C, 5E

Grammar Practice

Verbs 7

- Gerunds
- Infinitives
- Participles

Write whether each underlined word or phrase is a *gerund*, a *participle*, or an *infinitive*.

Example: 1. gerund

(1) Playing the piano is an acquired skill. The piano is a popular instrument because it is relatively easy **(2)** to learn. Most people enjoy the piano's **(3)** inviting sound.

Many great pianists had excellent teachers. Franz Liszt, the famous pianist and composer, enjoyed **(4)** teaching young students. **(5)** Studying with Carl Czerny, an accomplished student of Beethoven, Liszt became a very capable teacher.

Usually, learning how **(6)** to play the piano involves **(7)** taking lessons from an **(8)** experienced professional. A good teacher knows how **(9)** to make practice fun. First, you will practice scales and chords and learn simple melodies. Before long, you will read music and learn **(10)** to create your own compositions.

Model

Model the following sentences to practice using infinitives, gerunds, and participles.

The best way to live is by not knowing what will happen to you at the end of the day.

—Donald Barthelme

Good communication is just as stimulating as black coffee, and just as hard to sleep after.

—Anne Morrow Lindbergh

Adjective

An **adjective** describes or modifies a noun or a pronoun. The articles *a, an,* and *the* are also adjectives.

> **The young driver peeked through the big steering wheel.**
> (*The* and *young* modify *driver; the* and *big* modify *steering wheel.*)

756.1 Types of Adjectives

A **proper adjective** is created from a proper noun and is capitalized.

> **In Canada** (proper noun), **you will find many cultures and climates.**
>
> **Canadian** (proper adjective) **winters can be harsh.**

A **predicate adjective** follows a form of the "be" verb (or other linking verb) and describes the subject.

> **Late autumn seems grim to those who love summer.** (*Grim* modifies *autumn.*)

NOTE: Some words can be either adjectives or pronouns (*that, these, all, each, both, many, some,* and so on). These words are adjectives when they come before the nouns they modify; they are pronouns when they stand alone.

> **Jiao made both goals.** (*Both* modifies *goals;* it is an adjective.)
>
> **Both were scored in the final period.** (*Both* stands alone; it is a pronoun.)

756.2 Forms of Adjectives

Adjectives have three forms: *positive, comparative,* and *superlative.*

- The **positive form** describes a noun or a pronoun without comparing it to anyone or anything else.

  > **The first game was long and tiresome.**

- The **comparative form** (*-er, more,* or *less*) compares two persons, places, things, or ideas.

  > **The second game was longer and more tiresome than the first.**

- The **superlative form** (*-est, most,* or *least*) compares three or more persons, places, things, or ideas.

  > **The third game was the longest and most tiresome of all.**

NOTE: Use *more* and *most* (or *less* and *least*)—instead of adding a suffix—with many adjectives of two or more syllables.

Positive	Comparative	Superlative
big	**bigger**	**biggest**
helpful	**more helpful**	**most helpful**
painful	**less painful**	**least painful**

ELPS 2C, 2I, 3B, 3C, 3E, 3F, 3H, 4C

Grammar Practice

Adjectives

Forms of Adjectives

For each sentence below, write the adjective and its form (positive, comparative, or superlative). Some sentences contain more than one adjective. (For this activity, ignore any proper adjective.)

Example: Odysseus is one of the most famous characters in Greek mythology.
most famous (superlative)

1. Also known as Ulysses, he was king of a smaller Greek island called Ithaca.
2. He was a suitor of Helen of Troy, the most beautiful woman on earth.
3. Some believe that he was more resourceful than other Greek warriors.
4. It was his idea to build a huge, hollow horse made of wood to sneak Greek soldiers into the city of Troy.
5. When the Trojans saw the big horse, they believed that it would bring them good luck.
6. The Trojan horse gave the Greeks an easier way to enter and destroy the city.
7. Odysseus is probably most renowned for his long journey back from Troy.
8. The trip was more difficult than Odysseus could ever have imagined.

Learning Language

Work with a partner to make a list of at least six adjectives. Take turns describing objects using the comparative form of adjectives on your list. Have your partner change the adjective from comparative to superlative form. Listen carefully to make sure that the correct form of each adjective has been used. Discuss and correct as needed.

Adverb

An **adverb** describes or modifies a verb, an adjective, or another adverb.

> **She sneezed loudly.** (*Loudly* modifies the verb *sneezed.*)
>
> **Her sneezes are really dramatic.** (*Really* modifies the adjective *dramatic.*)
>
> **The sneeze exploded very noisily.** (*Very* modifies the adverb *noisily.*)

An adverb usually tells *when, where, how,* or *how much.*

758.1 Types of Adverbs

Adverbs can be cataloged in four basic ways: *time, place, manner,* and *degree.*

Time (These adverbs tell *when, how often,* and *how long.*)

today, yesterday **daily, weekly** **briefly, eternally**

Place (These adverbs tell *where, to where,* and *from where.*)

here, there **nearby, beyond** **backward, forward**

Manner (These adverbs often end in *ly* and tell *how* something is done.)

precisely **effectively** **regally** **smoothly** **well**

Degree (These adverbs tell *how much* or *how little.*)

substantially **greatly** **entirely** **partly** **too** **much**

NOTE: Some adverbs can be written with or without the *ly* ending. When in doubt, use the *ly* form.

slow, slowly **loud, loudly** **fair, fairly** **tight, tightly** **quick, quickly**

758.2 Forms of Adverbs

Adverbs of manner have three forms: *positive, comparative,* and *superlative.*

- The **positive form** describes a verb, an adjective, or another adverb without comparing it to anyone or anything else.

  Model X vacuum cleans well and runs quietly.

- The **comparative form** (*-er, more,* or *less*) compares how two things are done.

  Model Y vacuum cleans better and runs more quietly than model X does.

- The **superlative form** (*-est, most,* or *least*) compares how three or more things are done.

  Model Z vacuum cleans best and runs most quietly of all.

Irregular Forms

Positive	Comparative	Superlative
well	better	best
fast	faster	fastest
remorsefully	more remorsefully	most remorsefully

Grammar Practice

Adverbs

Types of Adverbs

For each sentence below, write the adverb as well as its type (time, place, manner, degree). The number of adverbs in each sentence is given in parenthesis.

Example: Today, all new cars are equipped with air bags. *(1)*
today (time)

1. An air bag's inflation system is much like a solid rocket booster. *(1)*
2. The system has a device inside that tells the bag when to inflate. *(1)*
3. A solid propellant burns extremely rapidly to create a large amount of hot gas. *(2)*
4. It quickly inflates the bag, causing it to explode from its container at speeds up to 200 mph. *(1)*
5. The purpose of the air bag is to restrain the driver or passenger immediately with little or no damage to his or her body. *(1)*
6. They prevent a person from moving forward too fast in a collision. *(3)*
7. After the air bag is entirely inflated, the gas escapes through tiny holes. *(1)*
8. Used air bags should always be replaced by factory technicians. *(1)*

Model

Model the sentence below to practice using types of adverbs.

He lay down low to the race, whining eagerly, his splendid body flashing forward, leap by leap, in the wan white moonlight.

—Jack London, *Call of the Wild*

ELPS 4C, 5E

Preposition

A **preposition** is the first word (or group of words) in a prepositional phrase. It shows the relationship between its object (a noun or a pronoun that follows the preposition) and another word in the sentence. The first noun or pronoun following a preposition is its object.

> **To make a mustache, Natasha placed the hairy caterpillar under her nose.**
> (*Under* shows the relationship between the verb, *placed*, and the object of the preposition, *nose*.)
>
> **The drowsy insect clung obediently to the girl's upper lip.**
> (The first noun following the preposition *to* is *lip; lip* is the object of the preposition.)

760.1 Prepositional Phrases

A **prepositional phrase** includes the preposition, the object of the preposition, and the modifiers of the object. A prepositional phrase functions as an adverb or as an adjective.

> **Some people run away from caterpillars.**
> (The phrase functions as an adverb and modifies the verb *run*.)
>
> **However, little kids with inquisitive minds enjoy their company.**
> (The phrase functions as an adjective and modifies the noun *kids*.)

NOTE: A preposition is always followed by an object; if there is no object, the word is an adverb, not a preposition.

> **Natasha never played with caterpillars before.** (The word *before* is not followed by an object; therefore, it functions as an adverb that modifies *played*, a verb.)

Common Prepositions

aboard	before	from	of	save
about	behind	from among	off	since
above	below	from between	on	subsequent to
according to	beneath	from under	on account of	through
across	beside	in	on behalf of	throughout
across from	besides	in addition to	onto	till
after	between	in back of	on top of	to
against	beyond	in behalf of	opposite	together with
along	by	in front of	out	toward
alongside	by means of	in place of	out of	under
along with	concerning	in regard to	outside of	underneath
amid	considering	inside	over	until
among	despite	inside of	over to	unto
apart from	down	in spite of	owing to	up
around	down from	instead of	past	upon
aside from	during	into	prior to	up to
at	except	like	regarding	with
away from	except for	near	round	within
because of	for	near to	round about	without

Grammar Practice

Prepositions

Write the prepositional phrases from the sentences below.

Example: According to some people, the creature called Bigfoot lives in the forests of Washington and Oregon.
according to some people, in the forests, of Washington and Oregon

1. Since a 1959 magazine article, people have searched for solid evidence of this hairy humanoid creature's existence.
2. In 1967, Roger Patterson saw and filmed what he called a Sasquatch.
3. The animal moved over a riverbank and disappeared into the trees.
4. Many people around the world say they have seen a similar beast.
5. In Asia, this being, called a Yeti, is usually seen at 10,000 feet.
6. Presumably, a man standing beside a Bigfoot would look small.
7. Serious Bigfoot searchers say the animal remains elusive because it moves during the night.
8. Despite all the sightings, no solid proof of such a creature has ever been found.

Model

Model the following sentences to practice using prepositional phrases as adjectives.

Love is like an hourglass, with the heart filling up as the brain empties.
—Jules Renard

Life isn't a matter of milestones but of moments.
—Rose Fitzgerald Kennedy

ELPS 4C, 5E

Conjunction

A **conjunction** connects individual words or groups of words. There are three kinds of conjunctions: *coordinating, correlative,* and *subordinating.*

762.1 Coordinating Conjunctions

Coordinating conjunctions usually connect a word to a word, a phrase to a phrase, or a clause to a clause. The words, phrases, or clauses joined by a coordinating conjunction are equal in importance or are of the same type.

I could see from the look on my sister's face that she was disappointed and wanted to come with me, but my parents said she had to stay home.

(*And* connects the two parts of a compound predicate; *but* connects two independent clauses that could stand on their own.)

762.2 Correlative Conjunctions

Correlative conjunctions are conjunctions used in pairs.

They were not only exhausted by the day's journey but also sunburned.

762.3 Subordinating Conjunctions

Subordinating conjunctions connect two clauses that are *not* equally important, thereby showing the relationship between them. A subordinating conjunction connects a dependent clause to an independent clause in order to complete the meaning of the dependent clause.

A brown trout will study the bait before he eats it. (The clause *before he eats it* is dependent. It depends on the rest of the sentence to complete its meaning.)

Kinds of Conjunctions

Coordinating: **and, but, or, nor, for, yet, so**

Correlative: **either, or; neither, nor; not only, but also; both, and; whether, or**

Subordinating: **after, although, as, as if, as long as, as though, because, before, if, in order that, provided that, since, so that, that, though, till, unless, until, when, where, whereas, while**

NOTE: Relative pronouns (see 734.1 and 736.2) and conjunctive adverbs (see 656.2) can also connect clauses.

Interjection

An **interjection** communicates strong emotion or surprise. Punctuation—a comma or an exclamation point—sets off an interjection from the rest of the sentence.

Oh no! The TV broke. Good grief! I have nothing to do! Yipes, I'll go mad!

Grammar Practice

Conjunctions

Number your paper from 1 to 11. Write the conjunctions you find in the following paragraph and label them *coordinating, subordinating,* or *correlative*. (Write both correlative conjunctions as one answer.)

Example: 1. although; subordinating

The Afrikaans language is attributed to the Dutch, although many other languages influenced it over time. Words and phrases of shipwrecked sailors found their way into the language, and when slaves arrived from eastern regions, they contributed an Oriental dialect. Soon, the language was neither Dutch nor any other known language. It had become unique after the new accents, dialects, and words were added. Today, Afrikaans is the first language of almost 60 percent of South Africa's whites, but it is spoken by more than 90 percent of the mixed-race population. Afrikaans is spoken not only in South Africa but also in the Republic of Namibia and in Zimbabwe. Afrikaans is the only language in the world that has a monument dedicated to it (in Paarl, Western Cape Province, South Africa), yet it is not the only official language of South Africa—there are nine others!

Model

Model the following sentences to practice using interjections effectively.

With a disgusted look on her face, Lakendra exclaimed, "Ugh! I can't eat this!"

Crikey, is that all?

—Alan Grayson, *Mile End*

TEKS 10.17C
ELPS 4E, 5E, 5F

Understanding Sentences

Constructing Sentences

A **sentence** is made up of one or more words that express a complete thought. Sentences begin with a capital letter; they end with a period, a question mark, or an exclamation point.

What should we do this afternoon? We could have a picnic. No, I hate the ants!

Using Subjects and Predicates

A sentence usually has a **subject** and a **predicate.** The subject is the part of the sentence about which something is said. The predicate, which contains the verb, is the part of the sentence that says something about the subject.

We write from aspiration and antagonism, as well as from experience.
—Ralph Waldo Emerson

764.1 The Subject

The **subject** is the part of the sentence about which something is said. The subject is always a noun; a pronoun; or a word, clause, or phrase that functions as a noun (such as a gerund or a gerund phrase or an infinitive).

Wolves howl. (noun)
They howl for a variety of reasons. (pronoun)
To establish their turf may be one reason. (infinitive phrase)
Searching for "lost" pack members may be another. (gerund phrase)
That wolves and dogs are similar animals seems obvious. (noun clause)

- A **simple subject** is the subject without its modifiers.
  Most wildlife biologists disapprove of crossbreeding wolves and dogs.
- A **complete subject** is the subject with all of its modifiers.
  Most wildlife biologists disapprove of crossbreeding wolves and dogs.
- A **compound subject** is composed of two or more simple subjects.
  Wise breeders and owners know that wolf-dog puppies can display unexpected, destructive behaviors.

764.2 Delayed Subject

In sentences that begin with *There* or *It* followed by a form of the "be" verb, the subject comes after the verb. The subject is also delayed in questions.

There was nothing in the refrigerator. (The subject is *nothing*; the verb is *was*.)
Where is my sandwich? (The subject is *sandwich*; the verb is *is*.)

TEKS 10.17C
ELPS 4E, 5E, 5F

Practice

Constructing Sentences 1

- **Simple, Complete, and Compound Subjects**
- **Delayed Subjects**

Write the complete subject of each sentence. Circle the simple subject or subjects.

Example: There is an art fair on the county grounds this weekend.
an art fair

1. Various artists are setting up their tents near the Picasso statue.
2. The Lakefront Art Fair is the best festival of the summer.
3. Colorful hot-air balloons float in the air, inviting people to the visit the event.
4. The bands and food tents are popular with the crowd.
5. There is a children's play area near the restrooms.
6. The fair, consisting of more than 100 vendors, attracts thousands of visitors each year.
7. The chamber of commerce spends a lot of time to put it together.
8. Pottery, paintings, and sculpture are featured items at the fair.
9. Is your sister-in-law looking for a special piece of art?
10. Most visitors come away with several purchases.

Model

Model the following sentences to practice using delayed subjects.

There was such a glory over everything.
—Harriet Tubman

Hasn't the fine line between sanity and madness gotten finer?
—George Price

TEKS 10.17C
ELPS 4E, 5E, 5F

766.1 Predicates

The **predicate** is the part of the sentence that shows action or says something about the subject.

Giant squid do exist.

- A **simple predicate** is the verb without its modifiers.

  One giant squid measured nearly 60 feet long.

- A **complete predicate** is the simple predicate with all its modifiers.

  One giant squid measured nearly 60 feet long.
  (*Measured* is the simple predicate; *nearly 60 feet long* modifies *measured*.)

- A **compound predicate** is composed of two or more simple predicates.

  A squid grasps its prey with tentacles and bites it with its beak.

NOTE: A sentence can have a **compound subject** and a **compound predicate.**

Both sperm whales and giant squid live and occasionally clash in the deep waters off New Zealand's South Island.

- A **direct object** is part of the predicate and receives the action of the verb. (See **744.2**.)

  Sperm whales sometimes eat giant squid.
  (The direct object *giant squid* receives the action of the verb *eat* by answering the question *whales eat what*?)

NOTE: The **direct object** may be compound.

In the past, whalers harvested oil, spermaceti, and ambergris from slain sperm whales.

766.2 Understood Subjects and Predicates

Either the subject or the predicate may be "missing" from a sentence, but both must be clearly **understood.**

Who is in the hot-air balloon?
(*Who* is the subject; *is in the hot-air balloon* is the predicate.)

No one.
(*No one* is the subject; the predicate *is in the hot-air balloon* is understood.)

Get out of the way!
(The subject *you* is understood; *get out of the way* is the predicate.)

TEKS 10.17C
ELPS 4E, 5E, 5F

Practice

Constructing Sentences 2

■ **Simple, Complete, and Compound Predicates**

Write the complete predicate of each sentence. Circle the simple predicate or predicates.

Example: The flatness of the Great Plains allows dry, cold air to collide with warm, moist air.
(allows) dry, cold air to collide with warm, moist air

1. Most tornadoes form along the front between these air masses.
2. Meteorologists call this "Tornado Alley" and include in it parts of Texas, Oklahoma, Kansas, and Nebraska.
3. Many cities in Tornado Alley enforce stronger building codes.
4. States in Tornado Alley can experience millions of dollars in damage each year.
5. Who is responsible for paying for the damage?
6. The federal government often provides disaster aid.
7. Storm chasers travel throughout Tornado Alley and search for storms.
8. The chasers sometimes find themselves in dangerous situations.
9. Spotters used binoculars, barometers, and other simple forecasting methods to predict a tornado's proximity.
10. The sophisticated computer systems in current use accurately predict and pinpoint a storm.

Model

Model the following sentence to practice using a compound predicate.

> **We learn and grow and are transformed not so much by what we do but by why and how we do it.**
>
> —Sharon Salzberg, "The Power of Intention"

TEKS 10.17A(i)
ELPS 4C, 5E

Using Phrases

A **phrase** is a group of related words that function as a single part of speech. The sentence below contains a number of phrases.

Finishing the race will require running up some steep slopes.

finishing the race (This gerund phrase functions as a subject noun.)

will require (This phrase functions as a verb.)

running up some steep slopes (This gerund phrase acts as an object noun.)

768.1 Types of Phrases

- An **appositive phrase,** which follows a noun or a pronoun and renames it, consists of a noun and its modifiers. An appositive adds new information about the noun or pronoun it follows.

  The Trans-Siberian Railroad, the world's longest railway, stretches from Moscow to Vladivostok. (The appositive phrase renames *Trans-Siberian Railroad* and provides new information.)

- A **verbal phrase** is a phrase based on one of the three types of verbals: *gerund, infinitive,* or *participle.* (See **754.1**, **754.2**, and **754.3**.)

  - A **gerund phrase** consists of a gerund and its modifiers. The whole phrase functions as a noun.

    Spotting the tiny mouse was easy for the hawk.
    (The gerund phrase is used as the subject of the sentence.)

    Dinner escaped by ducking under a rock.
    (The gerund phrase is the object of the preposition *by.*)

  - An **infinitive phrase** consists of an infinitive and its modifiers. The whole phrase functions either as a noun, an adjective, or an adverb.

    To shake every voter's hand was the candidate's goal.
    (The infinitive phrase functions as a noun used as the subject.)

    Your efforts to clean the chalkboard are appreciated.
    (The infinitive phrase is used as an adjective modifying *efforts.*)

    Please watch carefully to see the difference.
    (The infinitive phrase is used as an adverb modifying *watch.*)

  - A **participial phrase** consists of a past or present participle and its modifiers. The whole phrase functions as an adjective.

    Following his nose, the beagle took off like a jackrabbit.
    (The participial phrase modifies the noun *beagle.*)

    The raccoons, warned by the rustling, took cover.
    (The participial phrase modifies the noun *raccoons.*)

Practice

Constructing Sentences 3

- Appositive Phrases
- Verbal Phrases

Identify each underlined phrase as an *appositive, gerund, infinitive,* or *participial phrase.*

Example: Ice fishing on the lake at this time of year is dangerous.
gerund phrase

1. Lucinda's goal of becoming class president was finally accomplished.
2. John Steinbeck, the famous American author, never graduated from college.
3. Dirk postponed cleaning the garage so he could go to the movies.
4. When he got his driver's license, Geoff wanted to buy a used car.
5. Refusing to accept defeat, Luis limped over the finish line.
6. The student chosen to compete will travel to Washington, D.C.
7. To continue his education, Reggie borrowed money from his uncle.
8. Working hard usually pays off.
9. Keleigh kept the secret to prevent anyone from telling Mr. Bain.
10. *Araucaria heterophylla,* the Norfolk Island pine, is a popular houseplant.

Model

Model the following sentence to practice using appositive phrases.

Everyone agreed that my father, my Baba, had built the most beautiful house in the Wazir Akbar Khan district, a new and affluent neighborhood in the northern part of Kabul.

—Khaled Hossein, *The Kite Runner*

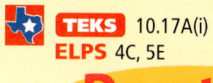

ELPS 4C

Using Phrases *(continued)*

- A **verb phrase** consists of a main verb preceded by one or more helping verbs.

  Snow has been falling for days. (*Has been falling* is a verb phrase.)

- A **prepositional phrase** is a group of words beginning with a preposition and ending with a noun or a pronoun. Prepositional phrases function mainly as adjectives and adverbs.

  Reach for that catnip ball behind the couch. (The prepositional phrase *behind the couch* is used as an adjective modifying *catnip ball.*)

  Zach won the wheelchair race in record time. (*In record time* is used as an adverb modifying the verb *won.*)

- An **absolute phrase** consists of a noun and a participle (plus the participle's object, if there is one, and any modifiers). An absolute phrase functions as a modifier that adds information to the entire sentence. Absolute phrases are always set off with commas.

  Its wheels clattering rhythmically over the rails, the train rolled into town. (The noun *wheels* is modified by the present participle *clattering.* The entire phrase modifies the rest of the sentence.)

Using Clauses

A **clause** is a group of related words that has both a subject and a predicate.

770.1 Independent and Dependent Clauses

An **independent clause** presents a complete thought and can stand alone as a sentence; a **dependent clause** (also called a *subordinate clause*) does not present a complete thought and cannot stand alone as a sentence.

Sparrows make nests in cattle barns (independent clause) **so that they can stay warm during the winter** (dependent clause).

770.2 Types of Dependent Clauses

There are three basic types of dependent clauses: *adverb, noun,* and *adjective.*

- An **adverb clause** is used like an adverb to modify a verb, an adjective, or an adverb. Adverb clauses begin with a subordinating conjunction. (See 762.3.)

  If I study hard, I will pass this test. (The adverb clause modifies the verb *will pass.*)

- A **noun clause** is used in place of a noun.

  However, the teacher said that the essay questions are based only on the last two chapters. (The noun clause functions as a direct object.)

- An **adjective clause** modifies a noun or a pronoun.

  Tomorrow's test, which covers the entire book, is half essay and half short answers. (The adjective clause modifies the noun *test.*)

Practice

Constructing Sentences 4

- Verb Phrases
- Prepositional Phrases
- Absolute Phrases

Identify the underlined part of each sentence as a *prepositional phrase*, an *absolute phrase*, or a *verb phrase*.

Example: All things considered, the Wildcats were headed for the finals.
absolute phrase

1. I could hear Min and Lissa whispering in the next room.
2. We will meet at Gerald's Diner at 4:30.
3. The full moon lighting his way, my brother followed the tracks through the field.
4. Once her speech was over, Heather did feel more relaxed.
5. His heart pounding like a jackhammer, Ty slam-dunked the ball.
6. Stuart reviewed his notes before the test.
7. Her hands and feet stinging from the cold, Danielle left the bleachers and went inside.
8. The baby clinging to the old woman had been making mewling noises for at least half an hour.

Learning Language

Work with a partner and take turns reading aloud the information about clauses and phrases on pages 768 and 770. Listen carefully as your partner reads one section. Take notes and then summarize the information. Ask your partner to listen carefully and take notes as you read. Your partner should then summarize those sections. Ask each other questions as you finish reading each section to ensure that you both understand the text and the summaries. When you have finished, copy each other's summaries and check them against the text.

TEKS 10.17C
ELPS 4C, 5E, 5F

Using Sentence Variety

A **sentence** may be classified according to the type of statement it makes, the way it is constructed, and its arrangement of words.

772.1 Kinds of Sentences

Sentences can make five basic kinds of sentences: *declarative, interrogative, imperative, exclamatory,* or *conditional.*

- **Declarative sentences** make statements. They tell us something about a person, a place, a thing, or an idea.

  The Statue of Liberty stands in New York Harbor.

  For over a century, it has greeted immigrants and visitors to America.

- **Interrogative sentences** ask questions.

  Did you know that the Statue of Liberty is made of copper and stands more than 150 feet tall?

  Are we allowed to climb all the way to the top?

- **Imperative sentences** make commands. They often contain an understood subject *(you)* as in the examples below.

  Go see the Statue of Liberty.

  After a few weeks of physical conditioning, climb its 168 stairs.

- **Exclamatory sentences** communicate strong emotion or surprise.

  Climbing 168 stairs is not a dumb idea!

  Just muster some of that old pioneering spirit, that desire to try something new, that never-say-die attitude that made America great!

- **Conditional sentences** express wishes ("if . . . then" statements) or conditions contrary to fact.

  If I could design a country's flag, I would use six colors behind a sun, a star, and a moon.

  I would feel as if I were representing many cultures in my design.

Practice

Kinds of Sentences

Sentence Variety

Write the kind of statement each sentence in the following paragraph makes: *declarative, interrogative, imperative, exclamatory,* or *conditional.*

Example: 1. *declarative*

(1) The earth's magnetic field has flipped many times in geologic history, and scientists think it is poised to flip again. **(2)** Think about what that means. **(3)** Compasses will point to the South Pole instead of to the North Pole. **(4)** What other effects would a flip have? **(5)** It most likely would confuse many types of migratory birds and sea creatures who use the earth's magnetic fields to find their way. **(6)** It would also leave the earth temporarily unprotected from some of the solar wind filtered out by the current magnetic field. **(7)** A solar flare could then disrupt communications and damage the ozone layer. **(8)** There is a trade-off, though. **(9)** If there were no magnetic field, people would be lucky enough to see auroras almost every night. **(10)** That would be cool!

Model

Model the following conditional sentences.

If you cannot convince them, confuse them.

—Harry S. Truman

If you aren't fired with enthusiasm, you will be fired with enthusiasm.

—Vince Lombardi

TEKS 10.17C
ELPS 4C, 5E, 5F

774.1 Types of Sentence Constructions

A sentence may be *simple, compound, complex,* or *compound-complex.* It all depends on the relationship between independent and dependent clauses.

- A **simple sentence** can have a single subject or a compound subject. It can have a single predicate or a compound predicate. However, a simple sentence has only one independent clause, and it has no dependent clauses.

  My back aches.
  (single subject; single predicate)

  My teeth and my eyes hurt.
  (compound subject; single predicate)

  My throat and nose feel sore and look red.
  (compound subject; compound predicate)

  I must have caught the flu from the sick kids in class.
  (independent clause with two phrases: *from the sick kids* and *in class*)

- A **compound sentence** consists of two independent clauses. The clauses must be joined by a comma and a coordinating conjunction or by a semicolon.

  I usually don't mind missing school, but this is not fun.

  I feel too sick to watch TV; I feel too sick to eat.

NOTE: The comma can be omitted when the clauses are very short.

  I wept and I wept.

- A **complex sentence** contains one independent clause (in black) and one or more dependent clauses (in red).

  When I get back to school, I'm actually going to appreciate it.
  (dependent clause; independent clause)

  I won't even complain about math class, although I might be talking out of my head because I'm feverish.
  (independent clause; two dependent clauses)

- A **compound-complex sentence** contains two or more independent clauses (in black) and one or more dependent clauses (in red).

  Yes, I have a bad flu, and because I need to get well soon, I won't think about school just yet.
  (two independent clauses; one dependent clause)

TEKS 10.17C
ELPS 4C, 5E, 5F

Practice

Types of Sentence Constructions

Types of Sentences

Identify each of the following sentences as a *simple, compound, complex,* or *compound-complex* sentence.

Example: 1. simple

(1) How do auroras form? **(2)** The solar wind contains charged particles that make the air glow when they blast into Earth's atmosphere. **(3)** The aurora borealis (or northern lights) and the aurora australis (southern lights) can take many different forms. **(4)** Sometimes simple lines appear across the sky, or pillars form at different points in the sky. **(5)** These lines or pillars can broaden into curtains of light, which wave back and forth overhead. **(6)** Lucky observers see more exotic forms. **(7)** Some aurora forms are petal shapes like giant blooming flowers, and others expand across the sky like slow-motion fireworks. **(8)** White aurora lights are most common, but when the solar wind is especially favorable, more vibrant colors such as purple, violet, green, and orange may appear. **(9)** Whatever colors they display or form they take, the lights of the aurora are always a sight to behold. **(10)** People who live in extreme north or south locales know this; they can see auroras almost 200 days a year!

Model

Model the following complex sentences.

When we blame ourselves, we feel that no one else has a right to blame us.

—Oscar Wilde, *The Picture of Dorian Gray*

Forgive me my nonsense as I also forgive the nonsense of those who think they talk sense.

—Robert Frost

TEKS 10.17C
ELPS 4C, 5E, 5F

776.1 Arrangements of Sentences

Depending on the arrangement of the words and the placement of emphasis, a sentence may also be classified as *loose, balanced, periodic,* or *cumulative.*

- A **loose sentence** expresses the main thought near the beginning and adds explanatory material as needed.

  We hauled out the boxes of food and set up the camp stove, all the time battling the hot wind that would not stop, even when we screamed into the sky.

  Jet airplanes do the seemingly impossible—moving us across countries and over oceans, transporting us to new continents, all within just a few hours.

- A **balanced sentence** is constructed so that it emphasizes a similarity or a contrast between two or more of its parts (words, phrases, or clauses).

  The wind in our ears drove us crazy and pushed us on.
  (The similar wording emphasizes the main idea in this sentence.)

  Experience is not what happens to you; it is what you do with what happens to you.

  —Aldous Huxley

- A **periodic sentence** is one that postpones the crucial or most surprising idea until the end.

  Following my mother's repeated threats to ground me for life, I decided it was time to propose a compromise.

  There is only one way to achieve happiness on this terrestrial ball—and that is to have either a clear conscience or no conscience at all.

  —Ogden Nash, *I'm a Stranger Here Myself*

- A **cumulative sentence** places the general idea in the middle of the sentence with modifying clauses and phrases coming before and after.

  With careful thought and extra attention to detail, I wrote out my plan for being a model teenager, a teen who cared about neatness and reliability.

  With careful planning and diligence, students who finish high school and graduate from college will end up in high-paying, satisfying jobs, an accomplishment we all admire and to which we all aspire.

TEKS 10.17C
ELPS 4C, 5E, 5F

Practice

Arrangements of Sentences

- **Sentence Arrangements**

Classify each of the following sentences as *loose, balanced, periodic,* or *cumulative.*

Example: From Chicago to Milwaukee it was cloudy, but north of Milwaukee it was clear.
balanced

1. The restaurant was nice, but the food was terrible.
2. The three of us climbed to the top of the hill and found the best spot, all the while darkness falling upon us, and then the fireworks began.
3. Suddenly, without a word and for no reason, Joshua bolted out the open door.
4. The energetic horses ran hard, following each other through the tall grass, occasionally slowing to catch their breath and then hurrying on toward the horizon.
5. With grass in his hair, dirt between his fingers, and mud all over his face, Oscar triumphantly held up the football.
6. After the ice storm, the woods looked hauntingly beautiful, as though diamonds had melted on the trees.
7. Although we were hungry, exhausted, and covered in mud, we continued to follow the moose tracks.
8. Some students study at home; others study at the public library.
9. Maria considered William a good friend—one who was trustworthy, honest, and reliable.

Model

Model the following balanced sentence.

We may brave human laws, but we cannot resist natural ones.
—Jules Verne, *20,000 Leagues Under the Sea*

ELPS 4C, 5E

Getting Sentence Parts to Agree

Agreement of Subject and Verb

A verb must agree in number (singular or plural) with its subject.

The student was proud of her quarter grades.

NOTE: Do not be confused by words that come between the subject and verb.

The manager, as well as the players, is required to display good sportsmanship. (*Manager*, not *players*, is the subject.)

778.1 Compound Subjects

Compound subjects joined by *or* or *nor* take a singular verb.

Neither Bev nor Kendra is going to the street dance.

NOTE: When one of the subjects joined by *or* or *nor* is singular and one is plural, the verb must agree with the subject nearer the verb.

Neither Miguel nor his friends are singing in the band anymore. (The plural subject *friends* is nearer the verb, so the plural verb *are* is correct.)

Compound subjects connected with *and* require a plural verb.

Strength and balance are necessary for gymnastics.

778.2 Delayed Subjects

Delayed subjects occur when the verb comes before the subject in a sentence. In these inverted sentences, the delayed subject must agree with the verb.

There are many hardworking students in our schools.
There is present among many young people today a will to succeed.
(*Students* and *will* are the true subjects of these sentences, not *there*.)

778.3 "Be" Verbs

When a sentence contains a form of the "be" verb—and a noun comes before and after that verb—the verb must agree with the subject, not the *complement* (the noun coming after the verb).

The cause of this problem was the bad brakes.
The bad brakes were the cause of this problem.

778.4 Special Cases

Some nouns that are **plural in form but singular in meaning** take a singular verb: *mumps, measles, news, mathematics, economics, gallows, shambles.*

Measles is still considered a serious disease in many parts of the world.

Some nouns that are plural in form but singular in meaning take a plural verb: *scissors, trousers, tidings.*

The scissors are missing again.

Practice

Agreement of Subject and Verb 1

- **Subject-Verb Agreement**

For each sentence, write the correct verb from the choice given in parentheses.

Example: The problem with both computers *(was, were)* their memory cards.
was

1. Mr. Valero *(are, is)* planning a quiz for this Friday.
2. There *(are, is)* rumors circulating that David will be the starting quarterback on Friday.
3. *(Do, Does)* this skin cream really prevent acne?
4. The result of last week's drills *(was, were)* a seminar on fire safety.
5. Either Serena or Kim and Tyler Garcia *(take, takes)* the gerbils home over holiday breaks.
6. The news of his accident *(was, were)* not surprising.
7. There *(are, is)* remaining one medium-sized sweatshirt with the team logo.
8. Dale Earnhardt, Jr., and Kyle Bush *(are, is)* popular race-car drivers.
9. Neither DeWayne nor Kevin *(are, is)* going with us to the stadium.
10. *(Have, Has)* the fireworks started yet?

Model

Model the following sentences to practice subject-verb agreement with special-case nouns.

Your glasses need a good cleaning.

The mathematics is not there until we put it there.
—Sir Arthur Eddington

Agreement of Subject and Verb *(continued)*

780.1 Collective Nouns

Collective nouns *(faculty, committee, team, congress, species, crowd, army, pair, squad)* take a singular verb when they refer to a group as a unit; collective nouns take a plural verb when they refer to the individuals within the group.

> **The favored team is losing, and the crowd is getting ugly.** (Both *team* and *crowd* are considered units in this sentence, requiring the singular verb *is*.)
>
> **The pair were finally reunited after 20 years apart.**
> (Here, *pair* refers to two individuals, so the plural verb *were* is required.)

780.2 Indefinite Pronouns

Some **indefinite pronouns** are singular: *each, either, neither, one, everybody, another, anybody, everyone, nobody, everything, somebody,* and *someone*. They require a singular verb.

> **Everybody is invited to the cafeteria for refreshments.**

Some **indefinite pronouns** are plural: *both, few, many,* and *several*.

> **Several like chocolate cake. Many ask for ice cream, too.**

Some **indefinite pronouns** are singular or plural: *all, any, most, none,* and *some*.

NOTE: Do not be confused by words or phrases that come between the indefinite pronoun and the verb.

> **One of the participants is** (not *are*) **going to have to stay late to clean up.**

A Closer Look

As stated above, some **indefinite pronouns** can be either singular or plural: *all, any, most, none,* and *some*. These pronouns are singular if the number of the noun in the prepositional phrase is singular; they are plural if the noun is plural.

> **Most of the food complaints are coming from the seniors.**
> (*Complaints* is plural, so *most* is plural.)
>
> **Most of the tabletop is sticky with melted ice cream.**
> (*Tabletop* is singular, so *most* is singular.)

780.3 Relative Pronouns

When a **relative pronoun** *(who, which, that)* is used as the subject of a clause, the number of the verb is determined by the antecedent of the pronoun. (The antecedent is the word to which the pronoun refers.)

> **This is one of the books that are required for class.** (The relative pronoun *that* requires the plural verb *are* because its antecedent, *books,* is plural.)

NOTE: To test this type of sentence for agreement, read the "of" phrase first.

> **Of the books that are required for geography class, this is one.**

Practice

Agreement of Subject and Verb 2

- Subject-Verb Agreement

For each underlined verb, state the reason it does not agree with its subject.

Example: 1. Were is plural, and its subject, one, is singular.

One of Edna Ferber's most popular works **(1)** were the novel *So Big*. (This is one book that **(2)** are required reading for literature class.) Some students **(3)** wonders about the author's reasons for writing the book. In one interview, Ferber answered: "I wrote my book because I wanted to write it more than anything in the world."

Many readers are aware that *So Big* won a Pulitzer Prize for literature. The main characters, Selina Peake DeJong and her son, Dirk "So Big" DeJong, **(4)** makes the story memorable. The pair **(5)** faces many challenges. Selina is a widow who **(6)** are forced to make her way in a male-dominated world. Dirk experiences many changes as he grows into a young man.

The novels *Showboat* and *Giant* **(7)** is other well-known works by Edna Ferber. Some of her fans **(8)** believes that she was the greatest novelist of her day.

Model

Model the following sentence to practice subject-verb agreement.

He had preconceived ideas about everything, and his idea about Americans was that they should be engineers or mechanics.

—Willa Cather, *Alexander's Bridge*

ELPS 4C, 5E

Agreement of Pronoun and Antecedent

A pronoun must agree in number, person, and gender with its *antecedent.* (The *antecedent* is the word to which the pronoun refers.)

> **Cal brought his gerbil to school.** (The antecedent of *his* is *Cal.* Both the pronoun and its antecedent are singular, third person, and masculine; therefore, the pronoun is said to "agree" with its antecedent.)

782.1 Agreement in Number

Use a **singular pronoun** to refer to such antecedents as *each, either, neither, one, anyone, anybody, everyone, everybody, somebody, another, nobody,* and *a person.*

> **Neither of the brothers likes his (not their) room.**

Two or more singular antecedents joined by *or* or *nor* are also referred to by a **singular pronoun.**

> **Either Connie or Sue left her headset in the library.**

If one of the antecedents joined by *or* or *nor* is singular and one is plural, the pronoun should agree with the nearer antecedent.

> **Neither the manager nor the players were crazy about their new uniforms.**

Use a **plural pronoun** to refer to plural antecedents as well as compound subjects joined by *and.*

> **Jared and Carlos are finishing their assignments.**

782.2 Agreement in Gender

Use a **masculine** or **feminine pronoun** depending upon the gender of the antecedent.

> **Is either Connor or Gloria bringing his or her baseball glove?**

When *a person* or *everyone* is used to refer to both sexes or either sex, you will have to choose whether to offer optional pronouns or rewrite the sentence.

> **A person should be allowed to choose her or his own footwear.**
> (optional pronouns)
>
> **People should be allowed to choose their own footwear.**
> (rewritten in plural form)

Practice

Agreement of Pronoun and Antecedent

- **Pronoun-Antecedent Agreement**

For each sentence below, first write the antecedent of the pronoun that appears later in the sentence. Then replace the incorrect pronoun with one that agrees with the antecedent. If the pronoun is correct as is, write "C."

Example: Should students always know the basics about how to maintain her computers?
students, their

1. Everyone should know how to delete files and save his documents to the network drive.
2. Tamyra and Ricardo know a lot about maintaining her computers.
3. Both of them keep his computers running smoothly.
4. The computer lab tech helps students with problems they can't fix.
5. Neither Tamyra nor Ricardo could help Arturo with their problem.
6. Arturo's computer was freezing up, and the lab tech fixed them.
7. The tech said that Arturo probably needs a new monitor for his computer.
8. Ricardo just got a new flat-screen monitor for their computer at home.
9. Most students at our school know how to fix his computers when something minor goes wrong.

Model

Model the following sentence to practice pronoun-antecedent agreement.

My parents gave up entirely their wandering life and fixed themselves in their native country.

—Mary Shelley, *Frankenstein*

TEKS 10.17C
ELPS 4C, 5E, 5F

Diagramming Sentences

A **graphic diagram** of a sentence is a picture of how the words in that sentence are related and how they fit together to form a complete thought.

784.1 Simple Sentence with One Subject and One Verb

Chris fishes.

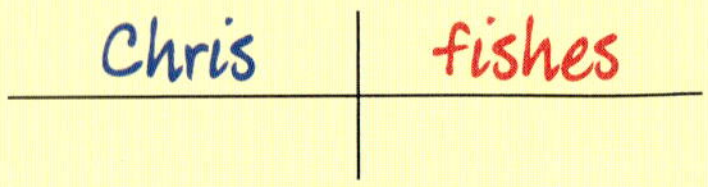

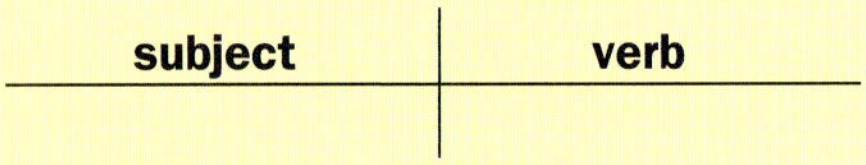

784.2 Simple Sentence with a Predicate Adjective

Fish are delicious.

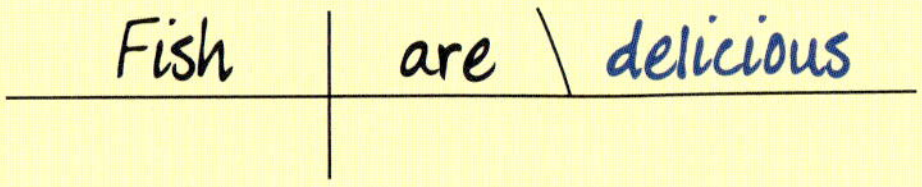

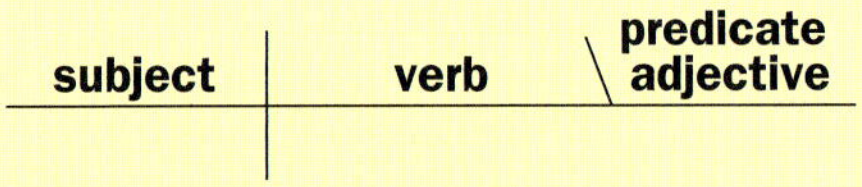

784.3 Simple Sentence with a Predicate Noun and Adjectives

Fishing is my favorite hobby.

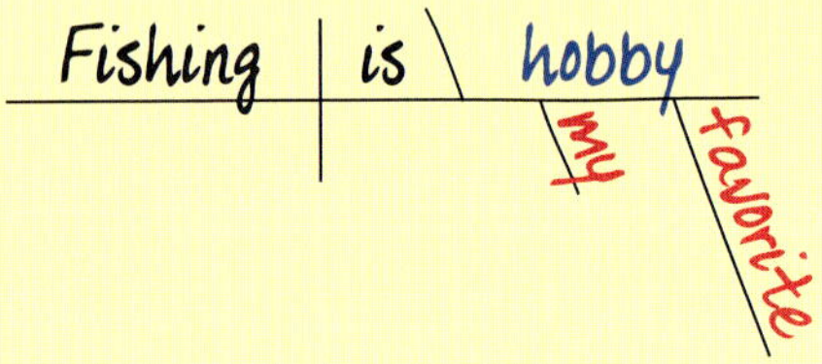

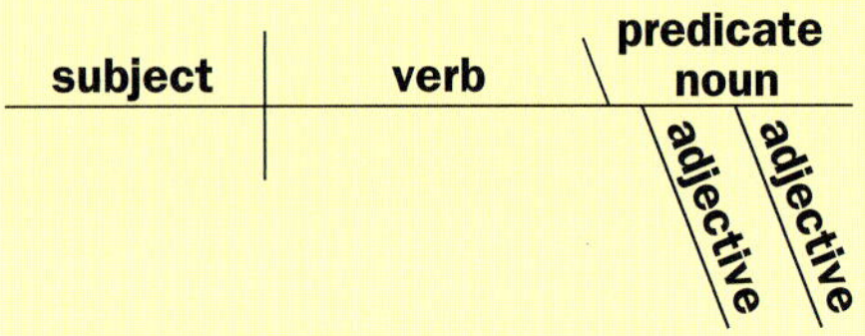

NOTE: When possessive pronouns *(my, his, their, etc.)* are used as adjectives, they are placed on a diagonal line under the word they modify.

784.4 Simple Sentence with an Indirect and Direct Object

My grandpa gave us a trout.

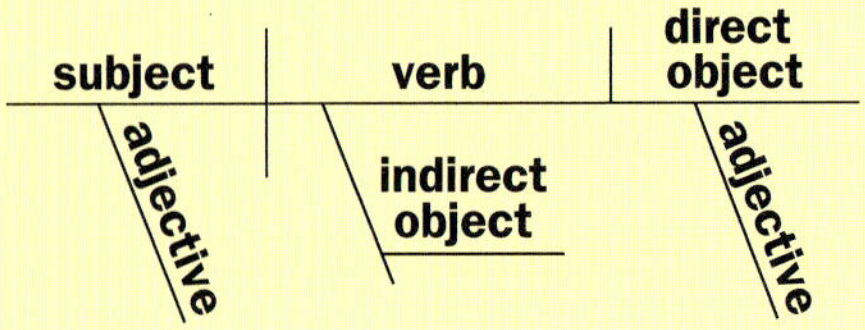

NOTE: Articles *(a, an, the)* are adjectives and are placed on a diagonal line under the word they modify.

TEKS 10.17C
ELPS 4C, 5E, 5F

Practice

Sentence Diagramming 1

- **Diagramming Sentences**

Diagram the following sentences.

Example: Wind is powerful.

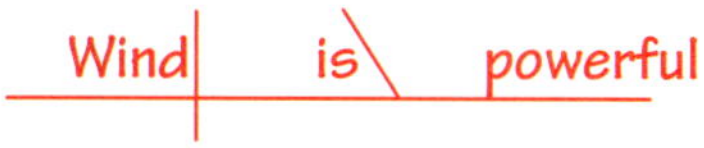

1. Wind turbines generate electricity.
2. This power is a clean energy source.
3. The turbine blades are huge.
4. My uncle made us a small wind turbine.
5. Our neighbors are glad.
6. We give them our excess power.
7. No wind means no power.
8. Wind is supplementary power.

Model

Model the following sentences to practice writing sentences with a direct object and with an indirect object.

Never give a party if you will be the most interesting person there.
—Mickey Friedman

Beauty is in the eye of the beholder, and it may be necessary from time to time to give a stupid or misinformed beholder a black eye.
—Miss Piggy

Diagramming Sentences *(continued)*

786.1 Simple Sentence with a Prepositional Phrase

I like fishing by myself.

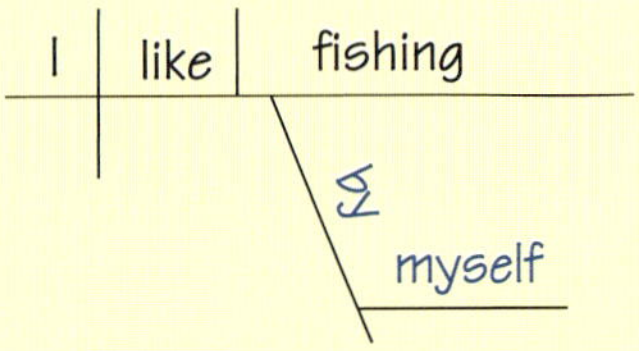

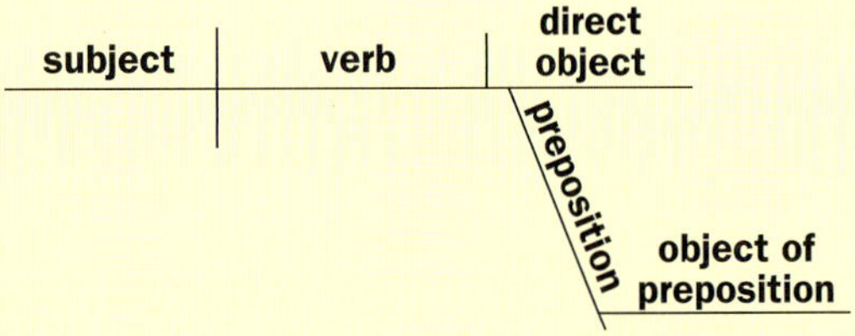

786.2 Simple Sentence with a Compound Subject and Verb

The team and fans clapped and cheered.

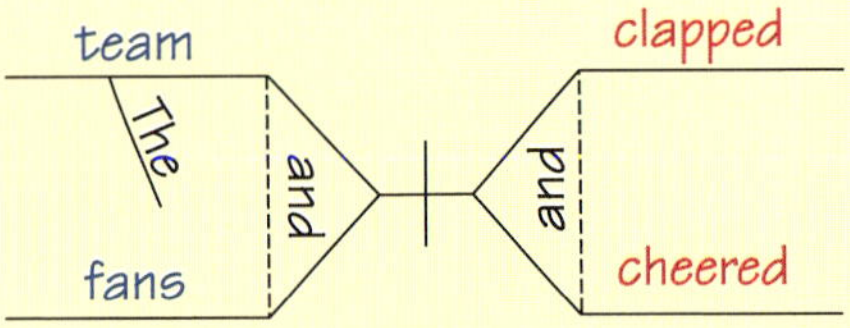

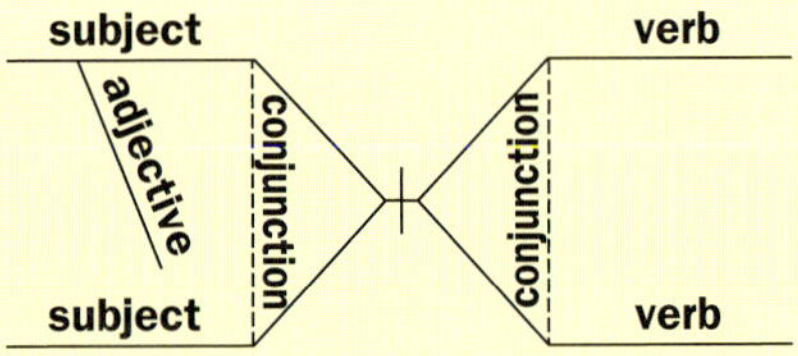

786.3 Compound Sentence

The team scored, and the crowd cheered wildly.

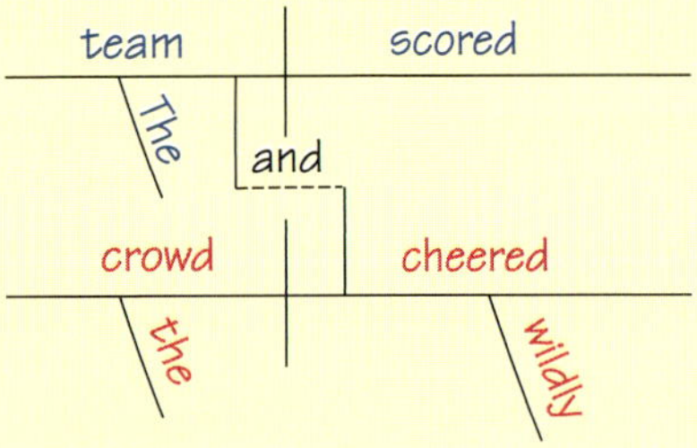

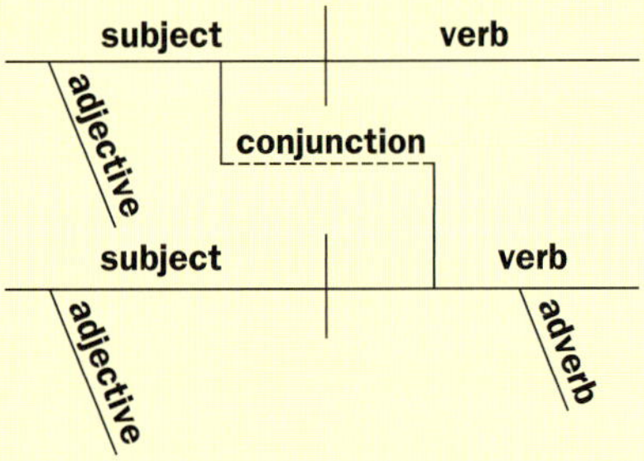

786.4 Complex Sentence with a Subordinate Clause

Before Erin scored, the crowd sat quietly.

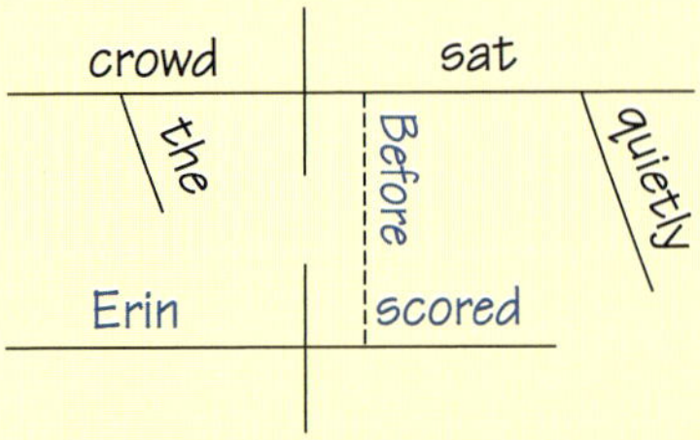

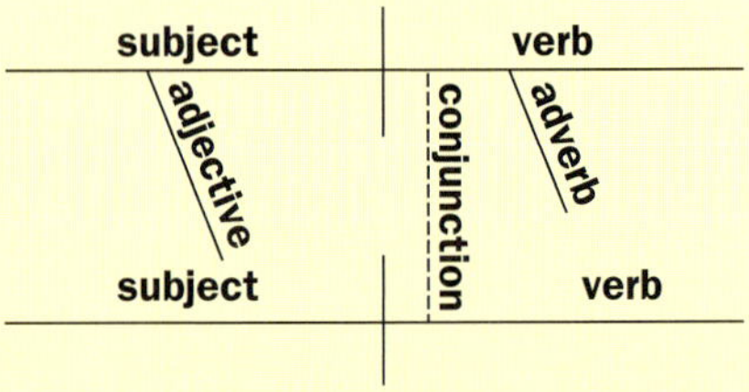

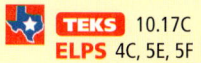

Practice

Sentence Diagramming 2

- Diagramming Sentences

Diagram the following sentences.

Example: The small boy on the swing emitted a squeal of delight.

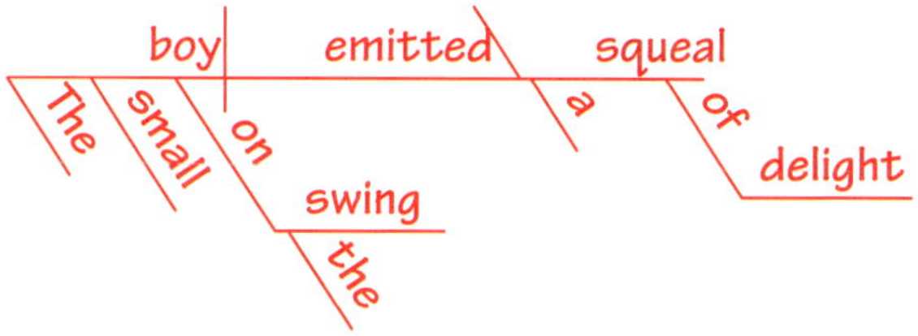

1. After the hawk landed, the rabbit ran across the field.
2. I put three new batteries in the silver flashlight.
3. Gene and Valeria planned and completed the school's mural.
4. My school won the state tournament, and my cousin's school captured third place.
5. The police and firefighters pushed and pulled the damaged crate.
6. All the students were gone, so the janitor locked the door.
7. Although the book was long, everyone wanted a copy.
8. The girl on the snowboard flew down the hill.

Model

Model the following sentences to practice writing compound and complex sentences.

Stay committed to your decisions, but stay flexible in your approach.
—Tom Robbins

The whole world opened to me when I learned to read.
—Mary McLeod Bethune

Texas Essential Knowledge and Skills for English Language Arts

The English Language Arts and Reading TEKS specify the skills you need to master by the end of English II. To help you understand what is required of you, we have provided a list of the skills you will practice and learn during this school year. The second column shows where these TEKS are addressed in this program.

TEKS 10.13 Writing/Writing Process

Students use elements of the writing process (planning, drafting, revising, editing, and publishing) to compose text. Students are expected to:

A plan a first draft by selecting the correct genre for conveying the intended meaning to multiple audiences, determining appropriate topics through a range of strategies (e.g., discussion, background reading, personal interests, interviews), and developing a thesis or controlling idea;	pages 4, 5, 9, 10, 15, 80, 85–88, 124, 131, 138, 143–148, 182, 184, 189, 198, 202, 238, 240, 256, 260, 264, 306, 307, 313, 315, 322, 328, 329, 337, 338, 372, 381, 382, 384, 385, 391, 450, 452, 456, 460, 462, 464, 472, 474, 476, 484, 486, 492–494, 496. 604, 611, 618–623, 630
B structure ideas in a sustained and persuasive way (e.g., using outlines, note taking, graphic organizers, lists) and develop drafts in timed and open-ended situations that include transitions and the rhetorical devices used to convey meaning;	pages 9, 10, 18, 19, 21, 92–96, 100, 101, 126, 131–133, 148, 150–154, 163, 180, 181, 183, 184, 189–191, 196, 197, 199, 200, 203, 206–210, 214, 224, 236, 237, 247–249, 257, 258, 266–270, 273, 274, 276, 304, 306, 309, 314–317, 341, 392, 405, 414, 415, 450–452, 456, 457, 460, 464, 465, 467–470, 472, 474–476, 478–481, 484–486, 488, 489, 492, 496, 497, 499, 500, 506–513, 600–605, 607–611, 613, 614, 624–629, 631, 632, 636, 637
C revise drafts to improve style, word choice, figurative language, sentence variety, and subtlety of meaning after rethinking how well questions of purpose, audience, and genre have been addressed;	pages 9, 11, 22–25, 98, 99, 102–105, 110, 111, 127, 134, 156–163, 185, 186, 192, 212–219, 224, 226, 243, 244, 250, 272–279, 284, 286, 302, 310, 318, 330, 343, 351, 355, 357, 411–413, 416–419, 424, 456, 460, 466, 472, 474, 476, 477, 484, 487, 492, 498, 506, 509, 510, 512, 513, 579, 584, 587, 604, 611, 615 pages 74, 91, 118, 126, 127, 172, 175, 176, 221, 224
D edit drafts for grammar, mechanics, and spelling; and	pages 9, 11, 26, 27, 108, 109, 112, 128, 134, 166, 167, 169, 170, 186, 192, 222, 223, 225, 226, 244, 250, 282, 283, 285, 286, 310, 318, 330, 343, 351, 355, 357, 422, 423, 456, 460, 466, 472, 474, 476, 477, 480, 484, 487, 492, 498, 506, 509, 510, 512, 513, 604, 615, 640, 641
E revise final draft in response to feedback from peers and teacher and publish written work for appropriate audiences.	pages 9, 11, 28–30, 50, 53, 54, 70–72, 75–77, 113, 128, 159, 171, 186, 227, 244, 287, 310, 428, 476, 611

*Page References in *Student Edition*
*Page References in *SkillsBook*

TEKS 10.14 Writing/Literary Texts

Students write literary texts to express their ideas and feelings about real or imagined people, events, and ideas. Students are responsible for at least two forms of literary writing. Students are expected to:

A write an engaging story with a well-developed conflict and resolution, interesting and believable characters, a range of literary strategies (e.g., dialogue, suspense) and devices to enhance the plot, and sensory details that define mood or tone;	pages 3, 81–89, 93–96, 98, 99, 102, 104, 105, 126, 133, 135, 323–329, 611, 636, 637
B write a poem using a variety of poetic techniques (e.g., structural elements, figurative language) and a variety of poetic forms (e.g., sonnets, ballads); and	pages 3, 348–357
C write a script with an explicit or implicit theme and details that contribute to a definite mood or tone.	pages 3, 334, 336–346, 452–455, 502

TEKS 10.15 Writing/Expository and Procedural Texts

Students write expository and procedural or work-related texts to communicate ideas and information to specific audiences for specific purposes. Students are expected to:

A write an analytical essay of sufficient length that includes: (i) effective introductory and concluding paragraphs and a variety of sentence structures; (ii) rhetorical devices, and transitions between paragraphs; (iii) a thesis or controlling idea; (iv) an organizing structure appropriate to purpose, audience, and context; (v) relevant evidence and well-chosen details, and (vi) distinctions about the relative value of specific data, facts, and ideas that support the thesis statement;	pages 140–148, 150–154, 156–163, 169, 170, 180–184, 190, 191, 236–238, 240, 241, 257, 258, 262–264, 266, 270, 272, 274–276, 304, 306–310, 360, 362, 363, 373, 378, 391, 395, 401, 406, 414, 415, 417, 450, 451, 477, 486–489, 582, 590, 605, 628, 629, 631, 636, 637
B write procedural or work-related documents (e.g., instructions, e-mails, correspondence, memos, project plans) that include: (i) organized and accurately conveyed information; (ii) reader-friendly formatting techniques; and (iii) anticipation of readers' questions;	pages 3, 506–513, 607

*Page References in *Student Edition*
*Page References in *SkillsBook*

C write an interpretative response to an expository or a literary text (e.g., essay or review) that: (i) extends beyond a summary and literal analysis; (ii) addresses the writing skills for an analytical essay and provides evidence from the text using embedded quotations; and (iii) analyzes the aesthetic effects of an author's use of stylistic or rhetorical devices; and	pages 253, 255, 257, 258, 261–264, 266, 268–270, 272, 274–277, 299–301, 304–309, 315–317, 373, 414–417, 636, 637
D produce a multimedia presentation (e.g., documentary, class newspaper, docudrama, infomercial, visual or textual parodies, theatrical production) with graphics, images, and sound that conveys a distinctive point of view and appeals to a specific audience.	pages 171, 430–434, 437–441, 452, 455, 501, 503

TEKS 10.16 Writing/Persuasive Texts

Students write persuasive texts to influence the attitudes or actions of a specific audience on specific issues. Students are expected to write an argumentative essay to the appropriate audience that includes:

A a clear thesis or position based on logical reasons supported by precise and relevant evidence;	pages 196, 197, 199, 200, 203, 207, 209, 210, 212, 214, 216–218, 236, 237, 239, 240, 248, 249, 476–478, 630
B consideration of the whole range of information and views on the topic and accurate and honest representation of these views (i.e., in the author's own words and not out of context);	pages 199, 200, 204, 206, 209, 213, 214, 219, 238, 240, 247, 476–479
C counter-arguments based on evidence to anticipate and address objections;	pages 200, 204, 206, 209, 210, 213, 237, 241, 242, 247–249, 476, 477
D an organizing structure appropriate to the purpose, audience, and context;	pages 197, 199, 200, 206, 215, 236, 237, 476–479
E an analysis of the relative value of specific data, facts, and ideas; and	pages 197, 199, 200, 209, 215, 236, 237, 241, 248, 249, 477–479
F a range of appropriate appeals (e.g., descriptions, anecdotes, case studies, analogies, illustrations).	pages 242, 477, 478

*Page References in *Student Edition*
*Page References in *SkillsBook*

TEKS 10.17 Oral and Written Conventions/Conventions

Students understand the function of and use the conventions of academic language when speaking and writing. Students will continue to apply earlier standards with greater complexity. Students are expected to:

A use and understand the function of the following parts of speech in the context of reading, writing, and speaking:
- (i) more complex active and passive tenses and verbals (gerunds, infinitives, participles);
- (ii) restrictive and nonrestrictive relative clauses; and
- (iii) reciprocal pronouns (e.g., each other, one another);

pages 46, 109–111, 166–170, 223, 282, 283, 310, 422, 423, 477, 487, 590, 734, 736, 737

pages 14, 15, 85, 88, 95–98, 101, 106, 129, 130, 134, 206, 211, 214, 222

B identify and use the subjunctive mood to express doubts, wishes, and possibilities; and

pages 222, 226, 286, 752, 753

pages 104, 105

C use a variety of correctly structured sentences (e.g., compound, complex, compound-complex).

pages 46, 47, 112, 128, 170, 186, 192, 224, 244, 250, 284, 310, 318, 424, 456, 460, 466, 472, 474, 476, 477, 480, 484, 487, 492, 498, 506, 509, 510, 512, 513, 587–593, 596, 604, 615, 764–767, 772–777, 784–787

pages 126–128, 136–138, 140–145, 161–171, 175, 176, 219–221, 224

TEKS 10.18 Oral and Written Conventions/Handwriting, Capitalization, and Punctuation

Students write legibly and use appropriate capitalization and punctuation conventions in their compositions. Students are expected to:

A use conventions of capitalization; and

pages 46, 112, 128, 170, 186, 192, 226, 244, 250, 286, 310, 318, 456, 460, 466, 472, 474, 476, 477, 480, 484, 487, 492, 498, 506, 509, 510, 512, 513, 520, 570, 615, 640, 641, 682–687

pages 5, 6, 39–44, 69, 70, 195, 196, 200–202, 227

B use correct punctuation marks including:
- (i) comma placement in nonrestrictive phrases, clauses, and contrasting expressions;
- (ii) quotation marks to indicate sarcasm or irony; and
- (iii) dashes to emphasize parenthetical information.

pages 46, 112, 128, 169, 170, 186, 192, 225, 226, 244, 250, 285, 286, 310, 318, 425, 456, 460, 466, 472, 474, 476, 477, 480, 484, 487, 492, 498, 506, 509, 510, 512, 513, 582, 592, 604, 615, 640, 641, 643–681

pages 3–38, 69, 70, 161, 162, 166, 167, 169, 189, 190–195, 202, 220, 225–227, 229–232

*Page References in *Student Edition*
*Page References in *SkillsBook*

TEKS 10.19 Oral and Written Conventions/Spelling

Students spell correctly. Students are expected to spell correctly, including using various resources to determine and check correct spellings.

pages 46, 112, 128, 170, 186, 226, 244, 250, 286, 310, 318, 425, 456, 460, 466, 472, 474, 476, 477, 480, 484, 487, 492, 498, 506, 509, 510, 512, 513, 520, 604, 615, 640, 641, 688–691, ,698–703, 710–729

pages 49–70, 197, 199–203, 227

TEKS 10.20 Research/Research Plan

Students ask open-ended research questions and develop a plan for answering them. Students are expected to:

A brainstorm, consult with others, decide upon a topic, and formulate a major research question to address the major research topic; and	pages 380, 382, 383, 462, 494
B formulate a plan for engaging in research on a complex, multi-faceted topic.	pages 362–370, 372, 380, 384, 462, 494

TEKS 10.21 Research/Gathering Sources

Students determine, locate, and explore the full range of relevant sources addressing a research question and systematically record the information they gather. Students are expected to:

A follow the research plan to compile data from authoritative sources in a manner that identifies the major issues and debates within the field of inquiry;	pages 360–370, 374–377, 379, 380, 385, 404, 463, 495
B organize information gathered from multiple sources to create a variety of graphics and forms (e.g., notes, learning logs); and	pages 362, 363, 367, 381, 383–386, 390, 392, 393, 463, 495
C paraphrase, summarize, quote, and accurately cite all researched information according to a standard format (e.g., author, title, page number).	pages 374, 375, 379, 387–389, 396, 403, 404, 456, 463, 472, 473, 492, 493, 495, 633

*Page References in *Student Edition*
*Page References in *SkillsBook*

TEKS 10.22 Research/Synthesizing Information

Students clarify research questions and evaluate and synthesize collected information. Students are expected to:

A	modify the major research question as necessary to refocus the research plan;	pages 394, 400, 464, 496
B	evaluate the relevance of information to the topic and determine the reliability, validity, and accuracy of sources (including Internet sources) by examining their authority and objectivity; and	pages 376, 377, 394, 397–399, 464, 496
C	critique the research process at each step to implement changes as the need occurs and is identified.	pages 400, 416, 417, 464, 466, 496, 498

TEKS 10.23 Research/Organizing and Presenting Ideas

Students organize and present their ideas and information according to the purpose of the research and their audience. Students are expected to synthesize the research into a written or an oral presentation that:

A	marshals evidence in support of a clear thesis statement and related claims;	pages 401–406, 430–433, 435, 437, 465, 467–469, 497, 499, 500
B	provides an analysis for the audience that reflects a logical progression of ideas and a clearly stated point of view;	pages 402–406, 430–433, 435, 437, 465, 467, 468, 497, 499, 500
C	uses graphics and illustrations to help explain concepts where appropriate;	pages 72, 374, 430, 432–436, 465, 473, 497, 638, 639
D	uses a variety of evaluative tools (e.g., self-made rubrics, peer reviews, teacher and expert evaluations) to examine the quality of the research; and	pages 403, 466, 469, 498
E	uses a style manual (e.g., *Modern Language Association, Chicago Manual of Style*) to document sources and format written materials.	pages 396, 403, 404, 407–410, 432, 433, 465, 467, 470, 493, 497, 499, 500

*Page References in *Student Edition*
*Page References in *SkillsBook*

English Language Proficiency Standards

The English Language Proficiency Standards (ELPS) outline expectations for students who are learning English. The chart below, which contains a selected list of the ELPS, includes descriptions of activities and interactions that will help you develop your knowledge of English. It also provides you with information on where these skills are specifically addressed in this program.

ELPS 2 Cross-curricular Second Language Acquisition/Listening

The ELL listens to a variety of speakers including teachers, peers, and electronic media to gain an increasing level of comprehension of newly acquired language in all content areas. ELLs may be at the beginning, intermediate, advanced, or advanced high stage of English language acquisition in listening. In order for the ELL to meet grade-level learning expectations across the foundation and enrichment curriculum, all instruction delivered in English must be linguistically accommodated (communicated, sequenced, and scaffolded) commensurate with the student's level of English language proficiency. The student is expected to:

D	monitor understanding of spoken language during classroom instruction and interactions and seek clarification as needed;	pages 48, 51, 516–518, 524, 525, 527, 531 page 86

ELPS 3 Cross-curricular Second Language Acquisition/Speaking

The ELL speaks in a variety of modes for a variety of purposes with an awareness of different language registers (formal/informal) using vocabulary with increasing fluency and accuracy in language arts and all content areas. ELLs may be at the beginning, intermediate, advanced, or advanced high stage of English language acquisition in speaking. In order for the ELL to meet grade-level learning expectations across the foundation and enrichment curriculum, all instruction delivered in English must be linguistically accommodated (communicated, sequenced, and scaffolded) commensurate with the student's level of English language proficiency. The student is expected to:

A	practice producing sounds of newly acquired vocabulary such as long and short vowels, silent letters, and consonant clusters to pronounce English words in a manner that is increasingly comprehensible;	pages 527, 531, 533, 539, 545, 551, 557, 563
G	express opinions, ideas, and feelings ranging from communicating single words and short phrases to participating in extended discussions on a variety of social and grade-appropriate academic topics;	pages 2, 5, 9, 52, 53, 72, 223, 348, 517, 518, 527, 529, 531, 533, 536, 537, 539, 540, 542, 543, 545, 549, 554, 555, 560–562, 566, 567, 733, 751 page 88
H	narrate, describe, and explain with increasing specificity and detail as more English is acquired;	pages 48, 517, 518, 527, 531, 537, 539, 540, 543, 545, 549, 555, 561, 562, 567, 608, 727, 751, 757

*Page References in *Student Edition*
*Page References in *SkillsBook*

ELPS 4 Cross-curricular Second Language Acquisition/Reading

The ELL reads a variety of texts for a variety of purposes with an increasing level of comprehension in all content areas. ELLs may be at the beginning, intermediate, advanced, or advanced high stage of English language acquisition in reading. In order for the ELL to meet grade-level learning expectations across the foundation and enrichment curriculum, all instruction delivered in English must be linguistically accommodated (communicated, sequenced, and scaffolded) commensurate with the student's level of English language proficiency. For kindergarten and first grade, certain of these student expectations apply to text read aloud for students not yet at the stage of decoding written text. The student is expected to:

C develop basic sight vocabulary, derive meaning of environmental print, and comprehend English vocabulary and language structures used routinely in written classroom materials;	pages 109, 193, 223, 251, 445, 520, 526, 527, 530, 531, 533–535, 539, 546, 547, 551, 553, 557, 559, 563, 565, 605, 606, 636, 637, 710–729 pages 61–68, 70, 199

ELPS 5 Cross-curricular Second Language Acquisition/Writing

The ELL writes in a variety of forms with increasing accuracy to effectively address a specific purpose and audience in all content areas. ELLs may be at the beginning, intermediate, advanced, or advanced high stage of English language acquisition in writing. In order for the ELL to meet grade-level learning expectations across foundation and enrichment curriculum, all instruction delivered in English must be linguistically accommodated (communicated, sequenced, and scaffolded) commensurate with the student's level of English language proficiency. For kindergarten and first grade, certain of these student expectations do not apply until the student has reached the stage of generating original written text using a standard writing system. The student is expected to:

B write using newly acquired basic vocabulary and content-based grade-level vocabulary;	pages 2, 10, 52, 533, 539, 545 pages 85–87, 117, 178
G narrate, describe, and explain with increasing specificity and detail to fulfill content area writing needs as more English is acquired.	pages 4, 5, 37–40, 44, 47, 59, 160, 161, 184, 450, 452, 460, 486, 551, 557, 563, 571, 575, 601, 602 pages 8, 24, 31, 52, 85, 87, 99, 101, 126, 127

*Page References in *Student Edition*
*Page References in *SkillsBook*

Credits

Text:

P. 521: Copyright © 2010 by Houghton Mifflin Harcourt Publishing Company. Adapted and reproduced by permission from *The American Heritage College Dictionary, Fourth Edition.*

Photos:

P. 348, 353 (top), **356** (top) ©Ablestock.com/Jupiter Images; **352** (top) ©Comstock/Getty Images; **352** (bottom), **356** (bottom) ©Photodisc/Getty Images; **353** (bottom) ©Corbis; **356** (middle) ©tbkmedia.de/Alamy; **536** ©Vicki Kerr/UpperCut Images/Getty Images; **542** ©Ian Shaw/Alamy; **548** ©Yellow Dog Productions/Getty Images; **554** ©image 100/Jupiter; **560** ©Inti St Clair/Digital Vision/Getty Images; **566** ©Thinkstock Images/Getty Images; **endsheet, 598** ©Ablestock.com/Jupiter; **618** (top, bottom right) ©Photodisc/Getty Images; **618** (bottom left) ©Photos.com/Jupiter Images.

Index

The index will help you find specific information in this book. Entries in italics are from the "Using the Right Word" section. The colored boxes contain information you will use often.

A

B

C

E

G

H

I

J

K

L

M

O

P

Q

S

U

V